INSIDE ALGEBRA

TEACHER GUIDE VOLUME 1

Larry Bradsby

Cambium LEARNING® Group | Voyager

4 5 6 7 8   WEB   14 13 12 11

ISBN 13: 978-1-60697-263-2
ISBN 10: 1-60697-263-4
188795/04-11

Printed in the United States of America

Published and distributed by

4093 Specialty Place • Longmont, CO 80504 • (303) 651-2829
www.voyagerlearning.com

Table of Contents • Volume 1

Table of Contents • Volume 1

Table of Contents • Volume 1

Table of Contents • Volume 2

Table of Contents • Volume 2

9 CHAPTER

Using Factoring **767**

Table of Contents • Volume 2

A Balanced Way to Teach Algebra

Inside Algebra is a balanced approach to teaching algebra. The four-step lesson design is a powerful tool that weaves:

- **Concept Development Activities** that build conceptual understanding through concrete modeling experiences

- **Practice Activities** that support new learning through games and small group activities

- **Problem-Solving Activities** that build problem-solving skills through relevant, real-world connections

- **Progress-Monitoring Activities** that help build computational fluency and monitor student understanding

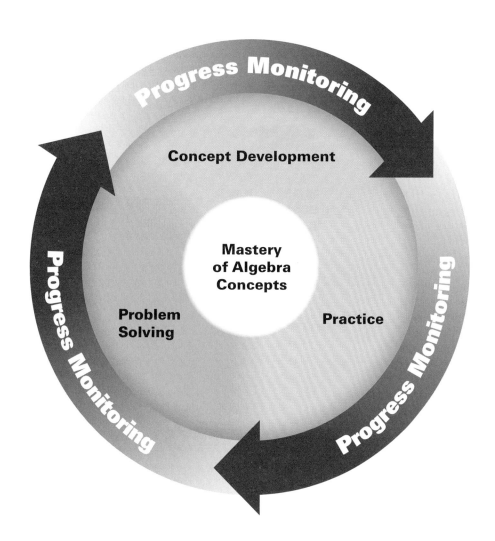

INSIDE ALGEBRA

Supports a Balanced Approach to Instruction Recommended by the National Mathematics Advisory Panel

The National Mathematics Advisory Panel (NMP) recommends that teachers employ a balanced approach to teaching algebra focused on conceptual understanding, developing fluency in procedures and number operations, and building strong problem-solving skills. These three aspects of learning mathematics are the focus of every *Inside Algebra* objective.

Students develop conceptual understanding.

Concept Development Activities

- Utilize manipulatives (provided with program)
- Provide concrete modeling experiences

Practice Activities

- Strengthen understanding of newly learned concepts
- Provide peer interaction through small group activities and games

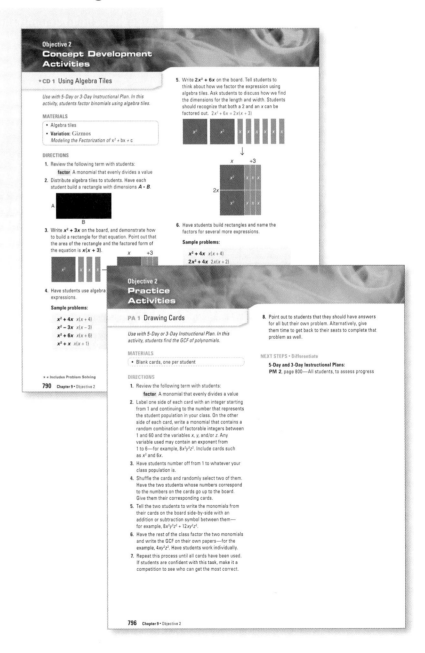

Students increase computational fluency.

Progress-Monitoring Activities

- Develop automaticity in basic skills
- Provide information to adjust instruction
- Build fluency with one-minute drills

Algebra Skill Builders (online resource)

Students build problem-solving skills.

Problem-Solving Activities

- Allow synthesis of a variety of skills
- Reinforce problem-solving strategies
- Provide real-world relevance

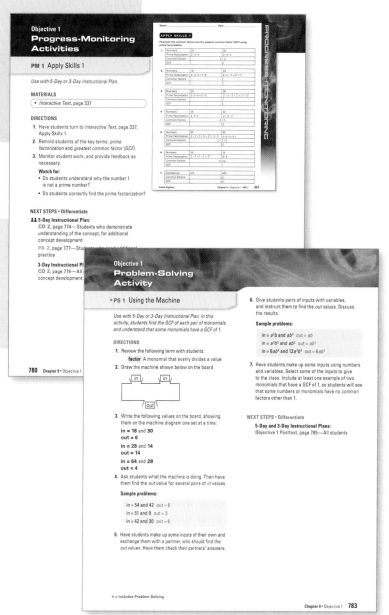

Addresses all Major Topics of Algebra Recommended by the National Mathematics Advisory Panel

Algebra, according to the National Mathematics Advisory Panel, is the gateway to higher learning success. A student's performance in algebra has a strong correlation to their success in upper-level mathematics. A solid algebraic foundation also correlates strongly with access to college, graduation from college, and earning potential. In fact, a student who completes Algebra II is more than twice as likely to graduate from college.

INSIDE
ALGEBRA
Develops Mastery of These Algebra Concepts

Foundational Skills

The National Mathematics Advisory Panel says:
"The coherence and sequential nature of mathematics dictate the foundational skills that are necessary for the learning of algebra. The most important foundational skill not presently developed appears to be proficiency with fractions (including decimals, percents, and negative fractions)."

Chapters 1–2

Pre-Algebra Skills

- Using operations with rational numbers
- Locating, comparing, and ordering real numbers
- Finding the square root of a number
- Using variables to represent specific values
- Using variables to write general statements
- Using mathematical properties and order of operations
- Using proportions to solve problems
- Graphing ordered pairs and relations
- Finding the domain and range of a relation

Basic Algebra

The National Mathematics Advisory Panel says:
"The Panel recommends that school algebra be consistently understood in terms of the Major Topics of School Algebra..." (Symbols and Expressions, Linear Equations, Quadratic Equations, Functions, Algebra of Polynomials, Combinatorics and Finite Probability)

Chapters 3–10

Basic Algebra Skills

- Writing and solving equations in one and two variables

- Graphing linear equations

- Identifying functions from a graph, table, or equation

- Writing equations in standard, point-slope, and slope-intercept form, and converting between forms

- Solving and graphing linear inequalities

- Solving systems of linear equations and inequalities

- Adding, subtracting, and multiplying polynomials

- Factoring polynomials

- Solving quadratic polynomial equations using a variety of methods

Advanced Algebra

The National Mathematics Advisory Panel says:
"...research shows that completion of Algebra II correlates significantly with success in college and earnings from employment. In fact, students who complete Algebra II are more than twice as likely to graduate from college compared to students with less mathematical preparation."

Chapters 11–12

Additional Algebra Skills

- Using operations with rational expressions

- Simplifying rational expressions

- Solving rational equations

- Dividing polynomials

- Simplifying radical expressions

- Using operations with radical expressions

- Solving equations involving radicals

- Using the Pythagorean theorem to solve problems

- Using coordinate geometry to solve problems

Skills build sequentially to mastery.

Delivers Content Through Explicit Instruction as Recommended by the National Mathematics Advisory Panel

Inside Algebra supports students through explicit instruction organized in a clear, consistent manner.

Explicit instruction is supported by clearly defined concepts and skills. A variety of activities help students learn and recognize the relationships between those concepts and skills.

This support is integrated into each of the 12 chapters in *Inside Algebra*, which are organized into objectives and activities. This includes:

- 60 objectives
- More than 500 activities

Instructional Design of Each Objective

Every objective in *Inside Algebra* begins with a pretest. Students complete a combination of Concept Development, Practice, and Progress-Monitoring activities before completing one or more Problem-Solving activities that synthesize student learning and provide relevant applications. A posttest measures student mastery of the objective.

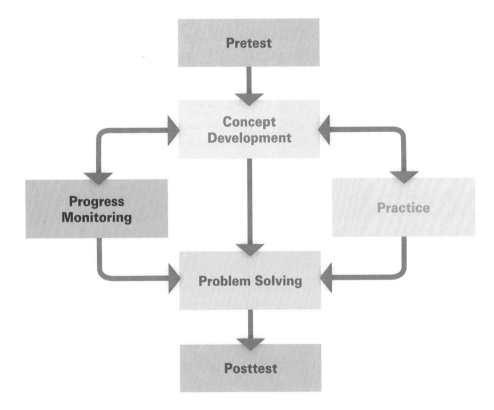

Teacher Materials

Teacher Guides: Two-Volume Set

Teacher Placement Guide
Guides teachers in administering and scoring the placement test

VPORT® Online Data Management System

Online Resources

Access to Selected ExploreLearning Gizmos

Algebra Skill Builders Blackline Masters

Student Materials

Student *Interactive Text*

Assessment Book

Student Placement Test

Access to Selected ExploreLearning Gizmos

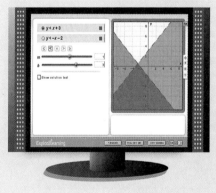

Placement Test Pinpoints Skill Levels

Inside Algebra placement is based on students' skill levels. Before instruction begins, the Placement Test is administered to all students being considered for the *Inside Algebra* program. Student results determine placement into one of two entry points:

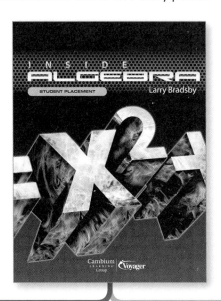

| Chapter 1 Variables and Expressions | Chapter 3 Solving Linear Equations |

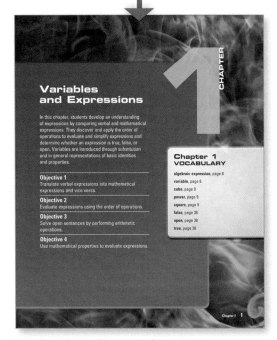

Teacher Guide, Chapter 1 Opener, page 1

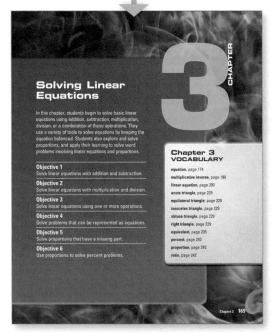

Teacher Guide, Chapter 3 Opener, page 169

The Comprehensive Assessment System Tracks and Monitors Student Growth From Placement to Mastery

This user-friendly assessment system provides teachers with the measures they need to accurately place students and monitor their progress though the curriculum. It furnishes the teacher with the data necessary to inform instruction to ensure each student meets his or her goals.

Placement Test	Ongoing Assessment	VPORT® Online Data Management System

- Daily Application
- Objective Pretests
- Objective Posttests
- Chapter Tests
- Extension Activities
- Reinforcement Activities

Placement

Based on students' demonstrated understanding of key mathematics concepts and skills, data from the *Inside Algebra* Placement Test accurately place students at one of the two entry points of the curriculum.

Ongoing Assessments

Regular assessment of student mastery of the concepts and skills taught in the curriculum ensures that teachers can adjust pacing or instruction to meet the needs of individual students.

VPORT Online Data Management System

This user-friendly data management system allows teachers and administrators to record, track, and report student test results. Reports can be generated at the individual, class, building, and district levels.

Easy to Access Data Informs Differentiation During Instruction. . .

Inside Algebra offers multiple opportunities to assess, reinforce, and differentiate instruction to promote mastery of each objective.

- **After each Objective Pretest** teachers use data to select an appropriate instructional plan for the class.

- **Throughout each instructional plan** teachers use informal assessment data to identify groups for acceleration or differentiation, providing a second layer of differentiation to support a range of learners.

- **After each Objective Posttest** teachers use data to identify students who may need additional instruction, either one-on-one or in small groups.

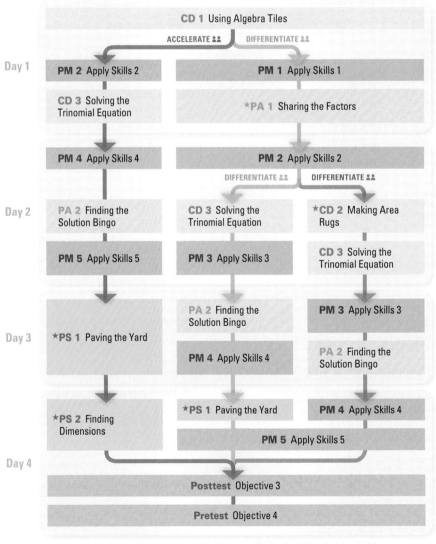

CD = Concept Development   PM = Progress Monitoring   PS = Problem Solving
PA = Practice Activity   ★ = Includes Problem Solving

. . .And After Assessment

Extensions and reinforcements are provided in every chapter.

After administering the Chapter Test, teachers determine differentiation using student data by:

- Scoring the Chapter Test by objective and reviewing student scores.
- Identifying differentiation needs.
- Establishing small groups for extension or reinforcement.

Students who demonstrated **mastery and score at or above 80 percent** on the Chapter Test complete extension activities individually or in pairs.

Students who demonstrated **mastery but score below 80 percent** on the Chapter Test complete independent reinforcement activities in pairs or small groups.

ExploreLearning Gizmos provide relevant, real-world activities.

Students who **did not demonstrate mastery on any or all the objectives on the objective posttests** or the Chapter Test complete teacher-guided reinforcement activities in a small group.

Retest students who scored below 80 percent using the Chapter Test, Form B, from the online resources.

Differentiation Planner (Chapter 9)

Students who demonstrated mastery on every objective posttest and scored 80% or above on the chapter test

Extend learning using:

- **Gizmos** Use the *Quadratics in Polynomial Form—Activity A* Gizmo with the Extension Activity. Have students work in pairs or individually to complete the activity.

Students who demonstrated mastery on every objective posttest but scored below 80% on the chapter test

Reinforce learning using:

- **Gizmos** Use the *Modeling the Factorization of* $x^2 + bx + c$ Gizmo with the Reinforcement Activity. Have students work in pairs or small groups to complete the activity.
- Additional Activities from the online resources.
- Algebra Skill Builders for Chapter 9 from the online resources.

Students who did not demonstrate mastery on any or all of the objective posttests or the chapter test

Reinforce learning using:

- **Gizmos** Present the *Modeling the Factorization of* $x^2 + bx + c$ Gizmo to students in small groups using the instruction on page 861.
- Additional Activities from the online resources.
- Algebra Skill Builders for Chapter 9 from the online resources.

Retest—Administer Chapter 9 Test, Form B, from the online resources to students who scored below 80 percent on Form A when time allows.

Provides Enhanced Instruction for English Language Learners

Inherent in the structure of *Inside Algebra* are strategies that enhance instruction for English Language Learners.

- **Simple and easily understood** instruction improves student comprehension.

- **Explicit vocabulary instruction** in the activities emphasizes the language of math.

- **Open-ended and short response prompts** encourage students to apply their reasoning skills through the use of brief constructed responses.

- **Small group activities and games** provide a nonthreatening form of communication.

- **Formal and informal assessments** monitor student growth to measure students' increasing understanding and proficiency.

Teaches the Language of Math

Throughout *Inside Algebra*, students are increasingly responsible for understanding and applying math vocabulary as they:

- collaborate with peers

- justify their thinking on mathematical tasks and problem solving

- demonstrate their understanding and proficiency in math on high stakes assessments

Promotes Flexible Grouping

A variety of grouping models are used throughout the *Inside Algebra* program.

- Flexible grouping models may be teacher-led or student-centered.

- Whole class, small group, pairs, and individual models are recommended depending on the nature of the activity.

Provides Multiple Modeling Activities

Teachers' use of modeling is an essential element in promoting understanding. The use of verbal explanations that include simple language and sentence structure combined with visual models of the information being presented allow students to use different modalities of learning as they work in *Inside Algebra*. *Inside Algebra* uses:

- Pictorial representation to help students visualize concepts

- Hands-on manipulatives to make concepts more complete

- ExploreLearning Gizmos for interactive learning

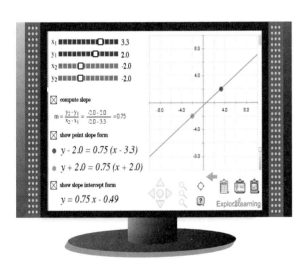

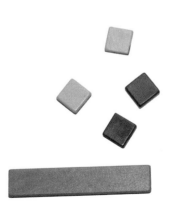

The activities of *Inside Algebra* include tools that help students connect their hands-on experiences with the pictorial representations, then relate these to the symbolic representations of algebra.

Supports Teachers and Students With Relevant Technology

Explore**learning** • **Gizmos**
Enhance Concept Development

Gizmos provide fun, interactive simulations to help students visualize and understand important concepts.

Teachers use ExploreLearning Gizmos to model concepts in lesson activities.

Students use ExploreLearning Gizmos during end-of-chapter differentiation activities to make connections between algebra and the real world.

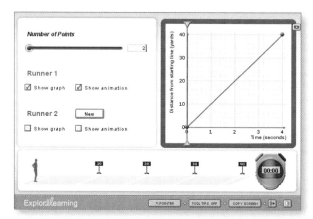

VPORT Tracks Student Progress

Inside Algebra includes the VPORT online data management system that allows educators to collect and report student results. Using VPORT, teachers, schools, and districts can:

- Input scores from all assessments
- View individual student scores
- Print a variety of reports for multiple uses

Online Resources Provide Daily Teacher Support

- Complete online *Teacher Guide*
- Blackline Masters
- Student Extension Activity Pages
- Student Reinforcement Activity Pages
- Alternate Form B Chapter Tests
- Algebra Skill Builder Masters
- Additional Activity Resources

Introduce the chapter.

Each chapter of *Inside Algebra* is focused on helping students master the concepts and skills necessary for future success. Chapters are organized into objectives, which students master through Concept Development, Practice, Progress-Monitoring, and Problem-Solving activities.

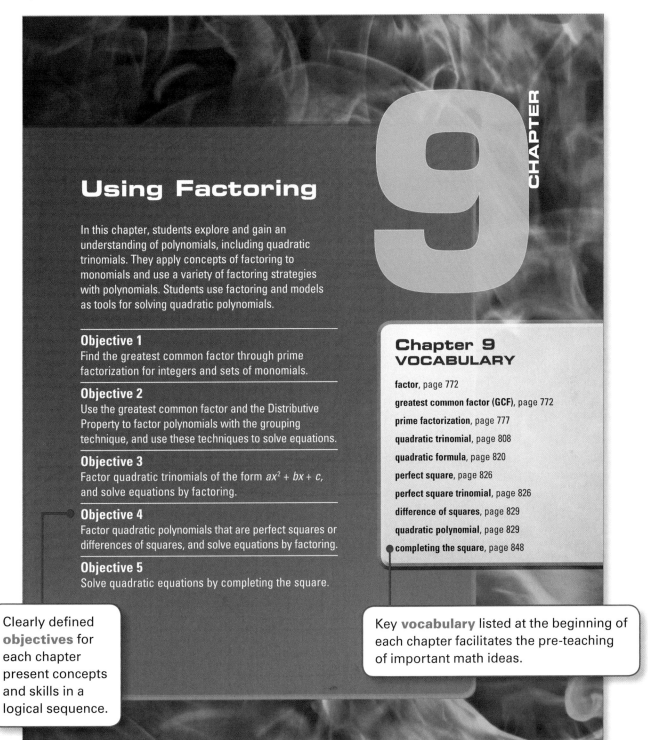

CHAPTER 9

Using Factoring

In this chapter, students explore and gain an understanding of polynomials, including quadratic trinomials. They apply concepts of factoring to monomials and use a variety of factoring strategies with polynomials. Students use factoring and models as tools for solving quadratic polynomials.

Objective 1
Find the greatest common factor through prime factorization for integers and sets of monomials.

Objective 2
Use the greatest common factor and the Distributive Property to factor polynomials with the grouping technique, and use these techniques to solve equations.

Objective 3
Factor quadratic trinomials of the form $ax^2 + bx + c$, and solve equations by factoring.

Objective 4
Factor quadratic polynomials that are perfect squares or differences of squares, and solve equations by factoring.

Objective 5
Solve quadratic equations by completing the square.

Chapter 9 VOCABULARY

factor, page 772

greatest common factor (GCF), page 772

prime factorization, page 777

quadratic trinomial, page 808

quadratic formula, page 820

perfect square, page 826

perfect square trinomial, page 826

difference of squares, page 829

quadratic polynomial, page 829

completing the square, page 848

Clearly defined **objectives** for each chapter present concepts and skills in a logical sequence.

Key **vocabulary** listed at the beginning of each chapter facilitates the pre-teaching of important math ideas.

Using Factoring, Teacher Guide, Chapter 9

Administer the pretest for each objective.

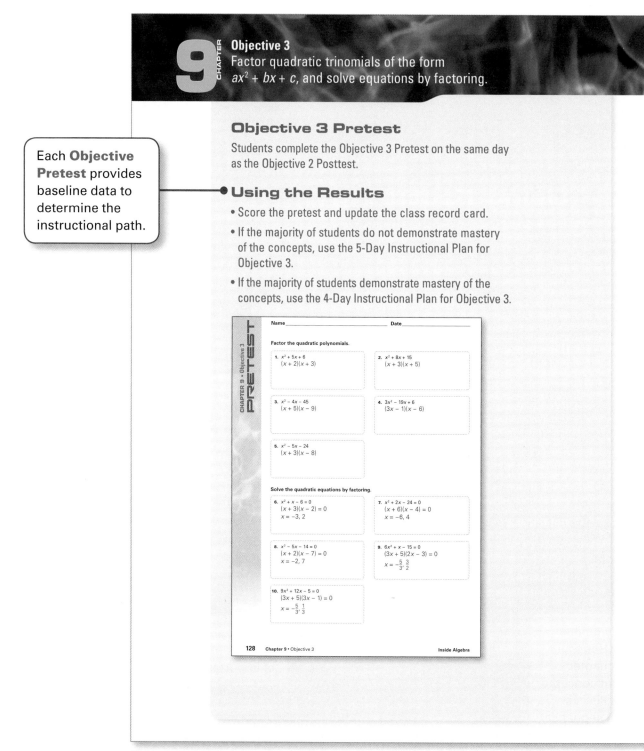

9 CHAPTER

Objective 3
Factor quadratic trinomials of the form
$ax^2 + bx + c$, and solve equations by factoring.

Objective 3 Pretest

Students complete the Objective 3 Pretest on the same day as the Objective 2 Posttest.

Using the Results

- Score the pretest and update the class record card.
- If the majority of students do not demonstrate mastery of the concepts, use the 5-Day Instructional Plan for Objective 3.
- If the majority of students demonstrate mastery of the concepts, use the 4-Day Instructional Plan for Objective 3.

> Each **Objective Pretest** provides baseline data to determine the instructional path.

CHAPTER 9 • Objective 3
PRETEST

Name_____ Date_____

Factor the quadratic polynomials.

1. $x^2 + 5x + 6$
$(x + 2)(x + 3)$

2. $x^2 + 8x + 15$
$(x + 3)(x + 5)$

3. $x^2 - 4x - 45$
$(x + 5)(x - 9)$

4. $3x^2 - 19x + 6$
$(3x - 1)(x - 6)$

5. $x^2 - 5x - 24$
$(x + 3)(x - 8)$

Solve the quadratic equations by factoring.

6. $x^2 + x - 6 = 0$
$(x + 3)(x - 2) = 0$
$x = -3, 2$

7. $x^2 + 2x - 24 = 0$
$(x + 6)(x - 4) = 0$
$x = -6, 4$

8. $x^2 - 5x - 14 = 0$
$(x + 2)(x - 7) = 0$
$x = -2, 7$

9. $6x^2 + x - 15 = 0$
$(3x + 5)(2x - 3) = 0$
$x = -\frac{5}{3}, \frac{3}{2}$

10. $9x^2 + 12x - 5 = 0$
$(3x + 5)(3x - 1) = 0$
$x = -\frac{5}{3}, \frac{1}{3}$

128   Chapter 9 • Objective 3   **Inside Algebra**

Using Factoring, Teacher Guide, Chapter 9

Goals and Activities

Objective 3 Goals ●———————

The following activities, when used with the instructional plans on pages 806 and 807, enable students to:

- Factor the quadratic polynomial $x^2 + 6x - 16$ to get $(x - 2)(x + 8)$
- Solve the quadratic equation $x^2 + 5x - 14 = 0$ to get $x = 2, -7$

Objective Goals provide specific examples of the skills and concepts students are expected to learn through the Objective Activities.

Objective 3 Activities ●———————

A color-coded **objective overview** outlines the different types of activities provided to meet the Objective Goals.

Concept Development Activities

CD 1 Using Algebra Tiles, page 808	**★CD 2** Making Area Rugs, page 810	**CD 3** Solving the Trinomial Equation, page 811

Practice Activities

★PA 1 Sharing the Factors, page 812	**PA 2** Finding the Solution Bingo, page 813

Progress-Monitoring Activities

PM 1 Apply Skills 1, page 814	**PM 2** Apply Skills 2, page 815	**PM 3** Apply Skills 3, page 816	**PM 4** Apply Skills 4, page 817	**PM 5** Apply Skills 5, page 818

★Problem-Solving Activities

★PS 1 Paving the Yard, page 819	**★PS 2** Finding Dimensions, page 820

Ongoing Assessment

Posttest Objective 3, page 821

Pretest Objective 4, page 822

CD = Concept Development PM = Progress Monitoring PS = Problem Solving
PA = Practice Activity ★ = Includes Problem Solving

INSIDE
How Does **ALGEBRA** Work?

Determine the appropriate instructional path based on pretest results.

> Two distinct **instructional plans** provide explicit guidance in the selection of appropriate activities for differentiation.

CHAPTER 9

Objective 3
Instructional Plans

> When the majority of students **do not demonstrate mastery** on the Objective Pretest, an **intensified Instructional Plan** provides additional activities.

5-Day Instructional Plan

Use the 5-Day Instructional Plan when pretest results indicate that students would benefit from a slower pace. This plan is used when the majority of students need more time or did not demonstrate mastery on the pretest. This plan does not include all activities.

Day 1
- **CD 1** Using Algebra Tiles
- ★**PA 1** Sharing the Factors

Day 2
- **PM 1** Apply Skills 1
- ★**CD 2** Making Area Rugs

Day 3
- **PM 2** Apply Skills 2
- **CD 3** Solving the Trinomial Equation
- **PM 3** Apply Skills 3

Day 4
- **PA 2** Finding the Solution Bingo
- **PM 4** Apply Skills 4

ACCELERATE 👥 DIFFERENTIATE 👥

> **Differentiation** occurs through alternate activities based on whether students demonstrate understanding of the concept or need additional support.

Day 5
- **PM 5** Apply Skills 5
- ★**PS 1** Paving the Yard

- **PM 5** Apply Skills 5

- **Posttest** Objective 3
- **Pretest** Objective 4

CD = Concept Development   PM = Progress Monitoring   PS = Problem Solving
PA = Practice Activity   ★ = Includes Problem Solving

Using Factoring, Teacher Guide, Chapter 9

When the majority of students **demonstrate mastery** on the Objective Pretest, a **streamlined Instructional Plan** provides an alternate pathway for when the class can move through the activities at a faster pace.

4-Day Instructional Plan

Use the 4-Day Instructional Plan when pretest results indicate that students can move through the activities at a faster pace. This plan is ideal when the majority of students demonstrate mastery on the pretest.

Differentiation occurs through alternate activities based on whether students demonstrate understanding of the concept or need additional support.

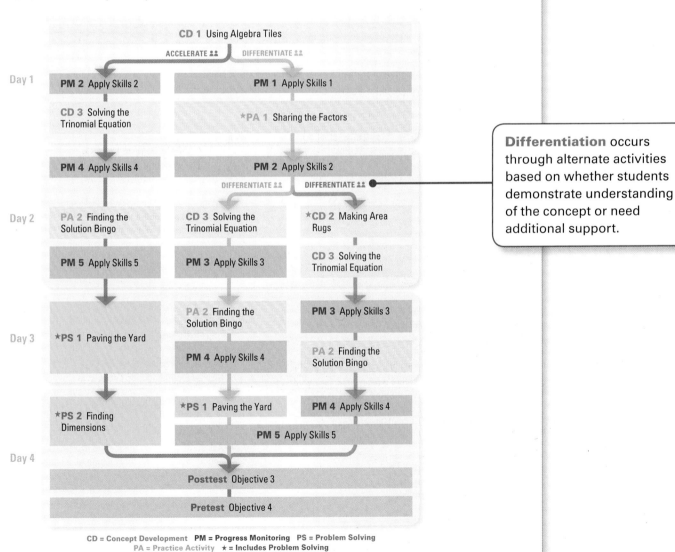

CD = Concept Development PM = Progress Monitoring PS = Problem Solving
PA = Practice Activity ★ = Includes Problem Solving

Provide instruction for content mastery.

Demonstrate conceptual understanding through Concept Development and Practice Activities.

Concept Development Activities use manipulatives to develop algebraic thinking and provide concrete representations of abstract concepts.

Consistent lesson format provides explicit direction for teachers to present instruction to support student mastery.

Objective 3
Concept Development Activities

CD 1 Using Algebra Tiles

Use with 5-Day or 4-Day Instructional Plan. In this activity, students factor quadratic trinomials using algebra tiles.

MATERIALS

- Algebra tiles, one set for every two students
- **Variation:** Gizmos
  Modeling the Factorization of $x^2 + bx + c$

DIRECTIONS

1. Review the following term with students:

   factor A monomial that evenly divides a value

2. Review how to find the product of two binomials using algebra tiles; for example, write $(x + 1)(x + 2)$ on the board and use the following rectangle to discuss:

   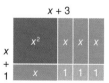

   Be sure students see that
   $(x + 1)(x + 2) = x^2 + 3x + 2$.

3. Discuss the following term with students:

   quadratic trinomial A polynomial of the form $ax^2 + bx + c$

4. Next, show students that to find factors of a trinomial, they should make a rectangle out of the given trinomial. In other words, work backward from what is shown in Step 2. Write $x^2 + 4x + 3$ on the board, and use algebra tiles to factor the trinomial. Show students how to determine the dimensions of the overall rectangle. $(x + 1)(x + 3)$

ExploreLearning Gizmos provide alternate presentations of concepts using interactive simulations and virtual manipulatives.

Variation: Gizmos For this activity, use the tiles in the Gizmo *Modeling the Factorization of* $x^2 + bx + c$ to model the factoring of these quadratic expressions.

Modeling the Factorization of $x^2 + bx + c$

5. Write several polynomials on the board, and have students use algebra tiles to find the factors. Call on students to give you the factors they found and write them under the appropriate polynomials.

   Sample problems:

   $x^2 + 5x + 6$ $(x + 2)(x + 3)$
   $x^2 + 4x + 4$ $(x + 2)^2$
   $x^2 + x - 6$ $(x - 2)(x + 3)$
   $x^2 + 6x + 5$ $(x + 1)(x + 5)$

6. Demonstrate how to factor $x^2 + 5x + 6$. $(x + 2)(x + 3)$ Discuss the relationship between the numbers (5 and 6) and the factors (2 and 3). Make sure students recognize that $2 + 3 = 5$ and $2 \cdot 3 = 6$. Use the model to show why the relationship exists. Repeat this process for all polynomials on the board.

7. Ask students to find the factors of $x^2 + 7x + 10$ and $x^2 + x - 12$. Allow students to use the algebra tiles if they need the model to find the factors.
   $x^2 + 7x + 10 = (x + 2)(x + 5)$, $x^2 + x + 12 = (x - 3)(x + 4)$

   Note: If students need more practice multiplying binomials, refer to Chapter 8, Objective 5.

Using Factoring, Teacher Guide, Chapter 9

Objective 3
Practice Activities

PA 2 Finding the Solution Bingo

Use with 5-Day or 4-Day Instructional Plan. In this activity, students factor quadratic trinomials.

MATERIALS

- Blackline Master 38
- Game markers to cover squares

DIRECTIONS

1. Review the following terms with students:

   factor A monomial that evenly divides a value

   quadratic trinomial A polynomial of the form $ax^2 + bx + c$

2. Distribute one copy of Blackline Master 38, 4 × 4 Bingo Card, to each student. Have each student put the numbers **−3, −2, −1, 0, 1, 2, 3** at random in the squares of the bingo card. Point out that they will have to repeat some numbers to fill the 16 squares.

3. Write an equation on the board, selected at random from the list below. Tell students to solve the equation and cover the squares that have the solution(s) with their markers. Have students write the equations and solutions on a piece of paper to hand in at the end of the activity.

	Equations to Use	Solutions		Equations to Use	Solutions
1.	$x^2 + 3x + 2 = 0$	−2, −1	14.	$x^2 − 2x − 3 = 0$	−1, 3
2.	$x^2 − 4x + 3 = 0$	3, 1	15.	$x^2 − x − 2 = 0$	2, −1
3.	$x^2 − 4x + 4 = 0$	2	16.	$x^2 − 5x + 6 = 0$	3, 2
4.	$x^2 + x − 6 = 0$	−3, 2	17.	$x^2 + 2x − 3 = 0$	−3, 1
5.	$x^2 + x − 2 = 0$	−2, 1	18.	$x^2 + 4x + 3 = 0$	−3, −1
6.	$x^2 + 2x + 1 = 0$	−1	19.	$x^2 + 5x + 6 = 0$	−3, −2
7.	$x^2 + 6x + 9 = 0$	−3	20.	$x^2 + 2x = 0$	−2, 0
8.	$x^2 − x − 6 = 0$	3, −2	21.	$x^2 − 4 = 0$	−2, 2
9.	$x^2 − 2x = 0$	0, 2	22.	$x^2 + 3x = 0$	0, −3
10.	$x^2 + 4x + 4 = 0$	−2	23.	$x^2 − 2x + 1 = 0$	1
11.	$x^2 + x = 0$	0, −1	24.	$x^2 − 3x + 2 = 0$	1, 2
12.	$x^2 − 6x + 9 = 0$	3	25.	$x^2 − 4x + 4 = 0$	2
13.	$x^2 − 3x = 0$	0, 3			

4. Continue with other equations. The first student to get four markers in a row should call out, "Bingo!" If the student's answers are correct, that student is the winner.

5. Alternatively, continue play until a student covers all the squares on his or her card.

NEXT STEPS • Differentiate

5-Day Instructional Plan:
PM 4, page 817—All students, to assess progress

4-Day Instructional Plan:
PM 5, page 818—Students who are on the accelerated path, to assess progress

PM 4, page 817—Students who are on the differentiated path, to assess progress

Name _____ Date _____

38

4 × 4 BINGO CARD

Monitor progress toward mastering the objective.

Progress-Monitoring Activities determine differentiation through alternate activities as they build fluency with basic algebra skills.

Informal assessment strategies such as **ask for, watch for,** and **listen for** provide further insight into student progress.

Objective 3
Progress-Monitoring Activities

PM 1 Apply Skills 1

Use with 5-Day or 4-Day Instructional Plan.

MATERIALS

- *Interactive Text*, page 346

DIRECTIONS

1. Have students turn to *Interactive Text*, page 346, Apply Skills 1.
2. Remind students of the key terms: *quadratic trinomial* and *factor*.
3. Monitor student work, and provide feedback as necessary.

● **Watch for:**
  - Do students factor the trinomials using algebra tiles to complete the rectangle?
  - Do any students try an algebraic method?

NEXT STEPS • Differentiate

5-Day Instructional Plan:
CD 2, page 810—All students, for additional concept development and problem solving

4-Day Instructional Plan:
PA 1, page 812—All students, for additional practice and problem solving

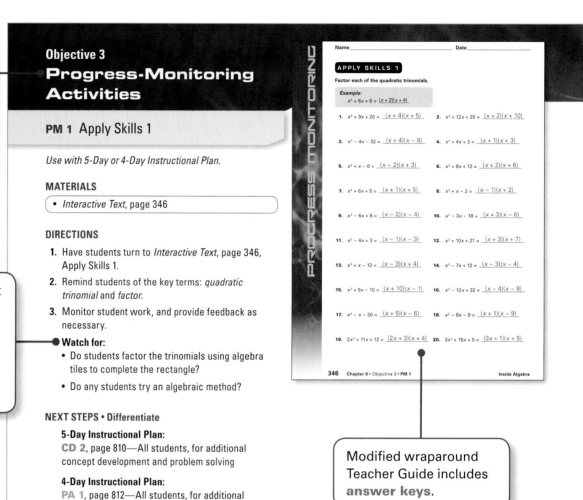

PROGRESS MONITORING

Name _____ Date _____

APPLY SKILLS 1

Factor each of the quadratic trinomials.

Example:
$x^2 + 6x + 8 = (x + 2)(x + 4)$

1. $x^2 + 9x + 20 = (x + 4)(x + 5)$
2. $x^2 + 12x + 20 = (x + 2)(x + 10)$
3. $x^2 - 4x - 32 = (x + 4)(x - 8)$
4. $x^2 + 4x + 3 = (x + 1)(x + 3)$
5. $x^2 + x - 6 = (x - 2)(x + 3)$
6. $x^2 + 8x + 12 = (x + 2)(x + 6)$
7. $x^2 + 6x + 5 = (x + 1)(x + 5)$
8. $x^2 + x - 2 = (x - 1)(x + 2)$
9. $x^2 - 6x + 8 = (x - 2)(x - 4)$
10. $x^2 - 3x - 18 = (x + 3)(x - 6)$
11. $x^2 - 4x + 3 = (x - 1)(x - 3)$
12. $x^2 + 10x + 21 = (x + 3)(x + 7)$
13. $x^2 + x - 12 = (x - 3)(x + 4)$
14. $x^2 - 7x + 12 = (x - 3)(x - 4)$
15. $x^2 + 9x - 10 = (x + 10)(x - 1)$
16. $x^2 - 12x + 32 = (x - 4)(x - 8)$
17. $x^2 - x - 30 = (x + 5)(x - 6)$
18. $x^2 - 8x - 9 = (x + 1)(x - 9)$
19. $2x^2 + 11x + 12 = (2x + 3)(x + 4)$
20. $3x^2 + 16x + 5 = (3x + 1)(x + 5)$

346 Chapter 9 • Objective 3 • PM 1   **Inside Algebra**

Modified wraparound Teacher Guide includes **answer keys**.

Using Factoring, Teacher Guide, Chapter 9

Build problem-solving skills and demonstrate relevance.

> **Problem-Solving Activities** reinforce problem-solving strategies and reflective thinking as students synthesize cumulative skills.

Objective 3
Problem-Solving Activities

★PS 2 Finding Dimensions

Use with 4-Day Instructional Plan. In this activity, students apply what they know about quadratic equations to solve word problems.

DIRECTIONS

1. Discuss the following term with students:

   quadratic formula $x = \frac{-b \pm \sqrt{b^2 - 4ac}}{2a}$ where $ax^2 + bx + c = 0$

2. Read the following scenario to students:

A small calf needs to be kept away from the herd of cattle because of an infection. The rancher has fences made of	280 square feet

   tubing that can be put up quickly. The calf will need 280 square feet of grazing land. The tube frame will be six feet longer than it is wide. Find the dimensions of the fence.

3. Guide students as they write an equation based on the information they know. Remind students to solve the equation to find the actual dimensions of the area.

   $x(x + 6) = 280$ sq. ft.
   $x^2 + 6x = 280$
   $x^2 + 6x - 280 = 0$
   $(x - 14)(x + 20) = 0$
   $x = 14, -20$; dimensions cannot be negative so the fence is 14 ft. by 20 ft.

4. Tell students to find the dimensions if the calf only needs 160 square feet of grazing land.

   $x(x + 6) = 160$ sq. ft.
   $x^2 + 6x = 160$
   $x^2 + 6x - 160 = 0$
   $(x - 10)(x + 16) = 0$
   $x = 10, -16$; dimensions cannot be negative so the fence is 10 ft. by 16 ft.

5. Read the following scenario to students:

A rectangular garden (16 feet by 21 feet) has a uniform rock path around it. If the total area of the garden and path is 500 square feet, what is the width of the path?	Total area = 500 square feet 21 ft. 16 ft.

6. Guide students as they write an equation based on the information they know. Remind students to solve the equation to find the actual dimensions of the area.

   $l \cdot w = 500$ sq. ft.
   $(21 + x + x)(16 + x + x) = 500$
   $(21 + 2x)(16 + 2x) = 500$
   $4x^2 + 74x + 336 = 500$
   $4x^2 + 74x - 164 = 0$
   $2x^2 + 37x - 82 = 0$
   $(2x + 41)(x - 2) = 0$
   $x = -\frac{41}{2}$ or 2; measurement must be positive so the width of the path is 2 ft.

> **Examples** of student solutions showcase one possible strategy that students may use to solve the problem.

NEXT STEPS • Differentiate

4-Day Instructional Plan:
Objective 3 Posttest, page 821—All students

★ = Includes Problem Solving

Administer the posttest for each objective.

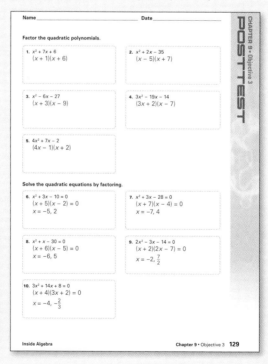

Chapter 9
Objective 3
Ongoing Assessment

Each **Objective Posttest** measures student growth in mastering the objective and identifies concepts that may need reinforcement.

• Objective 3 Posttest

Discuss with students the key concepts in Objective 3. Following the discussion, administer the Objective 3 Posttest to all students.

Using the Results

- Score the posttest and update the class record card.
- Provide reinforcement for students who do not demonstrate mastery of the concepts through individual or small-group reteaching of key concepts.

Name _____ Date _____

CHAPTER 9 • Objective 3 POSTTEST

Factor the quadratic polynomials.

1. $x^2 + 7x + 6$
   $(x + 1)(x + 6)$

2. $x^2 + 2x - 35$
   $(x - 5)(x + 7)$

3. $x^2 - 6x - 27$
   $(x + 3)(x - 9)$

4. $3x^2 - 19x - 14$
   $(3x + 2)(x - 7)$

5. $4x^2 + 7x - 2$
   $(4x - 1)(x + 2)$

Solve the quadratic equations by factoring.

6. $x^2 + 3x - 10 = 0$
   $(x + 5)(x - 2) = 0$
   $x = -5, 2$

7. $x^2 + 3x - 28 = 0$
   $(x + 7)(x - 4) = 0$
   $x = -7, 4$

8. $x^2 + x - 30 = 0$
   $(x + 6)(x - 5) = 0$
   $x = -6, 5$

9. $2x^2 - 3x - 14 = 0$
   $(x + 2)(2x - 7) = 0$
   $x = -2, \frac{7}{2}$

10. $3x^2 + 14x + 8 = 0$
    $(x + 4)(3x + 2) = 0$
    $x = -4, -\frac{2}{3}$

Inside Algebra   Chapter 9 • Objective 3   **129**

Using Factoring, Teacher Guide, Chapter 9

Complete all objectives in the chapter.

Flexible pacing meets the needs of a variety of learners.

For each objective, teachers select the appropriate instructional plan to meet the needs of students.

- In some objectives teachers will follow a more accelerated plan.
- In other objectives, assessment scores will necessitate the use of the longer Instructional Plan.

When using individual activities as a supplement, teachers may consider using Concept Development Activities followed by Progress-Monitoring Activities.

- Concept Development Activities take an average of 20 minutes to complete.
- Progress-Monitoring Activities take approximately 10 to 15 minutes to complete.

The pacing structure for *Inside Algebra* is unique.

- The strength of *Inside Algebra* comes from its flexibility. Teachers are encouraged to choose instructional plans based on student need and not time considerations.
- Each objective is focused on mastery of the concepts and not a specific time frame.
- Taking the time necessary to reach mastery is beneficial for students.

The chart below outlines the minimum amount of time required to complete each chapter using the shorter Instructional Plan for each objective.

Chapter											
1	**2**	**3**	**4**	**5**	**6**	**7**	**8**	**9**	**10**	**11**	**12**
14 days	18 days	20 days	17 days	17 days	18 days	17 days	17 days	19 days	14 days	17 days	18 days
Total: 206 Days											

The chart below outlines an alternative pacing for students who would benefit from an additional 15 to 20 days of instruction beyond the minimum time required.

Summer School	School Year
Chapter 1	Chapters 2–12
Total: 221 Days	

Using only the longer instructional plans, it will take students two full years to complete *Inside Algebra*.

After completing the chapter, review chapter objectives.

The **Chapter Review** consolidates key concepts to reinforce objectives and provides the opportunity to monitor student learning.

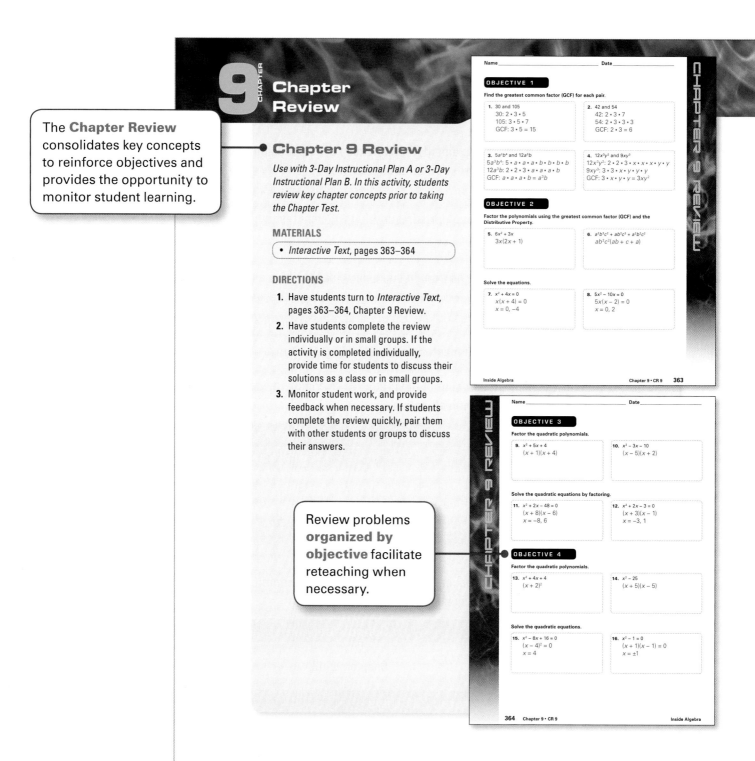

CHAPTER 9

Chapter Review

Chapter 9 Review

Use with 3-Day Instructional Plan A or 3-Day Instructional Plan B. In this activity, students review key chapter concepts prior to taking the Chapter Test.

MATERIALS

- *Interactive Text*, pages 363–364

DIRECTIONS

1. Have students turn to *Interactive Text*, pages 363–364, Chapter 9 Review.

2. Have students complete the review individually or in small groups. If the activity is completed individually, provide time for students to discuss their solutions as a class or in small groups.

3. Monitor student work, and provide feedback when necessary. If students complete the review quickly, pair them with other students or groups to discuss their answers.

Review problems **organized by objective** facilitate reteaching when necessary.

Name _____ Date _____

CHAPTER 9 REVIEW

OBJECTIVE 1

Find the greatest common factor (GCF) for each pair.

1. 30 and 105
30: $2 \cdot 3 \cdot 5$
105: $3 \cdot 5 \cdot 7$
GCF: $3 \cdot 5 = 15$

2. 42 and 54
42: $2 \cdot 3 \cdot 7$
54: $2 \cdot 3 \cdot 3 \cdot 3$
GCF: $2 \cdot 3 = 6$

3. $5a^3b^4$ and $12a^3b$
$5a^3b^4$: $5 \cdot a \cdot a \cdot a \cdot b \cdot b \cdot b \cdot b$
$12a^3b$: $2 \cdot 2 \cdot 3 \cdot a \cdot a \cdot a \cdot b$
GCF: $a \cdot a \cdot a \cdot b = a^3b$

4. $12x^3y^2$ and $9xy^3$
$12x^3y^2$: $2 \cdot 2 \cdot 3 \cdot x \cdot x \cdot x \cdot y \cdot y$
$9xy^3$: $3 \cdot 3 \cdot x \cdot y \cdot y \cdot y$
GCF: $3 \cdot x \cdot y \cdot y = 3xy^2$

OBJECTIVE 2

Factor the polynomials using the greatest common factor (GCF) and the Distributive Property.

5. $6x^2 + 3x$
$3x(2x + 1)$

6. $a^3b^3c^2 + ab^2c^3 + a^2b^2c^2$
$ab^2c^2(ab + c + a)$

Solve the equations.

7. $x^2 + 4x = 0$
$x(x + 4) = 0$
$x = 0, -4$

8. $5x^2 - 10x = 0$
$5x(x - 2) = 0$
$x = 0, 2$

Inside Algebra   Chapter 9 · CR 9   **363**

Name _____ Date _____

CHAPTER 9 REVIEW

OBJECTIVE 3

Factor the quadratic polynomials.

9. $x^2 + 5x + 4$
$(x + 1)(x + 4)$

10. $x^2 - 3x - 10$
$(x - 5)(x + 2)$

Solve the quadratic equations by factoring.

11. $x^2 + 2x - 48 = 0$
$(x + 8)(x - 6)$
$x = -8, 6$

12. $x^2 + 2x - 3 = 0$
$(x + 3)(x - 1)$
$x = -3, 1$

OBJECTIVE 4

Factor the quadratic polynomials.

13. $x^2 + 4x + 4$
$(x + 2)^2$

14. $x^2 - 25$
$(x + 5)(x - 5)$

Solve the quadratic equations.

15. $x^2 - 8x + 16 = 0$
$(x - 4)^2 = 0$
$x = 4$

16. $x^2 - 1 = 0$
$(x + 1)(x - 1) = 0$
$x = \pm 1$

364   Chapter 9 · CR 9   Inside Algebra

Chapter Review, Teacher Guide, Chapter 9

Administer the Chapter Test.

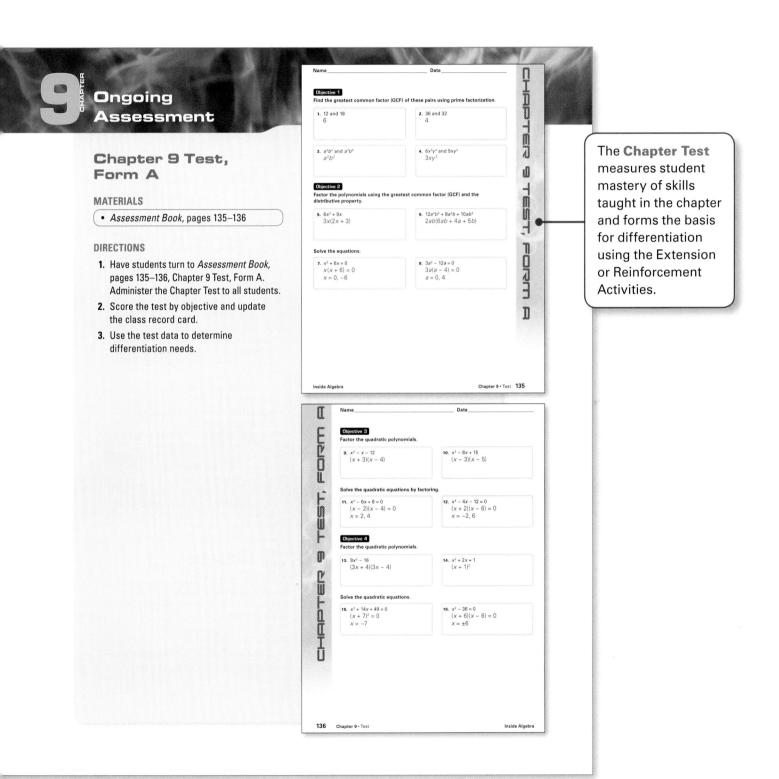

Ongoing Assessment

Chapter 9 Test, Form A

MATERIALS

- *Assessment Book*, pages 135–136

DIRECTIONS

1. Have students turn to *Assessment Book,* pages 135–136, Chapter 9 Test, Form A. Administer the Chapter Test to all students.

2. Score the test by objective and update the class record card.

3. Use the test data to determine differentiation needs.

Name _____ Date _____

CHAPTER 9 TEST, FORM A

Objective 1
Find the greatest common factor (GCF) of these pairs using prime factorization.

1. 12 and 18
6

2. 36 and 32
4

3. a^2b^2 and a^2b^5
a^2b^2

4. $6x^3y^4$ and $9xy^3$
$3xy^2$

Objective 2
Factor the polynomials using the greatest common factor (GCF) and the distributive property.

5. $6x^2 + 9x$
$3x(2x + 3)$

6. $12a^2b^2 + 8a^3b + 10ab^2$
$2ab(6ab + 4a + 5b)$

Solve the equations.

7. $x^2 + 6x = 0$
$x(x + 6) = 0$
$x = 0, -6$

8. $3a^2 - 12a = 0$
$3a(a - 4) = 0$
$a = 0, 4$

Inside Algebra   Chapter 9 · Test **135**

Name _____ Date _____

CHAPTER 9 TEST, FORM A

Objective 3
Factor the quadratic polynomials.

9. $x^2 - x - 12$
$(x + 3)(x - 4)$

10. $x^2 - 8x + 15$
$(x - 3)(x - 5)$

Solve the quadratic equations by factoring.

11. $x^2 - 6x + 8 = 0$
$(x - 2)(x - 4) = 0$
$x = 2, 4$

12. $x^2 - 4x - 12 = 0$
$(x + 2)(x - 6) = 0$
$x = -2, 6$

Objective 4
Factor the quadratic polynomials.

13. $9x^2 - 16$
$(3x + 4)(3x - 4)$

14. $x^2 + 2x + 1$
$(x + 1)^2$

Solve the quadratic equations.

15. $x^2 + 14x + 49 = 0$
$(x + 7)^2 = 0$
$x = -7$

16. $x^2 - 36 = 0$
$(x + 6)(x - 6) = 0$
$x = \pm6$

136 Chapter 9 · Test   Inside Algebra

The **Chapter Test** measures student mastery of skills taught in the chapter and forms the basis for differentiation using the Extension or Reinforcement Activities.

Chapter Test, Teacher Guide, Chapter 9

Use Chapter Test results to identify students for differentiation.

The color-coded **Differentiation Planner** quickly identifies whether students need extension or reinforcement based on the results of the Chapter Test.

9 CHAPTER

Ongoing Assessment

For students who have mastered objectives, **Extension Activities** use ExploreLearning Gizmos in real-life applications to engage and extend their knowledge of chapter objectives.

For students who have not completely mastered objectives, **Reinforcement Activities** use ExploreLearning Gizmos in either student-centered or teacher-led activities that scaffold instruction for chapter objectives.

Differentiation

MATERIALS

- **Gizmos** *Quadratics in Polynomial Form—Activity A* Gizmo
- **Gizmos** Extension Activity pages
- **Gizmos** *Modeling the Factorization of* $x^2 + bx + c$ Gizmo
- **Gizmos** Reinforcement Activity page
- Additional Activities
- Algebra Skill Builders for Chapter 9
- Chapter Test, Form B

DIRECTIONS

1. Review Chapter 9 Test, Form A, with the class.
2. Use the results from Chapter 9 Test, Form A, to identify students for reinforcement or extension.
3. After students have been identified for extension or reinforcement, break students into appropriate groups. See pages 859–861 for detailed differentiated instruction.

Differentiation Planner

Students who demonstrated mastery on every objective posttest and scored 80% or above on the chapter test

Extend learning using:

- **Gizmos** Use the *Quadratics in Polynomial Form—Activity A* Gizmo with the Extension Activity. Have students work in pairs or individually to complete the activity.

Students who demonstrated mastery on every objective posttest but scored below 80% on the chapter test

Reinforce learning using:

- **Gizmos** Use the *Modeling the Factorization of* $x^2 + bx + c$ Gizmo with the Reinforcement Activity. Have students work in pairs or small groups to complete the activity.
- Additional Activities from the online resources.
- Algebra Skill Builders for Chapter 9 from the online resources.

Students who did not demonstrate mastery on any or all of the objective posttests or the chapter test

Reinforce learning using:

- **Gizmos** Present the *Modeling the Factorization of* $x^2 + bx + c$ Gizmo to students in small groups using the instruction on page 861.
- Additional Activities from the online resources.
- Algebra Skill Builders for Chapter 9 from the online resources.

Retest—Administer Chapter 9 Test, Form B, from the online resources to students who scored below 80 percent on Form A when time allows.

NEXT STEPS • Pretest

- Administer Chapter 10, Objective 1 Pretest, page 864, to all students.

Differentiation, Teacher Guide, Chapter 9

Launch Extension Activity to differentiate.

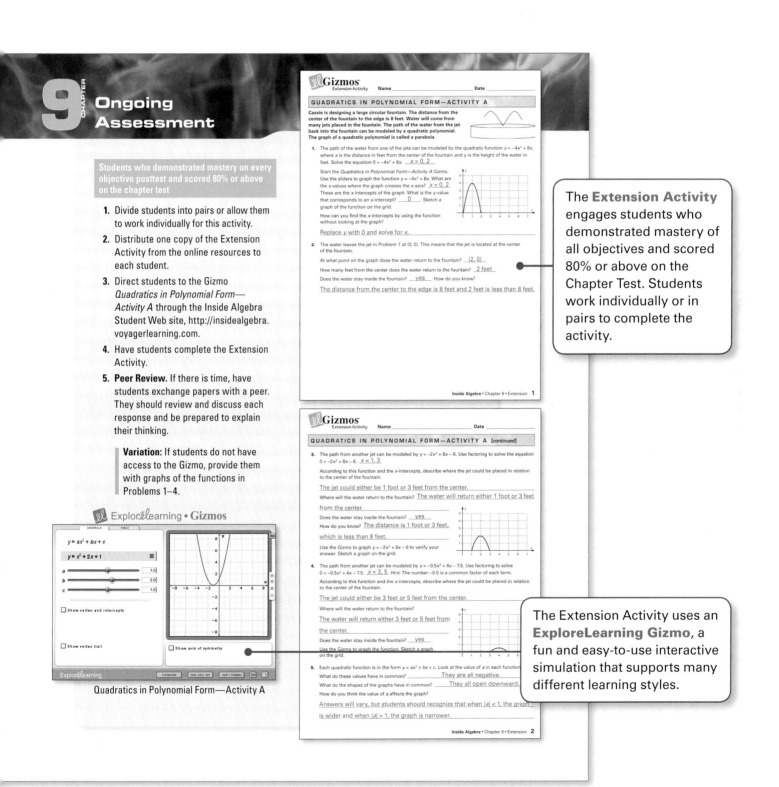

9 CHAPTER
Ongoing Assessment

Students who demonstrated mastery on every objective posttest and scored 80% or above on the chapter test

1. Divide students into pairs or allow them to work individually for this activity.

2. Distribute one copy of the Extension Activity from the online resources to each student.

3. Direct students to the Gizmo *Quadratics in Polynomial Form—Activity A* through the Inside Algebra Student Web site, http://insidealgebra.voyagerlearning.com.

4. Have students complete the Extension Activity.

5. **Peer Review.** If there is time, have students exchange papers with a peer. They should review and discuss each response and be prepared to explain their thinking.

   Variation: If students do not have access to the Gizmo, provide them with graphs of the functions in Problems 1–4.

Quadratics in Polynomial Form—Activity A

The **Extension Activity** engages students who demonstrated mastery of all objectives and scored 80% or above on the Chapter Test. Students work individually or in pairs to complete the activity.

The Extension Activity uses an **ExploreLearning Gizmo**, a fun and easy-to-use interactive simulation that supports many different learning styles.

Launch student-centered reinforcement to differentiate.

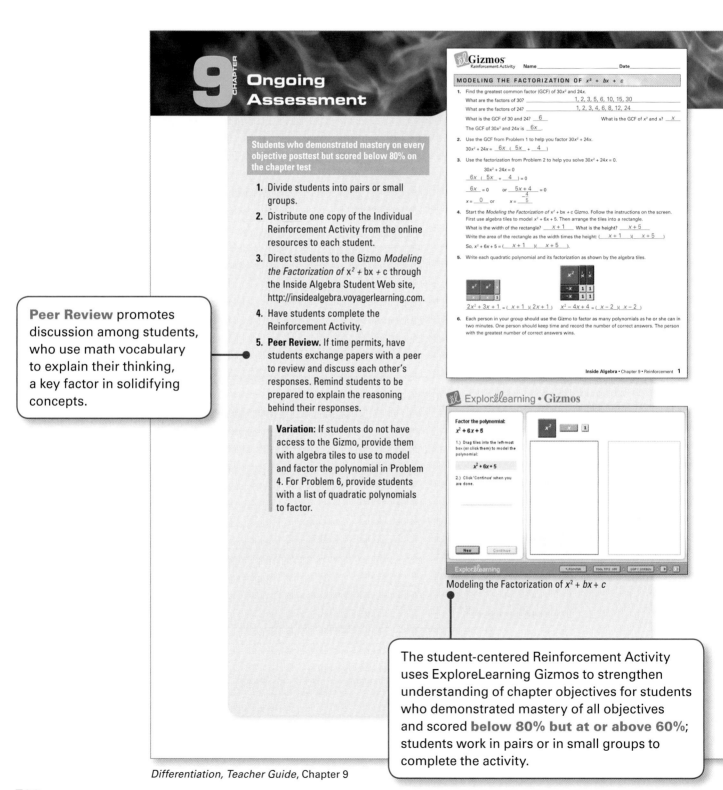

Peer Review promotes discussion among students, who use math vocabulary to explain their thinking, a key factor in solidifying concepts.

9 CHAPTER
Ongoing Assessment

Students who demonstrated mastery on every objective posttest but scored below 80% on the chapter test

1. Divide students into pairs or small groups.

2. Distribute one copy of the Individual Reinforcement Activity from the online resources to each student.

3. Direct students to the Gizmo *Modeling the Factorization of* x^2 + bx + c through the Inside Algebra Student Web site, http://insidealgebra.voyagerlearning.com.

4. Have students complete the Reinforcement Activity.

5. **Peer Review.** If time permits, have students exchange papers with a peer to review and discuss each other's responses. Remind students to be prepared to explain the reasoning behind their responses.

   Variation: If students do not have access to the Gizmo, provide them with algebra tiles to use to model and factor the polynomial in Problem 4. For Problem 6, provide students with a list of quadratic polynomials to factor.

Modeling the Factorization of x^2 + bx + c

The student-centered Reinforcement Activity uses ExploreLearning Gizmos to strengthen understanding of chapter objectives for students who demonstrated mastery of all objectives and scored **below 80% but at or above 60%**; students work in pairs or in small groups to complete the activity.

Differentiation, Teacher Guide, Chapter 9

Use the teacher Reinforcement Activity to differentiate.

> The teacher-led Reinforcement Activity uses ExploreLearning Gizmos and accompanying teacher directions to reteach key objectives for students who **did not demonstrate mastery of any or all objectives.**

9 CHAPTER Ongoing Assessment

Students who did not demonstrate mastery on any or all of the objective posttests or the chapter test

Note: The Gizmo is not needed to answer Problems 1–3, 5, and 6.

1. Ask students to find the greatest common factor (GCF) of $30x^2$ and $24x$.
   - Ask students to name the factors of 30 and 24. 30: 1, 2, 3, 5, 6, 10, 15, 30; 24: 1, 2, 3, 4, 6, 8, 12, 24 Ask for the common factors. 1, 2, 3, 6 Ask for the greatest common factor. 6
   - Ask students to name the greatest common factor of x^2 and x. x
   - Ask students to name the GCF of $30x^2$ and $24x$. $6x$

2. Ask students to factor $30x^2 + 24x$. Have students use their answer to Problem 1.
   - Ask students what $6x$ is multiplied by to get $30x^2$. $5x$ Ask students what $6x$ is multiplied by to get $24x$. 4
   - Ask students to use the Distributive Property and state the factored expression. $30x^2 + 24x = 6x(5x + 4)$

3. Ask students to solve $30x^2 + 24x = 0$. Use the answer to Problem 2. Remind students of the Zero Product Property.
   - Ask students what two equations they need to solve the problem. $6x = 0$ and $5x + 4 = 0$
   - Ask students to solve the equations. $x = 0$ and $x = -\frac{4}{5}$

4. Start the *Modeling the Factorization of* $x^2 + bx + c$ Gizmo.
   - Ask students to name the tiles needed to model $x^2 + 6x + 5$. Drag tiles into the left box as they answer. one x^2 tile, six x tiles, five unit tiles

   - Ask students to help you arrange the tiles into a rectangle to factor the expression. As you drag tiles into the right box, point out the width and height written along the top and left sides of the box.
   - After the rectangle is formed, ask students for the factors. $(x + 5)$ and $(x + 1)$

5. Arrange algebra tiles into a rectangle to show $2x^2 + 3x + 1 = (x + 1)(2x + 1)$. First ask students to name the expression shown by the tiles. $2x^2 + 3x + 1$ Next, ask them to name factors given by the length and width of the rectangle. $(x + 1)$ and $(2x + 1)$

6. Repeat the process in Problem 5 with $x^2 - 4x + 4 = (x - 2)(x - 2)$.

   Variation: If students do not have access to the Gizmo, use a blackboard or overhead projector and algebra tiles to complete the activity.

> The **Variation** describes how to complete the differentiation activities if the teacher or the students cannot access ExploreLearning Gizmos.

ExploreLearning • Gizmos

Modeling the Factorization of $x^2 + bx + c$

Developed With Instructional Strategies Grounded in Research

The evidence that students are not understanding algebra has sparked new research into what works and what does not work in algebra instruction. This research has raised concerns about the absence of important aspects of algebra instruction in many widely used curricula.

Larry Bradsby, past president of the National Council of Supervisors of Mathematics, created *Inside Algebra* with a team of experienced algebra instructors in order to respond to these concerns. Research findings on how students learn algebra and what components and methods in algebra instruction are likely to be effective validate the approach to instruction embodied in *Inside Algebra*. Each objective in the curriculum is supported by instructional strategies that have foundations in research.

Concept Development

Students are often taught that algebra is a sequence of steps rather than a set of concepts that can be meaningful and useful to them. As a consequence, students tend to memorize algorithms and miss the underlying concept. Equipped only with fragmented understanding, students often become confused when the problems they encounter become increasingly complex.

A more effective approach to teaching algebra is to teach concepts, emphasizing the "how" and "why" of what students are doing: how to solve problems, why they are using certain techniques, how and why the concept they have learned relates to new problems, and various procedures for solving them. Once students have mastered the concepts, they can move on to employing, combining, and relating multiple concepts when they are presented with more complex problems (Witzel et al., 2001).

Inside Algebra was designed using the philosophy that students must learn the concepts behind the skills before they are expected to apply skills and problem-solving strategies. Consequently, students are taught why a specific technique is appropriate as well as how to solve the problem. The Concept Development Activities in each objective align with various student needs. These activities utilize manipulatives and other hands-on approaches to provide students with concrete modeling experiences.

Practice Activities

In order to gain a true understanding of concepts and mastery of skills, students need focused practice time (Marzano, Pickering & Polluck, 2001). Practice gives students the chance to shape the skills they have learned into a conceptual understanding. If this does not occur, students may develop gaps in their learning and superficial understandings that will interfere with their ability to apply what they have learned to more complex problems, causing frustration and failure (Mathematical Sciences Education Board, 1990; Witzel et al., 2001).

Inside Algebra uses Practice Activities to reinforce concept learning and prepare students for more complex problem-solving exercises. The practice activities include games, projects, and problem solving for independent and group practice. This range of choices allows teachers to offer students practice opportunities that are closely aligned with their specific learning needs. Continuous practice is strongly supported in *Inside Algebra* in order to build understanding while strengthening motivation and confidence through personal success.

Focus on Objectives

Most students develop a deeper understanding of algebraic content when their learning is structured around an objective-based approach. In a well-designed, objective-based approach, students master objectives in a logical sequence in which new learning builds on the foundation of prior learning. This approach is consistent with the hierarchical structure of algebraic knowledge, and the designation of objectives gives students a focus so they are able to retain meaningful information and filter out information that is not relevant.

Objective-based teaching has been shown to be especially useful for teaching students with learning disabilities, because these students often have substantial difficulty retaining information (Ysseldyke, Thurlow, Langenfeld, Nelson, Teelucksingh & Seyfarth, 1998). Teaching to objectives and using a variety of activities until mastery is achieved is more likely to ensure student success than a lesson-based approach.

Inside Algebra is completely objective based, providing ongoing and differentiated activities to meet various student needs. Objectives are listed in a logical sequence and are clearly defined for students so learners always have a goal to reach and a focus to maintain. Several activities are provided for each objective so students have as much opportunity to practice as they might need. The activities vary in approach, offering individual as well as small-group and whole-class instruction; multisensory, hands-on activities; problem solving; and real-life challenges. This range of approaches empowers more students to absorb information naturally—in ways that are most comfortable and effective for them.

Explicit Instruction

When curricular design clearly defines concepts and skills and identifies the relationships between those concepts and skills, it is considered explicit (Woodward, 1991). Research findings show that more explicit math instruction improves student achievement (Montague, 1997). In one study, for example, a highly explicit math curriculum produced greater student achievement than a less explicit curriculum (Jitendra, Kameenui & Carnine, 1994). In another study involving secondary students with learning disabilities, students made greater improvement in the acquisition, application, maintenance, and generalization of information through explicit instruction than through traditional instruction (Montague, 1997).

Inside Algebra employs explicit instruction as a vital element of its design. Concepts and skills are clearly defined and students are provided with examples of all concepts so that relationships between the concepts and the skills are clear and explicit.

Hands-on and Manipulative-based Activities

Hands-on activities can make math relevant and interesting to students. Giving students the opportunity to work through abstract algebraic concepts with manipulatives and hands-on activities helps them see how concepts can be translated into real life. This instructional strategy is both engaging and accessible for most students (Devlin, 2000; Maccini & Gagnon, 2000). As a result, students are more interested in the concepts being taught—they can see how they make sense in concrete terms and they can grasp the content more easily. Many students, especially those with learning disabilities, need hands-on manipulatives and visual representations to help them understand abstract algebraic concepts.

Inside Algebra employs a variety of hands-on activities and manipulatives as tools for developing an understanding of abstract concepts. Every objective is supported by hands-on activities that quickly engage students and help them view concepts from a concrete perspective. Each activity includes detailed instructions and goals, enabling students to stay on task and understand the purpose behind the activity.

Cooperative Learning

Cooperative learning, or group investigation, denotes an instructional arrangement for teaching academic and collaborative skills to small, heterogeneous groups of students (Rich, 1993). Cooperative learning is supported by the NCTM (1991) and has been shown to benefit mathematics achievement in students with and without learning disabilities (Slavin, Leavy & Madden, 1984). Cooperative learning has also been shown to promote peer acceptance (Johnson & Johnson, 1986).

Inside Algebra offers many activities that involve dividing the class into small groups in which students interact in instructionally relevant ways and focus on explicit goals. Students are grouped heterogeneously so various levels of mathematical ability or achievement and social interaction skills are represented in each group. This approach promotes social acceptance and nurturance as well as a deeper understanding of algebra. Students collaboratively translate, explain, discuss, and solve problems and concepts in their own terms, thus deepening their understanding of the content.

Problem Solving

Problem-solving activities can foster deep and lasting learning in algebra. Problem solving also provides students with opportunities for self-evaluation through reflection on their strategies. When using a problem-solving approach, teachers should guide students through the activities with step-by-step directions—identifying problem areas for various students, helping students understand the significance of each step, and drawing attention to relationships between abstract and concrete concepts (Witzel et al., 2001; Miller & Mercer, 1997).

Inside Algebra provides Problem-Solving Activities to help students understand each objective. These activities require students to synthesize a variety of skills, solidify their understanding of concepts, and engage them in problem-solving strategies and reflective thinking. Additionally, many of the Practice Activities rely on problem-solving strategies and techniques.

Ongoing Assessment

Frequent assessment of student learning, with reference to student performance on specific tasks, is essential to effective instruction. Curriculum-based assessment, in which each student's progress is measured as she or he moves through the curriculum, generates data that can inform teachers' evaluations of student learning and progress. Teachers can use these data to develop an accurate assessment of each student's progress and design appropriate instructional interventions for students who are falling behind. Thus, the collection of data on student progress improves both instruction and student learning (Jones, Wilson & Bhojwani, 1997).

Inside Algebra's approach is based on setting objectives, diagnosing student comprehension, using this diagnosis to select appropriate instructional plans, evaluating students' understanding during and after learning, and recording data on student progress. Students are given a pretest to determine their learning needs. Teachers then use student performance on activities to monitor their progress. At the end of each objective, students are given a posttest to assess levels of mastery. To ensure that all students are successful, opportunities for further instruction are provided for students who have not achieved mastery.

References

Devlin, K. (2000). *Finding the inner mathematician*. The Chronicle of Higher Education, 46, B5.

Jitendra, A. K., Kameenui, E., & Carnine, D. (1994). An exploratory evaluation of dynamic assessment of the role of basals on comprehension of mathematical operations. *Education and Treatment of Children*, 17, 139–162.

Johnson, D. W., & Johnson, R. T. (1986). Mainstreaming and cooperative learning strategies. *Exceptional Children*, 52(6), 553–561.

Jones, E., Wilson, R., & Bhojwani S. (1997). Mathematics instruction for secondary students with learning disabilities. *Journal of Learning Disabilities*, 30(2), 151–163.

Maccini, P., & Gagnon, J. C. (2000). Best practices for teaching mathematics to secondary students with special needs. *Focus on Exceptional Children*, 32(5) 1–21.

Marzano, R. J., Pickering, D. J., & Polluck, J. E. (2001). *Classroom instruction that works: Research-based strategies for increasing student achievement*. Alexandria, VA: McREL/Association for Supervision and Curriculum Development (ASCD).

Mathematical Sciences Education Board. (1990). *Reshaping school mathematics*. Washington, D.C.: National Academy Press.

Miller, S. P., & Mercer, C. D. (1997). Educational aspects of mathematical disabilities. *Journal of Learning Disabilities*, 30(1), 47–56.

Montague, M. (1997). Cognitive strategy instruction in mathematics for students with learning disabilities. *Journal of Learning Disabilities*. 30(2), 164–178.

National Council of Teachers of Mathematics (NCTM). (1991). *Professional standards for teaching mathematics*. Reston, VA: NCTM.

Rich, Y. (1993). *Education and instruction in the heterogeneous class*. Springfield, IL: Charles C. Thomas.

Slavin, R. E., Leavey, M. B., & Madden, N. A. (1984). Combining cooperative learning and individualized instruction: Effects on student mathematics achievement, attitudes, and behaviors. *The Elementary School Journal*, 84(4), 409–422.

Wilson, C. L., & Sindelar, P. T. (1991). Direct instruction in math word problems: Students with learning disabilities. *Exceptional Children*, 57, 512–519.

Witzel, B., Smith, S. W., & Brownell, M. T. (2001). How can I help students with learning disabilities in algebra? *Intervention in School and Clinic*, 37(2), 101–104.

Woodward, J. (1991). Procedural knowledge in mathematics: The role of the curriculum. *Journal of Learning Disabilities*, 24, 242–251.

Ysseldyke, J. E., Thurlow, M. L., Langenfeld, K. L., Nelson, J. R., Teelucksingh, E., & Seyfarth, A. (1998). Educational results for students with disabilities: What do the data tell us? (Technical Rep. No. 23). Minneapolis, MN: National Center on Educational Outcomes.

Implementation Results

In a large urban New Mexico school district during the 2007–2008 school year, students with learning disabilities used *Inside Algebra* as the primary math program. In the implementation, students completed at least four lessons per week and teachers consistently used all the lesson components. Students showed an average improvement of 110%.

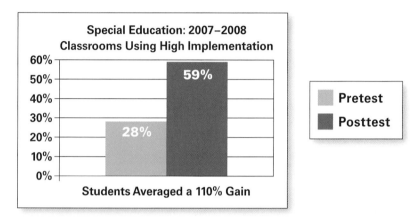

Special Education: 2007–2008
Classrooms Using High Implementation

Pretest 28%
Posttest 59%

Students Averaged a 110% Gain

In another implementation in the same district, students identified as low-achieving based on state assessment scores and at risk of failing algebra used *Inside Algebra* during the 2006–2007 school year. Of the more than 100 students, some used *Inside Algebra* as their core algebra program and others first attended their *Inside Algebra* classroom and then attended an additional session utilizing a traditional algebra program. The Pretest and Posttest scores for this group indicate that students showed remarkable gains.

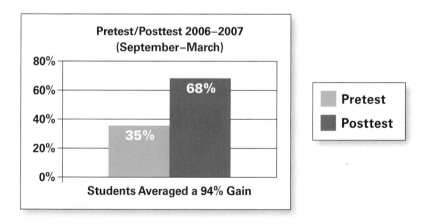

Pretest/Posttest 2006–2007
(September–March)

Pretest 35%
Posttest 68%

Students Averaged a 94% Gain

Scope and Sequence

Chapter 1—Variables and Expressions

Objective 1: Translate verbal expressions into mathematical expressions and vice versa.
Objective 2: Evaluate expressions using the order of operations.
Objective 3: Solve open sentences by performing arithmetic operations.
Objective 4: Use mathematical properties to evaluate expressions.

Chapter 2—Exploring Rational Numbers

Objective 1: Graph rational numbers on the number line.
Objective 2: Add and subtract rational numbers.
Objective 3: Compare and order rational numbers.
Objective 4: Multiply and divide rational numbers.
Objective 5: Find the principal square root of a number.

Chapter 3—Solving Linear Equations

Objective 1: Solve linear equations with addition and subtraction.
Objective 2: Solve linear equations with multiplication and division.
Objective 3: Solve linear equations using one or more operations.
Objective 4: Solve problems that can be represented as equations.
Objective 5: Solve proportions that have a missing part.
Objective 6: Use proportions to solve percent problems.

Chapter 4—Graphing Relations and Functions

Objective 1: Graph ordered pairs and relations.
Objective 2: Identify the domain, range, and the inverse of a relation.
Objective 3: Determine the range for a given domain of a relation.
Objective 4: Graph linear equations.
Objective 5: Determine whether a relation is a function, and find a value for a given function.

Chapter 5—Analyzing Linear Equations

Objective 1: Determine the slope given a line on a graph or two points on the line.
Objective 2: Write the equation of a line in standard form given two points on the line.
Objective 3: Draw a best-fit line, and find the equation of the best-fit line for a scatter plot.
Objective 4: Write linear equations in slope-intercept form to find the slope, x-intercept, and y-intercept, and sketch the graph.
Objective 5: Use the slope of lines to determine if two lines are parallel or perpendicular.

Chapter 6—Solving Linear Inequalities

Objective 1: Solve and graph the solution set of inequalities with addition and subtraction.
Objective 2: Solve and graph the solution set of inequalities with multiplication and division.
Objective 3: Solve and graph the solution set of inequalities using more than one operation.
Objective 4: Solve and graph the solution set of compound inequalities and inequalities involving absolute value.
Objective 5: Graph inequalities in the coordinate plane.

Chapter 7—Solving Systems of Linear Equations and Inequalities

Objective 1: Solve systems of equations by graphing.
Objective 2: Determine whether a system of equations has one solution, no solutions, or infinitely many solutions.
Objective 3: Solve systems of equations using the substitution method.
Objective 4: Solve systems of equations by eliminating one variable.
Objective 5: Solve systems of inequalities by graphing.

Chapter 8—Exploring Polynomials

Objective 1: Multiply and divide monomials and simplify expressions.
Objective 2: Write numbers in scientific notation and find products and quotients of these numbers.
Objective 3: Add and subtract polynomials and express the answer so the powers of the terms are in descending order.
Objective 4: Multiply a polynomial by a monomial and arrange the terms in descending order by powers.
Objective 5: Multiply two binomials and simplify the expressions, including special products of $(a + b)(a + b)$ and $(a + b)(a - b)$.

Chapter 9—Using Factoring

Objective 1: Find the greatest common factor through prime factorization for integers and sets of monomials.
Objective 2: Use the greatest common factor and the Distributive Property to factor polynomials with the grouping technique, and use these techniques to solve equations.
Objective 3: Factor quadratic trinomials of the form $ax^2 + bx + c$, and solve equations by factoring.
Objective 4: Factor quadratic polynomials that are perfect squares or differences of squares, and solve equations by factoring.
Objective 5: Solve quadratic equations by completing the square.

Chapter 10—Exploring Quadratic and Exponential Functions

Objective 1: Graph parabolas, and find the coordinates of the vertex and axis of symmetry.
Objective 2: Estimate the roots of a quadratic equation by graphing the associated function.
Objective 3: Solve quadratic equations by factoring or using the quadratic formula.
Objective 4: Graph exponential functions, and solve problems using the graphs.

Chapter 11—Exploring Rational Expressions and Equations

Objective 1: Simplify rational expressions.
Objective 2: Multiply and divide rational expressions.
Objective 3: Divide a polynomial by a binomial.
Objective 4: Add and subtract rational expressions.
Objective 5: Solve equations involving rational expressions.

Chapter 12—Exploring Radical Expressions and Equations

Objective 1: Simplify and perform operations with radical expressions.
Objective 2: Solve equations with radical expressions.
Objective 3: Use the Pythagorean theorem to solve problems.
Objective 4: Find the distance between two points in the coordinate plane.
Objective 5: Find the unknown measures of the sides of similar triangles.

Inside Algebra is aligned to the National Council of Teachers of Mathematics' *Principles and Standards for School Mathematics* (2000).

Key to Standards:
2.1–2.4: Algebra Content Standards; 6: Problem Solving; 7: Reasoning and Proof; 8: Communication; 9: Connections; 10: Representation

Objective	NCTM Standards
Chapter 1	
Objective 1	2.2, 6, 7, 8, 9, 10
Objective 2	2.1, 6, 7, 8, 9, 10
Objective 3	2.2, 6, 7, 8, 9, 10
Objective 4	2.1, 2.2, 2.3, 6, 7, 8, 9, 10
Chapter 2	
Objective 1	2.1, 6, 7, 8, 9, 10
Objective 2	2.1, 6, 7, 8, 9, 10
Objective 3	2.1, 6, 7, 8, 9, 10
Objective 4	2.1, 6, 7, 8, 9, 10
Objective 5	2.1, 6, 7, 8, 9, 10
Chapter 3	
Objective 1	2.2, 2.3, 6, 7, 8, 9, 10
Objective 2	2.2, 2.3, 6, 7, 8, 9, 10
Objective 3	2.2, 2.3, 6, 7, 8, 9, 10
Objective 4	2.2, 2.3, 6, 7, 8, 9, 10
Objective 5	2.2, 2.3, 6, 7, 8, 9, 10
Objective 6	2.2, 2.3, 6, 7, 8, 9, 10
Chapter 4	
Objective 1	2.1, 2.3, 6, 7, 8, 9, 10
Objective 2	2.1, 6, 7, 8, 9, 10
Objective 3	2.1, 6, 7, 8, 9, 10
Objective 4	2.1, 2.3, 6, 7, 8, 9, 10
Objective 5	2.1, 2.3, 6, 7, 8, 9, 10
Chapter 5	
Objective 1	2.2, 2.4, 6, 7, 8, 9, 10
Objective 2	2.2, 2.3, 6, 7, 8, 9, 10
Objective 3	2.3, 6, 7, 8, 9, 10
Objective 4	2.2, 2.3, 6, 7, 8, 9, 10
Objective 5	2.3, 6, 7, 8, 9, 10
Chapter 6	
Objective 1	2.2, 2.3, 2.4, 6, 7, 8, 9, 10
Objective 2	2.2, 6, 7, 8, 9, 10
Objective 3	2.2, 2.3, 6, 7, 8, 9, 10
Objective 4	2.2, 6, 7, 8, 9, 10
Objective 5	2.2, 2.4, 6, 7, 8, 9, 10

Objective	NCTM Standards
Chapter 7	
Objective 1	2.1, 2.2, 2.3, 2.4, 6, 7, 8, 9, 10
Objective 2	2.1, 2.2, 2.4, 6, 7, 8, 9, 10
Objective 3	2.1, 2.2, 2.3, 6, 7, 8, 9, 10
Objective 4	2.1, 2.3, 6, 7, 8, 9, 10
Objective 5	2.1, 2.2, 2.3, 2.4, 6, 7, 8, 9, 10
Chapter 8	
Objective 1	2.1, 2.2, 6, 7, 8, 9, 10
Objective 2	2.1, 2.2, 6, 7, 8, 9, 10
Objective 3	2.1, 2.2, 6, 7, 8, 9, 10
Objective 4	2.1, 2.2, 6, 7, 8, 9, 10
Objective 5	2.1, 2.2, 6, 7, 8, 9, 10
Chapter 9	
Objective 1	2.1, 2.2, 6, 7, 8, 9, 10
Objective 2	2.1, 2.2, 6, 7, 8, 9, 10
Objective 3	2.1, 2.2, 2.3, 6, 7, 8, 9, 10
Objective 4	2.1, 2.2, 2.3, 6, 7, 8, 9, 10
Objective 5	2.1, 2.2, 2.3, 6, 7, 8, 9, 10
Chapter 10	
Objective 1	2.1, 2.2, 2.3, 2.4, 6, 7, 8, 9, 10
Objective 2	2.1, 2.2, 2.3, 2.4, 6, 7, 8, 9, 10
Objective 3	2.1, 2.2, 6, 7, 8, 9, 10
Objective 4	2.1, 2.2, 2.3, 2.4, 6, 7, 8, 9, 10
Chapter 11	
Objective 1	2.1, 2.2, 6, 7, 8, 9, 10
Objective 2	2.1, 2.2, 6, 7, 8, 9, 10
Objective 3	2.1, 2.2, 6, 7, 8, 9, 10
Objective 4	2.1, 2.2, 6, 7, 8, 9, 10
Objective 5	2.1, 2.2, 2.3, 6, 7, 8, 9, 10
Chapter 12	
Objective 1	2.1, 2.2, 6, 7, 8, 9, 10
Objective 2	2.1, 2.2, 6, 7, 8, 9, 10
Objective 3	2.1, 2.2, 2.3, 2.4, 6, 7, 8, 9, 10
Objective 4	2.1, 2.2, 6, 7, 8, 9, 10
Objective 5	2.1, 2.2, 6, 7, 8, 9, 10

Variables and Expressions

In this chapter, students develop an understanding of expressions by comparing verbal and mathematical expressions. They discover and apply the order of operations to evaluate and simplify expressions and determine whether an expression is true, false, or open. Variables are introduced through substitution and in general representations of basic identities and properties.

Objective 1
Translate verbal expressions into mathematical expressions and vice versa.

Objective 2
Evaluate expressions using the order of operations.

Objective 3
Solve open sentences by performing arithmetic operations.

Objective 4
Use mathematical properties to evaluate expressions.

Chapter 1
VOCABULARY

Objective 1

Translate verbal expressions into mathematical expressions and vice versa.

Objective 1 Pretest

Students complete the Objective 1 Pretest at least one day before beginning Objective 1.

Using the Results

- Score the pretest and update the class record card.

- If the majority of students do not demonstrate mastery of the concepts, use the 4-Day Instructional Plan for Objective 1.

- If the majority of students demonstrate mastery of the concepts, use the 3-Day Instructional Plan for Objective 1.

Name _____ Date _____

Write a mathematical expression for each written expression.

1. The product of nine and twelve reduced by sixteen $9 \cdot 12 - 16$

2. Eight squared minus the quantity of four times six $8^2 - (4 \cdot 6)$

3. Seven increased by the product of thirteen and the number x

    $7 + 13x$

4. Ten multiplied by the quantity x plus seven $10(x + 7)$

5. The product of two and the square of x $2x^2$

Write a verbal expression for each mathematical expression.

6. $7 + (9 \cdot 3)$

    the sum of seven and the quantity nine times three

7. $(14 + 24) \cdot (7 - 2)$

    the product of the quantity fourteen plus twenty-four and the
    quantity seven minus two

8. $x^2 - 17$

    x squared minus seventeen

9. $(2y)^2$

    two times y, the quantity squared

10. $2 \cdot 17 - 5$

    two times seventeen minus five

Inside Algebra　　　　　　　　　　Chapter 1 • Objective 1　　**1**

CHAPTER 1 • Objective 1

PRETEST

Goals and Activities

Objective 1 Goals

The following activities, when used with the instructional plans on pages 4 and 5, enable students to:

- Write *three times nineteen decreased by twenty-seven* as

    3 · 19 − 27

- Write 29 − 3 · 7 as **twenty-nine minus three times seven**

Objective 1 Activities

Concept Development Activities

★CD 1 Finding Different Verbal Expressions for One Mathematical Expression, page 6

CD 2 Finding Different Verbal Expressions for One Mathematical Expression Involving Two Operations and Grouping Symbols, page 8

Practice Activities

★PA 1 Matching Verbal and Mathematical Expressions—Part 1, page 9

★PA 2 Matching Verbal and Mathematical Expressions—Part 2, page 10

PA 3 Writing Equivalent Verbal and Mathematical Expressions, page 12

Progress-Monitoring Activities

PM 1 Apply Skills 1, page 13

PM 2 Apply Skills 2, page 14

PM 3 Apply Skills 3, page 15

★Problem-Solving Activity

★PS 1 Creating Closely Related Verbal and Mathematical Expressions, page 16

Ongoing Assessment

Posttest Objective 1, page 17

Pretest Objective 2, page 18

CD = Concept Development   PM = Progress Monitoring   PS = Problem Solving
PA = Practice Activity   ★ = Includes Problem Solving

Instructional Plans

4-Day Instructional Plan

Use the 4-Day Instructional Plan when pretest results indicate that students would benefit from a slower pace. This plan is used when the majority of students need more time or did not demonstrate mastery on the pretest. This plan does not include all activities.

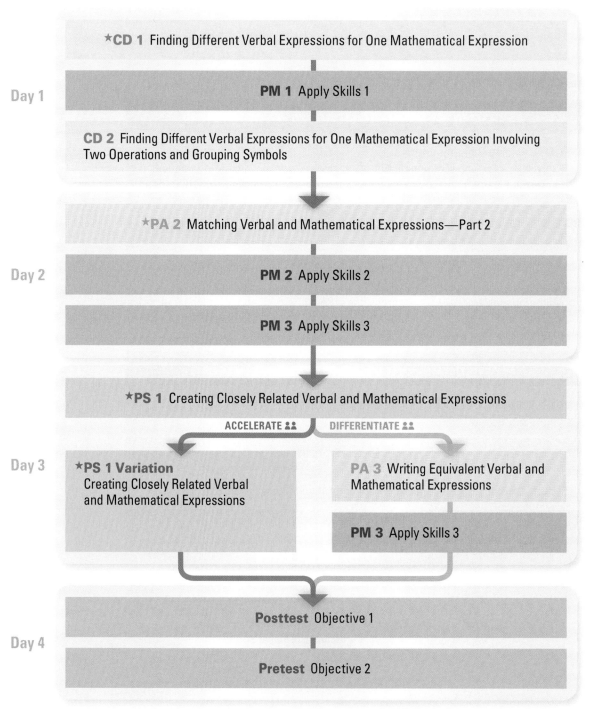

Day 1

★**CD 1** Finding Different Verbal Expressions for One Mathematical Expression

PM 1 Apply Skills 1

CD 2 Finding Different Verbal Expressions for One Mathematical Expression Involving Two Operations and Grouping Symbols

Day 2

★**PA 2** Matching Verbal and Mathematical Expressions—Part 2

PM 2 Apply Skills 2

PM 3 Apply Skills 3

Day 3

★**PS 1** Creating Closely Related Verbal and Mathematical Expressions

ACCELERATE ▲▲   DIFFERENTIATE ▲▲

★**PS 1 Variation** Creating Closely Related Verbal and Mathematical Expressions

PA 3 Writing Equivalent Verbal and Mathematical Expressions

PM 3 Apply Skills 3

Day 4

Posttest Objective 1

Pretest Objective 2

CD = Concept Development   PM = Progress Monitoring   PS = Problem Solving
PA = Practice Activity   ★ = Includes Problem Solving

3-Day Instructional Plan

Use the 3-Day Instructional Plan when pretest results indicate that students can move through the activities at a faster pace. This plan is ideal when the majority of students demonstrate mastery on the pretest. This plan does not include all activities.

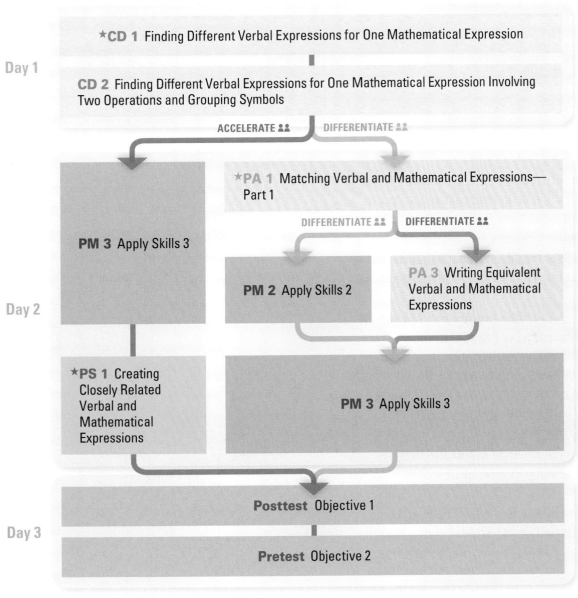

CD = Concept Development   PM = Progress Monitoring   PS = Problem Solving
PA = Practice Activity   ★ = Includes Problem Solving

Concept Development Activities

★ CD 1 Finding Different Verbal Expressions for One Mathematical Expression

Use with 4-Day or 3-Day Instructional Plan. In this activity, students verbally express simple mathematical expressions in multiple ways.

MATERIALS

- *Interactive Text*, page 3

DIRECTIONS

1. Have students turn to *Interactive Text*, page 3, Expressions 1, for this activity.

2. Call on different students to read aloud the verbal expressions for the mathematical expressions. Some problems may have to be repeated, depending on class size.

3. Skip to Step 5 for maximum inductive reasoning practice. Do Step 4 if the class seems to need more help.

4. Use the information from Expressions 1 to identify five or six different ways the addition of two numbers, such as the mathematical expression $5 + 2$, could be represented verbally. Do not identify the different ways of stating multiplication and subtraction. Let students discover them while performing Steps 5–7.

5. Write a new mathematical expression that uses multiplication on the board or overhead transparency.

6. Ask students to come to the board one at a time to write a different verbal expression for this new mathematical expression. Continue this process until four or five different but equivalent verbal expressions have been written for the new mathematical expression.

Name _____ Date _____

EXPRESSIONS 1

Mathematical Expression	Example Equivalent Verbal Expression
$3 + 9$	three plus nine
$7 \cdot 52$	seven times fifty-two
$18 - 3$	the difference of eighteen and three
$\left(\frac{1}{2}\right) + \left(\frac{3}{4}\right)$	one-half increased by three-fourths
$5\% \cdot 12$	five percent of twelve
$29 - 17$	twenty-nine minus seventeen
$25 + 13$	the sum of twenty-five and thirteen
$5 \cdot (-45)$	the product of five and negative forty-five
$84 - 33$	eighty-four reduced by thirty-three
$9 + 5$	the addends nine and five
$10 - 6$	six less than ten
$21 + 43$	forty-three more than twenty-one
$27 \cdot 86$	twenty-seven multiplied by eighty-six
$7 - 13$	thirteen subtracted from seven
$9 + 5$	five added to nine
$23 - (-4)$	twenty-three subtract a negative four

★ = Includes Problem Solving

7. Repeat the process in Steps 5 and 6 using a new expression each time that involves addition, multiplication, or subtraction. The expressions should involve only one operation.

Sample problems:

9 + 7
- nine *plus* seven
- the *sum of* nine and seven
- nine *added to* seven
- nine *increased by* seven
- seven *more than* nine

13 · 6
- thirteen *times* six
- *the product of* thirteen and six
- thirteen *by* six
- thirteen *multiplied by* six

27 − 9
- *the difference of* twenty-seven and nine
- twenty-seven *reduced by* nine
- nine *subtracted from* twenty-seven
- twenty-seven *minus* nine
- nine *less than* twenty-seven
- twenty-seven *subtract* nine

NEXT STEPS • Differentiate

4-Day Instructional Plan:
PM 1, page 13—All students, to assess progress

3-Day Instructional Plan:
CD 2, page 8—All students, for additional concept development

Objective 1

Concept Development Activities

CD 2 Finding Different Verbal Expressions for One Mathematical Expression Involving Two Operations and Grouping Symbols

Use with 4-Day or 3-Day Instructional Plan. In this activity, students verbally express more complex mathematical expressions in multiple ways.

MATERIALS

- *Interactive Text*, page 4

DIRECTIONS

1. Have students turn to *Interactive Text*, page 4, Expressions 2, for this activity.

2. Discuss the following terms with students:

   variable A letter or symbol used to represent a value or set of values

   algebraic expression An expression that includes variables

3. Call on different students to read aloud the verbal expressions for the mathematical expressions. Some problems may have to be repeated, depending on class size.

4. Divide the class into groups of four.

5. Assign each group a mathematical expression involving at least two operations and at least one pair of grouping symbols.

   Sample problems:

   $3(x - 7) - 19$ $\qquad$ $2(8 - 6)$

   $5 + 2(4x - 3x)$ $\qquad$ $(2 + 15) - 9 \cdot 3$

   | **Variation: Create Your Own** In Step 5, ask the groups to make up their own expressions.

6. Ask each group to write at least three different verbal expressions for their mathematical expression.

7. Ask one member of each group, one group at a time, to write the mathematical expression and the three different verbal expressions on the board.

8. Ask the other groups to evaluate the work of the group at the board. Offer extra credit points to each group that finds errors in the work on the board; offer extra credit points to the group at the board if there are no errors.

NEXT STEPS • Differentiate

4-Day Instructional Plan:
PA 2, page 10—All students, for additional practice and problem solving

3-Day Instructional Plan:
PM 3, page 15—Students who demonstrate understanding of the concepts, to assess progress

PA 1, page 9—Students who need additional practice

Name _____ Date _____

EXPRESSIONS 2

Mathematical Expression	Example Equivalent Verbal Expression
$9 - 2x$	two times x subtracted from nine
	two times x less than nine
	nine subtract the product of two and x
$3x - (x - 2)$	the product of three and x reduced by the quantity x decreased by two
	the quantity x minus two subtracted from three times x
	three multiplied by x subtract the quantity x reduced by two
$(x + 3)(x - 3)$	the quantity x increased by three multiplied by the quantity x decreased by three
	the quantity x plus three times the quantity x minus three
	the product of the quantity three added to x and the quantity three subtracted from x
$(5\%)(9 + 4)$	five percent of the quantity nine increased by four
	the product of five percent and the quantity nine plus four
	five percent of the quantity nine plus four
$3(x - 7) - 4$	three times the quantity x reduced by seven, minus four
	the product of three and the quantity x minus seven, subtract four
	the difference of three times the quantity x minus seven and four
$x - 3(x + 1)$	three times the quantity x plus one subtracted from x
	x minus three times the quantity x increased by one
	three times the quantity x plus one, less than x

4   Chapter 1 • Objective 1 • **CD 2**   Inside Algebra

---

8   Chapter 1 • Objective 1

Objective 1
Practice Activities

★ PA 1 Matching Verbal and Mathematical Expressions—Part 1

Use with 3-Day Instructional Plan. In this activity, students recognize when verbal expressions and mathematical expressions are equivalent.

MATERIALS

- *Interactive Text*, pages 5–6

DIRECTIONS

1. Have students work in groups of two.

2. Have students turn to *Interactive Text*, pages 5–6, Matching Verbal and Mathematical Expressions.

3. Discuss the following terms with students:

   power A number or variable that indicates repeated multiplication; x^y is the product of y copies of x

   square A number or variable raised to the second power; the product of two equal factors

   cube A number or variable raised to the third power

4. Have each pair of students solve the problems in the activity. Call on various groups to list their answers on the board.

5. Encourage other students to raise their hands and object if they disagree with the answer given.

6. Ask pairs of students to discuss the problems for which there are major disagreements.

7. Call on pairs of students to verbally justify the answer they think is correct. Discuss related examples until there is class agreement.

NEXT STEPS • Differentiate

👥 **3-Day Instructional Plan:**
   PM 2, page 14—Students who demonstrate understanding of the concepts, to assess progress

   PA 3, page 12—Students who need additional practice

★ = Includes Problem Solving

MATCHING VERBAL AND MATHEMATICAL EXPRESSIONS—PARTS 1 AND 2

Match each mathematical expression with the correct verbal expression.

Verbal Expression

1. three times nineteen ___aa___
2. the product of x and five plus four ___j___
3. the product of x and the quantity five increased by four ___w___
4. x plus five times x minus five ___f___
5. nine plus eleven minus four ___z___
6. five hundredths of seventeen ___u___
7. x plus two squared ___y___
8. x plus y, the quantity cubed ___ee___
9. five dollars increased by one and ninety-five hundredths dollars ___p___
10. two plus five, the quantity squared ___bb___
11. four-tenths of x, minus nine ___hh___
12. the product of the quantity x plus five and the quantity x minus five ___e___
13. eighteen ___ii___
14. nine decreased by seventeen ___a___
15. one-fifth of seventy-five percent ___kk___
16. the product of seven-hundredths and nine-hundredths ___m___
17. seven-hundredths percent times nine percent ___g___
18. seventy-nine hundredths minus the quantity of nine times five hundred forty-five thousandths ___v___
19. five-ninths of the quantity F minus thirty-two ___b___
20. x plus two, the quantity squared ___gg___

Mathematical Expression

a. $9 - 17$
b. $\left(\frac{5}{9}\right)(F - 32)$
c. $(7\%)(\$29.45)$
d. $(5\%)(17)$
e. $(x + 5)(x - 5)$
f. $x + 5x - 5$
g. $(0.07\%)(9\%)$
h. 16
i. $0.4(x - 9)$
j. $5x + 4$
k. $\left(\frac{1}{2}\right)(33\%)(120)$
l. $9 + \left(\frac{1}{2}\right)9$
m. $0.07(0.09)$
n. $-9 - 9$
o. $x + 5(x + 5)$
p. $\$5.00 + \$1.95$
q. $3x - 4$
r. $\left(\frac{9}{5}\right)C + 32$
s. $-9 - (-9)$
t. $4 - 4$

MATCHING VERBAL AND MATHEMATICAL EXPRESSIONS—PARTS 1 AND 2 *(continued)*

Verbal Expression

21. x plus five times the quantity x plus five ___o___
22. negative nine decreased by nine ___n___
23. three times the quantity x minus four ___ff___
24. four decreased by four ___t___
25. fifty percent of one-half ___nn___
26. five percent of seventeen ___d___
27. sixteen ___h___
28. nine increased by half of that same number ___l___
29. zero divided by nine ___jj___
30. seven percent of twenty-nine and forty-five hundredths dollars ___c___
31. nine-fifths of C increased by thirty-two ___r___
32. half of x plus three subtract half of x subtract three ___dd___
33. negative nine minus negative nine ___s___
34. four-tenths of the quantity x minus nine ___i___
35. one-half of the sum of eleven, twelve, and thirteen ___ll___
36. one-third of x increased by thirteen ___mm___
37. half of the quantity x plus three, decreased by half of the quantity x minus three ___cc___
38. half of thirty-three percent of one hundred twenty ___k___
39. zero ___x___
40. three times x minus four ___q___

Mathematical Expression

u. $0.05(17)$
v. $0.79 - 9(0.545)$
w. $x(5 + 4)$
x. 0
y. $x + 2^2$
z. $9 + 11 - 4$
aa. $3(19)$
bb. $(2 + 5)^2$
cc. $\left(\frac{1}{2}\right)(x + 3) - \left(\frac{1}{2}\right)(x - 3)$
dd. $\left(\frac{1}{2}\right)x + 3 - \left(\frac{1}{2}\right)x - 3$
ee. $(x + y)^3$
ff. $3(x - 4)$
gg. $(x + 2)^2$
hh. $0.4x - 9$
ii. 18
jj. $\frac{0}{9}$
kk. $\left(\frac{1}{5}\right)75\%$
ll. $\left(\frac{1}{2}\right)(11 + 12 + 13)$
mm. $\left(\frac{1}{3}\right)x + 13$
nn. $50\%\left(\frac{1}{2}\right)$

Practice Activities

★PA 2 Matching Verbal and Mathematical Expressions—Part 2

Use with 4-Day Instructional Plan. In this activity, students recognize when verbal expressions and mathematical expressions are equivalent.

MATERIALS

- *Interactive Text*, pages 5–6
- Blackline Masters 1–2
- Container for trimmed mathematical expressions
- Scissors

DIRECTIONS

1. Cut out the mathematical expressions on Blackline Masters 1–2, Matching Verbal and Mathematical Expressions.

2. Put the slips of paper in a container.

3. Have students turn to *Interactive Text*, pages 5–6, Matching Verbal and Mathematical Expressions.

4. Discuss the following terms with students:

   power A number or variable that indicates repeated multiplication; x^y is the product of y copies of x

   square A number or variable raised to the second power; the product of two equal factors

   cube A number or variable raised to the third power

5. Have students take turns drawing one slip.

6. Have students find the verbal expression in the *Interactive Text* that matches their selection and have them write the matching verbal expression on the slip. List each answer on the board or overhead.

★ = Includes Problem Solving

10 Chapter 1 • Objective 1

Name _____ Date _____

1

MATCHING VERBAL AND MATHEMATICAL EXPRESSIONS

$9 - 17$	nine decreased by seventeen
$\left(\frac{5}{9}\right)(F - 32)$	five-ninths of the quantity F minus thirty-two
$(7\%)(\$29.45)$	seven percent of twenty-nine and forty-five hundredths dollars
$(5\%)(17)$	five percent of seventeen
$(x + 5)(x - 5)$	the product of the quantity x plus five and the quantity x minus five
$x + 5x - 5$	x plus five times x minus five
$(0.07\%)(9\%)$	seven-hundredths percent times nine percent
16	sixteen
$0.4(x - 9)$	four-tenths of the quantity x minus nine
$5x + 4$	the product of x and five plus four
$\left(\frac{1}{2}\right)(33\%)(120)$	half of thirty-three percent of one hundred twenty
$9 + \left(\frac{1}{2}\right)9$	nine increased by half of that same number
$0.07(0.09)$	the product of seven-hundredths and nine-hundredths
$-9 - 9$	negative nine decreased by nine
$x + 5(x + 5)$	x plus five times the quantity x plus five
$\$5.00 + \$1.95$	five dollars increased by one and ninety-five one-hundredths dollars
$3x - 4$	three times x minus four
$\left(\frac{9}{5}\right)C + 32$	nine-fifths of C increased by thirty-two
$-9 - (-9)$	negative nine minus negative nine

Name _____ Date _____

2

MATCHING VERBAL AND MATHEMATICAL EXPRESSIONS *(continued)*

$4 - 4$	four decreased by four
$0.05(17)$	five one-hundredths of seventeen
$0.79 - 9(0.545)$	seventy-nine hundredths minus the quantity of nine times five hundred forty-five thousandths
0	zero
$x + 2^2$	x plus two squared
$9 + 11 - 4$	nine plus eleven minus four
$3(19)$	three times nineteen
$(2 + 5)^2$	two plus five, the quantity squared
$\left(\frac{1}{2}\right)(x + 3) - \left(\frac{1}{2}\right)(x - 3)$	half of the quantity x plus three, decreased by half of the quantity x minus three
$\left(\frac{1}{2}\right)x + 3 - \left(\frac{1}{2}\right)x - 3$	half of x plus three subtract half of x subtract three
$(x + y)^3$	x plus y, the quantity cubed
$3(x - 4)$	three times the quantity x minus four
$(x + 2)^2$	x plus two, the quantity squared
$0.4x - 9$	four-tenths of x, minus nine
18	eighteen
$\left(\frac{0}{9}\right)$	zero divided by nine
$\left(\frac{1}{5}\right)75\%$	one-fifth of seventy-five percent
$\left(\frac{1}{2}\right)(11 + 12 + 13)$	one-half of the sum of eleven, twelve, and thirteen
$\left(\frac{1}{3}\right)x + 13$	one-third of x increased by thirteen
$50\%\left(\frac{1}{2}\right)$	fifty percent of one-half

7. Encourage other students to raise their hands and object if they disagree with the answer given.

8. Discuss the problems for which there are major disagreements.

9. Invite students to verbally justify the answer they think is correct.

NEXT STEPS • Differentiate

4-Day Instructional Plan:
PM 2, page 14—All students, to assess progress

MATCHING VERBAL AND MATHEMATICAL EXPRESSIONS—PARTS 1 AND 2

Match each mathematical expression with the correct verbal expression.

Verbal Expression

1. three times nineteen ___aa___
2. the product of x and five plus four ___j___
3. the product of x and the quantity five increased by four ___w___
4. x plus five times x minus five ___f___
5. nine plus eleven minus four ___z___
6. five hundredths of seventeen ___u___
7. x plus two squared ___y___
8. x plus y, the quantity cubed ___ee___
9. five dollars increased by one and ninety-five hundredths dollars ___p___
10. two plus five, the quantity squared ___bb___
11. four-tenths of x, minus nine ___hh___
12. the product of the quantity x plus five and the quantity x minus five ___e___
13. eighteen ___ii___
14. nine decreased by seventeen ___a___
15. one-fifth of seventy-five percent ___kk___
16. the product of seven-hundredths and nine-hundredths ___m___
17. seven-hundredths percent times nine percent ___g___
18. seventy-nine hundredths minus the quantity of nine times five hundred forty-five thousandths ___v___
19. five-ninths of the quantity F minus thirty-two ___b___
20. x plus two, the quantity squared ___gg___

Mathematical Expression

a. $9 - 17$
b. $\left(\frac{5}{9}\right)(F - 32)$
c. $(7\%)(\$29.45)$
d. $(5\%)(17)$
e. $(x + 5)(x - 5)$
f. $x + 5x - 5$
g. $(0.07\%)(9\%)$
h. 16
i. $0.4(x - 9)$
j. $5x + 4$
k. $\left(\frac{1}{2}\right)(33\%)(120)$
l. $9 + \left(\frac{1}{2}\right)9$
m. $0.07(0.09)$
n. $-9 - 9$
o. $x + 5(x + 5)$
p. $\$5.00 + \$1.95$
q. $3x - 4$
r. $\left(\frac{9}{5}\right)C + 32$
s. $-9 - (-9)$
t. $4 - 4$

MATCHING VERBAL AND MATHEMATICAL EXPRESSIONS—PARTS 1 AND 2 *(continued)*

Verbal Expression

21. x plus five times the quantity x plus five ___o___
22. negative nine decreased by nine ___n___
23. three times the quantity x minus four ___ff___
24. four decreased by four ___t___
25. fifty percent of one-half ___nn___
26. five percent of seventeen ___d___
27. sixteen ___h___
28. nine increased by half of that same number ___l___
29. zero divided by nine ___jj___
30. seven percent of twenty-nine and forty-five hundredths dollars ___c___
31. nine-fifths of C increased by thirty-two ___r___
32. half of x plus three subtract half of x subtract three ___dd___
33. negative nine minus negative nine ___s___
34. four-tenths of the quantity x minus nine ___i___
35. one-half of the sum of eleven, twelve, and thirteen ___ll___
36. one-third of x increased by thirteen ___mm___
37. half of the quantity x plus three, decreased by half of the quantity x minus three ___cc___
38. half of thirty-three percent of one hundred twenty ___k___
39. zero ___x___
40. three times x minus four ___q___

Mathematical Expression

u. $0.05(17)$
v. $0.79 - 9(0.545)$
w. $x(5 + 4)$
x. 0
y. $x + 2^2$
z. $9 + 11 - 4$
aa. $3(19)$
bb. $(2 + 5)^2$
cc. $\left(\frac{1}{2}\right)(x + 3) - \left(\frac{1}{2}\right)(x - 3)$
dd. $\left(\frac{1}{2}\right)x + 3 - \left(\frac{1}{2}\right)x - 3$
ee. $(x + y)^3$
ff. $3(x - 4)$
gg. $(x + 2)^2$
hh. $0.4x - 9$
ii. 18
jj. $\frac{0}{9}$
kk. $\left(\frac{1}{5}\right)75\%$
ll. $\left(\frac{1}{2}\right)(11 + 12 + 13)$
mm. $\left(\frac{1}{3}\right)x + 13$
nn. $50\%\left(\frac{1}{2}\right)$

Practice Activities

PA 3 Writing Equivalent Verbal and Mathematical Expressions

Use with 4-Day or 3-Day Instructional Plan. In this activity, students recognize when verbal expressions and mathematical expressions are equivalent.

MATERIALS

- *Interactive Text*, page 7

DIRECTIONS

1. Have students work in pairs.

2. Have students turn to *Interactive Text*, page 7, Writing Verbal and Mathematical Expressions.

3. Ask each student pair to complete the activity by filling in the missing verbal and mathematical expressions.

4. Have each pair exchange papers with another pair when they are finished and ask them to check each other's work.

5. When all student pairs are finished with their checking, ask one pair to write an incorrect answer they found along with their correction on the board.

6. Discuss as many examples as possible in this way, using data generated by the students.

7. Have the class reach consensus on the correct answer for each example presented.

NEXT STEPS • Differentiate

4-Day and 3-Day Instructional Plans:
PM 3, page 15—All students, to assess progress

WRITING VERBAL AND MATHEMATICAL EXPRESSIONS

Write the equivalent verbal or mathematical expressions in the corresponding spaces.

	Verbal Expression	Mathematical Expression
1.	seven hundredths multiplied by the quantity x plus one	$0.07(x + 1)$
2.	the product of twenty-nine and x increased by the quantity x plus seven	$29x + (x + 7)$
3.	seventeen minus the product of three and x minus the quantity three minus x	$17 - 3x - (3 - x)$
4.	the product of seven-hundredths and x reduced by five	$0.07x - 5$
5.	the quantity x minus seven multiplied by the quantity three times x plus four	$(x - 7)(3x + 4)$
6.	x times y times z minus the quantity nine minus seven	$xyz - (9 - 7)$
7.	seventeen increased by nine decreased by x decreased by the product of three and x	$17 + 9 - x - 3x$
8.	the quantity x minus five multiplied by the quantity x plus five	$(x - 5)(x + 5)$
9.	x minus the product of five and x increased by 5	$x - 5x + 5$
10.	seventeen reduced by the product of six and x	$17 - 6x$
11.	forty-three minus nine	$43 - 9$
12.	nine times x minus seventeen plus three	$9x - 17 + 3$
13.	nine times x minus seventeen multiplied by the quantity x plus three	$9x - 17(x + 3)$

Inside Algebra   Chapter 1 • Objective 1 • PA 3 **7**

Objective 1
Progress-Monitoring Activities

PM 1 Apply Skills 1

Use with 4-Day Instructional Plan.

MATERIALS

- *Interactive Text*, page 8

DIRECTIONS

1. Have students turn to *Interactive Text*, page 8, Apply Skills 1.

2. Remind students of the key term: *variable*.

3. Monitor student work, and provide feedback as necessary.

   Watch for:

   - Do students see that the phrase *the quantity* means to take the associated part of the number sentence as a whole?

   - Do students write the mathematical expression in the correct order?

   - Do students understand implied multiplication?

   - Do students use strategies such as underlining to understand the verbal expressions?

NEXT STEPS • Differentiate

4-Day Instructional Plan:
CD 2, page 8—All students, for additional concept development

---

APPLY SKILLS 1

Write the equivalent mathematical expression for the given verbal expression.

Verbal Expression	Mathematical Expression
1. seven plus three	$7 + 3$
2. six subtracted from nine	$9 - 6$
3. the product of two and seven	$2 \cdot 7$
4. ten increased by seven	$10 + 7$
5. five plus two times nine	$5 + 2 \cdot 9$
6. four times seven minus twenty	$4 \cdot 7 - 20$
7. five times the quantity three plus one	$5(3 + 1)$
8. x increased by three	$x + 3$
9. six subtracted from y	$y - 6$
10. the product of two and a	$2a$
11. x added to seven	$7 + x$
12. five plus two times y	$5 + 2y$
13. four times x minus twenty	$4x - 20$
14. five times the quantity x plus one	$5(x + 1)$
15. the quantity x plus four multiplied by eight	$(x + 4)8$
16. the sum of seven and nine times x	$7 + 9x$
17. the quantity of x minus two times the quantity of x plus one	$(x - 2)(x + 1)$
18. six plus four times x minus seventeen	$6 + 4x - 17$

PM 2 Apply Skills 2

Use with 4-Day or 3-Day Instructional Plan.

MATERIALS

- *Interactive Text*, page 9

DIRECTIONS

1. Have students turn to *Interactive Text*, page 9, Apply Skills 2.

2. Remind students of the key terms: *power*, *square*, and *cube*.

3. Monitor student work, and provide feedback as necessary.

   Watch for:

   - Do students correctly represent parentheses with grouping words?

   - Do students use strategies such as underlining to understand the mathematical expressions?

NEXT STEPS • Differentiate

4-Day and 3-Day Instructional Plans:
PM 3, page 15—All students, for additional progress assessment

---

Name _____ Date _____

APPLY SKILLS 2

Write an equivalent verbal expression for the given mathematical expression.

Mathematical Expression	Verbal Expression
1. $7 + 8$	seven plus eight
2. $2x$	two times x
3. $2 \cdot 3 + 1$	two times three plus one
4. $3 \cdot 6 - 1$	three times six minus one
5. $5x - 4$	five times x minus four
6. $3x^2$	three times x squared
7. $3(x + 1)^2$	three times the quantity x plus one, squared
8. $2^2 - 4$	two squared minus four
9. $(x + 2)^2$	the quantity x plus two, squared
10. $x + 2^2$	x plus two squared
11. $5x - 9$	five times x minus nine
12. $x^2 + y^2$	x squared plus y squared
13. $(x + y)^2$	x plus y, the quantity squared
14. $7x^2 + 2x + 3$	seven times x squared plus two times x plus three
15. $3x^2 + 4y - 5$	three times x squared plus four times y minus five

Progress-Monitoring Activities

PM 3 Apply Skills 3

Use with 4-Day or 3-Day Instructional Plan.

MATERIALS

- *Interactive Text*, page 10

DIRECTIONS

1. Have students turn to *Interactive Text,* page 10, Apply Skills 3.

2. Remind students of the key terms: *power*, *square*, and *cube*.

3. Monitor student work, and provide feedback as necessary.

   Watch for:
   - Do students write *x*2 when they mean x^2 or $2x$?
   - Do students try to simplify the problem before matching?

NEXT STEPS • Differentiate

👥 4-Day Instructional Plan:

PS 1, page 16—Students who are completing the activity for the first time, to develop problem-solving skills

Objective 1 Posttest, page 17—Students who are completing the activity for the second time

👥 3-Day Instructional Plan:

PS 1, page 16—Students who are on the accelerated path, to develop problem-solving skills

Objective 1 Posttest, page 17—Students who are on the differentiated path

---

Name _____ Date _____

APPLY SKILLS 3

Fill in the missing equivalent verbal or mathematical expressions.

	Verbal Expression	Mathematical Expression
1.	thirteen increased by the factors two and two	$13 + 2(2)$
2.	five plus two cubed, the quantity times two decreased by five	$(5 + 2^3)2 - 5$
3.	five percent of seven percent of thirteen	$(5\%)(7\%)13$
4.	seven times three minus four	$7(3) - 4$
5.	the product of nine and seven, the quantity squared	$[9(7)]^2$
6.	three squared decreased by the product of seventeen and negative two	$3^2 - 17(-2)$
7.	the difference between the sum of seven and nine and the sum of nine and eleven	$(7 + 9) - (9 + 11)$
8.	five minus seven, the quantity multiplied by two	$(5 - 7)2$
9.	fifty-two thousandths times nine and ninety-eight hundredths dollars	$0.052(\$9.98)$
10.	seven and five-tenths percent of one dollar and ninety-five cents	$(7.5\%)(\$1.95)$
11.	the product of three and seven increased by nine	$3(7) + 9$
12.	three times the sum of seven and nine	$3(7 + 9)$
13.	two cubed minus seven squared	$2^3 - 7^2$
14.	two cubed minus seven, the quantity squared	$(2^3 - 7)^2$

Problem-Solving Activity

★ PS 1 Creating Closely Related Verbal and Mathematical Expressions

Use with 4-Day or 3-Day Instructional Plan. In this activity, students will correctly verbalize similar mathematical expressions.

MATERIALS

- Large sheets of chart paper or newsprint
- Marking pens
- Blank 3 × 5 inch cards

DIRECTIONS

1. Divide the class into groups of three.
2. Give each group one sheet of chart paper and a marking pen.
3. Direct each group to write two closely related mathematical expressions on the chart paper, one at the top and one in the middle.

   Sample answers:

   $(x + 5)(x - 5)$ and $(x + 5x - 5)$

   $3(x + 3) - 3(x - 3)$ and $3x + 3 - 3x - 3$

4. Post each group's chart paper on the wall, and distribute four blank 3 × 5 inch cards to each group.
5. Ask each group to study another group's work and write an equivalent verbal expression for each mathematical expression on separate 3 × 5 inch cards. Have the groups tape the cards on the newsprint below the corresponding mathematical expression.
6. Have the groups move on to another group's newsprint and repeat Step 5. Each group should write a different verbal expression.
7. Ask each group to check the cards on their own newsprint. The groups should mark a large C by each correct card. They should mark a large X by each incorrect card.

8. Have the class discuss the incorrect cards on each newsprint and come to consensus about the correct answer. They should then, if necessary, post a new card with the correct verbal expression.

   | **Variation:** Reverse the process on another day, starting with student-generated verbal expressions and moving to mathematical expressions.

NEXT STEPS • Differentiate

👥 4-Day Instructional Plan:

PS 1 Variation, page 16—Students who demonstrate understanding of the concept to develop problem-solving skills

PA 3, page 12—Students who need additional practice

4-Day Instructional Plan (Variation):

Objective 1 Posttest, page 17—All students

3-Day Instructional Plan:

Objective 1 Posttest, page 17—All students

★ = Includes Problem Solving

Objective 1 Posttest

Discuss with students the key concepts in Objective 1. Following the discussion, administer the Objective 1 Posttest to all students.

Using the Results

- Score the posttest and update the class record card.

- Provide reinforcement for students who do not demonstrate mastery of the concepts through individual or small-group reteaching of key concepts.

Name _____ Date _____

Write a mathematical expression for each written expression.

1. Six times the quantity of nine minus six _____ $6(9 - 6)$ _____

2. The sum of eight squared and the quantity four times eleven

   _____ $8^2 + (4 \cdot 11)$ _____

3. Three times x minus seven _____ $3x - 7$ _____

4. Nine multiplied by x squared _____ $9x^2$ _____

5. The product of the quantity x plus five and the quantity x minus five

   _____ $(x + 5)(x - 5)$ _____

Write a verbal expression for each mathematical expression.

6. $(8 + 4) \cdot 8 + 4$

   the quantity eight plus four times eight plus four _____

7. $(4 + 5) \cdot (2 + 17)$

   the product of the quantity four plus five and the quantity two

   plus seventeen _____

8. $3(x + 2)$

   three times the quantity x plus two _____

9. $(x + 2)^2$

   x plus two, the quantity squared _____

10. $3x + 5$

    three times x increased by five _____

Inside Algebra   Chapter 1 • Objective 1   **3**

CHAPTER 1 • Objective 1
POSTTEST

Objective 2
Evaluate expressions using the order of operations.

Objective 2 Pretest

Students complete the Objective 2 Pretest on the same day as the Objective 1 Posttest.

Using the Results

- Score the pretest and update the class record card.

- If the majority of students do not demonstrate mastery of the concepts, use the 5-Day Instructional Plan for Objective 2.

- If the majority of students demonstrate mastery of the concepts, use the 3-Day Instructional Plan for Objective 2.

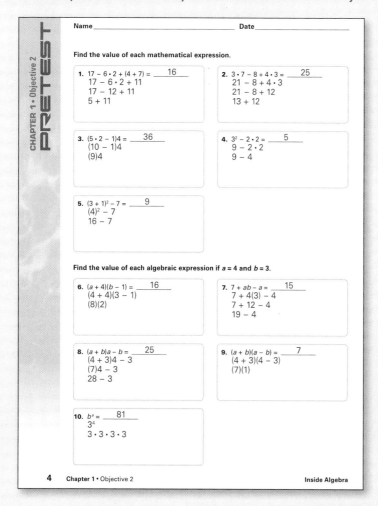

Name _____ Date _____

CHAPTER 1 • Objective 2
PRETEST

Find the value of each mathematical expression.

1. $17 - 6 \cdot 2 + (4 + 7) = $ ___16___
$17 - 6 \cdot 2 + 11$
$17 - 12 + 11$
$5 + 11$

2. $3 \cdot 7 - 8 + 4 \cdot 3 = $ ___25___
$21 - 8 + 4 \cdot 3$
$21 - 8 + 12$
$13 + 12$

3. $(5 \cdot 2 - 1)4 = $ ___36___
$(10 - 1)4$
$(9)4$

4. $3^2 - 2 \cdot 2 = $ ___5___
$9 - 2 \cdot 2$
$9 - 4$

5. $(3 + 1)^2 - 7 = $ ___9___
$(4)^2 - 7$
$16 - 7$

Find the value of each algebraic expression if $a = 4$ and $b = 3$.

6. $(a + 4)(b - 1) = $ ___16___
$(4 + 4)(3 - 1)$
$(8)(2)$

7. $7 + ab - a = $ ___15___
$7 + 4(3) - 4$
$7 + 12 - 4$
$19 - 4$

8. $(a + b)a - b = $ ___25___
$(4 + 3)4 - 3$
$(7)4 - 3$
$28 - 3$

9. $(a + b)(a - b) = $ ___7___
$(4 + 3)(4 - 3)$
$(7)(1)$

10. $b^a = $ ___81___
3^4
$3 \cdot 3 \cdot 3 \cdot 3$

4 Chapter 1 • Objective 2   Inside Algebra

18 Chapter 1 • Objective 2

Goals and Activities

Objective 2 Goals

The following activities, when used with the instructional plans on pages 20 and 21, enable students to:

- Evaluate the expression $14 - 6 \cdot 2 + 8 - 10$ to get **0**
- Evaluate the expression $5 \cdot 5 - 3 - 7 \cdot 2$ to get **8**

Objective 2 Activities

Concept Development Activities

★**CD 1** Understanding the Order of Operations in Addition and Multiplication, page 22	**CD 2** Writing Powers and Division as Forms of Multiplication, page 24	★**CD 3** Substituting Values for Variables, page 25	★**CD 4** Inserting Grouping Symbols to Correct Equations, page 26

Practice Activities

PA 1 Practicing the Four Operations With Operation Bingo, page 27	**PA 2** Calculating Correctly Without Parentheses, page 28

Progress-Monitoring Activities

PM 1 Apply Skills 1, page 29	**PM 2** Apply Skills 2, page 30	**PM 3** Apply Skills 3, page 31

★Problem-Solving Activity

★**PS 1** Inserting Parentheses to Get Different Values, page 32

Ongoing Assessment

Posttest Objective 2, page 33

Pretest Objective 3, page 34

CD = Concept Development   PM = Progress Monitoring   PS = Problem Solving
PA = Practice Activity   ★ = Includes Problem Solving

Instructional Plans

5-Day Instructional Plan

Use the 5-Day Instructional Plan when pretest results indicate that students would benefit from a slower pace. This plan is used when the majority of students need more time or did not demonstrate mastery on the pretest.

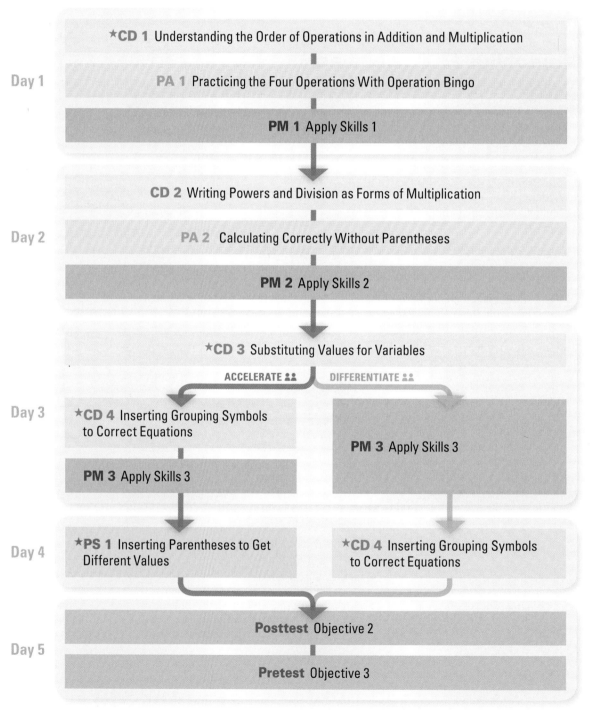

Day 1
★CD 1 Understanding the Order of Operations in Addition and Multiplication
PA 1 Practicing the Four Operations With Operation Bingo
PM 1 Apply Skills 1

Day 2
CD 2 Writing Powers and Division as Forms of Multiplication
PA 2 Calculating Correctly Without Parentheses
PM 2 Apply Skills 2

Day 3
★CD 3 Substituting Values for Variables
ACCELERATE / DIFFERENTIATE
★CD 4 Inserting Grouping Symbols to Correct Equations
PM 3 Apply Skills 3
PM 3 Apply Skills 3

Day 4
★PS 1 Inserting Parentheses to Get Different Values
★CD 4 Inserting Grouping Symbols to Correct Equations

Day 5
Posttest Objective 2
Pretest Objective 3

CD = Concept Development PM = Progress Monitoring PS = Problem Solving
PA = Practice Activity ★ = Includes Problem Solving

3-Day Instructional Plan

Use the 3-Day Instructional Plan when pretest results indicate that students can move through the activities at a faster pace. This plan is ideal when the majority of students demonstrate mastery on the pretest. This plan does not include all activities.

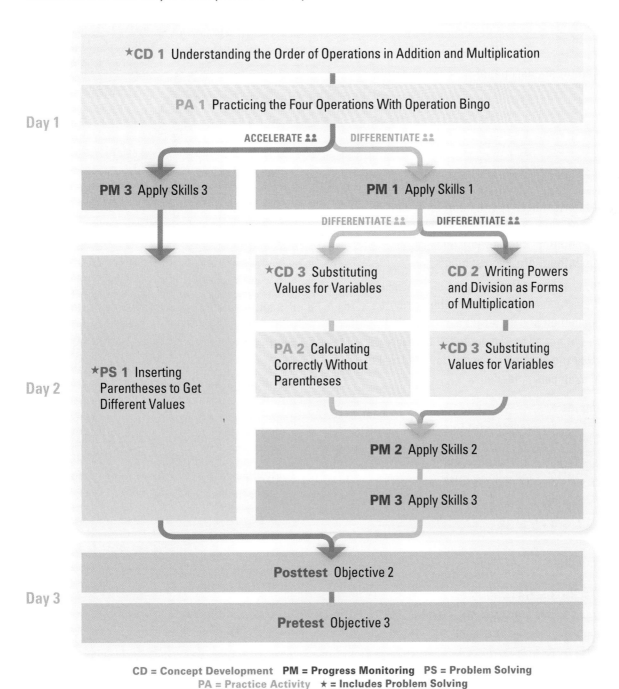

Day 1

★CD 1 Understanding the Order of Operations in Addition and Multiplication

PA 1 Practicing the Four Operations With Operation Bingo

ACCELERATE ▲▲   DIFFERENTIATE ▲▲

PM 3 Apply Skills 3   PM 1 Apply Skills 1

DIFFERENTIATE ▲▲   DIFFERENTIATE ▲▲

Day 2

★PS 1 Inserting Parentheses to Get Different Values

★CD 3 Substituting Values for Variables

PA 2 Calculating Correctly Without Parentheses

CD 2 Writing Powers and Division as Forms of Multiplication

★CD 3 Substituting Values for Variables

PM 2 Apply Skills 2

PM 3 Apply Skills 3

Day 3

Posttest Objective 2

Pretest Objective 3

CD = Concept Development   PM = Progress Monitoring   PS = Problem Solving
PA = Practice Activity   ★ = Includes Problem Solving

Concept Development Activities

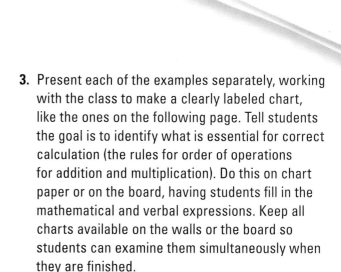

★ CD 1 Understanding the Order of Operations in Addition and Multiplication

Use with 5-Day or 3-Day Instructional Plan. In this activity, students derive rules for the correct order to do multiplication, addition, and subtraction.

MATERIALS

- At least one sheet of chart paper for each example (10 or more)
- Markers
- Tape

DIRECTIONS

1. Explain to students that they will be determining the order of operations in numerical expressions involving only addition, subtraction, and multiplication without grouping symbols.

2. On the board, write as many examples as possible, both correct examples that contain all the attributes of correct calculation and incorrect examples that contain some but not all the attributes of correct calculation. Use the examples given below and make up additional examples if needed.

   Correct examples:

   $3 \cdot 5 - 4 + 2 \cdot 3 = 17$
   $2 + 3 \cdot 5 - 6 + 1 - 5 + 2 \cdot 8 = 23$
   $9 - 7 + 3 \cdot 2 \cdot 3 - 14 + 5 \cdot 2 = 16$
   $5 \cdot 5 + 2 \cdot 7 - 20 + 2 \cdot 3 = 25$
   $2 \cdot 3 + 3 \cdot 4 + 4 \cdot 5 = 38$

   Incorrect examples:

   $2 \cdot 7 + 1 + 3 \cdot 3 = 54$
   $1 + 2 \cdot 5 - 10 + 6 + 3 \cdot 4 - 10 = 46$
   $11 - 7 + 5 \cdot 3 - 1 - 2 \cdot 4 = 96$
   $2 \cdot 2 + 3 \cdot 4 - 15 + 3 \cdot 4 = 64$
   $2 + 3 \cdot 3 + 4 \cdot 4 + 5 = 65$

3. Present each of the examples separately, working with the class to make a clearly labeled chart, like the ones on the following page. Tell students the goal is to identify what is essential for correct calculation (the rules for order of operations for addition and multiplication). Do this on chart paper or on the board, having students fill in the mathematical and verbal expressions. Keep all charts available on the walls or the board so students can examine them simultaneously when they are finished.

★ = Includes Problem Solving

Correct example: $3 \cdot 5 - 4 + 2 \cdot 3 = 17$

Mathematical Evaluation Process	Verbal Statement of Evaluation Process
$3 \cdot 5 - 4 + 2 \cdot 3 = 15 - 4 + 2 \cdot 3$	⟵ Multiply 3 times 5 and replace that operation with 15.
$= 15 - 4 + 6$	⟵ Multiply 2 times 3 and replace that operation with 6.
$= 11 + 6$	⟵ Add 15 and negative 4 and replace that operation with 11.
$= 17$	⟵ Add 11 and 6 and replace that operation with 17.

Incorrect example: $2 \cdot 7 + 1 + 3 \cdot 3 = 54$

Mathematical Evaluation Process	Verbal Statement of Evaluation Process
$2 \cdot 7 + 1 + 3 \cdot 3 = 14 + 1 + 3 \cdot 3$	⟵ Multiply 2 times 7 and replace that operation with 14.
$= 15 + 3 \cdot 3$	⟵ Add 14 and 1 and replace that operation with 15.
$= 18 \cdot 3$	⟵ Add 15 and 3 and replace that operation with 18.
$= 54$	⟵ Multiply 18 by 3 and replace that operation with 54.

Correct example: $2 + 3 \cdot 5 - 6 + 1 - 5 + 2 \cdot 8 = 23$

Mathematical Evaluation Process	Verbal Statement of Evaluation Process
$2 + 3 \cdot 5 - 6 + 1 - 5 + 2 \cdot 8$	
$= 2 + 15 - 6 + 1 - 5 + 2 \cdot 8$	⟵ Multiply 3 times 5 and replace that operation with 15.
$= 2 + 15 - 6 + 1 - 5 + 16$	⟵ Multiply 2 times 8 and replace that operation with 16.
$= 17 - 6 + 1 - 5 + 16$	⟵ Add 2 and 15 and replace that operation with 17.
$= 11 + 1 - 5 + 16$	⟵ Add 17 and negative 6 and replace that operation with 11.
$= 12 - 5 + 16$	⟵ Add 11 and 1 and replace that operation with 12.
$= 7 + 16$	⟵ Add 12 and negative 5 and replace that operation with 7.
$= 23$	⟵ Add 7 and 16 and replace that operation with 23.

4. After students have studied all the charts, ask them to write a definition or rule for the correct calculation of an expression involving addition and multiplication. By studying all the charts together, students should be able to induce the rules.

Listen for:

- First, perform all multiplications in order from left to right.

- Second, go back and perform all additions or subtractions in order from left to right.

NEXT STEPS • Differentiate

5-Day and 3-Day Instructional Plans:
PA 1, page 27—All students, for additional practice

Objective 2
Concept Development Activities

CD 2 Writing Powers and Division as Forms of Multiplication

Use with 5-Day or 3-Day Instructional Plan. In this activity, students correctly rewrite division and powers using multiplication.

DIRECTIONS

1. Divide the class into pairs of students.

2. Write the problem $3^2 \cdot 5 + 2 \cdot 3 + 7 + 20 \div 5$ on the board or on a transparency.

3. Have one student in each pair rewrite the expression in an equivalent form using only multiplication and addition. $3 \cdot 3 \cdot 5 + 2 \cdot 3 + 7 + 20 \cdot \frac{1}{5}$

4. Have the other student in the pair evaluate the expression. $45 + 6 + 7 + 4 = 62$

5. Choose a student pair at random to show their work on the board, with each student showing his or her own part.

6. Ask the class for corrections if necessary.

7. Repeat Steps 3–6 using another problem from the list below.

   Sample problems:

$3 + 6 \cdot 2^3 \div 3$ 19	$17 + 3 \cdot 2^3 \div 6$ 21
$5^2 \cdot 3 \div 5 + 6$ 21	$16 \div 8 \cdot 2^3 + 5$ 21
$2^3 + 3^2 + 4 \cdot 2$ 25	$5 \div 5 + 2^2 \div 4$ 2
$21 \cdot 3 \div 7 \div 9$ 1	$24 \div 6 \cdot 6 \div 8$ 3
$3^2 \cdot 2^2 \div 36 + 1$ 2	$3 \cdot 5^2 \cdot 2 \div 5 \div 30$ 1
$2^2 + 3^2 \cdot 2 + 5^2$ 47	$5^2 \cdot 4 \div 10 \cdot 2$ 20
$2^3 \cdot 3^2 \div 3$ 24	

NEXT STEPS • Differentiate

5-Day Instructional Plan:
PA 2, page 28—All students, for additional practice

3-Day Instructional Plan:
CD 3, page 25—All students, for additional concept development and problem solving

Concept Development Activities

★ CD 3 Substituting Values for Variables

Use with 5-Day or 3-Day Instructional Plan. In this activity, students substitute values for variables.

DIRECTIONS

1. Review some formulas students have had previously in mathematics, such as the ones below.

   Area formulas:
   Rectangle $A = lw$
   Square $A = s^2$
   Triangle $A = \frac{1}{2}bh$

   Perimeter formulas:
   Rectangle $P = 2l + 2w$
   Square $P = 4s$
   Triangle $P = a + b + c$

   Distance formula:
   Distance $D = r\,(\text{rate}) \cdot t\,(\text{time})$

2. Discuss the fact that to find the solution to this kind of problem, we need to substitute values for the variables; for example, to find the area of a rectangle ($A = lw$), we need to know the length (l) and the width (w). Tell students to think of a classroom with the dimensions 40 ft. by 30 ft., that is, $l = 40$ ft. and $w = 30$ ft. Have them use the formula, $A = lw$, to find the area.
   $A = 40$ ft. $\cdot\ 30$ ft. $= 1,200$ sq. ft.

3. Ask students to find the perimeter of the same classroom. $P = 2l + 2w$, when $l = 40$ ft. and $w = 30$ ft.; $P = 2(40) + 2(30) = 140$ ft.

4. Present another example, such as finding the value of A if $A = s^2$ and $s = 7$ ft. $A = 49$ sq. ft.

5. Discuss finding the value of an expression by substitution. If a variable is repeated in an expression, the same value is used each time; for example, in evaluating the expression $3x + yx$ when $x = 6$ and $y = 2$, we get $3(6) + (2)(6) = 30$. We must substitute the value 6 for both x's.

6. Present other examples if students seem confused.

   Sample problems:

   Find the perimeter of a square when $s = 7$ in.
   $P = 4 \cdot 7 = 28$ in.

   Find the distance when $r = 2$ miles per hour and $t = 3$ hours $D = 2 \cdot 3 = 6$ miles

NEXT STEPS • Differentiate

👥 5-Day Instructional Plan:
CD 4, page 26—Students who demonstrate understanding of the concept, for additional concept development and problem solving

PM 3, page 31—Students who need additional support, to assess progress

👥 3-Day Instructional Plan:
PA 2, page 28—Students who demonstrated understanding on Apply Skills 1, for additional practice

PM 2, page 30—All other students, to assess progress

★ = Includes Problem Solving

Concept Development Activities

★CD 4 Inserting Grouping Symbols to Correct Equations

Use with 5-Day Instructional Plan. In this activity, students insert grouping symbols to correct equations.

DIRECTIONS

1. Review the order of operations: (1) inside grouping symbols first; (2) exponents left to right; (3) multiplications and divisions left to right; (4) additions and subtractions left to right.

2. Present the eight incorrect problems shown below, and have students insert grouping symbols to make the equations correct. Remind students that the order of the grouping symbols, when they are embedded, is { [( )] }.

Incorrect example:	Example corrected:
$3 \cdot 6 + 4 = 30$	$3 \cdot (6 + 4) = 30$
$5 + 2 \cdot 3 = 21$	$(5 + 2) \cdot 3 = 21$
$2 + 3 \cdot 4 + 5 = 45$	$(2 + 3) \cdot (4 + 5) = 45$
$2(3 + 4) + 2 \cdot 3 = 48$	$[2(3 + 4) + 2] \cdot 3 = 48$
$2 + 3 \cdot 6 - 5 \cdot 4 = 100$	$\{[(2 + 3) \cdot 6] - 5\} \cdot 4 = 100$
$6 \cdot 5 - 3 + 3 \cdot 2 = 30$	$[6 \cdot (5 - 3) + 3] \cdot 2 = 30$
$2 \cdot 2 + 3 \cdot 4 - 15 + 3 \cdot 4 = 64$	$\{[(2 \cdot 2 + 3) \cdot 4 - 15] + 3\} \cdot 4 = 64$
$2 + 3 \cdot 3 + 4 \cdot 4 + 5 = 65$	$[2 + (3 \cdot 3) + 4] \cdot 4 + 5 = 65$

NEXT STEPS • Differentiate

👥 5-Day Instructional Plan:

PM 3, page 31—Students who are on the accelerated path, to assess progress

Objective 2 Posttest, page 33—Students who are on the differentiated path

★ = Includes Problem Solving

Practice Activities

PA 1 Practicing the Four Operations With Operation Bingo

Use with 5-Day or 3-Day Instructional Plan. In this activity, students correctly use the order of operations to solve problems involving parentheses.

MATERIALS

- Blackline Master 3
- Blackline Master 38
- Game markers to cover squares
- Overhead projector or board

DIRECTIONS

1. Give each student a copy of Blackline Master 38, 4 × 4 Bingo Card.

2. Ask students to write the following numbers in any squares they choose at random: 0, 1, 2, 9, 11, 12, 15, 18, 21, 24, 27, 32, 41, 43, 49, 68.

3. Make a transparency of Blackline Master 3, Operation Bingo, and show students the problems one at a time or write the problems one at a time on an overhead transparency or the board. Each student should use a marker to cover the square with the number that is the correct answer to each problem. The first student to get four markers in a row says "Bingo!" Check the answers to determine if the four in a row is a bingo. Do *not* write supplied answers on the board.

4. Repeat using the remaining problems or make new ones with the answers from Step 2.

NEXT STEPS • Differentiate

5-Day Instructional Plan:
PM 1, page 29—All students, to assess progress

3-Day Instructional Plan:
PM 3, page 31—Students who demonstrate understanding of the concept, to assess progress

PM 1, page 29—Students who need additional support, to assess progress

---

1. $4 \cdot (2 + 6) = 32$
2. $7 \cdot (8 - 5) + 3 = 24$
3. $(12 - 8) \cdot 3 = 12$
4. $5 \cdot 7 - 6 \cdot 4 = 11$
5. $(8 - 3) \cdot 2 \div 5 = 2$
6. $9 \div 3 \cdot 1 + 6 = 9$
7. $9 \div 3 \cdot (1 + 6) = 21$
8. $20 - 10 \div 2 = 15$
9. $12 \div 4 - 21 \div 7 = 0$
10. $3 + 4 \cdot 6 = 27$
11. $39 + 74 - 16 \cdot 4 = 49$
12. $(8 - 2) \cdot (7 - 4) = 18$
13. $17 - 6 \cdot 2 - 4 = 1$
14. $26 + 5 \cdot 4 - 3 = 43$
15. $10 \cdot 10 - 4 \cdot 8 = 68$
16. $[(6 - 4) \cdot 3] + 5 \cdot 7 = 41$

Objective 2
Practice Activities

PA 2 Calculating Correctly Without Parentheses

Use with 5-Day or 3-Day Instructional Plan. In this activity, students correctly use the order of operations to solve multiple-operation problems without parentheses.

MATERIALS

- *Interactive Text*, page 11

DIRECTIONS

1. Have students turn to *Interactive Text*, page 11, No Parentheses.

2. Ask students to individually complete the problems on the page.

3. Work the problems that are unclear to students on the board or overhead.

4. Have each student make up two problems that involve at least two different operations and no parentheses. Have them work the problems that they made up following the order of operations.

5. Exchange the problems with other students in the class. Have students work the problems to see if the given answer is correct.

NEXT STEPS • Differentiate

5-Day and 3-Day Instructional Plans:
PM 2, page 30—All students, to assess progress

NO PARENTHESES

Find the correct value for each expression.

Incorrect Values	Correct Values
1. $2 \cdot 9 + 6 = 30$	$2 \cdot 9 + 6 = 24$
2. $6 + 2 \cdot 5 + 9 = 49$	$6 + 2 \cdot 5 + 9 = 25$
3. $3 - 2 \cdot 5 + 9 = -4$	$3 - 2 \cdot 5 + 9 = 2$
4. $5 + 1 \cdot 2 + 4 = 36$	$5 + 1 \cdot 2 + 4 = 11$
5. $2 + 3 \cdot 3 + 4 \cdot 4 + 5 = 65$	$2 + 3 \cdot 3 + 4 \cdot 4 + 5 = 32$
6. $4 + 3 \cdot 3 + 5 \cdot 4 = 41$	$4 + 3 \cdot 3 + 5 \cdot 4 = 33$
7. $1 + 2 \cdot 3 + 4 \cdot 5 + 6 = 35$	$1 + 2 \cdot 3 + 4 \cdot 5 + 6 = 33$
8. $7 \cdot 2 - 6 \cdot 2 + 4 = 20$	$7 \cdot 2 - 6 \cdot 2 + 4 = 6$
9. $6 - 4 + 8 \cdot 2 + 3 - 7 = 16$	$6 - 4 + 8 \cdot 2 + 3 - 7 = 14$
10. $7 - 2 + 5 \cdot 3 = 0$	$7 - 2 + 5 \cdot 3 = 20$
11. $5 \cdot 3 - 2 + 7 = 12$	$5 \cdot 3 - 2 + 7 = 20$
12. $6 \cdot 2 \cdot 4 - 7 = 6$	$6 \cdot 2 \cdot 4 - 7 = 41$
13. $9 - 7 + 4 \cdot 7 = 42$	$9 - 7 + 4 \cdot 7 = 30$
14. $6 + 3 \cdot 4 - 4 \cdot 2 = 28$	$6 + 3 \cdot 4 - 4 \cdot 2 = 10$
15. $6 \cdot 5 - 8 + 3 \cdot 4 = 100$	$6 \cdot 5 - 8 + 3 \cdot 4 = 34$

Objective 2
Progress-Monitoring Activities

PM 1 Apply Skills 1

Use with 5-Day or 3-Day Instructional Plan.

MATERIALS

- *Interactive Text*, page 12

DIRECTIONS

1. Have students turn to *Interactive Text*, page 12, Apply Skills 1.

2. Monitor student work, and provide feedback as necessary.

   Watch for:
   - Do students multiply before adding?
   - Do students understand parentheses?

NEXT STEPS • Differentiate

5-Day Instructional Plan:
CD 2, page 24—All students, for additional concept development

👥 3-Day Instructional Plan:
CD 3, page 25—Students who demonstrate understanding of the concept, to extend understanding and develop problem-solving skills

CD 2, page 24—Students who need additional concept development

---

Name _____ Date _____

APPLY SKILLS 1

Evaluate the expressions using the order of operations.

Example:
$11 - 2 \cdot 3 =$ ___5___

1. $3 \cdot 6 - 2 =$ ___16___
2. $5^2 + 9 =$ ___34___
3. $5 + 4 \cdot 6 =$ ___29___
4. $18 - 7 \cdot 2 + 7 =$ ___11___
5. $3 \cdot 6 + 9 \cdot 4 =$ ___54___
6. $8 + 3 + 6 \cdot 2 =$ ___23___
7. $17 - 3 \cdot 5 =$ ___2___
8. $28 - 6 \cdot 4 + 5 =$ ___9___
9. $3.6 \cdot 4 - 6.2 =$ ___8.2___

Evaluate the expressions.

Example:
$(2 \cdot 3) + 9 =$ ___15___

10. $7 + (2 \cdot 6) =$ ___19___
11. $(9 - 4) + (4 \cdot 3) =$ ___17___
12. $15 - 7 + (6 \cdot 2) =$ ___20___
13. $6 \cdot (7 - 4) + 12 =$ ___30___
14. $(3 + 7) \cdot (9 - 3) =$ ___60___
15. $7 + (12 - 4) - 2 =$ ___13___
16. $35 \cdot (17 - 7) + 13 =$ ___363___
17. $40 - 11 \cdot 3 =$ ___7___
18. $42 - 6 \cdot 2 + 7 =$ ___37___
19. $14 + 3 \cdot (6 - 4) =$ ___20___
20. $3.8 \cdot 4 - 1.6 =$ ___13.6___

Objective 2
Progress-Monitoring Activities

PM 2 Apply Skills 2

Use with 5-Day or 3-Day Instructional Plan.

MATERIALS

- *Interactive Text*, page 13

DIRECTIONS

1. Have students turn to *Interactive Text*, page 13, Apply Skills 2.

2. Monitor student work, and provide feedback as necessary.

   Watch for:
   - Do students remember how to square numbers?
   - Do students work from left to right, performing operations in the correct order?

NEXT STEPS • Differentiate

5-Day Instructional Plan:
CD 3, page 25—All students, for additional concept development and problem solving

3-Day Instructional Plan:
PM 3, page 31—All students, for additional progress assessment

---

Name _____ Date _____

APPLY SKILLS 2

Evaluate each expression using the order of operations.

Example:
$6 \cdot (7 - 3) + 4 =$ ___28___
$6 \cdot 4 + 4$
$24 + 4$

1. $11 - 4 \cdot 2 =$ ___3___
   $11 - 8$

2. $(15 - 4) \cdot 6 =$ ___66___
   $11 \cdot 6$

3. $3 + 12 - 3^2 =$ ___6___
   $3 + 12 - 9$

4. $8^2 - (4 \cdot 8) =$ ___32___
   $64 - 32$

5. $8 + 4 \cdot 3 - 5 =$ ___15___
   $8 + 12 - 5$

6. $27 - (6 + 8) =$ ___13___
   $27 - 14$

7. $(3 + 8)(9 - 4) =$ ___55___
   $11 \cdot 5$

8. $6 \cdot (4 - 2) + 5 =$ ___17___
   $6 \cdot 2 + 5$
   $12 + 5$

9. $8^2 + 2 \cdot 5 - 8 =$ ___66___
   $64 + 10 - 8$

10. $(3 + 7)^2 =$ ___100___
    10^2

11. $(6 + 3)(6 - 3) =$ ___27___
    $9 \cdot 3$

12. $4 + (7 - 2)^2 + 3 =$ ___32___
    $4 + 5^2 + 3$
    $4 + 25 + 3$

13. $(6 + 3)^2 - (6 - 3)^2 =$ ___72___
    $9^2 - 3^2$
    $81 - 9$

14. $8 \cdot (11 - 7) \cdot (3 + 4) =$ ___224___
    $8 \cdot 4 \cdot 7$

15. $3^2 + 17 - 4 \cdot 3 =$ ___14___
    $9 + 17 - 12$

16. $8 + 4^2 - 3^2 =$ ___15___
    $8 + 16 - 9$

17. $5 \cdot 3^2 + (17 - 15)^3 =$ ___53___
    $5 \cdot 9 + 2^3$
    $45 + 8$

Inside Algebra   Chapter 1 • Objective 2 • PM 2   **13**

Progress-Monitoring Activities

PM 3 Apply Skills 3

Use with 5-Day or 3-Day Instructional Plan.

MATERIALS

- *Interactive Text*, page 14

DIRECTIONS

1. Have students turn to *Interactive Text*, page 14, Apply Skills 3.

2. Monitor student work, and provide feedback as necessary.

   Watch for:
   - Do students understand implied multiplication?
   - Do students substitute before solving?

NEXT STEPS • Differentiate

👥 5-Day Instructional Plan:

PS 1, page 32—Students who are on the accelerated path, to develop problem-solving skills

CD 4, page 26—Students who are on the differentiated path, for additional concept development and problem solving

👥 3-Day Instructional Plan:

PS 1, page 32—Students who are on the accelerated path, to develop problem-solving skills

Objective 2 Posttest, page 33—Students who are on the differentiated path

---

PROGRESS MONITORING

Name _____ Date _____

APPLY SKILLS 3

Find the value of each expression if $x = 2$, $y = 6$, and $z = 4$.

Example:
$(x + y)z = $ __32__
$(2 + 6)4$

1. $xy = $ __12__
   $2(6)$

2. $2x + y = $ __10__
   $2(2) + 6$

3. $6 + xz = $ __14__
   $6 + 2(4)$

4. $xy - z = $ __8__
   $2(6) - 4$

5. $4 + x(y - z) = $ __8__
   $4 + 2(6 - 4)$

6. $\frac{1}{2}(2x + z) = $ __4__
   $\frac{1}{2}(2 \cdot 2 + 4)$

7. $xyz = $ __48__
   $2(6)(4)$

8. $(6 + x)x - z = $ __12__
   $(6 + 2)2 - 4$

9. $x^2 + y^2 = $ __40__
   $2^2 + 6^2$

Find the value of each expression if $a = 3$, $b = 6$, and $c = 4$.

Example:
$2b - 4 = $ __8__
$2 \cdot 6 - 4$

10. $8 - 2a = $ __2__
    $8 - 2(3)$

11. $16 - a^2 + c = $ __11__
    $16 - 3^2 + 4$

12. $ab - 4 = $ __14__
    $3(6) - 4$

13. $7 - b \div a + c = $ __9__
    $7 - 6 \div 3 + 4$

14. $b - 2a + 7 = $ __7__
    $6 - 2(3) + 7$

15. $3b - 4c = $ __2__
    $3(6) - 4(4)$

16. $\frac{b + 3c}{a} = $ __6__
    $\frac{6 + 3(4)}{3}$

17. $(a + c)^2 = $ __49__
    $(3 + 4)^2$

18. $a + b + c - 2a = $ __7__
    $3 + 6 + 4 - 2(3)$

19. $(b - c) \cdot a = $ __6__
    $(6 - 4) \cdot 3$

20. $3(b - a) + 12 = $ __21__
    $3(6 - 3) + 12$

14   Chapter 1 • Objective 2 • PM 3   Inside Algebra

Objective 2
Problem-Solving Activity

Inserting Parentheses to Get Different Values

Use with 5-Day or 3-Day Instructional Plan. In this activity, students recognize how grouping symbols can change the value of an expression.

DIRECTIONS

1. Divide the class into pairs of students.

2. Write **3 − 2 • 4 + 7 • 3** on the board.

3. Ask each pair to find the value of the expression. 16

4. Challenge the student pairs to insert one or more pairs of parentheses in such a way that the value of the expression changes.

5. Call on one student pair to put their new expression on the board along with the correct value.
   Many answers are possible, for example,
   $(3 − 2) • 4 + (7 • 3) = 25$, and $3 − 2(4 + 7) • 3 = −63$.

6. Ask the class to check the value to see if it is correct. If the value that the pair found is correct, leave it on the board. If the value that the pair found is incorrect, have the class agree on the correct solution.

7. Move to a new spot on the board and repeat Steps 4–6 as long as student pairs come up with new expressions. Be sure to leave each example on the board. When the class can find no new ways of writing each expression, start this activity over with a new expression.

Sample problems:

$$3 − 2 • 4 + 7 • 3 = 16$$
$$(3 − 2) • 4 + 7 • 3 = 25$$
$$3 − 2 • (4 + 7) • 3 = −63$$
$$3 − 2 • [4 + (7 • 3)] = −47$$
$$3 − [2 • (4 + 7)] • 3 = −63$$
$${3 − [2 • (4 + 7)]} • 3 = −57$$

Variation: Different Numbers Give students five different numbers (e.g., 2–6). Have students write as many different problems (different answers) as they can using all five numbers without using parentheses. The order of the numbers and operations may change.

NEXT STEPS • Differentiate

5-Day and 3-Day Instructional Plans:
Objective 2 Posttest, page 33—All students

★ = Includes Problem Solving

Ongoing Assessment

Objective 2 Posttest

Discuss with students the key concepts in Objective 2. Following the discussion, administer the Objective 2 Posttest to all students.

Using the Results

- Score the posttest and update the class record card.

- Provide reinforcement for students who do not demonstrate mastery of the concepts through individual or small-group reteaching of key concepts.

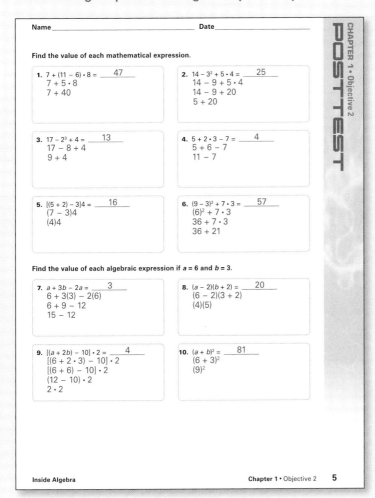

Name _____ Date _____

Find the value of each mathematical expression.

1. $7 + (11 - 6) \cdot 8 =$ ___47___
$7 + 5 \cdot 8$
$7 + 40$

2. $14 - 3^2 + 5 \cdot 4 =$ ___25___
$14 - 9 + 5 \cdot 4$
$14 - 9 + 20$
$5 + 20$

3. $17 - 2^3 + 4 =$ ___13___
$17 - 8 + 4$
$9 + 4$

4. $5 + 2 \cdot 3 - 7 =$ ___4___
$5 + 6 - 7$
$11 - 7$

5. $[(5 + 2) - 3]4 =$ ___16___
$(7 - 3)4$
$(4)4$

6. $(9 - 3)^2 + 7 \cdot 3 =$ ___57___
$(6)^2 + 7 \cdot 3$
$36 + 7 \cdot 3$
$36 + 21$

Find the value of each algebraic expression if $a = 6$ and $b = 3$.

7. $a + 3b - 2a =$ ___3___
$6 + 3(3) - 2(6)$
$6 + 9 - 12$
$15 - 12$

8. $(a - 2)(b + 2) =$ ___20___
$(6 - 2)(3 + 2)$
$(4)(5)$

9. $[(a + 2b) - 10] \cdot 2 =$ ___4___
$[(6 + 2 \cdot 3) - 10] \cdot 2$
$[(6 + 6) - 10] \cdot 2$
$(12 - 10) \cdot 2$
$2 \cdot 2$

10. $(a + b)^2 =$ ___81___
$(6 + 3)^2$
$(9)^2$

Inside Algebra   Chapter 1 • Objective 2   **5**

Objective 3 Pretest

Students complete the Objective 3 Pretest on the same day as the Objective 2 Posttest.

Using the Results

- Score the pretest and update the class record card.
- If the majority of students do not demonstrate mastery of the concepts, use the 4-Day Instructional Plan for Objective 3.
- If the majority of students demonstrate mastery of the concepts, use the 3-Day Instructional Plan for Objective 3.

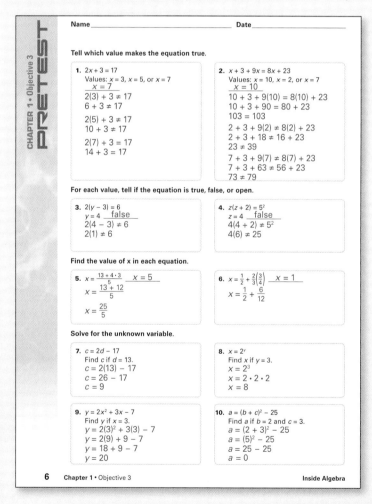

Name _____ Date _____

Tell which value makes the equation true.

1. $2x + 3 = 17$
Values: $x = 3$, $x = 5$, or $x = 7$
$\underline{x = 7}$
$2(3) + 3 \neq 17$
$6 + 3 \neq 17$

$2(5) + 3 \neq 17$
$10 + 3 \neq 17$

$2(7) + 3 = 17$
$14 + 3 = 17$

2. $x + 3 + 9x = 8x + 23$
Values: $x = 10$, $x = 2$, or $x = 7$
$\underline{x = 10}$
$10 + 3 + 9(10) = 8(10) + 23$
$10 + 3 + 90 = 80 + 23$
$103 = 103$
$2 + 3 + 9(2) \neq 8(2) + 23$
$2 + 3 + 18 \neq 16 + 23$
$23 \neq 39$
$7 + 3 + 9(7) \neq 8(7) + 23$
$7 + 3 + 63 \neq 56 + 23$
$73 \neq 79$

For each value, tell if the equation is true, false, or open.

3. $2(y - 3) = 6$
$y = 4$ $\underline{\text{false}}$
$2(4 - 3) \neq 6$
$2(1) \neq 6$

4. $z(z + 2) = 5^2$
$z = 4$ $\underline{\text{false}}$
$4(4 + 2) \neq 5^2$
$4(6) \neq 25$

Find the value of x in each equation.

5. $x = \frac{13 + 4 \cdot 3}{5}$ $\underline{x = 5}$
$x = \frac{13 + 12}{5}$
$x = \frac{25}{5}$

6. $x = \frac{1}{2} + \frac{2}{3}\left(\frac{3}{4}\right)$ $\underline{x = 1}$
$x = \frac{1}{2} + \frac{6}{12}$

Solve for the unknown variable.

7. $c = 2d - 17$
Find c if $d = 13$.
$c = 2(13) - 17$
$c = 26 - 17$
$c = 9$

8. $x = 2^y$
Find x if $y = 3$.
$x = 2^3$
$x = 2 \cdot 2 \cdot 2$
$x = 8$

9. $y = 2x^2 + 3x - 7$
Find y if $x = 3$.
$y = 2(3)^2 + 3(3) - 7$
$y = 2(9) + 9 - 7$
$y = 18 + 9 - 7$
$y = 20$

10. $a = (b + c)^2 - 25$
Find a if $b = 2$ and $c = 3$.
$a = (2 + 3)^2 - 25$
$a = (5)^2 - 25$
$a = 25 - 25$
$a = 0$

6 Chapter 1 • Objective 3

Inside Algebra

Goals and Activities

Objective 3 Goals

The following activities, when used with the instructional plans on pages 36 and 37, enable students to:

- Find the value of x when $x = \dfrac{19 - 7 \cdot 3}{2}$ to be **$x = -1$**

- Find the value of y when $y = 2x - 7$ and $x = 3$ to be **$y = -1$**

Objective 3 Activities

Concept Development Activities

CD 1 Deciding Whether a Mathematical Statement Is True, False, or Open— Part 1, page 38	**CD 2** Deciding Whether a Mathematical Statement Is True, False, or Open— Part 2, page 39	**CD 3** Evaluating Equations, page 40

Practice Activities

PA 1 Rolling the Value for Equations, page 41	**PA 2** Solving Inequalities, page 42

Progress-Monitoring Activities

PM 1 Apply Skills 1, page 43	**PM 2** Apply Skills 2, page 44	**PM 3** Apply Skills 3, page 45

*Problem-Solving Activities

★PS 1 Developing a Formula, page 46	**★PS 2** Converting Temperatures: Celsius to Fahrenheit and Vice Versa, page 47

Ongoing Assessment

Posttest Objective 3, page 49

Pretest Objective 4, page 50

CD = Concept Development   PM = Progress Monitoring   PS = Problem Solving
PA = Practice Activity   ★ = Includes Problem Solving

Instructional Plans

4-Day Instructional Plan

Use the 4-Day Instructional Plan when pretest results indicate that students would benefit from a slower pace. This plan is used when the majority of students need more time or did not demonstrate mastery on the pretest. This plan does not include all activities.

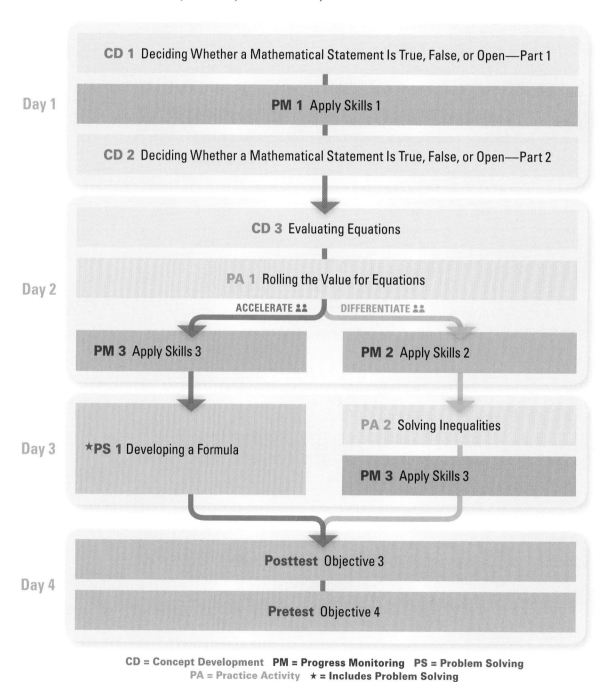

CD 1 Deciding Whether a Mathematical Statement Is True, False, or Open—Part 1

Day 1

PM 1 Apply Skills 1

CD 2 Deciding Whether a Mathematical Statement Is True, False, or Open—Part 2

CD 3 Evaluating Equations

Day 2

PA 1 Rolling the Value for Equations

ACCELERATE   DIFFERENTIATE

PM 3 Apply Skills 3   **PM 2** Apply Skills 2

PA 2 Solving Inequalities

Day 3   **★PS 1** Developing a Formula

PM 3 Apply Skills 3

Posttest Objective 3

Day 4

Pretest Objective 4

CD = Concept Development   PM = Progress Monitoring   PS = Problem Solving
PA = Practice Activity   ★ = Includes Problem Solving

3-Day Instructional Plan

Use the 3-Day Instructional Plan when pretest results indicate that students can move through the activities at a faster pace. This plan is ideal when the majority of students demonstrate mastery on the pretest. This plan does not include all activities.

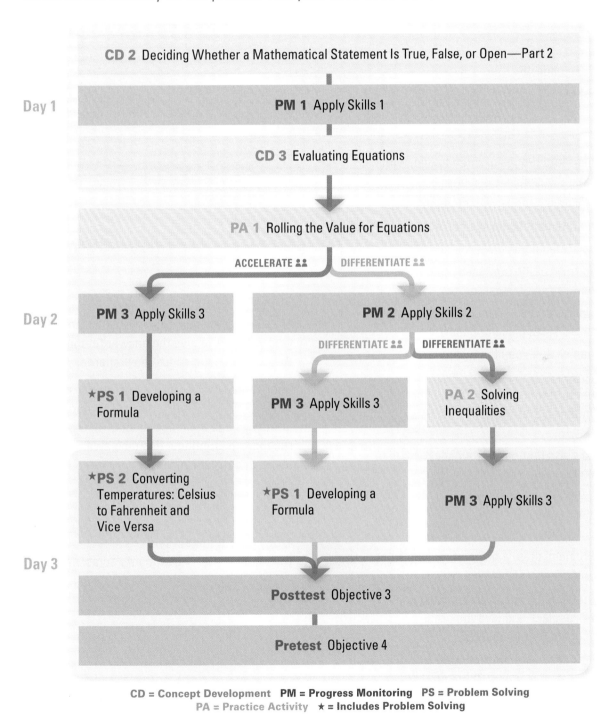

Day 1

CD 2 Deciding Whether a Mathematical Statement Is True, False, or Open—Part 2

PM 1 Apply Skills 1

CD 3 Evaluating Equations

PA 1 Rolling the Value for Equations

ACCELERATE 👥   DIFFERENTIATE 👥

Day 2

PM 3 Apply Skills 3

PM 2 Apply Skills 2

DIFFERENTIATE 👥   DIFFERENTIATE 👥

★**PS 1** Developing a Formula

PM 3 Apply Skills 3

PA 2 Solving Inequalities

★**PS 2** Converting Temperatures: Celsius to Fahrenheit and Vice Versa

★**PS 1** Developing a Formula

PM 3 Apply Skills 3

Day 3

Posttest Objective 3

Pretest Objective 4

CD = Concept Development   PM = Progress Monitoring   PS = Problem Solving
PA = Practice Activity   ★ = Includes Problem Solving

Concept Development Activities

CD 1 Deciding Whether a Mathematical Statement Is True, False, or Open—Part 1

Use with 4-Day Instructional Plan. In this activity, students learn the difference between true, false, and open statements.

MATERIALS

- *Interactive Text*, page 15
- Small pieces of paper for students' names

DIRECTIONS

1. Divide the class into groups of three to five, with as many groups the same size as possible.

2. Discuss the following terms with students:

   true The statement is always correct

   false The statement is always incorrect

   open The truth of the statement cannot be determined without further information

3. Ask each member of each group to write his or her name on a small piece of paper.

4. Collect the names and keep them separated by group.

5. Have students turn to *Interactive Text*, page 15, Deciding Whether a Statement Is True, False, or Open—Part 1.

6. Explain to the class that each group must come to consensus on their answer to each problem in the activity. Ask the groups to complete the activity.

7. After the groups are finished, review the problems in the following way:

   - For each problem, draw a name at random from a given group.

   - The student whose name is drawn must come to the front of the class and give the group's answer and the rationale for the answer.

   - If the group's answer is correct, each member of the group gets five points. If the group's answer is incorrect, each member of the group loses five points.

DECIDING WHETHER A STATEMENT IS TRUE, FALSE, OR OPEN—PART 1

Identify each statement as True, False, or Open.

- True: The statement is true.
- False: The statement is false.
- Open: The truth value of the statement cannot be determined without further information; hence, the statement is open.

Statements:

1. William Jefferson Clinton is now president of the United States of America.
   __false__

2. He is a 12-year-old student. __open__

3. Thanksgiving is always on a Thursday in the United States. __true__

4. George W. Bush is a former governor of Texas. __true__

5. He was in the oil business. __open__

6. Today's date is January 24, 2001. __false__

7. It is a Wednesday. __open__

8. Ford is the name of an automobile manufacturing company. __true__

9. The company is based in this country. __open__

10. Benjamin Franklin, the founding father who signed the Declaration of Independence, was also once president of the United States. __false__

11. He was a printer. __open__

12. Five added to seven is thirteen. __false__

13. It is twelve. __open__

14. The square of twenty-five is six hundred twenty-five. __true__

15. Labor Day is always celebrated in the spring in the United States. __false__

Note: This structure keeps the group interdependent during the group discussion because no one knows who will have to give the answer for the group. All the group members must be prepared.

8. Repeat the process for each problem, each time drawing a name from a different group. When every group has had a chance to answer, draw names at random and continue, this time awarding one point for each correct response.

NEXT STEPS • Differentiate

4-Day Instructional Plan:
PM 1, page 43—All students, to assess progress

Concept Development Activities

CD 2 Deciding Whether a Mathematical Statement Is True, False, or Open—Part 2

Use with 4-Day or 3-Day Instructional Plan. In this activity, students determine if a mathematical statement is true, false, or open.

MATERIALS

- *Interactive Text*, page 16
- Small pieces of paper for students' names

DIRECTIONS

1. Divide the class into groups of three to five, with as many groups the same size as possible.

2. Discuss the following terms with students:

   true The statement is always correct

   false The statement is always incorrect

   open The truth of the statement cannot be determined without further information

3. Ask each member of each group to write his or her name on a small piece of paper.

4. Collect the names and keep them separated by group.

5. Have students turn to *Interactive Text*, page 16, Deciding Whether a Statement Is True, False, or Open—Part 2.

6. Explain to the class that each group must come to consensus on their answer to each problem in the activity. Ask the groups to complete the activity.

7. After the groups are finished, review the problems in the following way:

   - For each problem, draw a name at random from a given group.

   - The student whose name is drawn must come to the front of the class and give the group's answer and the rationale for the answer.

   - If the group's answer is correct, each member of the group gets five points. If the group's answer is incorrect, each member of the group loses five points.

Note: This structure keeps the group interdependent during the group discussion because no one knows who will have to give the answer for the group. All the group members must be prepared.

8. Repeat the process for each problem, each time drawing a name from a different group. When every group has had a chance to answer, draw names at random and continue, this time awarding one point for each correct response.

NEXT STEPS • Differentiate

4-Day Instructional Plan:
CD 3, page 40—All students, for additional concept development

3-Day Instructional Plan:
PM 1, page 43—All students, to assess progress

Name_____ **Date**_____

DECIDING WHETHER A STATEMENT IS TRUE, FALSE, OR OPEN—PART 2

Identify each statement as True, False, or Open.

- True: The statement is true.
- False: The statement is false.
- Open: The truth value of the statement cannot be determined without further information; hence, the statement is open.

Statements:

1. Nine increased by seven is twenty-two. __false__

2. When an unknown number is reduced by five, the result is one hundred seven. __open__

3. The square of twenty is four hundred. __true__

4. Five multiplied by the quantity of seven plus two is forty-five. __true__

5. $x + 7 = 13$ __open__

6. $5 = 6$ __false__

7. $a(b + 4) = 29$ __open__

8. $0.5(9 + 7) = 8$ __true__

9. $x + 5 = x + 3 + 2$ __true__

10. Three plus five times seven is fifty-six. __false__

11. Three plus five times seven is thirty-eight. __true__

12. $3 + (5)(2) + 4 = 34$ __false__

13. It should be seventeen. __open__

14. $(2)(2)(2) > 7$ __true__

15. $2 + (2)(2) > 7$ __false__

Concept Development Activities

CD 3 Evaluating Equations

Use with 4-Day or 3-Day Instructional Plan. In this activity, students correctly evaluate an equation.

DIRECTIONS

1. Review the following term with students:

   open The truth value of the statement cannot be determined without further information

2. Explain to the class that a sentence such as $x + 3 = 12$ is an open sentence. It is not true or false until a value is substituted for x. Ask students whether the sentence is true or false if x is 4. False Tell them to explain their answers and tell what value makes the sentence true. $4 + 3 \neq 12$; $x = 9$ makes the sentence true.

3. Point out that some open sentences have more than one variable. To illustrate this point, say, "Suppose the cost of a telephone call is 75¢ plus 7¢ per minute. This can be represented by $C = 75 + 7m$." Write this statement on the board. Explain that you can find the cost (C) if you know the minutes (m). With the class, figure out the cost of a 20-minute telephone call, substituting 20 for m. Continue with other values for m, such as 60 minutes and 10 minutes.

4. Work some other examples on the board.

   Sample problems:

   Which of the following values makes the sentence $2x + 4 = 14$ true? $x = \{3, 4, \boxed{5}, 6\}$

   Evaluate: $x = \dfrac{3 \cdot 8 - 4}{2}$ $x = 10$

   Find d when r is **60** and $d = 14r$. $d = 840$

   Evaluate $2x - 7 + 3y$ if $x = 2$ and $y = 3$. 6

NEXT STEPS • Differentiate

4-Day and 3-Day Instructional Plans:

PA 1, page 41—All students, for additional practice

PA 1 Rolling the Value for Equations

Use with 4-Day or 3-Day Instructional Plan. In this activity, students determine whether substituting a particular value for a variable makes an equation true or false.

MATERIALS

- Blackline Master 4 or blank cards
- Dice, one per group

DIRECTIONS

1. Divide the class into groups of five. Give each group one die.

2. Duplicate and cut apart the cards on Blackline Master 4, Rolling the Value for Equations, and give one set of cards to each group. Alternatively, give each group six blank cards. Make a transparency of Blackline Master 4, and have students write each equation on the blank cards, one per card.

3. Have each group shuffle their cards, place them facedown, and turn the first card over.

4. In each group, have each person, in turn, roll the die and remember the number he or she rolled. If the number was already rolled by someone else in the group, the player should continue rolling until he or she has a number that no one else in the group has.

5. Explain the game rules to students.

   - Each player substitutes his or her number in the open sentence showing on the card and determines if the resulting statement is true or false.

   - Each person in the group reports his or her result, and the group records the number that makes the sentence true.

   - The next card is turned over, and the process is repeated. The activity continues until all six cards are used.

6. Conduct a class discussion about the equations and what makes an equation true. Ask students how many numbers they think will make the equation true. one

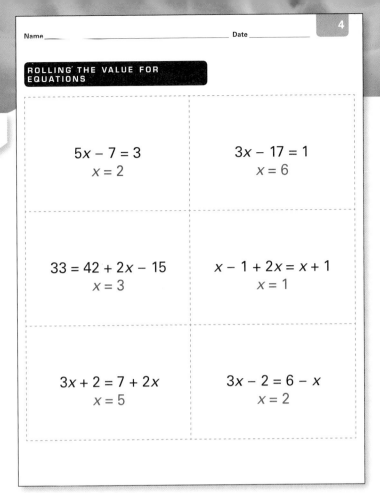

Name _____ Date _____

ROLLING THE VALUE FOR EQUATIONS

$5x - 7 = 3$ $x = 2$	$3x - 17 = 1$ $x = 6$
$33 = 42 + 2x - 15$ $x = 3$	$x - 1 + 2x = x + 1$ $x = 1$
$3x + 2 = 7 + 2x$ $x = 5$	$3x - 2 = 6 - x$ $x = 2$

NEXT STEPS • Differentiate

4-Day and 3-Day Instructional Plans:
   PM 3, page 45—Students who demonstrate understanding of the concept, to assess progress
   PM 2, page 44—Students who need additional support, to assess progress

Practice Activities

PA 2 Solving Inequalities

Use with 4-Day or 3-Day Instructional Plan. In this activity, students determine whether substituting a particular value for a variable makes an inequality true or false.

MATERIALS

- Blackline Master 5 or blank cards
- Dice, one per group

DIRECTIONS

1. Divide the class into groups of five. Give each group one die.

2. Duplicate and cut apart the cards on Blackline Master 5, Solving Inequalities, and give one set of cards to each group. Alternatively, give each group six blank cards. Make a transparency of Blackline Master 5, and ask students to write the inequalities on the blank cards, one equation per card.

3. Review inequalities such as **$2x - 1 > 4$** with the class. Ask students to substitute 2 for x and check if the inequality is true. no Ask students if it is true if you substitute 4 for x. yes

4. Have a student from each group shuffle the cards, place them facedown, and turn the first card over.

5. In each group, have each person, in turn, roll the die and remember the number he or she rolled. If the number was already rolled by someone else in the group, the player should continue rolling until he or she has a number that no one else in the group has.

6. Explain the game rules to students.

   - Each player substitutes his or her number in the open sentence showing on the card and determines if the resulting statement is true or false.

   - Each person in the group reports his or her result, and the group records the numbers that make the sentence true.

   - The next card is turned over, and the process is repeated. The activity continues until all six cards are used.

7. Conduct a class discussion about the inequalities and what numbers make them true. Ask students whether there are other numbers that would make the inequality true. yes

NEXT STEPS • Differentiate

4-Day and 3-Day Instructional Plans:
PM 3, page 45—All students, to assess progress

SOLVING INEQUALITIES

$5x - 7 < 5$ $x = 1, 2$	$3x - 13 > 1$ $x = 5, 6$
$50 > 42 + 2x$ $x = 1, 2, 3$	$2x - 5 > 3$ $x = 5, 6$
$3x - 2 < x + 7$ $x = 1, 2, 3, 4$	$2x < x + 3$ $x = 1, 2$

Progress-Monitoring Activities

PM 1 Apply Skills 1

Use with 4-Day or 3-Day Instructional Plan.

MATERIALS

- *Interactive Text*, page 17

DIRECTIONS

1. Have students turn to *Interactive Text*, page 17, Apply Skills 1.

2. Remind students of the key terms: *true*, *false*, and *open*.

3. Monitor student work, and provide feedback as necessary.

   Watch for:
   - Do students understand that open questions might be true?
   - Do students understand the concept of mathematical truth?

NEXT STEPS • Differentiate

4-Day Instructional Plan:
CD 2, page 39—All students, for additional concept development

3-Day Instructional Plan:
CD 3, page 40—All students, for additional concept development

---

Name _____ Date _____

Determine if each given statement is True, False, or Open. Place an X in the correct column.

	Statement	True	False	Open
1.	It is behind the barn next to the tractor.			X
2.	In the order of the days of the week, Thursday always comes after Wednesday and before Friday.	X		
3.	When x is added to twenty-seven, the sum can be thirty.	X		
4.	When twenty-seven is added to three, the sum can be forty.		X	
5.	George Washington was the first president of the United States of America.	X		
6.	He lived in South Carolina.			X
7.	For any real number x, $x > 5$.		X	
8.	For any real number x, $x + 5 = 22$.		X	
9.	For any real number x, if $x = 7$, then $x + 5 = 12$.	X		
10.	$2(5 + 4) - 7 = 7$		X	
11.	$3(4 - 3) + 6 = 9$	X		
12.	For any real number called x, $3(x + 5) = 3x + 15$.	X		
13.	For any real number called x, $5(x + 7) = 5x + 12$.		X	
14.	$[2 + 6(9 - 7)2^2]3 + 3 = 51$		X	
15.	$[2 + 6(9 - 7)2^2]3 + 3 = 153$	X		
16.	Now is the time for a man to come to the aid of his country.			X
17.	Tom Cruise is a movie star.	X		
18.	He starred in more than five movies.			X
19.	Tom is not married.			X

Progress-Monitoring Activities

PM 2 Apply Skills 2

Use with 4-Day or 3-Day Instructional Plan.

MATERIALS

- *Interactive Text*, page 18

DIRECTIONS

1. Have students turn to *Interactive Text*, page 18, Apply Skills 2.

2. Remind students of the key terms: *true*, *false*, and *open*.

3. Monitor student work, and provide feedback as necessary.

   Watch for:

   - Do students understand the concept of identity?

   - Do students use number sense to determine when a problem can be marked true or false without checking?

NEXT STEPS • Differentiate

4-Day Instructional Plan:

PA 2, page 42—All students, for additional practice

👥 3-Day Instructional Plan:

PM 3, page 45—Students who demonstrate understanding of the concept, for additional progress assessment

PA 2, page 42—Students who need additional practice

Name _____ Date _____

APPLY SKILLS 2

Label the statement as True, False, or Open when each of the values is used for the variable.

Statement	$x = 2$	$x = 3$	$x = 5$
1. William Jefferson Clinton had x terms as president of the United States of America.	true	false	false
2. $x - 3 = x - 3$	true	true	true
3. $x + 5 = x + 7$	false	false	false
4. $x + 7 = 2x + 5$	true	false	false
5. $3(x + 2) = 3x + 6$	true	true	true
6. $x - 5 = 0$	false	false	true
7. TV programs can be received on channel x in this city.	open	open	open
8. $x + 7 < 2x + 9$	true	true	true
9. $x\left(\frac{1}{x}\right) = 1$	true	true	true
10. $x + x + x = 0$	false	false	false
11. $(x - 5)(2x) = 0$	false	false	true
12. A triangle has x sides.	false	true	false
13. $3^x = 27$	false	true	false
14. $3x + 18 = 11x + 2$	true	false	false
15. $2x - 7 = x + 2$	false	false	false
16. x subtracted from 13 is 8.	false	false	true
17. The product of the quantities $x + 2$ and $x - 2$ is zero.	true	false	false

Objective 3
Progress-Monitoring Activities

PM 3 Apply Skills 3

Use with 4-Day or 3-Day Instructional Plan.

MATERIALS

- *Interactive Text*, page 19

DIRECTIONS

1. Have students turn to *Interactive Text*, page 19, Apply Skills 3.

2. Monitor student work, and provide feedback as necessary.

   Watch for:
   - Do any students struggle with the arithmetic?
   - Do students substitute before solving?

NEXT STEPS • Differentiate

👥 4-Day Instructional Plan:

PS 1, page 46—Students who are on the accelerated path, to develop problem-solving skills

Objective 3 Posttest, page 48—Students who are on the differentiated path

👥 3-Day Instructional Plan:

PS 1, page 46—Students who are on the accelerated path, to develop problem-solving skills

PS 1, page 46—Students on the differentiated path who demonstrated understanding of the concepts in Apply Skills 2, to develop problem-solving skills

Objective 3 Posttest, page 48—All other students

APPLY SKILLS 3

Use substitution to find the solution for each formula.

Example:
$P = 2l + 2w$
$l = 14$ ft., $w = 8$ ft.
$P = 2(14) + 2(8)$
$P = \underline{\ 44 \text{ ft.}\ }$

1. $A = \frac{1}{2}(b_1 + b_2) \cdot h$
$b_1 = 9,\ b_2 = 11,\ h = 6$
$A = \underline{\ 60\ }$
$A = \frac{1}{2}(9 + 11)\ \ 6$

2. $y = x^2 + 3x + 1$
$x = 4$
$y = \underline{\ 29\ }$
$y = (4)^2 + 3(4) + 1$

3. $V = \pi r^2 h$
$\pi = 3.14,\ r = 6,\ h = 5$
$V = \underline{\ 565.2\ }$
$V = 3.14(6)^2 \cdot 5$

4. $C = \frac{5}{9}(F - 32)$
$F = 77$
$C = \underline{\ 25\ }$
$C = \frac{5}{9}(77 - 32)$

5. $y = \frac{a^2 - b^2}{a - b}$
$a = 6,\ b = 1$
$y = \underline{\ 7\ }$
$y = \frac{(6)^2 - (1)^2}{6 - 1}$

6. $y = (x + 3)^2$
$x = 5$
$y = \underline{\ 64\ }$
$y = (5 + 3)^2$

7. $P = (5\%)(3)(400)$
$P = \underline{\ 60\ }$
$P = (0.05)(3)(400)$

8. $y = 2x + 6 - x$
$x = 11$
$y = \underline{\ 17\ }$
$y = 2(11) + 6 - 11$

Problem-Solving Activities

★PS 1 Developing a Formula

Use with 4-Day or 3-Day Instructional Plan. In this activity, students discover a formula by asking a series of yes or no questions.

MATERIALS

• Blackline Master 6

DIRECTIONS

1. Make a transparency of Blackline Master 6, Developing a Formula, or write on the overhead or board:

Case 1	$\frac{x}{2}$	$\frac{y}{4}$	$\frac{z}{7}$	$\frac{A}{21}$

2. Explain that the value of *A* was calculated by using the values of *x*, *y*, and *z* and that a method of calculation (formula) was used. Tell the class they are to find the method of calculation (formula) used in this case by following this procedure:

   • Any student may raise his or her hand and ask any question about the formula as long as it can be answered "yes" or "no."

   • The rest of the class members may not talk during this process but must listen to the questions and answers. Call on every student who wants to ask a question until the class indicates it wants to caucus (talk as a group).

   • During the caucus, you will accept no more questions, but the class members may discuss what they know. This discussion process must be managed by the class with you being silent.

   • If the class discovers it wants to ask more questions, the caucus will be stopped and the "yes/no" questioning resumed.

   • The process continues until the class can state how the calculation was made by stating a rule in the form of a "yes/no" question.

   • Ask someone in the class to present the verbal rule as an algebraic formula.

3. Have the class use this procedure to find the formula for Case 1. $\frac{x+y}{2} \cdot z$

DEVELOPING A FORMULA

	x	*y*	*z*	*A*
Case 1	2	4	7	21
Case 2	4	3	5	7
Case 3	9	3	8	48
Case 4	0.5	3.5	7	11
Case 5	13	17	5	75
Case 6	2	6	7	9

4. Repeat the process for the other cases.

	x	*y*	*z*	*A*	
Case 2	4	3	5	7	$xy - z$
Case 3	9	3	8	48	
Case 4	0.5	3.5	7	11	$x + y + z$
Case 5	13	17	5	75	
Case 6	2	6	7	9	$(x - y + z)^2$

5. Cases 1, 3, and 5 can be solved with the same formula. See if the students can find it using the "yes/no" questions.

NEXT STEPS • Differentiate

4-Day Instructional Plan:
Objective 3 Posttest, page 48—All students

👥 3-Day Instructional Plan:
PS 2, page 47—Students who are on the accelerated path, for additional problem solving

Objective 3 Posttest, page 48—Students who are on the differentiated path

★ = Includes Problem Solving

Problem-Solving Activities

★ **PS 2** Converting Temperatures: Celsius to Fahrenheit and Vice Versa

Use with 3-Day Instructional Plan. In this activity, students convert temperatures from Celsius to Fahrenheit and vice versa.

MATERIALS

- *Interactive Text*, pages 20–21

DIRECTIONS

1. Have students work individually on this assignment.

2. Have students turn to *Interactive Text*, pages 20–21, Converting Celsius to Fahrenheit Temperatures, and complete the problems.

3. If necessary, discuss the difference between Fahrenheit and Celsius temperatures.

NEXT STEPS • Differentiate

3-Day Instructional Plan:
Objective 3 Posttest, page 48—All students

★ = Includes Problem Solving

PROBLEM SOLVING

Name _____ Date _____

CONVERTING CELSIUS TO FAHRENHEIT TEMPERATURES

Most European countries and most of the world use the Celsius scale for measuring temperature. When Americans are traveling outside of the United States, they will get the weather forecast in Celsius. In order to understand the Celsius temperature, it is helpful to convert the temperature to our Fahrenheit scale.

The formula for conversion from Celsius (C) to Fahrenheit (F) is $F = \frac{9}{5}C + 32$

Use the formula to convert each temperature.

> **Example:**
> If the temperature is 30° Celsius, what is the equivalent Fahrenheit temperature?
> $F = \frac{9}{5}(30) + 32$
> $F = 54 + 32 = 86$
> 86°F

1. The temperature in Paris is reported at 15° Celsius. What is the equivalent Fahrenheit temperature?
   $F = \frac{9}{5}(15) + 32$
   $F = 27 + 32$
   59°F

2. The winter temperature in London is 5° Celsius. What is that in Fahrenheit?
   $F = \frac{9}{5}(5) + 32$
   $F = 9 + 32$
   41°F

3. What is the Fahrenheit temperature for −5° Celsius?
   $F = \frac{9}{5}(-5) + 32$
   $F = -9 + 32$
   23°F

4. What Celsius temperature would be a comfortable room temperature? Most Americans keep their room temperature between 68° and 75° Fahrenheit.
   $C = \frac{5}{9}(F - 32)$
   $C = \frac{5}{9}(68 - 32)$ to $\frac{5}{9}(75 - 32)$
   20°C to 23.9°C

20   Chapter 1 • Objective 3 • PS 2   Inside Algebra

PROBLEM SOLVING

Name _____ Date _____

CONVERTING CELSIUS TO FAHRENHEIT TEMPERATURES   *(continued)*

5. If the temperature in Berlin is 0° Celsius, what is that in Fahrenheit?
   $F = \frac{9}{5}(0) + 32$
   32°F

6. What would be the Fahrenheit temperature for 100° Celsius?
   $F = \frac{9}{5}(100) + 32$
   $F = 180 + 32$
   212°F

7. Dublin reported a reading of 25° Celsius. What is that in Fahrenheit?
   $F = \frac{9}{5}(25) + 32$
   $F = 45 + 32$
   77°F

8. A temperature of 35° Celsius was reported in Lisbon. How hot is that in Fahrenheit?
   $F = \frac{9}{5}(35) + 32$
   $F = 63 + 32$
   95°F

9. How cold in Fahrenheit is a temperature of −25° Celsius?
   $F = \frac{9}{5}(-25) + 32$
   $F = -45 + 32$
   −13°F

10. About what temperature in Fahrenheit is 14° Celsius?
    $F = \frac{9}{5}(14) + 32$
    $F = 25.2 + 32$
    57.2°F

Inside Algebra   Chapter 1 • Objective 3 • PS 2   21

This page intentionally left blank

Ongoing Assessment

Objective 3 Posttest

Discuss with students the key concepts in Objective 3. Following the discussion, administer the Objective 3 Posttest to all students.

Using the Results

• Score the posttest and update the class record card.

• Provide reinforcement for students who do not demonstrate mastery of the concepts through individual or small-group reteaching of key concepts.

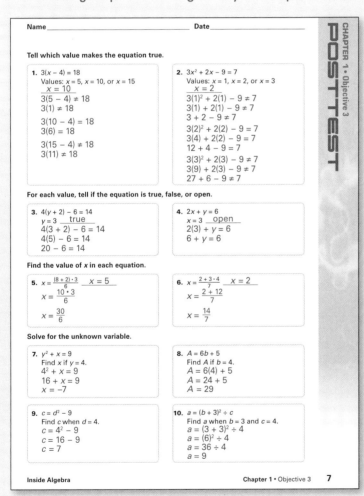

Objective 4 Pretest

Students complete the Objective 4 Pretest on the same day as the Objective 3 Posttest.

Using the Results

- Score the pretest and update the class record card.
- If the majority of students do not demonstrate mastery of the concepts, use the 5-Day Instructional Plan for Objective 4.
- If the majority of students demonstrate mastery of the concepts, use the 3-Day Instructional Plan for Objective 4.

CHAPTER 1 • Objective 4 PRETEST

Name _____ Date _____

Evaluate the mathematical expressions by using properties to make the computation as easy as possible.

1. $25 + (134 + 75) =$ ___234___
$25 + 75 + 134$
$100 + 134$

2. $(18 \cdot 7) \cdot (13 \cdot 0) =$ ___0___
$(18 \cdot 7 \cdot 13)0$

3. $(17 \cdot 8) + (17 \cdot 2) =$ ___170___
$17(8 + 2)$
$17(10)$

4. $\left[\frac{5}{6}(2 + 7)\right] \cdot \frac{6}{5} =$ ___9___
$\left[\frac{5}{6}(9)\right] \cdot \frac{6}{5}$
$\frac{6}{5} \cdot \frac{5}{6} \cdot 9$
$1 \cdot 9$

5. $5 \cdot 17 \cdot 20 =$ ___1,700___
$5 \cdot 20 \cdot 17$
$100 \cdot 17$

6. $\frac{3 + 7}{4} \cdot \frac{4}{10} =$ ___1___
$\frac{3 + 7}{10}$
$\frac{10}{10}$

7. $123 \cdot 4 =$ ___492___
$400 + 80 + 12$

8. $[3(4 + 5) + 2] \cdot 0 =$ ___0___

9. $(4 - 2)(13 + 1) \cdot 1 =$ ___28___
$(4 - 2)(13 + 1)$
$(2)(14)$

10. $9(2 + 3) =$ ___45___
$9(5)$

8   Chapter 1 • Objective 4   Inside Algebra

Goals and Activities

Objective 4 Goals

The following activities, when used with the instructional plans on pages 52 and 53, enable students to:

- Evaluate the expression $3\left(\dfrac{9+7}{5}\right) \cdot 5\left(\dfrac{9+7}{3}\right)$ to get **256**

- Evaluate the expression $6 \cdot \left[\dfrac{1}{2}(5+7)\right]$ to get **36**

Objective 4 Activities

Concept Development Activities

★**CD 1** Learning Mathematical Properties, page 54	**CD 2** Identifying Simple Instances of Mathematical Properties, page 56	★**CD 3** Using the Distributive Property With Mathematical Expressions, page 58

Practice Activities

PA 1 Computing and Naming a Property, page 60	**PA 2** Sharing Properties, page 62

Progress-Monitoring Activities

PM 1 Apply Skills 1, page 64	**PM 2** Apply Skills 2, page 65	**PM 3** Apply Skills 3, page 66

★Problem-Solving Activity

★**PS 1** Playing the Mathematical Properties Game, page 67

Ongoing Assessment

Posttest Objective 4, page 69

Review Chapter 1 Review, page 70

CD = Concept Development PM = Progress Monitoring PS = Problem Solving
PA = Practice Activity ★ = Includes Problem Solving

Instructional Plans

5-Day Instructional Plan

Use the 5-Day Instructional Plan when pretest results indicate that students would benefit from a slower pace. This plan is used when the majority of students need more time or did not demonstrate mastery on the pretest.

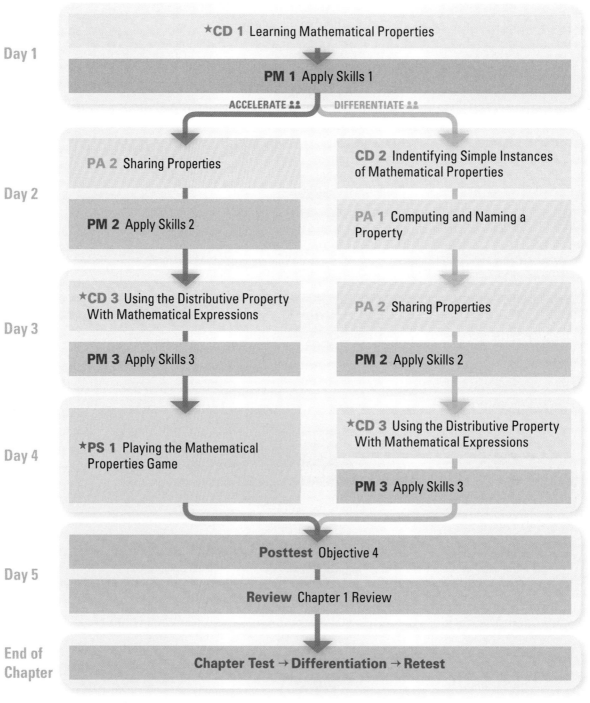

Day 1
★**CD 1** Learning Mathematical Properties
PM 1 Apply Skills 1

ACCELERATE 👥   DIFFERENTIATE 👥

Day 2
PA 2 Sharing Properties
PM 2 Apply Skills 2

CD 2 Indentifying Simple Instances of Mathematical Properties
PA 1 Computing and Naming a Property

Day 3
★**CD 3** Using the Distributive Property With Mathematical Expressions
PM 3 Apply Skills 3

PA 2 Sharing Properties
PM 2 Apply Skills 2

Day 4
★**PS 1** Playing the Mathematical Properties Game

★**CD 3** Using the Distributive Property With Mathematical Expressions
PM 3 Apply Skills 3

Day 5
Posttest Objective 4
Review Chapter 1 Review

End of Chapter
Chapter Test → Differentiation → Retest

CD = Concept Development   PM = Progress Monitoring   PS = Problem Solving
PA = Practice Activity   ★ = Includes Problem Solving

3-Day Instructional Plan

Use the 3-Day Instructional Plan when pretest results indicate that students can move through the activities at a faster pace. This plan is ideal when the majority of students demonstrate mastery on the pretest. This plan does not include all activities.

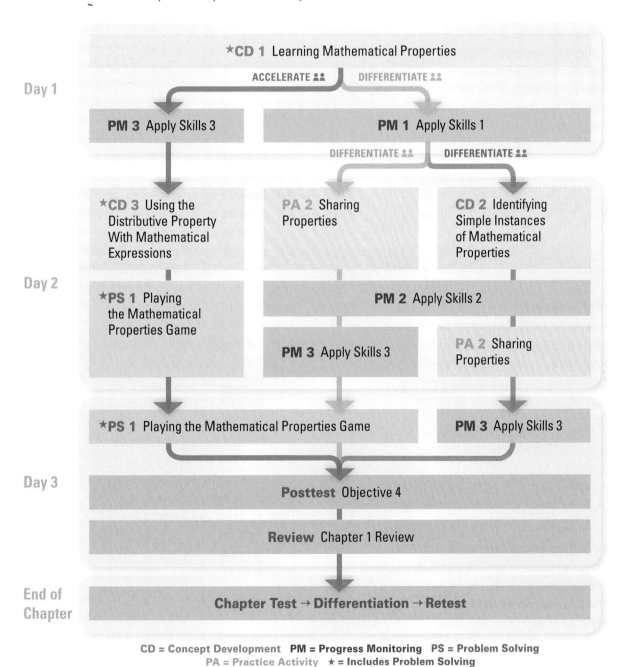

Day 1

★**CD 1** Learning Mathematical Properties

ACCELERATE 👥   DIFFERENTIATE 👥

PM 3 Apply Skills 3   **PM 1** Apply Skills 1

DIFFERENTIATE 👥   DIFFERENTIATE 👥

Day 2

★**CD 3** Using the Distributive Property With Mathematical Expressions

PA 2 Sharing Properties

CD 2 Identifying Simple Instances of Mathematical Properties

★**PS 1** Playing the Mathematical Properties Game

PM 2 Apply Skills 2

PM 3 Apply Skills 3

PA 2 Sharing Properties

Day 3

★**PS 1** Playing the Mathematical Properties Game   **PM 3** Apply Skills 3

Posttest Objective 4

Review Chapter 1 Review

End of Chapter

Chapter Test → Differentiation → Retest

CD = Concept Development   PM = Progress Monitoring   PS = Problem Solving
PA = Practice Activity   ★ = Includes Problem Solving

★**CD 1** Learning Mathematical Properties

Use with 5-Day or 3-Day Instructional Plan. In this activity, students give examples that demonstrate mathematical properties.

DIRECTIONS

1. Explain to students that there are properties in mathematics that are used over and over in algebra. It is important for all students to understand these properties and to be able to use them in a variety of ways. The following steps discuss these properties.

2. **Additive Identity:** $a + 0 = a$. Ask students for an example (e.g., $3 + 0 = 3$). Most students will see this as obvious because they have been adding zero since kindergarten. Give students the problem $8 + 3 - 3 = ?$ Discuss that $3 - 3 = 0$, so $8 + 3 - 3 = 8$. It is an application of $a + 0 = a$. Also discuss a problem such as $x + 1 + 1 + 1 - 1 - 1 - 1 = ?$ Again, $1 + (-1)$ is the same as zero, so the answer is x.

3. **Multiplicative Identity:** $a \cdot 1 = a$. Ask students for an example (e.g., $6 \cdot 1 = 6$). Ask if everyone believes this property is true for all numbers. Ask if anyone can give a counterexample. Students know it is true and have been using the property since third grade. Give students the problem $\frac{2}{3} \cdot \frac{3}{3} = ?$ Most students will give $\frac{6}{9}$, which is a correct response, but the answer could also be $\frac{2}{3}$ because $\frac{3}{3}$ is the same as 1, and $\frac{2}{3} \cdot 1 = \frac{2}{3}$. Both are names for the same number. This property will be used in algebra with different names for 1. Ask, "What is the answer to the problem $14 \cdot \frac{1}{2} \cdot 2 = ?$" Note that $\frac{1}{2} \cdot 2 = 1$, so the answer is 14.

4. **Multiplicative Property of Zero:** $a \cdot 0 = 0$. Ask students for an example (e.g., $8 \cdot 0 = 0$). Ask whether the students believe this is true for all numbers or if they can find a counterexample. In algebra, we may see a problem such as $9 \cdot (3 - 3) = ?$ Since $3 - 3 = 0$, $9 \cdot 0 = 0$. Another example to discuss is if $a \cdot b = 0$, what do we know about a or b?

5. **Multiplicative Inverse:** $\frac{a}{b} \cdot \frac{b}{a} = 1$, $(a \neq 0, b \neq 0)$. Ask students for an example (e.g., $\frac{2}{3} \cdot \frac{3}{2} = 1$). Ask students why this is true. When multiplying a number by its inverse, the numerator and denominator in the result are equal.

Examples:

$$\frac{6 \cdot 7}{\frac{3}{8}} = \frac{6 \cdot 7 \cdot \frac{8}{3}}{\frac{3}{8} \cdot \frac{8}{3}} = \frac{6 \cdot 7 \cdot \frac{8}{3}}{1} = 112$$

$$\frac{1}{2} \cdot \frac{5}{6} \cdot 2 = ?$$

Since $\frac{1}{2} \cdot 2 = 1$, we have $1 \cdot \frac{5}{6} = \frac{5}{6}$.

6. **Distributive Property:** $a \cdot (b + c) = a \cdot b + a \cdot c$. Ask students for an example [e.g., $4 \cdot (5 + 9) = 4 \cdot 5 + 4 \cdot 9$]. Discuss how to multiply numbers such as $15 \cdot 24$ by using the distributive property: $15 \cdot 24 = 15 \cdot (20 + 4) = 15 \cdot 20 + 15 \cdot 4 = 300 + 60 = 360$. Another example to discuss is $3(N + 4) = 3N + 3 \cdot 4 = 3N + 12$. A third example is $6 \cdot 7 + 6 \cdot 3 = 6 \cdot (7 + 3) = 6 \cdot 10 = 60$.

7. **Commutative Property of Addition:** $a + b = b + a$. Ask students for an example [e.g., $(11 + 15) = (15 + 11)$]. This property indicates that you can add in any order. For example, $6 + 17 + 4 + 11 = (6 + 4) + 17 + 11 = 38$. Explain that problems can be made easier if you look for sums that are easy for you. Discuss that this property works only for problems that are all addition. Discuss examples such as $6 \cdot 8 + 9 + 2 \neq 6 \cdot 10 + 9$. Ask students for the answer to $14 + 19 + 6 + 1 = ?$ Ask students how you can arrange the addends to make it easy. $(14 + 6) + (19 + 1) = 20 + 20 = 40$

★ = Includes Problem Solving

8. **Commutative Property of Multiplication:**
$a \cdot b = b \cdot a$. Ask students for an example (e.g., $6 \cdot 9 = 9 \cdot 6$). Discuss that this property indicates that the order of multiplication can be changed. For example, $5 \cdot 21 \cdot 4 = 5 \cdot 4 \cdot 21$. Students should watch for problems that can be made easier by changing the order. Discuss that this property works for problems containing all products, but *not* for those with a mixture of operations, such as $8 \cdot 4 + 2 \cdot 5 \neq 8 \cdot 5 \cdot 4 + 2$.

9. **Associative Property of Addition:**
$(a + b) + c = a + (b + c)$. Ask students for an example [e.g., $(5 + 8) + 3 = 5 + (8 + 3)$]. This property shows that we can add different groupings if the problem is all addition. Show that combining this property with the commutative property allows rearrangement of terms to make a sum easier to find. For example, $(8 + 17) + 3 = 8 + (17 + 3) = 8 + 20 = 28$. Another example is $(7 + 19) + 1 + (5 + 3) = (7 + 3) + (19 + 1) + 5 = 10 + 20 + 5 = 35$.

10. **Associative Property of Multiplication:**
$(a \cdot b) \cdot c = a \cdot (b \cdot c)$. Ask students for an example [e.g., $(9 \cdot 8) \cdot 12 = 9 \cdot (8 \cdot 12)$]. Discuss that this property shows that we can multiply different groupings of numbers if the problem is all multiplication. Show that combining this property with the commutative property of multiplication allows rearrangement of factors to make the product easier to find. For example, $4 \cdot 18 \cdot 25 = (4 \cdot 25) \cdot 18 = 100 \cdot 18 = 1,800$. Another example is $(5 \cdot 17) \cdot 2 = (2 \cdot 5) \cdot 17 = 10 \cdot 17 = 170$.

11. Ask students how they would rearrange the following problems to make them easy to solve. Have them name the properties they would use.

Sample problems:

$(7 + 29) + 3 = ?$ 39, associative or commutative properties of addition

$(81 + 3) - 3 = ?$ 81, associative property of addition and additive identity

$\frac{2}{3} \cdot \left(\frac{3}{2} \cdot \frac{1}{8} \right) = ?$ $\frac{1}{8}$, associative property of multiplication, multiplicative inverse, multiplicative identity

$(9 \cdot 8) + (9 \cdot 2) = ?$ 90, distributive property

$(47 + 9) + (13 + 11) = ?$ 80, associative property of addition

NEXT STEPS • Differentiate

5-Day Instructional Plan:
PM 1, page 64—All students, to assess progress

3-Day Instructional Plan:
PM 3, page 66—Students who demonstrate understanding of the concepts, to assess progress
PM 1, page 64—Students who need additional support, to assess progress

Concept Development Activities

CD 2 Identifying Simple Instances of Mathematical Properties

Use with 5-Day or 3-Day Instructional Plan. In this activity, students identify the mathematical property being demonstrated.

MATERIALS

- *Interactive Text*, pages 22–23
- Blackline Master 7
- Blackline Master 8 or blank cards

DIRECTIONS

1. Make a transparency of Blackline Master 7, Identifying Simple Instances of Mathematical Properties, or list the following formulas and properties on a transparency master. Discuss and review the properties, giving an example of each.

Formula	Property
$a + 0 = a$	Additive Identity
$a \cdot 1 = a$	Multiplicative Identity
$a \cdot 0 = 0$	Multiplicative Property of Zero
$\frac{a}{b} \cdot \frac{b}{a} = 1$ $(a \neq 0, b \neq 0)$	Multiplicative Inverse
$a \cdot (b + c) = a \cdot b + a \cdot c$	Distributive Property
$a + b = b + a$	Commutative Property of Addition
$a \cdot b = b \cdot a$	Commutative Property of Multiplication
$(a + b) + c = a + (b + c)$	Associative Property of Addition
$(a \cdot b) \cdot c = a \cdot (b \cdot c)$	Associative Property of Multiplication

---

Name _____ Date _____

7

IDENTIFYING SIMPLE INSTANCES OF MATHEMATICAL PROPERTIES

	Formula	Property
a.	$a + 0 = a$	Additive Identity
b.	$a \cdot 1 = a$	Multiplicative Identity
c.	$a \cdot 0 = 0$	Multiplicative Property of Zero
d.	$\frac{a}{b} \cdot \frac{b}{a} = 1$, $(a \neq 0, b \neq 0)$	Multiplicative Inverse
e.	$a \cdot (b + c) = a \cdot b + a \cdot c$	Distributive Property
f.	$a + b = b + a$	Commutative Property of Addition
g.	$a \cdot b = b \cdot a$	Commutative Property of Multiplication
h.	$(a + b) + c = a + (b + c)$	Associative Property of Addition
i.	$(a \cdot b) \cdot c = a \cdot (b \cdot c)$	Associative Property of Multiplication

---

Name _____ Date _____

8

IDENTIFYING SIMPLE INSTANCES OF MATHEMATICAL PROPERTIES *(continued)*

$a + 0 = a$ Additive Identity	$a \cdot 1 = a$ Multiplicative Identity	$a \cdot 0 = 0$ Multiplicative Property of Zero
$\frac{a}{b} \cdot \frac{b}{a} = 1$, $(a \neq 0, b \neq 0)$ Multiplicative Inverse	$a \cdot (b + c) = a \cdot b + a \cdot c$ Distributive Property	$a + b = b + a$ Commutative Property of Addition
$a \cdot b = b \cdot a$ Commutative Property of Multiplication	$(a + b) + c = a + (b + c)$ Associative Property of Addition	$(a \cdot b) \cdot c = a \cdot (b \cdot c)$ Associative Property of Multiplication

2. Duplicate and cut out the cards on Blackline Master 8, Identifying Simple Instances of Mathematical Properties, or write the formula and property on blank cards, one per card.

3. Have students work in groups of four. Have students turn to *Interactive Text*, pages 22–23, Identifying Properties, and have students complete the table as a group.

4. Choose a group at random and ask them to select one of the property cards.

5. Ask one member of that group to identify one instance of that property from the list on the blackline master and to state the formula and the values for the variable(s).

6. Ask another member of that group to identify another instance of that property from the list on the blackline master and to state the formula and the values for the variable(s).

7. Repeat this process until a student indicates that there are no more instances of that property on the blackline master.

8. Repeat Steps 4–7 with another group.

   Note: Not every student in each group needs to be called on. This is acceptable because the group is responsible for working all the problems on the blackline master, and all members should be prepared.

NEXT STEPS • Differentiate

5-Day Instructional Plan:
PA 1, page 60—All students, for additional practice

3-Day Instructional Plan:
PM 2, page 65—All students, to assess progress

Name_____ Date_____

IDENTIFYING PROPERTIES

Identify each instance of a mathematical property by name and formula statement, and give the corresponding values of the variables in the formula statement. Use *a*, *b*, and *c* as the variables, and use · as the symbol for multiplication. See the first entry for an example. Some properties will not use all three variables.

Problem	Name of Property	Formula of Property	a	b	c
Example: $3(0.5 + 7) = 3(0.5) + 3(7)$	Distributive	$a \cdot (b + c) = a \cdot b + a \cdot c$	3	0.5	7
1. $137(5\%) = (5\%)(137)$	Commutative (×)	$a(b) = (b)(a)$	137	5%	—
2. $12 + 0 = 12$	Identity (+)	$a + 0 = a$	12	—	—
3. $\frac{4}{3}\left(\frac{3}{4}\right) = 1$	Inverse (×)	$\frac{a}{b}\left(\frac{b}{a}\right) = 1$	4	3	—
4. $(7 \cdot 4) \cdot 5 = 7 \cdot (4 \cdot 5)$	Associative (×)	$(a \cdot b) \cdot c = a \cdot (b \cdot c)$	7	4	5
5. $173(1) = 173$	Identity (×)	$a(1) = a$	173	—	—
6. $1.05 + 2.23 = 2.23 + 1.05$	Commutative (+)	$a + b = b + a$	1.05	2.23	—
7. $973 \cdot 0 = 0$	Multiplicative Property of Zero	$a \cdot 0 = 0$	973	—	—
8. $(1 + 2) + 3 = 1 + (2 + 3)$	Associative (+)	$(a + b) + c = a + (b + c)$	1	2	3
9. $19.98 + 0 = 19.98$	Identity (+)	$a + 0 = a$	19.98	—	—
10. $1.79 + 2.19 = 2.19 + 1.79$	Commutative (+)	$a + b = b + a$	1.79	2.19	—
11. $(0.2 \cdot 0.4)6 = 0.2(0.4 \cdot 6)$	Associative (×)	$(a \cdot b)c = a(b \cdot c)$	0.2	0.4	6
12. $4,972.03 \cdot 0 = 0$	Multiplicative Property of Zero	$a \cdot 0 = 0$	4,972.03	—	—
13. $30.33 \cdot 0.76 = 0.76 \cdot 30.33$	Commutative (×)	$a \cdot b = b \cdot a$	30.33	0.76	—

Name_____ Date_____

IDENTIFYING PROPERTIES   *(continued)*

Problem	Name of Property	Formula of Property	a	b	c
14. $13(5 + 2) = 13 \cdot 5 + 13 \cdot 2$	Distributive	$a(b + c) = a \cdot b + a \cdot c$	13	5	2
15. $(2 + 3) + 9 = 2 + (3 + 9)$	Associative (+)	$(a + b) + c = a + (b + c)$	2	3	9
16. $3.14159 \cdot 1 = 3.14159$	Identity (×)	$a \cdot 1 = a$	3.14159	—	—
17. $13 + 0 = 13$	Identity (+)	$a + 0 = a$	13	—	—
18. $29 \cdot 0 = 0$	Multiplicative Property of Zero	$a \cdot 0 = 0$	29	—	—
19. $75 \cdot 1 = 75$	Identity (×)	$a \cdot 1 = a$	75	—	—
20. $(2 \cdot 7) \cdot 5 = 2 \cdot (7 \cdot 5)$	Associative (×)	$(a \cdot b) \cdot c = a \cdot (b \cdot c)$	2	7	5
21. $(2 \cdot 7)5 = 2(7 \cdot 5)$	Commutative (×)	$(a \cdot b)c = a(b \cdot c)$	2	7	5
22. $2(0.5) = 1$	Inverse (×)	$a\left(\frac{1}{a}\right) = 1$	2	—	—
23. $0.5(2) = 2(0.5)$	Commutative (×)	$a(b) = b(a)$	0.5	2	—
24. $2(5 + 3) = 2(5) + 2(3)$	Distributive	$a(b + c) = a(b) + a(c)$	2	5	3
25. $4.98 + 2.673 = 2.673 + 4.98$	Commutative (+)	$a + b = b + a$	4.98	2.673	—
26. $5(7 + 6) = (7 + 6)5$	Commutative (×)	$a(b + c) = (b + c)a$	5	7	6
27. $3 \cdot 17 = 3 \cdot 10 + 3 \cdot 7$	Distributive	$a(b + c) = a(b) + a(c)$	3	10	7
28. $(5\% \cdot 275) \cdot 1 = (5\%)(275)$	Identity (×)	$(a \cdot b)1 = (a)(b)$	5%	275	—
29. $(a + b)c = c(a + b)$	Commutative (×)	$(a + b)c = c(a + b)$	—	—	—

Concept Development Activities

★ CD 3 Using the Distributive Property With Mathematical Expressions

Use with 5-Day or 3-Day Instructional Plan. In this activity, students write a mathematical expression for a word problem using the Distributive Property.

MATERIALS

- Blackline Masters 9–12

DIRECTIONS

1. Discuss with students the following property: *Distributive Property* $a \cdot (b + c) = a \cdot b + a \cdot c$

2. Explain that there may be more than two addends; for example, $3(9 + 5 + 2 + 7) = 3(9) + 3(5) + 3(2) + 3(7)$.

3. Cut one copy of Blackline Masters 9–12, Mathematical Expressions Using the Distributive Property, into horizontal strips, separating each row of the matrix from every other row.

4. Place the separated rows from the matrix into a hat and have each student draw out one row.

5. Ask students to solve the problem they have drawn.

6. Have each student find the other student in the class who has the same situation but instructions to develop an expression in a different form.

7. Ask the student pairs to check each other's work.

8. Replace the rows from the matrix into the hat and have the students draw again, repeating Steps 5–7. Most students should get a different problem than they had previously.

9. Repeat the process several times until all members of the class understand the two models for calculation represented by the distributive property.

10. Ask the student pairs from the last pairing to write a word problem of their own that requires both types of modeling using the distributive property.

11. Have the groups exchange problems, solve the problems, and check each other's work.

★ = Includes Problem Solving

MATHEMATICAL EXPRESSIONS USING THE DISTRIBUTIVE PROPERTY

Read each scenario and write a mathematical expression to solve the problem.

John has five pieces of plywood, each 8 feet long. The widths of the individual pieces are 1 foot, 2 feet, 3 feet, 4 feet, and 5 feet, respectively. John is going to lay the pieces side by side to make a flat rectangular surface that is 8 feet long and as wide as possible.	Write a mathematical expression that represents the total area of the flat surface and *does not require* calculation of the area of the individual pieces.	$8(1 + 2 + 3 + 4 + 5) =$ 120 square feet
John has five pieces of plywood, each 8 feet long. The widths of the individual pieces are 1 foot, 2 feet, 3 feet, 4 feet, and 5 feet, respectively. John is going to lay the pieces side by side to make a flat rectangular surface that is 8 feet long and as wide as possible.	Write a mathematical expression that represents the total area of the flat surface that *requires* calculation of the area of each individual piece.	$8(1) + 8(2) + 8(3) + 8(4) + 8(5) =$ 120 square feet
Mary purchases one comb for $1.95, one lip gloss for $5.98, and one set of false fingernails for $13.50. The sales tax rate is 7%.	Write a mathematical expression that represents the total sales tax on Mary's purchases and *does not require* calculation of the tax on each individual item.	$(7\%)(\$1.95 + \$5.98 + \$13.50) = \$1.50$ in sales tax
Mary purchases one comb for $1.95, one lip gloss for $5.98, and one set of false fingernails for $13.50. The sales tax rate is 7%.	Write a mathematical expression that represents the total sales tax on Mary's purchases that *requires* calculation of the tax on each individual item.	$7\%(\$1.95) + 7\%(\$5.98) + 7\%(\$13.50) = \$1.50$ in sales tax
A real estate developer is leasing a new 17-story building to national corporations. Each corporation must lease full floors. The rent for an entire floor is $22,973 per month. An insurance company leases four floors. An oil company leases nine floors. The Antique Boutique leases the first two floors. The top two floors are leased to a local restaurant for a dining room and kitchens.	Write a mathematical expression that represents the total rent to be collected each month by the developer and *does not require* calculation of the rent paid by each renter each month.	$\$22,973(4 + 9 + 2 + 2) = \$390,541$ per month

---

MATHEMATICAL EXPRESSIONS USING THE DISTRIBUTIVE PROPERTY *(continued)*

A real estate developer is leasing a new 17-story building to national corporations. Each corporation must lease full floors. The rent for an entire floor is $22,973 per month. An insurance company leases four floors. An oil company leases nine floors. The Antique Boutique leases the first two floors. The top two floors are leased to a local restaurant for a dining room and kitchens.	Write a mathematical expression that represents the total rent to be collected each month by the developer that *requires* calculation of the rent paid by each renter each month.	$\$22,973(4) + \$22,973(9) + \$22,973(2) + \$22,973(2) = \$390,541$ per month
During a business recession, a car dealer decides to discount each new car 20%. The original prices were as follows: Car 1, $23,795; Car 2, $19,750; Car 3, $45,999. On Saturday, the dealer sells one of each.	Write a mathematical expression that represents the total amount of money taken in by the dealer on Saturday and *does not require* calculation of the sale price of each individual car.	$80\%(\$23,795 + \$19,750 + \$45,999) = \$71,635.20$
During a business recession, a car dealer decides to discount each new car 20%. The original prices were as follows: Car 1, $23,795; Car 2, $19,750; Car 3, $45,999. On Saturday, the dealer sells one of each.	Write a mathematical expression that represents the total amount of money taken in by the dealer on Saturday that *requires* calculation of the sale price of each individual car.	$80\%(\$23,795) + 80\%(\$19,750) + 80\%(\$45,999) = \$71,635.20$
During a business recession, a car dealer decides to discount each new car 20%. The original prices were as follows: Car 1, $23,795; Car 2, $19,750; Car 3, $45,999. On Saturday, the dealer sells one of each.	Write a mathematical expression that represents the total amount of money lost by the dealer on Saturday and *does not require* calculation of the amount lost on each individual car.	$20\%(\$23,795 + \$19,750 + \$45,999) = \$17,908.80$
During a business recession, a car dealer decides to discount each new car 20%. The original prices were as follows: Car 1, $23,795; Car 2, $19,750; Car 3, $45,999. On Saturday, the dealer sells one of each.	Write a mathematical expression that represents the total amount of money lost by the dealer on Saturday that *requires* calculation of the amount lost on each individual car.	$20\%(\$23,795) + 20\%(\$19,750) + 20\%(\$45,999) = \$17,908.80$
John purchases four items at the local hobby shop. The regular prices are one tube of glue at $2, one block of balsa wood at $4, one file at $17, and one set of decals at $5. The shop is having a 25% off sale, and the sales tax rate is 5%.	Write a mathematical expression that represents the total amount of John's bill and *does not require* calculation of the sale price or the sales tax on an individual item.	$0.75(\$2 + \$4 + \$17 + \$5) + 0.05[0.75(\$2 + \$4 + \$17 + \$5)] = \$22.05$

Name_____ Date_____

MATHEMATICAL EXPRESSIONS USING THE DISTRIBUTIVE PROPERTY *(continued)*

John purchases four items at the local hobby shop. The regular prices are one tube of glue at $2, one block of balsa wood at $4, one file at $17, and one set of decals at $5. The shop is having a 25% off sale, and the sales tax rate is 5%.	Write a mathematical expression that represents the total amount of John's bill that *requires* calculation of the sale price including sales tax for each individual item.	[(0.75 • $2) + 0.05 (0.75 • $2)] + [(0.75 • $4) + 0.05(0.75 • $4)] + [(0.75 • $17) + 0.05 (0.75 • $17)] + [(0.75 • $5) + 0.05(0.75 • $5)] = $22.05
Three dump trucks belonging to a trucking company are carrying gravel to the same local construction site. The weight of the gravel in each truck is 5,795 pounds, 5,992 pounds, and 5,699 pounds. The Department of Transportation has stopped the three trucks because they are overloaded. The load in each truck must be reduced by 15% by removing gravel from each truck before it can proceed.	Write a mathematical expression that represents the total amount of gravel that a trucking company must unload but *does not require* calculation of the amount to be removed from each individual truck.	15%(5,795 + 5,992 + 5,699) = 2,622.9 lbs.
Three dump trucks belonging to a trucking company are carrying gravel to the same local construction site. The weight of the gravel in each truck is 5,795 pounds, 5,992 pounds, and 5,699 pounds. The Department of Transportation has stopped the three trucks because they are overloaded. The load in each truck must be reduced by 15% by removing gravel from each truck before it can proceed.	Write a mathematical expression that represents the total amount of gravel that a trucking company must unload that *requires* calculation of the amount to be removed from each individual truck.	15%(5,795) + 15% (5,992) + 15%(5,699) = 2,622.9 lbs.
Three dump trucks belonging to a trucking company are carrying gravel to the same local construction site. The weight of the gravel in each truck is 5,795 pounds, 5,992 pounds, and 5,699 pounds. The Department of Transportation has stopped the three trucks because they are overloaded. The load in each truck must be reduced by 15% by removing gravel from each truck before it can proceed.	Write a mathematical expression that represents the total amount of gravel that will be delivered to the construction site, after unloading gravel from each truck, and *does not require* calculation of the amount remaining in each individual truck after unloading.	85%(5,795 + 5,992 + 5,699) = 14,863.1 lbs.

Name_____ Date_____

MATHEMATICAL EXPRESSIONS USING THE DISTRIBUTIVE PROPERTY *(continued)*

Three dump trucks belonging to a trucking company are carrying gravel to the same local construction site. The weight of the gravel in each truck is 5,795 pounds, 5,992 pounds, and 5,699 pounds. The Department of Transportation has stopped the three trucks because they are overloaded. The load in each truck must be reduced by 15% by removing gravel from each truck before it can proceed.	Write a mathematical expression that represents the total amount of gravel that will be delivered to the construction site, after unloading gravel from each truck, that *requires* calculation of the amount remaining in each individual truck after unloading.	85%(5,795) + 85%(5,992) + 85%(5,699) = 14,863.1 lbs.
Mr. Jones goes to the dentist for major dental work. The procedures and the costs are one filling, $150; one gold crown, $790; and one implant, $4,550. Due to the extent of the work done, the dentist gives Mr. Jones a 15% discount.	Write a mathematical expression that represents the total cost of the dental work and *does not require* calculation of the discounted price of each procedure.	85%($150 + $790 + $4,550) = $4,666.50
Mr. Jones goes to the dentist for major dental work. The procedures and the costs are one filling, $150; one gold crown, $790; and one implant, $4,550. Due to the extent of the work done, the dentist gives Mr. Jones a 15% discount.	Write a mathematical expression that represents the total cost of the dental work that *requires* calculation of the discounted price of each procedure.	85%($150) + 85%($790) + 85%($4,550) = $4,666.50
Three local elementary schools have enrollments of 573 students, 691 students, and 472 students. Due to new home construction, the superintendent is expecting a 15% increase in enrollment at each school in September.	Write a mathematical expression that represents the projected total combined enrollment of the three schools in September and *does not require* calculation of the projected enrollments of each individual school.	15%(573 + 691 + 472) + 573 + 691 + 472 = 1,996 students
Three local elementary schools have enrollments of 573 students, 691 students, and 472 students. Due to new home construction, the superintendent is expecting a 15% increase in enrollment at each school in September.	Write a mathematical expression that represents the projected total combined enrollment of the three schools in September that *requires* calculation of the projected enrollments of each individual school.	15%(573) + 15%(691) + 15%(472) + 573 + 691 + 472 = 1,996 students

NEXT STEPS • Differentiate

5-Day Instructional Plan:
PM 3, page 66—All students, to assess progress

3-Day Instructional Plan:
PS 1, page 67—All students, to develop problem-solving skills

Practice Activities

PA 1 Computing and Naming a Property

Use with 5-Day Instructional Plan. In this activity, students make problems easier using mathematical properties.

MATERIALS

- Blackline Masters 13–16 or blank cards

DIRECTIONS

1. Have students work in groups of four.

2. Discuss with students the following properties and identities:

   Associative Property of Addition
   $(a + b) + c = a + (b + c)$

   Associative Property of Multiplication
   $(a \cdot b) \cdot c = a \cdot (b \cdot c)$

   Commutative Property of Addition
   $a + b = b + a$

   Commutative Property of Multiplication
   $a \cdot b = b \cdot a$

   Distributive Property
   $a \cdot (b + c) = a \cdot b + a \cdot c$

   Multiplicative Identity
   $a \cdot 1 = a$

   Multiplicative Inverse
   $\frac{a}{b} \cdot \frac{b}{a} = 1 \ (a \neq 0, b \neq 0)$

   Multiplicative Property of Zero
   $a \cdot 0 = 0$

3. Duplicate and cut out the cards on Blackline Masters 13–16, Computing and Naming a Property. Make sure Blackline Masters 13 and 14 are back-to-back and Blackline Masters 15 and 16 are back-to-back. Alternatively, write each equation and its solution on either side of a blank card.

4. After all the cards have been made, have the students mix them up with the fronts (problems) facing up.

Name _____ Date _____ 13

COMPUTING AND NAMING A PROPERTY

$(77 + 7) + 3 =$ 87; associative (+)	$20 \cdot (59 \cdot 5) =$ 5,900; commutative (×) or associative (×)	$38 \cdot (14 \cdot 0) =$ 0; multiplicative property of zero, associative (×)
$13 + 8 + 7 + 2 =$ 30; commutative (+) or associative (+)	$19,876 \cdot 1 =$ 19,876; multiplicative identity	$\frac{3}{4} \cdot \left(\frac{4}{3} \cdot 8\right) =$ 8; multiplicative inverse, associative (×)
$\frac{3}{5} + \left(\frac{1}{8} + \frac{2}{5}\right) =$ $1\frac{1}{8}$; commutative (+), associative (+)	$19(8) + 19(2) =$ 190; distributive	$(18 \cdot 7) \cdot 1 \cdot (14 \cdot 0) =$ 0; multiplicative property of zero, commutative (×), associative (×)

Name _____ Date _____ 14

COMPUTING AND NAMING A PROPERTY *(continued)*

0; multiplicative property of zero, associative (×)	5,900; commutative (×) or associative (×)	87; associative (+)
8; multiplicative inverse, associative (×)	19,876; multiplicative identity	30; commutative (+) or associative (+)
0; multiplicative property of zero, commutative (×), associative (×)	190; distributive	$1\frac{1}{8}$; commutative (+), associative (+)

5. Have students take turns finding the answers by making the problems as easy as possible using the properties. Students can use paper and pencil. Along with the answer, they should name one property they used to find the answer. For example, for the problem $7 + 4 \cdot \frac{1}{4} + 6 \cdot 0 = ?$ the answer is 8, and the properties used are the Multiplicative Property of Zero and Multiplicative Inverse.

6. Award each student two points for a correct answer and one point for a correct property. Each group should keep a tally for the students in the group.

7. Once the students have completed the deck, instruct them to shuffle the deck and continue.

NEXT STEPS • Differentiate

5-Day Instructional Plan:
PA 2, page 62—All students, for additional practice

COMPUTING AND NAMING A PROPERTY *(continued)*

$9 + 2 + 8 + 1 =$ 20; commutative (+), associative (+)	$\left(\frac{1}{9} + \frac{3}{8}\right) + \frac{5}{8} =$ $1\frac{1}{9}$; associative (+)	$\frac{5}{6} + 0 + \frac{2}{6} =$ $1\frac{1}{6}$; additive identity
$64 + (75 + 36) =$ 175; commutative (+), associative (+)	$(29 + 1) + 0 =$ 30; additive identity	$\frac{4}{5} \cdot \left(12 \cdot \frac{5}{4}\right) =$ 12; multiplicative inverse
$(1.5 + 13.83) + 0.5 =$ 15.83; commutative (+), associative (+)	$(41 \cdot 6) + (9 \cdot 6) =$ 300; distributive	$(348 + 35) + 65 =$ 448; associative (+)

COMPUTING AND NAMING A PROPERTY *(continued)*

$1\frac{1}{6}$; additive identity	$1\frac{1}{9}$; associative (+)	20; commutative (+), associative (+)
12; multiplicative inverse	30; additive identity	175; commutative (+), associative (+)
448; associative (+)	300; distributive	15.83; commutative (+), associative (+)

Practice Activities

PA 2 Sharing Properties

Use with 5-Day or 3-Day Instructional Plan. In this activity, students identify the mathematical property used in an equation.

MATERIALS

- *Interactive Text*, page 24
- Blackline Master 17

DIRECTIONS

1. Write the nine basic math properties from Blackline Master 17, Sharing Properties, on the board or make an overhead transparency of Blackline Master 17.

2. Have students turn to *Interactive Text*, page 24, Properties. Have each student write a numerical example of any property he or she chooses. For example, $9 \cdot 14 = 14 \cdot 9$.

3. Divide the class into groups of four and have the members of each group identify one another's properties.

4. Discuss how a quantity can serve as a variable. For example, we can make $a = (3 + 9)$ and $b = (13 + 24)$, so for the property $a + b = b + a$, we could write $(3 + 9) + (13 + 24) = (13 + 24) + (3 + 9)$.

5. Have each student write another numerical example of any property using quantities for the variables.

6. Have the members of each group identify one another's properties. Then, have them exchange their four examples with other groups for identification.

7. Have each group make a problem as difficult as possible using one of the properties of their choice.

8. Have each group exchange their problem with another group for identification. All members of a group should be able to explain the property their problem models.

SHARING PROPERTIES

a. $a + 0 = a$

b. $a \cdot 1 = a$

c. $a \cdot 0 = 0$

d. $\dfrac{a}{b} \cdot \dfrac{b}{a} = 1,\ (a \neq 0,\ b \neq 0)$

e. $a \cdot (b + c) = a \cdot b + a \cdot c$

f. $a + b = b + a$

g. $a \cdot b = b \cdot a$

h. $(a + b) + c = a + (b + c)$

i. $(a \cdot b) \cdot c = a \cdot (b \cdot c)$

NEXT STEPS • Differentiate

5-Day Instructional Plan:

PM 2, page 65—All students, to assess progress

3-Day Instructional Plan:

PM 2, page 65—Students who demonstrated understanding on PM 1, to assess progress

PM 3, page 66—All other students, to assess progress

Name_____ Date_____

PROPERTIES

Write a numerical example of each property.

Answers will vary.
Sample answers are given.

1. $a + 0 = a$
$3.1 + 0 = 3.1$

2. $a \cdot 1 = a$
$1{,}580 \cdot 1 = 1{,}580$

3. $a \cdot 0 = 0$
$79 \cdot 0 = 0$

4. $\frac{a}{b} \cdot \frac{b}{a} = 1$
$a \neq 0,\ b \neq 0$
$\frac{11}{12} \cdot \frac{12}{11} = 1$

5. $a \cdot (b + c) = a \cdot b + a \cdot c$
$37 \cdot (8 + 15) = 37 \cdot 8 + 37 \cdot 15$

6. $a + b = b + a$
$547 + 339 = 339 + 547$

7. $a \cdot b = b \cdot a$
$82 \cdot 91 = 91 \cdot 82$

8. $(a + b) + c = a + (b + c)$
$(16 + 23) + 7 = 16 + (23 + 7)$

9. $(a \cdot b) \cdot c = a \cdot (b \cdot c)$
$(11 \cdot 14) \cdot 25 = 11 \cdot (14 \cdot 25)$

24   Chapter 1 • Objective 4 • PA 2   Inside Algebra

Progress-Monitoring Activities

PM 1 Apply Skills 1

Use with 5-Day or 3-Day Instructional Plan.

MATERIALS

- *Interactive Text*, page 25

DIRECTIONS

1. Have students turn to *Interactive Text*, page 25, Apply Skills 1.

2. Monitor student work, and provide feedback as necessary.

   Watch for:

   - Do students rewrite problems to get multiples of 10?

   - Do students avoid multiplying when finding the product of several numbers and zero?

NEXT STEPS • Differentiate

👥 5-Day and 3-Day Instructional Plans:

PA 2, page 62—Students who demonstrate understanding of the concept, for additional practice

CD 2, page 56—Students who need additional concept development

---

Name _____ Date _____

Rewrite each mathematical expression so it will be easy to compute, then compute the answer.

Example:

$(5 \cdot 53) \cdot 20 = (5 \cdot 20) \cdot 53 = 100 \cdot 53 = 5,300$

1. $(16 + 37) + 4 = \underline{(16 + 4) + 37 = 20 + 37 = 57}$

2. $\frac{3}{4} \cdot \left(\frac{2}{5} \cdot \frac{4}{3}\right) = \underline{\frac{2}{5} \cdot \left(\frac{3}{4} \cdot \frac{4}{3}\right) = \frac{2}{5} \cdot 1 = \frac{2}{5}}$

3. $35 + 22 + 5 + 8 = \underline{(35 + 5) + (22 + 8) = 40 + 30 = 70}$

4. $47 \cdot 69 \cdot 0 \cdot 97 = \underline{(47 \cdot 69 \cdot 97) \cdot 0 = 0}$

5. $(14 \cdot 7) + (14 \cdot 3) = \underline{14(7 + 3) = 14(10) = 140}$

6. $(17 + 8) \cdot (5 + 5) = \underline{(5 + 5) \cdot (17 + 8) = 10 \cdot 25 = 250}$

7. $4 \cdot (51 \cdot 25) = \underline{51(4 \cdot 25) = 51 \cdot 100 = 5,100}$

8. $2.4 + 7.7 + 5.6 + 0.3 = \underline{(2.4 + 5.6) + (7.7 + 0.3) = 8 + 8 = 16}$

9. $\frac{3}{4} \cdot (17 \cdot 4) = \underline{17 \cdot \left(\frac{3}{4} \cdot 4\right) = 17 \cdot 3 = 51}$

10. $\frac{5}{8} + \left(\frac{2}{9} + \frac{3}{8}\right) = \underline{\left(\frac{5}{8} + \frac{3}{8}\right) + \frac{2}{9} = 1 + \frac{2}{9} = 1\frac{2}{9}}$

11. $(9 \cdot 67) \cdot (12 \cdot 0) = \underline{(9 \cdot 67 \cdot 12) \cdot 0 = 0}$

12. $(6 + 17) + (4 + 3) = \underline{(6 + 4) + (17 + 3) = 10 + 20 = 30}$

13. $(2 \cdot 8) \cdot 5 = \underline{(2 \cdot 5) \cdot 8 = 10 \cdot 8 = 80}$

14. $\frac{3}{8} \cdot \left(15 \cdot \frac{8}{3}\right) = \underline{15 \cdot \left(\frac{3}{8} \cdot \frac{8}{3}\right) = 15 \cdot 1 = 15}$

15. $17 + (83 + 68) = \underline{(17 + 83) + 68 = 100 + 68 = 168}$

Progress-Monitoring Activities

PM 2 Apply Skills 2

Use with 5-Day or 3-Day Instructional Plan.

MATERIALS

- *Interactive Text*, page 26

DIRECTIONS

1. Have students turn to *Interactive Text*, page 26, Apply Skills 2.
2. Monitor student work, and provide feedback as necessary.

   Watch for:
   - Do students apply the Associative Property of Addition?
   - Do students apply the Commutative Property of Addition and Commutative Property of Multiplication to make problems easier?

NEXT STEPS • Differentiate

5-Day Instructional Plan:
CD 3, page 58—All students, for additional concept development and problem solving

3-Day Instructional Plan:
PM 3, page 66—Students who demonstrated understanding on PM 1, for additional progress assessment

PA 2, page 62—All other students, for additional practice

Name _____ Date _____

APPLY SKILLS 2

Compute the answers using properties to make the computation easier. Name one property you used.

Problem		Property Used
1.	$(15 \cdot 7) \cdot 0 = \underline{0}$	Multiplicative Property of Zero
2.	$\frac{5}{8} \cdot \left(19 \cdot \frac{8}{5}\right) = \underline{19}$	Commutative (×) or Inverse (×)
3.	$(47 + 3) + (-3) = \underline{47}$	Associative (+) or Additive Identity
4.	$(8 \cdot 7) + (8 \cdot 3) = \underline{80}$	Distributive
5.	$20 + 7.4 + 80 = \underline{107.4}$	Commutative (+)
6.	$(29 + 17) + (13 + 21) = \underline{80}$	Associative (+)
7.	$25 \cdot (17 - 6) \cdot 4 = \underline{1{,}100}$	Commutative (×)
8.	$40 \cdot (11 \cdot 5) = \underline{2{,}200}$	Commutative (×)
9.	$\frac{5}{6} + \left(\frac{1}{7} + \frac{1}{6}\right) = \underline{1\frac{1}{7}}$	Commutative (+)
10.	$(16 \cdot 7) \cdot (12 \cdot 0) = \underline{0}$	Multiplicative Property of Zero
11.	$9 + 7 + 3 + 8 + 1 + 2 = \underline{30}$	Commutative (+)
12.	$5 \cdot (37 \cdot 2) = \underline{370}$	Commutative (×) or Associative (×)
13.	$5 \cdot 40 \cdot 1 = \underline{200}$	Associative (×) or Multiplicative Identity
14.	$44 + 17 + 56 + 83 = \underline{200}$	Commutative (+) or Associative (+)

26   Chapter 1 • Objective 4 • PM 2   Inside Algebra

Progress-Monitoring Activities

PM 3 Apply Skills 3

Use with 5-Day or 3-Day Instructional Plan.

MATERIALS

- *Interactive Text*, pages 27–28

DIRECTIONS

1. Have students turn to *Interactive Text*, pages 27–28, Apply Skills 3.

2. Monitor student work, and provide feedback as necessary.

   Watch for:
   - Do students understand the difference between the commutative and the associative properties?
   - Are students able to treat variables as if they were constants?
   - Do students apply the Distributive Property?

NEXT STEPS • Differentiate

👥 5-Day Instructional Plan:

PS 1, page 67—Students who are on the accelerated path, to develop problem-solving skills

Objective 4 Posttest, page 69—Students who are on the differentiated path

👥 3-Day Instructional Plan:

CD 3, page 58—Students who are on the accelerated path, for additional concept development and problem solving

PS 1, page 67—Students who demonstrated understanding on PM 1, to develop problem-solving skills

Objective 4 Posttest, page 69—All other students

Name_____ Date_____

APPLY SKILLS 3

Each of the equalities illustrates a mathematical property. Name the property.

1. $(x + 2) + 0 = (x + 2)$
   Additive Identity

2. $(\$4.98)1 = \$4.98$
   Multiplicative Identity

3. $(7x)9 = 7(x9)$
   Associative Property of Multiplication

4. $(589\%)(0) = 0$
   Multiplicative Property of Zero

5. $\left(\frac{x+2}{9}\right)\left(\frac{9}{x+2}\right) = 1$, when $x \neq -2$
   Multiplicative Inverse

6. $3(x^2 + 2x + 7) = (x^2 + 2x + 7)3$
   Commutative Property of Multiplication

7. $(x + 5)(x + 9) = (x + 5)x + (x + 5)9$
   Distributive Property

8. $(x + 7) + 5 = x + (7 + 5)$
   Associative Property of Addition

9. $x + (7 + 5) = (7 + 5) + x$
   Commutative Property of Addition

10. $29(x + 4) = (x + 4)29$
    Commutative Property of Multiplication

11. $(x - 5)x = x(x - 5)$
    Commutative Property of Multiplication

12. $x(x + 9) = x^2 + x9$
    Distributive Property

Name_____ Date_____

APPLY SKILLS 3 *(continued)*

Each of the equalities is the result of applying more than one mathematical property. Name, in order, all the mathematical properties used to transform the left-hand side of the equality into the right-hand side of the equality.

13. $x(x + 7) = x^2 + 7x$
    Distributive Property, $x^2 + x7$
    Commutative Property of Multiplication, $x^2 + 7x$

14. $5 + x(x + 2) = x^2 + 2x + 5$
    Commutative Property of Addition, $x(x + 2) + 5$
    Distributive Property, $x^2 + x2 + 5$
    Commutative Property of Multiplication, $x^2 + 2x + 5$

15. $(5 - 5)\left(\frac{1}{2}\right) = 0$
    Substitution, $0\left(\frac{1}{2}\right)$
    Commutative Property of Multiplication, $\left(\frac{1}{2}\right)0$
    Multiplicative Property of Zero, 0

16. $x(2x + 3x + 7 + 2) = 5x^2 + 9x$
    Distributive Property, $x[x(2 + 3) + 7 + 2]$
    Substitution, $x[x(5) + 9]$
    Distributive Property, $x^2 5 + 9x$
    Commutative Property of Multiplication, $5x^2 + 9x$

Problem-Solving Activity

★ PS 1 Playing the Mathematical Properties Game

Use with 5-Day or 3-Day Instructional Plan. In this activity, students increase their familiarity with mathematical properties.

MATERIALS

- *Interactive Text*, page 24
- Blackline Masters 18–26 or blank cards

DIRECTIONS

1. Divide the class into groups of two to six students.

2. Discuss with students the following properties and identities:

   Associative Property of Addition
   $(a + b) + c = a + (b + c)$

   Associative Property of Multiplication
   $(a \cdot b) \cdot c = a(b \cdot c)$

   Commutative Property of Addition
   $a + b = b + a$

   Commutative Property of Multiplication
   $a \cdot b = b \cdot a$

   Distributive Property
   $a \cdot (b + c) = a \cdot b + a \cdot c$

   Multiplicative Identity
   $a \cdot 1 = a$

   Multiplicative Inverse
   $\frac{a}{b} \cdot \frac{b}{a} = 1 \ (a \neq 0, \ b \neq 0)$

   Multiplicative Property of Zero
   $a \cdot 0 = 0$

3. Duplicate and cut out the cards on Blackline Masters 18–26 and give one set of cards to each group. Alternatively, give each group 81 blank cards and have the students make decks of cards as described at right, one deck per group.

★ = Includes Problem Solving

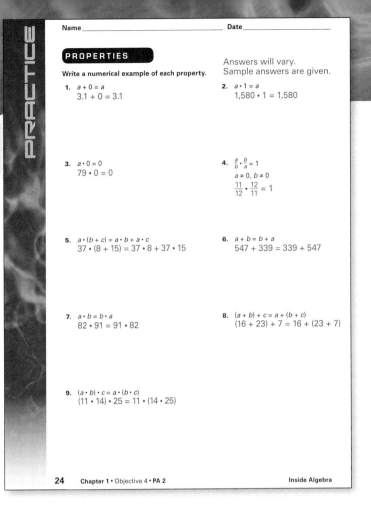

PROPERTIES

Write a numerical example of each property.

Answers will vary. Sample answers are given.

1. $a + 0 = a$
   $3.1 + 0 = 3.1$

2. $a \cdot 1 = a$
   $1{,}580 \cdot 1 = 1{,}580$

3. $a \cdot 0 = 0$
   $79 \cdot 0 = 0$

4. $\frac{a}{b} \cdot \frac{b}{a} = 1$
   $a \neq 0, \ b \neq 0$
   $\frac{11}{12} \cdot \frac{12}{11} = 1$

5. $a \cdot (b + c) = a \cdot b + a \cdot c$
   $37 \cdot (8 + 15) = 37 \cdot 8 + 37 \cdot 15$

6. $a + b = b + a$
   $547 + 339 = 339 + 547$

7. $a \cdot b = b \cdot a$
   $82 \cdot 91 = 91 \cdot 82$

8. $(a + b) + c = a + (b + c)$
   $(16 + 23) + 7 = 16 + (23 + 7)$

9. $(a \cdot b) \cdot c = a \cdot (b \cdot c)$
   $(11 \cdot 14) \cdot 25 = 11 \cdot (14 \cdot 25)$

24 Chapter 1 • Objective 4 • PA 2   Inside Algebra

Deck of 81 playing cards with the following symbols:

16 cards with the symbol   **a**

10 cards with the symbol   **b**

6 cards with the symbol   **c**

6 cards with the symbol   **(**

6 cards with the symbol   **)**

12 cards with the symbol   **×**

9 cards with the symbol   **+**

9 cards with the symbol   **=**

3 cards with the symbol   **0**

2 cards with the symbol   **1**

1 card with the symbol $\dfrac{a}{b}$

1 card with the symbol $\dfrac{b}{a}$

4. Have students turn to *Interactive Text*, page 24, Properties.

5. Explain the game rules to students.

   - The object of this game is for each player to use the cards to compose as many real number property statements as possible and to use all his or her cards.

   - Each group selects one player to be the first dealer. The dealer shuffles the cards and deals eight cards to each player. The remaining cards are placed facedown in the middle of the table.

   - Play begins to the left of the dealer and moves clockwise. At each player's turn, the player draws a card from the deck on the table. The player can then do any one of the following:

     - Place at least three cards from his or her own hand faceup on the table to begin one mathematical property statement reading from left to right. The statement must be one of those listed on the blackline master, and each property statement may be used no more than once by any player in each game.

     - Use as many cards from his or her hand as possible to continue the statements made by any player. A player can play on more than one other player's statements. However, the player must have started a statement himself or herself in a previous turn before playing on any other player's statement.

     - Pass without playing any cards.

   - The play continues until one player has used all his or her cards and has at least one complete property statement on the table in front of himself or herself. If the player has started more than one property statement, all his or her property statements must be complete. Otherwise, the player must continue to draw cards and play.

   - The winner is the first player to obtain a score of 100 or more.

     Note: Each mathematical property statement from the *Interactive Text* can appear only once during the game for any one player.

6. Explain that scoring is as follows for each individual:

   - 20 points awarded for all cards played and all completed statements.

   - 10 points awarded for each completed statement.

   - 5 points subtracted for each statement started but not completed.

   - 1 point subtracted for each card held when another player goes out.

NEXT STEPS • Differentiate

5-Day Instructional Plan:
Objective 4 Posttest, page 69—All students

👥 3-Day Instructional Plan:
PS 1, page 67—Students on the accelerated path who are doing this activity for the first time

Objective 4 Posttest, page 69—All other students

Objective 4 Posttest

Discuss with students the key concepts in Objective 4. Following the discussion, administer the Objective 4 Posttest to all students.

Using the Results

• Score the posttest and update the class record card.

• Provide reinforcement for students who do not demonstrate mastery of the concepts through individual or small-group reteaching of key concepts.

Name _____ Date _____

Evaluate the mathematical expressions by using properties to make the computation as easy as possible.

1. $40 + (217 + 60) =$ ___317___
$40 + 60 + 217$
$100 + 217$

2. $8 \cdot (9 \cdot 3) \cdot 0 =$ ___0___
$(8 \cdot 9 \cdot 3) \cdot 0$

3. $(14 \cdot 7) + (14 \cdot 3) =$ ___140___
$14(7 + 3)$
$14(10)$

4. $\left[\frac{1}{4} \cdot (5 + 12)\right] \cdot 4 =$ ___17___
$\left(\frac{1}{4} \cdot 17\right) \cdot \frac{4}{1}$
$\frac{4}{4} \cdot 17$
$1 \cdot 17$

5. $10 \cdot 132 =$ ___1,320___

6. $(5 \cdot 9) + (5 \cdot 11) =$ ___100___
$5(9 + 11)$
$5(20)$

7. $\frac{1}{17}(9 + 8) =$ ___1___
$\frac{1}{17}(17)$
$\frac{1}{17} \cdot \frac{17}{1}$
$\frac{17}{17}$

8. $7(3.14159) + 3(3.14159) =$ ___31.4159___
$3.14159(7 + 3)$
$3.14159(10)$

9. $5\%(81) + 5\%(19) =$ ___5___
$5\%(81 + 19)$
$5\%(100)$

10. $13(100 + 20 + 5) =$ ___1,625___
$1,300 + 260 + 65$

Inside Algebra   Chapter 1 • Objective 4   **9**

Chapter Review

Chapter 1 Review

Use with 5-Day or 3-Day Instructional Plan. In this activity, students review key chapter concepts prior to taking the Chapter Test.

MATERIALS

- *Interactive Text*, pages 29–30

DIRECTIONS

1. Have students turn to *Interactive Text*, pages 29–30, Chapter 1 Review.

2. Have students complete the review individually or in small groups. If the activity is completed individually, provide time for students to discuss their solutions as a class or in small groups.

3. Monitor student work, and provide feedback when necessary. If students complete the review quickly, pair them with other students or groups to discuss their answers.

Name _____ Date _____

OBJECTIVE 1

Write a mathematical expression for each written expression.

1. The product of six and fifteen ___ $6 \cdot 15$ ___

2. The sum of twelve and three times seven ___ $12 + 3 \cdot 7$ ___

Write a verbal expression for each mathematical expression.

3. $17 - 4 \cdot 2$

___seventeen minus four times two or the difference of___

___seventeen and four times two___

4. $3^2 + 9$

___three squared plus nine or the sum of three squared and nine___

OBJECTIVE 2

Find the value of each mathematical expression.

5. $7 + 2 \cdot 5 - 3 =$ ___ 14 ___
$7 + 10 - 3$
$17 - 3$

6. $12 - 5 + 6 - 3 =$ ___ 10 ___
$7 + 6 - 3$
$13 - 3$

7. Evaluate $6 + b \cdot 3$ when $b = 5$.
___ 21 ___
$6 + 5 \cdot 3$
$6 + 15$

8. $40 - (5 + 3) \cdot 3 =$ ___ 16 ___
$40 - 8 \cdot 3$
$40 - 24$

Inside Algebra   Chapter 1 • CR 1   **29**

Name _____ Date _____

OBJECTIVE 3

Solve.

9. True or false: $5x - 6 = 14$ if $x = 5$?
___false___
$5(5) - 6 = 14$
$25 - 6 \neq 14$

10. Find A if $A = \frac{1}{2}bh$ and $b = 7$ and $h = 6$. ___ 21 ___
$A = \frac{1}{2}(7)(6)$
$A = \frac{1}{2}(42)$

11. Find x if $x = y^2 + y + 2$ and $y = 4$.
___ 22 ___
$x = 4^2 + 4 + 2$
$x = 16 + 4 + 2$
$x = 20 + 2$

12. What number for x makes $x - 9 = 3$ true? ___ 12 ___
$x - 9 + 9 = 3 + 9$

OBJECTIVE 4

Evaluate the mathematical expressions by using properties to make the computation as easy as possible.

13. $(19 + 30) + 70 =$ ___ 119 ___
$30 + 70 + 19$
$100 + 19$

14. $(6 \cdot 8) + (6 \cdot 22) =$ ___ 180 ___
$6(8 + 22)$
$6(30)$

15. $(40 + 38) + (60 + 2) =$ ___ 140 ___
$(40 + 60) + (38 + 2)$
$100 + 40$

16. $28 + 17 - 8 =$ ___ 37 ___
$28 - 8 + 17$
$20 + 17$

30   Chapter 1 • CR 1   Inside Algebra

1 CHAPTER

Ongoing Assessment

Chapter 1 Test, Form A

MATERIALS

- *Assessment Book*, pages 11–12

DIRECTIONS

1. Have students turn to *Assessment Book*, pages 11–12, Chapter 1 Test, Form A. Administer the Chapter Test to all students.

2. Score the test by objective and update the class record card.

3. Use the test data to determine differentiation needs.

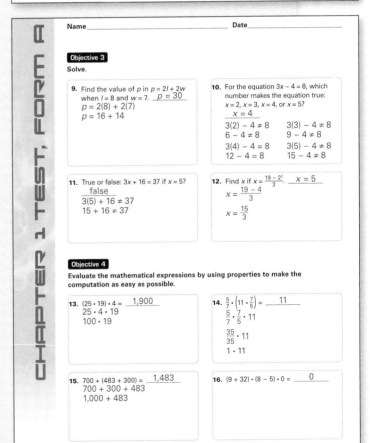

Name _____ Date _____

Write a mathematical expression for each written expression.

1. The sum of nine and five times seven _____$9 + 5 \cdot 7$_____

2. The product of eleven and x squared _____$11 \cdot x^2$ or $11x^2$_____

Write a verbal expression for each mathematical expression.

3. $(4 + 8) - (6 - 3)$

   the quantity four plus eight minus the quantity six minus three

4. $25 - 8 \cdot (4 - 2)$

   twenty-five minus eight times the quantity four minus two

Objective 2

Find the value of each mathematical expression.

5. $8 \cdot 3 - 6 + 3 \cdot 4 =$ _____30_____
   $24 - 6 + 3 \cdot 4$
   $24 - 6 + 12$
   $18 + 12$

6. $9 \cdot (4 + 3) - (5 \cdot 7) =$ _____28_____
   $9 \cdot 7 - 35$
   $63 - 35$

7. $3 + 6^2 \div 9 =$ _____7_____
   $3 + 36 \div 9$
   $3 + 4$

8. Evaluate $3 \cdot (a - b) + 7$ when $a = 5$ and $b = 3$. _____13_____
   $3 \cdot (5 - 3) + 7$
   $3 \cdot 2 + 7$
   $6 + 7$

Inside Algebra   Chapter 1 • Test   11

Name _____ Date _____

Objective 3

Solve.

9. Find the value of p in $p = 2l + 2w$ when $l = 8$ and $w = 7$. _____$p = 30$_____
   $p = 2(8) + 2(7)$
   $p = 16 + 14$

10. For the equation $3x - 4 = 8$, which number makes the equation true: $x = 2$, $x = 3$, $x = 4$, or $x = 5$?
    _____$x = 4$_____
    $3(2) - 4 \neq 8$ $3(3) - 4 \neq 8$
    $6 - 4 \neq 8$ $9 - 4 \neq 8$
    $3(4) - 4 = 8$ $3(5) - 4 \neq 8$
    $12 - 4 = 8$ $15 - 4 \neq 8$

11. True or false: $3x + 16 = 37$ if $x = 5$?
    _____false_____
    $3(5) + 16 \neq 37$
    $15 + 16 \neq 37$

12. Find x if $x = \frac{19 - 2^2}{3}$. _____$x = 5$_____
    $x = \frac{19 - 4}{3}$
    $x = \frac{15}{3}$

Objective 4

Evaluate the mathematical expressions by using properties to make the computation as easy as possible.

13. $(25 \cdot 19) \cdot 4 =$ _____1,900_____
    $25 \cdot 4 \cdot 19$
    $100 \cdot 19$

14. $\frac{5}{7} \cdot \left(11 \cdot \frac{7}{5}\right) =$ _____11_____
    $\frac{5}{7} \cdot \frac{7}{5} \cdot 11$
    $\frac{35}{35} \cdot 11$
    $1 \cdot 11$

15. $700 + (483 + 300) =$ _____1,483_____
    $700 + 300 + 483$
    $1,000 + 483$

16. $(9 + 32) \cdot (8 - 5) \cdot 0 =$ _____0_____

12   Chapter 1 • Test   Inside Algebra

Differentiation

MATERIALS

- **Gizmos** *Fido's Flower Bed (Perimeter and Area)* Gizmo
- **Gizmos** Extension Activity pages
- **Gizmos** *Using Algebraic Expressions* Gizmo
- **Gizmos** Reinforcement Activity page
- Additional Activities
- Algebra Skill Builders for Chapter 1
- Chapter Test, Form B

DIRECTIONS

1. Review Chapter 1 Test, Form A, with the class.

2. Use the results from Chapter 1 Test, Form A, to identify students for reinforcement or extension.

3. After students have been identified for extension or reinforcement, break students into appropriate groups. See pages 73–75 for detailed differentiated instruction.

Differentiation Planner

Students who demonstrated mastery on every objective posttest and scored 80% or above on the chapter test

Extend learning using:

- **Gizmos** Use the *Fido's Flower Bed (Perimeter and Area)* Gizmo with the Extension Activity. Have students work in pairs or individually to complete the activity.

Students who demonstrated mastery on every objective posttest but scored below 80% on the chapter test

Reinforce learning using:

- **Gizmos** Use the *Using Algebraic Expressions* Gizmo with the Reinforcement Activity. Have students work in pairs or small groups to complete the activity.
- Additional Activities from the online resources.
- Algebra Skill Builders for Chapter 1 from the online resources.

Students who did not demonstrate mastery on any or all of the objective posttests or the chapter test

Reinforce learning using:

- **Gizmos** Present the *Using Algebraic Expressions* Gizmo to students in small groups using the instruction on page 75.
- Additional Activities from the online resources.
- Algebra Skill Builders for Chapter 1 from the online resources.

Retest—Administer Chapter 1 Test, Form B, from the online resources to students who scored below 80 percent on Form A when time allows.

NEXT STEPS • Pretest

- Administer Chapter 2, Objective 1 Pretest, page 78, to all students.

Ongoing Assessment

CHAPTER 1

Students who demonstrated mastery on every objective posttest and scored 80% or above on the chapter test

1. Divide students into pairs or allow them to work individually for this activity.

2. Distribute one copy of the Extension Activity from the online resources to each student.

3. Direct students to the Gizmo *Fido's Flower Bed (Perimeter and Area)* through the Inside Algebra Student Web site, http://insidealgebra.voyagerlearning.com.

4. Have students complete the Extension Activity.

5. **Peer Review.** If there is time, have students exchange papers with a peer. They should review and discuss each response, and be prepared to explain their thinking.

> **Variation:** If students do not have access to the Gizmo, provide them with grid paper so they can model the possible lengths and widths of gardens in Problem 2. Tell them each grid square is 1 yard long and 1 yard wide and has an area of 1 square yard. Students can check the area and perimeter of their gardens using the grid.

Explore Learning • Gizmos

Fido's Flower Bed (Perimeter and Area)

Gizmos
Extension Activity   Name_____   Date_____

FIDO'S FLOWER BED (PERIMETER AND AREA)

Sienna and Anthony are making a rectangular flower garden. They will surround the garden with a fence. The area of the garden must be exactly 16 square yards. They need to know how much sod and fencing is needed to build the garden.

1. The area of a rectangle is found by multiplying the length by the width. Let *l* represent the length of a rectangle. Let *w* represent the width. What mathematical expression is used to compute the area of a rectangle?

   $A =$ ___*lw* or *l • w*___

2. Sienna and Anthony need to find all possible whole number lengths and widths for the garden. One possibility is that the garden is 1 yard wide and 16 yards long as shown in the table. Start the *Fido's Flower Bed* Gizmo. Drag pieces of sod from the sod supply to make different rectangular gardens. Find the remaining two possible lengths and widths for the garden.

Width (yards)	1	__2__	__4__
Length (yards)	16	__8__	__4__
Area (square yards)	1 • 16 = 16	__2__ • __8__ = 16	__4__ • __4__ = 16

To find how much fencing is needed, Sienna and Anthony must find the perimeter of the garden.

3. Sienna finds the perimeter by adding the quantity 2 times the length to the quantity 2 times the width.

   Let *l* represent the length of a rectangle. Let *w* represent the width.

   What mathematical expression matches Sienna's verbal expression? __(2*l*) + (2*w*)__

4. Anthony finds the perimeter by multiplying 2 by the quantity of the sum of the length and the width.

   Let *l* represent the length of a rectangle. Let *w* represent the width.

   What mathematical expression matches Anthony's verbal expression? __2(*l* + *w*)__

5. Are both Sienna and Anthony correct? Explain your reasoning.

   Yes; the Distributive Property shows that 2(*l* + *w*) = 2*l* + 2*w*.

Gizmos
Extension Activity   Name_____   Date_____

FIDO'S FLOWER BED (PERIMETER AND AREA) *(continued)*

6. Use either Sienna's or Anthony's way of finding the perimeter of each garden from Problems 3 and 4. The first perimeter is already found. You can check your answers by dragging the fencing to surround your gardens in the Gizmo.

Width (yards)	1	2	4
Length (yards)	16	8	4
Area (square yards)	16	16	16
Perimeter (yards)	2(1) + 2(16) = 34 or 2(1 + 16) = 34	2(2) + 2(8) = 20 or 2(2 + 8) = 20	2(4) + 2(4) = 16 or 2(4 + 4) = 16

7. Which length and width could Sienna and Anthony choose so they use the least amount of fencing?

   length = 4 yards, width = 4 yards

8. What kind of geometric figure did they choose? __square__

9. Let *s* represent the side length of a square.

   What expression in simplest form can you write for the perimeter of a square? __4*s*__

   What expression in simplest form can you write for the area of a square? __*s*²__

10. Sienna and Anthony design the gardens at right. The perimeters increase in a pattern. If the pattern continues, what will be the perimeter of Garden 4?

    __20 yards__

    Garden 1   Garden 2   Garden 3

    Perimeter = 8 yards   Perimeter = 12 yards   Perimeter = 16 yards

11. How many times greater is the perimeter of Garden 3 than the perimeter of Garden 1? __2__

12. How many times greater is the area of Garden 3 than the area of Garden 1? __4__

Ongoing Assessment

USING ALGEBRAIC EXPRESSIONS

1. Start the *Using Algebraic Expressions* Gizmo. You should see the mathematical expression $3 + x$. This expression has three parts. What are the three parts? ___3, +, x___

2. What word do you write for the number 3? ___three___ Drag this tile down into the work space. Notice that both the mathematical expression and the verbal expression appear below the work space. Use this display to check your work.

3. What word do you write for the operation +? ___plus___ Drag this tile down into the work space.

4. Look at the tiles that are left in the bin. What words do you write for the variable x? ___a number___ Drag this tile down into the work space.

5. What verbal expression matches the mathematical expression $3 + x$? ___three plus a number___

6. What is the value of $3 + x$ when $x = 19$? ___22___

7. What number for x makes $3 + x = 10$ true? ___7___

8. What property allows you to write $3 + x$ as $x + 3$? ___Commutative Property of Addition___

9. Each person in your group should use the Gizmo to model as many expressions as he or she can in two minutes. One person should keep time and record the number of correct answers. The person with the greatest number of correct answers wins.

10. Write the mathematical symbol that corresponds to each tile.

a number	x	divided by	$\div$
minus	$-$	more than	$+$
plus	$+$	subtracted from	$-$
times	$\times$ or $\cdot$		

Students who demonstrated mastery on every objective posttest but scored below 80% on the chapter test

1. Divide students into pairs or small groups.

2. Distribute one copy of the Individual Reinforcement Activity from the online resources to each student.

3. Direct students to the Gizmo *Using Algebraic Expressions* through the Inside Algebra Student Web site, http://insidealgebra.voyagerlearning.com.

4. Have students complete the Reinforcement Activity.

5. **Peer Review.** If time permits, have students exchange papers with a peer to review and discuss each other's responses. Remind students to be prepared to explain the reasoning behind their responses.

Variation: If students do not have access to the Gizmo, tell them that the words *a number* can be used to represent x in Problem 4. For Problem 9, write different mathematical and verbal expressions on the board. Students should write their answers on a sheet of paper. Once they are done, write the answers on the board and have students grade each other's papers.

Explorelearning • **Gizmos**

Model the expression: $3 + x$

three	minus	times	divided by
a number	seven	plus	one

(Drag tiles from the bin above into the workspace below to build your expression.)

HINT

NEW

Explorelearning   POINTER   TOOL TIPS OFF   COPY SCREEN

Using Algebraic Expressions

Students who did not demonstrate mastery on any or all of the objective posttests or the chapter test

1. Use the *Using Algebraic Expressions* Gizmo. The expression 3 + *x* should appear first. Ask students to identify the three parts of the expression. 3, +, *x*

2. Ask students to find the verbal expression for 3 + *x*. Use these steps to scaffold instruction. Drag tiles down into the work space as students complete each step. Point out that both the mathematical and verbal expressions appear below the work space.

   - Ask students to name the tile that matches the number 3. three

   - Ask students to name the tile that matches the operation +. plus

   - Ask students to name the tile that matches the variable *x*. a number

   - Ask students to say the verbal expression that matches 3 + *x*. three plus a number

   Note: The Gizmo is not needed to answer Problems 3–5.

3. Ask students to find the value of 3 + *x* when *x* = 19. 22

4. Ask students to name the value for *x* that makes 3 + *x* = 10 true. 7

5. Ask students which property allows them to write 3 + *x* as *x* + 3. Commutative Property of Addition

6. The "New" button creates new mathematical and verbal expressions. Have several students go up to the board. Use the Gizmo to create a new expression. The student who first translates the expression correctly on the board wins. Repeat this process with different groups of students.

7. Point to the tiles in the bin on the Gizmo screen and have them say the symbol or words indicated by the tiles.

   Variation: If students do not have access to the Gizmo, use a blackboard or overhead projector to complete the activity.

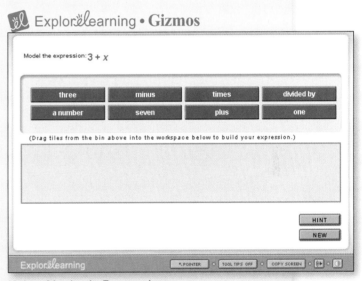

ExploreLearning • **Gizmos**

Using Algebraic Expressions

Ongoing Assessment

Chapter 1 Test, Form B

MATERIALS

- Chapter 1 Test, Form B, from the Online Resources, pages 1–2

DIRECTIONS

1. Have students turn to Chapter 1 Test, Form B, pages 1–2, from the Online Resources. Administer the Chapter Test to all students.

2. Score the test by objective and update the class record card.

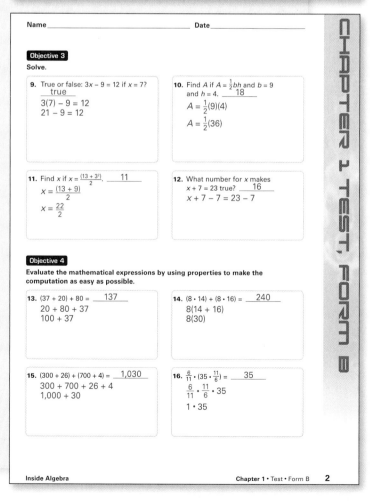

Name _____ Date _____

Objective 1

Write a mathematical expression for each written expression.

1. The product of three and eighteen _____ $3 \cdot 18$ _____

2. The sum of seven and four times thirteen _____ $7 + 4 \cdot 13$ _____

Write a verbal expression for each mathematical expression.

3. $16 - 6 \cdot 3$

   sixteen minus six times three or the difference of sixteen and six times three

4. $32 - (5^2 + 7)$

   thirty-two minus the quantity five squared plus seven or the difference of thirty-two and the sum of five squared and seven

Objective 2

Find the value of each mathematical expression.

5. $8 + 3 \cdot 4 - 9 = $ _____ 11 _____
   $8 + 12 - 9$
   $20 - 9$

6. $15 - 4 + 7 - 2 = $ _____ 16 _____
   $11 + 7 - 2$
   $18 - 2$

7. Evaluate $7 + g \cdot 2$ when $g = 5$.
   _____ 17 _____
   $7 + 5 \cdot 2$
   $7 + 10$

8. $50 - (7 + 3) \cdot 4 = $ _____ 10 _____
   $50 - 10 \cdot 4$
   $50 - 40$

Inside Algebra   Chapter 1 • Test • Form B   1

Name _____ Date _____

Objective 3

Solve.

9. True or false: $3x - 9 = 12$ if $x = 7$?
   _____ true _____
   $3(7) - 9 = 12$
   $21 - 9 = 12$

10. Find A if $A = \frac{1}{2}bh$ and $b = 9$ and $h = 4$. _____ 18 _____
    $A = \frac{1}{2}(9)(4)$
    $A = \frac{1}{2}(36)$

11. Find x if $x = \frac{(13 + 3^2)}{2}$. _____ 11 _____
    $x = \frac{(13 + 9)}{2}$
    $x = \frac{22}{2}$

12. What number for x makes $x + 7 = 23$ true? _____ 16 _____
    $x + 7 - 7 = 23 - 7$

Objective 4

Evaluate the mathematical expressions by using properties to make the computation as easy as possible.

13. $(37 + 20) + 80 = $ _____ 137 _____
    $20 + 80 + 37$
    $100 + 37$

14. $(8 \cdot 14) + (8 \cdot 16) = $ _____ 240 _____
    $8(14 + 16)$
    $8(30)$

15. $(300 + 26) + (700 + 4) = $ _____ 1,030 _____
    $300 + 700 + 26 + 4$
    $1,000 + 30$

16. $\frac{6}{11} \cdot (35 \cdot \frac{11}{6}) = $ _____ 35 _____
    $\frac{6}{11} \cdot \frac{11}{6} \cdot 35$
    $1 \cdot 35$

Inside Algebra   Chapter 1 • Test • Form B   2

Exploring Rational Numbers

In this chapter, students learn about the properties of rational numbers and their relationship to integers. They use these properties to perform basic operations with rational numbers and to use a number line to compare and order sets of rational numbers. Students also learn to find square roots and to identify the principal square root of a number.

Objective 1
Graph rational numbers on the number line.

Objective 2
Add and subtract rational numbers.

Objective 3
Compare and order rational numbers.

Objective 4
Multiply and divide rational numbers.

Objective 5
Find the principal square root of a number.

Chapter 2
VOCABULARY

Objective 1
Graph rational numbers on the number line.

Objective 1 Pretest

Students complete the Objective 1 Pretest at least one day before beginning Objective 1.

Using the Results

- Score the pretest and update the class record card.
- If the majority of students do not demonstrate mastery of the concepts, use the 5-Day Instructional Plan for Objective 1.
- If the majority of students demonstrate mastery of the concepts, use the 3-Day Instructional Plan for Objective 1.

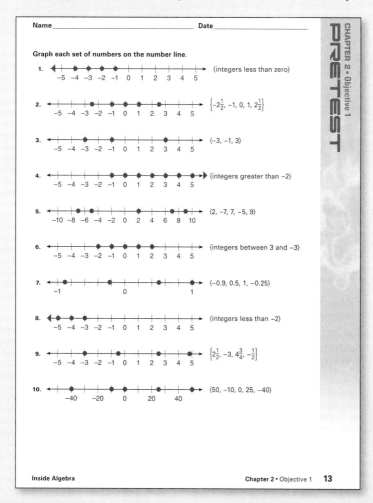

Goals and Activities

Objective 1 Goals

The following activities, when used with the instructional plans on pages 80 and 81, enable students to:

- Graph the set {–1, 1, 2} on the number line as

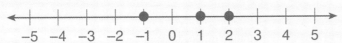

- Graph the set {–1$\frac{1}{2}$, 0.5, 2} on the number line as

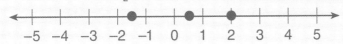

- Graph the set {integers between 2 and –2} on the number line as

Objective 1 Activities

Concept Development Activities

CD 1 Developing Number Lines, page 82

CD 2 Graphing on the Number Line, page 84

Practice Activity

★**PA 1** Graphing It, page 85

Progress-Monitoring Activities

PM 1 Apply Skills 1, page 86

PM 2 Apply Skills 2, page 87

PM 3 Apply Skills 3, page 88

★Problem-Solving Activities

★**PS 1** Plotting Data—Part 1, page 89

★**PS 2** Plotting Data—Part 2, page 90

Ongoing Assessment

Posttest Objective 1, page 91

Pretest Objective 2, page 92

CD = Concept Development   PM = Progress Monitoring   PS = Problem Solving
PA = Practice Activity   ★ = Includes Problem Solving

2 CHAPTER

5-Day Instructional Plan

Use the 5-Day Instructional Plan when pretest results indicate that students would benefit from a slower pace. This plan is used when the majority of students need more time or did not demonstrate mastery on the pretest.

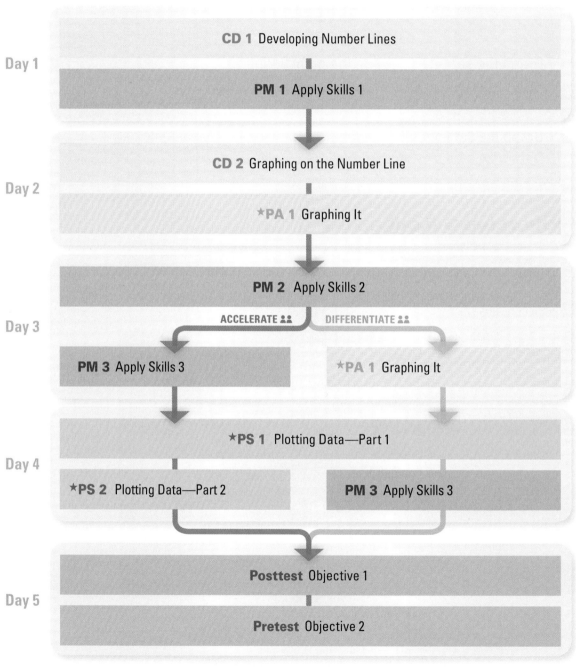

Day 1
CD 1 Developing Number Lines
PM 1 Apply Skills 1

Day 2
CD 2 Graphing on the Number Line
★PA 1 Graphing It

Day 3
PM 2 Apply Skills 2
ACCELERATE 👥   DIFFERENTIATE 👥
PM 3 Apply Skills 3   **★PA 1** Graphing It

Day 4
★PS 1 Plotting Data—Part 1
★PS 2 Plotting Data—Part 2   **PM 3** Apply Skills 3

Day 5
Posttest Objective 1
Pretest Objective 2

CD = Concept Development   PM = Progress Monitoring   PS = Problem Solving
PA = Practice Activity   ★ = Includes Problem Solving

3-Day Instructional Plan

Use the 3-Day Instructional Plan when pretest results indicate that students can move through the activities at a faster pace. This plan is ideal when the majority of students demonstrate mastery on the pretest.

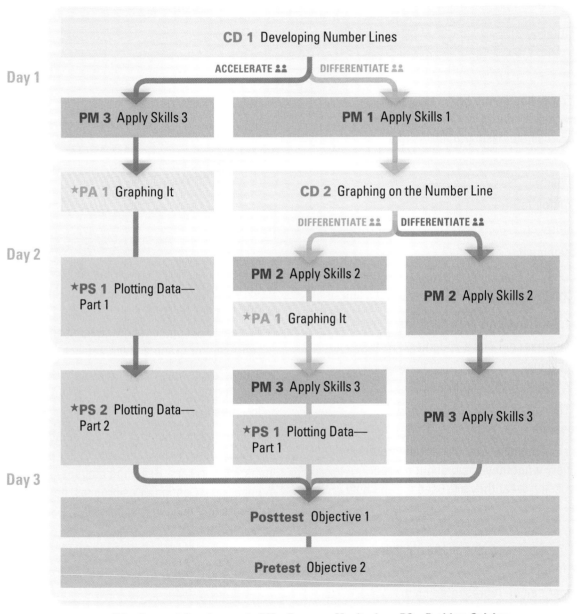

CD = Concept Development   PM = Progress Monitoring   PS = Problem Solving
PA = Practice Activity   ★ = Includes Problem Solving

Concept Development Activities

CD 1 Developing Number Lines

Use with 5-Day or 3-Day Instructional Plan. In this activity, students create a number line and locate integers on the line.

MATERIALS

- Blackline Master 27

DIRECTIONS

1. Draw a horizontal line on the board or overhead transparency. Ask students to name the figure. Have them discuss the basic properties of a line.

   Listen for:
   - It is unending.
   - It is a set of points.
   - It goes on forever.
   - Two points name it.

2. Distribute a copy of Blackline Master 27, Number Lines, to each student, or have students draw a line.

3. Discuss the following terms with students:

   finite A set that contains a specific number of values

   infinite A set that goes on forever

   integer The set of whole numbers and their opposites

4. Discuss the term **number line** with students. Have students review what they know about number lines by discussing what they are used for and how to make one.

   Listen for:
   - It is a tool used to represent all the numbers in graphic form.
   - Every number can be represented on it.
   - The integers are evenly spaced.
   - Both positive and negative numbers can be shown on it.

- Zero is between the positives and the negatives and is a member of neither set.
- We can use segments of the number line to represent or graph a given set.
- The arrows show it continues in both directions indefinitely because the positive and negative integers are infinite.

5. Mark zero on the number line on the board or transparency and mark off spaces for positive and negative numbers. Have one student find 3 on the number line. Continue this process, having other students find numbers, such as 6, 1, −3, −5, −10, or 9.

6. Discuss changes students need to make in the scale of the number line to graph a large number, such as 1,000. Demonstrate the concept on a number line.

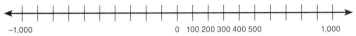

7. Make another number line on the board or overhead transparency. Mark integers −5 to 5. Have students make a new number line on their own papers and mark integers −5 to 5.

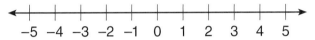

8. Ask a student volunteer to count the spaces from the 5 to the zero. Emphasize that 5 is five away from zero. Now ask a student to count the spaces from −5 to zero. Emphasize that −5 is also exactly five away from zero.

9. Discuss the following term with students:

> **absolute value** The distance of a number from zero on the number line; it is always a positive number

10. Write **|5| = 5** and **|−5| = 5** on the board. Explain to students that both 5 and −5 have an absolute value of 5 because both numbers are exactly five away from zero. Tell students that the straight lines tell us we should find the absolute value of those numbers. Demonstrate more examples if necessary.

Examples:

|−17| = 17 |264| = 264

|−264| = 264 |−58| = 58

11. Direct students back to the number line labeled with 5 and −5. Discuss how to locate numbers such as $1\frac{1}{2}$ and $-3\frac{3}{4}$ between the integers. Have students mark or graph the numbers 2, −4, 0, $1\frac{1}{2}$, and $-3\frac{3}{4}$ on the number line.

12. Tell students to make another number line from −5 to 5. Have them mark all integers greater than 1. See what alternatives students might use to graph this set. Discuss using an arrowhead to show that the pattern continues. The arrowhead symbol, ▶, means the integers continue forever. If necessary, demonstrate the concept on a number line.

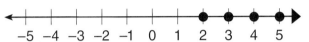

13. Have students try some other sets, such as {integers less than 4}, {integers between 3 and −4}, and {integers greater than −3}.

NEXT STEPS • Differentiate

5-Day Instructional Plan:
PM 1, page 86—All students, to assess progress

3-Day Instructional Plan:
PM 3, page 88—Students who demonstrate understanding of the concept, to assess progress
PM 1, page 86—Students who need additional support, to assess progress

CD 2 Graphing on the Number Line

Use with 5-Day or 3-Day Instructional Plan. In this activity, students create a number line and locate rational numbers on the line.

MATERIALS

- Blackline Master 27
- **Variation:** Gizmos
  Comparing and Ordering Integers

DIRECTIONS

1. Distribute a copy of Blackline Master 27, Number Lines, to each student, or have students draw several blank number lines.

2. Review the following term with students:

   integer The set of whole numbers and their opposites

3. Have students practice graphing sets by labeling individual number lines and graphing each of the following sets: {integers}, {negative integers}, {positive integers}, {positive integers between 9 and 25}, and {negative integers between −9 and −1}. Include other sets if students need more practice.

   Variation: Gizmos For this activity use the Gizmo *Comparing and Ordering Integers* as a class to demonstrate each set of integers.

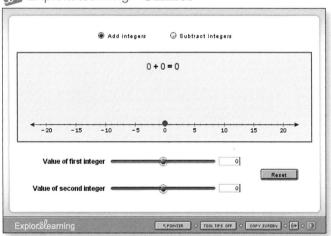

Comparing and Ordering Integers

4. Discuss the following term with students:

   rational number A number that can be expressed as the ratio of two integers

5. Give students some rational numbers to graph, such as $\frac{1}{8}$, $\frac{1}{4}$, 0.6, $\frac{3}{4}$, or 0.9.

   Point out that these numbers are located between 0 and 1. Explain that we may choose to use just that part of the number line if we wish.

6. Tell students not all numbers can be labeled or graphed at the same time. Explain that too many numbers are too close together. Demonstrate this concept by graphing halves, thirds, fourths, etc., on a number line. Explain that by selecting the appropriate scale, it is possible to picture numbers that are very close together. Show a number line with only twelfths to demonstrate this point.

7. Have students make a number line from −1 to 1. Tell them to graph the following set of numbers: {−0.8, −0.5, $−\frac{1}{4}$, $−\frac{1}{8}$, $\frac{1}{8}$, 0.5, $\frac{3}{4}$, 0.8}.

NEXT STEPS • Differentiate

5-Day Instructional Plan:
PA 1, page 85—All students, for additional practice and problem solving

3-Day Instructional Plan:
PM 2, page 87—All students, to assess progress

Practice Activity

★ PA 1 Graphing It

Use with 5-Day or 3-Day Instructional Plan. In this activity, students graph numbers on a number line, with duplication.

MATERIALS

- Blackline Master 27
- Dice, one per student

DIRECTIONS

1. Discuss the following terms with students:

   average The sum of the values in a set, divided by the number of values in the set

   median The center value in a set when all values are ordered by size

   mode The value in a set that appears most

2. Have students work in groups of two. Give each student a die. Distribute a copy of Blackline Master 27, Number Lines, to each student, or have students draw a blank number line. Have them label the number line from 1 to 6.

3. Explain the game rules.

   - Each student takes a turn rolling the die and graphing the number he or she rolls. Some rolls will be repeats.

   - Students continue to roll until they have graphed the numbers 1 through 6. The student who graphs all the numbers with the fewest number of die rolls wins.

   - Students keep track of the number of rolls it takes to complete the line.

4. After the game is over, work as a class to find the average number of rolls taken to complete the lines.

5. Repeat the activity with each student using two dice and a number line marked from 2 to 12. Have each student guess how many rolls it will take to get all 11 numbers graphed.

Name _____ Date _____

NUMBER LINES

NEXT STEPS • Differentiate

5-Day Instructional Plan:

PM 2, page 87—Students who are completing the activity for the first time, to assess progress

PS 1, page 89—Students who are completing the activity for the second time, to develop problem-solving skills

3-Day Instructional Plan:

PS 1, page 89—Students who are on the accelerated path, to develop problem-solving skills

PM 3, page 88—Students who are on the differentiated path, to assess progress

---

★ = Includes Problem Solving

6. Discuss changes students need to make in the scale of the number line to graph a large number, such as 1,000. Demonstrate the concept on a number line.

7. Make another number line on the board or overhead transparency. Mark integers –5 to 5. Have students make a new number line on their own papers and mark integers –5 to 5.

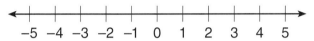

8. Ask a student volunteer to count the spaces from the 5 to the zero. Emphasize that 5 is five away from zero. Now ask a student to count the spaces from –5 to zero. Emphasize that –5 is also exactly five away from zero.

9. Discuss the following term with students:

   absolute value The distance of a number from zero on the number line; it is always a positive number

10. Write **|5| = 5** and **|–5| = 5** on the board. Explain to students that both 5 and –5 have an absolute value of 5 because both numbers are exactly five away from zero. Tell students that the straight lines tell us we should find the absolute value of those numbers. Demonstrate more examples if necessary.

    Examples:

|–17| = 17	**|264|** = 264
|–264| = 264	**|–58|** = 58

11. Direct students back to the number line labeled with 5 and –5. Discuss how to locate numbers such as $1\frac{1}{2}$ and $-3\frac{3}{4}$ between the integers. Have students mark or graph the numbers 2, –4, 0, $1\frac{1}{2}$, and $-3\frac{3}{4}$ on the number line.

12. Tell students to make another number line from –5 to 5. Have them mark all integers greater than 1. See what alternatives students might use to graph this set. Discuss using an arrowhead to show that the pattern continues. The arrowhead symbol, ▶, means the integers continue forever. If necessary, demonstrate the concept on a number line.

13. Have students try some other sets, such as {integers less than 4}, {integers between 3 and –4}, and {integers greater than –3}.

NEXT STEPS • Differentiate

5-Day Instructional Plan:
PM 1, page 86—All students, to assess progress

3-Day Instructional Plan:
PM 3, page 88—Students who demonstrate understanding of the concept, to assess progress
PM 1, page 86—Students who need additional support, to assess progress

Objective 1
Concept Development Activities

CD 2 Graphing on the Number Line

Use with 5-Day or 3-Day Instructional Plan. In this activity, students create a number line and locate rational numbers on the line.

MATERIALS

- Blackline Master 27
- **Variation:** Gizmos
  Comparing and Ordering Integers

DIRECTIONS

1. Distribute a copy of Blackline Master 27, Number Lines, to each student, or have students draw several blank number lines.

2. Review the following term with students:

   integer The set of whole numbers and their opposites

3. Have students practice graphing sets by labeling individual number lines and graphing each of the following sets: {integers}, {negative integers}, {positive integers}, {positive integers between 9 and 25}, and {negative integers between −9 and −1}. Include other sets if students need more practice.

   | **Variation:** Gizmos For this activity use the Gizmo *Comparing and Ordering Integers* as a class to demonstrate each set of integers.

 ExploreLearning • Gizmos

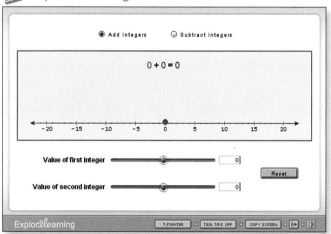

Comparing and Ordering Integers

4. Discuss the following term with students:

   rational number A number that can be expressed as the ratio of two integers

5. Give students some rational numbers to graph, such as $\frac{1}{8}$, $\frac{1}{4}$, 0.6, $\frac{3}{4}$, or 0.9.

   Point out that these numbers are located between 0 and 1. Explain that we may choose to use just that part of the number line if we wish.

6. Tell students not all numbers can be labeled or graphed at the same time. Explain that too many numbers are too close together. Demonstrate this concept by graphing halves, thirds, fourths, etc., on a number line. Explain that by selecting the appropriate scale, it is possible to picture numbers that are very close together. Show a number line with only twelfths to demonstrate this point.

7. Have students make a number line from −1 to 1. Tell them to graph the following set of numbers: {−0.8, −0.5, $-\frac{1}{4}$, $-\frac{1}{8}$, $\frac{1}{8}$, 0.5, $\frac{3}{4}$, 0.8}.

NEXT STEPS • Differentiate

5-Day Instructional Plan:
PA 1, page 85—All students, for additional practice and problem solving

3-Day Instructional Plan:
PM 2, page 87—All students, to assess progress

Objective 1
Practice Activity

★ PA 1 Graphing It

Use with 5-Day or 3-Day Instructional Plan. In this activity, students graph numbers on a number line, with duplication.

MATERIALS

- Blackline Master 27
- Dice, one per student

DIRECTIONS

1. Discuss the following terms with students:

   average The sum of the values in a set, divided by the number of values in the set

   median The center value in a set when all values are ordered by size

   mode The value in a set that appears most

2. Have students work in groups of two. Give each student a die. Distribute a copy of Blackline Master 27, Number Lines, to each student, or have students draw a blank number line. Have them label the number line from 1 to 6.

3. Explain the game rules.

   - Each student takes a turn rolling the die and graphing the number he or she rolls. Some rolls will be repeats.

   - Students continue to roll until they have graphed the numbers 1 through 6. The student who graphs all the numbers with the fewest number of die rolls wins.

   - Students keep track of the number of rolls it takes to complete the line.

4. After the game is over, work as a class to find the average number of rolls taken to complete the lines.

5. Repeat the activity with each student using two dice and a number line marked from 2 to 12. Have each student guess how many rolls it will take to get all 11 numbers graphed.

Name_____ Date_____

NUMBER LINES

NEXT STEPS • Differentiate

👥 5-Day Instructional Plan:

PM 2, page 87—Students who are completing the activity for the first time, to assess progress

PS 1, page 89—Students who are completing the activity for the second time, to develop problem-solving skills

👥 3-Day Instructional Plan:

PS 1, page 89—Students who are on the accelerated path, to develop problem-solving skills

PM 3, page 88—Students who are on the differentiated path, to assess progress

★ = Includes Problem Solving

Objective 1
Progress-Monitoring Activities

PM 1 Apply Skills 1

Use with 5-Day or 3-Day Instructional Plan.

MATERIALS

- *Interactive Text*, page 33

DIRECTIONS

1. Have students turn to *Interactive Text*, page 33, Apply Skills 1.

2. Remind students of the key terms: *finite*, *infinite*, and *integer*.

3. Monitor student work, and provide feedback as necessary.

   Watch for:
   - Do students understand the difference between finite and infinite sets?
   - Can students locate noninteger numbers on the number line?

NEXT STEPS • Differentiate

5-Day and 3-Day Instructional Plans:
CD 2, page 84—All students, for additional concept development

---

Name_____ Date_____

APPLY SKILLS 1

Use the number lines to solve each problem.

1. Using the number line below, put a dot on the following rational numbers: −3, 1, 5, −5, and 3.

2. How many numbers did you graph? <u>5</u>

3. Is the set finite or infinite? <u>finite</u>

4. Express the numbers as a set. <u>{−5, −3, 1, 3, 5}</u>

5. Using the number line below, graph this set of numbers: {−4, −3, −2, −1, . . .}.

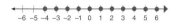

6. How many integers did you graph? <u>an infinite number</u>

7. Does the graphed set of numbers stop or continue on indefinitely?
   <u>continue on indefinitely</u>

8. Is the graphed set an infinite set or a finite set? <u>infinite</u>

9. Using the number line below, graph this set of numbers: {−6, −4.9, −3½, −1.75, 0, ½, 2, 3.4, 5}.

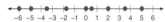

10. Using the number line below, graph this set of numbers: {integers between −5 and 6}.

Progress-Monitoring Activities

PM 2 Apply Skills 2

Use with 5-Day or 3-Day Instructional Plan. Some students on the 3-Day Plan may complete this activity early and move on to additional practice.

MATERIALS

- *Interactive Text*, page 34

DIRECTIONS

1. Have students turn to *Interactive Text*, page 34, Apply Skills 2.

2. Remind students of the key term: *integer*.

3. Monitor student work, and provide feedback as necessary.

   Watch for:

   - Do students know that the set of numbers between *x* and *y* does not include *x* or *y*?

   - Do students know what an integer is?

   - Do students include all values when writing the set in set notation?

NEXT STEPS • Differentiate

👥 5-Day Instructional Plan:

PM 3, page 88—Students who demonstrate understanding of the concept, to assess progress

PA 1, page 85—Students who need additional practice

👥 3-Day Instructional Plan:

PA 1, page 85—Students who complete the activity early, for additional practice and problem solving

PM 3, page 88—Students who use the full time allotted, for additional progress assessment

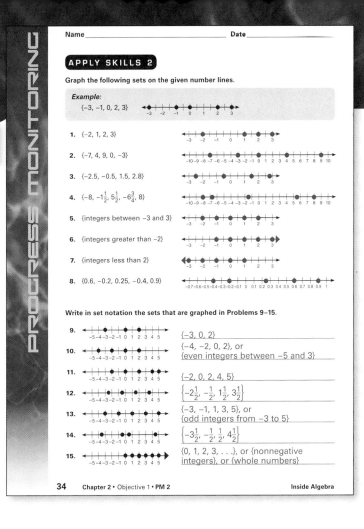

Objective 1
Progress-Monitoring Activities

PM 3 Apply Skills 3

Use with 5-Day or 3-Day Instructional Plan. Some students on the 3-Day Plan may complete this activity early and move on to additional problem solving.

MATERIALS

- *Interactive Text*, page 35

DIRECTIONS

1. Have students turn to *Interactive Text*, page 35, Apply Skills 3.

2. Remind students of the key term: *integer*.

3. Monitor student work, and provide feedback as necessary.

   Watch for:
   - Do students choose an appropriate scale for the data they need to graph?

   - Do students know that zero is even, but not positive or negative?

NEXT STEPS • Differentiate

👥 5-Day Instructional Plan:

   PS 1, page 89—Students who are on the accelerated path, to develop problem-solving skills

   Objective 1 Posttest, page 91—Students who are on the differentiated path

👥 3-Day Instructional Plan:

   PA 1, page 85—Students who are on the accelerated path, for additional practice and problem solving

   PS 1, page 89—Students on the differentiated path who complete the activity early, to develop problem-solving skills

   Objective 1 Posttest, page 91—All other students

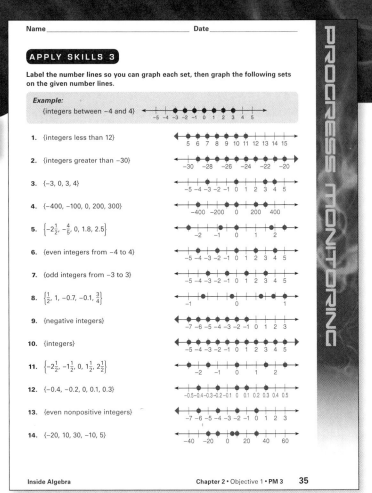

Objective 1
Problem-Solving Activities

★PS 1 Plotting Data—Part 1

Use with 5-Day or 3-Day Instructional Plan. In this activity, given the possible range of values, students choose a reasonable method of labeling a number line to accommodate collected data.

MATERIALS

- Blackline Master 27

DIRECTIONS

1. Divide the class into groups of two to four. Have one member of each group go to the other groups and collect numbers representing the day of the month of each group member's birthday (1 through 31).

2. Distribute one copy of Blackline Master 27, Number Lines, to each group, or have a student from each group draw a blank number line.

3. Have each group choose one student to be the recorder. He or she should graph the collected numbers on a number line. Tell students to think about the interval when deciding how to label the number line.

   Example:

4. Have recorders label any repeats, writing the number of repeats above the date.

5. Direct a discussion about the process of selecting the labeling for the number line. Groups may have an interval of 1, 2, 5, etc. Compare the number line graphs of the different groups.

6. Review the following terms with students:

   average The sum of the values, divided by the number of values

   mode The value that appears most

   median The center value when all values are ordered by size

7. Discuss the graphed data, including same birthdays, average, mode, and median. Ask students to discuss how these are related.

NEXT STEPS • Differentiate

👥 5-Day Instructional Plan:
 PS 2, page 90—Students who are on the accelerated path, for additional problem solving

 PM 3, page 88—Students who are on the differentiated path, to assess progress

👥 3-Day Instructional Plan:
 PS 2, page 90—Students who are on the accelerated path, for additional problem solving

 Objective 1 Posttest, page 91—Students who are on the differentiated path

★ = Includes Problem Solving

Name _____ Date _____

NUMBER LINES

27

Problem-Solving Activities

★ PS 2 Plotting Data—Part 2

Use with 5-Day or 3-Day Instructional Plan. In this activity, students choose a reasonable method of labeling a number line to accommodate collected data where the range of values is not given.

MATERIALS

- Blackline Master 27

DIRECTIONS

1. Divide the class into groups of two to four. Have one member of each group go to all the other groups and collect numbers representing the students' heights.

2. Distribute a copy of Blackline Master 27, Number Lines, to each group, or have students draw a blank number line.

3. Instruct students to convert the heights into inches when the groups look at the data. For example, 5 feet 3 inches = 63 inches. Explain that the recorder from each group should graph the collected numbers on a number line. Each group must think about intervals and decide how to label the number line.

   Example:

   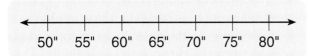

4. Review the following term with students:

   average The sum of the values, divided by the number of values

   Have each group determine the average height from the number line graph and write an explanation of how they reached this answer.

5. Have groups use calculators to find the average height and compare the value to the answer they got using the graph.

6. Direct a discussion about the process of determining the average height with a number line, and compare the methods of the different groups.

NEXT STEPS • Differentiate

5-Day and 3-Day Instructional Plans:
Objective 1 Posttest, page 91—All students

★ = Includes Problem Solving

NUMBER LINES

2 Ongoing Assessment

Objective 1 Posttest

Discuss with students the key concepts in Objective 1, then administer the Objective 1 Posttest to all students.

Using the Results

• Score the posttest and update the class record card.

• Provide reinforcement for students who do not demonstrate mastery of the concepts through individual or small-group reteaching of key concepts.

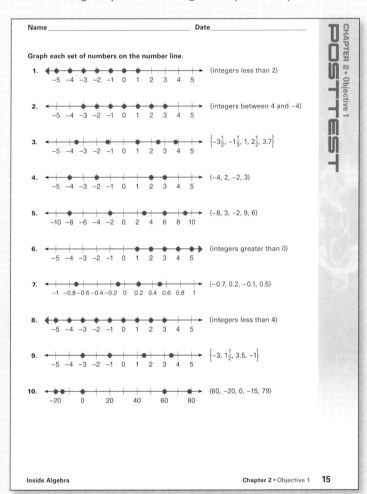

Objective 2
Add and subtract rational numbers.

Objective 2 Pretest

Students complete the Objective 2 Pretest on the same day as the Objective 1 Posttest.

Using the Results

- Score the pretest and update the class record card.

- If the majority of students do not demonstrate mastery of the concepts, use the 6-Day Instructional Plan for Objective 2.

- If the majority of students demonstrate mastery of the concepts, use the 4-Day Instructional Plan for Objective 2.

Name _____   Date _____

CHAPTER 2 • Objective 2
PRETEST

Simplify.

1. $-3 + (-2) =$ ___−5___

2. $-3 + 5 =$ ___2___

3. $0 - 3 =$ ___−3___

4. $3 + (-5) =$ ___−2___

5. $-3 - 7 =$ ___−10___

6. $-8 + 0 =$ ___−8___

7. $-3 + 7 =$ ___4___

8. $-0.3 + 0.5 =$ ___0.2___

9. $-\frac{1}{3} - \frac{1}{2} =$ ___$-\frac{5}{6}$___

10. $0.34 - 0.52 =$ ___−0.18___

16   Chapter 2 • Objective 2   Inside Algebra

Goals and Activities

Objective 2 Goals

The following activities, when used with the instructional plans on pages 94 and 95, enable students to:

- Simplify $4 + (-7)$ to get **−3**
- Simplify $4 - (-7)$ to get **11**
- Simplify $-2.3 - 5.1$ to get **−7.4**
- Simplify $-1\frac{1}{2} + 5\frac{1}{2}$ to get **4**

Objective 2 Activities

Concept Development Activities

CD 1 Using Tiles to Add, page 96	**CD 2** Adding Positives and Negatives, page 97	**CD 3** Using Tiles to Subtract, page 98	**CD 4** Adding and Subtracting on the Number Line, page 100

Practice Activities

PA 1 Finding Winter Temperature Changes, page 102	**★PA 2** Adding and Subtracting and the Contig Game, page 103	**PA 3** Adding and Graphing Numbers, page 104

Progress-Monitoring Activities

PM 1 Apply Skills 1, page 105	**PM 2** Apply Skills 2, page 106	**PM 3** Apply Skills 3, page 107	**PM 4** Apply Skills 4, page 108

★Problem-Solving Activities

★PS 1 Finding All the Answers, page 109	**★PS 2** Managing a Used Bookstore, page 110

Ongoing Assessment

Posttest Objective 2, page 111

Pretest Objective 3, page 112

CD = Concept Development PM = Progress Monitoring PS = Problem Solving
PA = Practice Activity ★ = Includes Problem Solving

6-Day Instructional Plan

Use the 6-Day Instructional Plan when pretest results indicate that students would benefit from a slower pace. This plan is used when the majority of students need more time or did not demonstrate mastery on the pretest.

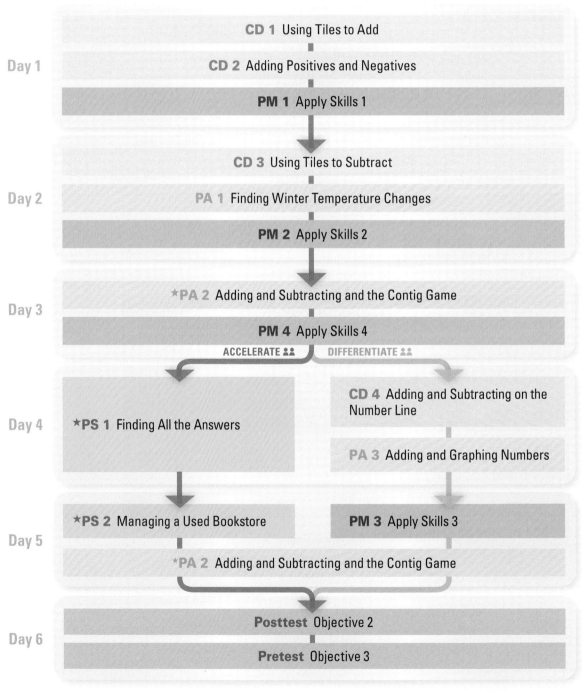

Day 1
CD 1 Using Tiles to Add
CD 2 Adding Positives and Negatives
PM 1 Apply Skills 1

Day 2
CD 3 Using Tiles to Subtract
PA 1 Finding Winter Temperature Changes
PM 2 Apply Skills 2

Day 3
★PA 2 Adding and Subtracting and the Contig Game
PM 4 Apply Skills 4

ACCELERATE 👥 DIFFERENTIATE 👥

Day 4
★PS 1 Finding All the Answers
CD 4 Adding and Subtracting on the Number Line
PA 3 Adding and Graphing Numbers

Day 5
★PS 2 Managing a Used Bookstore
PM 3 Apply Skills 3
★PA 2 Adding and Subtracting and the Contig Game

Day 6
Posttest Objective 2
Pretest Objective 3

CD = Concept Development PM = Progress Monitoring PS = Problem Solving
PA = Practice Activity ★ = Includes Problem Solving

4-Day Instructional Plan

Use the 4-Day Instructional Plan when pretest results indicate that students can move through the activities at a faster pace. This plan is ideal when the majority of students demonstrate mastery on the pretest. Not all activities are used in this plan.

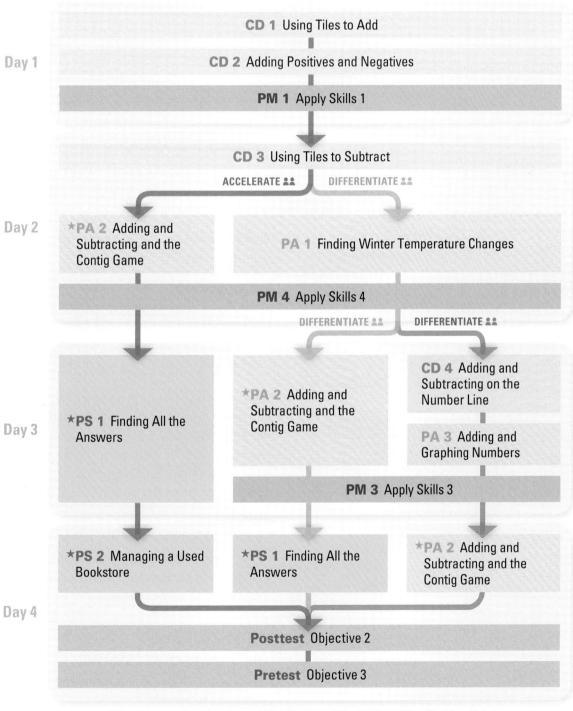

CD = Concept Development   PM = Progress Monitoring   PS = Problem Solving
PA = Practice Activity   ★ = Includes Problem Solving

Objective 2
Concept Development Activities

CD 1 Using Tiles to Add

Use with 6-Day or 4-Day Instructional Plan. In this activity, students understand the concept of zero pairs and create a general rule for adding two arbitrary numbers that may or may not have the same sign.

MATERIALS

- Objects of two colors, such as red and yellow tiles cut from construction paper, sprayed beans, or the algebra tiles
- **Variation: Gizmos**
  Adding and Subtracting Integers

DIRECTIONS

1. Have students form groups of two to four. Give each student 20 objects: 10 red and 10 yellow. Let red represent negative and yellow represent positive.

2. Establish the idea that a gain of one (+1) and a loss of one (−1) makes no gain at all, or zero gain. Write **+1 + (−1) = 0** on the board.

3. Demonstrate the concept of zero gain by showing some examples to the class.

Sample problems:

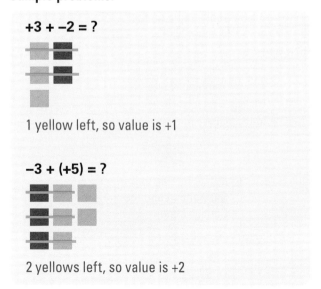

+3 + −2 = ?

1 yellow left, so value is +1

−3 + (+5) = ?

2 yellows left, so value is +2

Variation: Gizmos For this activity use the Gizmo *Adding and Subtracting Integers* as an alternate demonstration of the concept.

ExploreLearning • Gizmos

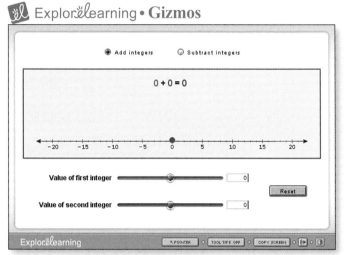

Adding and Subtracting Integers

4. Have students practice addition problems using the colored objects.

Sample problems:

−3 + (+2) = <u>−1</u>	**−4 + (+6) =** <u>+2</u>
+10 + (−3) = <u>+7</u>	**−4 + (−4) =** <u>−8</u>
+4 + (+3) = <u>+7</u>	**−7 + (+4) =** <u>−3</u>

5. Have some students in each group try to come up with general rules. Tell each group to write their own rule, or generalization. If students have trouble coming up with the generalization, have them use the tiles until they come up with it on their own. Have groups share the generalization they wrote.

Listen for:
- If the two numbers have like signs, find the sum.
- If the two numbers have unlike signs, find the difference and use the sign of the number with the larger absolute value.

NEXT STEPS • Differentiate

6-Day and 4-Day Instructional Plans:
CD 2, page 97—All students, for additional concept development

Objective 2
Concept Development Activities

CD 2 Adding Positives and Negatives

Use with 6-Day or 4-Day Instructional Plan. In this activity, students understand that adding a negative number is the same as subtracting a positive number.

MATERIALS

- *Interactive Text*, page 36

DIRECTIONS

1. Explain to students that we can use football to think about the addition and subtraction of positive and negative numbers. Point out that a running back on the offense of a football team strives to run with the ball to gain yardage and first downs for the team.

2. Point out that 10 yards are needed to get a first down, or another chance. Also explain that yards can be lost if the running back doesn't make it past the line of scrimmage, or starting point.

3. Explain that if we want to apply football to math, we think of yards gained by the running back as positive (+) yards, and yards lost as negative (–) yards. Thus, combinations of runs by a running back provide a good example of adding positives and negatives. For example, suppose that in four tries, or downs, a running back gains 5 (+5) yards, gains 3 (+3) yards, loses 2 (–2) yards, and gains $4\frac{1}{2}$ $\left(+4\frac{1}{2}\right)$ yards. We determine if the running back gained enough for a first down by calculating $(+5) + (+3) + (-2) + \left(+4\frac{1}{2}\right) = +10\frac{1}{2}$. In this case, the running back gained $10\frac{1}{2}$ yards, which is enough for a first down.

4. As a class, do a few more examples. Have students tell if the team gains enough yardage to make a first down in each situation.

Name_____ Date_____

FOOTBALL RUNNING BACK

The following are possible results of a running back's attempts to gain yardage.

a. gain of 1 yard	b. gain of 2 yards	c. gain of 3 yards
d. gain of 5 yards	e. gain of 8 yards	f. gain of 9 yards
g. loss of 1 yard	h. loss of 3 yards	i. loss of 5 yards

Use the gains and losses to complete the following steps for each series.

- Translate each series of four tries (downs) into an addition problem.
- Calculate the result as a positive or negative number.
- Answer the question: "Did the running back gain a first down?" (This means gaining 10 yards or more.)

Example:
a, c, d, h $(+1) + (+3) + (+5) + (-3) = +6$ Answer __no__

1. b, c, h, d $(+2) + (+3) + (-3) + (+5) = (+7)$ Answer __no__
2. e, i, g, f $(+8) + (-5) + (-1) + (+9) = (+11)$ Answer __yes__
3. g, d, b, d $(-1) + (+5) + (+2) + (+5) = (+11)$ Answer __yes__
4. f, i, h, e $(+9) + (-5) + (-3) + (+8) = (+9)$ Answer __no__
5. e, h, g, d $(+8) + (-3) + (-1) + (+5) = (+9)$ Answer __no__
6. f, i, b, e $(+9) + (-5) + (+2) + (+8) = (+14)$ Answer __yes__
7. e, g, h, i $(+8) + (-1) + (-3) + (-5) = (-1)$ Answer __no__

36   Chapter 2 • Objective 2 • CD 2   Inside Algebra

Sample problems:

Suppose the running back:

Gains 1 yard, loses 4 yards, gains $6\frac{1}{2}$ yards, and gains 5 yards. The team does not make a first down because it only gained a total of $8\frac{1}{2}$ yards.

Loses 2 yards, loses 1 yard, gains 9 yards, gains 4 yards. The team does make a first down because it gained a total of 10 yards.

Loses 5 yards, gains 5 yards, gains 6 yards, gains 7 yards. The team does make a first down because it gained a total of 13 yards.

5. Have students turn to *Interactive Text*, page 36, Football Running Back, to practice the idea of adding negatives and positives. For this exercise, explain that only running plays are used.

NEXT STEPS • Differentiate

6-Day and 4-Day Instructional Plans:
PM 1, page 105—All students, to assess progress

CD 3 Using Tiles to Subtract

Use with 6-Day or 4-Day Instructional Plan. In this activity, students understand that subtracting is taking away, regardless of whether a positive or negative number is subtracted. Students also use zero pairs in tile arithmetic.

MATERIALS

- Objects of two colors, such as red and yellow tiles cut from construction paper, sprayed beans, or the algebra tiles
- **Variation:** Gizmos *Adding and Subtracting Integers*

DIRECTIONS

1. Have students form groups of two to four. Give each student 20 objects: 10 red and 10 yellow. Let red represent negative and yellow represent positive.

2. Remind students that a gain of one (+1) and a loss of one (−1) makes no gain at all, or zero gain. Write **+1 + (−1) = 0, Additive Identity Property** on the board.

3. Demonstrate subtraction of two positives on the board. Make sure students understand that subtraction is taking away.

Sample problems:

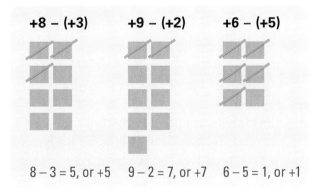

$$+8 - (+3) \qquad +9 - (+2) \qquad +6 - (+5)$$

$$8 - 3 = 5, \text{ or } +5 \qquad 9 - 2 = 7, \text{ or } +7 \qquad 6 - 5 = 1, \text{ or } +1$$

4. Next, demonstrate subtraction of two negatives by taking away.

Sample problems:

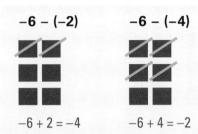

$$-6 - (-2) \qquad -6 - (-4)$$

$$-6 + 2 = -4 \qquad -6 + 4 = -2$$

5. Discuss the following term with students:

   zero pair A positive value and a negative value of equal magnitude that together equal zero

6. Write **+4 − (−3) = ?** on the board. Explain that to solve this problem, we start with four yellows, or positives, and no reds, or negatives.

Tell students we cannot take away three reds, or negatives, without introducing enough zero pairs. We have to add three zero pairs in order to have three reds to take away.

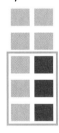

Point out that when we take away three reds, or negatives, we are left with seven yellows, or **+7**.

Write **+4 + (+3) = +7** on the board. Point out that this problem has the same answer as +4 − (−3).

7. Next demonstrate how to solve **+3 − (−1) = ?** on the board. Point out that we need to introduce one zero pair in order to have a red to take away.

We are left with four yellows, or **+4**.

8. Continue demonstrating the process, but as students catch on, have them take part in solving the problems. The goal is for students to see that subtracting is like adding the opposite.

Sample problems:

$$-6 - (-2) = -6 + (+2) = -4$$
$$-6 - (-4) = -6 + (+4) = -2$$
$$+4 - (-3) = +4 + (+3) = +7$$
$$+3 - (-1) = +3 + (+1) = +4$$

Variation: Gizmos For this activity use the Gizmo *Adding and Subtracting Integers* as an alternate demonstration of the concept of subtraction.

9. Have students try to come up with the general rule: **To subtract an integer, add its opposite.** it is okay if students come up with variations of this, as long as they understand the concept and can model why it is true.

NEXT STEPS • Differentiate

6-Day Instructional Plan:
PA **1**, page 102—All students, for additional practice

4-Day Instructional Plan:
PA **2**, page 103—Students who demonstrate understanding of the concept, for additional practice and problem solving

PA **1**, page 102—Students who need additional support

 Explorelearning • **Gizmos**

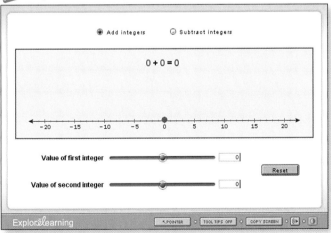

Adding and Subtracting Integers

Concept Development Activities

CD 4 Adding and Subtracting on the Number Line

Use with 6-Day or 4-Day Instructional Plan. In this activity, students understand that adding a positive or subtracting a negative means moving right on the number line, while subtracting a positive or adding a negative means moving left on the number line.

MATERIALS

- Blackline Master 27
- **Variation:** Gizmos
  Adding and Subtracting Integers

DIRECTIONS

1. Distribute a copy of Blackline Master 27, Number Lines, to each student, or have students draw a blank number line. Have them label the center 0 and go to at least 10 and −10.

2. Explain that when adding integers, positives go to the right of 0 and negatives go to the left of 0. Where we end tells us the answer.

Sample problems:

+3 + (−1) = +2

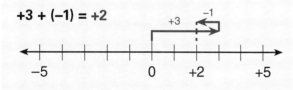

−5 + (+7) = +2

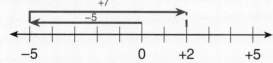

3. Ask students how subtraction can be shown. Explain that we must change direction for the number being subtracted. Make sure students understand that when subtracting a positive number, we move to the left, and when subtracting a negative number, we move to the right. Demonstrate a couple more examples, encouraging students to participate in the process.

Sample problems:

+3 − (−1) = +4

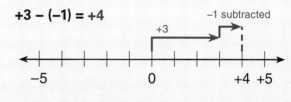

−3 − (−2) = −1

4. Demonstrate a problem with two positives, such as **+3 − (+1) = +2, or 3 − 1**, if students have trouble seeing why there is a change of direction. Show this on the number line. Starting at zero, move to the right to +3, then move one to the left because you are taking it away. This sets up the pattern for subtraction to change direction on the number line.

> **Variation:** Gizmos For this activity use the Gizmo *Adding and Subtracting Integers* to demonstrate addition and subtraction using a number line.

el Explor*e*learning • **Gizmos**

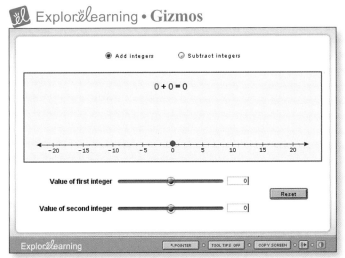

Adding and Subtracting Integers

5. Ask students to practice on the number lines with some problems, and/or make up some of their own. At this point, you may want to mix up addition and subtraction.

Sample problems:

−5 − (+5) = $\underline{-10}$	**−5 + (−3) =** $\underline{-8}$
+5 − (−4) = $\underline{+9}$	**+5 + (−4) =** $\underline{+1}$
+4 + (+3) = $\underline{+7}$	**−6 − (−3) =** $\underline{-3}$
−8 + (+13) = $\underline{+5}$	**−8 − (−15) =** $\underline{+7}$

NEXT STEPS • Differentiate

6-Day and 4-Day Instructional Plans:
PA 3, page 104—All students, for additional practice

Practice Activities

PA 1 Finding Winter Temperature Changes

Use with 6-Day or 4-Day Instructional Plan. In this activity, students use subtraction to find the distance between two values, which may or may not have the same sign.

MATERIALS

- *Interactive Text*, page 37

DIRECTIONS

1. Have students turn to *Interactive Text*, page 37, Winter Temperature Changes, which shows high and low temperatures for eight days.

2. Tell students the object of the activity is to show how subtraction is used to find the changes in temperature from one day to the next, or from the high temperature to the low temperature in a day.

3. Point out that changes in temperature can be negative, as in a decrease, or positive, as in an increase.

4. Demonstrate how to find the change in temperature from the high on Day 1 to the low on Day 1. Explain that moving left on the number line shows a decrease of 20 degrees or $-20°$. Stress that, mathematically, we subtract the first number from the second: Low of Day 1 – High of Day 1 = 5 – (+25) = 5 + (–25) = –20° (decrease of 20 degrees).

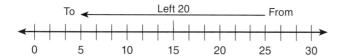

Have students find the change in temperature from the high of Day 1 to the low of Day 2. Make sure they see that the number line shows a decrease of 28 degrees, or –28° change from the high of Day 1

to the low of Day 2. We subtract the first number from the second: Low of Day 2 – High of Day 1 = –3 – (+25) = –3 + (–25) = –28° (decrease of 28 degrees).

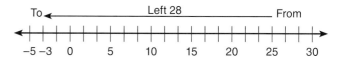

5. Have students form groups of two or three to find the changes in temperature on *Interactive Text*, page 37, Winter Temperature Changes. Point out that students are to express the changes as positive or negative numbers and they must show their work. Do more problems as a class if students need more practice.

NEXT STEPS • Differentiate

6-Day Instructional Plan:
PM 2, page 106—All students, to assess progress

4-Day Instructional Plan:
PM 4, page 108—All students, to assess progress

Practice page (Interactive Text, page 37)

Name _____ Date _____

WINTER TEMPERATURE CHANGES

Use the table to solve each problem. Show the change in temperature as positive or negative numbers.

Winter Temperature Changes		
Day	High Temp.	Low Temp.
1	25°F	5°F
2	20°F	–3°F
3	10°F	–11°F
4	–4°F	–15°F
5	33°F	16°F
6	50°F	22°F
7	20°F	4°F
8	12°F	–12°F

WORK SPACE

1. Find the change in temperature from the high of Day 2 to the low of Day 2. ____–23°F____
   1. –3 – 20

2. Find the change in temperature from the high of Day 3 to the low of Day 3. ____–21°F____
   2. –11 – 10

3. Find the change in temperature from the high of Day 1 to the low of Day 4. ____–40°F____
   3. –15 – 25

4. Find the change in temperature from the high of Day 5 to the low of Day 8. ____–45°F____
   4. –12 – 33

5. Find the change in temperature from the high of Day 8 to the low of Day 8. ____–24°F____
   5. –12 – 12

6. Find the change in temperature from the low of Day 4 to the high of Day 5. ____48°F____
   6. 33 – (–15)

Practice Activities

★PA 2 Adding and Subtracting and the Contig Game

Use with 6-Day or 4-Day Instructional Plan. In this activity, students correctly add and subtract positive and negative numbers and utilize number sense to form strategies for scoring the maximum number of points.

MATERIALS

- Blackline Master 28
- Red and white dice, six to each group (three pair)
- Game markers to cover squares

DIRECTIONS

1. Have students form groups of three or four.

2. Distribute six dice (three red and three white), one copy of Blackline Master 28, Contig Game Board 1, and markers to each group.

3. Explain the game rules.

   - Students take turns rolling three dice, any combination of red and white. Red represents negative numbers, and white represents positive numbers.

   - The object is to take the three rolled numbers and form a problem in addition and/or subtraction to equal one of the game board numbers that is not covered.

   - After each student takes a turn rolling the dice, he/she is awarded one point if that student is able to cover an answer on the board. Other students in the group verify their group members' answers.

   - Once an answer on the board is covered, it cannot be used again in rolls of other students in the group.

   - Additional points can be scored by covering a square that touches (is contiguous to) other covered answers, either at a corner or on a side. A student can earn as many as eight additional points in this manner.

★ = Includes Problem Solving

Name _____ Date _____

28

CONTIG GAME BOARD 1

Roll three dice to create an addition or subtraction problem equal to one of the numbers on the board. Place a marker on the answer. One point is awarded for each number covered, with additional points awarded if the number is next to any numbers already covered.

–17	–16	–15	–14	–13
–12	–11	–10	–9	–8
–7	–6	–5	–4	–3
–2	–1	0	+1	+2
+3	+4	+5	+6	+7
+8	+9	+10	+11	+12
+13	+14	+15	+16	+17

Example:

last chip played

In this case, the player gets three total points; two points are awarded because the marker is contiguous to two other markers, and one point is awarded for covering an empty square.

- Students can work individually or as a group to find the answer that scores the most points.

NEXT STEPS • Differentiate

6-Day Instructional Plan:
Objective 2 Posttest, page 111—All students

4-Day Instructional Plan:
PM 4, page 108—Students who are on the accelerated path, to assess progress

PM 3, page 107—Students on the differentiated path who demonstrated understanding on Apply Skills 4, to assess progress

Objective 2 Posttest, page 111—All other students

Practice Activities

PA 3 Adding and Graphing Numbers

Use with 6-Day or 4-Day Instructional Plan. In this activity, students use number sense to determine a strategy for optimal game play.

MATERIALS

- Blackline Master 27
- Dice of two different colors, four to each pair of students (two red and two white)

DIRECTIONS

1. Have students work in groups of two. Give each pair of students four dice (two red and two white). Distribute a copy of Blackline Master 27, Number Lines, to each student, or have students draw a blank number line. Tell them to label the number line from −8 to 8.

2. Explain the game rules.

   - Students take turns rolling the four dice. The white dice denote positive integers and the red dice denote negative integers.

   - The roller can select any two of the four dice and use the sum as a point to be graphed. For example, if the roll comes up 3, 4, −1, −4, the students can select 3 and 4 to graph 7, or 3 and −1 to graph 2, etc.

   - Students should continue to roll until all the numbers −8 through 8 have been graphed. The student who graphs all the numbers first wins.

3. Have students repeat the activity a few times, then discuss any strategies they used. For example, they may be covering −8, −7, −6, 6, 7, and 8 first.

4. Repeat the game but let students add the numbers on 2, 3, or 4 of the dice to get the numbers to graph on the number line.

Name _____ Date _____

NUMBER LINES

NEXT STEPS • Differentiate

6-Day and 4-Day Instructional Plans:
PM 3, page 107—All students, to assess progress

Objective 2
Progress-Monitoring Activities

PM 1 Apply Skills 1

Use with 6-Day or 4-Day Instructional Plan.

MATERIALS

- *Interactive Text*, page 38

DIRECTIONS

1. Have students turn to *Interactive Text*, page 38, Apply Skills 1.

2. Remind students of the key term: *zero pair*.

3. Monitor student work, and provide feedback as necessary.

   Watch for:
   - Do students understand how to make zero pairs?

   - Do students get a smaller answer when subtracting a positive from a negative?

NEXT STEPS • Differentiate

6-Day and 4-Day Instructional Plans:
CD 3, page 98—All students, for additional concept development

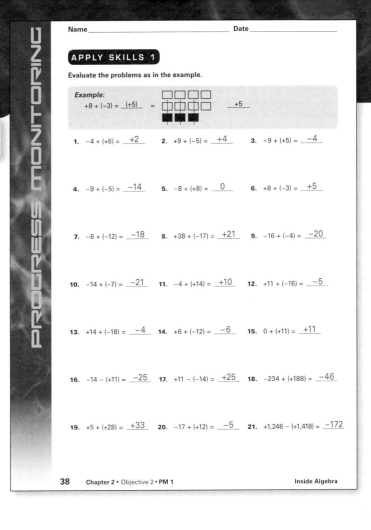

Progress-Monitoring Activities

PM 2 Apply Skills 2

Use with 6-Day Instructional Plan.

MATERIALS

- *Interactive Text*, pages 39–40

DIRECTIONS

1. Have students turn to *Interactive Text*, pages 39–40, Apply Skills 2.

2. Remind students of the key term: *zero pair*.

3. Monitor student work, and provide feedback as necessary.

   Watch for:
   - Do students see that subtraction is the same as adding the opposite?
   - Do students get a smaller answer when subtracting a positive from a negative?

NEXT STEPS • Differentiate

6-Day Instructional Plan:

PA 2, page 103—All students, for additional practice and problem solving

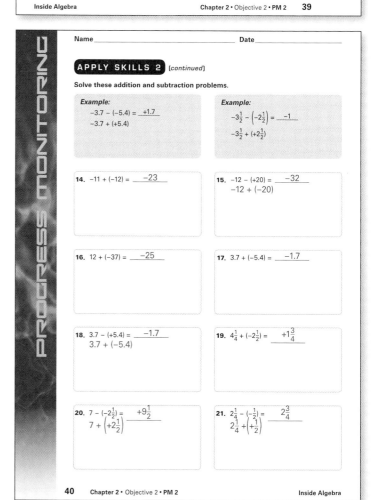

Name _____ Date _____

APPLY SKILLS 2

Study the two examples, then complete the remainder of the subtraction problems.

Example:
$4 - (-3) = \underline{\;4 + (+3)\;} = \underline{\;7\;}$

Example:
$-5 - (-2) = \underline{\;-5 + (+2)\;} = \underline{\;-3\;}$

1. $-3 - (-5) = -3 + (+5) = \underline{\;+2\;}$
2. $-3 - (+5) = -3 + \underline{\;(-5)\;} = \underline{\;-8\;}$
3. $15 - (-15) = \underline{\;15 + (+15)\;} = \underline{\;+30\;}$
4. $-15 - (-15) = \underline{\;-15 + (+15)\;} = \underline{\;0\;}$
5. $-15 - (+15) = \underline{\;-15 + (-15)\;} = \underline{\;-30\;}$
6. $15 - (+15) = \underline{\;15 + (-15)\;} = \underline{\;0\;}$
7. $25 - (-11) = \underline{\;25 + (+11)\;} = \underline{\;+36\;}$
8. $-25 - (-11) = \underline{\;-25 + (+11)\;} = \underline{\;-14\;}$
9. $-25 - (+11) = \underline{\;-25 + (-11)\;} = \underline{\;-36\;}$
10. $25 - (+11) = \underline{\;25 + (-11)\;} = \underline{\;+14\;}$
11. $13 - (-12) = \underline{\;13 + (+12)\;} = \underline{\;+25\;}$
12. $-13 - (-12) = \underline{\;-13 + (+12)\;} = \underline{\;-1\;}$
13. $-13 - (+12) = \underline{\;-13 + (-12)\;} = \underline{\;-25\;}$

Inside Algebra   Chapter 2 • Objective 2 • PM 2   39

Name _____ Date _____

APPLY SKILLS 2 (continued)

Solve these addition and subtraction problems.

Example:
$-3.7 - (-5.4) = \underline{\;+1.7\;}$
$-3.7 + (+5.4)$

Example:
$-3\frac{1}{2} - \left(-2\frac{1}{2}\right) = \underline{\;-1\;}$
$-3\frac{1}{2} + \left(+2\frac{1}{2}\right)$

14. $-11 + (-12) = \underline{\;-23\;}$

15. $-12 - (+20) = \underline{\;-32\;}$
$-12 + (-20)$

16. $12 + (-37) = \underline{\;-25\;}$

17. $3.7 + (-5.4) = \underline{\;-1.7\;}$

18. $3.7 - (+5.4) = \underline{\;-1.7\;}$
$3.7 + (-5.4)$

19. $4\frac{1}{4} + \left(-2\frac{1}{2}\right) = \underline{\;+1\frac{3}{4}\;}$

20. $7 - \left(-2\frac{1}{2}\right) = \underline{\;+9\frac{1}{2}\;}$
$7 + \left(+2\frac{1}{2}\right)$

21. $2\frac{1}{4} - \left(-\frac{1}{2}\right) = \underline{\;2\frac{3}{4}\;}$
$2\frac{1}{4} + \left(+\frac{1}{2}\right)$

40   Chapter 2 • Objective 2 • PM 2   Inside Algebra

Objective 2
Progress-Monitoring Activities

PM 3 Apply Skills 3

Use with 6-Day or 4-Day Instructional Plan.

MATERIALS

- *Interactive Text*, page 41

DIRECTIONS

1. Have students turn to *Interactive Text*, page 41, Apply Skills 3.

2. Monitor student work, and provide feedback as necessary.

   Watch for:
   - Do students see numbers as being distances toward or away from zero?
   - Do students realize they simply change direction when they see a minus sign?

NEXT STEPS • Differentiate

6-Day Instructional Plan:
PA 2, page 103—All students, for additional practice and problem solving

4-Day Instructional Plan:
PS 1, page 109—Students who demonstrated understanding on PM 4, to develop problem-solving skills

PA 2, page 103—All other students, for additional practice and problem solving

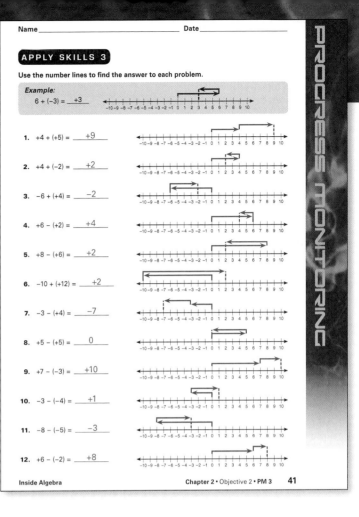

Objective 2
Progress-Monitoring Activities

PM 4 Apply Skills 4

Use with 6-Day or 4-Day Instructional Plan.

MATERIALS

- *Interactive Text*, pages 42–43

DIRECTIONS

1. Have students turn to *Interactive Text*, pages 42–43, Apply Skills 4.

2. Monitor student work, and provide feedback as necessary.

   Watch for:

   - Do students notice the operation to be performed in each problem?

   - Do students see that subtraction is the same as adding the opposite?

   - Do students get a smaller answer when subtracting a positive from a negative?

NEXT STEPS • Differentiate

6-Day Instructional Plan:

PS 1, page 109—Students who demonstrate understanding of the concept, to develop problem-solving skills

CD 4, page 100—Students who need additional concept development

4-Day Instructional Plan:

PS 1, page 109—Students who are on the accelerated path, to develop problem-solving skills

PA 2, page 103—Students on the differentiated path who demonstrate understanding of the concept, for additional practice and problem solving

CD 4, page 100—All other students, for additional concept development

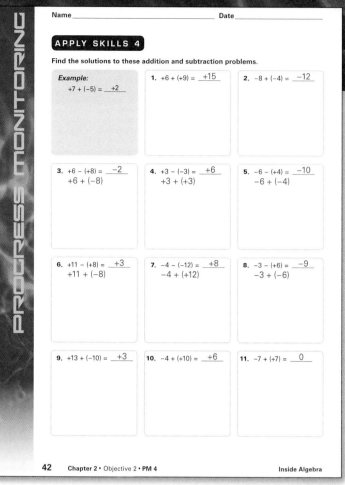

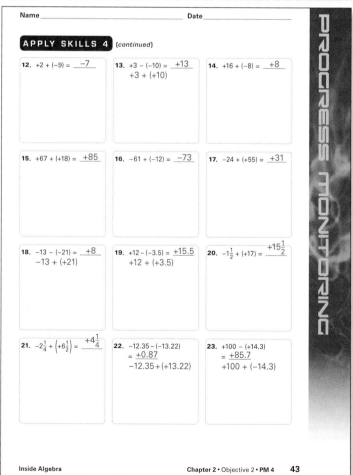

Objective 2
Problem-Solving Activities

★PS 1 Finding All the Answers

Use with 6-Day or 4-Day Instructional Plan. In this activity, students add and subtract positive and negative numbers.

MATERIALS

- Three dice to each group, two of one color and one of another color, such as two red and one white

DIRECTIONS

1. Have students form groups of two or three.
2. Explain the game rules.
   - Students take turns rolling the dice. Two red dice represent negative numbers and one white die represents positive numbers.
   - Using as many combinations of addition and subtraction, order, and grouping as they can, students should work together as a group to see how many answers they can form.

   Example:

   > If the numbers 4, −3, and −2 are rolled, there are several possibilities.
   > $4 + (−3) + (−2) = −1$
   > $4 + (−3) − (−2) = 4 + (−3) + (2) = 3$
   > $4 − (−3) − (−2) = 4 + (3) + (2) = 9$
   > $4 − [−3 + (−2)] = 4 − (−5) = 4 + (5) = 9$ (same answer as above)

3. Because many answers are possible, set a time limit of about three to five minutes.
4. Discuss strategies with students for finding different answers.
5. Repeat the process as time permits.

   Variation: Give all students the same three numbers and see which group can come up with the greatest number of different problems and answers.

NEXT STEPS • Differentiate

6-Day Instructional Plan:
PS 2, page 110—All students, for additional problem solving

4-Day Instructional Plan:
PS 2, page 110—Students who are on the accelerated path, for additional problem solving

Objective 2 Posttest, page 111—Students who are on the differentiated path

★ = Includes Problem Solving

Problem-Solving Activities

★ PS 2 Managing a Used Bookstore

Use with 6-Day or 4-Day Instructional Plan. In this activity, students add and subtract positive and negative numbers.

MATERIALS

- *Interactive Text*, page 44

DIRECTIONS

1. Tell students that in this activity, they calculate how much money a used bookstore owner has after one hour of buying and selling books.

2. Have students turn to *Interactive Text*, page 44, Used Bookstore.

3. Encourage students to write their subtotals after each addition.

NEXT STEPS • Differentiate

6-Day Instructional Plan:
PA 2, page 103—All students, for additional practice and problem solving

4-Day Instructional Plan:
Objective 2 Posttest, page 111—All students

Name _____ Date _____

USED BOOKSTORE

Jeff owns a used bookstore. He buys used books at half off the paid price. He sells the used books at a markup from the paid price. To keep track of his transactions, he records a purchase of a book as a negative number and a sale of a book as a positive number.

Listed below is one hour's worth of transactions. What was his final total for the hour?

Transaction	Ledger
Example: Purchased a book for $5.00	-5
Example: Sold a book for $7.00	+7
Sold a book for $3.00	+3
Purchased a book for $6.00	−6
Sold a book for $11.00	+11
Sold a book for $9.00	+9
Sold a book for $10.00	+10
Purchased a book for $6.00	−6
Purchased a book for $7.00	−7
Sold a book for $9.00	+9
Purchased a book for $5.00	−5
Purchased a book for $6.00	−6
Sold a book for $8.00	+8
Sold a book for $8.00	+8
Sold a book for $7.00	+7
Purchased a book for $6.00	−6
Sold a book for $12.00	+12
Total:	+43

★ = Includes Problem Solving

Objective 2

Ongoing Assessment

Objective 2 Posttest

Discuss with students the key concepts in Objective 2. Following the discussion, administer the Objective 2 Posttest to all students.

Using the Results

- Score the posttest and update the class record card.
- Provide reinforcement for students who do not demonstrate mastery of the concepts through individual or small-group reteaching of key concepts.

Name ____________________ Date ____________________

CHAPTER 2 • Objective 2

POSTTEST

Simplify.

1. $-5 + (-4) =$ -9
2. $-5 + 14 =$ 9
3. $-1 - 1 =$ -2
4. $5 + (-14) =$ -9
5. $-15 + 7 =$ -8
6. $-3 + 0 =$ -3
7. $-15 - 7 =$ -22
8. $\frac{2}{5} - \frac{1}{2} =$ $-\frac{1}{10}$
9. $-0.4 + 0.5 =$ 0.1
10. $-0.35 + (-0.28) =$ -0.63

Inside Algebra Chapter 2 • Objective 2 17

Objective 3 Pretest

Students complete the Objective 3 Pretest on the same day as the Objective 2 Posttest.

Using the Results

• Score the pretest and update the class record card.

• If the majority of students do not demonstrate mastery of the concepts, use the 5-Day Instructional Plan for Objective 3.

• If the majority of students demonstrate mastery of the concepts, use the 3-Day Instructional Plan for Objective 3.

CHAPTER 2 • Objective 3
PRETEST

Name _____   Date _____

Arrange the numbers in order from the smallest to the largest.

1. 1, −3, 0, −2, 2, −4, −5

   $\underline{-5, -4, -3, -2, 0, 1, 2}$

2. −8, 4, −3, 8, −5, 13

   $\underline{-8, -5, -3, 4, 8, 13}$

3. −5, 7, −1, 1, 3, −10

   $\underline{-10, -5, -1, 1, 3, 7}$

4. $-\frac{1}{2}$, 0.9, −0.3, 0.31, −0.9, $-\frac{3}{4}$

   $\underline{-0.9, -\frac{3}{4}, -\frac{1}{2}, -0.3, 0.31, 0.9}$

Place the symbol <, >, or = between each pair of numbers to make the sentence true.

5. −3 $\underline{<}$ 10

6. −3.1 $\underline{>}$ −4

7. $\frac{3}{4}$ $\underline{<}$ $\frac{4}{5}$

8. 0.31 $\underline{>}$ 0.2

9. −0.31 $\underline{<}$ −0.2

10. −21 $\underline{>}$ −22

18   Chapter 2 • Objective 3   Inside Algebra

Goals and Activities

Objective 3 Goals

The following activities, when used with the instructional plans on pages 114 and 115, enable students to:

- Make the sentence $\frac{1}{4}$ __ $\frac{1}{3}$ true by inserting a **<**

- Make the sentence -2.8 __ -3 true by inserting a **>**

- Make the sentence -10 __ 25 true by inserting a **<**

- Arrange the numbers 3, -2.4, -3, 2.4, 0 in order from smallest to largest as **-3, -2.4, 0, 2.4, 3**

Objective 3 Activities

Concept Development Activities	
CD 1 Modeling Number Lines, page 116	**★CD 2** Ranking Temperatures, page 118

Practice Activities		
PA 1 Rolling a Fraction, page 119	**PA 2** Computing Profits and Losses, page 120	**PA 3** Comparing Numbers, page 121

Progress-Monitoring Activities		
PM 1 Apply Skills 1, page 122	**PM 2** Apply Skills 2, page 123	**PM 3** Apply Skills 3, page 124

★Problem-Solving Activities	
★PS 1 Finding Closer Fractions, page 125	**★PS 2** Analyzing Temperatures, page 126

Ongoing Assessment
Posttest Objective 3, page 127
Pretest Objective 4, page 128

CD = Concept Development PM = Progress Monitoring PS = Problem Solving
PA = Practice Activity ★ = Includes Problem Solving

Instructional Plans

5-Day Instructional Plan

Use the 5-Day Instructional Plan when pretest results indicate that students would benefit from a slower pace. This plan is used when the majority of students need more time or did not demonstrate mastery on the pretest.

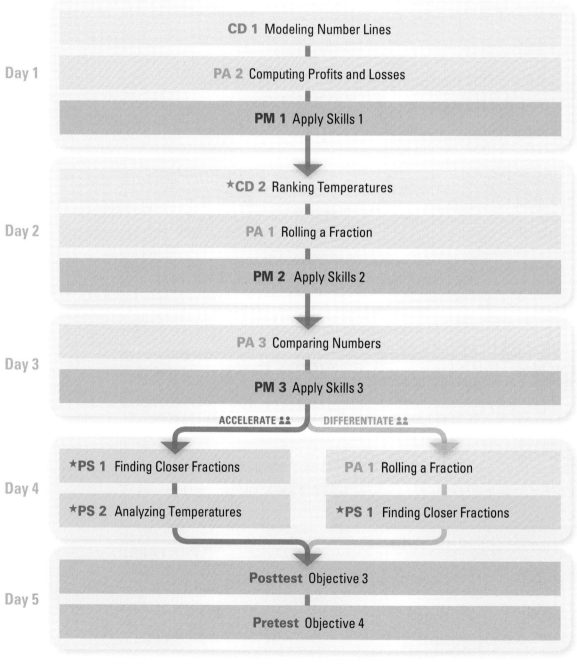

Day 1
- **CD 1** Modeling Number Lines
- **PA 2** Computing Profits and Losses
- **PM 1** Apply Skills 1

Day 2
- ★**CD 2** Ranking Temperatures
- **PA 1** Rolling a Fraction
- **PM 2** Apply Skills 2

Day 3
- **PA 3** Comparing Numbers
- **PM 3** Apply Skills 3

ACCELERATE / DIFFERENTIATE

Day 4
- ★**PS 1** Finding Closer Fractions
- ★**PS 2** Analyzing Temperatures

- **PA 1** Rolling a Fraction
- ★**PS 1** Finding Closer Fractions

Day 5
- **Posttest** Objective 3
- **Pretest** Objective 4

CD = Concept Development   PM = Progress Monitoring   PS = Problem Solving
PA = Practice Activity   ★ = Includes Problem Solving

3-Day Instructional Plan

Use the 3-Day Instructional Plan when pretest results indicate that students can move through the activities at a faster pace. This plan is ideal when the majority of students demonstrate mastery on the pretest.

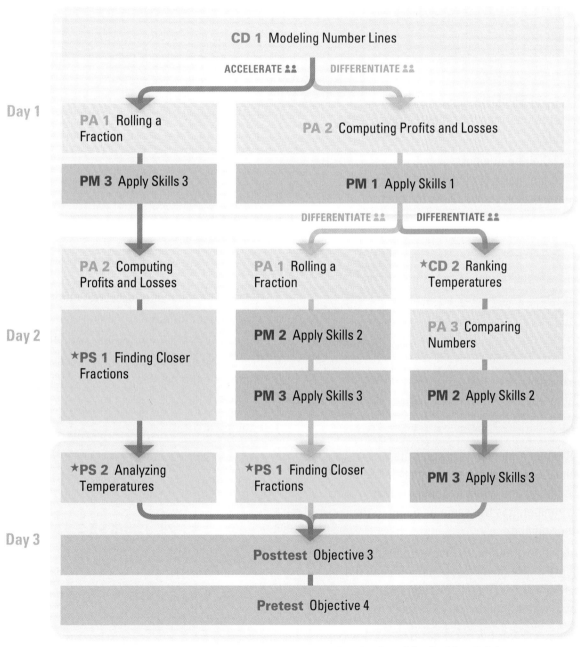

CD = Concept Development   PM = Progress Monitoring   PS = Problem Solving
PA = Practice Activity   ★ = Includes Problem Solving

Objective 3
Concept Development Activities

CD 1 Modeling Number Lines

NUMBER LINES

Use with 5-Day or 3-Day Instructional Plan. In this activity, students understand that when given any two numbers on a number line, the one to the right is always greater.

MATERIALS

- Blackline Master 27

DIRECTIONS

1. Distribute a copy of Blackline Master 27, Number Lines, to each student, or have students draw a blank number line.

2. Have students label the numbers −8 to 8 on the number line and plot pairs of numbers. As students graph each number pair, discuss how to compare the numbers.

   Examples:

   2 and 6 Stress that the number to the right on the number line is always greater, so $6 > 2$.

   −3 and 2 Point out that positive numbers are always greater than negative numbers, so $2 > -3$, or $-3 < 2$.

   −3 and −6 Explain that since −3 is farther to the right on the number line, −3 is larger, so $-3 > -6$, or $-6 < -3$.

3. Point out that when a number is greater than another number, it is the same as being to the right of the other number, and when a number is less than another number, it is the same as being to the left of the other number.

4. Use number lines to graph more number pairs and involve students as you discuss the positions on the number line. Make sure students understand how position affects order and comparative values.

   Examples:

   $-8 \; \underline{<} \; 1$ $\dfrac{3}{4} \; \underline{<} \; \dfrac{9}{10}$

   $-5.2 \; \underline{>} \; -5.3$ $0.4 \; \underline{>} \; -4$

5. Review the following term with students:

   rational number A number that can be expressed as the ratio of two integers

6. Present some examples in which several rational numbers must be placed in order from smallest to largest.

   Examples:

   3, −1, −2, $1\frac{1}{2}$, −1.4, and 2.1
   $-2, -1.4, -1, 1\frac{1}{2}, 2.1, 3$

   −3, $-\frac{1}{2}$, 4, $-2\frac{5}{6}$, $\frac{1}{4}$, and −6.2
   $-6.2, -3, -2\frac{5}{6}, -\frac{1}{2}, \frac{1}{4}, 4$

   −5.5, 0.7, −5.6, 5.5, 4.5, and 5
   $-5.6, -5.5, 0.7, 4.5, 5, 5.5$

7. Explain to students that they can think of an alligator to help them remember the order of rational numbers. The alligator's mouth represents the inequality sign, and the alligator always eats the larger number. So if the numbers are 5 and 6, the inequality would be $5 < 6$. The alligator is eating the larger number, 6.

NEXT STEPS • Differentiate

5-Day Instructional Plan:

PA 2, page 120—All students, for additional practice

3-Day Instructional Plan:

PA 1, page 119—Students who demonstrate understanding of the concept, for additional practice

PA 2, page 120—Students who need additional support

Objective 3
Concept Development Activities

★ **CD 2** Ranking Temperatures

Use with 5-Day or 3-Day Instructional Plan. In this activity, students write number sentences using comparison operators.

MATERIALS

• Blackline Master 29

DIRECTIONS

1. Divide students into pairs. Distribute one copy of Blackline Master 29, Winter Temperature Changes, to each pair.

2. Ask each pair to compare high temperatures by writing as many number sentences as it can using < or >.

Sample problems:

Day 1 high to Day 2 high $25° > 20°$
Day 2 high to Day 3 high $20° > 10°$
Day 3 high to Day 4 high $10° > -4°$
Day 4 high to Day 5 high $-4° < 33°$

3. When the pairs are done comparing the high temperatures, have them do the same for the low temperatures.

Sample problems:

Day 1 low to Day 2 low $5° > -3°$
Day 2 low to Day 3 low $-3° > -11°$
Day 8 low to Day 3 low $-12° < -11°$
Day 4 low to Day 6 low $-15° < 22°$

4. As a bonus question, ask pairs to rank the high temperatures in order from coldest (smallest) to warmest (largest). When this task is complete, ask them to do the same with the low temperatures.
High temperatures: $-4°$, $10°$, $12°$, $20°$, $20°$, $25°$, $33°$, $50°$
Low temperatures: $-15°$, $-12°$, $-11°$, $-3°$, $4°$, $5°$, $16°$, $22°$

29

WINTER TEMPERATURE CHANGES

Day	High Temp.	Low Temp.
1	25°F	5°F
2	20°F	−3°F
3	10°F	−11°F
4	−4°F	−15°F
5	33°F	16°F
6	50°F	22°F
7	20°F	4°F
8	12°F	−12°F

5. Ask students to discuss whether they can write a sentence in which the low temperature for a day is greater than the high temperature for another day.
Listen for:
• Day 1 low greater than Day 4 high: $5° > -4°$
• Day 6 low greater than Day 8 high: $22° > 12°$
• Other correct comparisons

NEXT STEPS • Differentiate

5-Day Instructional Plan:
PA 1, page 119—All students, for additional practice

3-Day Instructional Plan:
PA 3, page 121—All students, for additional practice

★ = Includes Problem Solving

Objective 3
Practice Activities

PA 1 Rolling a Fraction

Use with 5-Day or 3-Day Instructional Plan. In this activity, students write comparative sentences using fractions.

MATERIALS

- Blackline Master 27
- Two dice per group, one red and one white
- Paper to keep track of sentences produced

DIRECTIONS

1. Divide the class into groups of two. Give each group one white die and one red die. Distribute a copy of Blackline Master 27, Number Lines, to each group, or have students draw a blank number line.

2. Have students label one number line from −6 to 6.

3. Explain the game rules.

   - In each group, one student will roll the dice twice. For each roll, the red die will represent the numerator of a fraction and the white die will represent the denominator. For the first roll, the numbers on the dice are positive numbers. On the second roll, fractions are negative.

   - The other student in the pair will find, label, and plot the fractions on the number line and write on a sheet of paper a comparative sentence using the two fractions from the two rolls of the dice.

Examples:

Student	Roll Number	Sign of Fractions	Red Die Numerator	White Die Denominator	Sentence
First Turns					
Student 1	Roll 1	+	3	4	$\frac{3}{4} > \frac{1}{6}$
Student 1	Roll 2	+	1	6	
Student 2	Roll 1	+	6	5	$\frac{6}{5} < \frac{5}{2}$
Student 2	Roll 2	+	5	2	

NEXT STEPS • Differentiate

5-Day Instructional Plan:
PM 2, page 123—All students, to assess progress

3-Day Instructional Plan:
PM 3, page 124—Students who are on the accelerated path, to assess progress

PM 2, page 123—Students who are on the differentiated path, to assess progress

Student	Roll Number	Sign of Fractions	Red Die Numerator	White Die Denominator	Sentence
Second Turns					
Student 1	Roll 1	−	3	3	$-\frac{3}{3} < -\frac{1}{6}$
Student 1	Roll 2	−	1	6	
Student 2	Roll 1	−	2	3	$-\frac{2}{3} > -\frac{5}{1}$
Student 2	Roll 2	−	5	1	

Practice Activities

PA 2 Computing Profits and Losses

Use with 5-Day or 3-Day Instructional Plan. In this activity, students understand that profits are positive earnings and losses are negative earnings.

MATERIALS

- *Interactive Text*, page 45

DIRECTIONS

1. Divide the class into groups of two. Have students turn to *Interactive Text*, page 45, Profits and Losses.

2. Explain to students that profits are positive earnings and losses are negative earnings.

3. Discuss how running a school store can result in a profit or a loss.

   Example:

   > Earnings of −$3.50 would actually be a loss of $3.50.

4. Have student pairs fill in the blanks on the Profits and Losses page and complete Problems 2 and 3.

5. Discuss the graphing of each number and the sequence of the numbers. Make sure students correctly graph the profits and losses. If students need help ordering the numbers, refer them to the number line.

NEXT STEPS • Differentiate

5-Day Instructional Plan:
PM 1, page 122—All students, to assess progress

👥 **3-Day Instructional Plan:**
PS 1, page 125—Students who are on the accelerated path, to develop problem-solving skills

PM 1, page 122—Students who are on the differentiated path, to assess progress

---

PROFITS AND LOSSES

Solve the problems using the table, which shows several days of profits and/or losses for a school store.

1. Fill in the blanks by writing each profit or loss as a positive or negative rational number.

Day	Profit or Loss Amount	Rational Number (+ or −)
1	Profit $5.55	+5.55
2	Loss $6.10	−6.10
3	Profit $3.45	+3.45
4	Loss $3.95	−3.95
5	Profit $7.00	+7.00
6	Loss $4.35	−4.35
7	Profit $2.25	+2.25
8	Profit $4.80	+4.80

2. Graph each rational number on the number line below.

3. Arrange the rational numbers from smallest (largest losses) to largest (largest profits).

   −6.10, −4.35, −3.95, +2.25, +3.45, +4.80, +5.55, +7.00

Practice Activities

PA 3 Comparing Numbers

Use with 5-Day or 3-Day Instructional Plan. In this activity, students compare and order numbers using a number line.

DIRECTIONS

1. Tell students to work individually on this activity.

2. Write the numbers **3**, $1\frac{1}{4}$, **−2.7**, **2.3**, **2.7**, $-1\frac{1}{4}$, **−3**, and **−2.3** on the board or overhead.

3. Have students draw a number line from −3 to 3, with an interval of $\frac{1}{2}$.

4. Have them graph each of the numbers given in Step 2. For the fractions, students may use calculators to change them to a decimal equivalent.

5. Discuss the plotting of the numbers on the number line and check for the correct sequence. −3, −2.7, −2.3, $-1\frac{1}{4}$, $1\frac{1}{4}$, 2.3, 2.7, 3

6. Ask students to write 5 to 10 comparative sentences with pairs of the given numbers, starting at the left.

   Sample answers:

   $3 > 1\frac{1}{4}$ $1\frac{1}{4} > -2.7$ **−2.7 < 2.3**

7. Have students rank the numbers from smallest to largest. It is already done on the number line, but it can be used to show students how they can do a sequence from a number line.

NEXT STEPS • Differentiate

5-Day Instructional Plan:
PM 3, page 124—All students, to assess progress

3-Day Instructional Plan:
PM 2, page 123—All students, to assess progress

Objective 3
Progress-Monitoring Activities

PM 1 Apply Skills 1

Use with 5-Day or 3-Day Instructional Plan.

MATERIALS

- *Interactive Text*, page 46

DIRECTIONS

1. Have students turn to *Interactive Text*, page 46, Apply Skills 1.

2. Monitor student work, and provide feedback as necessary.

   Watch for:
   - Do students understand that all negative numbers are smaller than all positive numbers?
   - Do students see that the number farther right on the number line is always greater?

NEXT STEPS • Differentiate

5-Day Instructional Plan:
CD 2, page 118—All students, for additional concept development and problem solving

👥 3-Day Instructional Plan:
PA 1, page 119—Students who demonstrate understanding of the concept, for additional practice

CD 2, page 118—Students who need additional concept development

---

Solve.

1. Graph these integers on the number line below: 5, 0, −3, −1, −2, 4, 3.

   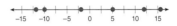

   $-5 \quad -4 \quad -3 \quad -2 \quad -1 \quad 0 \quad 1 \quad 2 \quad 3 \quad 4 \quad 5$

2. Rank the numbers in Problem 1 from smallest to largest.

   −3, −2, −1, 0, 3, 4, 5

3. Place the inequality symbol > or < between each pair of numbers to make a true sentence.

   a. 5 _>_ 0   b. 0 _>_ −3   c. −3 _<_ −1

   d. −1 _>_ −2   e. −2 _<_ 4   f. 4 _>_ 3

4. Place these low temperatures on the number line below.

January 1	−10°	January 2	−12°
January 3	−2°	January 4	5°
January 5	12°	January 6	16°

   $-15 \quad -10 \quad -5 \quad 0 \quad 5 \quad 10 \quad 15$

5. Rank the low temperatures from Problem 4 from smallest (or coldest) to largest (or warmest).

   −12°, −10°, −2°, 5°, 12°, 16°

Progress-Monitoring Activities

PM 2 Apply Skills 2

Use with 5-Day or 3-Day Instructional Plan.

MATERIALS

- *Interactive Text*, page 47

DIRECTIONS

1. Have students turn to *Interactive Text*, page 47, Apply Skills 2.

2. Monitor student work, and provide feedback as necessary.

   Watch for:
   - Do students understand that all negative numbers are smaller than all positive numbers?
   - Do students see that numbers that are farther left on the number line are smaller?
   - Do students remember to check place value on Problems 14 and 15?

NEXT STEPS • Differentiate

5-Day Instructional Plan:
PA 3, page 121—All students, for additional practice

3-Day Instructional Plan:
PM 3, page 124—All students, to assess progress

APPLY SKILLS 2

Rearrange each set of numbers from smallest to largest.

1. −5, 5, 10, −10, 9, −9, −3   −10 , −9 , −5 , −3 , 5 , 9 , 10

2. 3, 2, 0, −2, −3, 1   −3 , −2 , 0 , 1 , 2 , 3

3. 1, −3, 5, −5, 3, −1   −5 , −3 , −1 , 1 , 3 , 5

4. −100, −101, −99, 99, 100, −98   −101, −100, −99, −98, 99, 100

5. $-1\frac{1}{2}$, $1\frac{1}{2}$, 2, 1, −2, −1, 0   −2 , $-1\frac{1}{2}$, −1 , 0 , 1 , $1\frac{1}{2}$, 2

Place the symbol <, >, or = between each pair of numbers to make a true statement.

6. −1 _<_ 1

7. −1 _<_ 0

8. −1 _>_ −2

9. −1 _>_ $-1\frac{1}{2}$

10. −1 _<_ $-\frac{1}{2}$

11. −1 _>_ −1.1

12. −13 _<_ −12

13. −13 _>_ −14

14. 0.13 _<_ 13.1

15. −0.13 _>_ −13.1

16. −4 _<_ −3

17. 4 _>_ 3

18. 14 _>_ 13

19. −14 _<_ −13

20. −1 _<_ 100

Objective 3
Progress-Monitoring Activities

PM 3 Apply Skills 3

Use with 5-Day or 3-Day Instructional Plan.

MATERIALS

- *Interactive Text*, page 48

DIRECTIONS

1. Have students turn to *Interactive Text*, page 48, Apply Skills 3.

2. Monitor student work, and provide feedback as necessary.

   Watch for:

   - Can students use a number line to find which number is larger?

   - Do students see profits as positive numbers and losses as negative numbers?

NEXT STEPS • Differentiate

👥 5-Day Instructional Plan:

PS 1, page 125—Students who demonstrate understanding of the concept, to develop problem-solving skills

PA 1, page 119—Students who need additional practice

👥 3-Day Instructional Plan:

PA 2, page 120—Students who are on the accelerated path, for additional practice

PS 1, page 125—Students on the differentiated path who demonstrated understanding on PM 1, to develop problem-solving skills

Objective 3 Posttest, page 127—All other students

Name_____ Date_____

APPLY SKILLS 3

Rearrange the following numbers from smallest to largest.

1. $-3, 5, -4, 4, -5$ $\underline{-5}$ $\underline{-4}$ $\underline{-3}$ $\underline{4}$ $\underline{5}$

2. $-\frac{1}{2}, \frac{2}{3}, -\frac{1}{4}, \frac{1}{2}$ $\underline{-\frac{1}{2}}$ $\underline{-\frac{1}{4}}$ $\underline{\frac{1}{2}}$ $\underline{\frac{2}{3}}$

3. $0.3, -0.1, -0.2, 0.2$ $\underline{-0.2}$ $\underline{-0.1}$ $\underline{0.2}$ $\underline{0.3}$

4. $-4, -\frac{21}{5}, -3.95, -\frac{15}{4}$ $\underline{-\frac{21}{5}}$ $\underline{-4}$ $\underline{-3.95}$ $\underline{-\frac{15}{4}}$

5. $0, -\frac{5}{5}, \frac{5}{5}, -\frac{10}{5}, \frac{10}{5}$ $\underline{-\frac{10}{5}}$ $\underline{-\frac{5}{5}}$ $\underline{0}$ $\underline{\frac{5}{5}}$ $\underline{\frac{10}{5}}$

Place the symbol <, >, or = between each pair of numbers to make a true statement (calculator may be used).

6. $-4 \underline{<} -\frac{15}{4}$ 7. $-3.95 \underline{>} -4$ 8. $0 \underline{>} -1$

9. $4 \underline{=} \frac{16}{4}$ 10. $-\frac{1}{2} \underline{<} -\frac{1}{4}$ 11. $\frac{1}{2} \underline{>} \frac{1}{4}$

12. $-3 \underline{>} -4$ 13. $0.30 \underline{<} 0.4$ 14. $0 \underline{>} -\frac{1}{4}$

15. $-\frac{1}{4} \underline{=} -\frac{4}{16}$ 16. $\frac{5}{16} \underline{<} \frac{3}{8}$ 17. $-\frac{1}{2} \underline{<} -\frac{7}{16}$

Solve.

18. Place these profits or losses on the number line below: loss of $10.50, profit of $5.75, loss of $7.25, loss of $6.75, profit of $4.50.

    ```
    ←●—●—●———————●●——————→
    -10   -5    0    5    10
    ```

19. Rank the five numbers in Problem 18 from smallest to largest.

    loss of $10.50, loss of $7.25, loss of $6.75,

    profit of $4.50, profit of $5.75

20. Was the total of all five numbers a profit or a loss? Of how much? (Express as a rational number.)

    loss of $14.25

48   Chapter 2 • Objective 3 • PM 3   Inside Algebra

Objective 3
Problem-Solving Activities

★ PS 1 Finding Closer Fractions

Use with 5-Day or 3-Day Instructional Plan. In this activity, students name fractions that lie between two other rational numbers.

MATERIALS

- *Interactive Text*, page 49
- Calculators

DIRECTIONS

1. Draw a number line on the board with tenths marked on it.

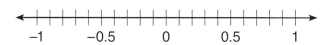

2. Write the fraction $\frac{2}{5}$ on the board. Ask students if they can locate it on the number line and plot it. Students may use calculators to change it to a decimal number.

3. Ask students to name a fraction that is closer to 0 than $\frac{2}{5}$. Answers can be fractions or decimal numbers.

   Listen for:

   - $\frac{1}{5}$
   - $\frac{1}{4}$
   - $\frac{1}{3}$
   - Other correct numbers

4. Have students name a fraction that is closer to 1 than $\frac{2}{5}$. Answers can be fractions or decimal numbers.

   Listen for:

   - $\frac{3}{5}$
   - $\frac{8}{10}$
   - $\frac{4}{6}$
   - Other correct numbers

★ = Includes Problem Solving

CLOSER

Finish the table. Answers will vary. Sample answers are given.

	Fraction	Find a Fraction Closer to:	Answer
1.	0.85	1	$\frac{9}{10}$
2.	$\frac{1}{9}$	0	$\frac{1}{10}$
3.	$-\frac{4}{5}$	0	$-\frac{2}{5}$
4.	$-\frac{4}{5}$	−1	$-\frac{9}{10}$
5.	$\frac{7}{8}$	1	$\frac{9}{10}$
6.	$-\frac{2}{3}$	−1	$-\frac{3}{4}$
7.	0.99	1	$\frac{999}{1,000}$
8.	0.01	0	$\frac{5}{1,000}$
9.	−0.1	0	$-\frac{1}{100}$

5. Discuss students' responses. Have students explain why the fractions they named are closer to 0 or 1.

6. Have students turn to *Interactive Text*, page 49, Closer, and complete the table.

NEXT STEPS • Differentiate

5-Day and 3-Day Instructional Plans:
   PS 2, page 126—Students who are on the accelerated path, for additional problem solving

   Objective 3 Posttest, page 127—Students who are on the differentiated path

Problem-Solving Activities

★ PS 2 Analyzing Temperatures

Use with 5-Day or 3-Day Instructional Plan. In this activity, students compare numbers and graph the numbers on a number line.

MATERIALS

- An almanac or a book on climate from the school library

DIRECTIONS

1. Review the following term with students:

   average The sum of the values in a set, divided by the number of values in the set

2. Have students work individually, or in small groups, to use an almanac or book on climate to find the average monthly temperatures for at least five different cities.

3. Have students make a chart that shows average high and low temperatures. Tell students they must include at least two cities that have negative temperatures.

4. When the chart is complete, have students graph, rank, and compare the average temperatures.

NEXT STEPS • Differentiate

5-Day and 3-Day Instructional Plans:
Objective 3 Posttest, page 127—All students

★ = Includes Problem Solving

Objective 3 Posttest

Discuss with students the key concepts in Objective 3.
Following the discussion, administer the Objective 3
Posttest to all students.

Using the Results

• Score the posttest and update the class record card.

• Provide reinforcement for students who do not
demonstrate mastery of the concepts through individual
or small-group reteaching of key concepts.

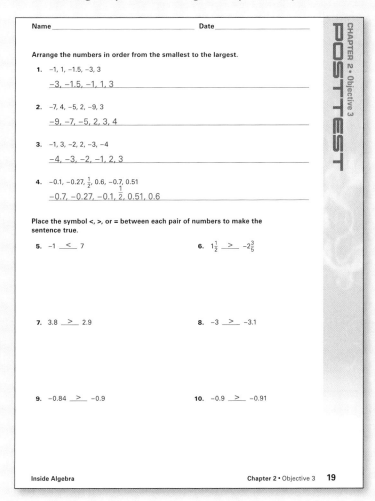

Name _____ Date _____

CHAPTER 2 • Objective 3
POSTTEST

Arrange the numbers in order from the smallest to the largest.

1. −1, 1, −1.5, −3, 3

  −3, −1.5, −1, 1, 3

2. −7, 4, −5, 2, −9, 3

  −9, −7, −5, 2, 3, 4

3. −1, 3, −2, 2, −3, −4

  −4, −3, −2, −1, 2, 3

4. −0.1, −0.27, $\frac{1}{2}$, 0.6, −0.7, 0.51

  −0.7, −0.27, −0.1, $\frac{1}{2}$, 0.51, 0.6

Place the symbol <, >, or = between each pair of numbers to make the sentence true.

5. −1 $\underline{\ <\ }$ 7   **6.** $1\frac{1}{2}$ $\underline{\ >\ }$ $-2\frac{3}{5}$

7. 3.8 $\underline{\ >\ }$ 2.9   **8.** −3 $\underline{\ >\ }$ −3.1

9. −0.84 $\underline{\ >\ }$ −0.9   **10.** −0.9 $\underline{\ >\ }$ −0.91

Inside Algebra   Chapter 2 • Objective 3   **19**

Objective 4
Multiply and divide rational numbers.

Objective 4 Pretest

Students complete the Objective 4 Pretest on the same day as the Objective 3 Posttest.

Using the Results

- Score the pretest and update the class record card.
- If the majority of students do not demonstrate mastery of the concepts, use the 5-Day Instructional Plan for Objective 4.
- If the majority of students demonstrate mastery of the concepts, use the 3-Day Instructional Plan for Objective 4.

CHAPTER 2 • Objective 4 PRETEST

Name _____ Date _____

Simplify.

1. $(-5) \cdot (2) =$ ___−10___

2. $\frac{-15}{-3} =$ ___5___

$$-3\overline{)-15}^{\,5}$$

3. $-5 \cdot (-13) =$ ___65___

4. $7 \cdot (-13) =$ ___−91___

5. $-12 \cdot (-5) =$ ___60___

6. $-60 \div (-5) =$ ___12___

$$-5\overline{)-60}^{\,12}$$

7. $\frac{60}{-12} =$ ___−5___

$$-12\overline{)60}^{\,-5}$$

8. $-48 \div 12 =$ ___−4___

$$12\overline{)-48}^{\,-4}$$

9. $-5.2 \cdot (-3.1) =$ ___16.12___

10. $\left(\frac{3}{4}\right) \div \left(-\frac{9}{10}\right) = \frac{-30}{36}$ or $-\frac{5}{6}$

$$\left(\frac{3}{4}\right) \cdot \left(-\frac{10}{9}\right)$$

20 **Chapter 2 • Objective 4**   **Inside Algebra**

Goals and Activities

Objective 4 Goals

The following activities, when used with the instructional plans on pages 130 and 131, enable students to:

- Simplify $-3 \cdot 4$ to get **-12**
- Simplify $\left(\frac{2}{3}\right) \cdot \left(-\frac{4}{5}\right)$ to get $-\frac{8}{15}$
- Simplify $-10 \div (-5)$ to get **2**
- Simplify $\left(\frac{2}{3}\right) \div \left(-\frac{4}{5}\right)$ to get $-\frac{10}{12}$ or $-\frac{5}{6}$

Objective 4 Activities

Concept Development Activities		
CD 1 Multiplying Positive and Negative Numbers, page 132	**CD 2** Using Inverse Operations, page 134	★**CD 3** Multiplying Integers, page 135

Practice Activities	
★**PA 1** Multiplying and the Contig Game, page 136	**PA 2** Multiplying and Dividing to Become a Millionaire, page 137

Progress-Monitoring Activities			
PM 1 Apply Skills 1, page 138	**PM 2** Apply Skills 2, page 139	**PM 3** Apply Skills 3, page 140	**PM 4** Apply Skills 4, page 141

★Problem-Solving Activity
★**PS 1** Filling in the Blanks, page 142

Ongoing Assessment
Posttest Objective 4, page 143
Pretest Objective 5, page 144

CD = Concept Development   PM = Progress Monitoring   PS = Problem Solving
PA = Practice Activity   ★ = Includes Problem Solving

5-Day Instructional Plan

Use the 5-Day Instructional Plan when pretest results indicate that students would benefit from a slower pace. This plan is used when the majority of students need more time or did not demonstrate mastery on the pretest.

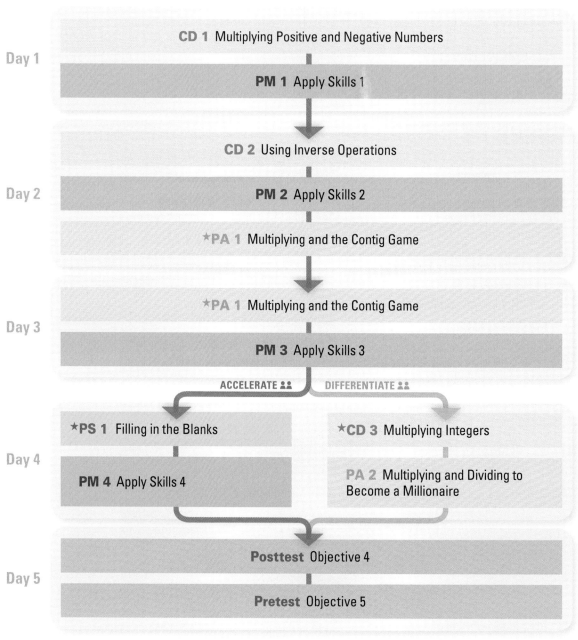

Day 1
- **CD 1** Multiplying Positive and Negative Numbers
- **PM 1** Apply Skills 1

Day 2
- **CD 2** Using Inverse Operations
- **PM 2** Apply Skills 2
- **★PA 1** Multiplying and the Contig Game

Day 3
- **★PA 1** Multiplying and the Contig Game
- **PM 3** Apply Skills 3

ACCELERATE 👥   DIFFERENTIATE 👥

Day 4
- **★PS 1** Filling in the Blanks
- **PM 4** Apply Skills 4

- **★CD 3** Multiplying Integers
- **PA 2** Multiplying and Dividing to Become a Millionaire

Day 5
- **Posttest** Objective 4
- **Pretest** Objective 5

CD = Concept Development   PM = Progress Monitoring   PS = Problem Solving
PA = Practice Activity   ★ = Includes Problem Solving

3-Day Instructional Plan

Use the 3-Day Instructional Plan when pretest results indicate that students can move through the activities at a faster pace. This plan is ideal when the majority of students demonstrate mastery on the pretest. This plan does not include all activities.

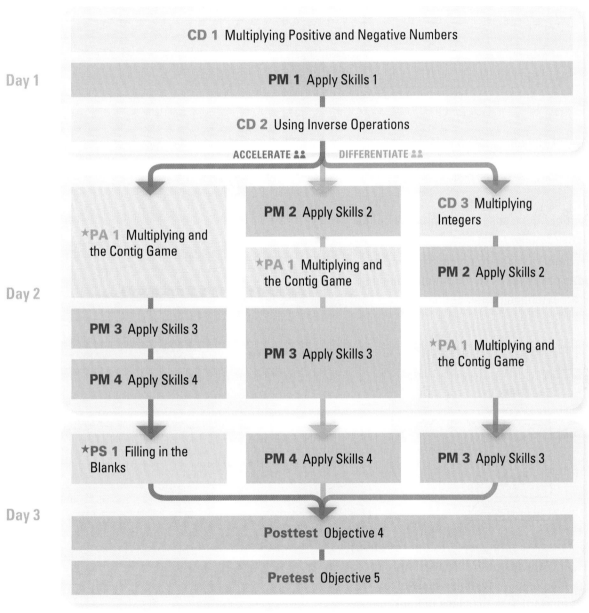

Day 1

CD 1 Multiplying Positive and Negative Numbers

PM 1 Apply Skills 1

CD 2 Using Inverse Operations

ACCELERATE 👥👥   DIFFERENTIATE 👥👥

Day 2

★PA 1 Multiplying and the Contig Game

PM 3 Apply Skills 3

PM 4 Apply Skills 4

PM 2 Apply Skills 2

★PA 1 Multiplying and the Contig Game

PM 3 Apply Skills 3

CD 3 Multiplying Integers

PM 2 Apply Skills 2

★PA 1 Multiplying and the Contig Game

Day 3

★PS 1 Filling in the Blanks

PM 4 Apply Skills 4

PM 3 Apply Skills 3

Posttest Objective 4

Pretest Objective 5

CD = Concept Development   PM = Progress Monitoring   PS = Problem Solving
PA = Practice Activity   ★ = Includes Problem Solving

Objective 4
Concept Development Activities

CD 1 Multiplying Positive and Negative Numbers

Use with 5-Day or 3-Day Instructional Plan. In this activity, students understand that adding a positive looks like subtracting a negative, and adding a negative looks like subtracting a positive.

MATERIALS

- *Interactive Text*, pages 50–51

DIRECTIONS

1. On the board, sketch the pump and tank as shown in the picture, or have students look at the picture on page 50 of the *Interactive Text*.

   Develop the idea of a pump that can pump water into (+) or out of (−) a transparent tank, making the water level rise or fall.

2. Add a video camera to the drawing. Explain that these devices can be used to record the pumping activity for an extended period of time.

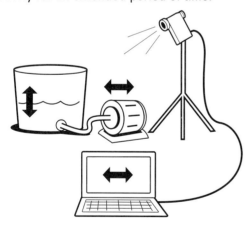

3. Have students turn to *Interactive Text*, pages 50–51, Pump, Tank, and Movie, for this activity. Introduce the concept of a computer that can play the movie backward or forward. Ask the class to think about what happens to the water level when the movie of the tank filling (+) is played backward (−). Students should recognize that it will look like the level is going down (−). Thus, a positive times a negative is a negative.

PUMP, TANK, AND MOVIE

- A pump can pump water into or out of a tank at different rates in gallons per minute (gal./min.).
- The tank is transparent, so the level of water can be seen.
- A digital video camera records the tank level rising and falling for a long period of time.
- The movie can be played either forward or backward on the computer.

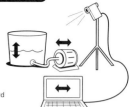

Complete the table by indicating in the last column whether the water level went up or down and whether this would represent a positive or negative number.

	Pump Direction	Movie Direction	Observed Result in Water Level
1.	in (+)	forward (+)	up (+)
2.	in (+)	backward (−)	down (−)
3.	out (−)	forward (+)	down (−)
4.	out (−)	backward (−)	up (+)

PUMP, TANK, AND MOVIE   *(continued)*

Complete the table by indicating in the last column whether the water is rising or falling and by how much. Follow the example given in the first row.

	Pump Direction	Observed Result in Direction	Water Level
	Example:		
	in, 6 gal./min.	forward for 6 min.	rising, 36 gal., ≈ +36
5.	in, 6 gal./min.	backward for 2 min.	falling, 12 gal., = −12
6.	out, 6 gal./min.	forward for 2 min.	falling, 12 gal., = −12
7.	out, 6 gal./min.	backward for 3 min.	rising, 18 gal., = +18
8.	in, 5 gal./min.	backward for 3 min.	falling, 15 gal., = −15
9.	out, 5 gal./min.	backward for 4 min.	rising, 20 gal., = +20
10.	out, 7 gal./min.	backward for 5 min.	rising, 35 gal., = +35
11.	out, 7 gal./min.	forward for 5 min.	falling, 35 gal., = −35
12.	in, 12 gal./min.	forward for $3\frac{1}{2}$ min.	rising, 42 gal., = +42
13.	out, 12 gal./min.	forward for $3\frac{1}{2}$ min.	falling, 42 gal., = −42
14.	out, 12 gal./min.	backward for $5\frac{1}{3}$ min.	rising, 64 gal., = +64
15.	in, 12 gal./min.	backward for 4.5 min.	falling, 54 gal., = −54

4. Go through the other possibilities, and have students fill in the answers for Problems 1–4 as each type of problem is discussed.

Sample problems:

The tank is filling (+) and the movie is running forward (+). (+)

The tank level is falling (−) and the movie is running forward (+). (−)

The tank level is falling (−) and the movie is running backward (−). (+)

5. As soon as students see the observed results as positive or negative, begin to introduce numbers. Discuss the examples shown in the chart.

Pumping Direction	Tape Direction	Observed Change in Level
In three gallons per minute (+)	Forward for four minutes (+)	Up twelve gallons (+12)
In three gallons per minute (+)	Backward for four minutes (−)	Down twelve gallons (−12)
Out three gallons per minute (−)	Backward for four minutes (−)	Up twelve gallons (+12)

6. Show students that these scenarios can be written as mathematical sentences. Write **+3 • (+4) = +12**, **+3 • (−4) = −12**, and **−3 • (−4) = +12** on the board.

7. As students complete *Interactive Text*, pages 50–51, tell them to think about the mathematical sentence each scenario represents.

NEXT STEPS • Differentiate

5-Day and 3-Day Instructional Plans:
PM 1, page 138—All students, to assess progress

Concept Development Activities

CD 2 Using Inverse Operations

Use with 5-Day or 3-Day Instructional Plan. In this activity, students use their knowledge of multiplication to divide. They see that they get a positive answer with like signs and a negative answer with unlike signs.

DIRECTIONS

1. Discuss the following term with students:

   inverse operations Pairs of operations that undoes each other and share an inverse relation

   Remind students that multiplication and division are inverse operations. Explain that one undoes the other. Write if **2 • 6 = 12**, then **12 ÷ 6 = 2** or **12 ÷ 2 = 6** on the board.

2. Present the problem **9 • 4 = 36** to students. Have them give the inverse operation problems related to it. $36 \div 9 = 4$ and $36 \div 4 = 9$

3. Have students discuss why these are related problems and all three equations result in a true sentence.

4. Have students write related sentences for inverse operations using integers. Give problems to students and ask them to write the related division sentences.

   Sample problems:

6 • 7 = 42	$42 \div 6 = 7, 42 \div 7 = 6$
−5 • 8 = −40	$-40 \div 8 = -5, -40 \div (-5) = 8$
7 • (−4) = −28	$-28 \div (-4) = 7, -28 \div 7 = -4$
−4 • (−9) = 36	$36 \div (-4) = -9, 36 \div (-9) = -4$

5. Give students verbal sentences, and have them think of mathematical sentences to model each verbal sentence. Remind students to include the answer.

   Sample problems:

   > Answers will vary. Sample answers are given.
   >
   > A positive number divided by a positive number.
   > $54 \div 6 = 9$
   >
   > A negative number divided by a positive number.
   > $-54 \div 6 = -9$
   >
   > A negative number divided by a negative number.
   > $-54 \div (-6) = 9$
   >
   > A positive number divided by a negative number.
   > $54 \div (-6) = -9$

6. Ask students to generalize about the value when doing division. Make sure they understand it is the same generalization as for multiplication; like signs yield a positive answer and unlike signs yield a negative answer.

NEXT STEPS • Differentiate

   5-Day Instructional Plan:
   PM 2, page 139—All students, to assess progress

👥 **3-Day Instructional Plan:**
   PA 1, page 136—Students who demonstrate fluency in multiplying positive and negative numbers

   PM 2, page 139—Students who need additional practice but do not require additional concept development

   CD 3, page 135—Students who need additional concept development

Concept Development Activities

★ CD 3 **Multiplying Integers**

Use with 5-Day or 3-Day Instructional Plan. In this activity, students apply their knowledge that multiplication is consecutive additions. Students are reminded that the product of two negatives is a positive.

DIRECTIONS

1. Review the following term with students:

   integer The set of whole numbers and their opposites

2. Have students work individually on this activity. Have each student write **4 • (−3)** on a sheet of paper.

3. Ask students to discuss the meaning of the number sentence. Lead them to the conclusion that multiplying is consecutive additions. Students should recognize that 4 • (−3) means adding four negative threes, or **(−3) + (−3) + (−3) + (−3) = −12.**
   $4 \cdot (-3) = -12$

4. Have students write **−2 • 3** on their papers. By the Commutative Property of Multiplication, this is the same as **3 • (−2)**. Explain that it can be thought of as **(−2) + (−2) + (−2) = −6**, or three negative twos.

5. Point out that these arguments work well for multiplying unlike signs or two positive numbers, but they do not work for multiplying two negatives. Have students look at a number pattern and complete the last number sentence.

Sample problems:

$-3 \cdot 4 = -12$	$-3 \cdot 2 = -6$
$-3 \cdot 1 = -3$	$-3 \cdot 0 = 0$
$-3 \cdot (-1) = \underline{\;3\;}$	$-3 \cdot (-2) = \underline{\;6\;}$

If students have difficulty, remind them of the pattern in the answers. Most students should see that −3 • (−1) must equal 3, and likewise, −3 • (−2) = 6. Lead students to the conclusion that multiplying two negatives must yield a positive.

6. Ask students to make up their own pattern to show that the product of two negatives must be a positive.

NEXT STEPS • Differentiate

5-Day Instructional Plan:
PA 2, page 137—All students, for additional practice

3-Day Instructional Plan:
PM 2, page 139—All students, to assess progress

★ = Includes Problem Solving

Practice Activities

★ PA 1 Multiplying and the Contig Game

Use with 5-Day or 3-Day Instructional Plan. In this activity, students perform basic mathematical operations on positive and negative numbers.

MATERIALS

- Blackline Master 30
- Game markers to cover squares
- Red dice and white dice, two of each color per group

DIRECTIONS

1. Have students form groups of two to four. Give each group two red dice and two white dice; one copy of Blackline Master 30, Contig Game Board 2; and enough markers to cover each square on the game board.

2. Explain the game rules.
   - Each student in the group rolls a die. The student with the highest number goes first. That student selects three dice to roll. Red denotes negative numbers, and white denotes positive numbers. The student's choice should depend on whether the student desires a positive or a negative answer.
   - The object of the game is to create a problem with the numbers rolled that has an answer corresponding to one of the unoccupied squares on the game board. The student may use any of the four operations (+, −, ×, ÷) and may use the numbers rolled in any order.

   Examples:

   If a student rolls 3, −2, and −4 some possible combinations are:

   $3 + (-2) - (-4) = 5$

   $3 \cdot (-2) \cdot (-4) = 24$

   $3 \cdot (-4 \div -2) = 6$

   $-4 \cdot [-2 - 3] = 20$

CONTIG GAME BOARD 2

Roll three dice to create a problem equal to one of the numbers on the board. Place a marker on the answer. One point is awarded for each number covered, with additional points awarded if the number is next to any numbers already covered.

+1	−2	+3	−4	+5	−6	+7	−8
+9	−10	+11	−12	+13	−14	+15	−16
+17	−18	+19	−20	+21	−22	+23	−24
+25	−26	+27	−28	+29	−30	+31	−32
+33	−34	+35	−36	+37	−38	+39	−40
+41	−42	+44	−45	+48	−50	+54	−55
+60	−64	+66	−72	+75	−80	+90	−96
+100	−108	+120	−125	+144	−150	+180	−216

- Once a player creates a problem, that player writes the problem on paper, and the other players check to see if the answer is correct. If the answer is correct, the player puts a marker on that square. The square can be used only once.

- One point is awarded for placing a marker on an unoccupied square. One additional point is awarded for each touching, or contiguous, square that has a marker on it.

- A tally is kept for each student. At each turn, a student is allowed to use only one problem to determine where his or her marker goes on the game board. The student selects one problem from all the possibilities.

3. Set a time limit to complete a turn and to end the game. For example, a player may have one minute to find a problem to use, and the game may last for 25 minutes.

NEXT STEPS • Differentiate

5-Day and 3-Day Instructional Plans:
PM 3, page 140—All students, to assess progress

★ = Includes Problem Solving

Practice Activities

PA 2 Multiplying and Dividing to Become a Millionaire

Use with 5-Day Instructional Plan. In this activity, students perform basic mathematical operations on positive and negative numbers.

DIRECTIONS

1. Discuss the following term with students:

   reciprocal The reciprocal of a number a is a number b such that $a \cdot b = 1$

2. Remind students they can use reciprocals to help them solve difficult problems. When dividing fractions, they write the reciprocal of the second fraction and multiply, rather than dividing.

   Sample problems:

   $$\frac{4}{7} \div \frac{1}{2} = \frac{4}{7} \cdot \frac{2}{1} = \frac{8}{7}$$
   $$16 \div \frac{1}{4} = 16 \cdot \frac{4}{1} = 64$$
   $$0.75 \div \frac{2}{24} = 0.75 \cdot \frac{24}{2} = 9$$

3. Explain the game rules.

   - The goal is for the class to become math millionaires by answering the questions correctly.

   - The class starts at the 100 point level and everyone answers the first sample question.

   - After each question, the teacher will select a student to give the answer. If the student is correct, the class continues to the next level. If the student is incorrect, the class does the second sample question for the current value.

   - If the class incorrectly answers both sample questions for the current value, other sets can be generated by following the examples given and changing the digits.

   - Each student should write answers on his or her paper, seeing how high he or she can go without a mistake.

4. Decide whether you will allow students to use calculators. It is preferable for them to use four function calculators rather than scientific or graphic calculators.

Value	Sample Question 1	Sample Question 2
100	$-3 \cdot 6 = -18$	$-5 \cdot 8 = -40$
200	$-11 \cdot (-6) = 66$	$-14 \cdot (-6) = 84$
300	$-46 \cdot 19 = -874$	$47 \cdot (-24) = -1{,}128$
500	$-2{,}020 \div (-5) = 404$	$-6{,}325 \div (-5) = 1{,}265$
1,000	$-1{,}403 \div 61 = -23$	$703 \div (-37) = -19$
2,000	$1.5 \cdot (-2.7) = -4.05$	$1.6 \cdot (-3.7) = -5.92$
4,000	$-63.6 \div (-1.2) = 53$	$-64.8 \div (-1.8) = 36$
8,000	$138 \div (-0.0005) = -276{,}000$	$164 \div (-0.0004) = -410{,}000$
16,000	$-24 \cdot (-6) \div 8 = 18$	$-32 \cdot 9 \div (-12) = 24$
32,000	$-\frac{1}{4} \cdot \frac{2}{5} = -\frac{1}{10}$	$-\frac{1}{6} \cdot \frac{3}{4} = -\frac{1}{8}$
64,000	$2\frac{4}{5} \div 1\frac{1}{2} = 1\frac{13}{15}$	$4\frac{3}{4} \div 1\frac{1}{8} = 4\frac{2}{9}$
125,000	$-12 \div 0.75 \div \left(-\frac{2}{5}\right) = 40$	$-16 \div 0.25 \div \left(-\frac{1}{5}\right) = 320$
250,000	$-8 \cdot \left(-1\frac{4}{5}\right) \div (-10) = -1.44$	$-12 \cdot \left(-1\frac{1}{4}\right) \div 8 = 1.875$
500,000	$-0.67 \cdot 2\frac{1}{4} \div 0.15 = -10.05$	$-0.38 \cdot 4\frac{1}{5} \div 0.12 = -13.3$
1,000,000	$-\frac{1}{3} \cdot 0.825 \div 1.1 = -0.25$	$\frac{2}{3} \cdot -0.942 \div -\frac{2}{5} = 1.57$

NEXT STEPS • Differentiate

5-Day Instructional Plan:
Objective 4 Posttest, page 143—All students

Progress-Monitoring Activities

PM 1 Apply Skills 1

Use with 5-Day or 3-Day Instructional Plan.

MATERIALS

- *Interactive Text*, pages 52–53

DIRECTIONS

1. Have students turn to *Interactive Text*, pages 52–53, Apply Skills 1.

2. Monitor student work, and provide feedback as necessary.

   Watch for:

   - Do students see that the product of two numbers with the same sign is positive?

   - Do students see that the product of two numbers with different signs is negative?

NEXT STEPS • Differentiate

5-Day and 3-Day Instructional Plans:
CD 2, page 134—All students, for additional concept development

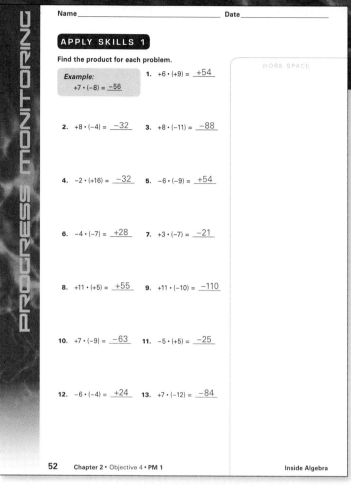

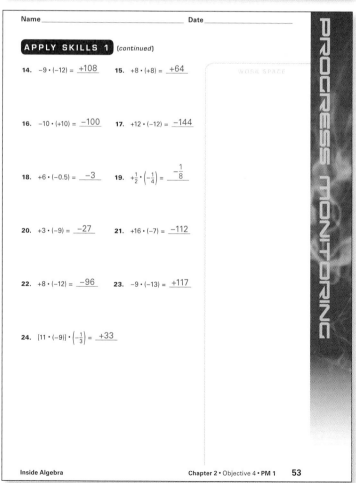

PM 2 Apply Skills 2

Use with 5-Day or 3-Day Instructional Plan.

MATERIALS

- *Interactive Text*, pages 54–55

DIRECTIONS

1. Have students turn to *Interactive Text*, pages 54–55, Apply Skills 2.

2. Monitor student work, and provide feedback as necessary.

   Watch for:
   - Do students see that the quotient of two numbers with the same sign is positive?
   - Do students see that the quotient of two numbers with different signs is negative?

NEXT STEPS • Differentiate

5-Day and 3-Day Instructional Plans:
PA 1, page 136—All students, for additional practice and problem solving

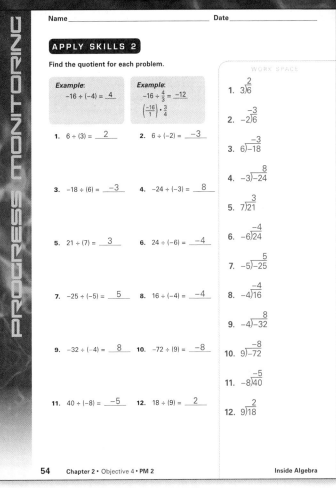

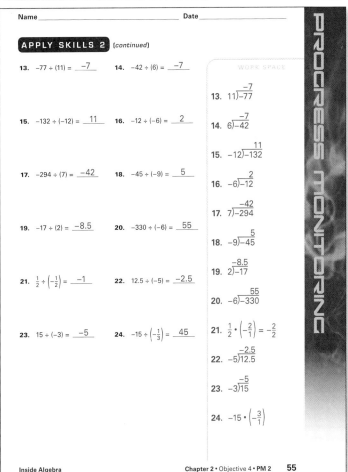

Progress-Monitoring Activities

PM 3 Apply Skills 3

Use with 5-Day or 3-Day Instructional Plan.

MATERIALS

- *Interactive Text*, pages 56–57

DIRECTIONS

1. Have students turn to *Interactive Text*, pages 56–57, Apply Skills 3.

2. Monitor student work, and provide feedback as necessary.

   Watch for:

   - Do students realize multiplication and division have the same sign rules?

   - Do students realize they can solve the multiplication and division problems first, then review the negative and positive signs to determine the sign of the answer?

NEXT STEPS • Differentiate

👥 5-Day Instructional Plan:

PS 1, page 142—Students who demonstrate understanding of the concept, to develop problem-solving skills

CD 3, page 135—Students who need additional concept development

👥 3-Day Instructional Plan:

PM 4, page 141—Students who are on the accelerated path, to assess progress

PM 4, page 141—Students on the differentiated path who have not completed CD 3, to assess progress

Objective 4 Posttest, page 143—All other students

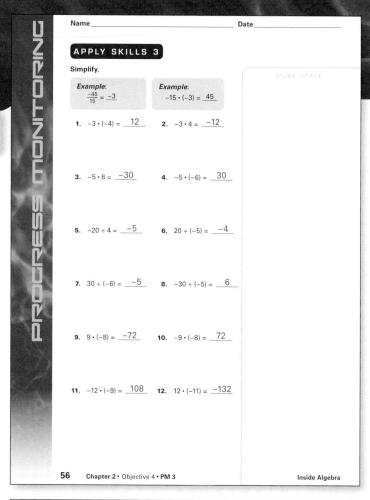

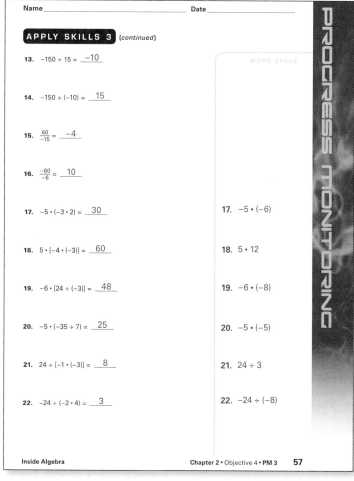

Objective 4
Progress-Monitoring Activities

PM 4 Apply Skills 4

Use with 5-Day or 3-Day Instructional Plan.

MATERIALS

- *Interactive Text*, pages 58–59

DIRECTIONS

1. Have students turn to *Interactive Text*, pages 58–59, Apply Skills 4.

2. Monitor student work, and provide feedback as necessary.

   Watch for:
   - Do students realize multiplication and division have the same sign rules?
   - Do students realize they can solve the multiplication and division problems first, then review the negative and positive signs to determine the sign of the answer?

NEXT STEPS • Differentiate

5-Day Instructional Plan:
Objective 4 Posttest, page 143—All students

3-Day Instructional Plan:
PS 1, page 142—Students who are on the accelerated path, to develop problem-solving skills

Objective 4 Posttest, page 143—Students who are on the differentiated path

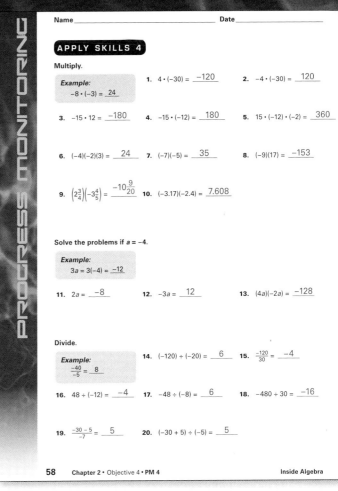

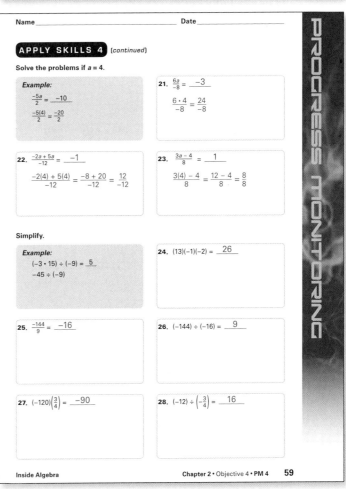

Problem-Solving Activity

★ PS 1 Filling in the Blanks

Use with 5-Day or 3-Day Instructional Plan. In this activity, students develop number sense while discovering a strategy for completing the puzzle.

MATERIALS

- *Interactive Text*, page 60

DIRECTIONS

1. Review the following term with students:

   integer The set of whole numbers and their opposites

2. Have students discuss the rules for multiplication and division of integers, including both positive and negative integers.

   Listen for:
   - A positive multiplied or divided by a positive equals a positive.
   - A positive multiplied or divided by a negative equals a negative.
   - A negative multiplied or divided by a negative equals a positive.

3. Draw the Fill in the Blanks diagram on the board. Include only the blocks, operation signs, first integer (5), and the answer blocks. Do not show the solution to students.

4. Instruct students to use any integers –9 through 9 to complete the equations so each row and column has the value indicated. Tell students each integer can be used only once.

5. Explain that to get the first row, we have to solve **5 × __ ÷ __ = –20**, and to get the first column, we have to solve **5 × __ ÷ __ = –10**.

6. Remind students that for an equation to have a negative answer, an odd number of factors would have to be negative. In each case described in Step 4, one of the missing integers must be negative.

7. Discuss the strategy of working backwards by using inverse relationships with multiplication and division.

8. Allow students to experiment with a variety of numbers until they find combinations that work. Caution them that their solutions must also solve the equations of the other rows and columns. For example, even though 5 × 4 ÷ (–1) = –20 is a solution for the first row, it does not work with the other rows and columns. Encourage students by pointing out that once they find the correct equations for the first row and first column, the other squares should be easier to complete.

9. Have students turn to *Interactive Text*, page 60, Fill in the Blanks. Review the directions as a class. Students may work individually or in teams.

NEXT STEPS • Differentiate

5-Day Instructional Plan:
PM 4, page 141—All students, for additional practice

3-Day Instructional Plan:
Objective 4 Posttest, page 143—All students

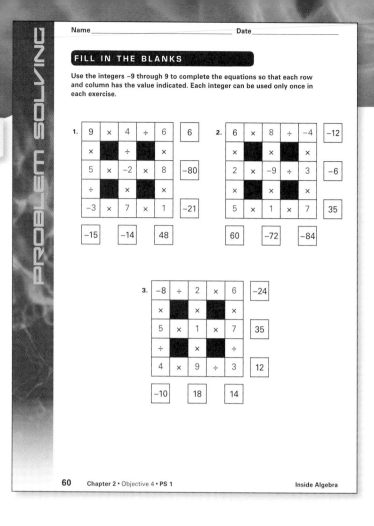

Objective 4 Posttest

Discuss with students the key concepts in Objective 4. Following the discussion, administer the Objective 4 Posttest to all students.

Using the Results

• Score the posttest and update the class record card.

• Provide reinforcement for students who do not demonstrate mastery of the concepts through individual or small-group reteaching of key concepts.

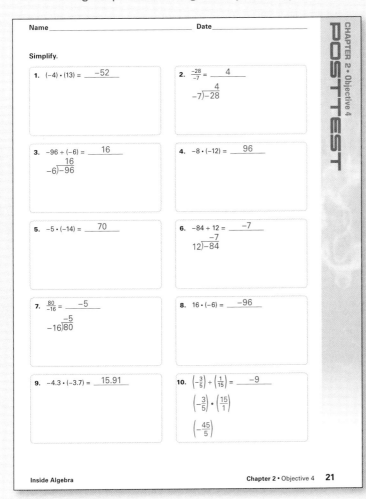

Name _____ Date _____

Simplify.

1. $(-4) \cdot (13) =$ ___−52___

2. $\frac{-28}{-7} =$ ___4___

$-7\overline{)-28}$ with 4 above

3. $-96 \div (-6) =$ ___16___

$-6\overline{)-96}$ with 16 above

4. $-8 \cdot (-12) =$ ___96___

5. $-5 \cdot (-14) =$ ___70___

6. $-84 \div 12 =$ ___−7___

$12\overline{)-84}$ with −7 above

7. $\frac{80}{-16} =$ ___−5___

$-16\overline{)80}$ with −5 above

8. $16 \cdot (-6) =$ ___−96___

9. $-4.3 \cdot (-3.7) =$ ___15.91___

10. $\left(-\frac{3}{5}\right) \div \left(\frac{1}{15}\right) =$ ___−9___

$\left(-\frac{3}{5}\right) \cdot \left(\frac{15}{1}\right)$

$\left(-\frac{45}{5}\right)$

Inside Algebra   Chapter 2 • Objective 4   **21**

CHAPTER 2 • Objective 4 POSTTEST

Objective 5
Find the principal square root of a number.

Objective 5 Pretest

Students complete the Objective 5 Pretest on the same day as the Objective 4 Posttest.

Using the Results

• Score the pretest and update the class record card.

• If the majority of students do not demonstrate mastery of the concepts, use the 5-Day Instructional Plan for Objective 5.

• If the majority of students demonstrate mastery of the concepts, use the 3-Day Instructional Plan for Objective 5.

CHAPTER 2 • Objective 5 — PRETEST

Name_____ Date_____

Find the square roots. Calculators may be used. Round to the nearest $\frac{1}{100}$ when the expression is irrational.

1. $\sqrt{9}$ = ___3___

2. $\pm\sqrt{81}$ = ___± 9___

3. $\sqrt{49}$ = ___7___

4. $-\sqrt{36}$ = ___-6___

5. $-\sqrt{100}$ = ___-10___

6. $\sqrt{400}$ = ___20___

7. $\pm\sqrt{900}$ = ___± 30___

8. $\sqrt{45}$ = ___6.71___

9. $\sqrt{21}$ = ___4.58___

10. $\sqrt{140}$ = ___11.83___

22   Chapter 2 • Objective 5   Inside Algebra

Goals and Activities

Objective 5 Goals

The following activities, when used with the instructional plans on pages 146 and 147, enable students to:

- Find the square root of 4 ($\sqrt{4}$) to be **2**

- Find the square root of 1 ($\sqrt{1}$) to be **1**

- Find the square roots of 16 ($\pm\sqrt{16}$) to be **±4**

- Find the negative square root of 100 ($-\sqrt{100}$) to be **−10**

Objective 5 Activities

Concept Development Activities		
CD 1 Using the Computing Machine, page 148	**CD 2** Building Squares, page 149	**CD 3** Estimating Square Roots, page 150

Practice Activities		
*****PA 1** Estimating, Then Calculating, page 152	**PA 2** Playing $\sqrt{\text{Roll It}}$ Bingo, page 153	**PA 3** Playing $\sqrt{\text{Roll It}}$, page 154

Progress-Monitoring Activities		
PM 1 Apply Skills 1, page 155	**PM 2** Apply Skills 2, page 156	**PM 3** Apply Skills 3, page 157

*Problem-Solving Activities	
★**PS 1** Finding the Areas of Squares, page 158	★**PS 2** Orbiting, page 159

Ongoing Assessment
Posttest Objective 5, page 161
Pretest Chapter 3, Objective 1, page 162

CD = Concept Development PM = Progress Monitoring PS = Problem Solving
PA = Practice Activity ★ = Includes Problem Solving

2 CHAPTER

Instructional Plans

5-Day Instructional Plan

Use the 5-Day Instructional Plan when pretest results indicate that students would benefit from a slower pace. This plan is used when the majority of students need more time or did not demonstrate mastery on the pretest. This plan does not include all activities.

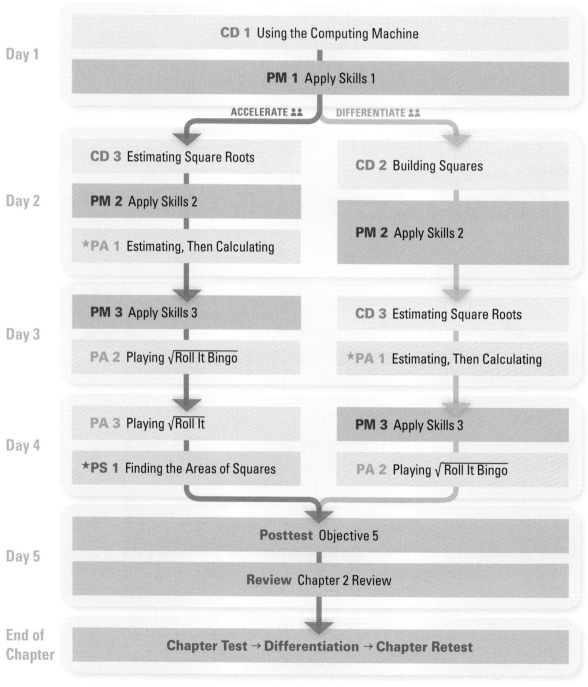

Day 1

CD 1 Using the Computing Machine

PM 1 Apply Skills 1

ACCELERATE 👥   DIFFERENTIATE 👥

Day 2

CD 3 Estimating Square Roots

PM 2 Apply Skills 2

★**PA 1** Estimating, Then Calculating

CD 2 Building Squares

PM 2 Apply Skills 2

Day 3

PM 3 Apply Skills 3

PA 2 Playing √Roll It Bingo

CD 3 Estimating Square Roots

★**PA 1** Estimating, Then Calculating

Day 4

PA 3 Playing √Roll It

★**PS 1** Finding the Areas of Squares

PM 3 Apply Skills 3

PA 2 Playing √Roll It Bingo

Day 5

Posttest Objective 5

Review Chapter 2 Review

End of Chapter

Chapter Test → Differentiation → Chapter Retest

CD = Concept Development   PM = Progress Monitoring   PS = Problem Solving
PA = Practice Activity   ★ = Includes Problem Solving

3-Day Instructional Plan

Use the 3-Day Instructional Plan when pretest results indicate that students can move through the activities at a faster pace. This plan is ideal when the majority of students demonstrate mastery on the pretest. This plan does not include all activities.

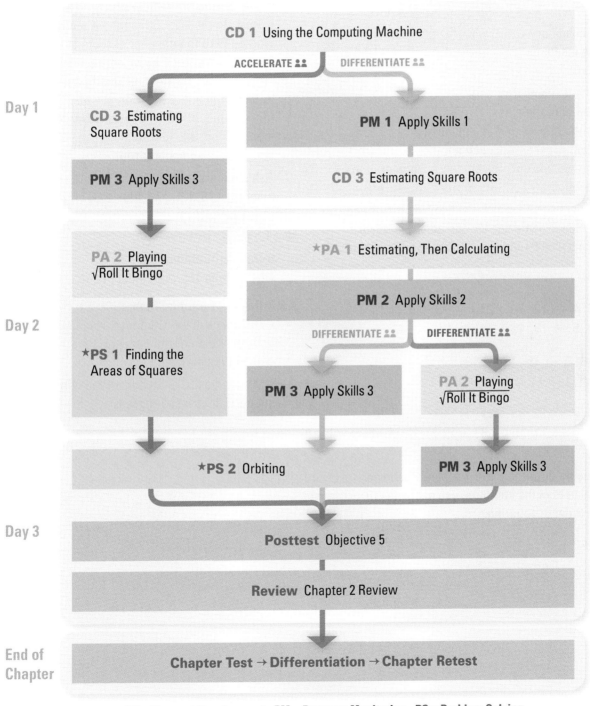

CD 1 Using the Computing Machine

ACCELERATE DIFFERENTIATE

Day 1

CD 3 Estimating Square Roots

PM 1 Apply Skills 1

PM 3 Apply Skills 3

CD 3 Estimating Square Roots

PA 2 Playing √Roll It Bingo

★**PA 1** Estimating, Then Calculating

PM 2 Apply Skills 2

DIFFERENTIATE DIFFERENTIATE

Day 2

★**PS 1** Finding the Areas of Squares

PM 3 Apply Skills 3

PA 2 Playing √Roll It Bingo

★**PS 2** Orbiting

PM 3 Apply Skills 3

Day 3

Posttest Objective 5

Review Chapter 2 Review

End of Chapter

Chapter Test → Differentiation → Chapter Retest

CD = Concept Development **PM = Progress Monitoring** **PS = Problem Solving**
PA = Practice Activity ★ = **Includes Problem Solving**

Concept Development Activities

CD 1 Using the Computing Machine

Use with 5-Day or 3-Day Instructional Plan. In this activity, students develop the concept of squaring and unsquaring (finding the square root of) a number.

DIRECTIONS

1. Draw the imaginary computing machine on the board.

2. Discuss the machine's capabilities with the class. Explain that when we put in a number, an operation is performed, and another number, or the answer, comes out. Tell students the operation can be changed.

3. Show students some examples of numbers for ins and outs. Ask them to determine the operation. Explain to students that 2 → 6 reads as, "2 goes to 6."

Examples:

> 2 → 6, 4 → 12, 7 → 21
> 3 → 9, 5 → 15, 15 → 45 ×3
>
> 7 → 14, 9 → 16, 12 → 19
> 3 → 10, 14 → 21, 100 → 107 +7
>
> 4 → 9, 7 → 15, 8 → 17
> 2 → 5, 5 → 11, 15 → 31 ×2 + 1

4. After students determine the machine's behavior for several sets of ins and outs, use examples to introduce them to squaring.

Examples:

> 2 → 4, 3 → 9, 4 → 16
> 5 → 25, 6 → 36, 7 → 49

5. Pretend the machine was dropped and damaged while it was set on squaring and the following results were then observed:
   9 → 3, 25 → 5, 81 → 9, 16 → 4
   Ask students to identify the operation. square root

6. Note that students may have an easier time remembering the radical sign ($\sqrt{}$) if they know its history. In the late 15th century, mathematicians worked with the concept of roots of numbers. The Latin word for root is *radix*, from which we get the word *radical*. At that time, mathematicians used the letter *r* to indicate the root, or *radix*, of a number; for example, *r*4 = 2. The letter *r* was written more loosely then, and looked more like $\sqrt{}$. Eventually, this became the symbol for root.

7. Ask students to identify the square roots for the numbers 4, 9, 121, and 400. 2, 3, 11, 20, respectively

NEXT STEPS • Differentiate

5-Day Instructional Plan:
PM 1, page 155—All students, to assess progress

3-Day Instructional Plan:
CD 3, page 150—Students who demonstrate understanding of the concept, for additional concept development

PM 1, page 155—Students who need additional support, to assess progress

Concept Development Activities

CD 2 Building Squares

Use with 5-Day Instructional Plan. In this activity, students develop an understanding of square numbers.

MATERIALS

- Objects, such as beans or colored chips

DIRECTIONS

1. Divide students into pairs and provide each pair with a pile of objects, such as beans or colored chips.

2. Discuss the following terms with students:

   square root One of two equal factors of a given number

   principal square root The positive square root of a number

   radical A symbol that indicates that one is to determine the square root

3. Have students build a square by placing the objects in a three by three array.

4. Discuss how this particular square is the square of three. Point out that there are three on each side and nine total. Thus, the square of three is nine, or $3^2 = 9$. Also, the array shows that the root of a square with nine objects is three, or $\sqrt{9} = 3$. The positive square root is often called the principal square root.

5. Have the class work together to try other squares until they are comfortable with the terms *square* and *square root*.

   Examples:

• •	$2^2 = 4$	Four is the square of two.
• •	$2 = \sqrt{4}$	Two is the square root of four.
• • • • • • • • • • • • • • • •	$4^2 = 16$	Sixteen is the square of four.
	$4 = \sqrt{16}$	Four is the square root of sixteen.

   NEXT STEPS • Differentiate

   5-Day Instructional Plan:
   PM 2, page 156—All students, to assess progress

Objective 5
Concept Development Activities

CD 3 Estimating Square Roots

Use with 5-Day or 3-Day Instructional Plan. In this activity, students find the principal square root of numbers and use the square root key on their calculators.

MATERIALS

- Calculators with square root keys
- **Variation:** Gizmos *Square Roots*

DIRECTIONS

1. Review the following terms with students:

    integer The set of whole numbers and their opposites

    principal square root The positive square root of a number

    square root One of two equal factors of a given number

2. Write $\sqrt{16}$ on the board. Ask students for the solution. Explain that 4 is the principal square root and $-\sqrt{16} = -4$ is the negative square root. Solving equations of the form $x^2 = 16$ will be done in Chapter 9.

3. Write $\sqrt{19}$ on the board. Ask students for the solution. Discuss different answers from the class. Point out that the answer is not an integer because $4^2 = 16$ and $5^2 = 25$. Therefore, the answer is between 4 and 5.

4. Draw a number line on the board. Ask the class to discuss where to graph $\sqrt{19}$ on the number line. If students are having difficulty, ask them to determine whether $\sqrt{19}$ is closer to 4 or 5. Note that 19 is closer to 16 than it is to 25.

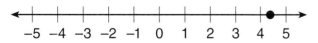

5. Have a few students guess at a decimal value to the nearest $\frac{1}{10}$ for $\sqrt{19}$. Suppose they guess 4.2. Have them multiply $4.2 \cdot 4.2 = 17.64$. Ask if another guess would come closer to 19. Try other values until the class is able to determine which is closest to 19. It is the decimal number 4.4.

    Examples:

    $4.3 \cdot 4.3 = 18.49$

    $4.4 \cdot 4.4 = 19.36$

    $4.5 \cdot 4.5 = 20.25$

    Variation: Gizmos For this activity use the Gizmo *Square Roots* to demonstrate finding the decimal value to the *nearest* $\frac{1}{10}$.

    ExploreLearning • **Gizmos**

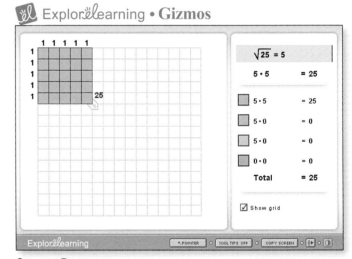

    Square Roots

6. Now show students how to use the $\sqrt{}$ key on the calculator. Have students practice by finding the square root of 19. Note that on some calculators, the square root sign should be entered first, and on other calculators, the number should be entered first. The display should show 4.358898944. To the nearest $\frac{1}{10}$ it is 4.4.

7. Discuss the following term with students:

   irrational number A number that cannot be expressed as the ratio of two integers

8. Point out that students will often find an irrational number when calculating the square root of a number. Explain that an estimate of the square root is often a sufficient answer.

9. Try some other examples. Have students estimate the answer and multiply it by itself on the calculator to find the approximate answer to the nearest $\frac{1}{100}$. Then use the $\sqrt{}$ key to check the estimate. Have students plot the examples on the number line.

   Sample problems:

$\sqrt{10} \approx 3.16$	$\sqrt{33} \approx 5.74$
$\sqrt{68} \approx 8.25$	$\sqrt{95} \approx 9.75$

10. Have students practice writing the square roots of numbers to the nearest $\frac{1}{100}$ using the $\sqrt{}$ key on the calculator.

    Sample problems:

$\sqrt{15} \approx 3.87$	$\sqrt{30} \approx 5.48$
$\sqrt{50} \approx 7.07$	$\sqrt{44} \approx 6.63$
$\sqrt{77} \approx 8.77$	$\sqrt{23} \approx 4.80$

11. Explain that it is important to have some approximate idea of an answer before using the calculator as a self-check because sometimes we push the wrong buttons on the calculator.

NEXT STEPS • Differentiate

👥 **5-Day Instructional Plan:**
PM 2, page 156—Students who are on the accelerated path, to assess progress

PA 1, page 152—Students who are on the differentiated path, for additional practice and problem solving

👥 **3-Day Instructional Plan:**
PM 3, page 157—Students who are on the accelerated path, to assess progress

PA 1, page 152—Students who are on the differentiated path, for additional practice and problem solving

Practice Activities

★PA 1 Estimating, Then Calculating

Use with 5-Day or 3-Day Instructional Plan. In this activity, students use estimation and multiplication to find square roots.

MATERIALS

- Interactive Text, page 61

DIRECTIONS

1. Divide students into groups of two to four. Have students turn to *Interactive Text*, page 61, Estimate, Then Calculate.

2. Review the following term with students:

   square root One of two equal factors of a given number

3. Designate one student in each group to be the checker. He or she will check to see if the others in the group got the square root correct to the nearest tenth. The checker should use the $\sqrt{\ }$ key on the calculator to check.

4. Explain that the other students in the group will have two minutes (modify this amount of time for your students' needs) to find the square root of each number with paper and pencil only. The checker will determine who is correct.

5. Tell students that one way for them to estimate the square roots is to graph the number on the number line and compare it to the perfect squares on each side.

   Example:

   Graph $\sqrt{40}$

   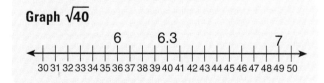

6. Have checkers award points to students who are correct. A winner can be determined in each group after the worksheet is complete.

   If you choose, the winners from each group can then compete against each other, tournament-style, doing additional problems.

ESTIMATE, THEN CALCULATE

Estimate the square root of each number using paper and pencil only, then have one student in your group find the correct answers using a calculator.

	Number	Estimate of √ to Nearest $\frac{1}{10}$	√ to Nearest $\frac{1}{10}$ by Calculator	Right	Wrong
1.	126		11.22		
2.	11		3.32		
3.	230		15.17		
4.	75		8.66		
5.	20		4.47		
6.	30		5.48		
7.	65		8.06		
8.	110		10.49		
9.	200		14.14		
10.	600		24.49		
11.	950		30.82		

Answers will vary.

---

7. Review the following terms with students:

   irrational number A number that cannot be expressed as the ratio of two integers

   rational number A number that can be expressed as the ratio of two integers

8. Help students develop an understanding of irrational square roots and their location between rational numbers.

   > **Variation: Use a Calculator** Allow all students to use calculators to do the computations for the multiplication of their best guess for each problem (e.g., 4.2 • 4.2). However, only the checker can use the $\sqrt{\ }$ key.

NEXT STEPS • Differentiate

5-Day Instructional Plan:
PM 3, page 157—All students, to assess progress

3-Day Instructional Plan:
PM 2, page 156—All students, to assess progress

★ = Includes Problem Solving

Practice Activities

PA 2 Playing $\sqrt{\text{Roll It}}$ Bingo

Use with 5-Day or 3-Day Instructional Plan. In this activity, students use estimation and multiplication to find square roots.

MATERIALS

- Blackline Master 31
- Pair of dice for caller
- Calculators, one per student
- Game markers to cover squares

DIRECTIONS

1. Distribute one copy of Blackline Master 31, Roll It Card, to each student.

2. Review the following term with students:

   square root One of two equal factors of a given number

3. Have students choose 16 numbers from the right side of the Roll It Card to randomly fill in the blanks on the cards. The numbers listed are the square roots of 1, 2, 3, 4, 5, 6, 8, 9, 10, 12, 15, 16, 18, 20, 24, 25, 30, and 36 to the nearest tenth, respectively.

4. Designate one student, or yourself, to be the caller. This person rolls the two dice. The product of the two numbers rolled is the number for which students have to find the square root. For example, if 4 and 6 are rolled, the caller announces the number 24, and that is the number for which students must find the square root using a calculator. The caller should record the number and its square root on a sheet of paper, and if a repeat of that number is rolled, the caller should roll again. Give students about 30 seconds between rolls (modify if necessary to meet your students' needs).

5. Tell students play proceeds until someone covers all the numbers in a row, across, down, or diagonally, and calls "Bingo!" The caller then confirms the bingo.

   > **Variation: Challenge** A more difficult version of this game could be produced by rolling three dice and using products of all three dice.

NEXT STEPS • Differentiate

5-Day Instructional Plan:

PA 3, page 154—Students who are on the accelerated path, for additional practice

Objective 5 Posttest, page 161—Students who are on the differentiated path

3-Day Instructional Plan:

PS 1, page 158—Students who are on the accelerated path, to develop problem-solving skills

PM 3, page 157—Students who are on the differentiated path, to assess progress

---

31

Name _____ Date _____

ROLL IT CARD

Fill in the card with the numbers to the right of the board. Each student should roll two dice, then find the product of these numbers. Find the square root of the product, and mark this number if it is on your card. Continue play until someone covers all the numbers in a row.

				1
				1.4
				1.7
				2
				2.2
				2.4
				2.8
				3
				3.2
				3.5
				3.9
				4
				4.2
				4.5
				4.9
				5
				5.5
				6

Practice Activities

PA 3 Playing $\sqrt{\text{Roll It}}$

Use with 5-Day Instructional Plan. In this activity, students find square roots.

MATERIALS

- Three dice
- Paper and pencil (no calculators) for each student
- One calculator for the caller

DIRECTIONS

1. Review the following term with students:

   square root One of two equal factors of a given number

2. Decide whether students will work individually or in groups for this activity.

3. Designate a caller. He or she will roll two or three dice. The product of the two or three numbers rolled is the number for which students must find the square root to the nearest tenth.

4. Establish a time limit, such as 30 seconds between rolls, but be flexible for more difficult numbers. After the time is up, the caller should read the correct answer to the nearest tenth.

5. Explain that correct answers earn one point. The first student to reach a certain predetermined point total wins the game.

   > **Variation: Different Numbers** A different set of numbers can be generated by taking the sum of the two, three, or more dice rolled.

NEXT STEPS • Differentiate

5-Day Instructional Plan:
PS 1, page 158—All students, to develop problem-solving skills

Objective 5
Progress-Monitoring Activities

PM 1 Apply Skills 1

Use with 5-Day or 3-Day Instructional Plan.

MATERIALS

- *Interactive Text*, page 62

DIRECTIONS

1. Have students turn to *Interactive Text*, page 62, Apply Skills 1.

2. Remind students of the key term: *square root*.

3. Monitor student work, and provide feedback as necessary.

   Watch for:
   - Do students understand the difference between square and square root?
   - Do students realize that the square of a number between zero and one will be smaller than the original number?

NEXT STEPS • Differentiate

5-Day Instructional Plan:

CD 3, page 150—Students who demonstrate understanding of the concept, to extend understanding

CD 2, page 149—Students who need additional concept development

3-Day Instructional Plan:

CD 3, page 150—All students, for additional concept development

---

Name_____ Date_____

APPLY SKILLS 1

Fill in the blanks to make true statements.

Example:
Since (3)(3) = 9, __9__ is the __square__ of 3, and __3__ is the square root of __9__.

1. Since (4)(4) = 16, __16__ is the __square__ of 4, and __4__ is the __square root__ of 16.

2. Since (6)(6) = 36, __36__ is the __square__ of __6__, and 6 is the __square root__ of 36.

3. Since (7)^2 = 49, 49 is the __square__ of __7__, and 7 is the square root of __49__.

4. Since (9)^2 = __81__, 81 is the square of __9__, and 9 is the square root of __81__.

5. Since $\frac{1}{4} \cdot \frac{1}{4} = \frac{1}{16}$, $\frac{1}{16}$ is the square of __$\frac{1}{4}$__, and __$\frac{1}{4}$__ is the square root of __$\frac{1}{16}$__.

6. Since (0.5)(0.5) = __0.25__, __0.25__ is the square of 0.5, and 0.5 is the square root of __0.25__.

7. Since $\left(\frac{2}{3}\right)^2 = \frac{4}{9}$, $\frac{4}{9}$ is the __square__ of $\frac{2}{3}$, and __$\frac{2}{3}$__ is the square root of __$\frac{4}{9}$__.

8. Since (2.5)^2 = __6.25__, __6.25__ is the square of 2.5, and 2.5 is the square root of __6.25__.

9. Write a similar statement involving 20 and (20)^2.
   Since 20^2 = 400, 400 is the square of 20, and 20 is the square root of 400.

10. Write another statement involving any number and its square.
    Answers will vary.

PM 2 Apply Skills 2

Use with 5-Day or 3-Day Instructional Plan:

MATERIALS

- *Interactive Text*, page 63

DIRECTIONS

1. Have students turn to *Interactive Text*, page 63, Apply Skills 2.

2. Remind students of the key term: *square root*.

3. Monitor student work, and provide feedback as necessary.

   Watch for:
   - Do students understand the idea of building a square?
   - Do students find the square root of a fraction by finding the square roots of the numerator and the denominator?

NEXT STEPS • Differentiate

👥 5-Day Instructional Plan:

   PA 1, page 152—Students who are on the accelerated path, for additional practice and problem solving

   CD 3, page 150—Students who are on the differentiated path, for additional concept development

👥 3-Day Instructional Plan:

   PM 3, page 157—Students who demonstrate understanding of the concept, to assess progress

   PA 2, page 153—Students who need additional practice

Name _____ Date _____

APPLY SKILLS 2

Solve.

1. The diagram shows that __9__ is the square of __3__, and __3__ is the square root of __9__.

2. The diagram shows that __16__ is the square of __4__, and __4__ is the square root of __16__.

3. The diagram shows that __36__ is the square of __6__, and __6__ is the square root of __36__.

4. $5 \cdot 5 = 5^2 = $ __25__

5. $\sqrt{25} = $ __5__

6. $(9)(9) = 9^2 = $ __81__

7. $\sqrt{81} = $ __9__

8. $(12)(12) = (12)^2 = $ __144__

9. $\sqrt{144} = $ __12__

10. $\frac{5}{6} \cdot \frac{5}{6} = \left(\frac{5}{6}\right)^2 = $ __$\frac{25}{36}$__

11. $\sqrt{\frac{25}{36}} = $ __$\frac{5}{6}$__

12. $\left(\frac{1}{7}\right)^2 = $ __$\frac{1}{49}$__

13. $\sqrt{\frac{1}{49}} = $ __$\frac{1}{7}$__

14. $(-11)(-11) = $ __121__

15. $-\sqrt{121} = $ __−11__

16. $(-15)^2 = $ __225__

17. $-\sqrt{0.49} = $ __−0.7__

18. $(1.5)^2 = $ __2.25__

19. $\pm\sqrt{100} = $ __±10__

20. $\left(\frac{6}{7}\right)^2 = $ __$\frac{36}{49}$__

21. $\sqrt{\frac{121}{144}} = $ __$\frac{11}{12}$__

22. $(8)^2 = $ __64__

23. $\sqrt{64} = $ __8__

24. $\sqrt{\frac{64}{25}} = $ __$\frac{8}{5}$__

Objective 5
Progress-Monitoring Activities

PM 3 Apply Skills 3

Use with 5-Day or 3-Day Instructional Plan.

MATERIALS

- *Interactive Text*, page 64

DIRECTIONS

1. Have students turn to *Interactive Text*, page 64, Apply Skills 3.

2. Remind students of the key terms: *irrational number* and *radical*.

3. Monitor student work, and provide feedback as necessary.

   Watch for:
   - Do students recognize that the answer is irrational if the number under the radical is not a perfect square?

   - Do students understand the meaning of the plus or minus sign ($\pm$)?

NEXT STEPS • Differentiate

5-Day Instructional Plan:
PA 2, page 153—All students, for additional practice

3-Day Instructional Plan:
PA 2, page 153—Students who are on the accelerated path, for additional practice

PS 2, page 159—Students on the differentiated path who demonstrated understanding on PM 2, to develop problem-solving skills

Objective 5 Posttest, page 161—All other students

Name_____ Date_____

APPLY SKILLS 3

Simplify the expressions. Estimate to the nearest $\frac{1}{100}$ when the expression is irrational. Use calculators only when you have to.

1. $3^2 = $ ___9___ 2. $5^2 = $ ___25___ 3. $7^2 = $ ___49___

4. $\sqrt{25} = $ ___5___ 5. $\sqrt{9} = $ ___3___ 6. $\sqrt{49} = $ ___7___

7. $6^2 = $ ___36___ 8. $13^2 = $ ___169___ 9. $15^2 = $ ___225___

10. $\sqrt{220} = $ ___14.83___ 11. $\sqrt{30} = $ ___5.48___ 12. $\sqrt{169} = $ ___13___

13. $-\sqrt{25} = $ ___−5___ 14. $\pm\sqrt{169} = $ ___±13___ 15. $\sqrt{\frac{25}{169}} = $ ___$\frac{5}{13}$___

16. $\sqrt{1.21} = $ ___1.1___ 17. $-\sqrt{0.49} = $ ___−0.7___ 18. $\pm\sqrt{1.44} = $ ___±1.2___

19. $\sqrt{45} = $ ___6.71___ 20. $-\sqrt{3} = $ ___−1.73___ 21. $\sqrt{7} = $ ___2.65___

22. $\sqrt{64} = $ ___8___ 23. $\sqrt{12} = $ ___3.46___ 24. $\pm\sqrt{600} = $ ___±24.49___

25. $\sqrt{100} = $ ___10___ 26. $-\sqrt{4,900} = $ ___−70___ 27. $\sqrt{77} = $ ___8.77___

28. $\sqrt{2} = $ ___1.41___ 29. $\sqrt{32} = $ ___5.66___ 30. $\pm\sqrt{8} = $ ___±2.83___

Objective 5
Problem-Solving Activities

★ PS 1 Finding the Areas of Squares

Use with 5-Day or 3-Day Instructional Plan. In this activity, students use the formula for the area of a square and estimate square roots.

DIRECTIONS

1. Draw a square with side *s* on the board or overhead. Review that the area of the square is $A = s^2$. Tell students that, for example, if the area of a square is 25 square inches, then side *s* is 5 inches.

$A = s^2$ | *s*

2. Have students find the lengths of the sides of several different squares when they are given the area.

   Examples:

   > *s* = __2__ ft. if *A* = 4 sq. ft.
   >
   > *s* = __8__ ft. if *A* = 64 sq. ft.
   >
   > *s* = __10__ yd. if *A* = 100 sq. yd.
   >
   > *s* = __12__ in. if *A* = 144 sq. in.
   >
   > Give the answer to question d in feet:
   >
   > *s* = __1__ ft.

3. Write *s* = __3.2__ **ft. if *A* = 10 sq. ft.** on the board. Tell students if they are puzzled about how to find the answer to this problem, they should think about if the answer is more or less than 3. Lead students to the answer by having them think about 3.1, then 3.2.

4. Have students practice more problems in the same way, rounding their answers to the nearest tenth.

   Sample problems:

   > $\sqrt{60} \approx 7.7$
   >
   > $\sqrt{150} \approx 12.2$
   >
   > $\sqrt{2{,}000} \approx 44.7$

5. Have students discuss whether the last two examples have exact answers. They do not have exact answers.

NEXT STEPS • Differentiate

5-Day Instructional Plan:
Objective 5 Posttest, page 161—All students

3-Day Instructional Plan:
PS 2, page 159—All students, for additional problem solving

Problem-Solving Activities

★ **PS 2** Orbiting

Use with 3-Day Instructional Plan. In this activity, students find the missing value in an ellipse.

MATERIALS

- *Interactive Text*, page 65

DIRECTIONS

1. Have students turn to *Interactive Text*, page 65, Orbits.

2. Draw a picture of an elliptical orbit on the board.

3. Explain that when a satellite is put into orbit, it has an elliptical route. One formula for an ellipse is $x^2 + y^2 = 1$, where x and y are coordinates. To find x, use the formula $x = \sqrt{1 - y^2}$ where $y \leq 1$. If $y = \frac{1}{2}$, then x would equal $\sqrt{1 - \left(\frac{1}{2}\right)^2} = \sqrt{1 - \left(\frac{1}{4}\right)} = \sqrt{\frac{3}{4}}$ which is about 0.87. So $x \approx 0.87$. Demonstrate how to check this.

   $x^2 + y^2 = 1$

   $0.87^2 + \frac{1}{2}^2 \approx 0.757 + 0.25 = 1.007$

   Point out that the answer is close.

4. Have students complete page 65 in the *Interactive Text*.

NEXT STEPS • Differentiate

3-Day Instructional Plan:
Objective 5 Posttest, page 161—All students

★ = Includes Problem Solving

Name _____ Date _____

ORBITS

Solve for *x* in the following ellipses.

Example:
Find x if $y = 0.2$
$x = \sqrt{1 - (0.2)^2}$
$x = \sqrt{0.96}$
$x \approx 0.98$

1. Find x if $y = 0.7$
$x = \sqrt{1 - (0.7)^2}$
$x = \sqrt{0.51}$
$x \approx 0.71$

2. Find x if $y = 0.5$
$x = \sqrt{1 - (0.5)^2}$
$x = \sqrt{0.75}$
$x \approx 0.87$

3. Find x if $y = 0.3$
$x = \sqrt{1 - (0.3)^2}$
$x = \sqrt{0.91}$
$x \approx 0.95$

4. Find x if $y = 0.9$
$x = \sqrt{1 - (0.9)^2}$
$x = \sqrt{0.19}$
$x \approx 0.44$

5. Find x if $y = 1$
$x = \sqrt{1 - (1)^2}$
$x = \sqrt{0}$
$x = 0$

6. Find x if $y = 0.33$
$x = \sqrt{1 - (0.33)^2}$
$x = \sqrt{0.8911}$
$x \approx 0.94$

7. Find x if $y = 0$
$x = \sqrt{1 - (0)^2}$
$x = \sqrt{1}$
$x = 1$

8. What would be true if $y = 2$?
Not possible. The x and y values for an ellipse must be at most one. Plugging $y = 2$ into the equation forces x to be the square root of −3.

Inside Algebra   Chapter 2 • Objective 5 • PS 2   **65**

PROBLEM SOLVING

This page intentionally left blank

Ongoing Assessment

Objective 5 Posttest

Discuss with students the key concepts in Objective 5. Following the discussion, administer the Objective 5 Posttest to all students.

Using the Results

• Score the posttest and update the class record card.

• Provide reinforcement for students who do not demonstrate mastery of the concepts through individual or small-group reteaching of key concepts.

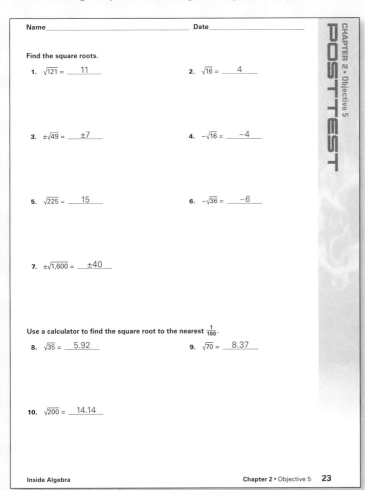

Name_____ Date_____

Find the square roots.

1. $\sqrt{121}$ = ___11___

2. $\sqrt{16}$ = ___4___

3. $\pm\sqrt{49}$ = ___±7___

4. $-\sqrt{16}$ = ___−4___

5. $\sqrt{225}$ = ___15___

6. $-\sqrt{36}$ = ___−6___

7. $\pm\sqrt{1,600}$ = ___±40___

Use a calculator to find the square root to the nearest $\frac{1}{100}$.

8. $\sqrt{35}$ = ___5.92___

9. $\sqrt{70}$ = ___8.37___

10. $\sqrt{200}$ = ___14.14___

Inside Algebra   Chapter 2 • Objective 5   **23**

CHAPTER 2 • Objective 5
POSTTEST

Chapter Review

Chapter 2 Review

Use with 5-Day or 3-Day Instructional Plan. In this activity, students review key chapter concepts prior to taking the Chapter Test.

MATERIALS

- *Interactive Text,* pages 67–68

DIRECTIONS

1. Have students turn to *Interactive Text,* pages 67–68, Chapter 2 Review.

2. Have students complete the review individually or in small groups. If the activity is completed individually, provide time for students to discuss their solutions as a class or in small groups.

3. Monitor student work, and provide feedback when necessary. If students complete the review quickly, pair them with other students or groups to discuss their answers.

Name _____ Date _____

OBJECTIVE 1

Graph each set of numbers on the number line.

1. {−3, 0, 5}

2. {$\frac{1}{2}$, 0.9, 1$\frac{1}{3}$, −0.2}

3. {integers greater than 1}

4. {−3, 2, 9}

OBJECTIVE 2

Simplify.

5. 3 + (−8) = ___−5___

6. 22 − 29 = ___−7___

7. −9.2 + 11.6 = ___2.4___

8. 14 − (−11) = ___25___

OBJECTIVE 3

Place the symbol <, >, or = between each pair of numbers to make the sentence true.

9. 5 __>__ −7

10. −3.6 __<__ 1.1

11. −3$\frac{1}{2}$ __=__ −3.5

Arrange the numbers in order from the smallest to the largest.

12. {−35, 6.35, 0, −11} −35, −11, 0, 6.35

Name _____ Date _____

OBJECTIVE 4

Simplify.

13. −24 ÷ 3 = ___−8___

$$\frac{-8}{3\overline{)-24}}$$

14. 6 · 9 = ___54___

15. −14 · (−5) = ___70___

16. 21 ÷ (−7) = ___−3___

$$\frac{-3}{-7\overline{)21}}$$

OBJECTIVE 5

Find the square roots. Calculators may be used. Round to the nearest $\frac{1}{100}$ when the expression is irrational.

17. −$\sqrt{36}$ = ___−6___

18. $\sqrt{81}$ = ___9___

19. ±$\sqrt{1}$ = ___±1___

20. $\sqrt{100}$ = ___10___

Ongoing Assessment

Chapter 2 Test, Form A

MATERIALS

- *Assessment Book,* pages 25–26

DIRECTIONS

1. Have students turn to *Assessment Book*, pages 25–26, Chapter 2 Test, Form A. Administer the Chapter Test to all students.

2. Score the test by objective and update the class record card.

3. Use the test data to determine differentiation needs.

Name_____ Date_____

Objective 1

Graph each set of numbers on the number line.

1. [number line: -3 to 7, points marked] $\{-3, 7, -1, 2\}$

2. [number line: -1 to 1, points marked] $\left\{\frac{3}{4}, -0.5, 0.1, -\frac{2}{3}\right\}$

3. [number line: -5 to 5, points marked] {integers greater than -3}

4. [number line: -30 to 20, points marked] $\{25, -10, 5, -30\}$

Objective 2

Simplify.

5. $-8 + (-13) = \underline{\quad -21 \quad}$

6. $5 - (-4) = \underline{\quad 9 \quad}$

7. $-27 - 17 = \underline{\quad -44 \quad}$

8. $3.7 + (-5.2) = \underline{\quad -1.5 \quad}$

Objective 3

Place the symbol <, >, or = between each pair of numbers to make the sentence true.

9. $10 \underline{\ >\ } -10$

10. $-3.2 \underline{\ <\ } 3.1$

11. $22 \underline{\ <\ } 22.5$

Arrange the numbers in order from the smallest to the largest.

12. $6, -11, 3\frac{1}{2}, -4, 14, -5.5$

$\underline{-11, -5.5, -4, 3\frac{1}{2}, 6, 14}$

Inside Algebra   Chapter 2 • Test   **25**

Name_____ Date_____

Objective 4

Simplify.

13. $-12 \cdot (7) = \underline{\quad -84 \quad}$

14. $-18 \div 3 = \underline{\quad -6 \quad}$

$3\overline{)-18}$ with -6 above

15. $-5 \cdot (-19) = \underline{\quad 95 \quad}$

16. $-36 \div (-12) = \underline{\quad 3 \quad}$

$-12\overline{)-36}$ with 3 above

Objective 5

Find the square roots. Calculators may be used. Round to the nearest $\frac{1}{100}$ when the expression is irrational.

17. $\sqrt{49} = \underline{\quad 7 \quad}$

18. $\sqrt{72} = \underline{\quad 8.49 \quad}$

19. $-\sqrt{81} = \underline{\quad -9 \quad}$

20. $\pm\sqrt{20} = \underline{\quad \pm 4.47 \quad}$

26   Chapter 2 • Test   Inside Algebra

Differentiation

MATERIALS

- **Gizmos** *Free Fall Tower* Gizmo
- **Gizmos** Extension Activity pages
- **Gizmos** *Adding and Subtracting Integers* Gizmo
- **Gizmos** Reinforcement Activity page
- Additional Activities
- Algebra Skill Builders for Chapter 2
- Chapter Test, Form B

DIRECTIONS

1. Review Chapter 2 Test, Form A, with the class.

2. Use the results from Chapter 2 Test, Form A, to identify students for reinforcement or extension.

3. After students have been identified for extension or reinforcement, break students into appropriate groups. See pages 165–167 for detailed differentiated instruction.

Differentiation Planner

Students who demonstrated mastery on every objective posttest and scored 80% or above on the chapter test

Extend learning using:

- **Gizmos** Use the *Free Fall Tower* Gizmo with the Extension Activity. Have students work in pairs or individually to complete the activity.

Students who demonstrated mastery on every objective posttest but scored below 80% on the chapter test

Reinforce learning using:

- **Gizmos** Use the *Adding and Subtracting Integers* Gizmo with the Reinforcement Activity. Have students work in pairs or small groups to complete the activity.
- Additional Activities from the online resources.
- Algebra Skill Builders for Chapter 2 from the online resources.

Students who did not demonstrate mastery on any or all of the objective posttests or the chapter test

Reinforce learning using:

- **Gizmos** Present the *Adding and Subtracting Integers* Gizmo to students in small groups using the instruction on page 167.
- Additional Activities from the online resources.
- Algebra Skill Builders for Chapter 2 from the online resources.

Retest—Administer Chapter 2 Test, Form B, from the online resources to students who scored below 80 percent on Form A when time allows.

NEXT STEPS • Pretest

- Administer Chapter 3, Objective 1 Pretest, page 170, to all students.

Ongoing Assessment

Students who demonstrated mastery on every objective posttest and scored 80% or above on the chapter test

1. Divide students into pairs or allow them to work individually for this activity.

2. Distribute one copy of the Extension Activity from the online resources to each student.

3. Direct students to the Gizmo *Free Fall Tower* through the Inside Algebra Student Web site, http://insidealgebra. voyagerlearning.com.

4. Have students complete the Extension Activity.

5. **Peer Review.** If there is time, have students exchange papers with a peer. They should review and discuss each response, and be prepared to explain their thinking.

Variation: The use of the Gizmo is required in Problems 7–9. If students do not have access to the Gizmo, they can use a calculator to estimate $\sqrt{2.04}$, $\sqrt{5.10}$, and $\sqrt{\frac{20}{4.9}}$. Explain to students that when objects of different weights are not subjected to air resistance, they reach the ground in the same amount of time when dropped from the same height. To demonstrate to students the effects of air resistance, drop a coffee filter and a baseball down a stairwell if possible.

Explore learning • Gizmos

Experiment

Drag objects to platforms. Press play to drop objects.

Ping pong ball
Golf ball
Soccer ball
Watermelon

Objects on the right have a parachute.

speed m/s

0.00 drop time (seconds)

Graph

Open parachute(s)

Choose atmosphere:
- Air
- Vacuum (no air)

speed m/s

0.00 drop time (seconds)

Free Fall Tower

Gizmos
Extension Activity   Name _____ Date _____

FREE FALL TOWER

Long ago, Galileo dropped objects from the Tower of Pisa to investigate how fast different objects fall to the ground. There is an expression that calculates the amount of time it takes an object to reach the ground. The time in seconds it takes an object to reach the ground once it drops can be found by using the expression $t = \sqrt{\frac{h}{4.9}}$, where h is the object's height in meters above the ground. This expression assumes that the object is not affected by air resistance.

1. The table shows different heights from which objects are dropped. Complete the second row of the table by dividing the height h by 4.9.

Height h (meters)	4.9	10	19.6	25	44.1
$\sqrt{\frac{h}{4.9}}$	$\sqrt{\frac{4.9}{4.9}} = \sqrt{1}$	$\sqrt{\frac{10}{4.9}} = \sqrt{2.04}$	$\sqrt{\frac{19.6}{4.9}} = \sqrt{4}$	$\sqrt{\frac{25}{4.9}} = \sqrt{5.10}$	$\sqrt{\frac{44.1}{4.9}} = \sqrt{9}$
Time (seconds)	1	1.43	2	2.26	3

2. Look at the square roots in the second row of the table above. Simplify the expressions that have exact answers. Write your answers in the third row of the table.

3. Graph your answers from Problem 2 on the number line. Write the square root expression above its point on the number line.

$\sqrt{1}$ $\sqrt{4}$ $\sqrt{9}$

0   1   2   3   4   5

4. As the height increases, what happens to the time it takes an object to fall?

The time increases.

5. Look at the square root expression for the time when the height is 10 meters.
What two consecutive perfect squares is 2.04 between? __1 and 4__
Between what two consecutive whole numbers should $\sqrt{2.04}$ be? __1 and 2__

6. Between what two consecutive whole numbers should $\sqrt{5.10}$ be? __2 and 3__ Why?

The number 5.10 is between the perfect squares 4 and 9, and the square root of 5.10 is between 2 and 3.

Gizmos
Extension Activity   Name _____ Date _____

FREE FALL TOWER (continued)

7. Start the *Free Fall Tower* Gizmo. Choose the "Vacuum (no air)" atmosphere.
Drag an object to a height of 10 meters, then hit the green play button.
How long does it take the object to drop? __1.43 seconds__
Hit the purple reset button. Drag a different object to a height of 10 meters. Hit the green play button.
How long does it take the object to drop? __1.43 seconds__
What do you notice about the two times? __They are the same.__ When an object is not affected by air resistance, does the object's weight affect the amount of time it takes the object to reach the ground? __no__
Record the time in the table in Problem 1.
Compare this time with the time you predicted in Problem 5.
Does this time agree with your prediction? __yes__
Hit the purple reset button. Drag an object to a height of 20 meters. Hit the green play button.
How long does it take the object to drop? __2.02 seconds__
Does doubling the height double the amount of time it takes the object to drop? __no__

8. Hit the purple reset button.
Drag an object to a height of 25 meters. How long does it take the object to drop?
__2.26 seconds__ Write this number in the table in Problem 1.
Compare this time with the time you predicted in Problem 6.
Does this time agree with your prediction? __yes__

9. In the Gizmo, choose the "Air" atmosphere. Drop all the objects from 25 meters. What do you notice about the drop times between the objects? How do these times compare with the times in Problem 8?

The heavier objects fall faster than the lighter objects. It took more time for the objects to reach the ground with air resistance than when there was no air resistance.

Ongoing Assessment

Students who demonstrated mastery on every objective posttest but scored below 80% on the chapter test

1. Divide students into pairs or small groups.

2. Distribute one copy of the Individual Reinforcement Activity from the online resources to each student.

3. Direct students to the Gizmo *Adding and Subtracting Integers* through the Inside Algebra Student Web site, http://insidealgebra.voyagerlearning.com.

4. Have students complete the Reinforcement Activity.

5. **Peer Review.** If time permits, have students exchange papers with a peer to review and discuss each other's responses. Remind students to be prepared to explain the reasoning behind their responses.

> **Variation:** If students do not have access to the Gizmo, provide them with copies of Blackline Master 27, Number Lines. Have them label the center 0 and go to at least 10 and –10. Students should use the number lines to complete Problems 2–6.

Gizmos
Reinforcement Activity   Name_____ Date_____

ADDING AND SUBTRACTING INTEGERS

1. Graph $\frac{1}{2}$, –3, 4.5, and $-1\frac{1}{2}$ on the number line. On the line, write the numbers in order from least to greatest.

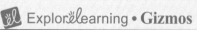

$-3, -1\frac{1}{2}, \frac{1}{2}, 4.5$

2. Use the *Adding and Subtracting Integers* Gizmo. Use the red slider to graph the first integer in the addition sentence. Use the blue slider to find the second integer. Use the "Reset" button to start a new sentence.

   a. $4 + \underline{\quad 5 \quad} = 9$ b. $-6 + \underline{\quad 9 \quad} = 3$ c. $-3 + \underline{\quad 1 \quad} = -2$

   d. $8 + \underline{\quad -3 \quad} = 5$ e. $-4 + \underline{\quad -2 \quad} = -6$ f. $5 + \underline{\quad -7 \quad} = -2$

3. Complete each sentence.
   When adding a positive integer, you move to the __right__ on the number line.
   When adding a negative integer, you move to the __left__ on the number line.

4. Select "Subtract integers." Use the red slider to graph the first integer. Use the blue slider to find the number that correctly completes each sentence.

   a. $2 - \underline{\quad 5 \quad} = -3$ b. $4 - \underline{\quad 3 \quad} = 1$ c. $-3 - \underline{\quad 4 \quad} = -7$

   d. $-2 - \underline{\quad -5 \quad} = 3$ e. $8 - \underline{\quad -2 \quad} = 10$ f. $-7 - \underline{\quad -2 \quad} = -5$

5. Complete each sentence.
   When subtracting a positive integer, you move to the __left__ on the number line.
   When subtracting a negative integer, you move to the __right__ on the number line.

6. Simplify.
   a. $-4 \cdot (-5) = \underline{\quad 20 \quad}$ b. $12 \div (-3) = \underline{\quad -4 \quad}$ c. $-7 \cdot 8 = \underline{\quad -56 \quad}$

7. Get together with another group and compete against one another. Each group has 45 seconds to guess whether the answers to the problems below will be positive or negative. Write + or – below each problem. After each group is done, find the answer to each problem. The group with the most correct guesses wins.

   $-10 + 7$ –3 $5 - (-3)$ 8 $7 \cdot 5$ 35 $-16 \div 4$ –4
   $3 + (-8)$ –5 $-11 - 5$ –16 $(-6) \div (-2)$ 3 $-3 \cdot 3$ –9
   $-4 - (-10)$ 6 $20 \div 5$ 4 $12 + (-7)$ 5 $-7 \cdot (-3)$ 21
   $2 \cdot (-1)$ –2 $-1 - (-4)$ 3 $20 \div (-2)$ –10 $7 + (-9)$ –2

ExploreLearning • Gizmos

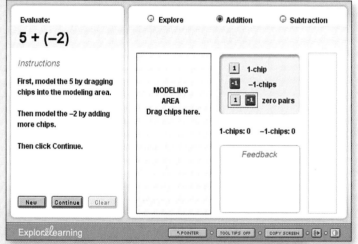

Adding and Subtracting Integers

Students who did not demonstrate mastery on any or all of the objective posttests or the chapter test

Note: The Gizmo is not needed to answer Problems 1, 4, and 5.

1. Ask students to draw a number line and graph $\frac{1}{2}$, −3, 4.5, and −$1\frac{1}{2}$. Tell them to use the number line to order the numbers from least to greatest.

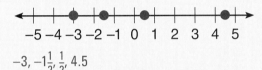

−3, −$1\frac{1}{2}$, $\frac{1}{2}$, 4.5

2. Start the *Adding and Subtracting Integers* Gizmo. Model the problems below. Use the red slider for the first addend. Have students tell you to stop moving the blue slider when the sum is found. After each problem, ask students to name the sign of the second addend and the direction moved when adding. After each set of problems, have students complete the statement.

- 4 + ___5___ = 9
  −6 + ___9___ = 3
  −3 + ___1___ = −2

- To add a positive integer, move to the ___right___ on the number line.

- 8 + ___−3___ = 5
  −4 + ___−2___ = −6
  5 + ___−7___ = −2

- To add a negative integer, move to the ___left___ on the number line.

3. Repeat the process from Problem 2 with the following problems:

- 2 − ___5___ = −3
  4 − ___3___ = 1
  −3 − ___4___ = −7

- To subtract a positive integer, move ___right___ on the number line.

- −2 − ___−5___ = 3
  8 − ___−2___ = 10
  −7 − ___−2___ = −5

- To subtract a negative integer, move ___left___ on the number line.

4. Review the rules of multiplying and dividing integers. Have students solve the following problems:
  −4 · (−5) = 20   12 ÷ (−3) = −4   −7 · 8 = −56

5. Write problems involving two integers with each operation on the board. Have students predict the sign of the answer without making the computation.

> **Variation:** If students do not have access to the Gizmo, use a blackboard or overhead projector to complete the activity.

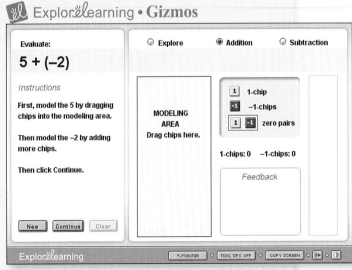

Adding and Subtracting Integers

2 CHAPTER

Ongoing Assessment

Chapter 2 Test, Form B

MATERIALS

- Chapter 2 Test, Form B, from the Online Resources, pages 1–2

DIRECTIONS

1. Have students turn to Chapter 2 Test, Form B, pages 1–2, from the Online Resources. Administer the Chapter Test to all students.

2. Score the test by objective and update the class record card.

Name_____ Date_____

Objective 1

Graph each set of numbers on the number line.

1.  {−5, 0, 2}

2. {−$\frac{1}{2}$, 0.7, 1$\frac{3}{4}$, 0.2}

3. {integers less than 2}

4. {−7, 4, 8}

Objective 2

Simplify.

5. $5 + (-3) =$ ___2___

6. $12 - 17 =$ ___−5___

7. $-7.3 + 10.8 =$ ___3.5___

8. $21 - (-8) =$ ___29___

Objective 3

Place the symbol <, >, or = between each pair of numbers to make the sentence true.

9. 3 _>_ -6

10. -7.2 _<_ 2.5

11. $4\frac{1}{4}$ _=_ 4.25

Arrange the numbers in order from the smallest to the largest.

12. $-12, 5.75, 0, -3$

___−12, −3, 0, 5.75___

Inside Algebra   Chapter 2 • Test • Form B   **1**

Name_____ Date_____

Objective 4

Simplify.

13. $-18 \div 2 =$ ___−9___

$$2\overline{)-18}^{\,-9}$$

14. $7 \cdot 8 =$ ___56___

15. $-16 \cdot (-4) =$ ___64___

16. $35 \div (-5) =$ ___−7___

$$-5\overline{)35}^{\,-7}$$

Objective 5

Find the square roots. Calculators may be used. Round to the nearest $\frac{1}{100}$ when the expression is irrational.

17. $-\sqrt{49} =$ ___−7___

18. $\sqrt{36} =$ ___6___

19. $\pm\sqrt{4} =$ ___±2___

20. $\sqrt{80} =$ ___8.94___

Inside Algebra   Chapter 2 • Test • Form B   **2**

Solving Linear Equations

In this chapter, students begin to solve basic linear equations using addition, subtraction, multiplication, division, or a combination of these operations. They use a variety of tools to solve equations by keeping the equation balanced. Students also explore and solve proportions, and apply their learning to solve word problems involving linear equations and proportions.

Objective 1
Solve linear equations with addition and subtraction.

Objective 2
Solve linear equations with multiplication and division.

Objective 3
Solve linear equations using one or more operations.

Objective 4
Solve problems that can be represented as equations.

Objective 5
Solve proportions that have a missing part.

Objective 6
Use proportions to solve percent problems.

Chapter 3
VOCABULARY

Objective 1 Pretest

Students complete the Objective 1 Pretest at least one day before beginning Objective 1.

Using the Results

- Score the pretest and update the class record card.

- If the majority of students do not demonstrate mastery of the concepts, use the 5-Day Instructional Plan for Objective 1.

- If the majority of students demonstrate mastery of the concepts, use the 3-Day Instructional Plan for Objective 1.

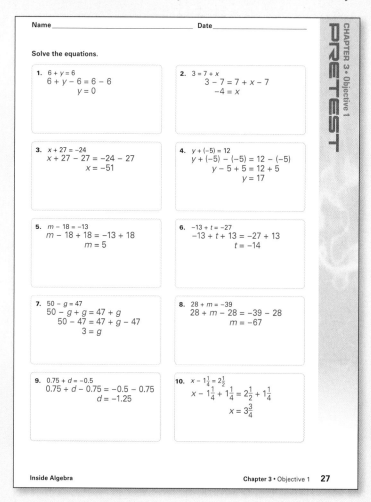

Name _____   Date _____

CHAPTER 3 • Objective 1
PRETEST

Solve the equations.

1. $6 + y = 6$
$6 + y - 6 = 6 - 6$
$y = 0$

2. $3 = 7 + x$
$3 - 7 = 7 + x - 7$
$-4 = x$

3. $x + 27 = -24$
$x + 27 - 27 = -24 - 27$
$x = -51$

4. $y + (-5) = 12$
$y + (-5) - (-5) = 12 - (-5)$
$y - 5 + 5 = 12 + 5$
$y = 17$

5. $m - 18 = -13$
$m - 18 + 18 = -13 + 18$
$m = 5$

6. $-13 + t = -27$
$-13 + t + 13 = -27 + 13$
$t = -14$

7. $50 - g = 47$
$50 - g + g = 47 + g$
$50 - 47 = 47 + g - 47$
$3 = g$

8. $28 + m = -39$
$28 + m - 28 = -39 - 28$
$m = -67$

9. $0.75 + d = -0.5$
$0.75 + d - 0.75 = -0.5 - 0.75$
$d = -1.25$

10. $x - 1\frac{1}{4} = 2\frac{1}{2}$
$x - 1\frac{1}{4} + 1\frac{1}{4} = 2\frac{1}{2} + 1\frac{1}{4}$
$x = 3\frac{3}{4}$

Inside Algebra   Chapter 3 • Objective 1   **27**

Objective 1
Goals and Activities

Objective 1 Goals

The following activities, when used with the instructional plans on pages 172 and 173, enable students to:

- Solve the equation $19 - x = 24$ for x to get $x = -5$
- Solve the equation $2d - (-3.7) = 4.2 + d$ to get $d = 0.5$

Objective 1 Activities

Concept Development Activities

CD 1 Adding and Subtracting With Algebra Tiles, page 174

CD 2 Using the Addition Property of Equality With Arithmetic, page 176

Practice Activities

PA 1 Finding the Solution Path, page 178

★PA 2 Banking the Money, page 179

★PA 3 Becoming a Math Millionaire, page 180

Progress-Monitoring Activities

PM 1 Apply Skills 1, page 181

PM 2 Apply Skills 2, page 182

★Problem-Solving Activities

★PS 1 Solving Real-Life Problems— Part 1, page 183

★PS 2 Solving Real-Life Problems— Part 2, page 184

Ongoing Assessment

Posttest Objective 1, page 185

Pretest Objective 2, page 186

CD = Concept Development PM = Progress Monitoring PS = Problem Solving
PA = Practice Activity ★ = Includes Problem Solving

5-Day Instructional Plan

Use the 5-Day Instructional Plan when pretest results indicate that students would benefit from a slower pace. This plan is used when the majority of students need more time or did not demonstrate mastery on the pretest.

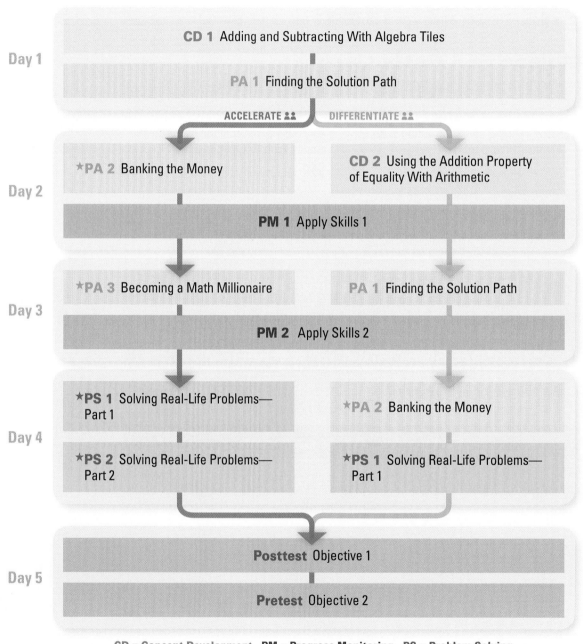

Day 1

CD 1 Adding and Subtracting With Algebra Tiles

PA 1 Finding the Solution Path

ACCELERATE 👥   DIFFERENTIATE 👥

Day 2

★**PA 2** Banking the Money

CD 2 Using the Addition Property of Equality With Arithmetic

PM 1 Apply Skills 1

Day 3

★**PA 3** Becoming a Math Millionaire

PA 1 Finding the Solution Path

PM 2 Apply Skills 2

Day 4

★**PS 1** Solving Real-Life Problems—Part 1

★**PS 2** Solving Real-Life Problems—Part 2

★**PA 2** Banking the Money

★**PS 1** Solving Real-Life Problems—Part 1

Day 5

Posttest Objective 1

Pretest Objective 2

CD = Concept Development   PM = Progress Monitoring   PS = Problem Solving
PA = Practice Activity   ★ = Includes Problem Solving

3-Day Instructional Plan

Use the 3-Day Instructional Plan when pretest results indicate that students can move through the activities at a faster pace. This plan is ideal when the majority of students demonstrate mastery on the pretest.

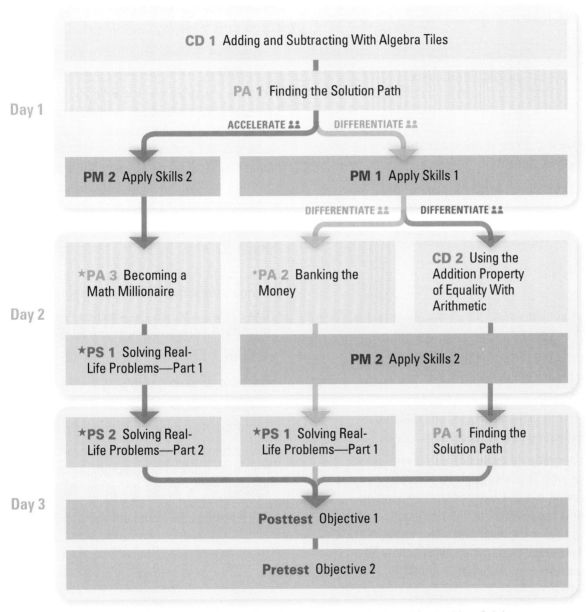

Day 1

CD 1 Adding and Subtracting With Algebra Tiles

PA 1 Finding the Solution Path

ACCELERATE   DIFFERENTIATE

PM 2 Apply Skills 2   **PM 1** Apply Skills 1

DIFFERENTIATE   DIFFERENTIATE

Day 2

★**PA 3** Becoming a Math Millionaire

★**PA 2** Banking the Money

CD 2 Using the Addition Property of Equality With Arithmetic

★**PS 1** Solving Real-Life Problems—Part 1

PM 2 Apply Skills 2

★**PS 2** Solving Real-Life Problems—Part 2

★**PS 1** Solving Real-Life Problems—Part 1

PA 1 Finding the Solution Path

Day 3

Posttest Objective 1

Pretest Objective 2

CD = Concept Development   PM = Progress Monitoring   PS = Problem Solving
PA = Practice Activity   ★ = Includes Problem Solving

Objective 1
Concept Development Activities

CD 1 Adding and Subtracting With Algebra Tiles

Use with 5-Day or 3-Day Instructional Plan. In this activity, students remember that a positive unit tile and a negative unit tile make up a zero pair. Students use zero pairs to solve algebra problems.

MATERIALS

• Algebra tiles, one set per pair of students

DIRECTIONS

1. Group students into pairs. Provide a set of algebra tiles for every two students.

2. Discuss what each piece in the set of algebra tiles represents.

   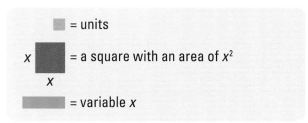

   The x^2 pieces are not used in this activity. Have students put them back in the container.

3. Explain that ▢ is usually referred to as a variable, or as *x*. It is the unknown, and the object is to find out what number it represents.

4. Explain that the variable piece has a different color on each side. One side is green ▭, which represents *x*, a positive or negative number, and the other is red ▭, which represents −*x*, the opposite of *x*. The unit piece also has a different color on each side. One side is yellow ▪, which represents 1, and the other is red ◼, which represents −1.

5. Ask students to think about the result when we combine, or add, 1 and −1. Model the answer by showing one yellow unit, which represents 1, and one red unit, which represents −1. Explain that one negative unit and one positive unit cancel each other out to make zero.

6. Show two yellow and two red units, and tell students to think about the result of adding 2 and −2. This is an important concept when using algebra tiles. Point out that one yellow unit and one red unit are a *zero pair*; that is, when 1 and −1 are combined, the result is zero. Make sure students see that 2 and −2 added together equal zero.

7. Discuss the following term with students:

   equation A statement that two quantities or mathematical expressions are equal

8. Write the equation **x + 1 = 8** on the board or the overhead. Explain that you want to find the value of a number (*x*) such that when 1 is added to it, the result is 8. Tell students to think about what the number is. Most students know the answer is 7: If you add 1 to 7, you get 8. However, this is a good problem for modeling the use of algebra tiles.

9. Tell students to model the problem using the tiles.

   ▭ ▪ **=** ▪ ▪ ▪ ▪ ▪ ▪ ▪ ▪

   Explain that two approaches can be used to determine what the ▭ represents.

   • One choice is to use the Addition Property of Equality, adding a negative one ◼ to both sides:

   ▭ ▪ ◼ **=** ▪ ▪ ▪ ▪ ▪ ▪ ▪ ▪ ◼

   Because ▪ ◼ is a zero pair, the model becomes

   ▭ **=** ▪ ▪ ▪ ▪ ▪ ▪ ▪

   Therefore, the model represents *x* = 7.

   • The other choice is to take away the same thing from both sides of the equation; for example,

   ▭ ✖ **=** ▪ ▪ ▪ ▪ ▪ ▪ ▪ ▪ ✖

   By removing a ▪ from each side, *x* = 7.

10. Model other equations using the tiles.

$x - 3 = 4$

Adding +3 to both sides yields

Again, three red tiles and three yellow tiles represent three zero pairs, or 0.

$x = 7$

11. Show the above model in algebraic terms.

$x - 3 = 4$

$x - 3 + 3 = 4 + 3$

$x + 0 = 7$

$x = 7$

12. Model other equations if students are still having difficulty with the concept. As you model the problems, show the algebraic work.

Sample problems:

$x + 2 = 1$ $x = -1$ $x - 4 = 2$ $x = 6$

$-x - 3 = 2$ $x = -5$ $4 - x = 0$ $x = 4$

$x + 3 = 2$ $x = -1$ $6 - x = -2$ $x = 8$

NEXT STEPS • Differentiate

5-Day and 3-Day Instructional Plans:

PA 1, page 178—All students, for additional practice

Objective 1
Concept Development Activities

Use with 5-Day or 3-Day Instructional Plan. In this activity, students understand that adding or subtracting the same amount from each side of an equation does not change whether the equation is true or false.

DIRECTIONS

1. Write these three math sentences on the board:

   $x + 4 = 9$ $7 = 7$ $6 = 5$

2. Remind students of the following key terms from Chapter 1: *true*, *false*, and *open*.

3. Review the following term with students:

   equation A statement that two quantities or mathematical expressions are equal

4. Ask the class which sentence is true. $7 = 7$
   Ask which sentence is open. $x + 4 = 9$
   Ask which sentence is false. $6 = 5$

5. Erase the first set of three sentences, and write these three sentences on the board.

   $7 = 7$ $7 + 2 = 7 + 3$ $7 + 3 = 7 + 3$

6. Ask the class which sentences are true and why.
   $7 = 7; 7 + 3 = 7 + 3$

   Point out that $7 + 3 = 7 + 3$ or $10 = 10$ is true and that $7 + 2 \neq 7 + 3$. Ask students to explain why the second sentence is false. Different amounts are added to each side.

7. Write the sentence **12 = 12** on the board or overhead. Be sure students understand it is a true sentence. Have the class tell you whether several other sentences are true or false. Write one sentence at a time on the board or overhead. When the class says true or false, ask a student why. Make sure the class understands that if the same amount is added to, or subtracted from, each side of an equation (=) that is *balanced*, the sentence is true. If a different amount is added to, or subtracted from, each side of a balanced equation, the sentence is false.

Sample problems:

$12 - 3 = 12 - 3$ true
$12 + 6 = 12 - 6$ false
$12 + 12 = 12 + 12$ true
$12 - 0 = 12 - 0$ true
$12 + 7 = 12 + 7$ true
$12 + 1 = 12 + 6$ false
$12 + (3 + 4) = 12 + (3 + 4)$ true
$12 - 8 = 12 - 8$ true
$12 - 4 = 12 + 4$ false
$12 - 7 = 12 + 7$ false

8. Now write $x + 4 = 18$ on the board. Ask students what type of sentence it is—true, false, or open. Tell students it is an open sentence because we don't know if it is true or false until we give x a value. Ask the class what value for x makes the sentence true. $x = 14$

9. Ask if the value for x (14) changes if 4 is subtracted from each side.

   $x + 4 - 4 = 18 - 4$
   $x + 0 = 14$
   $x = 14$

10. Ask if the value for x changes if 2 is added to one side and 3 to the other.

$$x + 4 + 2 = 18 + 3$$
$$x + 6 = 21$$

Point out that to make this sentence true, x would have to be 15.

11. Ask students why the value for x changed. Because the same amount was not added to, or subtracted from, each side.

Remind students that if $7 = 7$, then $7 + 2 \neq 7 + 3$. For the sentence to be true, the **same** amount must be added or subtracted.

12. Do another example with the class, such as $x - 2 = 15$. Add 2 to each side, then add a different amount to each side.

13. Have students discuss the Addition Property of Equality.

Listen for:

- The term *true* means that the statement is always true.

- The term *false* means that the statement is always false.

- The term *open* means that the truth of the statement cannot be determined without additional information.

- If the same amount is added to, or subtracted from, each side of an equation (=) that is *balanced*, the sentence is true.

- If a different amount is added to, or subtracted from, each side of a balanced equation, the sentence is false.

- An open sentence means we don't know if it is true or false until we give x a value.

NEXT STEPS • Differentiate

5-Day Instructional Plan:
PM 1, page 181—All students, to assess progress

3-Day Instructional Plan:
PM 2, page 182—All students, to assess progress

Practice Activities

PA 1 Finding the Solution Path

Use with 5-Day or 3-Day Instructional Plan. In this activity, students play a game that requires them to solve algebra problems.

MATERIALS

- Blackline Master 35
- Dice, one per group
- Game markers, one per student

DIRECTIONS

1. Divide the class into groups of four.

2. Distribute one copy of Blackline Master 35, Solve Game Board, to each group. Give each group one die. If possible, use dice that are numbered 1, 2, 3, 1, 2, 3. This will provide more practice.

3. Explain the game rules.

   - Tell everyone to put a marker on the start space. Students should take turns rolling the die to determine who goes first. The largest number goes first. Students in each group take turns moving, in clockwise order.

   - Have the first student roll the die and move his or her marker the number of spaces shown on the die. The student writes the problem shown on that space on a piece of paper, then works the problem.

   - The group checks each student's problem on his or her turn. If the student's answer is correct, the next person takes a turn. If the student's answer is incorrect, the student returns his or her marker to its previous spot.

   - Students might need to work a problem already worked by another student. If this happens, have them do their own work without looking back at the other player's problem.

   - Play continues until a player gets to the finish space. Students can repeat the game several times.

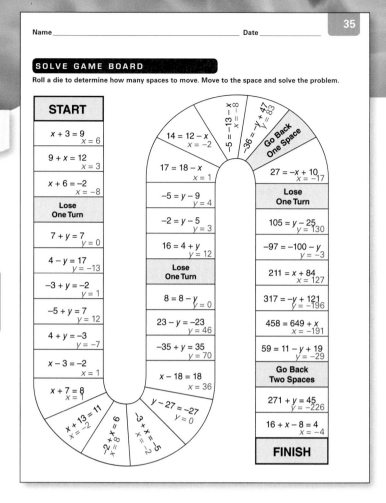

NEXT STEPS • Differentiate

👥 **5-Day Instructional Plan:**

PA 2, page 179–Students completing the activity for the first time who demonstrate understanding of the concept, for additional practice and problem solving

CD 2, page 176—Students who are doing this activity for the first time and need additional concept development

PM 2, page 182—Students who are doing this activity for the second time, to assess progress

👥 **3-Day Instructional Plan:**

PM 2, page 182—Students completing the activity for the first time who demonstrate understanding of the concept, to assess progress

PM 1, page 181—Students completing the activity for the first time who need additional support, to assess progress

Objective 1 Posttest, page 185—Students who are doing this activity for the second time

★ **PA 2** Banking the Money

Use with 5-Day or 3-Day Instructional Plan. In this activity, students solve algebra problems involving adding and subtracting negative numbers.

MATERIALS

- *Interactive Text*, page 71

DIRECTIONS

1. Review the following term with students:

   equation A statement that two quantities or mathematical expressions are equal

2. Have students work in groups of four. Have students turn to *Interactive Text*, page 71, Banking the Money, for this activity.

3. Explain the game rules.

   - Explain that a student from each group is to select an equation from Banking the Money. The more complex the equation, the more money it is worth. If an equation is solved correctly, the student can bank that amount of money on his or her register (paper).

   - Each student in the group solves the equation chosen by the player. If a group member thinks the equation was solved incorrectly by the player, that student can challenge the player. If the challenge is correct, the challenger gets double the money.

   - No equation can be used more than once in a game.

   - Students or groups of students can establish competitions.

Name_____ Date_____

BANKING THE MONEY

Use the equations to play Banking the Money.

$ Values	Equations	
$1.25	**1.** $23 + t = 16$ $t = -7$	**2.** $b - (-8) = 27$ $b = 19$
	3. $-14 = 32 + h$ $h = -46$	**4.** $99 = 47 + m$ $m = 52$
$2.75	**5.** $55 - n = 51$ $n = 4$	**6.** $-19 = 47 - t$ $t = 66$
	7. $113 = 999 + n$ $n = -886$	**8.** $15 = -5 + b$ $b = 20$
$3.85	**9.** $190 - x = 216$ $x = -26$	**10.** $-14 = 32 - (-d)$ $d = -46$
	11. $27 - y = 99$ $y = -72$	**12.** $\frac{3}{4} = d - 1\frac{1}{2}$ $d = 2\frac{1}{4}$
$4.80	**13.** $1.75 = m - 3.5$ $m = 5.25$	**14.** $\frac{14}{15} - t = \frac{4}{3}$ $t = -\frac{6}{15}$ or $-\frac{2}{5}$
	15. $1\frac{5}{7} = 2\frac{5}{21} - d$ $d = \frac{11}{21}$	**16.** $-1.998 = x - 3.123$ $x = 1.125$
$5.35	**17.** $17 - (-2x) = 19 - (-3x)$ $x = -2$	**18.** $y - (-14) = 2y - 9$ $y = 23$
	19. $42 - a = -2a + 99$ $a = 57$	**20.** $16 - (-d) = 132 + 2d$ $d = -116$

NEXT STEPS • Differentiate

👥 **5-Day Instructional Plan:**

PM 1, page 181—Students who are on the accelerated path, to assess progress

PS 1, page 183—Students who are on the differentiated path, to develop problem-solving skills

3-Day Instructional Plan:

PM 2, page 182—All students, to assess progress

★ = Includes Problem Solving

Practice Activities

★PA 3 Becoming a Math Millionaire

Use with 5-Day or 3-Day Instructional Plan. In this activity, students solve algebra problems involving adding and subtracting positive and negative numbers.

MATERIALS

- *Interactive Text*, page 72

DIRECTIONS

1. Review the following term with students:

   equation A statement that two quantities or mathematical expressions are equal

2. Divide the class into groups of five students each.

3. Explain the game rules.

   - Each of four students in the group completes an equation.

   - The fifth student acts as the master of ceremonies and directs the activity.

   - The goal of this activity is for students to try to become math millionaires by answering the questions correctly.

   - Students start at the $15,000 level, and with each correct answer, students continue to the next level.

   > **Variation:** This activity might also be conducted as a whole-class activity by asking each student to solve all four equations, looking for the correct answer.

4. Tell students to write their answers on a piece of paper, seeing how high they can go without a mistake.

5. Have students turn to *Interactive Text*, page 72, Become a Math Millionaire, and begin the game.

Name _____ Date _____

BECOME A MATH MILLIONAIRE

Use the equations to become a math millionaire.

$ Values	Equations	
$15,000	1. $5 = b - 2$ $b = 7$	2. $a - 5 = 13$ $a = 18$
	3. $32 - a = 19$ $a = 13$	4. $116 + a = 97$ $a = -19$
$35,000	5. $3.9 + a = 5.7$ $a = 1.8$	6. $x - (-13) = -14$ $x = -27$
	7. $32 = -121 - y$ $y = -153$	8. $\frac{1}{2} + m = -1\frac{1}{2}$ $m = -2$
$75,000	9. $18 = 89 + t$ $t = -71$	10. $-x - (-7) = 5$ $x = 2$
	11. $23 - y = -81$ $y = 104$	12. $-1 = -t + 4.14159$ $t = 5.14159$
$125,000	13. $14.9 = 3\frac{7}{10} + x$ $x = 11\frac{2}{10}$ or 11.2	14. $4{,}990 = 3.111 - n$ $n = -4{,}986.889$
	15. $\frac{17}{18} = \frac{35}{18} - x$ $x = \frac{18}{18}$ or 1	16. $-0.5 = 3\frac{3}{4} - d$ $d = 4\frac{1}{4}$ or 4.25
$250,000	17. $-\frac{3}{7} = \frac{4}{7} - y$ $y = \frac{7}{7}$ or 1	18. $\frac{4}{11} + a = -\frac{5}{8}$ $a = -\frac{87}{88}$
	19. $3\frac{5}{8} - d = 7\frac{3}{5}$ $d = -\frac{159}{40}$ or $-3\frac{39}{40}$	20. $1\frac{17}{18} - h = 0.75$ $h = \frac{43}{36}$ or $1\frac{7}{36}$
$500,000	21. $1.19 = 0.703 - x$ $x = -0.487$	22. $x + 3.07 + 2.5 = 1.8$ $x = -3.77$
	23. $-7.6 = 5.3 + x + 7.34$ $x = -20.24$	24. $\frac{1}{6} - x + \frac{1}{4} = -\frac{5}{8}$ $x = \frac{13}{24}$
$1,000,000	25. $x + 4 = x - 2$ no solution	26. $3x + 4.6 = x - 2.8 + x + 6.4 + x$ no solution
	27. $x - 6 + 4 = x - 3 + 1$ any number	28. $x + 2.43 = 1.64 + x + 0.79$ any number

---

NEXT STEPS • Differentiate

5-Day Instructional Plan:
PM 2, page 182—All students, to assess progress

3-Day Instructional Plan:
PS 1, page 183—All students, to develop problem-solving skills

---

★ = Includes Problem Solving

Objective 1
Progress-Monitoring Activities

PM 1 Apply Skills 1

Use with 5-Day or 3-Day Instructional Plan.

MATERIALS

- *Interactive Text*, pages 73–74

DIRECTIONS

1. Have students turn to *Interactive Text*, pages 73–74, Apply Skills 1.

2. Remind students of the key term: *equation*.

3. Monitor student work, and provide feedback as necessary.

   Watch for:
   - Do students solve equations (isolate the variable) by adding the opposite of one of the numbers to both sides of the equation?
   - Do students know they need to isolate the variable?

NEXT STEPS • Differentiate

👥 5-Day Instructional Plan:
  PA 3, page 180—Students who are on the accelerated path, for additional practice

  PA 1, page 178—Students who are on the differentiated path, for additional practice

👥 3-Day Instructional Plan:
  PA 2, page 179—Students who demonstrate understanding of the concept, for additional practice and problem solving

  CD 2, page 176—Students who need additional concept development

---

APPLY SKILLS 1

Solve each equation and check the answer.

Example:
$$x + 7 = 16$$
$$x + 7 - 7 = 16 - 7$$
$$x = 9$$
Check: $9 + 7 = 16$

1. $x - 2 = 8$
$$x - 2 + 2 = 8 + 2$$
$$x = 10$$

2. $3 + x = 6$
$$3 + x - 3 = 6 - 3$$
$$x = 3$$

3. $x + 11 = 1$
$$x + 11 - 11 = 1 - 11$$
$$x = -10$$

4. $2 + x = 12$
$$2 + x - 2 = 12 - 2$$
$$x = 10$$

5. $x - 3 = 14$
$$x - 3 + 3 = 14 + 3$$
$$x = 17$$

6. $4 + x - 10 = 14$
$$x - 6 + 6 = 14 + 6$$
$$x = 20$$

7. $6 + x = 14$
$$6 + x - 6 = 14 - 6$$
$$x = 8$$

8. $32 + x = 12$
$$32 + x - 32 = 12 - 32$$
$$x = -20$$

9. $x + 13 = -4$
$$x + 13 - 13 = -4 - 13$$
$$x = -17$$

APPLY SKILLS 1 *(continued)*

10. $4 = x - 7$
$$4 + 7 = x - 7 + 7$$
$$x = 11$$

11. $7 - x = 4$
$$7 - x - 7 = 4 - 7$$
$$-x = -3$$
$$x = 3$$

12. $4 + x = 2x$
$$4 + x - x = 2x - x$$
$$x = 4$$

13. $x - 16 = 17 + 13$
$$x - 16 + 16 = 30 + 16$$
$$x = 46$$

14. $104 + x = 212$
$$104 + x - 104 = 212 - 104$$
$$x = 108$$

15. $x + 7 = 0$
$$x + 7 - 7 = 0 - 7$$
$$x = -7$$

16. $6 - x = -9$
$$6 - x - 6 = -9 - 6$$
$$-x = -15$$
$$x = 15$$

17. $27 + x = 10$
$$27 + x - 27 = 10 - 27$$
$$x = -17$$

18. $2 = 12 + x$
$$2 - 12 = 12 + x - 12$$
$$x = -10$$

19. $x - 14 = -6$
$$x - 14 + 14 = -6 + 14$$
$$x = 8$$

Objective 1
Progress-Monitoring Activities

PM 2 Apply Skills 2

Use with 5-Day or 3-Day Instructional Plan.

MATERIALS

- *Interactive Text*, pages 75–76

DIRECTIONS

1. Have students turn to *Interactive Text*, pages 75–76, Apply Skills 2.

2. Remind students of the key term: *equation*.

3. Monitor student work, and provide feedback as necessary.

   Watch for:
   - Do students solve equations (isolate the variable) by adding the opposite of one of the numbers to both sides of the equation?
   - Do students know that the coefficient of the isolated variable should be positive?

NEXT STEPS • Differentiate

👥 5-Day Instructional Plan:

PS 1, page 183—Students who are on the accelerated path, to develop problem-solving skills

PA 2, page 179—Students who are on the differentiated path, for additional practice and problem solving

👥 3-Day Instructional Plan:

PA 3, page 180—Students who are on the accelerated path, for additional practice and problem solving

PS 1, page 183—Students on the differentiated path who demonstrated understanding on PM 1, to develop problem-solving skills

PA 1, page 178—All other students, for additional practice

Name_____ Date_____

APPLY SKILLS 2

Solve each equation and check the answer.

Example: $3.2 = 1.4 + x$
$3.2 - 1.4 = 1.4 + x - 1.4$
$1.8 = x$
Check: $3.2 = 1.4 + 1.8$
$3.2 = 3.2$

1. $a = -19 - 17$
$a = -36$

2. $a + 19 = -17$
$a + 19 - 19 = -17 - 19$
$a = -36$

3. $a + 17 = -19$
$a + 17 - 17 = -19 - 17$
$a = -36$

4. $x = 28 + (-47)$
$x = -19$

5. $47 = 28 + x$
$47 - 28 = 28 + x - 28$
$x = 19$

6. $-28 = -47 - x$
$-28 + 47 = -47 - x + 47$
$19 = -x$
$x = -19$

7. $-15 + d = -22$
$-15 + d + 15 = -22 + 15$
$d = -7$

8. $4.8 = 13.9 + m$
$4.8 - 13.9 = 13.9 + m - 13.9$
$m = -9.1$

9. $-7 = -19 + (-k)$
$-7 + 19 = -19 - k + 19$
$12 = -k$
$k = -12$

Inside Algebra   Chapter 3 • Objective 1 • PM 2   75

Name_____ Date_____

APPLY SKILLS 2 (continued)

10. $\frac{1}{6} + 2m = \frac{2}{3}$
$\frac{1}{6} + 2m - \frac{1}{6} = \frac{2}{3} - \frac{1}{6}$
$2m = \frac{1}{2}$
$m = \frac{1}{4}$

11. $t + (-9) = 18$
$t - 9 + 9 = 18 + 9$
$t = 27$

12. $g - 37 = 49$
$g - 37 + 37 = 49 + 37$
$g = 86$

13. $-142 = m + 217$
$-142 - 217 = m + 217 - 217$
$m = -359$

14. $s - 13.5 = -9.1$
$s - 13.5 + 13.5 = -9.1 + 13.5$
$s = 4.4$

15. $u - \left(-\frac{7}{8}\right) = \frac{15}{16}$
$u + \frac{7}{8} - \frac{7}{8} = \frac{15}{16} - \frac{7}{8}$
$u = \frac{1}{16}$

16. $\$4.18 = t - \$17.97$
$\$4.18 + \$17.97 =$
$t - \$17.97 + \$17.97$
$t = \$22.15$

17. $0.6 = y - 0.7$
$0.6 + 0.7 = y - 0.7 + 0.7$
$y = 1.3$

18. $4,987 + d = -7,289$
$4,987 + d - 4,987 =$
$-7,289 - 4,987$
$d = -12,276$

19. $x - \left(-\frac{27}{18}\right) = \frac{5}{9}$
$x + \frac{27}{18} - \frac{27}{18} = \frac{5}{9} - \frac{27}{18}$
$x = -\frac{17}{18}$

76   Chapter 3 • Objective 1 • PM 2   Inside Algebra

---

182 Chapter 3 • Objective 1

★PS 1 Solving Real-Life Problems—Part 1

Use with 5-Day or 3-Day Instructional Plan. In this activity, students translate verbal expressions into mathematical equations.

MATERIALS

- *Interactive Text*, page 77

DIRECTIONS

1. Review the following term with students:

   equation A statement that two quantities or mathematical expressions are equal

2. Tell students to work individually on this activity, and solve the word problems by writing equations.

3. Have students turn to *Interactive Text*, page 77, Real-Life Problems—Part 1, and complete the problems.

4. Note whether students choose addition or subtraction to write their equations.

NEXT STEPS • Differentiate

👥 **5-Day and 3-Day Instructional Plans:**

   PS 2, page 184—Students who are on the accelerated path, for additional problem solving

   Objective 1 Posttest, page 185—Students who are on the differentiated path

★ = Includes Problem Solving

Name _____ Date _____

REAL-LIFE PROBLEMS—PART 1

Write an equation to represent each problem. Solve the equation and check your solution.

WORK SPACE

1. Alicia has a job in her neighborhood pharmacy. Her earnings last week, less deductions of $1.50, were equal to $30. How much did she earn last week?

   $e - \$1.50 = \$30.00$

   She earned $31.50.

   1. $e - \$1.50 = \$30.00$
      $e = \$31.50$

2. The pharmacy where Alicia works has a great cosmetics department. Alicia wants to buy a complete array of skin products. Her last two weeks' pay totaled $58.00. After buying the skin products, she will have $14.85 left. How much did the skin products cost?

   $\$58.00 - s = \$14.85 \text{ or } s + \$14.85 = \$58.00$

   They cost $43.15.

   2. $\$58.00 - s = \$14.85$
      $s = \$43.15$

3. Alicia earns $6.45 each hour she works. She needs to work 4 hours to earn enough money to buy her little brother the skateboard he wants. She will have $1.80 remaining after buying the skateboard. How much does it cost?

   $4(\$6.45) = s + \$1.80$

   The skateboard costs $24.00.

   3. $4(\$6.45) = s + \$1.80$
      $s = \$24.00$

4. Alicia will receive a discount of $2.50 on the skateboard purchase because she is an employee. How much would the board cost a nonemployee?

   $n - \$2.50 = \$24.00$

   The board would cost $26.50.

   4. $n - \$2.50 = \$24.00$
      $n = \$26.50$

Objective 1
Problem-Solving Activities

★ PS 2 Solving Real-Life Problems—Part 2

Use with 5-Day or 3-Day Instructional Plan. In this activity, students translate verbal expressions into mathematical equations.

MATERIALS

- *Interactive Text*, page 78

DIRECTIONS

1. Review the following term with students:

   equation A statement that two quantities or mathematical expressions are equal

2. Tell students to solve the word problems in this activity by writing equations.

3. Have students turn to *Interactive Text*, page 78, Real-Life Problems—Part 2, and solve the problems.

4. Tell students to work individually on this assignment.

5. Note whether students choose addition or subtraction to write their equations.

NEXT STEPS • Differentiate

5-Day and 3-Day Instructional Plans:
Objective 1 Posttest, page 185—All students

★ = Includes Problem Solving

PROBLEM SOLVING

REAL-LIFE PROBLEMS—PART 2

Write an equation to represent each problem. Solve the equation and check your solution.

WORK SPACE

1. Carlos works in a sporting goods store on weekends. His earnings last Saturday, less $2.00 for deductions, were $35.00. How much did he earn on Saturday?

   $e - \$2.00 = \$35.00$

   He earned $37.00.

   1. $e - \$2.00 = \$35.00$
      $e = \$37.00$

2. This sporting goods store has an excellent skateboard department. Carlos wants to buy new wheels for his board. His last paycheck was for $38.00. He has $12 remaining after buying one set of wheels. How much did one set of wheels cost him?

   $w + \$12.00 = \$38.00$

   One set cost $26.00.

   2. $w + \$12.00 = \$38.00$
      $w = \$26.00$

3. The owner of the sporting goods store pays Carlos $6.40 for each hour he works. He needs to work 5 hours to earn enough money to buy his sister the in-line skates she wants for her birthday. Carlos will have $3.20 remaining after he buys the skates. How much will the skates cost Carlos?

   $5(\$6.40) = i + \$3.20$

   The skates cost $28.80.

   3. $5(\$6.40) = i + \$3.20$
      $i = \$28.80$

4. Carlos received an employee discount of $3.15 when he bought the skates. How much would the skates have cost someone who did not receive an employee discount?

   $c - \$3.15 = \$28.80$

   They would cost $31.95.

   4. $c - \$3.15 = \$28.80$
      $c = \$31.95$

Objective 1 Posttest

Discuss with students the key concepts in Objective 1.
Following the discussion, administer the Objective 1
Posttest to all students.

Using the Results

• Score the posttest and update the class record card.

• Provide reinforcement for students who do not
  demonstrate mastery of the concepts through individual
  or small-group reteaching of key concepts.

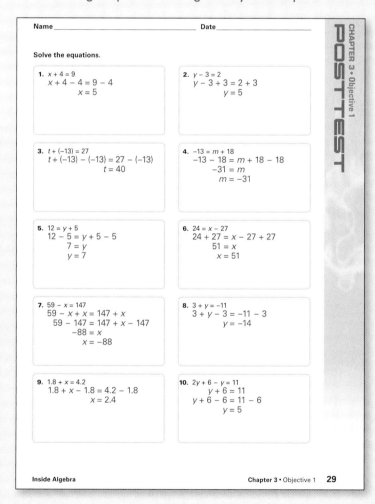

Name _____ Date _____

CHAPTER 3 • Objective 1
POSTTEST

Solve the equations.

1. $x + 4 = 9$
$x + 4 - 4 = 9 - 4$
$x = 5$

2. $y - 3 = 2$
$y - 3 + 3 = 2 + 3$
$y = 5$

3. $t + (-13) = 27$
$t + (-13) - (-13) = 27 - (-13)$
$t = 40$

4. $-13 = m + 18$
$-13 - 18 = m + 18 - 18$
$-31 = m$
$m = -31$

5. $12 = y + 5$
$12 - 5 = y + 5 - 5$
$7 = y$
$y = 7$

6. $24 = x - 27$
$24 + 27 = x - 27 + 27$
$51 = x$
$x = 51$

7. $59 - x = 147$
$59 - x + x = 147 + x$
$59 - 147 = 147 + x - 147$
$-88 = x$
$x = -88$

8. $3 + y = -11$
$3 + y - 3 = -11 - 3$
$y = -14$

9. $1.8 + x = 4.2$
$1.8 + x - 1.8 = 4.2 - 1.8$
$x = 2.4$

10. $2y + 6 - y = 11$
$y + 6 = 11$
$y + 6 - 6 = 11 - 6$
$y = 5$

Inside Algebra   Chapter 3 • Objective 1   **29**

Objective 2 Pretest

Students complete the Objective 2 Pretest on the same day as the Objective 1 Posttest.

Using the Results

- Score the pretest and update the class record card.

- If the majority of students do not demonstrate mastery of the concepts, use the 4-Day Instructional Plan for Objective 2.

- If the majority of students demonstrate mastery of the concepts, use the 3-Day Instructional Plan for Objective 2.

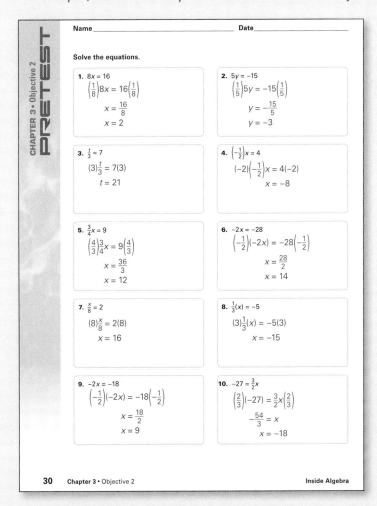

Name_____ Date_____

CHAPTER 3 • Objective 2
PRETEST

Solve the equations.

1. $8x = 16$

$$\left(\frac{1}{8}\right)8x = 16\left(\frac{1}{8}\right)$$

$$x = \frac{16}{8}$$

$$x = 2$$

2. $5y = -15$

$$\left(\frac{1}{5}\right)5y = -15\left(\frac{1}{5}\right)$$

$$y = -\frac{15}{5}$$

$$y = -3$$

3. $\frac{t}{3} = 7$

$$(3)\frac{t}{3} = 7(3)$$

$$t = 21$$

4. $\left(-\frac{1}{2}\right)x = 4$

$$(-2)\left(-\frac{1}{2}\right)x = 4(-2)$$

$$x = -8$$

5. $\frac{3}{4}x = 9$

$$\left(\frac{4}{3}\right)\frac{3}{4}x = 9\left(\frac{4}{3}\right)$$

$$x = \frac{36}{3}$$

$$x = 12$$

6. $-2x = -28$

$$\left(-\frac{1}{2}\right)(-2x) = -28\left(-\frac{1}{2}\right)$$

$$x = \frac{28}{2}$$

$$x = 14$$

7. $\frac{x}{8} = 2$

$$(8)\frac{x}{8} = 2(8)$$

$$x = 16$$

8. $\frac{1}{3}(x) = -5$

$$(3)\frac{1}{3}(x) = -5(3)$$

$$x = -15$$

9. $-2x = -18$

$$\left(-\frac{1}{2}\right)(-2x) = -18\left(-\frac{1}{2}\right)$$

$$x = \frac{18}{2}$$

$$x = 9$$

10. $-27 = \frac{3}{2}x$

$$\left(\frac{2}{3}\right)(-27) = \frac{3}{2}x\left(\frac{2}{3}\right)$$

$$-\frac{54}{3} = x$$

$$x = -18$$

Goals and Activities

Objective 2 Goals

The following activities, when used with the instructional plans on pages 188 and 189, enable students to:

- Solve the equation $3x = 18$ for x to get **$x = 6$**
- Solve the equation $\frac{x}{3} = 9$ for x to get **$x = 27$**

Objective 2 Activities

Concept Development Activities

CD 1 Reviewing Multiplicative Inverse, page 190

CD 2 Multiplying and Dividing With Algebra Tiles, page 191

CD 3 Using the Multiplication Property of Equality, page 193

Practice Activities

PA 1 Playing Multiplication and Division Equation Bingo, page 195

★PA 2 Solving the Guided Maze, page 196

Progress-Monitoring Activities

PM 1 Apply Skills 1, page 198

PM 2 Apply Skills 2, page 199

★Problem-Solving Activities

★PS 1 Solving and Writing Equations, page 200

★PS 2 Solving Equations With Phone Call Problems, page 201

Ongoing Assessment

Posttest Objective 2, page 203

Pretest Objective 3, page 204

CD = Concept Development   PM = Progress Monitoring   PS = Problem Solving
PA = Practice Activity   ★ = Includes Problem Solving

3 Instructional Plans

4-Day Instructional Plan

Use the 4-Day Instructional Plan when pretest results indicate that students would benefit from a slower pace. This plan is used when the majority of students need more time or did not demonstrate mastery on the pretest.

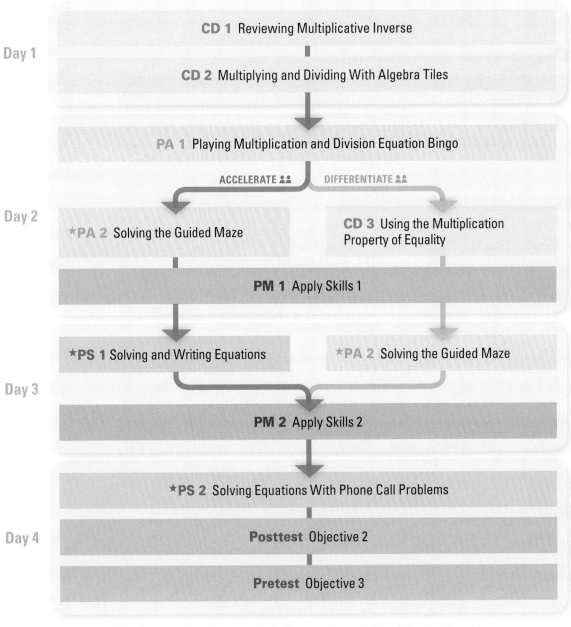

Day 1

CD 1 Reviewing Multiplicative Inverse

CD 2 Multiplying and Dividing With Algebra Tiles

PA 1 Playing Multiplication and Division Equation Bingo

ACCELERATE   DIFFERENTIATE

Day 2

★**PA 2** Solving the Guided Maze

CD 3 Using the Multiplication Property of Equality

PM 1 Apply Skills 1

Day 3

★**PS 1** Solving and Writing Equations

★**PA 2** Solving the Guided Maze

PM 2 Apply Skills 2

Day 4

★**PS 2** Solving Equations With Phone Call Problems

Posttest Objective 2

Pretest Objective 3

CD = Concept Development   PM = Progress Monitoring   PS = Problem Solving
PA = Practice Activity   ★ = Includes Problem Solving

3-Day Instructional Plan

Use the 3-Day Instructional Plan when pretest results indicate that students can move through the activities at a faster pace. This plan is ideal when the majority of students demonstrate mastery on the pretest.

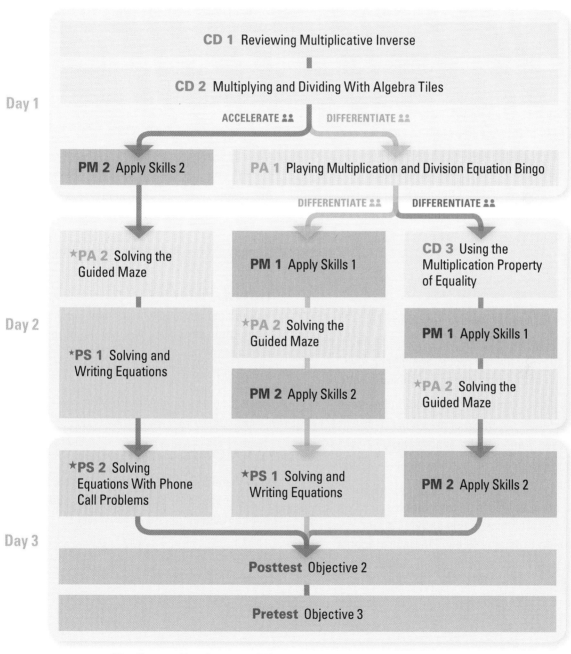

Day 1

CD 1 Reviewing Multiplicative Inverse

CD 2 Multiplying and Dividing With Algebra Tiles

ACCELERATE 👥   DIFFERENTIATE 👥

PM 2 Apply Skills 2   PA 1 Playing Multiplication and Division Equation Bingo

DIFFERENTIATE 👥   DIFFERENTIATE 👥

Day 2

★PA 2 Solving the Guided Maze

★PS 1 Solving and Writing Equations

PM 1 Apply Skills 1

★PA 2 Solving the Guided Maze

PM 2 Apply Skills 2

CD 3 Using the Multiplication Property of Equality

PM 1 Apply Skills 1

★PA 2 Solving the Guided Maze

Day 3

★PS 2 Solving Equations With Phone Call Problems

★PS 1 Solving and Writing Equations

PM 2 Apply Skills 2

Posttest Objective 2

Pretest Objective 3

CD = Concept Development   PM = Progress Monitoring   PS = Problem Solving
PA = Practice Activity   ★ = Includes Problem Solving

Objective 2
Concept Development Activities

CD 1 Reviewing Multiplicative Inverse

Use with 4-Day or 3-Day Instructional Plan. In this activity, students find reciprocals and simplify mathematical expressions.

MATERIALS

- *Interactive Text*, page 79

DIRECTIONS

1. Discuss the number **3** and its reciprocal $\frac{1}{3}$. Remind students that two numbers that yield 1 when multiplied together are called *reciprocals*. Point out that $3 \cdot \frac{1}{3} = 1$. Tell students there is another term for these types of numbers.

2. Discuss the following term with students:

   multiplicative inverse Numbers that multiply to equal one

3. Tell students to work individually on this short activity.

4. Have students turn to *Interactive Text*, page 79, Multiplicative Inverse.

5. Tell students to write the reciprocal or multiplicative inverse for each of the expressions in Problems 1–10.

6. Ask students if they remember the relation between the numerical factors in these expressions. The relation between 2 and $\frac{1}{2}$ in the expression $\frac{1}{2}(2x)$ is that they are reciprocals, or multiplicative inverses, of one another. Their product is always 1.

7. Before instructing students to complete the remainder of the problems in this activity, direct their attention to Problems 19 and 20. Have students discuss how they would answer these questions.

Name _____ Date _____

MULTIPLICATIVE INVERSE

Write the multiplicative inverse, or reciprocal, of each of the numbers below.

1. 27 $\frac{1}{27}$
2. -13 $-\frac{1}{13}$
3. $\frac{1}{7}$ 7
4. $-\frac{1}{5}$ -5

5. $\frac{4}{5}$ $\frac{5}{4}$ or $1\frac{1}{4}$
6. $-\frac{15}{16}$ $-\frac{16}{15}$ or $-1\frac{1}{15}$
7. $\frac{3}{4}$ $\frac{4}{3}$ or $1\frac{1}{3}$
8. $-\frac{3}{7}$ $-\frac{7}{3}$ or $-2\frac{1}{3}$

9. $\frac{5}{8}$ $\frac{8}{5}$ or $1\frac{3}{5}$
10. -1 -1

Write the simplest equivalent expression for each of the products below.

11. $\frac{1}{2}(2x)$ x
12. $3\left(\frac{1}{3}\right)x$ x
13. $\frac{1}{7}(7y)$ y
14. $8\left(\frac{1}{8}x\right)$ x

15. $\frac{2}{3}\left(\frac{3}{2}x\right)$ x
16. $-5\left(-\frac{1}{5}y\right)$ y
17. $-\frac{3}{2}\left(-\frac{2}{3}y\right)$ y
18. $\frac{1}{-9}(-9x)$ x

19. What can be said about any number and its reciprocal?

   Answers will vary.
   _____

20. How would you describe the multiplicative inverse of a number?

   Answers will vary.
   _____

By what number would you multiply each expression to get 1x or x as the final expression?

21. $2x$ $\frac{1}{2}$
22. $-5x$ $-\frac{1}{5}$
23. $17x$ $\frac{1}{17}$
24. $-8x$ $-\frac{1}{8}$

25. $\frac{1}{3}x$ 3
26. $-\frac{3}{4}x$ $-\frac{4}{3}$
27. $\frac{14}{15}x$ $\frac{15}{14}$
28. $\frac{2x}{3}$ $\frac{3}{2}$

Inside Algebra   Chapter 3 • Objective 2 • CD 1   **79**

Listen for:

- Two numbers that yield 1 when multiplied together are called reciprocals, or multiplicative inverses.

- $3 \cdot \frac{1}{3} = 1$

8. Have students complete Problems 11–28.

NEXT STEPS • Differentiate

4-Day and 3-Day Instructional Plans:
CD 2, page 191—All students, for additional concept development

Concept Development Activities

CD 2 Multiplying and Dividing With Algebra Tiles

Use with 4-Day or 3-Day Instructional Plan. In this activity, students use zero pairs to solve algebra problems.

MATERIALS

- Algebra tiles, one set per pair of students

DIRECTIONS

1. Group students into pairs. Give a set of algebra tiles to every two students.

2. Discuss what each piece in the set of algebra tiles represents.

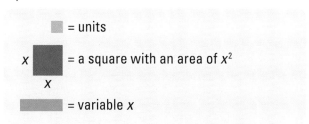

The x^2 pieces are not used in this activity. Have students put them back in the container.

3. Explain that we typically refer to the ▪ as a variable, or as x. It is the unknown, and the goal is to find out what number it represents.

4. Explain that the variable piece has a different color on each side. One side is green ▪, which represents x, a positive or negative number, and the other is red ▪, which represents $-x$, the opposite of x. The unit piece also has a different color on each side. One side is yellow ▪, which represents 1, and the other is red ▪, which represents -1.

5. Review the concept of zero pairs by demonstrating that three yellow tiles and three red tiles represent $3 + (-3)$. Each yellow and red pair represents a zero pair because $1 + (-1) = 0$. Therefore, ▪▪▪▪▪▪ represents three zero pairs, or zero.

6. Ask students how they would model $3x$ with algebra tiles.

   Have students model $3x$ as ▪▪▪ using green tiles.

   Have students model $-3x$ as ▪▪▪ using red tiles.

7. Review the following term with students:

   equation A statement that two quantities or mathematical expressions are equal

8. Write the equation **$3x = 6$** on the board or overhead. Show how to solve for the value of x using algebra tiles. Use green variable tiles and yellow unit tiles, which are both positive.

   Example:

   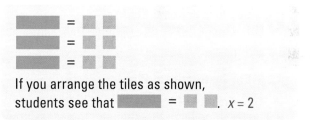

   If you arrange the tiles as shown, students see that ▪ = ▪▪. $x = 2$

9. Have students check the answer. $3(2) = 6$, or $6 = 6$

10. Model other equations using the tiles.

    Sample problem:

    $2x = 6$

    ▪ = ▪▪▪
    ▪ = ▪▪▪

    $x = 3$

11. Demonstrate how to check the solution.
    $2x = 6$
    $2(3) = 6$
    $6 = 6$

Concept Development Activities

12. Have students model and solve other equations using tiles.

Sample problems:

$5x = 15$ $x = 3$

$3x = -9$ $x = -3$

$-3x = 12$ $x = -4$

$3x = 12$ $x = 4$

$-2x = 8$ $x = -4$

$-3x = 3$ $x = -1$

NEXT STEPS • Differentiate

4-Day Instructional Plan:

PA 1, page 195—All students, for additional practice

3-Day Instructional Plan:

PM 2, page 199—Students who demonstrate understanding of the concept, to assess progress

PA 1, page 195—Students who need additional practice

Concept Development Activities

CD 3 Using the Multiplication Property of Equality

Use with 4-Day or 3-Day Instructional Plan. In this activity, students understand that multiplying or dividing by the same amount on each side of an equation does not change whether the equation is true or false.

MATERIALS

- Blackline Master 36

DIRECTIONS

1. Review the following term with students:

   equation A statement that two quantities or mathematical expressions are equal

2. Show examples of true, false, and open sentences.

   Examples:

   $9 = 9$ true

   $6 = 5$ false

   $x + 3 = 10$ open

3. Ask students to name an example of a true sentence. Write a sentence on the board or overhead. Have a volunteer multiply both sides by 3. Ask students if the sentence is true after both sides have been multiplied by 3.

   Examples:

   $6 = 6$
   $6 \cdot 3 = 6 \cdot 3$
   $18 = 18$ true

USING THE MULTIPLICATION PROPERTY OF EQUALITY

Determine whether each statement is true or false.

1. If $6 = 6$, then $6 \cdot 5 = 6 \cdot 5$ true

2. If $6 = 6$, then $6 \cdot (-2) = 6 \cdot (-2)$ true

3. If $6 = 6$, then $6 \cdot 4 = 6 \cdot 5$ false

4. If $6 = 6$, then $6 \cdot 3 = 6 \cdot (-2)$ false

5. If $5 = 5$, then $5 \cdot 4 = 5 \cdot 5$ false

6. If $7 = 7$, then $3 \cdot 7 = 7 \cdot 3$ true

7. If $14 = 14$, then $14 \cdot (-8) = 14 \cdot (-8)$ true

8. If $2 + 3 = 5$, then $6(2 + 3) = 6 \cdot 5$ true

9. If $8 - 3 = 10 - 5$, then $2(8 - 3) = 2(10 - 5)$ true

10. If $8 - 3 = 5$, then $7(8 - 3) = 5 - 7$ false

11. If $8 = 8$, then $\frac{1}{4}(8) = \frac{1}{4}(8)$ true

---

4. Make a transparency of Blackline Master 36, Using the Multiplication Property of Equality, or write the sentences on the board or overhead without the true and false designations.

5. Discuss which sentences are true. Explain that a true sentence remains true when each side of the equation is multiplied by the same number; that is, if $x = y$, then $x \cdot z = y \cdot z$. Point out that true sentences also remain true if each side is divided by the same number because division is the same as multiplying by the reciprocal.

   Example:

   If $x = y$, then $\frac{x}{z} = \frac{y}{z}$ $(z \neq 0)$.

Concept Development Activities

6. Demonstrate how to solve an open sentence. Explain that to keep the sentence true, we need to multiply or divide each side by the same amount.

   Sample problem:

   $$2x = 14$$
   $$\left(\tfrac{1}{2}\right)2x = 14\left(\tfrac{1}{2}\right)$$
   $$x = 7$$

7. Write a few open sentences on the board, and have students solve them.

   Sample problems:

   $$3x = 18 \quad x = 6$$
   $$-4x = 28 \quad x = -7$$
   $$\left(\tfrac{1}{2}\right)x = 18 \quad x = 36$$

8. Have students discuss the basic steps for solving open sentences.

   Listen for:
   - Multiplying or dividing by the same amount on each side of an equation does not change whether the equation is true or false.
   - A true sentence remains true if each side of the equation is multiplied by the same number.
   - If $x = y$, then $x \cdot z = y \cdot z$.

NEXT STEPS • Differentiate

4-Day and 3-Day Instructional Plans:
PM 1, page 198—All students, to assess progress

Practice Activities

PA 1 Playing Multiplication and Division Equation Bingo

Use with 4-Day or 3-Day Instructional Plan. In this activity, students quickly solve simple algebra problems.

MATERIALS

- Blackline Master 38
- Markers

DIRECTIONS

1. Distribute one copy of Blackline Master 38, 4 × 4 Bingo Card, to each student.

2. Have students write the following numbers randomly in the 16 squares. Tell them there are no free spaces. **–3, 18, –8, 21, –13, 9, –9, 25, –72, 36, –15, 6, –30, 8, 0, 4**

3. Write the problems below one at a time on the overhead or on the board. Do not write the answers. Have students solve each problem, then use a marker to cover the square that contains the correct answer.

$x = -3$ $x = -3$	$\frac{1}{2}x = 3$ $x = 6$
$\frac{1}{3}x = -3$ $x = -9$	$2x = 16$ $x = 8$
$2x = -60$ $x = -30$	$4x = 100$ $x = 25$
$-2x = 16$ $x = -8$	$\frac{x}{3} = 6$ $x = 18$
$\frac{x}{-6} = 12$ $x = -72$	$5x = 105$ $x = 21$
$118x = 0$ $x = 0$	$\frac{2x}{3} = 6$ $x = 9$
$-x = 13$ $x = -13$	$4x = 16$ $x = 4$
$\frac{-3x}{5} = 9$ $x = -15$	$\frac{x}{-4} = -9$ $x = 36$

4. Tell students the first person to get four markers in a row says, "Bingo!" Check the student's answers. If they are correct, he or she wins the game.

5. Repeat using the remaining problems or making new ones with the answers from Step 2.

---

4 × 4 BINGO CARD

NEXT STEPS • Differentiate

4-Day Instructional Plan:

PA 2, page 196—Students who demonstrate understanding of the concept, for additional practice and problem solving

CD 3, page 193—Students who need additional concept development

3-Day Instructional Plan:

PM 1, page 198—Students who demonstrate understanding of the concept, to assess progress

CD 3, page 193—Students who need additional concept development

Objective 2
Practice Activities

★PA 2 Solving the Guided Maze

Use with 4-Day or 3-Day Instructional Plan. In this activity, students solve equations and recognize their own errors.

MATERIALS

- *Interactive Text*, page 80
- Blackline Master 39

DIRECTIONS

1. Review the following term with students:

   equation A statement that two quantities or mathematical expressions are equal

2. Have students turn to *Interactive Text*, page 80, Guided Maze, for this activity.

3. Write the following equations on the board or overhead:

   1. $3x = -21$ $x = -7$ **2. $6x = 3$** $x = 0.5$

   3. $-4x = -32$ $x = 8$ **4. $-x = 6$** $x = -6$

   5. $\frac{1}{2}x = 2$ $x = 4$ **6. $4x = 3.2$** $x = 0.8$

   7. $5x = 15$ $x = 3$ **8. $\frac{x}{4} = 3$** $x = 12$

   9. $-48 = 12x$ $x = -4$ **10. $-0.7x = 10.5$** $x = -15$

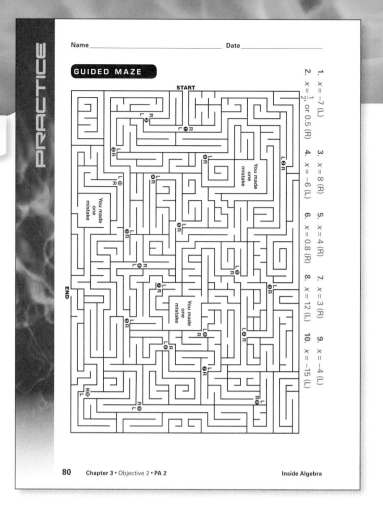

Name_____ Date_____

GUIDED MAZE

L	R
$\frac{1}{3}$	7
−6	3
−7	150
−8	4
1	8
1.5	0.8
2	0.5
12	6
−15	−1
−4	15

4. Make a transparency of Blackline Master 39, Guided Maze, or write the chart on the board or overhead.

5. Have students work the first equation given in Step 3, and find the answer in the L (left) or R (right) column of Blackline Master 39. The answer for this equation is in the L column. The students should then start the maze. When they get to the ❶, they should follow the L route because the answer to the equation is in the L column.

6. Tell students to solve the remaining equations in the order given. If students work each problem correctly and follow the path, they work through to the end of the maze.

NEXT STEPS • Differentiate

👥 **4-Day Instructional Plan:**

PM 1, page 198—Students who are on the accelerated path, to assess progress

PM 2, page 199—Students who are on the differentiated path, to assess progress

👥 **3-Day Instructional Plan:**

PS 1, page 200—Students who are on the accelerated path, to develop problem-solving skills

PM 2, page 199—Students who are on the differentiated path, to assess progress

Objective 2
Progress-Monitoring Activities

PM 1 Apply Skills 1

Use with 4-Day or 3-Day Instructional Plan.

MATERIALS

- *Interactive Text*, pages 81–82

DIRECTIONS

1. Have students turn to *Interactive Text*, pages 81–82, Apply Skills 1.

2. Remind students of the key terms: *equation* and *multiplicative inverse*.

3. Monitor student work, and provide feedback as necessary.

   Watch for:
   - Do students isolate the variable by multiplying by the inverse of the coefficient?
   - Do students know the coefficient of the isolated variable should be positive one?
   - Do students recognize when a problem has no solution?

NEXT STEPS • Differentiate

👥 4-Day Instructional Plan:

PS 1, page 200—Students who are on the accelerated path, to develop problem-solving skills

PA 2, page 196—Students who are on the differentiated path, for additional practice and problem solving

3-Day Instructional Plan:

PA 2, page 196—All students, for additional practice and problem solving

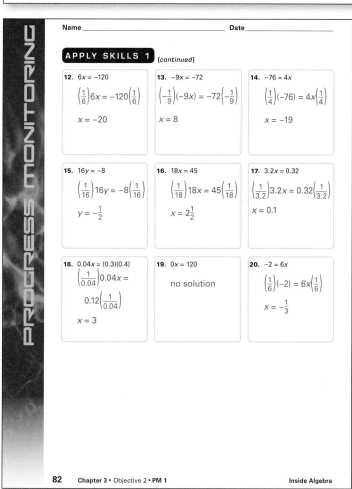

Name_____ Date_____

APPLY SKILLS 1

Solve each equation and check the answer.

Example:
$17x = -34$
$\left(\frac{1}{17}\right)17x = -34\left(\frac{1}{17}\right)$
$x = -2$
Check: $17(-2) = -34$

1. $4x = 12$
$\left(\frac{1}{4}\right)4x = (12)\left(\frac{1}{4}\right)$
$x = 3$

2. $-3y = 18$
$\left(-\frac{1}{3}\right)(-3y) = 18\left(-\frac{1}{3}\right)$
$y = -6$

3. $75 = 5x$
$\left(\frac{1}{5}\right)75 = 5x\left(\frac{1}{5}\right)$
$x = 15$

4. $-146 = 2y$
$\left(\frac{1}{2}\right)(-146) = 2y\left(\frac{1}{2}\right)$
$y = -73$

5. $3n = -210$
$\left(\frac{1}{3}\right)3n = -210\left(\frac{1}{3}\right)$
$n = -70$

6. $7x = \frac{3}{4}$
$\left(\frac{1}{7}\right)7x = \frac{3}{4}\left(\frac{1}{7}\right)$
$x = \frac{3}{28}$

7. $7.5x = 1.5$
$\left(\frac{1}{7.5}\right)7.5x = 1.5\left(\frac{1}{7.5}\right)$
$x = \frac{1}{5}$

8. $0.8y = 3.20$
$\left(\frac{5}{4}\right)0.8y = 3.20\left(\frac{5}{4}\right)$
$y = 4$

9. $-8.8 = 2.2x$
$\left(\frac{1}{2.2}\right)(-8.8) =$
$2.2x\left(\frac{1}{2.2}\right)$
$x = -4$

10. $5x = 480\left(\frac{1}{2}\right)$
$\left(\frac{1}{5}\right)5x = 240\left(\frac{1}{5}\right)$
$x = 48$

11. $18x = 36$
$\left(\frac{1}{18}\right)18x = 36\left(\frac{1}{18}\right)$
$x = 2$

Inside Algebra   Chapter 3 • Objective 2 • PM 1   **81**

Name_____ Date_____

APPLY SKILLS 1 *(continued)*

12. $6x = -120$
$\left(\frac{1}{6}\right)6x = -120\left(\frac{1}{6}\right)$
$x = -20$

13. $-9x = -72$
$\left(-\frac{1}{9}\right)(-9x) = -72\left(-\frac{1}{9}\right)$
$x = 8$

14. $-76 = 4x$
$\left(\frac{1}{4}\right)(-76) = 4x\left(\frac{1}{4}\right)$
$x = -19$

15. $16y = -8$
$\left(\frac{1}{16}\right)16y = -8\left(\frac{1}{16}\right)$
$y = -\frac{1}{2}$

16. $18x = 45$
$\left(\frac{1}{18}\right)18x = 45\left(\frac{1}{18}\right)$
$x = 2\frac{1}{2}$

17. $3.2x = 0.32$
$\left(\frac{1}{3.2}\right)3.2x = 0.32\left(\frac{1}{3.2}\right)$
$x = 0.1$

18. $0.04x = (0.3)(0.4)$
$\left(\frac{1}{0.04}\right)0.04x =$
$0.12\left(\frac{1}{0.04}\right)$
$x = 3$

19. $0x = 120$
no solution

20. $-2 = 6x$
$\left(\frac{1}{6}\right)(-2) = 6x\left(\frac{1}{6}\right)$
$x = -\frac{1}{3}$

82   Chapter 3 • Objective 2 • PM 1   Inside Algebra

Objective 2
Progress-Monitoring Activities

PM 2 Apply Skills 2

Use with 4-Day or 3-Day Instructional Plan.

MATERIALS

- *Interactive Text*, pages 83–84

DIRECTIONS

1. Have students turn to *Interactive Text*, pages 83–84, Apply Skills 2.

2. Remind students of the key terms: *equation* and *multiplicative inverse*.

3. Monitor student work, and provide feedback as necessary.

   Watch for:
   - Do students remove fractional coefficients by multiplication?
   - Do students utilize appropriate problem-solving strategies such as cross-multiplication and multiplicative inverse?

NEXT STEPS • Differentiate

4-Day Instructional Plan:
PS 2, page 201—All students, to develop problem-solving skills

3-Day Instructional Plan:
PA 2, page 196—Students who are on the accelerated path, for additional practice and problem solving

PS 1, page 200—Students on the differentiated path who demonstrated understanding on PA 1, to develop problem-solving skills

Objective 2 Posttest, page 203—All other students

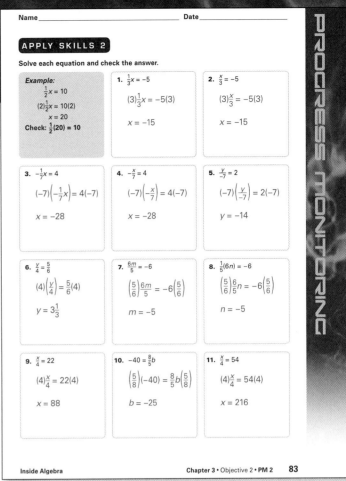

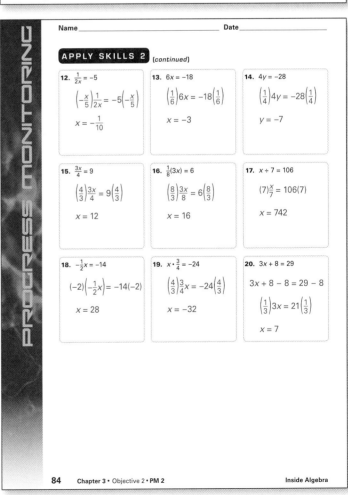

Problem-Solving Activities

★PS 1 Solving and Writing Equations

Use with 4-Day or 3-Day Instructional Plan. In this activity, students create algebra problems that yield a predefined solution.

MATERIALS

- *Interactive Text*, page 85

DIRECTIONS

1. Discuss the following term with students:

   linear equation The equation of a straight line

2. Tell students this activity involves solving simple linear equations. Tell them to work individually on this assignment.

3. Have students turn to *Interactive Text*, page 85, Solving and Writing Equations, and solve the problems.

4. Note whether students can answer Problem 3 without actually solving the equation.

NEXT STEPS • Differentiate

4-Day Instructional Plan:
PM 2, page 199—All students, to assess progress

👥 **3-Day Instructional Plan:**
PS 2, page 201—Students who are on the accelerated path, to develop problem-solving skills

Objective 2 Posttest, page 203—Students who are on the differentiated path

---

Name_____ Date_____

SOLVING AND WRITING EQUATIONS

Solve each equation for *x*.

1. $6x = 30$ $x = \underline{\ 5\ }$

   Write five equations whose solution is the same as that for $6x = 30$.
   Answers will vary. Sample answers are given.

   $9x = 45$

   $-3x = -15$

   $x + 7 = 12$

   $9 - x = 4$

   $7x - 4 = 31$

2. $4x = 6$ $x = \dfrac{6}{4}$ or $1\frac{1}{2}$ or 1.5

   Write five equations whose solution is the same as that for $4x = 6$.
   Answers will vary. Sample answers are given.

   $2x = 3$

   $10x = 15$

   $x - 2 = -\frac{1}{2}$

   $\frac{4}{6}x = 1$

   $3\frac{1}{3}x = 5$

Determine whether the solution to each equation is an integer.

3. $\frac{1}{2}x = 4$ <u>integer</u>

4. $4x = 2$ <u>not an integer</u>

5. $7x = 20$ <u>not an integer</u>

6. $-3x = 42$ <u>integer</u>

7. $30x = 100$ <u>not an integer</u>

8. $25x = 100$ <u>integer</u>

★ = Includes Problem Solving

Problem-Solving Activities

★ PS 2 Solving Equations With Phone Call Problems

Use with 4-Day or 3-Day Instructional Plan. In this activity, students write and solve mathematical equations for verbal expressions.

MATERIALS

- *Interactive Text*, page 86

DIRECTIONS

1. Review the following term with students:

   linear equation The equation of a straight line

2. Tell students that in this activity, they write and solve simple linear equations. Tell them to work individually on this assignment.

3. Have students turn to *Interactive Text*, page 86, Phone Calls, and solve the problems.

4. Note whether students write 7¢ as 0.07 in their equations.

NEXT STEPS • Differentiate

4-Day and 3-Day Instructional Plans:
Objective 2 Posttest, page 203—All students

Name _____ Date _____

PROBLEM SOLVING

PHONE CALLS

Find the solution to each problem.

1. A telephone company has a long-distance calling card that charges 7¢ per minute for any call anytime. Write an equation for the cost (*c*) of a call that lasts (*m*) minutes.

   $(7¢)m$, or $c = 0.07m$

2. For the charges in Problem 1, how much will a 10-minute phone call cost? (Solve for *c* when *m* = 10 minutes.)

   The call will cost 70¢.

3. How long can you talk if you want to spend only $3.50? (Solve for *m* when the total cost is $3.50.)

   You can talk for 50 minutes.

4. How long could you talk for $5.00? Write your equation and solve for *m*.

   You could talk for 71.43 minutes.

5. Write the equation for the cost of phone calls if the charge is 10¢ per minute.

   $c = (10¢)m$, or $c = 0.1m$

6. How long could you talk at 10¢ per minute if you wanted to spend only $5.00? Write the equation and solve for *m*.

   You could talk for 50 minutes.

7. Write the equation for a plan where the cost of a phone call is 14¢ per minute.

   $c = (14¢)m$, or $c = 0.14m$

WORK SPACE

2. $c = 0.07(10)$
   $c = 70¢$, or 0.70

3. $\left(\frac{1}{0.07}\right)0.07m = 3.50\left(\frac{1}{0.07}\right)$
   $m = 50$ min.

4. $\left(\frac{1}{0.07}\right)0.07m = 5.00\left(\frac{1}{0.07}\right)$
   $m = 71.43$ min.

6. $\left(\frac{1}{0.10}\right)0.10m = 5.00\left(\frac{1}{0.10}\right)$
   $m = 50$ min.

86 Chapter 3 • Objective 2 • PS 2   Inside Algebra

★ = Includes Problem Solving

This page intentionally left blank

Objective 2 Posttest

Discuss with students the key concepts in Objective 2. Following the discussion, administer the Objective 2 Posttest to all students.

Using the Results

• Score the posttest and update the class record card.

• Provide reinforcement for students who do not demonstrate mastery of the concepts through individual or small-group reteaching of key concepts.

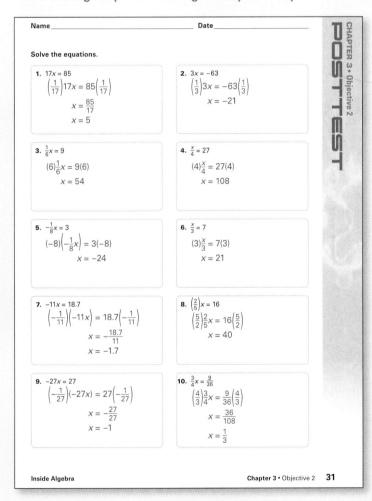

Name _____ Date _____

Solve the equations.

1. $17x = 85$

$\left(\frac{1}{17}\right)17x = 85\left(\frac{1}{17}\right)$

$x = \frac{85}{17}$

$x = 5$

2. $3x = -63$

$\left(\frac{1}{3}\right)3x = -63\left(\frac{1}{3}\right)$

$x = -21$

3. $\frac{1}{6}x = 9$

$(6)\frac{1}{6}x = 9(6)$

$x = 54$

4. $\frac{x}{4} = 27$

$(4)\frac{x}{4} = 27(4)$

$x = 108$

5. $-\frac{1}{8}x = 3$

$(-8)\left(-\frac{1}{8}x\right) = 3(-8)$

$x = -24$

6. $\frac{x}{3} = 7$

$(3)\frac{x}{3} = 7(3)$

$x = 21$

7. $-11x = 18.7$

$\left(-\frac{1}{11}\right)(-11x) = 18.7\left(-\frac{1}{11}\right)$

$x = -\frac{18.7}{11}$

$x = -1.7$

8. $\left(\frac{2}{5}\right)x = 16$

$\left(\frac{5}{2}\right)\frac{2}{5}x = 16\left(\frac{5}{2}\right)$

$x = 40$

9. $-27x = 27$

$\left(-\frac{1}{27}\right)(-27x) = 27\left(-\frac{1}{27}\right)$

$x = -\frac{27}{27}$

$x = -1$

10. $\frac{3}{4}x = \frac{9}{36}$

$\left(\frac{4}{3}\right)\frac{3}{4}x = \frac{9}{36}\left(\frac{4}{3}\right)$

$x = \frac{36}{108}$

$x = \frac{1}{3}$

Inside Algebra   Chapter 3 • Objective 2   **31**

Objective 3
Solve linear equations using one or more operations.

Objective 3 Pretest

Students complete the Objective 3 Pretest on the same day as the Objective 2 Posttest.

Using the Results

- Score the pretest and update the class record card.

- If the majority of students do not demonstrate mastery of the concepts, use the 5-Day Instructional Plan for Objective 3.

- If the majority of students demonstrate mastery of the concepts, use the 3-Day Instructional Plan for Objective 3.

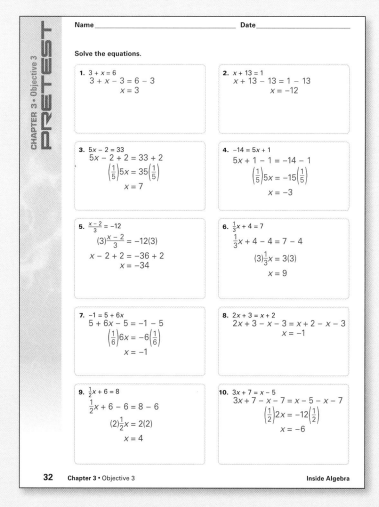

Name _____ Date _____

CHAPTER 3 • Objective 3
PRETEST

Solve the equations.

1. $3 + x = 6$
$3 + x - 3 = 6 - 3$
$x = 3$

2. $x + 13 = 1$
$x + 13 - 13 = 1 - 13$
$x = -12$

3. $5x - 2 = 33$
$5x - 2 + 2 = 33 + 2$
$\left(\frac{1}{5}\right)5x = 35\left(\frac{1}{5}\right)$
$x = 7$

4. $-14 = 5x + 1$
$5x + 1 - 1 = -14 - 1$
$\left(\frac{1}{5}\right)5x = -15\left(\frac{1}{5}\right)$
$x = -3$

5. $\frac{x-2}{3} = -12$
$(3)\frac{x-2}{3} = -12(3)$
$x - 2 + 2 = -36 + 2$
$x = -34$

6. $\frac{1}{3}x + 4 = 7$
$\frac{1}{3}x + 4 - 4 = 7 - 4$
$(3)\frac{1}{3}x = 3(3)$
$x = 9$

7. $-1 = 5 + 6x$
$5 + 6x - 5 = -1 - 5$
$\left(\frac{1}{6}\right)6x = -6\left(\frac{1}{6}\right)$
$x = -1$

8. $2x + 3 = x + 2$
$2x + 3 - x - 3 = x + 2 - x - 3$
$x = -1$

9. $\frac{1}{2}x + 6 = 8$
$\frac{1}{2}x + 6 - 6 = 8 - 6$
$(2)\frac{1}{2}x = 2(2)$
$x = 4$

10. $3x + 7 = x - 5$
$3x + 7 - x - 7 = x - 5 - x - 7$
$\left(\frac{1}{2}\right)2x = -12\left(\frac{1}{2}\right)$
$x = -6$

32   Chapter 3 • Objective 3   Inside Algebra

Goals and Activities

Objective 3 Goals

The following activities, when used with the instructional plans on pages 206 and 207, enable students to:

- Solve the equation $3x + 6 = -12$ for x to get $x = -6$
- Solve the equation $5 - x = 7$ for x to get $x = -2$
- Solve the equation $3x + 4 = x - 2$ for x to get $x = -3$

Objective 3 Activities

Concept Development Activities		
★**CD 1** Using Algebra Tiles—Part 1, page 208	★**CD 2** Using Algebra Tiles—Part 2, page 209	**CD 3** Identifying the Principal Operator, page 210

Practice Activities		
PA 1 Playing Equation Bingo, page 211	**PA 2** Playing Equation Rummy, page 212	★**PA 3** Making and Sharing Linear Equations, page 215

Progress-Monitoring Activities			
PM 1 Apply Skills 1, page 216	**PM 2** Apply Skills 2, page 217	**PM 3** Apply Skills 3, page 218	**PM 4** Apply Skills 4, page 219

★Problem-Solving Activities	
★**PS 1** Finding the Number, page 220	★**PS 2** Creating a Problem, page 221

Ongoing Assessment
Posttest Objective 3, page 223
Pretest Objective 4, page 224

CD = Concept Development   PM = Progress Monitoring   PS = Problem Solving
PA = Practice Activity   ★ = Includes Problem Solving

5-Day Instructional Plan

Use the 5-Day Instructional Plan when pretest results indicate that students would benefit from a slower pace. This plan is used when the majority of students need more time or did not demonstrate mastery on the pretest. This plan does not include all activities.

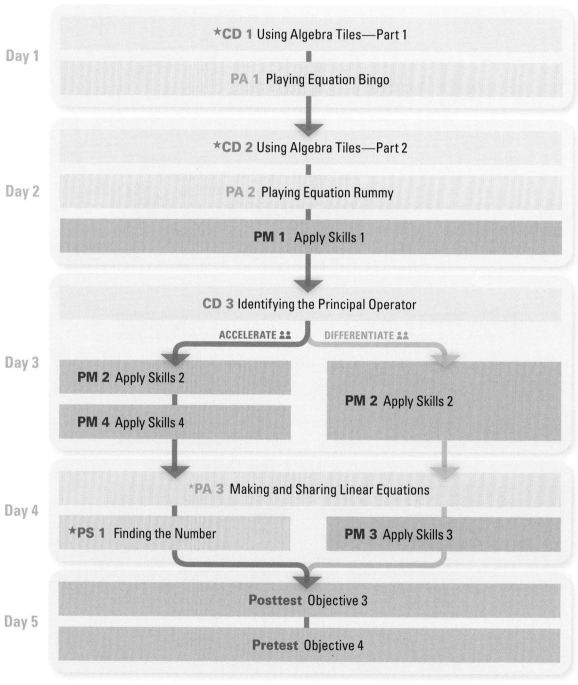

Day 1
★**CD 1** Using Algebra Tiles—Part 1

PA 1 Playing Equation Bingo

Day 2
★**CD 2** Using Algebra Tiles—Part 2

PA 2 Playing Equation Rummy

PM 1 Apply Skills 1

Day 3
CD 3 Identifying the Principal Operator

ACCELERATE ▐▐   DIFFERENTIATE ▐▐

PM 2 Apply Skills 2

PM 4 Apply Skills 4

PM 2 Apply Skills 2

Day 4
★**PA 3** Making and Sharing Linear Equations

★**PS 1** Finding the Number

PM 3 Apply Skills 3

Day 5
Posttest Objective 3

Pretest Objective 4

CD = Concept Development   **PM = Progress Monitoring**   PS = Problem Solving
PA = Practice Activity   ★ = Includes Problem Solving

3-Day Instructional Plan

Use the 3-Day Instructional Plan when pretest results indicate that students can move through the activities at a faster pace. This plan is ideal when the majority of students demonstrate mastery on the pretest.

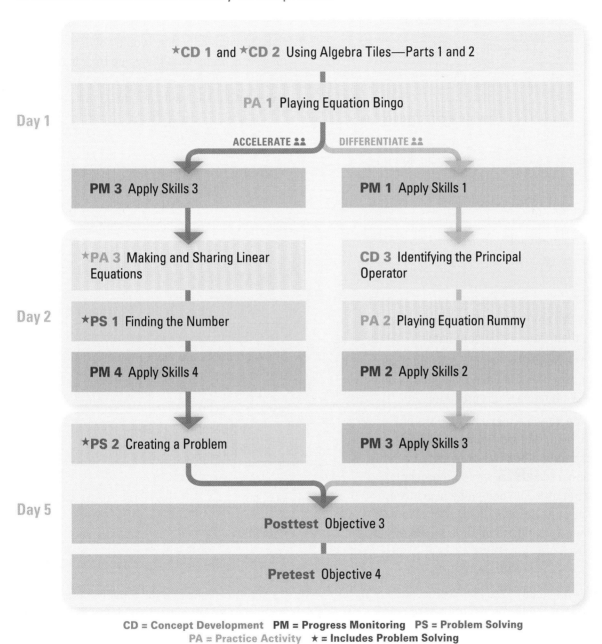

Day 1

★CD 1 and ★CD 2 Using Algebra Tiles—Parts 1 and 2

PA 1 Playing Equation Bingo

ACCELERATE · · · · DIFFERENTIATE · ·

PM 3 Apply Skills 3 · · · PM 1 Apply Skills 1

Day 2

★PA 3 Making and Sharing Linear Equations · · · CD 3 Identifying the Principal Operator

★PS 1 Finding the Number · · · PA 2 Playing Equation Rummy

PM 4 Apply Skills 4 · · · PM 2 Apply Skills 2

Day 5

★PS 2 Creating a Problem · · · PM 3 Apply Skills 3

Posttest Objective 3

Pretest Objective 4

CD = Concept Development   PM = Progress Monitoring   PS = Problem Solving
PA = Practice Activity   ★ = Includes Problem Solving

Objective 3
Concept Development Activities

★ **CD 1** Using Algebra Tiles—Part 1

Use with 5-Day or 3-Day Instructional Plan. In this activity, students understand that whatever is done to one side of an equation must also be done to the other.

MATERIALS

- Algebra tiles, one set for each pair of students

DIRECTIONS

1. Group students into pairs. Provide a set of algebra tiles for every two students.

2. Discuss what each piece in the set of algebra tiles represents.

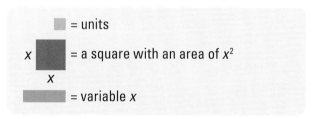

= units

x = a square with an area of x^2

= variable x

The x^2 pieces are not used in this activity. Have students put them back in the container.

3. Explain that the ▬▬▬ is usually referred to as a variable, or as x. It is the unknown, and the object is to find out what number it represents.

4. Explain that the variable piece has a different color on each side. One side is green ▬▬▬, which represents x, a positive or negative number, and the other is red ▬▬▬, which represents $-x$, the opposite of x. The unit piece also has a different color on each side. One side is yellow ▪, which represents 1, and the other is red ▪, which represents -1.

5. Review the concept of zero pairs by demonstrating that three yellow and three red tiles represent $3 + (-3)$. Each yellow and red pair represents a zero pair because $1 + (-1) = 0$. Therefore, ▪▪▪▪▪▪ represents three zero pairs, or 0.

6. Review the following term with students:

    equation A statement that two quantities or mathematical expressions are equal

★ = Includes Problem Solving

7. Write the equation **$2x + 3 = 7$** on the board or overhead. Have the students model the equation using the algebra tiles.

8. Ask students how they would solve the equation for x. Ask them what the value for x is that makes the sentence true. The usual steps are, first, to take away 3 from each side or add -3 to each side.

$$2x + 3 - 3 = 7 - 3$$
$$2x = 4$$

The next step is to divide the four remaining tiles into two sets.

So, $1x = 2$.

9. Show students the work they did using the algebra tiles to solve the equations.

$$2x + 3 = 7$$
$$2x + 3 - 3 = 7 - 3$$
$$2x = 4$$
$$\frac{2x}{2} = \frac{4}{2}$$
$$x = 2$$

10. Model and write the steps for solving other equations.

    Examples:

    $3x - 1 = 5$ $x = 2$ $4x + 1 = -11$ $x = -3$

11. Be sure to summarize the algebra steps using the Properties of Equality to solve the equations.

NEXT STEPS • Differentiate

5-Day Instructional Plan:
PA 1, page 211—All students, for additional practice

3-Day Instructional Plan:
CD 2, page 209—All students, for additional concept development and problem solving

Objective 3
Concept Development Activities

★CD 2 Using Algebra Tiles—Part 2

Use with 5-Day or 3-Day Instructional Plan. In this activity, students use algebra tiles to isolate variables in equations.

MATERIALS

- Algebra tiles, one set for each pair of students

DIRECTIONS

1. Group students into pairs. Provide a set of algebra tiles for every two students.

2. Review the following term with students:

   equation A statement that two quantities or mathematical expressions are equal

3. Write the equation $2x + 3 = x + 8$ on the board or overhead. Ask students to use their algebra tiles to make a model of the problem.

4. Ask students how to solve the problem. Write the steps as students describe how they would solve the equation. For example, first take away 3 from each side or add −3 to each side.

$$2x + 3 = x + 8$$
$$2x + 3 - 3 = x + 8 - 3$$
$$2x = x + 5$$

Next, take away an x from each side.

$$2x = x + 5$$
$$2x - x = x - x + 5$$
$$x = 5$$

5. Present other examples of equations with variables on each side for students to solve using the algebra tiles.

   Sample problems:

   $3x + 4 = x - 6$ $x = -5$
   $4x - 6 = x + 6$ $x = 4$
   $6 - x = x + 8$ $x = -1$

6. Have students write a paragraph describing how to solve an equation with variables on each side.

7. Discuss different ideas students generate, and determine whether these ideas always work. Note that it is usually necessary to add or subtract the constant before multiplying or dividing by the coefficient of the variable.

NEXT STEPS • Differentiate

5-Day Instructional Plan:
PA 2, page 212—All students, for additional practice

3-Day Instructional Plan:
PA 1, page 211—All students, for additional practice

★ = Includes Problem Solving

Concept Development Activities

CD 3 Identifying the Principal Operator

Use with 5-Day or 3-Day Instructional Plan. In this activity, students solve algebra equations by undoing the principal operator with the inverse operation.

DIRECTIONS

1. Explain to the class that in an algebraic expression, the last operation to be performed is called the *principal operator*. For example, the expression $3x + 6$ is an *indicated sum*. The principal operator is addition.

2. Ask students to name the principal operator in several expressions.

Examples:

> $3y - 4$ subtraction
>
> $4(x + 2)$ multiplication
>
> $(6x + 5) + x$ addition
>
> $\frac{3x - 6}{2}$ division
>
> $\frac{3x}{2} + 5$ addition
>
> $(2x - 4)2$ multiplication

3. Review the following term with students:

   equation A statement that two quantities or mathematical expressions are equal

4. Explain that an algebraic equation can be solved by undoing the principal operator with the inverse operation. Demonstrate this process for students by solving a couple of problems on the board.

Sample problems:

> $4x - 3 = 9$ $\qquad$ $\frac{x - 1}{2} = 7$
>
> $4x - 3 + 3 = 9 + 3$ $\qquad$ $2 \cdot \frac{x - 1}{2} = 7 \cdot 2$
>
> $4x = 12$ $\qquad$ $x - 1 = 14$
>
> $\frac{4x}{4} = \frac{12}{4}$ $\qquad$ $x - 1 + 1 = 14 + 1$
>
> $x = 3$ $\qquad$ $x = 15$

5. Have student volunteers work through several other examples. First, ask what the principal operator is, then ask how to undo the operation.

Sample problems:

> $3x - 4 = 14$ Add 4, then divide by 3; $x = 6$
>
> $\frac{1}{2}x + 3 = 11$ Subtract 3, then multiply by 2; $x = 16$
>
> $x - 27 = 14$ Add 27; $x = 41$
>
> $6 = 2x - 4$ Add 4, then divide by 2; $x = 5$
>
> $5 = \frac{x + 6}{3}$ Multiply by 3, then subtract 6; $x = 9$
>
> $6(x + 1) = 24$ Divide by 6, then subtract 1; $x = 3$
>
> $3(2x + 6) + 4 = 52$ Subtract 4, divide by 3, subtract 6, then divide by 2; $x = 5$
>
> $\frac{8 + 2x - 4}{3} = -2$ Multiply by 3, subtract 4, then divide by 2; $x = -5$

NEXT STEPS • Differentiate

5-Day Instructional Plan:
PM 2, page 217—All students, to assess progress

3-Day Instructional Plan:
PA 2, page 212—All students, for additional practice

PA 1 Playing Equation Bingo

Use with 5-Day or 3-Day Instructional Plan. In this activity, students quickly solve equations with a variable on both sides of the equal sign.

MATERIALS

- Blackline Master 38 and Blackline Master 41
- Markers

DIRECTIONS

1. Review the following term with students:

   equation A statement that two quantities or mathematical expressions are equal

2. Distribute a copy of Blackline Master 38, 4 × 4 Bingo Card, to each student.

3. Read aloud the following sixteen solutions, and ask students to write each one at random in the sixteen squares on their grids: **6, –7, 9, 5, –8, –1, 4, 7, –63, –80, 0, –31, 15, 1, no solution, 42**.

4. Make a transparency of Blackline Master 41, Equation Bingo, and put it on the overhead. Show students only one equation at a time by covering the others. Alternatively, write the equations from Blackline Master 41 on the board.

5. Allow time for students to solve each equation and cover the answer on their bingo card before you show the next equation. The first student to cover four answers in a row or column, straight or diagonally, shouts, "Bingo!" Check the student's solutions.

6. Continue the game until other students get bingo. Additionally, you can make new problems for the game that have the same solutions as the original problems.

NEXT STEPS • Differentiate

5-Day Instructional Plan:
CD 2, page 209—All students, for additional concept development and problem solving

3-Day Instructional Plan:
PM 3, page 218—Students who demonstrate understanding of the concept, to assess progress
PM 1, page 216—Students who need additional support, to assess progress

---

Name _____ Date _____ | 38

4 × 4 BINGO CARD

Name _____ Date _____ | 41

EQUATION BINGO

1. $5x = 3x + 12$ $x = 6$
2. $9y + 42 = 3y$ $y = -7$
3. $5m + 1 = 7m - 17$ $m = 9$
4. $-7x = 10 - 9x$ $x = 5$
5. $8x + 32 = 4x$ $x = -8$
6. $4z - 5 = 10z + 1$ $z = -1$
7. $6 - 3a = -14 + 2a$ $a = 4$
8. $0.7x + 0.3x = 2x - 7$ $x = 7$
9. $21 = \frac{d}{-3}$ $d = -63$
10. $-\frac{1}{4}x = 20$ $x = -80$
11. $2.2666x = 0$ $x = 0$
12. $\frac{3 + y}{7} = -4$ $y = -31$
13. $\frac{4x}{5} + 3 = x$ $x = 15$
14. $\frac{7 + y}{8} = y$ $y = 1$
15. $\frac{1}{4}(12b - 20) = 3b + 8$ no solution
16. $\frac{7(x - 2)}{2} = 6 + 2x + 8 + x$ $x = 42$

Practice Activities

PA 2 Playing Equation Rummy

Use with 5-Day or 3-Day Instructional Plan. In this activity, students solve equations.

MATERIALS

- Blackline Masters 42–47 or 48 blank cards for each group
- Marking pens

DIRECTIONS

1. Review the following term with students:

   equation A statement that two quantities or mathematical expressions are equal

2. Have students work in groups of three, four, or five players. Provide each group with marking pens.

3. Distribute one set of Blackline Masters 42–47, Equation Rummy, to each group. Alternatively, give each group 48 blank cards, and direct students to write an equation on each blank card from Blackline Masters 42–47.

4. Explain the game rules to students.

   - Each group shuffles their cards before dealing. Players are dealt ten, eight, or six cards, depending on the number of players in the group. The remaining cards are placed facedown, in a draw pile.

   - Each player solves the equations on the cards they have been dealt. Players should lay down any sets of three cards that have the same solution.

   - Once a set of three cards is on the table, any player, on his or her turn, can lay down cards with the same solution as the set.

   - Play begins with each player, in turn, drawing a card from the draw pile and solving the equation on that card. That player can either form a set of cards, add to an existing set, or discard a card.

Name _____ Date _____ 42

EQUATION RUMMY

$x = 21 - 8$ $x = 13$	$x + 8 = 21$ $x = 13$
$-x + 21 = 8$ $x = 13$	$x = 13$ $x = 13$
$5x - 13 = 52$ $x = 13$	$3(x - 15) = 9 - 15$ $x = 13$
$24 - \dfrac{2}{5}x = 64$ $x = -100$	$\dfrac{x + 60}{5} = -8$ $x = -100$

Name _____ Date _____ 43

EQUATION RUMMY   *(continued)*

$x - 15 = -2$ $x = 13$	$5x = 5(13)$ $x = 13$
$3x + 127 = -173$ $x = -100$	$\dfrac{3(x - 15)}{6} = -1$ $x = 13$
$5x - 13 = 4(13)$ $x = 13$	$3x + 120 = 12(-15)$ $x = -100$
$x + 93 = -7$ $x = -100$	$-39 = -3x$ $x = 13$

- The discards are available to any player who would like to draw one for his or her hand.
- Play continues clockwise, with each player taking a turn.
- Play ends when one player gets rid of all the cards in his or her hand. That player is declared the winner.

NEXT STEPS • Differentiate

5-Day Instructional Plan:
PM 1, page 216—All students, to assess progress

3-Day Instructional Plan:
PM 2, page 217—All students, to assess progress

EQUATION RUMMY *(continued)*

$-\left(\dfrac{1}{2}\right)(240) = x + (-20)$
$x = -100$

$-2x = 155 - (-45)$
$x = -100$

$3x - 45 = -6$
$x = 13$

$\dfrac{x}{350} = \dfrac{-2}{7}$
$x = -100$

$\dfrac{x}{80} = \dfrac{-5}{4}$
$x = -100$

$12 = \dfrac{2x + 80}{-10}$
$x = -100$

$\dfrac{x + 40}{15} = -4$
$x = -100$

$1 = \dfrac{-60}{x + 40}$
$x = -100$

EQUATION RUMMY *(continued)*

$\dfrac{27}{2} = -3x + 9$
$x = -\dfrac{3}{2}$

$2x + 4 = x - 2$
$x = -6$

$2x + 7 = -5$
$x = -6$

$-2x = 3$
$x = -\dfrac{3}{2}$

$1.5 = \dfrac{3x + 9}{3}$
$x = -\dfrac{3}{2}$

$5x - 18 = 3x - 30$
$x = -6$

$2(x + 1) = -\left(\dfrac{1}{3}\right)3$
$x = -\dfrac{3}{2}$

$2x = 4(x + 3)$
$x = -6$

46

Name _____ Date _____

EQUATION RUMMY *(continued)*

$2x = -12$ $x = -6$	$5x + 30 = 3x + 18$ $x = -6$
$-2(15 + x) = 3x$ $x = -6$	$\dfrac{2x - 3}{2} + 2 = 2x + 2$ $x = -\dfrac{3}{2}$
$2(x + 1) = -10$ $x = -6$	$\dfrac{x + 6}{5} = \dfrac{x + 6}{3}$ $x = -6$
$\dfrac{x - 3}{9} = -\dfrac{1}{2}$ $x = -\dfrac{3}{2}$	$\dfrac{12}{x + 3} = 8$ $x = -\dfrac{3}{2}$

Name _____ Date _____

EQUATION RUMMY *(continued)*

$2(x + 1) = 3x + 8$ $x = -6$	$\dfrac{9}{2} = 9 + 3x$ $x = -\dfrac{3}{2}$
$2(x + 3) = 3$ $x = -\dfrac{3}{2}$	$10x + 30 = 15$ $x = -\dfrac{3}{2}$
$3x + 6 = 2x$ $x = -6$	$2x - 3 = -6$ $x = -\dfrac{3}{2}$
$4(x + 3) = 3(4 + x) - 1\dfrac{1}{2}$ $x = -\dfrac{3}{2}$	$\dfrac{1}{2}(5 + 2x) = 1$ $x = -\dfrac{3}{2}$

Objective 3
Practice Activities

★PA 3 Making and Sharing Linear Equations

Use with 5-Day or 3-Day Instructional Plan. In this activity, students solve linear equations by substituting a value for the variable.

DIRECTIONS

1. Review the following terms with students:

   equation A statement that two quantities or mathematical expressions are equal

   linear equation The equation of a straight line

2. Have students select a number between −10 and 10. Have students write the simple equation $x =$ their number on a piece of paper, for example, $x = 3$.

3. Write $ax + b = ?$ on the board or overhead. Explain that the a and b can be any number students choose for writing a linear equation. Have students write an equation following the example.

   Sample answer:

   $4x + (−3) = ?$

   $a = 4$ and $b = −3$

4. Have students discuss how to find the solution. Make sure students see that they substitute their number for x into the equation. Have students write their equation on one sheet of paper and keep the solution on a different sheet of paper.

   Sample answer:

   If $x = 3$:

   $4(3) + (−3) = ?$

   $? = 9$

5. Repeat Steps 2–4 to come up with two more equations using the form $ax + b = ?$ writing the equations and solutions on separate sheets of paper.

6. Give students the general form $x + \frac{a}{b} = ?$. Have them create an equation of this form by selecting an x and numbers for a and b, then finding the ?. Read aloud some of their equations. Discuss how to ensure the answer is an integer.

7. Give students the general form $\frac{1}{a}x + b = ?$. Have students create an equation for this form, following the same procedures listed above.

8. Have students exchange their papers with the equations on them. Have students work the equations on the paper given to them and check the answers. Repeat exchanging papers as time allows. You might need to work some problems if the answers are different from the given answer.

NEXT STEPS • Differentiate

5-Day Instructional Plan:

PS 1, page 220—Students who are on the accelerated path, to develop problem-solving skills

PM 3, page 218—Students who are on the differentiated path, to assess progress

3-Day Instructional Plan:

PS 1, page 220—All students, to develop problem-solving skills

★ = Includes Problem Solving

Objective 3
Progress-Monitoring Activities

PM 1 Apply Skills 1

Use with 5-Day or 3-Day Instructional Plan.

MATERIALS

- *Interactive Text*, pages 87–88

DIRECTIONS

1. Have students turn to *Interactive Text*, pages 87–88, Apply Skills 1.

2. Remind students of the key term: *equation*.

3. Monitor student work, and provide feedback as necessary.

   Watch for:
   - Do students group like terms before solving?
   - Do students combine like terms before dividing by the coefficient?

NEXT STEPS • Differentiate

5-Day and 3-Day Instructional Plans:

CD 3, page 210—All students, for additional concept development

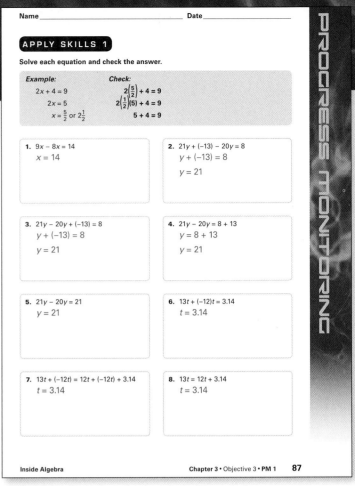

Name _____ Date _____

APPLY SKILLS 1

Solve each equation and check the answer.

Example: Check:
$2x + 4 = 9$ $2\left(\frac{5}{2}\right) + 4 = 9$
$2x = 5$ $2\left(\frac{1}{2}\right)(5) + 4 = 9$
$x = \frac{5}{2}$ or $2\frac{1}{2}$ $5 + 4 = 9$

1. $9x - 8x = 14$
$x = 14$

2. $21y + (-13) - 20y = 8$
$y + (-13) = 8$
$y = 21$

3. $21y - 20y + (-13) = 8$
$y + (-13) = 8$
$y = 21$

4. $21y - 20y = 8 + 13$
$y = 8 + 13$
$y = 21$

5. $21y - 20y = 21$
$y = 21$

6. $13t + (-12)t = 3.14$
$t = 3.14$

7. $13t + (-12t) = 12t + (-12t) + 3.14$
$t = 3.14$

8. $13t = 12t + 3.14$
$t = 3.14$

Inside Algebra   Chapter 3 • Objective 3 • PM 1   87

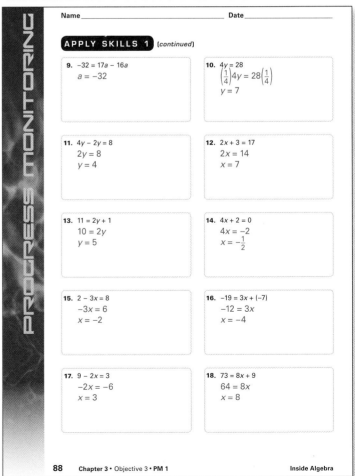

Name _____ Date _____

APPLY SKILLS 1 *(continued)*

9. $-32 = 17a - 16a$
$a = -32$

10. $4y = 28$
$\left(\frac{1}{4}\right)4y = 28\left(\frac{1}{4}\right)$
$y = 7$

11. $4y - 2y = 8$
$2y = 8$
$y = 4$

12. $2x + 3 = 17$
$2x = 14$
$x = 7$

13. $11 = 2y + 1$
$10 = 2y$
$y = 5$

14. $4x + 2 = 0$
$4x = -2$
$x = -\frac{1}{2}$

15. $2 - 3x = 8$
$-3x = 6$
$x = -2$

16. $-19 = 3x + (-7)$
$-12 = 3x$
$x = -4$

17. $9 - 2x = 3$
$-2x = -6$
$x = 3$

18. $73 = 8x + 9$
$64 = 8x$
$x = 8$

88   Chapter 3 • Objective 3 • PM 1   Inside Algebra

Progress-Monitoring Activities

PM 2 Apply Skills 2

Use with 5-Day or 3-Day Instructional Plan.

MATERIALS

- *Interactive Text*, page 89

DIRECTIONS

1. Have students turn to *Interactive Text*, page 89, Apply Skills 2.

2. Remind students of the key term: *equation*.

3. Monitor student work, and provide feedback as necessary.

   Watch for:
   - Do students see that Columns 1, 2, and 3 contain different forms of the same problem?
   - Do students recognize that they get the same solution to the problem in each column?

NEXT STEPS • Differentiate

👥 5-Day Instructional Plan:

PM 4, page 219—Students who finish the activity early, to assess progress

PA 3, page 215—Students who need additional practice

3-Day Instructional Plan:

PM 3, page 218—All students, to assess progress

Name_____ Date_____

APPLY SKILLS 2

Solve the equations in each row. Check your answers. Once you see a relationship between columns, state what the relationship is. You can shortcut the activity by solving only the equations in the right-hand column.

	Column 1	Column 2	Column 3	Solutions
1.	$5n - 9 = 71$	$5n = 71 + 9$	$5n = 80$	$n = 16$
2.	$4d + 9 = -3$	$4d = -3 - 9$	$4d = -12$	$d = -3$
3.	$3y - 4 = 14$	$3y = 14 + 4$	$3y = 18$	$y = 6$
4.	$2x - 1 = 11$	$2x = 12$	$\frac{1}{2}(2x) = \frac{1}{2}(12)$	$x = 6$
5.	$3p + 8 = -16$	$3p = -24$	$\frac{1}{3}(3p) = \frac{1}{3}(-24)$	$p = -8$
6.	$-2x + 5 = 19$	$-2x = 14$	$\left(-\frac{1}{2}\right)(-2x) = \left(-\frac{1}{2}\right)(14)$	$x = -7$
7.	$5n = 80$	$\frac{1}{5}(5n) = \frac{1}{5}(80)$		$n = 16$
8.	$\frac{x}{2} = 15$	$2\left(\frac{x}{2}\right) = 2(15)$		$x = 30$
9.	$\frac{1}{7}y = -3$	$7\left(\frac{1}{7}y\right) = (7)(-3)$		$y = -21$
10.	$\frac{a}{8} = \frac{3}{4}$	$8\left(\frac{a}{8}\right) = 8\left(\frac{3}{4}\right)$		$a = 6$
11.	$\frac{2+m}{7} = -3$	$7\left(\frac{2+m}{7}\right) = (7)(-3)$	$2 + m = -21$	$m = -23$
12.	$-\frac{2}{3}(2y + 4) = 8$	$-\frac{3}{2}\left(-\frac{2}{3}\right)(2y + 4) = \left(-\frac{3}{2}\right)8$	$2y + 4 = -12$	$y = -8$
13.	$7 = \frac{15 + 9x}{6}$	$(6)(7) = 6\left(\frac{15 + 9x}{6}\right)$	$42 = 15 + 9x$	$x = 3$

Inside Algebra | Chapter 3 • Objective 3 • PM 2 | **89**

Objective 3
Progress-Monitoring Activities

PM 3 Apply Skills 3

Use with 5-Day or 3-Day Instructional Plan.

MATERIALS

• *Interactive Text*, pages 90–91

DIRECTIONS

1. Have students turn to *Interactive Text*, pages 90–91, Apply Skills 3.

2. Remind students of the key term: *equation*.

3. Monitor student work, and provide feedback as necessary.

   Watch for:
   • Do students isolate the variable on one side of the equal sign and combine like terms?

   • Do students recognize when a problem has no solution?

NEXT STEPS • Differentiate

5-Day Instructional Plan:
Objective 3 Posttest, page 223—All students

3-Day Instructional Plan:
PA 3, page 215—Students who are on the accelerated path, for additional practice and problem solving

Objective 3 Posttest, page 223—Students who are on the differentiated path

---

Name _____ Date _____

APPLY SKILLS 3

Solve each equation and check the answer.

Example:

$$7x - 3 = 4x + 15$$
$$7x - 4x - 3 = 4x - 4x + 15$$
$$3x - 3 + 3 = 15 + 3$$
$$3x = 18$$
$$x = 6$$

Check:
$$7(6) - 3 = 4(6) + 15$$
$$42 - 3 = 24 + 15$$
$$39 = 39$$

1. $2x - 9 = 3 - x$
$2x - 9 + 9 = 3 - x + 9$
$2x + x = 12 - x + x$
$3x = 12$
$x = 4$

2. $4x + 5 = 2x + 7$
$4x + 5 - 2x = 2x + 7 - 2x$
$2x + 5 - 5 = 7 - 5$
$2x = 2$
$x = 1$

3. $4x + 12 = x + 3$
$4x + 12 - x = x + 3 - x$
$3x + 12 - 12 = 3 - 12$
$3x = -9$
$x = -3$

4. $2(x - 5) = 12$
$2x - 10 + 10 = 12 + 10$
$2x = 22$
$x = 11$

5. $24 = 4(y - 3)$
$24 + 12 = 4y - 12 + 12$
$36 = 4y$
$y = 9$

6. $\frac{1}{2}(28) = 2(3 + 2n)$
$14 - 6 = 6 + 4n - 6$
$8 = 4n$
$n = 2$

7. $7x + 4 = 9x + 24 - 2x$
$7x + 4 - 7x = 7x + 24 - 7x$
$4 = 24$
no solution

8. $3y + 9 = 4y + 15$
$3y + 9 - 3y = 4y + 15 - 3y$
$9 - 15 = y + 15 - 15$
$y = -6$

90   Chapter 3 • Objective 3 • PM 3   Inside Algebra

Name _____ Date _____

APPLY SKILLS 3 (continued)

9. $4x + 1 = 7x - 17$
$4x + 1 - 4x = 7x - 17 - 4x$
$1 + 17 = 3x - 17 + 17$
$18 = 3x$
$x = 6$

10. $-6x + 9 = -4x - 3$
$-6x + 9 + 6x = -4x - 3 + 6x$
$9 + 3 = 2x - 3 + 3$
$12 = 2x$
$x = 6$

11. $-3y - 8 = -5y + 12$
$-3y - 8 + 5y = -5y + 12 + 5y$
$2y - 8 + 8 = 12 + 8$
$2y = 20$
$y = 10$

12. $t - 7 = 3\frac{1}{2} + 2t$
$t - 7 - t = 3\frac{1}{2} + 2t - t$
$-7 - 3\frac{1}{2} = 3\frac{1}{2} + t - 3\frac{1}{2}$
$t = -10\frac{1}{2}$, or $-\frac{21}{2}$

13. $2x - 20 = 20$
$2x - 20 + 20 = 20 + 20$
$2x = 40$
$x = 20$

14. $3x + 5 = -7$
$3x + 5 - 5 = -7 - 5$
$3x = -12$
$x = -4$

15. $4x + 8 = 3x$
$4x + 8 - 4x = 3x - 4x$
$8 = -x$
$x = -8$

16. $7x = -2x + 18$
$7x + 2x = -2x + 18 + 2x$
$9x = 18$
$x = 2$

17. $-3x + 24 = 2x - 1$
$-3x + 24 + 3x = 2x - 1 + 3x$
$24 + 1 = 5x - 1 + 1$
$25 = 5x$
$x = 5$

18. $5(m - 5) = 45$
$5m - 25 + 25 = 45 + 25$
$5m = 70$
$m = 14$

Inside Algebra   Chapter 3 • Objective 3 • PM 3   91

Progress-Monitoring Activities

PM 4 Apply Skills 4

Use with 5-Day or 3-Day Instructional Plan.

MATERIALS

- *Interactive Text*, pages 92–93

DIRECTIONS

1. Have students turn to *Interactive Text*, pages 92–93, Apply Skills 4.

2. Remind students of the key term: *equation*.

3. Monitor student work, and provide feedback as necessary.

    Watch for:
    - Do students isolate the variable on one side of the equal sign and combine like terms?
    - Do students recognize when any real value is a solution to the problem?

NEXT STEPS • Differentiate

5-Day Instructional Plan:
PA 3, page 215—All students, for additional practice and problem solving

3-Day Instructional Plan:
PS 2, page 221—All students, to develop problem-solving skills

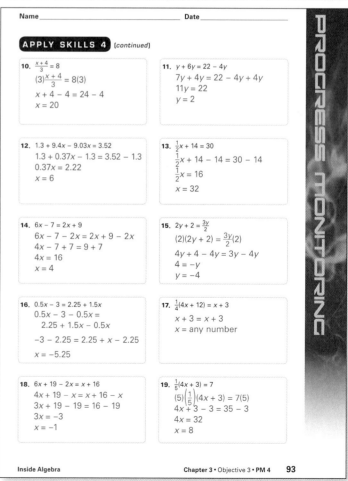

Problem-Solving Activities

★ PS 1 Finding the Number

Use with 5-Day or 3-Day Instructional Plan. In this activity, students solve more complex verbal algebraic expressions.

MATERIALS

- *Interactive Text*, page 94

DIRECTIONS

1. Review the following term with students:

   equation A statement that two quantities or mathematical expressions are equal

2. Tell students that in this activity, they will write equations given in verbal form.

3. Tell students to work individually on this assignment.

4. Have students turn to *Interactive Text*, page 94, Find the Number, and solve the problems.

5. Note whether students consistently use a variable to represent an unknown. When the same unknown is referred to several times in one sentence, it must be represented by the same variable each time.

NEXT STEPS • Differentiate

5-Day Instructional Plan:
Objective 3 Posttest, page 223—All students

3-Day Instructional Plan:
PM 4, page 219—All students, to assess progress

Name _____ Date _____

PROBLEM SOLVING

FIND THE NUMBER

Write an equation to represent each stated problem.
Solve the equation and check your solution.

WORK SPACE

1. A number decreased by twelve is twice the opposite of ten. Find the number.

   $n - 12 = 12(-10)$ _____ $n = -8$

2. The sum of two numbers is three times negative seven. If one of the numbers is negative twenty-four, what is the other number?

   $-24 + n = 3(-7)$ _____ $n = 3$

3. Two times the number forty-one added to twice another number is thirty-four. Find the other number.

   $2(41) + 2n = 34$ _____ $n = -24$

4. Negative six times a number is negative forty-eight. What is that number?

   $-6n = -48$ _____ $n = 8$

5. Three-fourths of a number added to fourteen is twenty-three. Find that number.

   $14 + \frac{3}{4}n = 23$ _____ $n = 12$

6. What is a number that when multiplied by three and decreased by twice itself equals fifty?

   $3n - 2n = 50$ _____ $n = 50$

7. If two and one-fourth of a number is the sum of negative four added to the opposite of one-half, what is the number?

   $2\frac{1}{4}n = -\frac{1}{2} + -4$ _____ $n = -2$

8. Four times a number divided by three is five more than that number divided by two. Find the value of that number.

   $\frac{4n}{3} = \frac{n}{2} + 5$ _____ $n = 6$

9. One-half added to three times a number is equal to one-half of the sum of seven added to eight times the number. What is that number?

   $3n + \frac{1}{2} = \frac{1}{2}(8n + 7)$ _____ $n = -3$

Work Space:

1. $n - 12 = 2(-10)$
   $n - 12 + 12 = -20 + 12$

2. $-24 + n = 3(-7)$
   $-24 + n + 24 = -21 + 24$

3. $2(41) + 2n = 34$
   $82 + 2n - 82 = 34 - 82$
   $\frac{1}{2}(2n) = (-48)\frac{1}{2}$

5. $14 + \frac{3}{4}n = 23$
   $14 + \frac{3}{4}n - 14 = 23 - 14$
   $\left(\frac{4}{3}\right)\frac{3}{4}n = 9\left(\frac{4}{3}\right)$

7. $2\frac{1}{4}n = -\frac{1}{2} + -4$
   $\frac{9}{4}n = -\frac{9}{2}$
   $\left(\frac{4}{9}\right)\frac{9}{4}n = -\frac{9}{2}\left(\frac{4}{9}\right)$

8. $\frac{4n}{3} = \frac{n}{2} + 5$
   $\frac{8n}{6} - \frac{3n}{6} = 5$

9. $3n + \frac{1}{2} = \frac{1}{2}(8n + 7)$
   $3n + \frac{1}{2} = 4n + 3.5$
   $3n + \frac{1}{2} - 3n =$
   $4n + 3.5 - 3n$
   $\frac{1}{2} - 3.5 = n + 3.5 - 3.5$

★ = Includes Problem Solving

Problem-Solving Activities

★ PS 2 Creating a Problem

Use with 3-Day Instructional Plan. In this activity, students develop number sense by finding possible values for problems with multiple solutions.

DIRECTIONS

1. Review the following term with students:

   equation A statement that two quantities or mathematical expressions are equal

2. Write the equation $ax + b = 12$ on the board or overhead. Ask the class to find values for a, b, and x so the sentence is true. Allow time for the class to work out solutions. $a \neq 0$, $b \neq 0$, $x \neq 0$

3. Group students into pairs. Have partners share their problems and check the answers.

   Ask:

   - How do you find out if the numbers that were chosen work? Substitute your solutions for the variables.

   - Can there be different answers? yes

   - How many different answers can there be? An infinite number

4. Make a list of some of the possible solutions.

a	b	x
3	3	3
2	2	5
1	8	4
-2	2	-5

5. Write the equation $ax + b = cx + d$ on the board or overhead. Ask students, in their pairs, to find values for a, x, b, c, and d that make the sentence true. Have the pairs try to find three different sets of numbers that make the sentence true.

a	b	c	d	x
3	-6	2	-2	4
2	8	3	11	-3
4	-2	3	-1	1

NEXT STEPS • Differentiate

3-Day Instructional Plan:
Objective 3 Posttest, page 223—All students

★ = Includes Problem Solving

This page intentionally left blank

Objective 3 Posttest

Discuss with students the key concepts in Objective 3. Following the discussion, administer the Objective 3 Posttest to all students.

Using the Results

• Score the posttest and update the class record card.

• Provide reinforcement for students who do not demonstrate mastery of the concepts through individual or small-group reteaching of key concepts.

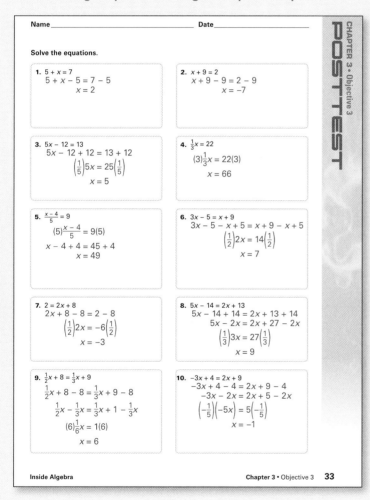

Name_____ Date_____

CHAPTER 3 • Objective 3
POSTTEST

Solve the equations.

1. $5 + x = 7$
$5 + x - 5 = 7 - 5$
$x = 2$

2. $x + 9 = 2$
$x + 9 - 9 = 2 - 9$
$x = -7$

3. $5x - 12 = 13$
$5x - 12 + 12 = 13 + 12$
$\left(\frac{1}{5}\right)5x = 25\left(\frac{1}{5}\right)$
$x = 5$

4. $\frac{1}{3}x = 22$
$(3)\frac{1}{3}x = 22(3)$
$x = 66$

5. $\frac{x-4}{5} = 9$
$(5)\frac{x-4}{5} = 9(5)$
$x - 4 + 4 = 45 + 4$
$x = 49$

6. $3x - 5 = x + 9$
$3x - 5 - x + 5 = x + 9 - x + 5$
$\left(\frac{1}{2}\right)2x = 14\left(\frac{1}{2}\right)$
$x = 7$

7. $2 = 2x + 8$
$2x + 8 - 8 = 2 - 8$
$\left(\frac{1}{2}\right)2x = -6\left(\frac{1}{2}\right)$
$x = -3$

8. $5x - 14 = 2x + 13$
$5x - 14 + 14 = 2x + 13 + 14$
$5x - 2x = 2x + 27 - 2x$
$\left(\frac{1}{3}\right)3x = 27\left(\frac{1}{3}\right)$
$x = 9$

9. $\frac{1}{2}x + 8 = \frac{1}{3}x + 9$
$\frac{1}{2}x + 8 - 8 = \frac{1}{3}x + 9 - 8$
$\frac{1}{2}x - \frac{1}{3}x = \frac{1}{3}x + 1 - \frac{1}{3}x$
$(6)\frac{1}{6}x = 1(6)$
$x = 6$

10. $-3x + 4 = 2x + 9$
$-3x + 4 - 4 = 2x + 9 - 4$
$-3x - 2x = 2x + 5 - 2x$
$\left(-\frac{1}{5}\right)(-5x) = 5\left(-\frac{1}{5}\right)$
$x = -1$

Inside Algebra   Chapter 3 • Objective 3   **33**

Objective 4
Solve problems that can be represented as equations.

Objective 4 Pretest

Students complete the Objective 4 Pretest on the same day as the Objective 3 Posttest.

Using the Results

- Score the pretest and update the class record card.

- If the majority of students do not demonstrate mastery of the concepts, use the 4-Day Instructional Plan for Objective 4.

- If the majority of students demonstrate mastery of the concepts, use the 3-Day Instructional Plan for Objective 4.

Name _____ Date _____

CHAPTER 3 • Objective 4
PRETEST

Find the solution to each problem.

1. Five times a number is 375. What is the number?

   75

2. One hundred twenty students are going on the New York field trip. This number represents one-third of the junior class. How many students are in the junior class?

   360 students

3. The sum of three consecutive integers is 171. What are the integers?

   The numbers are 56, 57, and 58.

4. The perimeter of a rectangle is 408 inches. If the length of one side is 70 inches, what is the measure of the other side? ($P = 2l + 2w$)

   134 inches

5. The three angles of a triangle add to a sum of 180°. If a right triangle has an angle of 63°, what is the measure of the third angle?

   27°

WORK SPACE

1. $5n = 375$
   $n = 75$

2. $\frac{1}{3}n = 120$
   $n = 360$

3. $n + (n + 1) + (n + 2) = 171$
   $3n + 3 = 171$
   $3n = 168$
   $n = 56$

4. $408 = 2(70) + 2w$
   $408 = 140 + 2w$
   $408 - 140 = 140 + 2w - 140$
   $268 = 2w$
   $134 = w$

5. $90° + 63° + x = 180°$
   $153° + x = 180°$
   $153° + x - 153° = 180° - 153°$
   $x = 27°$

34   Chapter 3 • Objective 4   Inside Algebra

Goals and Activities

Objective 4 Goals

The following activities, when used with the instructional plans on pages 226 and 227, enable students to solve these problems:

- Bill has $32 in his savings account. If he saves $7.50 per week toward a new $113 skateboard, how long will it take him to purchase the new skateboard?
  It will take 11 weeks.

- In an industrial setting with three wind towers, the first wind tower is 20 feet taller than the second, and the second is twice the height of the third. If the third tower is 97 feet high, what are the heights of the first and second towers?
  The first tower is 214 feet high, and the second tower is 194 feet high.

Objective 4 Activities

Concept Development Activities	
★**CD 1** Writing and Solving Classroom Problems, page 228	★**CD 2** Solving Problems Involving Geometry, page 229

Practice Activities	
★**PA 1** Writing Problems From Equations, page 231	**PA 2** Writing and Solving Number Theory Sentences, page 232

Progress-Monitoring Activities	
PM 1 Apply Skills 1, page 233	**PM 2** Apply Skills 2, page 234

★Problem-Solving Activity
★**PS 1** Writing Equivalent Equations and Finding Their Solutions, page 235

Ongoing Assessment
Posttest Objective 4, page 237
Pretest Objective 5, page 238

CD = Concept Development   PM = Progress Monitoring   PS = Problem Solving
PA = Practice Activity   ★ = Includes Problem Solving

4-Day Instructional Plan

Use the 4-Day Instructional Plan when pretest results indicate that students would benefit from a slower pace. This plan is used when the majority of students need more time or did not demonstrate mastery on the pretest.

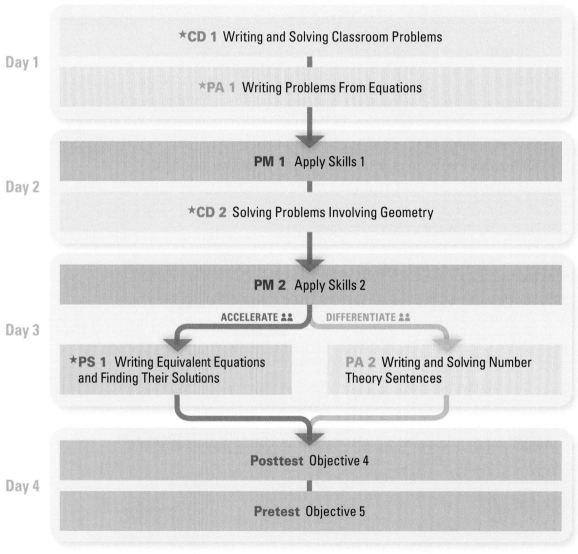

Day 1
★CD 1 Writing and Solving Classroom Problems
★PA 1 Writing Problems From Equations

Day 2
PM 1 Apply Skills 1
★CD 2 Solving Problems Involving Geometry

Day 3
PM 2 Apply Skills 2
ACCELERATE DIFFERENTIATE
★PS 1 Writing Equivalent Equations and Finding Their Solutions
PA 2 Writing and Solving Number Theory Sentences

Day 4
Posttest Objective 4
Pretest Objective 5

CD = Concept Development   PM = Progress Monitoring   PS = Problem Solving
PA = Practice Activity   ★ = Includes Problem Solving

3-Day Instructional Plan

Use the 3-Day Instructional Plan when pretest results indicate that students can move through the activities at a faster pace. This plan is ideal when the majority of students demonstrate mastery on the pretest.

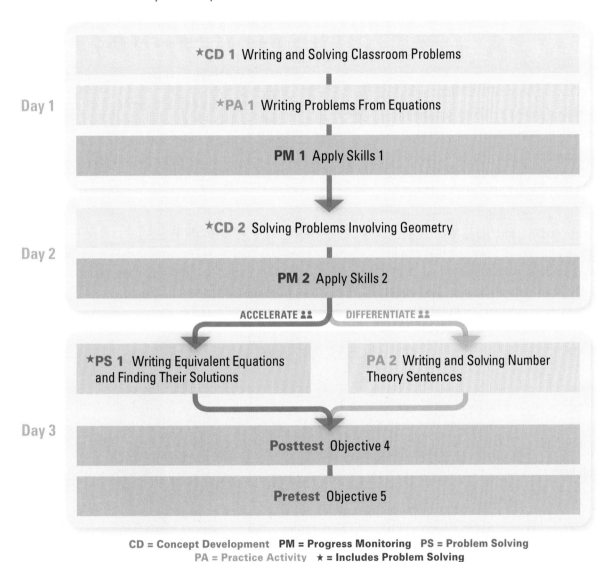

Day 1

★**CD 1** Writing and Solving Classroom Problems

★**PA 1** Writing Problems From Equations

PM 1 Apply Skills 1

Day 2

★**CD 2** Solving Problems Involving Geometry

PM 2 Apply Skills 2

ACCELERATE 👥   DIFFERENTIATE 👥

★**PS 1** Writing Equivalent Equations and Finding Their Solutions

PA 2 Writing and Solving Number Theory Sentences

Day 3

Posttest Objective 4

Pretest Objective 5

CD = Concept Development   PM = Progress Monitoring   PS = Problem Solving
PA = Practice Activity   ★ = Includes Problem Solving

★ CD 1 Writing and Solving Classroom Problems

Use with 4-Day or 3-Day Instructional Plan. In this activity, students describe real-life situations using algebraic sentences and translate these sentences into mathematical equations.

DIRECTIONS

1. Review the following term with students:

   equation A statement that two quantities or mathematical expressions are equal

2. Form an even number of groups. In this way, the problems each group creates can be exchanged with another group for solution and verification.

3. Have each group select a student to write down the problems the group generates. Tell students the groups should generate problems that can be expressed as mathematical equations and can be solved using the Principles of Equality. Point out that the challenge is to develop the greatest number of high-quality algebraic sentences that can be represented as mathematical equations that use only one variable.

4. Give students an idea of what is expected of them. Share examples that relate to the class, and work with them to develop word sentences that can be written as equations.

   Sample problems:

   > If there are 31 students in the classroom, and 26 are not bilingual, then how many are bilingual? $x + 26 = 31$, $x = 5$ There are 5 bilingual students.
   >
   > Ed is 4 inches taller than Janelle. If Janelle is 5 feet, 2 inches tall, how tall is Ed? $e - 4" = 5'2"$, $e = 5'6"$ Ed is 5 feet, 6 inches.
   >
   > A classroom has 7 rows of desks, and 5 of these rows have exactly 5 desks each. If the room contains 32 desks, how many desks are in the other two rows? $5(5) + d = 32$; or $32 - 5(5) = d$, $d = 7$ There are 7 desks in the last two rows.

5. Point out to students that the critical attribute of this activity is to have them check each answer to see that it correctly defines the variable condition.

6. Extend this activity to school or home situations. Direct each student to come to class with a sentence that describes a condition at home. The class can solve the problems together, or student pairs can exchange and solve problems.

   Sample problem:

   > There are 9 people living in my house. There are twice as many children as adults. How many adults live in my house? $9 = a + 2a$, $a = 3$ There are 3 adults.

NEXT STEPS • Differentiate

4-Day and 3-Day Instructional Plans:
PA 1, page 231—All students, for additional practice and problem solving

★ = Includes Problem Solving

Objective 4
Concept Development Activities

★ CD 2 Solving Problems Involving Geometry

Use with 4-Day or 3-Day Instructional Plan. In this activity, students remember that the angles of a triangle sum to 180°.

MATERIALS

- *Interactive Text*, page 95
- Paper from which to cut triangles
- Scissors
- Straightedge

DIRECTIONS

1. Review the following term with students:

   equation A statement that two quantities or mathematical expressions are equal

2. Tell students that in this activity, they will discover the relationship of the angles of a triangle. Tell students we use this relationship to solve word problems by creating and solving an equation.

3. Decide whether students will work individually or in small groups, and put students into groups, if applicable. Have students turn to *Interactive Text*, page 95, Problems Involving Geometry.

4. Review the different types of triangles in the *Interactive Text*. Have students discuss the properties of each triangle.

   Listen for:
   - Every triangle has three angles, and the angles add up to 180°.
   - An **isosceles triangle** has two sides of equal length. The angles opposite the equal sides are also equal.
   - An **obtuse triangle** has one angle that is obtuse, or greater than 90°. The longest side is always opposite the obtuse angle.
   - A **right triangle** is a triangle with one right angle, an angle that is exactly 90°.

★ = Includes Problem Solving

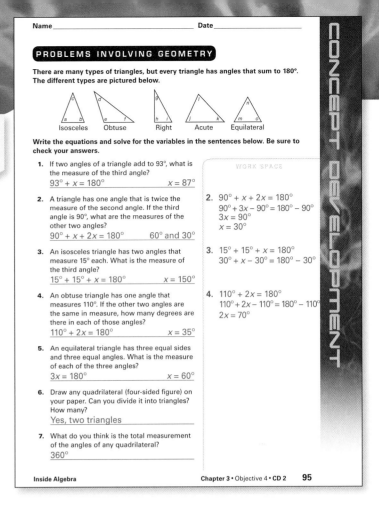

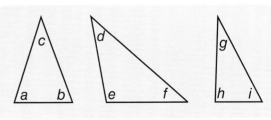

- An **acute triangle** is a triangle whose angles are all acute, or less than 90°.
- An **equilateral triangle** has all three sides equal in length. Its three angles are also equal and they are each 60°.

5. After the discussion, direct students to draw at least three triangles of any size and to label the angles sequentially from *a* to *i*.

   Example:

6. Have students choose one of their triangles, cut off its three angles, and arrange them on the straightedge. Students should be able to make a supposition that the three angles create a straight line, or add to 180°. Have them do the same with the other two triangles.

7. Have students complete Problems 1–5 in the *Interactive Text*.

8. Discuss the concept of the perimeters of triangles and quadrilaterals. Review the properties of the square, rectangle, and other quadrilaterals.

Listen for:

- Perimeter is the distance around a shape. It is found by adding all the sides.

- Quadrilaterals are shapes with four sides and four angles.

- Squares are four-sided figures, in which all four sides are equal in length and all four angles are 90°.

- Rectangles are four-sided figures, in which all four angles are 90° and opposite sides are equal in length.

9. Have students complete Problems 6–7 in the *Interactive Text*. Make sure students understand every quadrilateral is composed of two triangular shapes by connecting opposite vertices, and the sum of the angles of a quadrilateral is $2 \cdot 180 = 360°$.

NEXT STEPS • Differentiate

4-Day and 3-Day Instructional Plans:
PM 2, page 234—All students, to assess progress

Practice Activities

Writing Problems From Equations

Use with 4-Day or 3-Day Instructional Plan. In this activity, students write mathematical equations as verbal expressions.

DIRECTIONS

1. Review the following term with students:

   equation A statement that two quantities or mathematical expressions are equal

2. Write **$3x = 45$** on the board or overhead transparency. Discuss examples of sentences that represent this equation. Emphasize that you can use many sentences to represent any given equation.

   Examples:

   Madison's father is three times as old as she is. How old is Madison if her father is 45?

   If an integer is multiplied by three, the product is forty-five. What is the integer?

3. Write **$4y + 2 = 14$** on the board or overhead transparency. Tell students to come up with sentences that represent this equation. Ask students to read their sentences aloud to illustrate different ways of representing the same equation.

   Examples:

   Fourteen is two more than four times a number. What is the number?

   There are two more oranges than four times the number of apples. There are fourteen oranges. How many apples are there?

4. Divide students into small groups of three to four students.

5. Have each student in the group write a simple equation and share it with each other. Tell the other students to write a word sentence that represents that equation. Explain that as a group, students analyze each sentence to see that it satisfies the conditions of the equation. Give more example equations to students if they need help getting started.

Sample problems:

$2x - 7 = 5$ Five is seven less than twice a number.

$\frac{n}{3} = -2$ One-third of a number is negative two.

$j + (j + 2) = 12$ Twelve is the sum of two consecutive odd numbers. What is the smaller number?

$\frac{3}{4}y = 18$ Three multiplied by one-fourth of a number is 18. What is the number?

NEXT STEPS • Differentiate

4-Day and 3-Day Instructional Plans:
PM 1, page 233—All students, to assess progress

★ = Includes Problem Solving

Practice Activities

PA 2 Writing and Solving Number Theory Sentences

Use with 4-Day or 3-Day Instructional Plan. In this activity, students recall the concept of sets and make statements about consecutive integers.

MATERIALS

- *Interactive Text*, page 96

DIRECTIONS

1. Review the following term with students:

   equation A statement that two quantities or mathematical expressions are equal

2. Tell students that in this activity, they will generate equations from sentences about even or odd sequential integers. Explain that this activity will help them understand and solve equations from number theory sentences.

3. Review what is meant by *the set of integers*. Write **{…, –2, –1, 0, 1, 2, 3, …}** on the board or an overhead transparency. Have students analyze statements related to the set of integers and make conclusions about them.

   Sample problems:

   If *n* represents one of these integers, how would you express the next sequential integer? *n* + 1

   If *n* represents any integer, write an expression for an even integer. 2*n*

   If *n* is any integer in this set, what is an expression for any odd integer? (2*n* + 1) or (2*n* – 1)

   Write the set of four consecutive integers if the first one is *n*. *n*, *n* + 1, *n* + 2, *n* + 3

   How would you write the set of three consecutive even integers if *n* is even? *n*, *n* + 2, *n* + 4

   How would you express the set of an odd integer *n* and the next three consecutive odd integers? *n*, *n* + 2, *n* + 4, *n* + 6

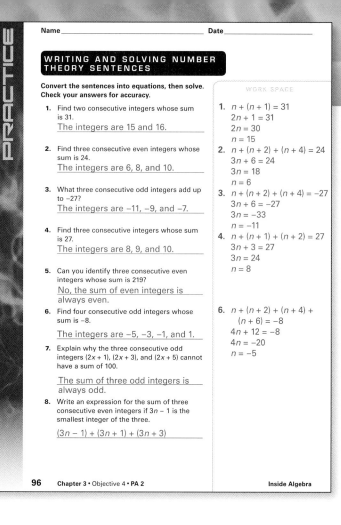

4. Review what is meant by *the set of even integers*. Write the set of even integers on the board or an overhead transparency. Have students analyze statements related to the set of even integers and make conclusions about them.

5. Review what is meant by *the set of odd integers*. Write the set of odd integers on the board or an overhead transparency. Have students analyze statements related to the set of odd integers and make conclusions about them.

6. Have students turn to *Interactive Text*, page 96, Writing and Solving Number Theory Sentences. Have students work in groups to convert the eight sentences into equations, then solve them. They should check their answers for accuracy.

NEXT STEPS • Differentiate

4-Day and 3-Day Instructional Plans:
Objective 4 Posttest, page 237—All students

Progress-Monitoring Activities

PM 1 Apply Skills 1

Use with 4-Day or 3-Day Instructional Plan.

MATERIALS

- *Interactive Text*, pages 97–98

DIRECTIONS

1. Have students turn to *Interactive Text*, pages 97–98, Apply Skills 1.

2. Remind students of the key term: *equation*.

3. Monitor student work, and provide feedback as necessary.

   Watch for:
   - Do students correctly interpret word problems as algebraic equations?
   - Do students recognize key terms that help them interpret the problem?
   - Do students recognize that a variable stands in for some unknown number?

NEXT STEPS • Differentiate

4-Day and 3-Day Instructional Plans:
CD 2, page 229—All students, for additional concept development and problem solving

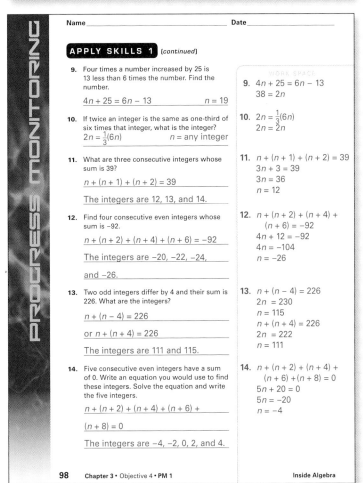

Name _____ **Date** _____

APPLY SKILLS 1

Write equations for each of the sentences, then answer the questions by solving the equations. Check your work.

WORK SPACE

1. The sum of twice a number and 32 is 78. What is the number?

   $2n + 32 = 78$ _____ $n = 23$

   1. $2n + 32 = 78$
      $2n = 46$

2. Two times a number added to 32 is 78. What is the number?

   $32 + 2n = 78$ _____ $n = 23$

   2. $32 + 2n = 78$
      $2n = 46$

3. Taking three times a given number, dividing it by two, and adding that result to eight gives the same result as multiplying the number by four and then subtracting the result from 32. What is the number?

   $8 + \frac{3n}{2} = 32 - 4n$ _____ $n = 4\frac{4}{11}$

   3. $8 + \frac{3n}{2} = 32 - 4n$
      $3n + 16 = 64 - 8n$
      $11n = 48$

4. The decimal 1.4 subtracted from a number is zero. What is the number?

   $n - 1.4 = 0$ _____ $n = 1.4$

   4. $n - 1.4 = 0$

5. An amount of money less $\frac{3}{4}$ of a dollar leaves $4\frac{1}{4}$. What was the original amount of money?

   $n - \frac{3}{4} = \$4\frac{1}{4}$ _____ $n = \$5.00$

   5. $n - \frac{3}{4} = 4\frac{1}{4}$

6. Find a number that is 96 greater than its opposite.

   $n - 96 = -n$ _____ $n = 48$

   6. $n - 96 = -n$
      $2n = 96$

7. Find a number whose product with 9 is the same as its sum with 56.

   $9n = n + 56$ _____ $n = 7$

   7. $9n = n + 56$
      $8n = 56$

8. Find a number that is 68 greater than three times its opposite.

   $n - 68 = -3n$ _____ $n = 17$

   8. $n - 68 = -3n$
      $4n = 68$

Inside Algebra   Chapter 3 • Objective 4 • PM 1   97

Name _____ **Date** _____

APPLY SKILLS 1 *(continued)*

9. Four times a number increased by 25 is 13 less than 6 times the number. Find the number.

   $4n + 25 = 6n - 13$ _____ $n = 19$

   9. $4n + 25 = 6n - 13$
      $38 = 2n$

10. If twice an integer is the same as one-third of six times that integer, what is the integer?

    $2n = \frac{1}{3}(6n)$ _____ $n =$ any integer

    10. $2n = \frac{1}{3}(6n)$
        $2n = 2n$

11. What are three consecutive integers whose sum is 39?

    $n + (n + 1) + (n + 2) = 39$

    The integers are 12, 13, and 14.

    11. $n + (n + 1) + (n + 2) = 39$
        $3n + 3 = 39$
        $3n = 36$
        $n = 12$

12. Find four consecutive even integers whose sum is –92.

    $n + (n + 2) + (n + 4) + (n + 6) = -92$

    The integers are –20, –22, –24, and –26.

    12. $n + (n + 2) + (n + 4) +$
        $(n + 6) = -92$
        $4n + 12 = -92$
        $4n = -104$
        $n = -26$

13. Two odd integers differ by 4 and their sum is 226. What are the integers?

    $n + (n - 4) = 226$

    or $n + (n + 4) = 226$

    The integers are 111 and 115.

    13. $n + (n - 4) = 226$
        $2n = 230$
        $n = 115$
        $n + (n + 4) = 226$
        $2n = 222$
        $n = 111$

14. Five consecutive even integers have a sum of 0. Write an equation you would use to find these integers. Solve the equation and write the five integers.

    $n + (n + 2) + (n + 4) + (n + 6) +$

    $(n + 8) = 0$

    The integers are –4, –2, 0, 2, and 4.

    14. $n + (n + 2) + (n + 4) +$
        $(n + 6) + (n + 8) = 0$
        $5n + 20 = 0$
        $5n = -20$
        $n = -4$

98   Chapter 3 • Objective 4 • PM 1   Inside Algebra

Progress-Monitoring Activities

PM 2 Apply Skills 2

Use with 4-Day or 3-Day Instructional Plan.

MATERIALS

- *Interactive Text*, pages 99–100

DIRECTIONS

1. Have students turn to *Interactive Text*, pages 99–100, Apply Skills 2.

2. Remind students of the key terms: *right triangle, obtuse triangle, acute triangle, equilateral triangle,* and *isosceles triangle.*

3. Monitor student work, and provide feedback as necessary.

   Watch for:
   - Do students correctly interpret word problems as algebraic equations?

   - Do students remember that the three angles of a triangle always add up to 180°?

   - Do students remember the difference between right, equilateral, and isosceles triangles?

NEXT STEPS • Differentiate

👥 4-Day and 3-Day Instructional Plans:

PS 1, page 235—Students who demonstrate understanding of the concept, to develop problem-solving skills

PA 2, page 232—Students who need additional practice

Name _____ Date _____

APPLY SKILLS 2

Write equations for each of the geometry sentences, then answer the questions by solving the equations. Check your work.

WORK SPACE

1. A triangle has three angles labeled A, B, and C. If ∠A measures 15° and ∠B measures 90°, what is the measure of ∠C?
   $15° + 90° + x = 180°$ $m∠C = 75°$

   1. $15° + 90° + x = 180°$
      $105° + x = 180°$
      $105° + x - 105° =$
      $180° - 105°$
      $x = 75°$

2. An isosceles triangle has two angles that measure 50°. What is the measure of the third angle?
   $2(50°) + x = 180°$ $x = 80°$

   2. $2(50°) + x = 180°$
      $100° + x = 180°$
      $100° + x - 100° =$
      $180° - 100°$

3. A right triangle has one angle that measures 52°. What are the measures of the other two angles?
   $52° + 90° + x = 180°$ $x = 38°$
   The angles are 90° and 38°.

   3. $52° + 90° + x = 180°$
      $142° + x = 180°$
      $142° + x - 142° =$
      $180° - 142°$

4. An equilateral triangle has three sides that are equal in length and three angles that are equal in measure. What is the measure of each angle of an equilateral triangle?
   $3x = 180°$ $x = 60°$

5. One angle of a triangle is three times the measure of another. If the third angle measures 80°, what are the measures of the other two angles?
   $x + 3x + 80° = 180°$ $x = 25°$
   The angles are 25° and 75°.

   5. $x + 3x + 80° = 180°$
      $4x + 80° = 180°$
      $4x + 80° - 80° =$
      $180° - 80°$
      $4x = 100°$
      $x = 25°$
      $3x = 75°$

6. An obtuse triangle is also isosceles. If the obtuse angle measures 120°, what is the measure of the other two angles?
   $120° + 2x = 180°$ $x = 30°$

   6. $120° + 2x = 180°$
      $120° + 2x - 120° =$
      $180° - 120°$
      $2x = 60°$

Name _____ Date _____

APPLY SKILLS 2 *(continued)*

Given the quadrilateral shown here, find the solution to the problems if ∠B = 60° and ∠E = 85°.

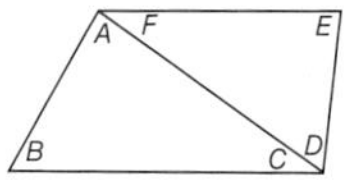

WORK SPACE

7. If ∠C measures 25°, what is the measure of ∠A?
   $∠A = 95°$

   7. $25° + 60° + ∠A = 180°$
      $85° + ∠A = 180°$

8. Find the measure of ∠D if ∠F measures 17°.
   $∠D = 78°$

   8. $17° + 85° + ∠D = 180°$
      $102° + ∠D = 180°$

9. If ∠A + ∠F = 115°, what is the sum of the measure of ∠C + ∠D?
   $∠C + ∠D = 100°$

   9. $115° + 60° + 85° +$
      $(∠C + ∠D) = 360°$
      $260° + ∠C + ∠D = 360°$

10. If ∠A + ∠F = 120° and ∠C = 40°, what is the measure of ∠D?
    $∠D = 55°$

    10. $120° + 60° + 40° + ∠D +$
        $85° = 360°$
        $305° + ∠D = 360°$

Problem-Solving Activity

★PS 1 Writing Equivalent Equations and Finding Their Solutions

Use with 4-Day or 3-Day Instructional Plan. In this activity, students solve algebra problems using several methods.

MATERIALS

- *Interactive Text*, pages 101–102

DIRECTIONS

1. Review the following term with students:

   equation A statement that two quantities or mathematical expressions are equal

2. Discuss the following term with students:

   equivalent Equal in value

3. Tell students that in this activity they will write word problems and demonstrate a firm understanding of them.

4. Tell students to work individually on this assignment.

5. Have students turn to *Interactive Text*, pages 101–102, Writing Equivalent Equations and Finding Their Solutions, and solve the problems.

6. Note whether students use equations to solve the algebra problems. Make sure students explain their reasoning using complete sentences.

NEXT STEPS • Differentiate

4-Day and 3-Day Instructional Plans:
Objective 4 Posttest, page 237—All students

★ = Includes Problem Solving

Name _____ Date _____

WRITING EQUIVALENT EQUATIONS AND FINDING THEIR SOLUTIONS

Answer each question using complete sentences.

1. Explain, in your own words, the steps you would take to solve the problem $\frac{2x + 4}{3} = 12$.

   Answers will vary. The solution is $x = 16$.

2. Write two equivalent equations for $\frac{2}{3}x + \frac{4}{3} = 12$ that lead to the solution of the equation.

   Answers will vary. The solution is $x = 16$.

3. Write two word sentences that are equivalent to, "The difference of a number and 14 is 38." Use the word "subtracted" in one sentence and the word "decreased" in the other.

   Answers will vary. Sample answers:

   14 subtracted from a number is 38.

   A number decreased by 14 is 38.

4. Explain how to solve $2p + 10 = 42$ if you have to undo the multiplication first.

   Answers will vary. The solution is $p = 16$.

5. Explain why undoing the multiplication first is inconvenient for solving the equation $7x - 4 = 24$.

   Answers will vary. Sample answer:

   7 does not divide evenly into 4 and 24, so dividing

   first means having to add fractions.

Name _____ Date _____

WRITING EQUIVALENT EQUATIONS AND FINDING THEIR SOLUTIONS *(continued)*

6. If 14 times a number added to 127 is the same as the difference between 13 times that number and 899, what is that number?

   $n = -1{,}026$

7. A number is decreased by 35, then that quantity is multiplied by 6, then the result is added to 87, and finally that result is divided by 3. The value of that expression is 49. Find that number.

   $n = 45$

8. You are eight years younger than your cousin Quinten. In four years you will be $\frac{2}{3}$ as old as he will be then. What are your ages now?

   Quinten is 20, and you are 12.

9. A city block is half as wide as it is long. If the distance around the block is 840 yards, what are the dimensions of the city block?

   It is 140 yards by 280 yards.

10. Your ongoing share of income for designing the Web page for a new company is $50 per week plus $0.05 per transaction. How many transactions per week must the site conduct for you to earn an average of $15 per day from this Web page, assuming a 5-day work week?

   $x = 500$ transactions per week

WORK SPACE

6. $127 + 14n = 13n - 899$
   $127 + 14n - 13n =$
   $\quad 13n - 899 - 13n$
   $127 + n - 127 =$
   $\quad -899 - 127$

7. $\frac{6(n - 35) + 87}{3} = 49$
   $6(n - 35) + 87 = 147$
   $6(n - 35) = 60$
   $n - 35 = 10$

8. $Q - 8 = \frac{2}{3}(Q + 4) - 4$
   $\frac{1}{3}Q = \frac{20}{3}$
   $Q = 20$

9. $2\left(\frac{1}{2}L\right) + 2L = 840$
   $3L = 840$
   $L = 280$

10. $\frac{\$50 + \$0.05x}{5} = \$15$
   $50 + 0.05x = 75$
   $0.05x = 25$

This page intentionally left blank

Objective 4 Posttest

Discuss with students the key concepts in Objective 4. Following the discussion, administer the Objective 4 Posttest to all students.

Using the Results

- Score the posttest and update the class record card.

- Provide reinforcement for students who do not demonstrate mastery of the concepts through individual or small-group reteaching of key concepts.

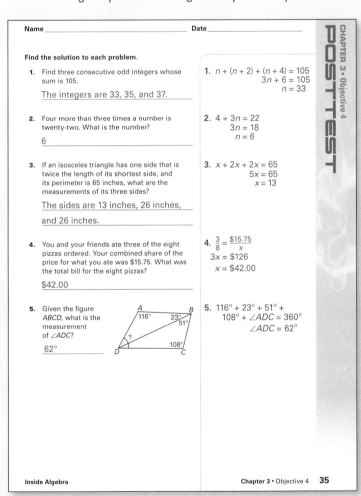

Name_____ Date_____

Find the solution to each problem.

1. Find three consecutive odd integers whose sum is 105.

    The integers are 33, 35, and 37.

2. Four more than three times a number is twenty-two. What is the number?

    6

3. If an isosceles triangle has one side that is twice the length of its shortest side, and its perimeter is 65 inches, what are the measurements of its three sides?

    The sides are 13 inches, 26 inches, and 26 inches.

4. You and your friends ate three of the eight pizzas ordered. Your combined share of the price for what you ate was $15.75. What was the total bill for the eight pizzas?

    $42.00

5. Given the figure $ABCD$, what is the measurement of $\angle ADC$?

    62°

CHAPTER 3 • Objective 4 **POSTTEST**

1. $n + (n + 2) + (n + 4) = 105$
   $3n + 6 = 105$
   $n = 33$

2. $4 + 3n = 22$
   $3n = 18$
   $n = 6$

3. $x + 2x + 2x = 65$
   $5x = 65$
   $x = 13$

4. $\dfrac{3}{8} = \dfrac{\$15.75}{x}$
   $3x = \$126$
   $x = \$42.00$

5. $116° + 23° + 51° + 108° + \angle ADC = 360°$
   $\angle ADC = 62°$

Inside Algebra

Chapter 3 • Objective 4 **35**

Objective 5 Pretest

Students complete the Objective 5 Pretest on the same day as the Objective 4 Posttest.

Using the Results

- Score the pretest and update the class record card.
- If the majority of students do not demonstrate mastery of the concepts, use the 4-Day Instructional Plan for Objective 5.
- If the majority of students demonstrate mastery of the concepts, use the 3-Day Instructional Plan for Objective 5.

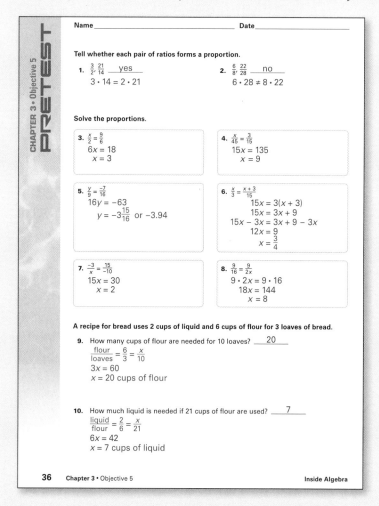

CHAPTER 3 • Objective 5 — PRETEST

Name _____ Date _____

Tell whether each pair of ratios forms a proportion.

1. $\frac{3}{2}, \frac{21}{14}$ ___yes___
$3 \cdot 14 = 2 \cdot 21$

2. $\frac{6}{8}, \frac{22}{28}$ ___no___
$6 \cdot 28 \neq 8 \cdot 22$

Solve the proportions.

3. $\frac{x}{2} = \frac{9}{6}$
$6x = 18$
$x = 3$

4. $\frac{x}{45} = \frac{3}{15}$
$15x = 135$
$x = 9$

5. $\frac{y}{9} = \frac{-7}{16}$
$16y = -63$
$y = -3\frac{15}{16}$ or -3.94

6. $\frac{x}{3} = \frac{x+3}{15}$
$15x = 3(x + 3)$
$15x = 3x + 9$
$15x - 3x = 3x + 9 - 3x$
$12x = 9$
$x = \frac{3}{4}$

7. $\frac{-3}{x} = \frac{15}{-10}$
$15x = 30$
$x = 2$

8. $\frac{9}{16} = \frac{9}{2x}$
$9 \cdot 2x = 9 \cdot 16$
$18x = 144$
$x = 8$

A recipe for bread uses 2 cups of liquid and 6 cups of flour for 3 loaves of bread.

9. How many cups of flour are needed for 10 loaves? ___20___
$\frac{flour}{loaves} = \frac{6}{3} = \frac{x}{10}$
$3x = 60$
$x = 20$ cups of flour

10. How much liquid is needed if 21 cups of flour are used? ___7___
$\frac{liquid}{flour} = \frac{2}{6} = \frac{x}{21}$
$6x = 42$
$x = 7$ cups of liquid

36   Chapter 3 • Objective 5   Inside Algebra

Objective 5 Goals

The following activities, when used with the instructional plans on pages 240 and 241, enable students to:

- Determine whether the ratios $\frac{2}{3}$ and $\frac{12}{18}$ form a proportion

  yes

- Determine whether the ratios $\frac{15}{30}$ and $\frac{1}{2}$ form a proportion

  yes

- Determine whether the ratios $\frac{15}{21}$ and $\frac{60}{105}$ form a proportion

  no

- Solve the proportion $\frac{2}{3} = \frac{8}{x}$ for x to get

  $x = 12$

- Solve the proportion $\frac{4}{w} = \frac{2}{10}$ for w to get

  $w = 20$

- Solve the proportion $\frac{x}{1.5} = \frac{2.4}{1.6}$ for x to get

  $x = 2.25$

Objective 5 Activities

Concept Development Activities

★**CD 1** Understanding Ratios and Chance, page 242	**CD 2** Solving a Proportion, page 244

Practice Activities

PA 1 Finding Equivalent Ratios to Solve Proportions, page 246	**PA 2** Playing the Proportion Game, page 249	**PA 3** Solving Recipe Proportions, page 250

Progress-Monitoring Activities

PM 1 Apply Skills 1, page 251	**PM 2** Apply Skills 2, page 252	**PM 3** Apply Skills 3, page 253

★Problem-Solving Activity

★**PS 1** Determining Body Proportions, page 254

Ongoing Assessment

Posttest Objective 5, page 255

Pretest Objective 6, page 256

CD = Concept Development   PM = Progress Monitoring   PS = Problem Solving
PA = Practice Activity   ★ = Includes Problem Solving

Instructional Plans

4-Day Instructional Plan

Use the 4-Day Instructional Plan when pretest results indicate that students would benefit from a slower pace. This plan is used when the majority of students need more time or did not demonstrate mastery on the pretest.

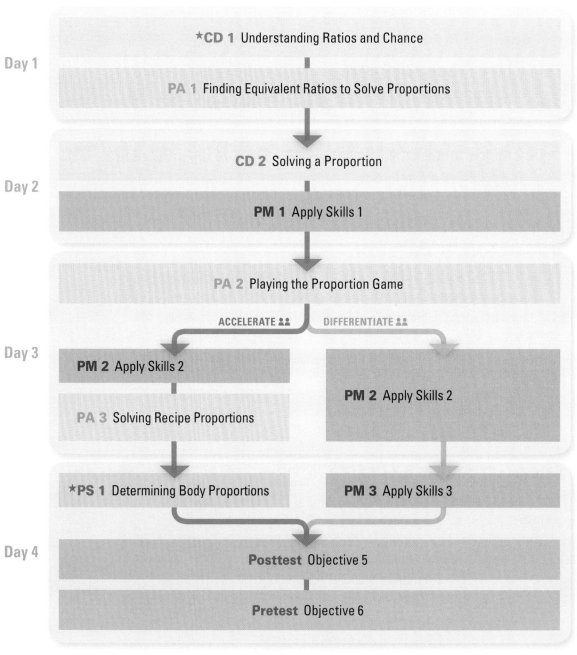

Day 1
- ★CD 1 Understanding Ratios and Chance
- PA 1 Finding Equivalent Ratios to Solve Proportions

Day 2
- CD 2 Solving a Proportion
- PM 1 Apply Skills 1

Day 3
- PA 2 Playing the Proportion Game

ACCELERATE | DIFFERENTIATE

- PM 2 Apply Skills 2
- PA 3 Solving Recipe Proportions

- PM 2 Apply Skills 2

Day 4
- ★PS 1 Determining Body Proportions
- PM 3 Apply Skills 3
- Posttest Objective 5
- Pretest Objective 6

CD = Concept Development   PM = Progress Monitoring   PS = Problem Solving
PA = Practice Activity   ★ = Includes Problem Solving

3-Day Instructional Plan

Use the 3-Day Instructional Plan when pretest results indicate that students can move through the activities at a faster pace. This plan is ideal when the majority of students demonstrate mastery on the pretest. This plan does not include all activities.

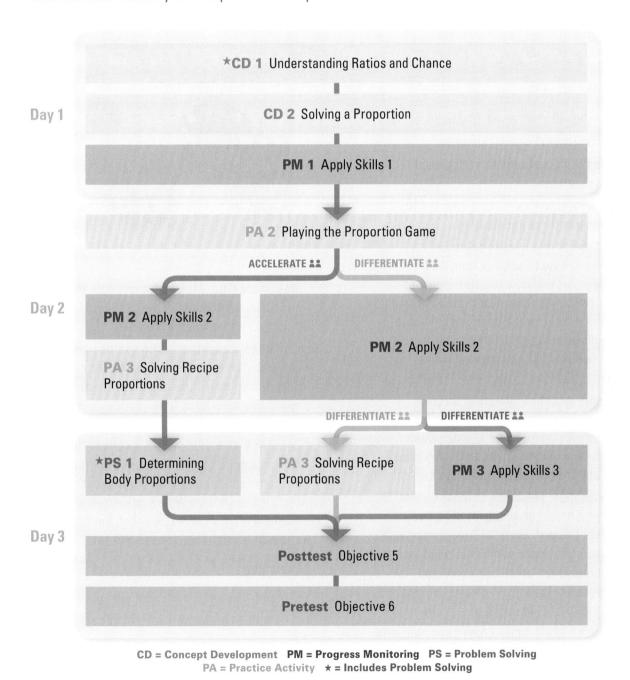

Day 1
- ★CD 1 Understanding Ratios and Chance
- CD 2 Solving a Proportion
- PM 1 Apply Skills 1

Day 2
- PA 2 Playing the Proportion Game

ACCELERATE ⚏ DIFFERENTIATE ⚏

- PM 2 Apply Skills 2
- PA 3 Solving Recipe Proportions

- PM 2 Apply Skills 2

DIFFERENTIATE ⚏ DIFFERENTIATE ⚏

- ★PS 1 Determining Body Proportions
- PA 3 Solving Recipe Proportions
- PM 3 Apply Skills 3

Day 3
- Posttest Objective 5
- Pretest Objective 6

CD = Concept Development PM = Progress Monitoring PS = Problem Solving
PA = Practice Activity ★ = Includes Problem Solving

Concept Development Activities

★ CD 1 Understanding Ratios and Chance

Use with 4-Day or 3-Day Instructional Plan. In this activity, students determine ratios using division.

MATERIALS

- Coins, dice, rolls of adding machine paper, or other objects

DIRECTIONS

1. Discuss the following terms with students:

   ratio A comparison of two numbers

   proportion An equation that states that two ratios are equal

   percent A ratio whose second term is 100; percent means parts per hundred

2. Explain to students that in developing an understanding of how to solve proportions with a missing part and how to solve problems involving percentages, they must first understand the concept of a ratio, or the comparison of two numbers by division. Approach this topic through information discovery of outcomes of events, or probability.

3. Divide students into small groups of three to four, and assign each group to a workstation. The number of workstations for this activity is determined by the number of students, the size of the groups, and the amount of materials available.

4. At each workstation, place one or more rolls of adding machine paper, or whatever object you choose to use. This activity will be illustrated with the use of adding machine paper. Ask all students to gather around one workstation while you demonstrate an example.

5. Tell students they are going to approximate how many times a roll of adding machine paper will land on its end when dropped. Point out to students that it is important to record the number of times the event was tried as well as the number of times it

was successful. Make sure students know that successful outcomes in the case of adding machine paper are those in which the roll lands on one end.

6. Explain to students that the events must be replicated as closely as possible; for example, the height from which the object is dropped should be about the same each time.

7. As you demonstrate, have students record the outcomes. Ask students to determine the ratio, or comparison of two numbers as a fraction, of successes to total attempts. Point out that ratios can also be written with a colon. Note that this example is only one experiment. Your result, although it might be close to this ratio, might differ.

Example:

Roll Dropped (Event or Attempt)	Landed on End (Successful Attempts)
~~HH~~ ~~HH~~ ~~HH~~ /	~~HH~~

In this example, the rolls were dropped from table height a total of 16 times with 5 successful outcomes (roll landed on one of its ends). $\frac{5}{16}$, or 5:16

8. Ask students to return to their own workstations and begin work. Each station should have a specific assignment.

   Examples:

   > Coins: How many times does a coin come up heads in a certain number of tosses? What is the ratio of heads to tosses? Heads to tails? Tails to tosses?

   > Dice: How many times does a specific number come up with a certain number of tosses of one die? What is that ratio? If two dice are used, how many times will the numbers rolled add to a certain sum? What are these ratios?

9. Have students increase the number of attempts once they begin to understand the ratios involved with their activities. Ask whether the ratios change significantly. Students should see that even though both ratios are not exactly the same, they are close to a mathematical probability of the event occurring.

10. Close this activity by asking students to write their ratios as fractions as well as with a colon. Explain that a ratio can also be written as a decimal number (as in a batting average or probability) or as a percentage. For workstations that have the same task, have students compare the ratios.

NEXT STEPS • Differentiate

4-Day Instructional Plan:
PA 1, page 246—All students, for additional practice

3-Day Instructional Plan:
CD 2, page 244—All students, for additional concept development

CD 2 Solving a Proportion

Use with 4-Day or 3-Day Instructional Plan. In this activity, students use proportions to solve for a variable.

MATERIALS

- Coins, dice, rolls of adding machine paper, or other objects

DIRECTIONS

1. Review the following terms with students:

    equation A statement that two quantities or mathematical expressions are equal

    equivalent Equal in value

    ratio A comparison of two numbers

    proportion An equation that states that two ratios are equal

2. Remind students of the exercise using adding machine paper rolls from the Concept Development Activity, Understanding Ratios and Chance.

3. Tell students that in the example from that lesson, the ratio of successful attempts to total events was $\frac{5}{16}$, or 5:16. Ask for the ratio of nonsuccessful occurrences to total events. $\frac{11}{16}$

4. Have students think about if the exercise with the adding machine paper rolls illustrated that the success ratio was $\frac{4}{16}$. Tell students to calculate how many successes would then be likely in four events. Demonstrate that you would use the equation $\frac{4}{16} = \frac{n}{4}$; so, there is likely to be one success.

$$\frac{4}{16} = \frac{n}{4}$$
$$4\left(\frac{4}{16}\right) = 4\left(\frac{n}{4}\right)$$
$$1 = n$$

5. Explain that the equation $\frac{4}{16} = \frac{1}{4}$, or an equality stating that two ratios are equal, is a proportion. Show that by using the Multiplication and Division Properties of Equality, a proportion can be solved using the cross-product.

$$\frac{a}{b} = \frac{c}{d}$$

$$\frac{a}{b} \bowtie \frac{c}{d}$$

ad = bc

The cross-product, *ad = bc*, is an equivalent equation to the original proportion.

6. Tell students it is called a cross-product because you can obtain the multipliers by making a cross (or X) in the proportion.

7. Ask what the probable successes of the adding machine paper roll landing on end would be after 20 trials, 40 trials, and 100 trials for a ratio of $\frac{1}{4}$. Respectively, 5, 10, and 25

8. Tell students to return to the ratios they generated with their groups in the activity Understanding Ratios and Chance. Give them several different scenarios, and have them write an equation to determine how many times a successful outcome would occur.

Sample problems:

Suppose a coin were tossed 20 times, and the real probability of heads occurring $\left(\frac{1}{2}\right)$ was discovered.

Double the number of trials.
$$\frac{10}{20} = \frac{n}{40}$$
$$n = 20$$

Triple the number of trials.
$$\frac{10}{20} = \frac{n}{60}$$
$$n = 30$$

Do a total of 100 trials.
$$\frac{10}{20} = \frac{n}{100}$$
$$n = 50$$

9. Have students imagine a die being tossed 30 times and the four appearing 5 of the 30 tosses, which is equivalent to odds of $\frac{5}{30}$, or $\frac{1}{6}$. Have students determine how many times they would expect the 4 to appear in several different scenarios of trial numbers.

Sample problems:

60 tosses	120 tosses	180 tosses
$\frac{1}{6} = \frac{n}{60}$	$\frac{1}{6} = \frac{n}{120}$	$\frac{1}{6} = \frac{n}{180}$
$n = 10$	$n = 20$	$n = 30$

10. Have students imagine that 25 thumbtacks are dropped, and eight of them land point down. Ask how many point-down tacks they would expect in several different scenarios of trial numbers.

Sample problems:

50 tacks	100 tacks	250 tacks
$\frac{8}{25} = \frac{n}{50}$	$\frac{8}{25} = \frac{n}{100}$	$\frac{8}{25} = \frac{n}{250}$
$n = 16$	$n = 32$	$n = 80$

11. Have students think about the results in Step 10 and write the ratio of thumbtacks that landed point-up. Ask them to determine how many tacks would land point up for different scenarios of trial numbers.

Sample answers:

The ratio for tacks that landed point-up is $\frac{17}{25}$.

200 tacks	150 tacks
$\frac{17}{25} = \frac{t}{200}$	$\frac{17}{25} = \frac{t}{150}$
$t = 136$	$t = 102$

NEXT STEPS • Differentiate

4-Day and 3-Day Instructional Plans:
PM 1, page 251—All students, to assess progress

Practice Activities

PA 1 Finding Equivalent Ratios to Solve Proportions

Use with 4-Day Instructional Plan. In this activity, students recognize equivalent ratios.

MATERIALS

- Blackline Masters 48–54, or 42 blank cards per group
- Markers

DIRECTIONS

1. Review the following terms with students:

    equivalent Equal in value

    ratio A comparison of two numbers

    proportion An equation that states that two ratios are equal

2. Divide the class into groups of three or four. Distribute one copy of Blackline Masters 48–54, Finding Equivalent Ratios to Solve Proportions, to each group. Alternatively, give each group 42 blank cards and have them write the information from Blackline Masters 48–54 on the cards.

3. Explain the game rules to students.

    - Each group designates a dealer, who shuffles the cards and deals six cards to each player (including himself or herself). The extra cards in the deck should be placed facedown in a pile on the table.

    - The object is for players to find sets of two, three, four, or more cards in their hands that are proportional.

    - Play proceeds from the dealer's left clockwise. At the beginning of his or her turn, each player draws one card from the facedown pile on the table.

    - When it is a player's turn, he or she places the matching cards faceup on the table and explains why the cards are proportional. If a player does not have a proportion, the play is passed to the player's left.

48

Name _____ Date _____

FINDING EQUIVALENT RATIOS TO SOLVE PROPORTIONS

$\dfrac{1}{2}$	$\dfrac{3}{10}$
$\dfrac{3}{5}$	$\dfrac{3}{8}$
$\dfrac{5}{8}$	$\dfrac{1}{4}$

- The first player to get rid of all his or her cards is the winner. Play then continues until the other players go out, or all the cards in the stack are drawn. The remaining players are ranked according to the number of cards remaining in their hands at the end of play.

    Variation: Proportions can be placed in the center of the playing area, and all players can, during their turns, play additional proportional cards on these matches.

NEXT STEPS • Differentiate

4-Day Instructional Plan:
CD 2, page 244—All students, for additional concept development

**FINDING EQUIVALENT RATIOS
TO SOLVE PROPORTIONS** *(continued)*

$\dfrac{2}{4}$	$\dfrac{6}{20}$
$\dfrac{6}{10}$	$\dfrac{6}{16}$
5:8	$\dfrac{3}{12}$

**FINDING EQUIVALENT RATIOS
TO SOLVE PROPORTIONS** *(continued)*

3:6	$\dfrac{9}{30}$
0.6	9:24
0.625	25%

**FINDING EQUIVALENT RATIOS
TO SOLVE PROPORTIONS** *(continued)*

50%	30%
15:25	0.375
$\dfrac{25}{40}$	100:400

**FINDING EQUIVALENT RATIOS
TO SOLVE PROPORTIONS** *(continued)*

0.5	0.3
60%	$37\dfrac{1}{2}\%$
62.5%	0.25

**FINDING EQUIVALENT RATIOS
TO SOLVE PROPORTIONS** *(continued)*

5:10	12:40
60:100	$\dfrac{12}{32}$
625:1,000	$\dfrac{25}{100}$

**FINDING EQUIVALENT RATIOS
TO SOLVE PROPORTIONS** *(continued)*

$\dfrac{5}{10}$	$\dfrac{15}{50}$
$\dfrac{9}{15}$	$\dfrac{18}{48}$
15:24	250:1,000

Objective 5
Practice Activities

PA 2 Playing the Proportion Game

Use with 4-Day or 3-Day Instructional Plan. In this activity, students solve proportions.

MATERIALS

- Blackline Master 55
- Dice
- Game marker pieces, one per student

DIRECTIONS

1. Review the following terms with students:

   ratio A comparison of two numbers

   proportion An equation that states that two ratios are equal

2. Divide the class into groups of about four students.

3. Distribute a copy of the Blackline Master 55, Proportion Game Board, to each group. Give each group one die. If possible, use dice numbered 1, 2, 3, 1, 2, 3, which will provide more practice for students.

4. Explain the game rules to students.

   - Members of each group take turns rolling the die. The student who rolls the largest number starts the game. The group continues taking turns clockwise.

   - Everyone in the group puts a game marker on the start space.

   - The first player rolls the die and moves his or her marker the number of spaces showing on the die. The student writes the problem in the space on which he or she lands on a separate piece of paper, then works the problem.

   - On each player's turn the group checks the player's work. If the answer is correct, the next player takes a turn. If it is incorrect, the student returns to the previous spot.

   - Students can work a problem that was previously done by another player. However, they should not look at work done by the earlier player.

   - Tell students to continue playing until the first player gets to the finish space.

5. For extra practice, have students repeat the activity several times.

NEXT STEPS • Differentiate

4-Day and 3-Day Instructional Plans:
PM 2, page 252—All students, to assess progress

Name _____ Date _____

PROPORTION GAME BOARD

START	$\frac{x}{6}=\frac{2}{3}$ $x=4$	$\frac{4}{n}=\frac{6}{15}$ $n=10$	$\frac{1}{2}=\frac{n}{10}$ $n=5$	$\frac{5}{4}=\frac{15}{x}$ $x=12$	$\frac{2}{m}=\frac{8}{12}$ $m=3$	$\frac{x}{16}=\frac{3}{4}$ $x=12$
						$\frac{y}{3}=\frac{4}{9}$ $y=1\frac{1}{3}$
$\frac{10}{3}=\frac{2}{x}$ $x=0.6$	$\frac{224}{8}=\frac{x}{13}$ $x=364$	$\frac{x}{121}=\frac{7}{16}$ $x=52\frac{15}{16}$	$\frac{-5}{7}=\frac{n}{28}$ $n=-20$	$\frac{2}{3}=\frac{10}{x}$ $x=15$	$\frac{2}{3}=\frac{4}{3x}$ $x=2$	
$\frac{21}{n}=\frac{7}{8}$ $n=24$						
$\frac{2x}{5}=\frac{8}{10}$ $x=2$	$\frac{-1}{n}=\frac{20}{62}$ $n=-3.1$	$\frac{4}{3g}=\frac{16}{9}$ $g=\frac{3}{4}$	$\frac{4n}{9}=\frac{24}{27}$ $n=2$	$\frac{1}{6}=\frac{2x}{36}$ $x=3$	$\frac{5}{3y}=\frac{15}{9}$ $y=1$	
						$\frac{2}{3}=\frac{14}{x}$ $x=21$
$\frac{12}{2y}=\frac{3}{6}$ $y=12$	$\frac{3x}{20}=\frac{3}{5}$ $x=4$	$\frac{3}{d}=\frac{21}{35}$ $d=5$	$\frac{x}{5}=\frac{5}{100}$ $x=0.25$	$\frac{17}{25}=\frac{m}{150}$ $m=102$	$\frac{3}{2}=\frac{3a}{10}$ $a=5$	
$\frac{x+2}{7}=\frac{5}{3}$ $x=9\frac{2}{3}$						
$\frac{7}{8}=\frac{x}{40}$ $x=35$	$\frac{3}{10}=\frac{x}{100}$ $x=30$	$\frac{25}{100}=\frac{12}{1x}$ $x=48$	$\frac{7}{x}=\frac{1}{9}$ $x=63$	$\frac{20}{3x}=\frac{4}{18}$ $x=30$	$\frac{a-2}{3}=\frac{20}{15}$ $a=6$	FINISH

Practice Activities

PA 3 Solving Recipe Proportions

Use with 4-Day or 3-Day Instructional Plan. In this activity, students use proportions to adjust the quantities in a recipe.

MATERIALS

- Recipes from various sources, for example, the cafeteria cook, a local baker, a home cookbook, cooking magazines, the food section of the local newspaper

DIRECTIONS

1. Review the following terms with students:

   ratio A comparison of two numbers

   proportion An equation that states that two ratios are equal

2. Divide students into small groups of three to four. Have each group bring in a recipe they want to use for this activity.

3. Write the following recipe on the board:

   Italian Bread Recipe (Makes three loaves)
   2 cups warm water
   1 teaspoon dry yeast
   2 tablespoons honey
   2 teaspoons salt
   6 cups flour

4. Ask students to think about what the recipe would be for making six loaves of bread. Demonstrate the process of converting each ingredient.

   $$\frac{\text{Original recipe}}{\text{New recipe}} = \frac{3 \text{ loaves}}{6 \text{ loaves}} = \frac{1}{2}$$

   For water: $\frac{1}{2} = \frac{2 \text{ cups}}{C \text{ cups}}$; so, $C = 4$ cups

   For yeast: $\frac{1}{2} = \frac{1 \text{ tsp}}{t \text{ tsp}}$; so, $t = 2$ tsp

   Other ingredients are determined similarly.

5. Assign each group a different quantity of loaves, and have them adjust the recipe accordingly.

6. Have groups turn their attention to the recipe they brought. If the recipe is one that serves fewer than 10 people, ask them to double the recipe. If the recipe is from the cafeteria, for example, and serves a large group of people, ask them to halve the recipe.

NEXT STEPS • Differentiate

4-Day Instructional Plan:
PS 1, page 254—All students, to develop problem-solving skills

3-Day Instructional Plan:
PS 1, page 254—Students who are on the accelerated path, to develop problem-solving skills

Objective 5 Posttest, page 255—Students who are on the differentiated path

Objective 5
Progress-Monitoring Activities

PM 1 Apply Skills 1

Use with 4-Day or 3-Day Instructional Plan.

MATERIALS

- *Interactive Text*, pages 103–104

DIRECTIONS

1. Have students turn to *Interactive Text*, pages 103–104, Apply Skills 1.

2. Remind students of the key terms: *ratio* and *proportion*.

3. Monitor student work, and provide feedback as necessary.

   Watch for:
   - Do students correctly use the cross-product to check if two ratios are proportional?
   - Do students use number sense to solve any problems without finding the cross-product?

NEXT STEPS • Differentiate

4-Day and 3-Day Instructional Plans:
PA 2, page 249—All students, for additional practice

APPLY SKILLS 1

The comparison of two numbers by division, $\frac{a}{b}$, is a ratio.

The equation formed by two equivalent ratios, $\frac{a}{b} = \frac{c}{d}$, is a proportion.

The cross product, $ad = bc$, can be shown as being equivalent by using the multiplication principle of equality. That is, if two ratios are equal, $\frac{a}{b} = \frac{c}{d}$, then $(bd)\frac{a}{b} = (bd)\frac{c}{d}$, and $ad = bc$, where ad and bc are cross products.

Using the cross product, show which of the pairs of ratios are proportions.

Example:
$\frac{1}{4}, \frac{2}{8}$
$1 \cdot 8 = 2 \cdot 4$
$8 = 8$, yes

1. $\frac{1}{2}, \frac{2}{4}$ ___4 = 4, yes___
   $1 \cdot 4 = 2 \cdot 2$

2. $\frac{4}{7}, \frac{7}{14}$ ___56 ≠ 49, no___
   $4 \cdot 14 \neq 7 \cdot 7$

3. $\frac{3}{8}, \frac{18}{48}$ ___144 = 144, yes___
   $3 \cdot 48 = 8 \cdot 18$

4. 7:13, 21:39 ___273 = 273, yes___
   $7 \cdot 39 = 13 \cdot 21$

5. $\frac{2.5}{6}, \frac{5}{11}$ ___27.5 ≠ 30, no___
   $2.5 \cdot 11 \neq 6 \cdot 5$

6. 3.7:37, 1:10 ___37 = 37, yes___
   $3.7 \cdot 10 = 37 \cdot 1$

APPLY SKILLS 1 (continued)

Solve the proportions.

Example:
$\frac{2}{5} = \frac{x}{20}$
$5x = 40$
$x = 8$

7. $\frac{x}{5} = \frac{15}{25}$
   $25x = 75$
   $x = 3$

8. $\frac{4}{7} = \frac{12}{x}$
   $4x = 84$
   $x = 21$

9. $\frac{9}{4t} = \frac{3}{8}$
   $72 = 12t$
   $t = 6$

10. $\frac{8}{5t} = \frac{2}{5}$
    $40 = 10t$
    $t = 4$

11. $\frac{3}{x} = \frac{15}{60}$
    $180 = 15x$
    $x = 12$

12. $\frac{x}{100} = \frac{49}{7}$
    $7x = 4,900$
    $x = 700$

13. $\frac{7}{8} = \frac{x}{40}$
    $280 = 8x$
    $x = 35$

14. $\frac{11}{x} = \frac{132}{24}$
    $264 = 132x$
    $x = 2$

15. $\frac{x}{5} = \frac{14}{20}$
    $20x = 70$
    $x = 3.5$

Objective 5
Progress-Monitoring Activities

PM 2 Apply Skills 2

Use with 4-Day or 3-Day Instructional Plan.

MATERIALS

- *Interactive Text*, pages 105–106

DIRECTIONS

1. Have students turn to *Interactive Text*, pages 105–106, Apply Skills 2.

2. Remind students of the key term: *proportion*.

3. Monitor student work, and provide feedback as necessary.

   Watch for:
   - Do students correctly use the cross-product to solve each proportion?
   - Do students use number sense to solve any problems without finding the cross-product?

NEXT STEPS • Differentiate

4-Day Instructional Plan:
PA 3, page 250—Students who are on the accelerated path, for additional practice

PM 3, page 253—Students who who are on the differentiated path, for progress assessment

3-Day Instructional Plan:
PA 3, page 250—Students who are on the accelerated path, for additional practice

PA 3, page 250—Students who are on the differentiated path, who demonstrate understanding, for additional practice

PM 3, page 253—All other students, for progress assessment

Name_____ Date_____

APPLY SKILLS 2

Solve the proportions.

1. $\frac{x}{9} = \frac{2}{3}$
   $3x = 18$
   $x = 6$

2. $\frac{20}{100} = \frac{4}{x}$
   $20x = 400$
   $x = 20$

3. $\frac{2}{x} = \frac{1}{15}$
   $1x = 30$
   $x = 30$

4. $\frac{5}{x} = \frac{1}{5}$
   $1x = 25$
   $x = 25$

5. $\frac{6}{21} = \frac{x}{7}$
   $21x = 42$
   $x = 2$

6. $\frac{1}{12} = \frac{10}{x}$
   $1x = 120$
   $x = 120$

7. $\frac{4}{x} = \frac{2}{9}$
   $2x = 36$
   $x = 18$

8. $\frac{x}{18} = \frac{5}{6}$
   $6x = 90$
   $x = 15$

9. $\frac{x}{24} = \frac{2}{3}$
   $3x = 48$
   $x = 16$

10. $\frac{15}{100} = \frac{3}{x}$
    $15x = 300$
    $x = 20$

Inside Algebra   Chapter 3 • Objective 5 • PM 2   105

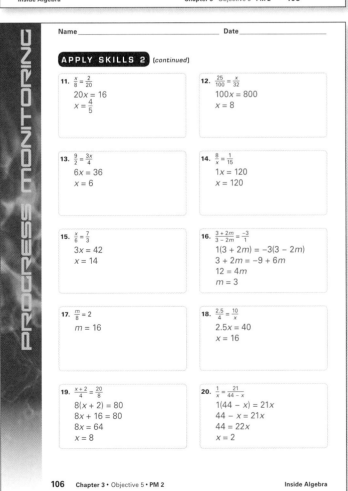

Name_____ Date_____

APPLY SKILLS 2 (continued)

11. $\frac{x}{8} = \frac{2}{20}$
    $20x = 16$
    $x = \frac{4}{5}$

12. $\frac{25}{100} = \frac{x}{32}$
    $100x = 800$
    $x = 8$

13. $\frac{9}{2} = \frac{3x}{4}$
    $6x = 36$
    $x = 6$

14. $\frac{8}{x} = \frac{1}{15}$
    $1x = 120$
    $x = 120$

15. $\frac{x}{6} = \frac{7}{3}$
    $3x = 42$
    $x = 14$

16. $\frac{3 + 2m}{3 - 2m} = \frac{-3}{1}$
    $1(3 + 2m) = -3(3 - 2m)$
    $3 + 2m = -9 + 6m$
    $12 = 4m$
    $m = 3$

17. $\frac{m}{8} = 2$
    $m = 16$

18. $\frac{2.5}{4} = \frac{10}{x}$
    $2.5x = 40$
    $x = 16$

19. $\frac{x + 2}{4} = \frac{20}{8}$
    $8(x + 2) = 80$
    $8x + 16 = 80$
    $8x = 64$
    $x = 8$

20. $\frac{1}{x} = \frac{21}{44 - x}$
    $1(44 - x) = 21x$
    $44 - x = 21x$
    $44 = 22x$
    $x = 2$

106   Chapter 3 • Objective 5 • PM 2   Inside Algebra

Objective 5
Progress-Monitoring Activities

PM 3 Apply Skills 3

Use with 4-Day or 3-Day Instructional Plan.

MATERIALS

- *Interactive Text*, page 107

DIRECTIONS

1. Have students turn to *Interactive Text*, page 107, Apply Skills 3.

2. Remind students of the key term: *proportion*.

3. Monitor student work, and provide feedback as necessary.

   Watch for:
   - Do students correctly use the cross-product to solve each proportion?

   - Do students use number sense to solve any problems without finding the cross-product?

NEXT STEPS • Differentiate

   4-Day and 3-Day Instructional Plans:
   Objective 5 Posttest, page 255—All students

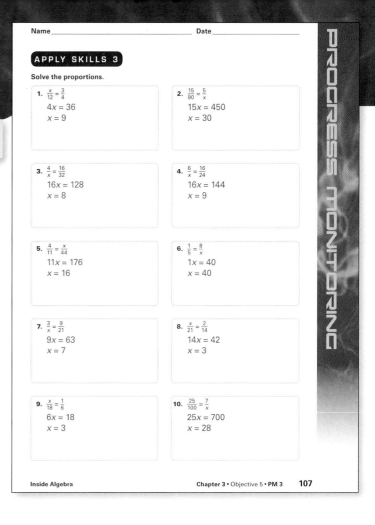

Objective 5
Problem-Solving Activity

★PS 1 Determining Body Proportions

Use with 4-Day or 3-Day Instructional Plan. In this activity, students make measurements and calculate proportions.

MATERIALS

- *Interactive Text*, page 108

DIRECTIONS

1. Review the following terms with students:

   ratio A comparison of two numbers

   proportion An equation that states that two ratios are equal

2. Tell students that in this activity, they calculate proportions.

3. Tell students to work individually on this assignment.

4. Have students turn to *Interactive Text*, page 108, Body Proportions, and solve the problems.

5. Note whether students realize the given proportions are averages. Most students are not exactly in the same proportion.

NEXT STEPS • Differentiate

4-Day and 3-Day Instructional Plans:
Objective 5 Posttest, page 255—All students

Name _____ Date _____

BODY PROPORTIONS

The height of the average human body, if divided into 16 units of measure, is approximately proportioned in these ratios:

Head	2:16
Neck to shoulder	1:16
Body	6:16
Thigh	3:16
Calf	3:16
Ankle and foot	1:16
Shoulder to waist	2:16
Arm	5:16
Shoulder to elbow	2:16
Elbow to wrist	2:16
Hand	1:16

1. Working in pairs, determine how close these ratios are to the actual proportions in your bodies. Measure your height and compute the proportions. For example, if your height is 64 inches, then your neck height would be calculated as $\frac{1}{16} = \frac{x}{64}$, or $x = 4$ inches.
   Answers will vary.

2. After the computations are completed, determine how closely your measurements conform to the proportions.
   Answers will vary.

★ = Includes Problem Solving

Objective 5 Posttest

Discuss with students the key concepts in Objective 5. Following the discussion, administer the Objective 5 Posttest to all students.

Using the Results

- Score the posttest and update the class record card.

- Provide reinforcement for students who do not demonstrate mastery of the concepts through individual or small-group reteaching of key concepts.

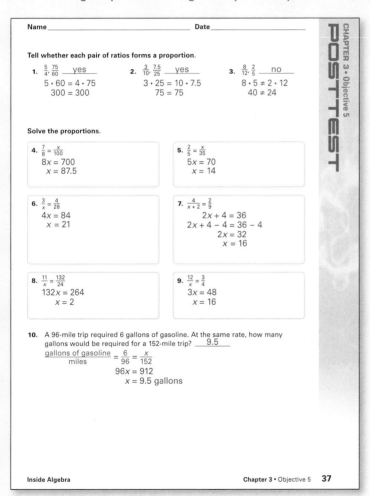

Name _____ Date _____

CHAPTER 3 • Objective 5

POSTTEST

Tell whether each pair of ratios forms a proportion.

1. $\frac{5}{4}, \frac{75}{60}$ ___yes___
$5 \cdot 60 = 4 \cdot 75$
$300 = 300$

2. $\frac{3}{10}, \frac{7.5}{25}$ ___yes___
$3 \cdot 25 = 10 \cdot 7.5$
$75 = 75$

3. $\frac{8}{12}, \frac{2}{5}$ ___no___
$8 \cdot 5 \neq 2 \cdot 12$
$40 \neq 24$

Solve the proportions.

4. $\frac{7}{8} = \frac{x}{100}$
$8x = 700$
$x = 87.5$

5. $\frac{2}{5} = \frac{x}{35}$
$5x = 70$
$x = 14$

6. $\frac{3}{x} = \frac{4}{28}$
$4x = 84$
$x = 21$

7. $\frac{4}{x+2} = \frac{2}{9}$
$2x + 4 = 36$
$2x + 4 - 4 = 36 - 4$
$2x = 32$
$x = 16$

8. $\frac{11}{x} = \frac{132}{24}$
$132x = 264$
$x = 2$

9. $\frac{12}{x} = \frac{3}{4}$
$3x = 48$
$x = 16$

10. A 96-mile trip required 6 gallons of gasoline. At the same rate, how many gallons would be required for a 152-mile trip? ___9.5___
$\frac{\text{gallons of gasoline}}{\text{miles}} = \frac{6}{96} = \frac{x}{152}$
$96x = 912$
$x = 9.5$ gallons

Inside Algebra   Chapter 3 • Objective 5   **37**

Objective 6
Use proportions to solve percent problems.

Objective 6 Pretest

Students complete the Objective 6 Pretest on the same day as the Objective 5 Posttest.

Using the Results

- Score the pretest and update the class record card.

- If the majority of students do not demonstrate mastery of the concepts, use the 4-Day Instructional Plan for Objective 6.

- If the majority of students demonstrate mastery of the concepts, use the 3-Day Instructional Plan for Objective 6.

CHAPTER 3 • Objective 6
PRETEST

Name_____ Date_____

Find the solution to each problem.

1. 25% of ___32___ is 8.

2. 6% of 1,000 is ___60___.

3. 30% of 120 is ___36___.

4. 14 is 10% of ___140___.

5. 20% off a watch selling for $28 equals how large a discount?
   ___$5.60___

6. ___60___ % of 70 is 42.

7. 13% of 35 is ___4.55___.

8. 5 is what percent of 20? ___25%___

9. 6 is 15 percent of what number? ___40___

10. If a bus with a capacity of 80 occupants is 85% full, how many more seats are available on the bus?

   ___12 seats are available.___

---

1. $(4)0.25x = 8(4)$
   $x = 32$

2. $0.06(1,000) = 60$

3. $0.30(120) = 36$

4. $(10)0.10x = 14(10)$
   $x = 140$

5. $0.20(28) = 5.60$

6. $\left(\frac{1}{70}\right)70x = 42\left(\frac{1}{70}\right)$
   $x = \frac{42}{70} = \frac{6}{10} = 60\%$

7. $0.13(35) = 4.55$

8. $\left(\frac{1}{20}\right)20x = 5\left(\frac{1}{20}\right)$
   $x = \frac{5}{20} = \frac{25}{100} = 25\%$

9. $\left(\frac{1}{0.15}\right)0.15x = 6\left(\frac{1}{0.15}\right)$
   $x = 40$

10. $0.15(80) = 12$

---

38 Chapter 3 • Objective 6

Inside Algebra

Goals and Activities

Objective 6 Goals

The following activities, when used with the instructional plans on pages 258 and 259, enable students to:

- Determine that 35% of 28 is **9.8**

- Determine that 21 is 6% of **350**

- Determine that the percent of $45 that is $5.40 is **12%**

- Create the proportion to find the saving on the purchase of a $36 item with a 7% discount as

$$\frac{7}{100} = \frac{n}{36}, \text{ or } 0.07 = \frac{n}{36}$$

Objective 6 Activities

Concept Development Activities

CD 1 Writing Percents as Ratios, page 260	**CD 2** Writing Percents as Proportions, page 261

Practice Activities

PA 1 Playing Dominoes, page 263	**★PA 2** Hunting in Newspapers, page 265

Progress-Monitoring Activities

PM 1 Apply Skills 1, page 266	**PM 2** Apply Skills 2, page 267	**PM 3** Apply Skills 3, page 268

★Problem-Solving Activity

★PS 1 Solving Everyday Problems, page 269

Ongoing Assessment

Posttest Objective 6, page 270

Pretest Chapter 4, Objective 1, page 271

CD = Concept Development   PM = Progress Monitoring   PS = Problem Solving
PA = Practice Activity   ★ = Includes Problem Solving

Instructional Plans

4-Day Instructional Plan

Use the 4-Day Instructional Plan when pretest results indicate that students would benefit from a slower pace. This plan is used when the majority of students need more time or did not demonstrate mastery on the pretest.

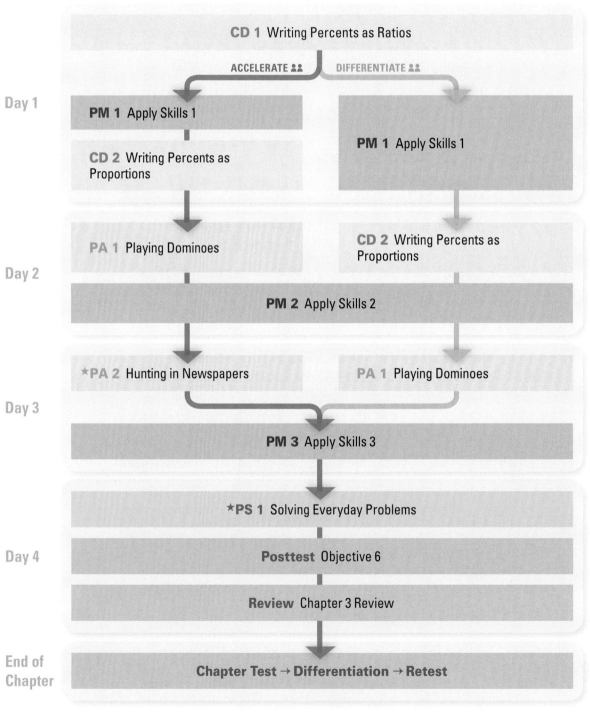

CD 1 Writing Percents as Ratios

ACCELERATE • DIFFERENTIATE

Day 1

PM 1 Apply Skills 1

CD 2 Writing Percents as Proportions

PM 1 Apply Skills 1

PA 1 Playing Dominoes

CD 2 Writing Percents as Proportions

Day 2

PM 2 Apply Skills 2

★PA 2 Hunting in Newspapers

PA 1 Playing Dominoes

Day 3

PM 3 Apply Skills 3

★PS 1 Solving Everyday Problems

Day 4

Posttest Objective 6

Review Chapter 3 Review

End of Chapter

Chapter Test → Differentiation → Retest

CD = Concept Development   PM = Progress Monitoring   PS = Problem Solving
PA = Practice Activity   ★ = Includes Problem Solving

3-Day Instructional Plan

Use the 3-Day Instructional Plan when pretest results indicate that students can move through the activities at a faster pace. This plan is ideal when the majority of students demonstrate mastery on the pretest.

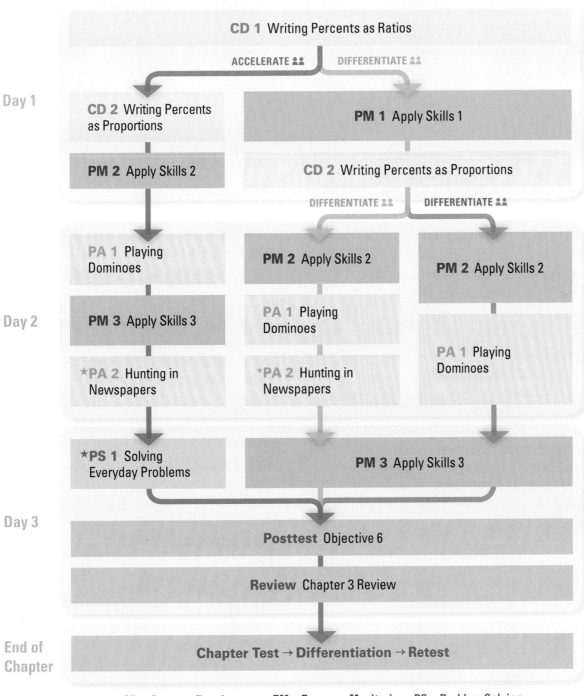

CD 1 Writing Percents as Ratios

ACCELERATE   DIFFERENTIATE

Day 1

CD 2 Writing Percents as Proportions

PM 1 Apply Skills 1

PM 2 Apply Skills 2

CD 2 Writing Percents as Proportions

DIFFERENTIATE   DIFFERENTIATE

Day 2

PA 1 Playing Dominoes

PM 2 Apply Skills 2

PM 2 Apply Skills 2

PM 3 Apply Skills 3

PA 1 Playing Dominoes

PA 1 Playing Dominoes

*★PA 2** Hunting in Newspapers

*★PA 2** Hunting in Newspapers

Day 3

*★PS 1** Solving Everyday Problems

PM 3 Apply Skills 3

Posttest Objective 6

Review Chapter 3 Review

End of Chapter

Chapter Test → Differentiation → Retest

CD = Concept Development   PM = Progress Monitoring   PS = Problem Solving
PA = Practice Activity   ★ = Includes Problem Solving

Concept Development Activities

CD 1 Writing Percents as Ratios

Use with 4-Day or 3-Day Instructional Plan. In this activity, students write percents by first writing a ratio with a denominator of 100.

DIRECTIONS

1. Review the following terms with students:

   ratio A comparison of two numbers

   proportion An equation that states that two ratios are equal

   percent A ratio whose second term is 100; percent means parts per hundred

2. Tell students this activity introduces percent, a ratio that compares a number to 100, to prepare for solving proportions involving percentages.

3. Ask students what they think a percent is. List as many plausible answers as reasonable on the board.

4. List areas for discussion that have units of 100 and lend themselves to percent calculations.

   Example:

   > one dollar = 100 cents
   > a football field = 100 yards in length
   > a flagpole = 100 units
   > one meter = 100 centimeters

5. Ask students to generate questions involving percentage for other class members to answer. This can be done in pairs with one student asking a partner the question and the partner responding. The roles can then be reversed.

Examples:

What percent of one dollar is a dime?

$$n\% = \frac{n}{100} = \frac{10\text{ cents}}{100\text{ cents}} = \frac{1}{10} = 0.1,\text{ or }10\%$$

A 32-yard gain is what percent of a football field?

$$n\% = \frac{n}{100} = \frac{32\text{ yd}}{100\text{ yd}} = \frac{32}{100} = 0.32,\text{ or }32\%$$

Twenty-five cents is what percent of a dollar?

$$n\% = \frac{n}{100} = \frac{25¢}{100¢} = 0.25,\text{ or }25\%$$

A business occupies nine floors of a 100-story building. What percent of the building is occupied by that business?

$$n\% = \frac{n}{100} = \frac{9\text{ floors}}{100\text{ floors}} = 0.09,\text{ or }9\%$$

The decimal $0.50 is what percent of a dollar?

$$n\% = \frac{n}{100} = \frac{50¢}{100¢} = 0.5,\text{ or }50\%$$

A quarterback breaks away for a 40-yard run. What percent of the playing field did the quarterback gain?

$$n\% = \frac{n}{100} = \frac{40\text{ yd.}}{100\text{ yd.}} = \frac{4}{10} = 0.4,\text{ or }40\%$$

6. Ask students to write proportions that represent these questions or provide other examples. With the examples based on 100 units, the proportions seem trivial, but they are important and easy for students to understand.

7. Be sure to discuss the corresponding decimal value of the percents students just worked with, such as 32 cents is $0.32, or 9% is $\frac{9}{100} = 0.09$.

NEXT STEPS • Differentiate

4-Day Instructional Plan:
PM 1, page 266—All students, to assess progress

3-Day Instructional Plan:
CD 2, page 261—Students who demonstrate understanding of the concept, for additional concept development

PM 1, page 266—Students who need additional support, to assess progress

Concept Development Activities

CD 2 Writing Percents as Proportions

Use with 4-Day or 3-Day Instructional Plan. In this activity, students use proportions to find percentages.

MATERIALS

- *Interactive Text*, page 109

DIRECTIONS

1. Review the following terms with students:

   ratio A comparison of two numbers

   proportion An equation that states that two ratios are equal

   percent A ratio whose second term is 100; percent means parts per hundred

2. Review the discoveries from the Concept Development activity, Writing Percents as Ratios. Review that $n\% = \frac{n}{100}$ and that n represents the decimal n-hundredths.

3. Have students turn to *Interactive Text*, page 109, Percent as Proportion, and complete the table of fractions, percents, and decimal numbers.

4. Note that just as any n in the table was written as a percentage, any number can be written as a percentage by using the solution of a proportion in which the ratios are part/whole; so, $n\% = \frac{n}{100} = \frac{part}{whole}$.

Sample problems:

The fraction $\frac{2}{5}$ is what percentage?

$\frac{2}{5} = \frac{n}{100}$

$2(100) = 5n$

$n = 40, \frac{n}{100} = 0.40$ or 40%

The fraction $\frac{2}{3}$ is what percentage?

$\frac{2}{3} = \frac{n}{100}$

$2(100) = 3n$

$n = 66\frac{2}{3}, \frac{n}{100} = 0.667$ or 66.7%

The decimal number 1.25 is what percentage?

$\frac{125}{100} = \frac{n}{100}$

$n = 125, \frac{n}{100} = 1.25$ or 125%

5. Explain that most percentage problems can be written as proportions because any percent can be written as a ratio: $\frac{n}{100}$.

Examples:

$40\% = \frac{40}{100}$

$15\% = \frac{15}{100}$

$6\% = \frac{6}{100}$

PERCENT AS PROPORTION

Complete the tables. Remember that $n\% = \frac{n}{100}$ and n represents the decimal n-hundredths.

n	1	3	5	10	17	25
$\frac{n}{100}$	$\frac{1}{100}$	$\frac{3}{100}$	$\frac{5}{100}$	$\frac{10}{100}$	$\frac{17}{100}$	$\frac{25}{100}$
$n\%$	1%	3%	5%	10%	17%	25%
n as a decimal number	0.01	0.03	0.05	0.10	0.17	0.25

n	43	72	98	100	125	250
$\frac{n}{100}$	$\frac{43}{100}$	$\frac{72}{100}$	$\frac{98}{100}$	$\frac{100}{100}$	$\frac{125}{100}$	$\frac{250}{100}$
$n\%$	43%	72%	98%	100%	125%	250%
n as a decimal number	0.43	0.72	0.98	1.00	1.25	2.50

Concept Development Activities

6. Have students apply the process to word problems.

Sample problems:

Your savings of $1,000 earns 6% interest. How much interest would you earn for one year?

$$\frac{n}{100} = \frac{part}{whole}$$

$$\frac{6}{100} = \frac{x}{1,000}$$

$100 \cdot x = 6 \cdot 1,000$

6% of 1,000 = 60, or $60 interest

You have a 20% off coupon and you want to buy a small TV that costs $250. How much will you save?

$$\frac{n}{100} = \frac{part}{whole}$$

$$\frac{20}{100} = \frac{s}{250}$$

$100 \cdot s = 20 \cdot 250$

20% of 250 = 50, or $50 savings

There is a 10% increase in the number of students in your class year. If there were 30 students last year, how many more are there this year?

$$\frac{n}{100} = \frac{part}{whole}$$

$$\frac{10}{100} = \frac{s}{30}$$

$100 \cdot s = 10 \cdot 30$

10% of 30 = 3, or 3 more students

7. Direct students to write the proportions for the problems in the table. Remind students of $\frac{n}{100} = \frac{part}{whole}$.

Problem	Proportion
13% of 200 = n	$\frac{13}{100} = \frac{n}{200}$
45% of 120 = n	$\frac{45}{100} = \frac{n}{120}$
16 = 20% of n	$\frac{16}{n} = \frac{20}{100}$
n% of 20 = 5	$\frac{n}{100} = \frac{5}{20}$
6 = 15% of n	$\frac{6}{n} = \frac{15}{100}$
n% of 150 = 27	$\frac{n}{100} = \frac{27}{150}$

NEXT STEPS • Differentiate

4-Day Instructional Plan:

PA 1, page 263—Students who are on the accelerated path, for additional practice

PM 2, page 267—Students who are on the differentiated path, to assess progress

3-Day Instructional Plan:

PM 2, page 267—All students, to assess progress

Practice Activities

PA 1 Playing Dominoes

Use with 4-Day or 3-Day Instructional Plan. In this activity, students find percentages.

MATERIALS

- Blackline Masters 56–58
- Scissors

DIRECTIONS

1. Review the following terms with students:

   ratio A comparison of two numbers

   proportion An equation that states that two ratios are equal

   percent A ratio whose second term is 100; percent means parts per hundred

2. Divide the students into groups of two to four players. Distribute a set of Blackline Masters 56–58, Dominoes for Percents as Proportions, to each group.

3. Have students cut the dominoes out of each sheet of paper.

4. Explain the game rules to students.

   - Mix the dominoes and place them facedown. Each player draws a total of 8, 6, or 5 dominoes at one time, depending on whether there are 2, 3, or 4 players in the group.

   - Designate one student as the first player and have play continue to the left.

   - The first player to draw a double lays that domino down. A double is a domino with the correct solution for the stated problem.

   Example:

   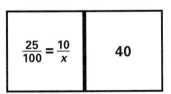

- Students use paper and pencil to solve the domino problems.

- Have players, in turn, attempt to play a domino that matches with one end of the played dominoes. Any player not having a play draws one domino from the extra dominoes and plays the drawn domino if it is playable.

- If a player plays a domino that does not connect correctly, he or she must take back the domino, draw a domino from the stack, and pass his or her turn.

- Play stops with the first person to use all his or her dominos being declared the winner, or play continues until all plays are exhausted.

Name _____ Date _____

DOMINOES FOR PERCENTS AS PROPORTIONS

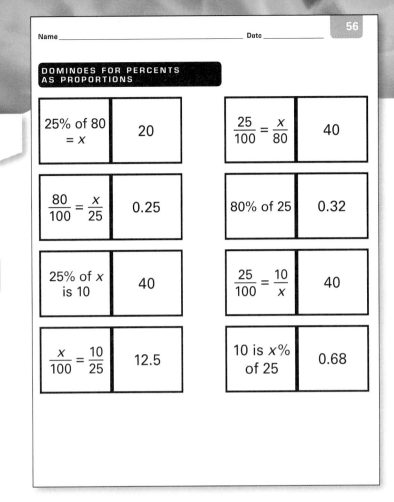

25% of 80 = x	20		$\dfrac{25}{100} = \dfrac{x}{80}$	40
$\dfrac{80}{100} = \dfrac{x}{25}$	0.25		80% of 25	0.32
25% of x is 10	40		$\dfrac{25}{100} = \dfrac{10}{x}$	40
$\dfrac{x}{100} = \dfrac{10}{25}$	12.5		10 is x% of 25	0.68

Problem-Solving Activities

5. A typical game array after a few plays might look like the example below. Note that doubles are played across the other dominoes, not end to end.

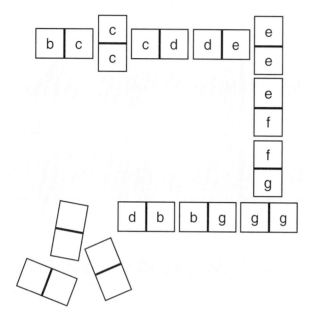

Variation: Give the dominoes to an individual student, and see if he or she can put all pieces in a domino configuration.

NEXT STEPS • Differentiate

👥 **4-Day Instructional Plan:**
PM 2, page 267—Students who are on the accelerated path, to assess progress

PM 3, page 268—Students who are on the differentiated path, to assess progress

👥 **3-Day Instructional Plan:**
PM 3, page 268—Students who are on the accelerated path, to assess progress

PA 2, page 265—Students on the differentiated path who demonstrate understanding early in the activity, for additional practice and problem solving

PM 3, page 268—All other students, to assess progress

Name _____ Date _____   57

DOMINOES FOR PERCENTS AS PROPORTIONS *(continued)*

$\frac{5}{100} = \frac{x}{72}$	3.6	5% of 72 is x	0.68
$\frac{72}{100} = \frac{x}{5}$	0.32	72% of 5 = x	12.5
32¢ is n% of \$1	0.32	$\frac{25}{100} = \frac{x}{1}$	40
$\frac{n}{68} = \frac{3}{300}$	3.6	$\frac{32}{100} = n$	0.25
50% of 0.5	0.25	n is 68% of \$1	0.68

Name _____ Date _____   58

DOMINOES FOR PERCENTS AS PROPORTIONS *(continued)*

x% of 300 is 60	12.5	0.32 = n%	3.6
$2n = \frac{16}{25}$	40	25% of 1	20
$n = \frac{68}{100}$	3.6	$\frac{n}{100} = \frac{37.5}{300}$	0.32
0.0025 = n%	0.68	0.0068 = n%	12.5
$3 = \frac{37.5}{n}$	20	0.125 = n%	0.25

Practice Activities

★PA 2 Hunting in Newspapers

Use with 4-Day or 3-Day Instructional Plan. In this activity, students develop fluency with percentages.

MATERIALS

- Daily newspapers, financial magazines

DIRECTIONS

1. Review the following terms with students:

   ratio A comparison of two numbers

   percent A ratio whose second term is 100; percent means parts per hundred

2. Have students find an article, advertisement, graph, or table that uses percentages. Students can do this at home, in the library, or in class with newspapers and magazines that the teacher provides.

3. Have students work in groups of four. Using typical numbers with the percentages they find, have students make up problems and present their problems to the other groups to solve.

   Sample problem:

   In the 2008 presidential election, 71% of United States citizens who were at least 18 years old were registered to vote. If there were 212 million citizens eligible to vote, how many registered to vote? about 151 million

NEXT STEPS • Differentiate

4-Day Instructional Plan:
PM 3, page 268—All students, to assess progress

3-Day Instructional Plan:
PS 1, page 269—Students who are on the accelerated path, to develop problem-solving skills

PM 3, page 268—Students who are on the differentiated path, to assess progress

★ = Includes Problem Solving

Progress-Monitoring Activities

PM 1 Apply Skills 1

Use with 4-Day or 3-Day Instructional Plan.

MATERIALS

- *Interactive Text*, page 110

DIRECTIONS

1. Have students turn to *Interactive Text*, page 110, Apply Skills 1.

2. Remind students of the key term: *percent*.

3. Monitor student work, and provide feedback as necessary.

   Watch for:
   - Do students convert between fractions, decimal numbers, and percents easily?

   - Do students recognize key terms that will help them interpret the problem?

NEXT STEPS • Differentiate

4-Day and 3-Day Instructional Plans:

CD 2, page 261—All students, for additional concept development

---

Name_____ Date_____

APPLY SKILLS 1

Find the solutions to the problems.

1. What percent of a dollar is one nickel? ___5%___

2. What decimal number is equivalent to 5 cents? ___0.05___

3. If n is 0.47, what is 0.47 as a percent? ___47%___

4. The fraction $\frac{60}{100}$ represents what percent? ___60%___
   What decimal number? ___0.60___

5. N is 78% of 100. What is the value of N? ___78___

6. What decimal number is equivalent to 78%? ___0.78___

7. The top 35 feet of a 100-foot high flagpole is repainted. What percent of the pole is repainted? If $\frac{35}{100}$ of the flagpole is repainted, what decimal number is represented? What percent of the pole is yet to be painted? What decimal number represents that percent? How many feet of the pole are yet to be painted?

   35% is repainted, or 0.35 of the flagpole. 65% is yet to be

   repainted, or 0.65 of the flagpole, or 65 feet.

8. What percent of one dollar is 100 cents? What decimal number represents 100% of one dollar?

   100%, 1.00

9. The Statue of Liberty is approximately 300 feet high, including the base upon which the statue stands. If the base is 150 feet high, what percent of the total height is the statue itself?

   50% | $h = 150 \div 300$
         $h = 0.5$

Objective 6
Progress-Monitoring Activities

PM 2 Apply Skills 2

Use with 4-Day or 3-Day Instructional Plan.

MATERIALS

- *Interactive Text*, pages 111–112

DIRECTIONS

1. Have students turn to *Interactive Text*, pages 111–112, Apply Skills 2.

2. Remind students of the key terms: *percent* and *proportion*.

3. Monitor student work, and provide feedback as necessary.

   Watch for:
   - Do students use proportions to solve percentage problems?
   - Do students realize that percentages can be greater than 100%?
   - Do students realize what a percentage greater than 100% represents?

NEXT STEPS • Differentiate

👥 4-Day Instructional Plan:

PA 2, page 265—Students who are on the accelerated path, for additional practice and problem solving

PA 1, page 263—Students who are on the differentiated path, for additional practice

3-Day Instructional Plan:

PA 1, page 263—All students, for additional practice

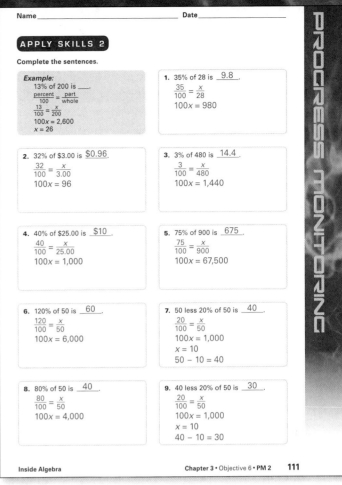

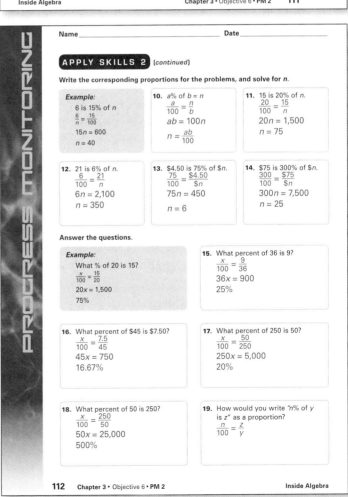

Progress-Monitoring Activities

PM 3 Apply Skills 3

Use with 4-Day or 3-Day Instructional Plan.

MATERIALS

- *Interactive Text*, pages 113–114

DIRECTIONS

1. Have students turn to *Interactive Text*, pages 113–114, Apply Skills 3.

2. Remind students of the key terms: *percent* and *proportion*.

3. Monitor student work, and provide feedback as necessary.

   Watch for:
   - Do students use proportions to solve percentage problems?
   - Do students mentally rewrite problems for easy solving?

NEXT STEPS • Differentiate

4-Day Instructional Plan:
PS 1, page 269—All students, to develop problem-solving skills

3-Day Instructional Plan:
PA 2, page 265—Students who are on the accelerated path, for additional practice and problem solving

Objective 6 Posttest, page 270—Students who are on the differentiated path

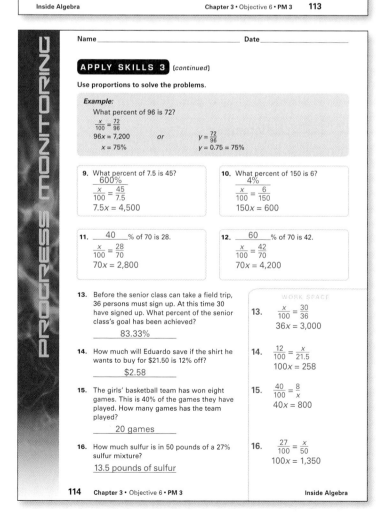

Problem-Solving Activity

★ **PS 1** Solving Everyday Problems

Use with 4-Day or 3-Day Instructional Plan. In this activity, students solve practical problems using percentages.

MATERIALS

- *Interactive Text*, pages 115–116

DIRECTIONS

1. Review the following terms with students:

   ratio A comparison of two numbers

   percent A ratio whose second term is 100; percent means parts per hundred

2. Tell students that in this activity, they solve everyday problems involving percentages.

3. Tell students to work individually on this assignment.

4. Have students turn to *Interactive Text*, pages 115–116, Everyday Problems, and solve the problems.

5. Note if students use the original price to find the percent difference when comparing two prices.

NEXT STEPS • Differentiate

4-Day and 3-Day Instructional Plans:
Objective 6 Posttest, page 270—All students

★ = Includes Problem Solving

Name_____ Date_____

PROBLEM SOLVING

EVERYDAY PROBLEMS

Find the solutions to the problems.

1. In a sale, a disk player that usually costs $120 is advertised for 30% off. How much is the sale price?

   The sale price is $84.00.

   WORK SPACE

   1. $120 \times 0.7 = 84.0$

2. A racing bicycle that regularly sells for $1,500 is advertised for $1,200. What is the percent of discount?

   The discount is 20%.

   2. $1{,}500 - 1{,}200 = 300$
   $\frac{300}{1{,}500} = \frac{1}{5} = 20\%$

3. A shirt that regularly sells for $22 is on sale for $18. A special sale is advertised at 40% off the regular price or 25% off the sale price. Which is the better deal?

   40% off the regular price

   ($13.20 versus $13.50)

   3. $22 \times 0.6 = 13.2$ $18 \times 0.75 = 13.50$

4. Last year 15,600 people attended a particular rock concert. This year, the attendance was down 6%. About how many people attended the concert this year?

   14,664 people

   4. $15{,}600 \cdot 0.94$

5. Members of a ski club are given 20% off their lift ticket price. What is the regular price of a lift ticket if a member is given an eight dollar discount?

   The regular price is $40.00.

   5. $\frac{0.2x}{0.2} = \frac{8}{0.2}$

Inside Algebra   Chapter 3 • Objective 6 • PS 1   **115**

Name_____ Date_____

PROBLEM SOLVING

EVERYDAY PROBLEMS   *(continued)*

6. The list price for a pair of in-line skates is $60, but they are on sale for $48. What is the percent of discount?

   The discount is 20%.

   WORK SPACE

   6. $60 - 48 = 12$
   $\frac{12}{60} = \frac{1}{5} = 20\%$

7. If you earn $6.50/hour at the Star Drive-in and are given a raise to $7.02, what is the percent of increase in wages that you were awarded?

   The increase is 8%.

   7. $7.02 - 6.50 = 0.52$
   $\frac{0.52}{6.50} = 8\%$

8. The basic monthly payment for Pablo's car is $425. With interest, that payment is $476. What is the interest rate?

   The interest rate is 12%.

   8. $476 - 425 = 51$
   $\frac{51}{425} = 12\%$

9. You paid $138 for a new driver to use with your golf clubs. I bought the same driver for $118.70. What percent more did you pay for your driver than I paid for mine?

   You paid 16.26% more.

   9. $138 - 118.70 = 19.30$
   $\frac{19.30}{118.70} = 16.26\%$

10. In Problem 9, what percent of your $138 price could you have saved by buying your driver where I bought mine?

    You could have saved 14%.

    10. $\frac{19.3}{138} = 14\%$

116   Chapter 3 • Objective 6 • PS 1   Inside Algebra

Objective 6 Posttest

Discuss with students the key concepts in Objective 6. Following the discussion, administer the Objective 6 Posttest to all students.

Using the Results

• Score the posttest and update the class record card.

• Provide reinforcement for students who do not demonstrate mastery of the concepts through individual or small-group reteaching of key concepts.

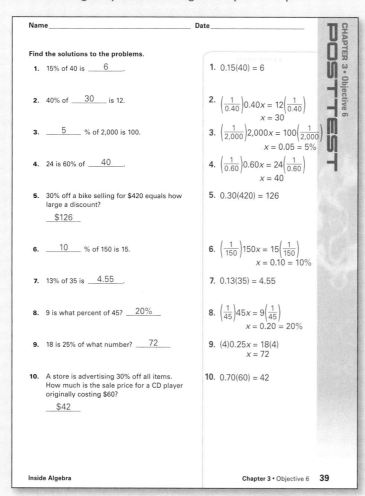

Name_____ Date_____

CHAPTER 3 • Objective 6
POSTTEST

Find the solutions to the problems.

1. 15% of 40 is ___6___.

2. 40% of ___30___ is 12.

3. ___5___ % of 2,000 is 100.

4. 24 is 60% of ___40___.

5. 30% off a bike selling for $420 equals how large a discount?
    ___$126___

6. ___10___ % of 150 is 15.

7. 13% of 35 is ___4.55___.

8. 9 is what percent of 45? ___20%___

9. 18 is 25% of what number? ___72___

10. A store is advertising 30% off all items. How much is the sale price for a CD player originally costing $60?
    ___$42___

1. $0.15(40) = 6$

2. $\left(\frac{1}{0.40}\right)0.40x = 12\left(\frac{1}{0.40}\right)$
   $x = 30$

3. $\left(\frac{1}{2,000}\right)2,000x = 100\left(\frac{1}{2,000}\right)$
   $x = 0.05 = 5\%$

4. $\left(\frac{1}{0.60}\right)0.60x = 24\left(\frac{1}{0.60}\right)$
   $x = 40$

5. $0.30(420) = 126$

6. $\left(\frac{1}{150}\right)150x = 15\left(\frac{1}{150}\right)$
   $x = 0.10 = 10\%$

7. $0.13(35) = 4.55$

8. $\left(\frac{1}{45}\right)45x = 9\left(\frac{1}{45}\right)$
   $x = 0.20 = 20\%$

9. $(4)0.25x = 18(4)$
   $x = 72$

10. $0.70(60) = 42$

Inside Algebra   Chapter 3 • Objective 6   **39**

Chapter Review

Chapter 3 Review

Use with 4-Day or 3-Day Instructional Plan. In this activity, students review key chapter concepts prior to taking the Chapter Test.

MATERIALS

- *Interactive Text*, pages 117–118

DIRECTIONS

1. Have students turn to *Interactive Text*, pages 117–118, Chapter 3 Review.

2. Have students complete the review individually or in small groups. If the activity is completed individually, provide time for students to discuss their solutions as a class or in small groups.

3. Monitor student work, and provide feedback when necessary. If students complete the review quickly, pair them with other students or groups to discuss their answers.

Name_____ Date_____

OBJECTIVE 1

Solve the equations.

1. $x = 6 - 18$
$x = -12$

2. $-4 + x = 11$
$x = 15$

3. $9 = x + 25$
$x = -16$

4. $x + 0.2 = 3.5$
$x = 3.3$

OBJECTIVE 2

Solve the equations.

5. If three x's are 18, what would one x be?
$x = 6$

6. $5x = 20$
$x = 4$

7. $\frac{x}{4} = -3$
$x = -12$

8. $\frac{2}{3} \cdot x = -6$
$x = -9$

OBJECTIVE 3

Solve the equations.

9. $2x + 3 = 13$
$x = 5$

10. $\frac{x}{4} - 16 = -11$
$x = 20$

11. $3x - 4 = x + 2$
$x = 3$

12. $\frac{2}{3}x - 4 = 12$
$x = 24$

Inside Algebra   Chapter 3 • CR 3   **117**

Name_____ Date_____

OBJECTIVE 4

Find the solution to each problem.

13. At a school dance, $\frac{1}{3}$ of the boys were wearing white shirts. If 26 boys were wearing white shirts, how many boys were at the dance?

__78 boys_____ $\frac{1}{3}x = 26$

14. The sum of three consecutive integers is −54. What are the integers?

__−17, −18, −19_____ $n + (n + 1) + (n + 2) = -54$
$3n + 3 + (-3) = -54 + (-3)$
$3n = -57$

OBJECTIVE 5

Solve the proportions.

15. $\frac{3}{x} = \frac{12}{20}$
$12x = 60$
$x = 5$

16. $\frac{2x}{-5} = \frac{16}{5}$
$10x = -80$
$x = -8$

17. $\frac{x}{100} = \frac{9}{4}$
$4x = 900$
$x = 225$

18. $\frac{15}{100} = \frac{6}{x}$
$15x = 600$
$x = 40$

OBJECTIVE 6

Find the solution to each problem.

19. __20__% of 120 is 24. $\frac{n}{100} = \frac{24}{120}$ $120n = 2,400$

20. 70% of 50 is __35__. $\frac{70}{100} = \frac{n}{50}$ $100n = 3,500$

21. 30% of __70__ is 21. $\frac{30}{100} = \frac{21}{n}$ $30n = 2,100$

22. A store is advertising that bikes are on sale for 25% off the regular price. What is the sale price for a $160 bike?

$\frac{25}{100} = \frac{n}{160}$ $100n = 4,000$ $n = 40$ $\$160 - \$40 = \$120$

118   Chapter 3 • CR 3   Inside Algebra

Ongoing Assessment

Chapter 3 Test, Form A

MATERIALS

- *Assessment Book*, pages 41–42

DIRECTIONS

1. Have students turn to *Assessment Book*, pages 41–42, Chapter 3 Test, Form A. Administer the Chapter Test to all students.

2. Score the test by objective and update the class record card.

3. Use the test data to determine differentiation needs.

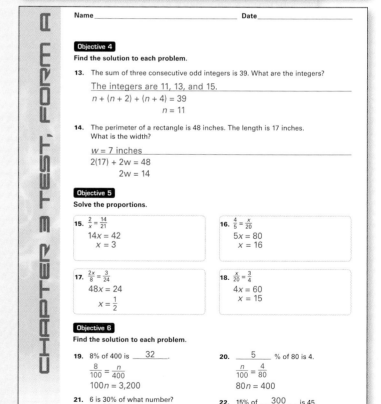

Name_____ Date_____

Objective 1

Solve the equations.

1. $x + 9 = 22$
$x = 13$

2. $-7 + n = 3$
$n = 10$

3. $21 - x = -10$
$x = 31$

4. $17 = n - 9$
$n = 26$

Objective 2

Solve the equations.

5. $6x = 96$
$x = 16$

6. $\frac{y}{7} = 40$
$y = 280$

7. $\frac{1}{5}x = 32$
$x = 160$

8. $30 = 8x$
$x = 3.75$, or $3\frac{3}{4}$

Objective 3

Solve the equations.

9. $5x + 9 = 44$
$x = 7$

10. $x + 6 = 3x - 14$
$x = 10$

11. $\frac{1}{2}x - 15 = -7$
$x = 16$

12. $-30 = 4x + 6$
$x = -9$

Inside Algebra   Chapter 3 • Test   **41**

Name_____ Date_____

Objective 4

Find the solution to each problem.

13. The sum of three consecutive odd integers is 39. What are the integers?
The integers are 11, 13, and 15.
$n + (n + 2) + (n + 4) = 39$
$n = 11$

14. The perimeter of a rectangle is 48 inches. The length is 17 inches. What is the width?
$w = 7$ inches
$2(17) + 2w = 48$
$2w = 14$

Objective 5

Solve the proportions.

15. $\frac{2}{x} = \frac{14}{21}$
$14x = 42$
$x = 3$

16. $\frac{4}{5} = \frac{x}{20}$
$5x = 80$
$x = 16$

17. $\frac{2x}{8} = \frac{3}{24}$
$48x = 24$
$x = \frac{1}{2}$

18. $\frac{x}{20} = \frac{3}{4}$
$4x = 60$
$x = 15$

Objective 6

Find the solution to each problem.

19. 8% of 400 is ___32___.
$\frac{8}{100} = \frac{n}{400}$
$100n = 3{,}200$

20. ___5___ % of 80 is 4.
$\frac{n}{100} = \frac{4}{80}$
$80n = 400$

21. 6 is 30% of what number?
___20___
$\frac{30}{100} = \frac{6}{n}$
$30n = 600$

22. 15% of ___300___ is 45.
$\frac{15}{100} = \frac{45}{n}$
$15n = 4{,}500$

42   Chapter 3 • Test   Inside Algebra

Ongoing Assessment

Differentiation

MATERIALS

- **Gizmos** *Beam to Moon* Gizmo
- **Gizmos** Extension Activity pages
- **Gizmos** *Solving Two-Step Equations* Gizmo
- **Gizmos** Reinforcement Activity page
- Additional Activities
- Algebra Skill Builders for Chapter 3
- Chapter Test, Form B

DIRECTIONS

1. Review Chapter 3 Test, Form A, with the class.

2. Use the results from Chapter 3 Test, Form A, to identify students for reinforcement or extension.

3. After students have been identified for extension or reinforcement, break students into appropriate groups. See pages 274–276 for detailed differentiated instruction.

Differentiation Planner

Students who demonstrated mastery on every objective posttest and scored 80% or above on the chapter test

Extend learning using:

- **Gizmos** Use the *Beam to Moon* Gizmo with the Extension Activity. Have students work in pairs or individually to complete the activity.

Students who demonstrated mastery on every objective posttest but scored below 80% on the chapter test

Reinforce learning using:

- **Gizmos** Use the *Solving Two-Step Equations* Gizmo with the Reinforcement Activity. Have students work in pairs or small groups to complete the activity.
- Additional Activities from the online resources.
- Algebra Skill Builders for Chapter 3 from the online resources.

Students who did not demonstrate mastery on any or all of the objective posttests or the chapter test

Reinforce learning using:

- **Gizmos** Present the *Solving Two-Step Equations* Gizmo to students in small groups using the instruction on page 276.
- Additional Activities from the online resources.
- Algebra Skill Builders for Chapter 3 from the online resources.

Retest—Administer Chapter 3 Test, Form B, from the online resources to students who scored below 80 percent on Form A when time allows.

NEXT STEPS • Pretest

- Administer Chapter 4, Objective 1 Pretest, page 280, to all students.

Ongoing Assessment

Students who demonstrated mastery on every objective posttest and scored 80% or above on the chapter test

1. Divide students into pairs or allow the to work individually for this activity.

2. Distribute one copy of the Extension Activity from the online resources to each student.

3. Direct students to the Gizmo *Beam to Moon* through the Inside Algebra Student Web site, http://insidealgebra. voyagerlearning.com.

4. Have students complete the Extension Activity.

5. **Peer Review.** If there is time, have students exchange papers with a peer. They should review and discuss each response and be prepared to explain their thinking.

Variation: If students do not have access to the Gizmo, provide them with the following information before they begin the Extension. An object that weighs 10 pounds on Earth weighs: 1.66 pounds on the Moon, 9.07 pounds on Venus, 3.77 pounds on Mars, and 0.58 pounds on Pluto.

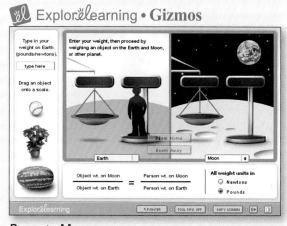

Beam to Moon

Gizmos
Extension Activity   Name_____ Date_____

BEAM TO MOON (RATIOS AND PROPORTIONS)

Did you know that an object's weight on Earth depends on Earth's gravitational force pulling the object down? Did you also know that an object's weight is different on different planets and the Moon? This is because larger planets have a greater gravitational force, which makes for greater weights on these planets.

1. The following proportion can be used to find a person's weight on the Moon.

$$\frac{\text{Object weight on Moon}}{\text{Object weight on Earth}} = \frac{\text{Person weight on Moon}}{\text{Person weight on Earth}}$$

Start the *Beam to Moon (Ratio and Proportions)* Gizmo. Suppose a person weighs 100 pounds. Enter this weight into the Gizmo. Notice how the proportion at the bottom of the screen changes.

2. To find your weight on the Moon, drag the watermelon to the scale on Earth, then to the scale on the Moon. What is the proportion now?

$$\frac{1.66}{10} = \frac{\text{Person weight on Moon}}{100}$$

Solve the proportion. What is the person's weight on the Moon? __16.6 pounds__ To check your answer, click "Beam Away."

3. What percent of 100 pounds is the person's weight on the Moon? Complete and solve the following proportion to find the answer.

$$\frac{n}{100} = \frac{16.6}{100}$$

The weight of a 100-pound person on the Moon is __16.6__% of his or her weight on Earth.

4. Click "Beam Home." A person weighs 200 pounds on Earth.

Find this person's weight on the Moon. _____33.2 pounds_____

What percent of this person's weight on Earth is the person's weight on the Moon?

16.6%

What does this tell you about the weight of any person on the Moon in relation to his or her weight on Earth?

The Moon weight is 16.6% of the Earth weight.

A dog weighs 60 pounds on Earth. Use the percentage you found in the previous question to find the weight of the dog on the Moon.

9.96 pounds

Inside Algebra • Chapter 3 • Extension   **1**

Gizmos
Extension Activity   Name_____ Date_____

BEAM TO MOON (RATIOS AND PROPORTIONS) (continued)

5. Click "Beam Home." Find the weight of the 100-pound person on different planets. Make sure you have 100 pounds entered as the weight on Earth, then change to the correct planet in the right pane of the screen. Next, drag the watermelon to the scale on Earth, then to the scale on the planet. Record the proportion in the table. Finally, click "Beam Away," and record the weight on the planet in the table.

Planet	Venus		Mars		Pluto	
Proportion	$\frac{9.07}{10}$	$=\frac{\text{Weight on Venus}}{100}$	$\frac{3.77}{10}$	$=\frac{\text{Weight on Mars}}{100}$	$\frac{0.58}{10}$	$=\frac{\text{Weight on Pluto}}{100}$
Weight (in pounds)	90.7		37.7		5.8	
Planet Weight as a Percent of Earth Weight	90.7%		37.7%		5.8%	

6. What percent of a person's Earth weight is his or her weight on Venus? On Mars? On Pluto? Record your answers in the table in Problem 5.

7. Which planet in Problem 5 is the largest? Which planet is the smallest? Explain how you found your answer.

Sample answer: Venus is the largest because its gravitational force is the

greatest. Pluto is the smallest because its gravitational force is the least.

8. Which is greater, the weight of an object on Pluto that weighs 200 pounds on Earth, or the weight of an object on Mars that weighs 30 pounds on Earth? Show your work.

200-pound object on Pluto:
$$\frac{0.58}{10} = \frac{x}{200}$$
$$116 = 10x$$
$$11.6 = x$$

30-pound object on Mars:
$$\frac{3.77}{10} = \frac{x}{30}$$
$$113.1 = 10x$$
$$11.31 = x$$

Because 11.6 pounds is greater than 11.31 pounds, the weight of the object on Pluto is greater.

Inside Algebra • Chapter 3 • Extension   **2**

Ongoing Assessment

Students who demonstrated mastery on every objective posttest but scored below 80% on the chapter test

1. Divide students into pairs or small groups.

2. Distribute one copy of the Individual Reinforcement Activity from the online resources to each student.

3. Direct students to the Gizmo *Solving Two-Step Equations* through the Inside Algebra Student Web site, http://insidealgebra.voyagerlearning.com.

4. Have students complete the Reinforcement Activity.

5. **Peer Review.** If time permits, have students exchange papers with a peer to review and discuss each others responses. Remind students to be prepared to explain the reasoning behind their responses.

> **Variation:** If students do not access to the Gizmo, have them use algebra tiles to model solving Problem 3. For Problem 4, write six different two-step equations on the board or overhead for students to solve.

Gizmos
Reinforcement Activity   Name _____ Date _____

SOLVING TWO-STEP EQUATIONS

1. Complete each step to solve each equation.

$$x + 3 = 8$$
$$x + 3 - \underline{3} = 8 - \underline{3}$$
$$x = \underline{5}$$

$$x - 5 = 7$$
$$x - 5 + \underline{5} = 7 + \underline{5}$$
$$x = \underline{12}$$

2. Complete each step to solve each equation.

$$4x = 20$$
$$4x \div \underline{4} = 20 \div \underline{4}$$
$$x = \underline{5}$$

$$\frac{x}{2} = 8$$
$$\frac{x}{2} \cdot \underline{2} = 8 \cdot \underline{2}$$
$$x = \underline{16}$$

3. Start the *Solving Two-Step Equations* Gizmo. Look at the equation $2x + 3 = 7$. This equation uses multiplication and addition.

   What operation undoes addition? _____ subtraction _____

   Drag the tile that undoes the addition. What is the equation that results? ___ $2x = 4$ ___

   What operation undoes multiplication? _____ division _____

   Drag the tile that undoes the multiplication. What is the solution to $2x + 3 = 7$? $x = \underline{2}$

4. Each person in your group should use the Gizmo to solve as many equations as he or she can in two minutes. One person should keep time and record the number of correct answers. The person with the greatest number of correct answers wins.

5. A store has a shirt on sale for 40% off of the regular price. What is the sale price for a $60 shirt?

   Complete the steps to find 40% of $60.

   This is the amount of discount.

   $$\frac{40}{100} = \frac{x}{60}$$
   $$2,400 = 100x$$
   $$24 = x$$

   Subtract the discount from the regular price.

   $$\$60 - \$\underline{24} = \$\underline{36}$$

ExploreLearning • Gizmos

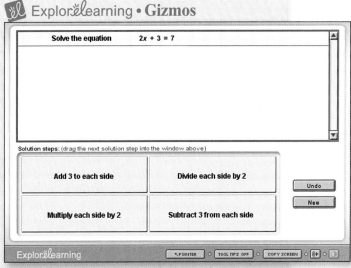

Solving Two-Step Equations

Students who did not demonstrate mastery on any or all of the objective posttests or the chapter test

The Gizmo is not needed in Problems 1–4.

1. Ask students to solve $x + 3 = 8$. Use these steps to scaffold instruction.

   • Ask students to name the operation given in the equation. addition Next, ask them what operation undoes addition. subtraction

   • Ask students to describe how subtraction is used to isolate x. subtract 3 from both sides

   • Ask students the result of subtracting 3 from 8. 5

   • Ask students to name the solution. 5

Repeat the process in Problem 1 with Problems 2–4.

2. Ask students to solve $x - 5 = 7$. 12

3. Ask students to solve $4x = 20$. 5

4. Ask students to solve $\frac{x}{2} = 8$. 16

5. Start the *Solving Two-Step Equations* Gizmo. Use the following steps to scaffold instruction:

   • Ask students to name the operations in $2x + 3 = 7$. multiplication; addition Next, ask them to name the principal operator. addition

   • Ask students what operation undoes addition. subtraction Drag the "Subtract 3 from each side" tile under the equation. Ask student to name the resulting equation. $2x = 4$

   • Ask students what operation undoes multiplication. division Next, ask whether dividing by 2 or by 4 isolates the variable. by 2 Drag the correct tile into the equation area.

   • Ask students to name the solution. 2

6. Have several students go up to the board. Use the "New" button to create a new equation. The student who solves the equations correctly first wins. Repeat with different groups of students.

   Variation: If students do not have access to the Gizmo, use a blackboard or overhead projector to complete the Activity. In Problem 6, create two-step equations for students to solve.

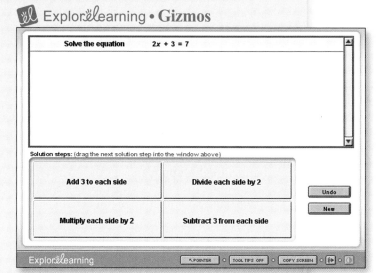

Solving Two-Step Equations

3 CHAPTER

Ongoing Assessment

Chapter 3 Test, Form B

MATERIALS

- Chapter 3 Test, Form B, from the Online Resources, pages 1–2

DIRECTIONS

1. Have students turn to Chapter 3 Test, Form B, pages 1–2, from the Online Resources. Administer the Chapter Test to all students.

2. Score the test by objective and update the class record card.

Name_____ Date_____

Objective 1

Solve the equations.

1. $x = 3 - 19$
   $x = -16$

2. $-6 + x = 14$
   $x = 20$

3. $7 = x + 17$
   $x = -10$

4. $x + 0.7 = 5.8$
   $x = 5.1$

Objective 2

Solve the equations.

5. $4x = 28$
   $x = 7$

6. $3x = 21$
   $x = 7$

7. $\frac{x}{3} = -8$
   $x = -24$

8. $\frac{3}{4} \cdot x = -9$
   $x = -12$

Objective 3

Solve the equations.

9. $3x + 2 = 11$
   $x = 3$

10. $\frac{x}{3} - 18 = -11$
    $x = 21$

11. $4x - 5 = x + 7$
    $x = 4$

12. $\frac{3}{5}x - 7 = 8$
    $x = 25$

Inside Algebra — Chapter 3 • Test • Form B — 1

Name_____ Date_____

Objective 4

Find the solution to each problem.

13. At a school dance, $\frac{2}{3}$ of the boys were wearing black shirts. If 36 boys were wearing black shirts, how many boys were at the dance?

    <u>54 boys</u>
    $\frac{2}{3}x = 36$

14. The sum of three consecutive integers is 48. What are the integers?

    <u>15, 16, 17</u>
    $n + (n + 1) + (n + 2) = 48 \qquad 3n + 3 + (-3) = 48 + (-3)$
    $3n = 45$

Objective 5

Solve the proportions.

15. $\frac{4}{x} = \frac{12}{21}$
    $12x = 84$
    $x = 7$

16. $\frac{3x}{-4} = \frac{12}{8}$
    $24x = -48$
    $x = -2$

17. $\frac{x}{120} = \frac{7}{3}$
    $3x = 840$
    $x = 280$

18. $\frac{24}{80} = \frac{12}{x}$
    $24x = 960$
    $x = 40$

Objective 6

Find the solution to each problem.

19. <u>30</u> % of 150 is 45.
    $\frac{n}{100} = \frac{45}{150}$
    $150n = 4,500$

20. 40% of 60 is <u>24</u> .
    $\frac{40}{100} = \frac{n}{60}$
    $100n = 2,400$

21. 25% of <u>68</u> is 17.
    $\frac{25}{100} = \frac{17}{n}$
    $25n = 1,700$

22. A store is advertising that bikes are on sale for 20% off the regular price. What is the sale price for a $180 bike?
    $\frac{20}{100} = \frac{n}{180}$
    $100n = 3,600$
    $n = 36$
    $\$180 - \$36 = \$144$

Inside Algebra — Chapter 3 • Test • Form B — 2

This page intentionally left blank

Graphing Relations and Functions

In this chapter, students graph ordered pairs, relations, and linear equations. They use tables, graphs, and sets to identify and write the domain, range, and inverse of a relation. Students also classify relations as functions and use function notation to find the value of a function at a specific point.

Objective 1
Graph ordered pairs and relations.

Objective 2
Identify the domain, range, and inverse of a relation.

Objective 3
Determine the range for a given domain of a relation.

Objective 4
Graph linear equations.

Objective 5
Determine whether a relation is a function, and find a value for a given function.

Chapter 4 VOCABULARY

Objective 1 Pretest

Students complete the Objective 1 Pretest at least one day before beginning Objective 1.

Using the Results

- Score the pretest and update the class record card.

- If the majority of students do not demonstrate mastery of the concepts, use the 4-Day Instructional Plan for Objective 1.

- If the majority of students demonstrate mastery of the concepts, use the 3-Day Instructional Plan for Objective 1.

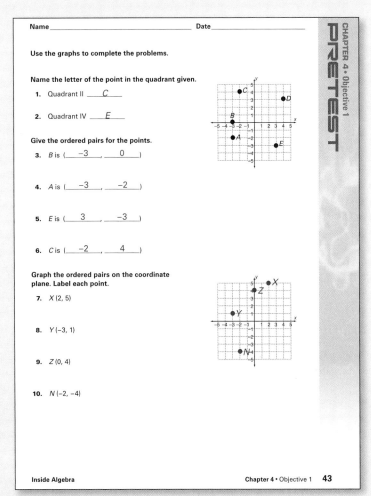

Name _____ Date _____

Use the graphs to complete the problems.

Name the letter of the point in the quadrant given.

1. Quadrant II _____C_____

2. Quadrant IV _____E_____

Give the ordered pairs for the points.

3. B is (___−3___ , ___0___)

4. A is (___−3___ , ___−2___)

5. E is (___3___ , ___−3___)

6. C is (___−2___ , ___4___)

Graph the ordered pairs on the coordinate plane. Label each point.

7. X (2, 5)

8. Y (−3, 1)

9. Z (0, 4)

10. N (−2, −4)

Inside Algebra   Chapter 4 • Objective 1   **43**

CHAPTER 4 • Objective 1
PRETEST

Goals and Activities

Objective 1 Goals

The following activities, when used with the instructional plans on pages 282 and 283, enable students to:

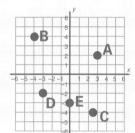

- Give the letter of the point in Quadrant III of the graph as **D**

- Give the letter of the point in Quadrant II of the graph as **B**

- Give the ordered pair for letter A as **(3, 2)**

- Give the ordered pair for letter C as $\left(2\frac{1}{2}, -4\right)$

Objective 1 Activities

Concept Development Activities	
★**CD 1** Finding Ordered Pairs in Graphs, page 284	★**CD 2** Graphing Maps, page 286

Practice Activities	
PA 1 Graphing Coordinates, page 287	**PA 2** Finding What Fits, page 288

Progress-Monitoring Activities	
PM 1 Apply Skills 1, page 289	**PM 2** Apply Skills 2, page 290

*Problem-Solving Activity
★**PS 1** Graphing Quadrants, page 291

Ongoing Assessment
Posttest Objective 1, page 293
Pretest Objective 2, page 294

CD = Concept Development   PM = Progress Monitoring   PS = Problem Solving
PA = Practice Activity   ★ = Includes Problem Solving

Instructional Plans

4-Day Instructional Plan

Use the 4-Day Instructional Plan when pretest results indicate that students would benefit from a slower pace. This plan is used when the majority of students need more time or did not demonstrate mastery on the pretest.

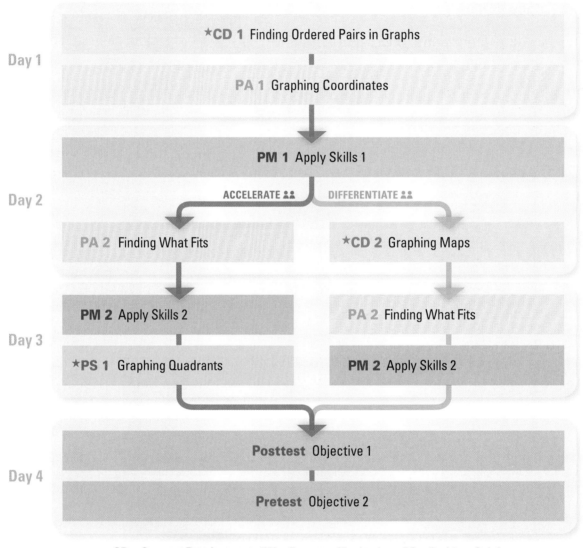

Day 1

★**CD 1** Finding Ordered Pairs in Graphs

PA 1 Graphing Coordinates

Day 2

PM 1 Apply Skills 1

ACCELERATE   DIFFERENTIATE

PA 2 Finding What Fits   ★**CD 2** Graphing Maps

Day 3

PM 2 Apply Skills 2   **PA 2** Finding What Fits

★**PS 1** Graphing Quadrants   **PM 2** Apply Skills 2

Day 4

Posttest Objective 1

Pretest Objective 2

CD = Concept Development   PM = Progress Monitoring   PS = Problem Solving
PA = Practice Activity   ★ = Includes Problem Solving

3-Day Instructional Plan

Use the 3-Day Instructional Plan when pretest results indicate that students can move through the activities at a faster pace. This plan is ideal when the majority of students demonstrate mastery on the pretest.

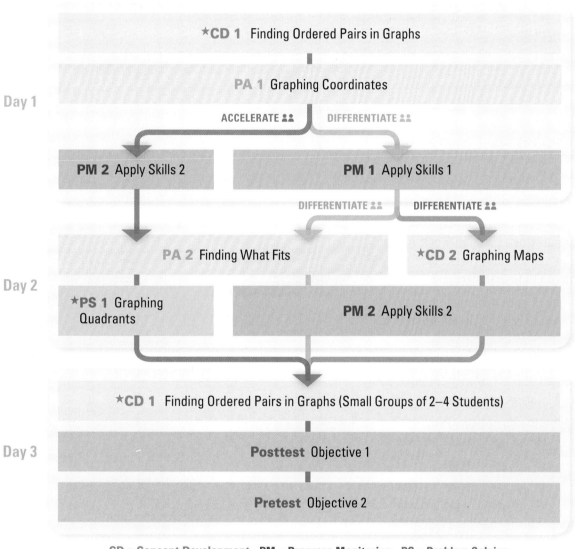

Day 1

★CD 1 Finding Ordered Pairs in Graphs

PA 1 Graphing Coordinates

ACCELERATE 👥   DIFFERENTIATE 👥

PM 2 Apply Skills 2

PM 1 Apply Skills 1

DIFFERENTIATE 👥   DIFFERENTIATE 👥

Day 2

PA 2 Finding What Fits

★CD 2 Graphing Maps

★PS 1 Graphing Quadrants

PM 2 Apply Skills 2

★CD 1 Finding Ordered Pairs in Graphs (Small Groups of 2–4 Students)

Day 3

Posttest Objective 1

Pretest Objective 2

CD = Concept Development   PM = Progress Monitoring   PS = Problem Solving
PA = Practice Activity   ★ = Includes Problem Solving

Objective 1
Concept Development Activities

★ CD 1 Finding Ordered Pairs in Graphs

Use with 4-Day or 3-Day Instructional Plan. In this activity, students gain experience placing ordered pairs in all quadrants of a graph.

MATERIALS

- *Interactive Text,* pages 121–122
- Blackline Master 59

DIRECTIONS

1. Make a transparency of Blackline Master 59, Graph Paper, marking 0 to 10 on the *x*- and *y*-axes. Distribute one copy of Blackline Master 59 to each student.

2. Discuss the following terms with students:

   ordered pair Two numbers that name the coordinates of a point on a graph, with the horizontal coordinate listed first and the vertical coordinate listed second

   x-coordinate The horizontal distance from the point of origin of a graph; in an ordered pair, this value is always written first

   y-coordinate The vertical distance from the point of origin of a graph; in an ordered pair, this value is always written second

3. Divide the class into two groups. Designate one group to be Team X and the other group to be Team O.

4. Explain the game rules to students.

   - The purpose of this activity is to be the first team to place four of its own points in a row on the grid. The four in a row can be horizontal, vertical, or diagonal.

   - The game will start with one student from each team choosing two whole numbers between 1 and 10. The first number represents the *x*-value, and the second represents the *y*-value of a point, making one ordered pair per team.

★ = Includes Problem Solving

284 Chapter 4 • Objective 1

GRAPH PAPER

Name _____ Date _____

WHO WON?

The tables show the ordered pairs selected by Team X and Team O for each game. Plot the points to determine who won each game (four in a row), and on what turn.

Game 1

Turn	1	2	3	4	5	6	7	8	9
X	(2, 3)	(3, 2)	(1, 4)	(0, 4)	(1, 5)	(1, 6)	(1, 3)	(0, 3)	(3, 3)
O	(2, 2)	(4, 1)	(0, 5)	(−1, 4)	(−2, 3)	(−3, 2)	(1, 2)	(0, 2)	(−1, 2)

1. Which team won? Team O _____
2. On what turn? 6 _____
3. List the ordered pairs that created the straight line. (0, 5), (−1, 4), (−2, 3),
   (−3, 2) _____

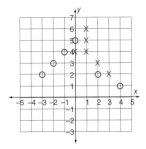

Inside Algebra   Chapter 4 • Objective 1 • CD 1   **121**

CONCEPT DEVELOPMENT

- Each ordered pair is plotted on the transparency and labeled with **X** for Team X or **O** for Team O.

- The teams will take turns naming ordered pairs for the teacher to plot.

- The teams must have an equal number of turns before a winner is announced.

- If both teams reach four points on the same turn, continue until one team has more points in a row after teams have had an equal number of turns.

5. If you choose, designate a team spokesperson for each team.

6. Write each ordered pair on the board in a chart with the headings **X** and **O** before graphing.

7. Emphasize how a point is graphed by counting aloud as you move across the x-axis and up the y-axis.

8. Continue the game until one team gets four points in a row. Ask the winning team to name the ordered pairs that formed the row and list them on the board.

> **Variation: Numbers** Make a grid marked from –5 to 5 on the x- and y-axes. Start by giving Team O the point (–1, 2). This will force the teams to use positive and negative coordinates on the grid.

9. Play several games until students understand how to get four points in a row and how to block their opponents.

10. Once students have a solid understanding of the process, divide the class into pairs, and have each pair play against another pair. Have each team write the ordered pair before plotting it. Circulate around the class to be sure students are naming and plotting the ordered pairs correctly.

11. Have students turn to *Interactive Text,* pages 121–122, Who Won? and complete the questions about the game.

> **Variation: Challenge** Teams must get five points in a row.

> **Variation: Different Numbers** The teacher picks the starting point for both teams.

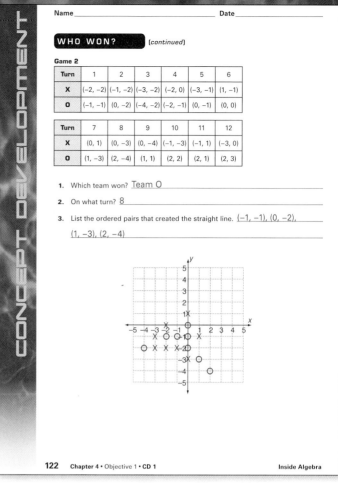

Name_____ Date_____

WHO WON? *(continued)*

Game 2

Turn	1	2	3	4	5	6
X	(–2, –2)	(–1, –2)	(–3, –2)	(–2, 0)	(–3, –1)	(1, –1)
O	(–1, –1)	(0, –2)	(–4, –2)	(–2, –1)	(0, –1)	(0, 0)

Turn	7	8	9	10	11	12
X	(0, 1)	(0, –3)	(0, –4)	(–1, –3)	(–1, 1)	(–3, 0)
O	(1, –3)	(2, –4)	(1, 1)	(2, 2)	(2, 1)	(2, 3)

1. Which team won? Team O

2. On what turn? 8

3. List the ordered pairs that created the straight line. (–1, –1), (0, –2), (1, –3), (2, –4)

NEXT STEPS • Differentiate

4-Day Instructional Plan:
PA 1, page 287—All students, for additional practice

3-Day Instructional Plan:
PA 1, page 287—Students who are completing this activity for the first time, for additional practice

Objective 1 Posttest, page 293—Students who are completing this activity for the second time

Concept Development Activities

★CD 2 Graphing Maps

Use with 4-Day or 3-Day Instructional Plan. In this activity, students identify the quadrants of a graph.

MATERIALS

- Blackline Master 59
- Rulers

DIRECTIONS

1. Review the following term with students:

   ordered pair Two numbers that name the coordinates of a point on a graph, with the horizontal coordinate listed first and the vertical coordinate listed second

2. Discuss the following terms with students:

   coordinate plane The plane determined by a horizontal number line, called the *x*-axis, and a vertical number line, called the *y*-axis, intersecting at a point called the origin

   quadrant One of four regions on a coordinate plane formed by the intersection of the *x*-axis and the *y*-axis

3. Split the classroom into four sections with an imaginary vertical line and an imaginary horizontal line. Ask students to give as many sets of names to these quadrants as they can, such as northeast, northwest, southeast, and southwest.

4. Assign each section a quadrant number: Quadrant I, Quadrant II, Quadrant III, and Quadrant IV.

5. Distribute one copy of Blackline Master 59, Graph Paper, to each student. Have students draw the quadrants, using the whole sheet. For each quadrant, they should draw the items it contains, such as tables, chairs, and desks.

6. As a class, have students decide on a scale for the coordinate plane. Using this scale, tell students to give an ordered pair for each of the different items in the room.

7. Have the class discuss why each student has different answers. Ask students what could be done to standardize the graphs, which are essentially maps of the room.

NEXT STEPS • Differentiate

4-Day Instructional Plan:
PA 2, page 288—All students, for additional practice

3-Day Instructional Plan:
PM 2, page 290—All students, to assess progress

★ = Includes Problem Solving

GRAPH PAPER

Practice Activities

PA 1 Graphing Coordinates

Use with 4-Day or 3-Day Instructional Plan. In this activity, students gain experience placing ordered pairs in all quadrants of a graph.

MATERIALS

- Blackline Master 59
- Rulers

DIRECTIONS

1. Review the following terms with students:

   coordinate plane The plane determined by a horizontal number line, called the *x*-axis, and a vertical number line, called the *y*-axis, intersecting at a point called the origin

   quadrant One of four regions on a coordinate plane formed by the intersection of the *x*-axis and the *y*-axis

2. Distribute one copy of Blackline Master 59, Graph Paper, to each student. Have students make a coordinate plane on the graph paper with the same scale in all four quadrants.

3. Have students draw their two initials on the graph paper using only straight lines and containing as many intersecting lines (integer coordinates) as possible. Tell half of the students to use Quadrants I and IV and the other half to use Quadrants II and III.

   Sample answers:

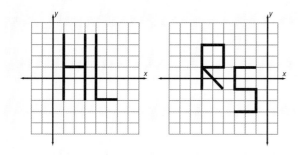

4. Ask each student to list the coordinates of the intersection points of their initials on notebook paper, making a separate list for each initial. Students should not indicate what the letters are. The points should be sequential, listed in the order used to draw each letter.

5. Collect the lists from the first half of the class, and mix the papers. Randomly give one list to each student in the second half of the class.

6. Collect the lists that the second half of the class made. Mix the papers, and randomly give one list to each student in the first half of the class.

7. Tell students to use their own graph paper to plot the points in the list they received and connect the points in the order given.

8. Have students find the person whose initials they graphed and check their work by comparing them to the original graphs.

NEXT STEPS • Differentiate

4-Day Instructional Plan:
PM **1**, page 289—All students, to assess progress

3-Day Instructional Plan:
PM **2**, page 290—Students who demonstrate understanding of the concept, to assess progress

PM **1**, page 289—Students who need additional support, to assess progress

Practice Activities

PA 2 Finding What Fits

Use with 4-Day or 3-Day Instructional Plan. In this activity, students solve for variables by using cross-multiplication and practice graphing ordered pairs.

MATERIALS

- *Interactive Text*, page 123
- Blackline Master 59

DIRECTIONS

1. Distribute one copy of Blackline Master 59, Graph Paper, to each student.

2. Review how to solve proportional equations.

   Sample problems:

   $\frac{3}{4} = \frac{1.5}{x}$ $x = 2$ $\frac{x}{10} = \frac{2}{2.5}$ $x = 8$ $\frac{6}{x} = \frac{30}{35}$ $x = 7$

3. Have students turn to *Interactive Text*, page 123, It Fits. Have students solve each proportion and indicate the value for each letter.

4. Tell students to use the values to find the ordered pairs at the bottom of the page and graph them on graph paper. Explain to students that the ordered pairs make a drawing when the points are connected.

5. Have students compare their pictures with one another. If different, have students check their ordered pairs and the solutions to the equations.

NEXT STEPS • Differentiate

4-Day Instructional Plan:
PM 2, page 290—All students, to assess progress

👥 **3-Day Instructional Plan:**
PS 1, page 291—Students who are on the accelerated path, to develop problem-solving skills

PM 2, page 290—Students who are on the differentiated path, to assess progress

---

Name _____ Date _____

59

GRAPH PAPER

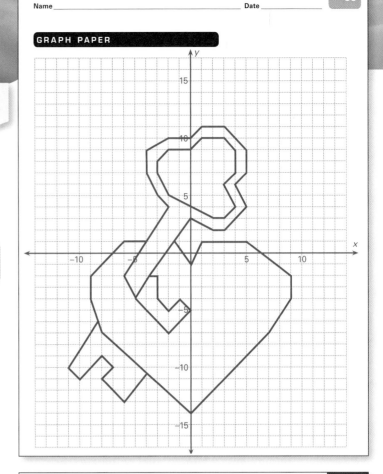

Name _____ Date _____

PRACTICE

IT FITS

Find the number that solves each equation. Use that number to replace the letter in the ordered pairs for the plots at the bottom of the page.

1. $\frac{2}{3} = \frac{A}{7.5}$ $3A = 15$
2. $\frac{B}{8} = \frac{1}{2}$ $2B = 8$
3. $\frac{10}{15} = \frac{2}{C}$ $10C = 30$
4. $\frac{D}{33} = \frac{1}{3}$ $3D = 33$
5. $\frac{E}{56} = \frac{1}{7}$ $7E = 56$
6. $\frac{2}{18} = \frac{F}{90}$ $18F = 180$
7. $\frac{2}{G} = \frac{6}{27}$ $6G = 54$
8. $\frac{H}{13} = \frac{3}{39}$ $39H = 39$
9. $\frac{25}{35} = \frac{5}{J}$ $25J = 175$
10. $\frac{-1}{K} = \frac{15}{30}$ $15K = -30$
11. $\frac{M}{15} = \frac{4}{10}$ $10M = 60$

A = 5
B = 4
C = 3
D = 11
E = 8
F = 10
G = 9
H = 1
J = 7
K = -2
M = 6

Plot the points and connect each point in order. Make all five plots on the same coordinate plane.

1st Plot:	2nd Plot:	3rd Plot:	4th Plot:	5th Plot:
(−6, K)	(−2, A)	(−8.5, −6)	(−5, −4)	(−4, H)
(−5, −4)	(2, C)	(−11, −10)	(−2, −7)	(−6, H)
(0, C)	(C, C)	(−10, −11)	(0, −5)	(−9, −2)
(2, 2)	(B, B)	(−8, −9)	(−1, −4)	(−9, −4)
(C, 2)	(C, M)	(−7, −10)	(−2, −5)	(−8, −7)
(A, B)	(B, J)	(−8, −11)	(−3, −4)	(0, −14)
(B, M)	(B, G)	(−6, −13)	(−3, −2)	(7, −7)
(A, J)	(C, F)	(−4, −10.5)	(−3.5, −2)	(G, −4)
(A, G)	(H, F)	STOP	STOP	(G, −2)
(C, D)	(0, G)	Pick up pencil	Pick up pencil	(A, H)
(H, D)	(−2, G)			(1, H)
(0, F)	(−3, E)			(0, −1)
(K, F)	(−3, J)			(−1.5, H)
(−4, G)	(−2, A)			STOP
(−4, J)	STOP			
(−3, A)	Pick up pencil			
(−2, B)				
(−6, −2)				
STOP				
Pick up pencil				

12. What picture did you get? key in heart

Inside Algebra   Chapter 4 • Objective 1 • PA 2   **123**

Objective 1
Progress-Monitoring Activities

PM 1 Apply Skills 1

Use with 4-Day or 3-Day Instructional Plan.

MATERIALS

- *Interactive Text*, page 124

DIRECTIONS

1. Have students turn to *Interactive Text,* page 124, Apply Skills 1.

2. Remind students of the key terms: *quadrant* and *ordered pair.*

3. Monitor student work, and provide feedback as necessary.

   Watch for:
   - Do students give the *x*-value first, followed by the *y*-value?
   - Do students correctly identify the four quadrants?

NEXT STEPS • Differentiate

👥 4-Day and 3-Day Instructional Plans:

PA 2, page 288—Students who demonstrate understanding of the concept, for additional practice

CD 2, page 286—Students who need additional concept development

---

Name _____ Date _____

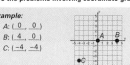

APPLY SKILLS 1

Solve the problems involving coordinate graphs.

Example:

A: (0 , 0)
B: (4 , 0)
C: (−4 , −4)

1. Name the ordered pairs for the labeled points.

   A: (−2 , 3)
   B: (1 , 1)
   C: (3 , 0)
   D: (1 , −2)
   E: (−2 , −4)

2. Plot the points listed below and label each point with its letter.

   A is (2, −3)
   B is (5, 0)
   C is (−3, −2)
   D is (−3, 4)
   E is (0, −1)

3. Name a point in Quadrant I. _B_
   What is its coordinate? (3 , 2)

4. Name a point in Quadrant IV. _D_
   What is its coordinate? (3 , −2)

5. Name a point in Quadrant II. _C_
   What is its coordinate? (−2 , 1)

Objective 1
Progress-Monitoring Activities

PM 2 Apply Skills 2

Use with 4-Day or 3-Day Instructional Plan.

MATERIALS

- *Interactive Text*, page 125

DIRECTIONS

1. Have students turn to *Interactive Text*, page 125, Apply Skills 2.

2. Remind students of the key term: *ordered pair*.

3. Monitor student work, and provide feedback as necessary.

   Watch for:
   - Do students remember that a square is also a rectangle and a parallelogram?
   - Do students recognize the difference between a parallelogram and a trapezoid?

NEXT STEPS • Differentiate

👥 4-Day Instructional Plan:

PS 1, page 291—Students who are on the accelerated path, to develop problem-solving skills

Objective 1 Posttest, page 293—Students who are on the differentiated path

👥 3-Day Instructional Plan:

PA 2, page 288—Students who are on the accelerated path, for additional practice

CD 1 (Small Groups), page 284—Students who are on the differentiated path, for additional concept development and problem solving

---

APPLY SKILLS 2

Plot the four ordered pairs on the graphs below them. Name the quadrilateral formed by connecting the four points. You may need to look up the definitions of quadrilateral, parallelogram, rectangle, trapezoid, and square.

Example:
(2, 2), (−2, 2), (−2, −2), (2, −2)

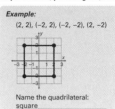

Name the quadrilateral:
square

1. (2, 3), (2, −1), (−3, 1), (−3, −3)

Name the quadrilateral:
parallelogram

2. (−3, −1), (−4, 2), (1, 2), (2, −1)

Name the quadrilateral:
parallelogram

3. (3, −1), (0, −4), (−3, −1), (0, 2)

Name the quadrilateral:
square

4. (0, 2), (2, −2), (−3, −2), (−2, 2)

Name the quadrilateral:
trapezoid

5. (2, 0), (0, −2), (−3, 1), (−1, 3)

Name the quadrilateral:
rectangle

Inside Algebra   Chapter 4 • Objective 1 • PM 2   **125**

Objective 1
Problem-Solving Activity

★ PS 1 Graphing Quadrants

Use with 4-Day or 3-Day Instructional Plan. In this activity, students identify the sign of the x *and* y *values in each quadrant.*

MATERIALS

- *Interactive Text,* page 126
- Blackline Master 59

DIRECTIONS

1. Review the following terms with students:

   coordinate plane The plane determined by a horizontal number line, called the *x*-axis, and a vertical number line, called the *y*-axis, intersecting at a point called the origin

   quadrant One of four regions on a coordinate plane formed by the intersection of the *x*-axis and the *y*-axis

   x-coordinate The horizontal distance from the point of origin of a graph; in an ordered pair, this value is always written first

   y-coordinate The vertical distance from the point of origin of a graph; in an ordered pair, this value is always written second

2. Discuss the following terms with students:

   parallel Lines that do not intersect; they are always the same distance apart

   perpendicular Lines that intersect at right angles

3. Distribute one copy of Blackline Master 59, Graph Paper, to each student, and have them use the full sheet to draw a coordinate plane and label the quadrants.

4. Have students turn to *Interactive Text,* page 126, Quadrant Graphing, and complete the exercises. Remind students that a line must be drawn with arrows at both ends to show that it goes on forever in both directions.

★ = Includes Problem Solving

Name _____ Date _____

GRAPH PAPER

Name _____ Date _____

PROBLEM SOLVING

QUADRANT GRAPHING

Answer the problems about coordinate graphs.

Answers will vary on all questions; sample answers are given.

Part A
1. Draw a coordinate plane on a piece of graph paper.
2. Draw a straight line through Quadrants I and IV only.
3. Label four points on the line with the letters *A*, *B*, *C*, and *D*.
4. Give the relation of this line. $x = 3$
5. What do you notice about the *x*-coordinates?
   They remain constant; they are positive.
6. What do you notice about the *y*-coordinates?
   They vary over all real values.

Part B
1. Draw a straight line through Quadrants III and II only.
2. Label four points on the line with the letters *W*, *X*, *Y*, and *Z*.
3. Give the relation of this line. $x = -6$
4. What do you notice about the *x*-coordinates?
   They remain constant; they are negative.
5. What do you notice about the *y*-coordinates?
   They vary over all real values.

Part C
1. Draw a straight line through Quadrants III, II, and I.
2. Label four points on the line with the letters *H*, *I*, *J*, and *K*.
3. Give the relation of this line. $y = 3x + 3$
4. What do you notice about the *x*-coordinates?
   They vary over all real values.
5. What do you notice about the *y*-coordinates?
   They vary over all real values and depend on *x*.

Part D
1. Draw a straight line through Quadrants IV, III, and II.
2. Label four points on the line with the letters *P*, *Q*, *R*, and *S*.
3. Give the relation of this line. $y = -x - 7$
4. What do you notice about the *x*-coordinates?
   They vary over all real values.
5. What do you notice about the *y*-coordinates?
   They vary over all real values and depend on *x*.

126 Chapter 4 • Objective 1 • PS 1   Inside Algebra

5. After students finish the exercises, have them discuss each of the four lines they created as a whole class or in small groups. Lead the discussion by asking questions about each line.

Examples:

> What is always true about the x-coordinate for the line?
>
> What is never true about the x-coordinate?
>
> What is sometimes true about the x-coordinate?
>
> What is always true about the y-coordinate?
>
> What is never true about the y-coordinate?
>
> What is sometimes true about the y-coordinate? Answers will vary, depending on the line discussed.

6. Direct students to notice the following:

- Whether the x- and y-coordinates are always positive or negative.

- Whether the x- and y-coordinates increase or decrease in value.

- Whether the line is parallel to an axis or sloped in one direction.

- Whether the line is perpendicular with one of the axes.

NEXT STEPS • Differentiate

4-Day Instructional Plan:
Objective 1 Posttest, page 293—All students

3-Day Instructional Plan:
CD 1 (Small Groups), page 284—All students, for additional concept development and problem solving

Objective 1 Posttest

Discuss with students the key concepts in Objective 1, then administer the Objective 1 Posttest to all students.

Using the Results

- Score the posttest and update the class record card.

- Provide reinforcement for students who do not demonstrate mastery of the concepts through individual or small-group reteaching of key concepts.

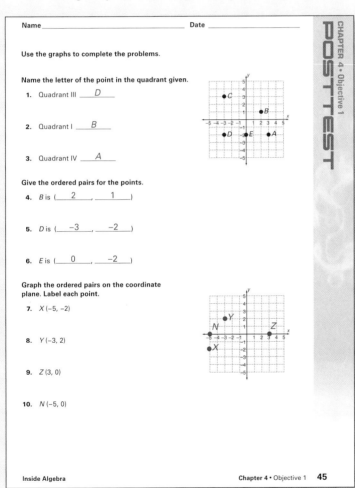

Name _____ Date _____

CHAPTER 4 • Objective 1
POSTTEST

Use the graphs to complete the problems.

Name the letter of the point in the quadrant given.

1. Quadrant III ___D___

2. Quadrant I ___B___

3. Quadrant IV ___A___

Give the ordered pairs for the points.

4. B is (___2___, ___1___)

5. D is (___−3___, ___−2___)

6. E is (___0___, ___−2___)

Graph the ordered pairs on the coordinate plane. Label each point.

7. X (−5, −2)

8. Y (−3, 2)

9. Z (3, 0)

10. N (−5, 0)

Inside Algebra   Chapter 4 • Objective 1   **45**

Objective 2
Identify the domain, range, and inverse of a relation.

Objective 2 Pretest

Students complete the Objective 2 Pretest on the same day as the Objective 1 Posttest.

Using the Results

• Score the pretest and update the class record card.

• If the majority of students do not demonstrate mastery of the concepts, use the 4-Day Instructional Plan for Objective 2.

• If the majority of students demonstrate mastery of the concepts, use the 3-Day Instructional Plan for Objective 2.

CHAPTER 4 • Objective 2
PRETEST

Name _____ Date _____

Answer the questions about relations.

1. How is the information in the table written as a set of ordered pairs called a relation?

x	y
5	2
–3	1
2	–3
–1	0
–4	–3

{(5, 2), (–3, 1), (2, –3), (–1, 0), (–4, –3)}

2. The domain of the relation in Problem 1 is which of the following?
   a. {5, 2, 1, 0}
   (b) {5, –3, 2, –1, –4}
   c. {2, 1, –3, 0 –3}
   d. {2, –3, –1, 0}

3. The range of the relation {(3, –1), (6, 2), (–2, –2), (0, 1)} is which of the following?
   a. {3, 6, –2, 0}
   (b) {–1, 2, –2, 1}
   c. {3, –1, 6, 2}
   d. {–1, . . . 1}

4. What is the inverse of the relation {(–3, 4), (0, 7), (2, 9), (–1, 6)}?

   {(4, –3), (7, 0), (9, 2), (6, –1)}

In Problems 5–7, the relation is {(2, 5), (0, 8), (–1, 3)}.

5. Write the inverse relation.

   {(5, 2), (8, 0), (3, –1)}

6. Write the domain of the inverse relation.

   {5, 8, 3}

7. Write the range of the inverse relation.

   {2, 0, –1}

Answer true or false for the relation {(–4, 2), (6, –8), (2, 0)}.

8. The range is {–4, 6, 0}. _____false_____

9. The domain is {–4, 6, 2}. _____true_____

10. The range is {(2, 0), (6, –8), (–4, 2)}. _____false_____

46 Chapter 4 • Objective 2   Inside Algebra

Objective 2 Goals

The following activities, when used with the instructional plans on pages 296 and 297, enable students to:

- Give the domain of the relation {(2, 3), (4, −1), (3, 0), (4, −3), (−2, −2)} as
  {2, 4, 3, 4, −2}

- Give the range of the relation {(2, 3), (4, −1), (3, 0), (4, −3), (−2, −2)} as
  {3, −1, 0, −3, −2}

- Give the inverse of the relation {(2, 3), (4, −1), (3, 0), (4, −3), (−2, −2)} as
  {(3, 2), (−1, 4), (0, 3), (−3, 4), (−2, −2)}

Objective 2 Activities

Concept Development Activities	
CD 1 Establishing Relationships, page 298	**★CD 2** Working for a Dollar, page 299

Practice Activities	
PA 1 Matching Ordered Pairs, page 301	**PA 2** Playing Definition Bingo, page 302

Progress-Monitoring Activities	
PM 1 Apply Skills 1, page 303	**PM 2** Apply Skills 2, page 304

★Problem-Solving Activities	
★PS 1 Finding the Information and Graphing It, page 305	**★PS 2** Valuing the Price of a Movie Ticket, page 306

Ongoing Assessment
Posttest Objective 2, page 307
Pretest Objective 3, page 308

CD = Concept Development   PM = Progress Monitoring   PS = Problem Solving
PA = Practice Activity   ★ = Includes Problem Solving

4 Instructional Plans

4-Day Instructional Plan

Use the 4-Day Instructional Plan when pretest results indicate that students would benefit from a slower pace. This plan is used when the majority of students need more time or did not demonstrate mastery on the pretest. This plan does not include all activities.

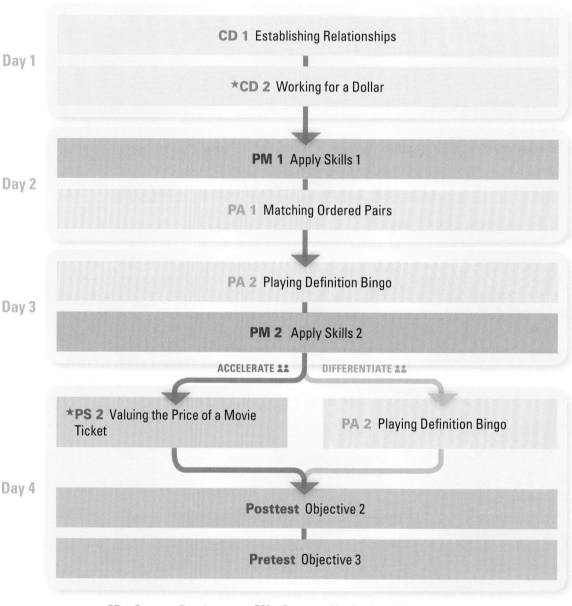

Day 1

CD 1 Establishing Relationships

★CD 2 Working for a Dollar

Day 2

PM 1 Apply Skills 1

PA 1 Matching Ordered Pairs

Day 3

PA 2 Playing Definition Bingo

PM 2 Apply Skills 2

ACCELERATE 👥👥   DIFFERENTIATE 👥👥

★PS 2 Valuing the Price of a Movie Ticket

PA 2 Playing Definition Bingo

Day 4

Posttest Objective 2

Pretest Objective 3

CD = Concept Development   PM = Progress Monitoring   PS = Problem Solving
PA = Practice Activity   ★ = Includes Problem Solving

3-Day Instructional Plan

Use the 3-Day Instructional Plan when pretest results indicate that students can move through the activities at a faster pace. This plan is ideal when the majority of students demonstrate mastery on the pretest. This plan does not include all activities.

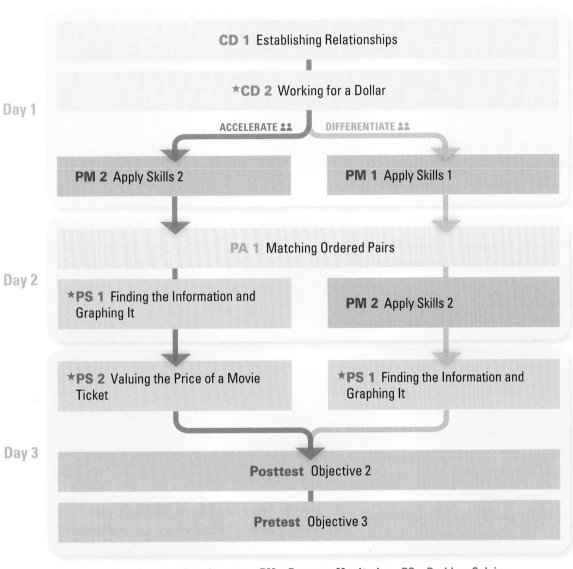

Day 1

CD 1 Establishing Relationships

★CD 2 Working for a Dollar

ACCELERATE · · / DIFFERENTIATE · ·

PM 2 Apply Skills 2

PM 1 Apply Skills 1

Day 2

PA 1 Matching Ordered Pairs

★PS 1 Finding the Information and Graphing It

PM 2 Apply Skills 2

Day 3

★PS 2 Valuing the Price of a Movie Ticket

★PS 1 Finding the Information and Graphing It

Posttest Objective 2

Pretest Objective 3

CD = Concept Development   PM = Progress Monitoring   PS = Problem Solving
PA = Practice Activity   ★ = Includes Problem Solving

Objective 2
Concept Development Activities

CD 1 Establishing Relationships

Use with 4-Day or 3-Day Instructional Plan. In this activity, students identify the domain, range, and inverse of a given relation.

MATERIALS

- Blackline Master 59

DIRECTIONS

1. Distribute one copy of Blackline Master 59, Graph Paper, to students.

2. Review the following terms with students:

   ordered pair Two numbers that name the coordinates of a point on a graph, with the horizontal coordinate listed first and the vertical coordinate listed second

   x-coordinate The horizontal distance from the point of origin of a graph; in an ordered pair, this value is always written first

   y-coordinate The vertical distance from the point of origin of a graph; in an ordered pair, this value is always written second

3. Discuss the following terms with students:

   relation A set of ordered pairs

   domain The possible values for x in a relation

   range The possible values for y in a relation

   inverse relation The set of ordered pairs obtained from switching the x- and y-values

4. Ask students to list six ordered pairs on their papers and define this list by giving it the name *relation*. Have them graph the ordered pairs they chose.

5. Tell students to list only the x-coordinate of each ordered pair and to name this list the *domain*.

6. Do the same for the y-coordinates. Have students name this list the *range*.

7. Have students use their original list of ordered pairs to write and graph the inverse relations. Have volunteers share their relation and its inverse relation. Ask the class to check the volunteers' work.

GRAPH PAPER

8. Reinforce students' understanding of relations by giving real-life examples.

   Example:

   There are two brothers, Jason and Jeremy. Jason is three years older than Jeremy. List the brothers' ages in terms of relations, when Jeremy is 5, 6, 7, 8, 9, and 10 years old.
   Domain: 5, 6, 7, 8, 9, 10   Range: 8, 9, 10, 11, 12, 13
   Relation: {(5, 8), (6, 9), (7, 10), (8, 11), (9, 12), (10, 13)}

9. Discuss what the inverse means in the case of the brothers. Challenge students to name the inverse relation. Remind students that the inverse gives the ordered pairs of the older compared to the younger at the different ages. Inverse Relation: {(8, 5), (9, 6), (10, 7), (11, 8), (12, 9), (13, 10)}

NEXT STEPS • Differentiate

4-Day and 3-Day Instructional Plans:
CD 2, page 299—All students, for additional concept development and problem solving

Objective 2
Concept Development Activities

★ CD 2 Working for a Dollar

Use with 4-Day or 3-Day Instructional Plan. In this activity, students represent a mathematical statement as a table and a graph.

MATERIALS

- Blackline Master 59

DIRECTIONS

1. Review the following terms with students:

   domain The possible values for x in a relation

   inverse relation The set of ordered pairs obtained from switching the x- and y-values

   ordered pair Two numbers that name the coordinates of a point on a graph, with the horizontal coordinate listed first and the vertical coordinate listed second

   range The possible values for y in a relation

   relation A set of ordered pairs

   ***x*-coordinate** The horizontal distance from the point of origin of a graph; in an ordered pair, this value is always written first

   ***y*-coordinate** The vertical distance from the point of origin of a graph; in an ordered pair, this value is always written second

2. At the top of their lined papers, have students write, "The clerk at the video store earns $6.00 per hour."

3. Ask students to write the ordered pairs that represent the hours and the amount earned up to 5 hours. Discuss with the class which should be the x-coordinate and which should be the y-coordinate. In this case, use the hours worked as the x-coordinate and the amount earned as the y-coordinate.

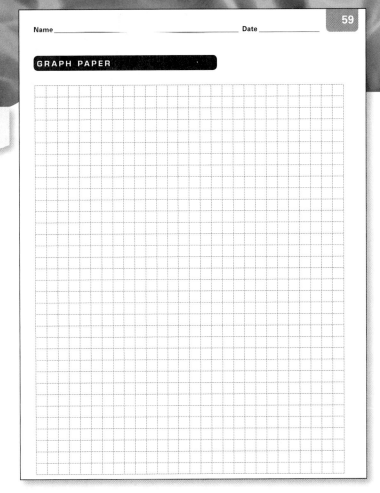

GRAPH PAPER

In 1 hour, $6 (1, 6)

In 2 hours, $12 (2, 12)

In 3 hours, $18 (3, 18)

In 4 hours, $24 (4, 24)

In 5 hours, $30 (5, 30)

4. Distribute one copy of Blackline Master 59, Graph Paper, to each student. Have students graph the ordered pairs.

5. Remind students that a relation is a set of ordered pairs. Discuss the domain and range of the relation.
   Domain: {1, 2, 3, 4, 5}
   Range: {6, 12, 18, 24, 30}

★ = Includes Problem Solving

Concept Development Activities

6. Ask students to make a table that shows the relation between hours worked and amount earned up to 5 hours. Include some fractional points, and make sure to graph these new points.

Sample problems:

Hours Worked	Amount Earned	Ordered Pair
$\frac{1}{2}$ hour	$3	$\left(\frac{1}{2}, 3\right)$
1 hour	$6	(1, 6)
$1\frac{1}{2}$ hour	$9	$\left(1\frac{1}{2}, 9\right)$
2 hours	$12	(2, 12)
$2\frac{1}{4}$ hours	$13.50	$\left(2\frac{1}{4}, 13.5\right)$
3 hours	$18	(3, 18)
$3\frac{3}{4}$ hours	$22.50	$\left(3\frac{3}{4}, 22.5\right)$
4 hours	$24	(4, 24)
$4\frac{1}{6}$ hours	$25	$\left(4\frac{1}{6}, 25\right)$
5 hours	$30	(5, 30)

7. Ask students to write a description under the graph of the information given in the visual presentation. Have them finish by giving the graph a title and axis labels.

8. Have students discuss which way of identifying relations is the easiest for employers to use with new employees.

9. Ask students to write the inverse relation and discuss how it is formed. Make sure students understand that the inverse relation represents the hours worked per dollars made, whereas the original relation represented money made per hour worked.

> **Variation: Different Numbers** Use weekly or monthly earnings for the activity.

NEXT STEPS • Differentiate

4-Day Instructional Plan:
PM 1, page 303—All students, to assess progress

3-Day Instructional Plan:
PM 2, page 304—Students who demonstrate understanding of the concept, to assess progress
PM 1, page 303—Students who need additional support, to assess progress

Practice Activities

PA 1 Matching Ordered Pairs

Use with 4-Day or 3-Day Instructional Plan. In this activity, students identify definitions of graph terminology.

MATERIALS

- *Interactive Text,* page 127

DIRECTIONS

1. Have students turn to *Interactive Text,* page 127, Relation Matching, for this activity.

2. Review the following terms with students:

   domain The possible values for *x* in a relation

   ordered pair Two numbers that name the coordinates of a point on a graph, with the horizontal coordinate listed first and the vertical coordinate listed second

   relation A set of ordered pairs

   ***x*-coordinate** The horizontal distance from the point of origin of a graph; in an ordered pair, this value is always written first

   ***y*-coordinate** The vertical distance from the point of origin of a graph; in an ordered pair, this value is always written second

3. Tell students to match the number with the correct letter and write the answer on the line.

   Example:

   Because the answer to Problem 1, domain, is *o,* the set of all first coordinates from the ordered pairs in a relation, students would write the letter *o* on the line.

4. Have students list the numbers 1 through 16 as the *x*-coordinates and the letters A through P as the *y*-coordinates and show a table of this relation.

   Example:

   For Problem 1, a 1 would go in the *x* column and an *o* would go in the *y* column.

x	*y*
1	*o*

RELATION MATCHING

Match each number with the correct letter, and write it on the line.

1. domain __o__
2. inverse __f__
3. quadrants __m__
4. Quadrant III __c__
5. the second number of an ordered pair that corresponds to the numbers on the *y*-axis __i__
6.
7. the plane that contains the *x*- and *y*-axes __g__
8. relation __a__
9. range __j__
10. the section of the coordinate plane that would have this ordered pair: (3, –5) __k__
11. the common endpoint of two rays (corner) __n__
12. *x*-axis __l__
13. Quadrant I __p__
14. upper left quadrant of a coordinate plane __d__
15. (*x*, *y*) __b__
16. the point formed by the intersection of the *x*-axis and the *y*-axis __e__

a. shows how the numbers in two sets of data are related
b. ordered pair
c. the section of the coordinate plane that has ordered pairs where both the *x*- and *y*-coordinates are negative
d. Quadrant II
e. origin
f. the switching of coordinates in each ordered pair of a relation
g. coordinate plane
h. graph
i. *y*-coordinate
j. the set of all second coordinates from the ordered pairs
k. Quadrant IV
l. the horizontal number line on the coordinate plane
m.
n. vertex
o. the set of all first coordinates from the ordered pairs in a relation
p. only positive values for both the *x*- and *y*-coordinates

---

5. Grade the activity using either the answers on the line or the table.

6. Share the correct answers with the class and allow students to correct any they missed. Tell students to fix the incorrect answers by writing the complete correct answer.

NEXT STEPS • Differentiate

4-Day Instructional Plan:
PA 2, page 302—All students, for additional practice

👥 3-Day Instructional Plan:
PS 1, page 305—Students who are on the accelerated path, to develop problem-solving skills

PM 2, page 304—Students who are on the differentiated path, to assess progress

Practice Activities

PA 2 Playing Definition Bingo

Use with 4-Day Instructional Plan. In this activity, students identify definitions of graph terminology.

MATERIALS

- *Interactive Text,* page 127
- Blackline Master 38
- Game markers to cover squares

DIRECTIONS

1. Distribute one copy of Blackline Master 38, 4 × 4 Bingo Card, to each student, and have students turn to *Interactive Text,* page 127, Relation Matching.

2. Choose one of the columns on Relation Matching, and have students randomly fill in the squares on the bingo card with the items in that column. When students are done, have them put away the *Interactive Text* so they cannot see the definitions in the other column.

3. Randomly choose one of the items on the opposite column, and write it on the board or overhead. Have students cover the matching descriptors on their bingo cards with markers.

4. Tell students that the first student to cover four answers in a row, column, or diagonal should shout, "Bingo!" Be sure to check that student's solution to confirm the bingo.

NEXT STEPS • Differentiate

👥 4-Day Instructional Plan:

PM 2, page 304—Students who are completing the activity for the first time, to assess progress

Objective 2 Posttest, page 307—Students who are completing the activity for the second time

---

Name _____ Date _____

4 × 4 BINGO CARD

Name _____ Date _____

RELATION MATCHING

Match each number with the correct letter, and write it on the line.

1. domain __o__
2. inverse __f__
3. quadrants __m__
4. Quadrant III __c__
5. the second number of an ordered pair that corresponds to the numbers on the *y*-axis __i__
6.

7. the plane that contains the *x*- and *y*-axes __g__
8. relation __a__
9. range __j__
10. the section of the coordinate plane that would have this ordered pair: (3, −5) __k__
11. the common endpoint of two rays (corner) __n__
12. *x*-axis __l__
13. Quadrant I __p__
14. upper left quadrant of a coordinate plane __d__
15. (*x, y*) __b__
16. the point formed by the intersection of the *x*-axis and the *y*-axis __e__

a. shows how the numbers in two sets of data are related
b. ordered pair
c. the section of the coordinate plane that has ordered pairs where both the *x*- and *y*-coordinates are negative
d. Quadrant II
e. origin
f. the switching of coordinates in each ordered pair of a relation
g. coordinate plane
h. graph
i. *y*-coordinate
j. the set of all second coordinates from the ordered pairs
k. Quadrant IV
l. the horizontal number line on the coordinate plane
m.
n. vertex
o. the set of all first coordinates from the ordered pairs in a relation
p. only positive values for both the *x*- and *y*-coordinates

PRACTICE

Progress-Monitoring Activities

PM 1 Apply Skills 1

Use with 4-Day or 3-Day Instructional Plan.

MATERIALS

- *Interactive Text*, page 128

DIRECTIONS

1. Have students turn to *Interactive Text*, page 128, Apply Skills 1.

2. Remind students of the key terms: *domain, range, ordered pair, relation,* and *inverse relation.*

3. Monitor student work, and provide feedback as necessary.

   Watch for:

   - Do students correctly write ordered pairs?

   - Given the domain for an equation, do students correctly find the range?

   - Do students correctly identify the inverse relation?

NEXT STEPS • Differentiate

4-Day and 3-Day Instructional Plans:

PA 1, page 301—All students, for additional practice

PROGRESS MONITORING

Name _____ Date _____

APPLY SKILLS 1

A video store charges $5.00 to rent a video for a weekend. The store gives a $5.00 discount if four or more videos are rented.

1. Make a table that shows this relation between the number of videos and the total cost for up to eight videos.

Number of Videos	Cost ($)
1	5
2	10
3	15
4	15
5	20
6	25
7	30
8	35

2. List the ordered pairs so that the number of videos is the domain.

   {(1, 5), (2, 10), (3, 15), (4, 15), (5, 20), (6, 25), (7, 30), (8, 35)}

3. Give the range of this relation. {5, 10, 15, 20, 25, 30, 35}

4. What is the inverse of this relation?

   {(5, 1), (10, 2), (15, 3), (15, 4), (20, 5), (25, 6), (30, 7), (35, 8)}

5. Graph the ordered pairs with the number of videos as the *x*-axis.

6. Write three questions that you could ask a classmate about information obtained from this relation.

   Questions will vary. Sample question: How many videos should you rent to get the lowest cost per video?

128 Chapter 4 • Objective 2 • PM 1   Inside Algebra

Progress-Monitoring Activities

PM 2 Apply Skills 2

Use with 4-Day or 3-Day Instructional Plan.

MATERIALS

- *Interactive Text*, pages 129–130

DIRECTIONS

1. Have students turn to *Interactive Text,* pages 129–130, Apply Skills 2.

2. Remind students of the key terms: *domain, range, relation,* and *inverse relation.*

3. Monitor student work, and provide feedback as necessary.

   Watch for:

   - Do students correctly identify the domain and the range?

   - Do students correctly write the inverse relation?

   - Do students correctly graph the relation?

NEXT STEPS • Differentiate

👥 4-Day Instructional Plan:

PS 2, page 306—Students who demonstrate understanding of the concept, to develop problem-solving skills

PA 2, page 302—Students who need additional practice

👥 3-Day Instructional Plan:

PA 1, page 301—Students who are on the accelerated path, for additional practice

PS 1, page 305—Students who are on the differentiated path, to develop problem-solving skills

---

APPLY SKILLS 2

The table below shows dollars earned for 1 to 5 hours of work.

Hours	Dollars Earned
1	5.25
2	10.50
3	15.75
4	21.00
5	26.25

1. The domain is represented by what? <u>hours worked</u>

   Give the domain: <u>{1, 2, 3, 4, 5}</u>

2. Give the range: <u>{5.25, 10.50, 15.75, 21.00, 26.25}</u>

3. What would the inverse relation be?

   <u>{(5.25, 1), (10.50, 2), (15.75, 3), (21.00, 4), (26.25, 5)}</u>

4. Write a math question that uses this relationship between the domain and the range.

   <u>Questions will vary. Sample question: How much is earned for</u>

   <u>6 hours of work?</u>

APPLY SKILLS 2 *(continued)*

5. Describe what you would have to do to figure out how much a person would earn if he or she worked $4\frac{1}{2}$ hours.

   <u>Multiply the hourly rate by 4.5, or divide the dollars earned</u>

   <u>for one hour by two and add the result to the dollars earned</u>

   <u>for four hours.</u>

6. Graph the relation.

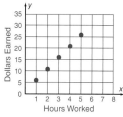

7. List the domain and range of the following relation: {(1, $4), (2, $7), (3, $10), (4, $13)}

   <u>domain {1, 2, 3, 4}   range {4, 7, 10, 13}</u>

8. Write the inverse of the relation in Problem 7.

   <u>{(4, 1), (7, 2), (10, 3), (13, 4)}</u>

9. Write a math problem that uses this relationship between the domain and the range.

   <u>Questions will vary. Sample question: How much will 7</u>

   <u>items cost?</u>

Problem-Solving Activities

★PS 1 Finding the Information and Graphing It

Use with 3-Day Instructional Plan. In this activity, students use real-life information in writing ordered pairs and their domains and ranges. They also graph the ordered pairs.

MATERIALS

- Recent almanac

DIRECTIONS

1. Review the following terms with students:

   domain The possible values for *x* in a relation

   ordered pair Two numbers that name the coordinates of a point on a graph, with the horizontal coordinate listed first and the vertical coordinate listed second

   range The possible values for *y* in a relation

   relation A set of ordered pairs

2. Choose one student to look for information in the almanac. The student should find two related sets of data that can be represented in a table or as ordered pairs. Have the student list the set of data he or she found on the board.

   Sample answers:

   > Prices of quantities related to years
   >
   > Height or weight related to age
   >
   > Months compared to average temperature
   >
   > Births or deaths by years

3. Have the other students rewrite the information as ordered pairs. Restrict the lists to no more than 10 ordered pairs.

4. Tell students to title the relation, list the domain, list the range, and graph the relationship.

5. Have students make and discuss predictions for the next two ordered pairs in the list.

6. Choose another student to look for a different set of related qualities in the almanac, and have the class repeat Steps 2–5.

NEXT STEPS • Differentiate

👥 3-Day Instructional Plan:

PS 2, page 306—Students who are on the accelerated path, for additional problem solving

Objective 2 Posttest, page 307—Students who are on the differentiated path

★ = Includes Problem Solving

Problem-Solving Activities

★ PS 2 Valuing the Price of a Movie Ticket

Use with 4-Day or 3-Day Instructional Plan. In this activity, students use information in a chart to determine the elements of a relation.

MATERIALS

- *Interactive Text*, page 131
- Blackline Master 59

DIRECTIONS

1. Review the following terms with students:

   domain The possible values for *x* in a relation

   ordered pair Two numbers that name the coordinates of a point on a graph, with the horizontal coordinate listed first and the vertical coordinate listed second

   range The possible values for *y* in a relation

   relation A set of ordered pairs

2. Divide students into groups of two or three, and distribute one copy of Blackline Master 59, Graph Paper, to each group.

3. Tell students to estimate how the price of a movie ticket has gone up from the year 1996 to the present by sketching a graph. Tell them that in 1996, a movie ticket cost about $4.40. Students should graph the point (1996, 4.4) and a second point representing the current year and ticket price, then draw a line through the points.

4. Have students turn to *Interactive Text*, page 131, Budget Movie Tickets, and compare their estimations to the information in the chart.

5. Have students work individually to complete *Interactive Text*, page 131, Budget Movie Tickets. Tell students to discuss the answers within their groups after everyone is done.

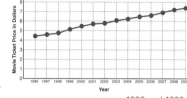

Name_____ Date_____

BUDGET MOVIE TICKETS

Answer the questions by referring to the chart below.

Year	Movie Ticket Price
1996	$4.40
1997	$4.60
1998	$4.70
1999	$5.10
2000	$5.40
2001	$5.65
2002	$5.80
2003	$6.05
2004	$6.20
2005	$6.40
2006	$6.55
2007	$6.90
2008	$7.20
2009	$7.40

1. What is the domain of the relation?

   {1996, 1997, 1998, 1999, 2000, 2001, 2002, 2003, 2004, 2005, 2006, 2007, 2008, 2009}

2. What is the range of the relation?

   {4.40, 4.60, 4.70, 5.10, 5.40, 5.65, 5.80, 6.05, 6.20, 6.40, 6.55, 6.90, 7.20, 7.40}

3. When graphing the relation, which data should be used on the *x*-axis?

   Year

Graph the relation, then use your graph to answer the questions below.

Budget Movie Tickets

4. Between which years did the price of tickets rise the least?

   1997 and 1998

5. Between which years did the price of tickets rise the most? 1998 and 1999

6. What is the highest and lowest range? $7.40 and $4.40

7. What adjustments would you need to make if you graphed the inverse?

   The price would be on the *x*-axis, and the year would be on the *y*-axis.

8. How much did the price of a ticket increase between 1999 and 2009?

   The price increased by $2.30 per ticket.

Inside Algebra   Chapter 4 • Objective 2 • PS 2   131

---

6. Tell students to extend their year scales to 2020 on the graphs they made on Blackline Master 59. Have students estimate what movies will cost by the year 2020 by extending the line they originally graphed.

7. Have each group discuss with the class what their estimate is and how they determined this. Encourage students to talk about how their graph helped them with the estimate.

NEXT STEPS • Differentiate

4-Day and 3-Day Instructional Plans:
Objective 2 Posttest, page 307—All students

★ = Includes Problem Solving

Objective 2 Posttest

Discuss with students the key concepts in Objective 2. Following the discussion, administer the Objective 2 Posttest to all students.

Using the Results

• Score the posttest and update the class record card.

• Provide reinforcement for students who do not demonstrate mastery of the concepts through individual or small-group reteaching of key concepts.

Name _____ Date _____

Answer the questions about relations.

1. How is the information in the table written as a set of ordered pairs called a relation?

x	y
2	5
1	−3
−3	2
0	−1
−3	−4

{(2, 5), (1, −3), (−3, 2), (0, −1), (−3, −4)}

2. The domain of the relation in Problem 1 is which of the following?
   a. {5, 2, 1, 0}   b. {5, −3, 2, −1, −4}
   c. {2, 1, −3, 0 −3}   d. {2, −3, −1, 0}

3. The range of the relation {(1, 0), (−2, −2), (2, 6), (−1, 3)} is which of the following?
   a. {1, 0, −2, 2, 6}   b. {0, −2, 6, 3}
   c. {1, −2, 2, −1}   d. {2, 6, −1, 3}

4. What is the inverse of the relation in Problem 1?
   {(5, 2), (−3, 1), (2, −3), (−1, 0), (−4, −3)}

In Problems 5–7, the domain of the relation is {−3, 2, 0} and the range is {0, 2, −3}.

5. Write the relation in a table.

x	y
−3	0
2	2
0	−3

6. Write the relation as ordered pairs.
   {(−3, 0), (2, 2), (0, −3)}

7. Write the inverse of the relation.
   {(0, −3), (2, 2), (−3, 0)}

Answer true or false for the relation {(6, −4), (3, 2), (−5, 0)}.

8. The domain is {6, 3, −5}. _____true_____

9. The range is {−4, 2, 0}. _____true_____

10. The inverse is {(6, 0), (3, 2), (−5, −4)}. _____false_____

Inside Algebra   Chapter 4 • Objective 2   **47**

---

4 CHAPTER

Objective 3
Determine the range for a given domain of a relation.

Objective 3 Pretest

Students complete the Objective 3 Pretest on the same day as the Objective 2 Posttest.

Using the Results

- Score the pretest and update the class record card.

- If the majority of students do not demonstrate mastery of the concepts, use the 5-Day Instructional Plan for Objective 3.

- If the majority of students demonstrate mastery of the concepts, use the 3-Day Instructional Plan for Objective 3.

Name _____ Date _____

CHAPTER 4 • Objective 3
PRETEST

Solve each problem based on the given information about the relation.

1. Complete the table of values. Find the solutions of the equation $x + y = 7$ when the domain is {3, –4, 0, 1}.

x	$x + y = 7$	y
3	$3 + y = 7$	4
–4	$-4 + y = 7$	11
0	$0 + y = 7$	7
1	$1 + y = 7$	6

2. Find the range for the equation $y = 2x - 1$ that has a domain of {0, –2, 3, –5}.

   {–1, –5, 5, –11}

3. Complete the table for any three values for x.

x	$2x + y = 2$	y
–1	$2(-1) + y = 2$	4
0	$2(0) + y = 2$	2
1	$2(1) + y = 2$	0

   Answers will vary.

4. Write the ordered pairs that satisfy the equation $2x + y = 2$ in Problem 3.

   {(–1, 4), (0, 2), (1, 0)}   Answers will vary.

Complete the ordered pairs to satisfy the relation $y = 5 - 2x$.

5. (1, _3_)

6. (2, _1_)

7. (–2, _9_)

Complete the table to satisfy the relation $2x + y = 5$.

	x	$2x + y = 5$	y
8.	0	$2(0) + y = 5$	5
9.	–1	$2(-1) + y = 5$	7
10.	2	$2(2) + y = 5$	1

48 Chapter 4 • Objective 3   Inside Algebra

Objective 3

Goals and Activities

Objective 3 Goals

The following activities, when used with the instructional plans on pages 310 and 311, enable students to:

- Find the ordered pairs that satisfy the relation $y = 2x + 1$ when the domain is $\{-1, 0, 1, 2\}$ to be **{(−1, −1), (0, 1), (1, 3), (2, 5)}**
- Complete the table of values given $x + y = -2$ for $x = -2, 0, 2, 4$ as

x	$x + y = -2$	y	(x, y)
−2	$-2 + y = -2$	0	(−2, 0)
0	$0 + y = -2$	−2	(0, −2)
2	$2 + y = -2$	−4	(2, −4)
4	$4 + y = -2$	−6	(4, −6)

Objective 3 Activities

Concept Development Activities

CD 1 Making Tables, page 312

CD 2 Determining the Domain and the Range, page 313

Practice Activities

PA 1 Forming Equations, page 314

PA 2 Matching Equivalent Cards, page 315

PA 3 Playing the Domain and Range Game, page 316

Progress-Monitoring Activities

PM 1 Apply Skills 1, page 317

PM 2 Apply Skills 2, page 318

PM 3 Apply Skills 3, page 319

*Problem-Solving Activity

*PS 1 Calculating Weight on Earth Versus Neptune, page 320

Ongoing Assessment

Posttest Objective 3, page 323

Pretest Objective 4, page 324

CD = Concept Development   PM = Progress Monitoring   PS = Problem Solving
PA = Practice Activity   ★ = Includes Problem Solving

5-Day Instructional Plan

Use the 5-Day Instructional Plan when pretest results indicate that students would benefit from a slower pace. This plan is used when the majority of students need more time or did not demonstrate mastery on the pretest.

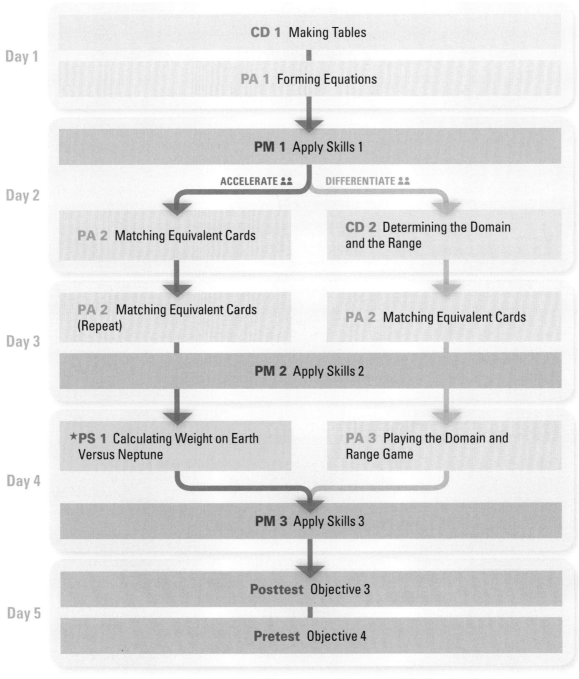

Day 1

CD 1 Making Tables

PA 1 Forming Equations

Day 2

PM 1 Apply Skills 1

ACCELERATE | DIFFERENTIATE

PA 2 Matching Equivalent Cards

CD 2 Determining the Domain and the Range

Day 3

PA 2 Matching Equivalent Cards (Repeat)

PA 2 Matching Equivalent Cards

PM 2 Apply Skills 2

Day 4

★PS 1 Calculating Weight on Earth Versus Neptune

PA 3 Playing the Domain and Range Game

PM 3 Apply Skills 3

Day 5

Posttest Objective 3

Pretest Objective 4

CD = Concept Development   PM = Progress Monitoring   PS = Problem Solving
PA = Practice Activity   ★ = Includes Problem Solving

3-Day Instructional Plan

Use the 3-Day Instructional Plan when pretest results indicate that students can move through the activities at a faster pace. This plan is ideal when the majority of students demonstrate mastery on the pretest. This plan does not include all activities.

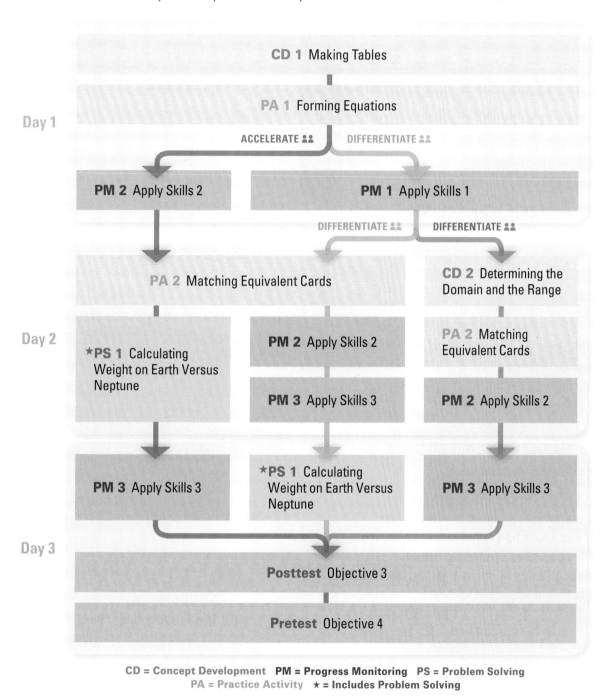

CD = Concept Development   PM = Progress Monitoring   PS = Problem Solving
PA = Practice Activity   ★ = Includes Problem Solving

Objective 3
Concept Development Activities

CD 1 Making Tables

Use with 5-Day or 3-Day Instructional Plan. In this activity, students understand that the domain is the independent variable and the range depends on the domain.

MATERIALS

- *Interactive Text,* page 132

DIRECTIONS

1. Review the following terms with students:

    domain The possible values for x in a relation

    relation A set of ordered pairs

2. Write **$2x + y = 6$** on the board or overhead.

3. Have students name some values for x. Make sure students recognize that there are an infinite number of values that can be used for x in this equation when there is no set value for y.

4. Explain that because there are an infinite number of values, we will restrict the domain and use only some values for x. Tell students that if we use only the integers from –4 to 2, the domain is **{–4, –3, –2, –1, 0, 1, 2}**.

5. Have students discuss the process for finding the y values when they know the x values.

    Listen for:
    - Replace the x in the equation with an x value.
    - Simplify the equation to solve for y.
    - Do this for each x value to find each y value.

6. Tell students that a table is a good way to find the y values. Have students turn to *Interactive Text,* page 132, Making Tables. Demonstrate the use of tables by working through the two problems on the board or an overhead transparency, while students complete the tables in their *Interactive Text.* Tell students that in tables, the domain should be listed first and should generally consist of evenly spaced values.

MAKING TABLES

Fill in each table.

1. Substitute for x and find y.
   $2x + y = 6$

x	y
–4	14
–3	12
–2	10
–1	8
0	6
1	4
2	2

2. Substitute for x and solve the equation for y, then list the values for y and write the ordered pairs (x, y).

x	$2x + y = 6$	y	(x, y)
–4	$2(–4) + y = 6$	14	$(–4, 14)$
–3	$2(–3) + y = 6$	12	$(–3, 12)$
–2	$2(–2) + y = 6$	10	$(–2, 10)$
–1	$2(–1) + y = 6$	8	$(–1, 8)$
0	$2(0) + y = 6$	6	$(0, 6)$
1	$2(1) + y = 6$	4	$(1, 4)$
2	$2(2) + y = 6$	2	$(2, 2)$

7. Have students try both examples of tables for the equation **$y = x - 2$**, when the domain is **{–2, –1, 0, 2, 6}**.

x	$y = x - 2$	y	(x, y)
–2	$y = (–2) – 2$	–4	$(–2, –4)$
–1	$y = (–1) – 2$	–3	$(–1, –3)$
0	$y = (0) – 2$	–2	$(0, –2)$
2	$y = (2) – 2$	0	$(2, 0)$
6	$y = (6) – 2$	4	$(6, 4)$

Note that the other table consists of the x and y columns in the table above.

NEXT STEPS • Differentiate

5-Day and 3-Day Instructional Plans:
PA 1, page 314—All students, for additional practice

Concept Development Activities

CD 2 Determining the Domain and the Range

Use with 5-Day or 3-Day Instructional Plan. In this activity, students understand that the domain is the independent variable, and the range depends on the domain.

DIRECTIONS

1. Review the following terms with students:

   domain The possible values for x in a relation

   range The possible values for y in a relation

   relation A set of ordered pairs

2. Remind students that the left column in a table is the x-value or domain, and the right column is the y-value or range.

3. Discuss the following terms with students:

   independent variable A variable whose value does not depend upon the value of another variable

   dependent variable A variable whose value is dependent upon the value of another variable

4. Explain to students that x, or the domain, is considered the independent variable, while y, or the range, is considered the dependent variable. Have students think of real-life examples of independent and dependent variables.

   Sample answers:

   The amount of tax one pays to the government every year during tax season depends on the amount of money one makes in a year. Independent variable: The amount of money you make; dependent variable: the amount of taxes you pay during tax season.

   The amount of crops a farmer has to sell in one year depends on the amount of seeds he plants. Independent variable: the amount of seeds a farmer plants; dependent variable: the amount of crops the farmer will have to sell.

5. Now give examples to students and have them identify which variable depends on the other.

   Sample problems:

   Distance is the rate of speed times the time traveled. If the rate is 55 mph, what is the distance? $D = r$ times t, or $D = 55 \cdot t$ Distance depends on the time.

   What is D (the distance) for 2 hours, 4 hours, and 10 hours? (2, 110), (4, 220), (10, 550) The domain is {2, 4, 10}. The range is {110, 220, 550}.

   If you work at a job and receive $5.25 per hour, then dollars earned is $5.25 times the number of hours worked. $d = 5.25$ times h, or $d = 5.25 \cdot h$ Dollars depend on the hours.

h	d	
8 hours	$42.00	The domain is {8, 12, 20, 40}.
12 hours	$63.00	
20 hours	$105.00	The range is {42, 63, 105, 210}
40 hours	$210.00	

6. Explain that because the domain is the independent variable and the range is the dependent variable, the range always depends on what is chosen for the domain. Tell students that the domain consists of possible values that can be substituted into the equation, while the range consists of the possible resulting values.

NEXT STEPS • Differentiate

5-Day and 3-Day Instructional Plans:
PA 2, page 315—All students, for additional practice

Practice Activities

PA 1 Forming Equations

Use with 5-Day or 3-Day Instructional Plan. In this activity, students find ordered pairs that are solutions to an equation.

MATERIALS

• Blackline Master 60

DIRECTIONS

1. Review the following terms with students:

   domain The possible values for *x* in a relation

   ordered pair Two numbers that name the coordinates of a point on a graph, with the horizontal coordinate listed first and the vertical coordinate listed second

   range The possible values for *y* in a relation

   relation A set of ordered pairs

2. Have students work in groups of three and designate themselves as Student 1, 2, or 3.

3. Tell Student 1 to give a domain value, Student 2 to give a range value, and Student 3 to give an equation that creates a solution using that ordered pair.

   Sample answer:

   Student 1 Domain = 3

   Student 2 Range = 4

   Student 3 $x + y = 7$, or $y = x + 1$

4. Have students rotate positions so that every student does each of the three tasks.

5. Distribute one copy of Blackline Master 60, Forming Equations, to each student. Tell students to make a table showing their solutions to the equation $2x + y = 6$. Have Student 1 give four values for the domain, have Student 2 substitute the value for *x* and find *y*, and have Student 3 give the ordered pair (*x, y*).

6. Have students make a table for the relation $y = -2x + 6$. Rotate student positions so that every student does each of the three tasks. Students will find the same answers as in Step 5 because the equations are the same.

7. Give students the relation $x \cdot y = 12$. Ask each student to find four ordered pairs to satisfy the equation. Have groups discuss the possible solutions. Answers will vary, but zero cannot be used as an answer. Possible solutions include {(1, 12), (−1, −12), (2, 6), (−2, −6), (3, 4), (−3, −4)}.

NEXT STEPS • Differentiate

5-Day Instructional Plan:
PM 1, page 317—All students, to assess progress

3-Day Instructional Plan:
PM 2, page 318—Students who demonstrate understanding of the concept, to assess progress

PM 1, page 317—Students who need additional support, to assess progress

---

60

Name_____ Date_____

FORMING EQUATIONS

1. Make a table showing the solutions to the equation $2x + y = 6$. Answers will vary.

x	2x + y = 6	y	(x, y)
−2	2 · (−2) + y = 6	10	(−2, 10)
−1	2 · (−1) + y = 6	8	(−1, 8)
0	2 · 0 + y = 6	6	(0, 6)
1	2 · 1 + y = 6	4	(1, 4)
2	2 · 2 + y = 6	2	(2, 2)

2. Make a table for the relation $y = -2x + 6$. The equations are the same, so students will find the same answers as Problem 1.

x	y = −2x + 6	y	(x, y)
−2	y = −2(−2) + 6	10	(−2, 10)
−1	y = −2(−1) + 6	8	(−1, 8)
0	y = −2(0) + 6	6	(0, 6)
1	y = −2(1) + 6	4	(1, 4)
2	y = −2(2) + 6	2	(2, 2)

Practice Activities

PA 2 Matching Equivalent Cards

Use with 5-Day or 3-Day Instructional Plan. In this activity, students recognize the same equation written two different ways and determine whether a set of ordered pairs represents solutions to the equation.

MATERIALS

- Blank 3×5 cards, three per student

DIRECTIONS

1. Review the following term with students:

   ordered pair Two numbers that name the coordinates of a point on a graph, with the horizontal coordinate listed first and the vertical coordinate listed second

2. Have each student make a set of three cards.

   - On the first card, the student should write an equation.

   - The second card should have the equation solved for y in terms of x.

   - The third card should have solutions as ordered pairs to the equation. There should be three ordered pairs.

   Sample answers:

Card 1	Card 2	Card 3
$x + y = 4$	$y = 4 - x$	$\{(2, 2), (3, 1), (4, 0)\}$
$2x + y = 3$	$y = 3 - 2x$	$\{(0, 3), (1, 1), (3, -3)\}$
$x - y = 6$	$y = x - 6$	$\{(7, 1), (0, -6), (6, 0)\}$
$2x + 2y = 4$	$y = 2 - x$	$\{(1, 1), (0, 2), (3, -1)\}$
$3x - y = 0$	$y = 3x - 0$	$\{(1, 3), (0, 0), (-2, -6)\}$
$x = y$	$y = x$	$\{(-1, -1), (0, 0), (3, 3)\}$

3. Collect all the cards, and without mixing them, count out enough sets of three for every student to have at least one card. Make sure the sets of three that each student made stay together when you count out the cards. Put the extra cards aside, and mix the deck of cards to be used.

4. Give each student one card randomly. If the number of students in your class is not a multiple of three, hold on to the extra cards in this deck. Because there should be enough cards to make three decks, extend the activity for two or three days. On subsequent days, hand out the cards as students come into class.

5. After each student has one card, have everyone stand. Instruct each student to find the other two students who have equivalent cards to form groups of three.

6. When students find their partners, have them exchange cards within their group and check one another's cards.

7. Explain to students that if all the cards were not used, some cards will not have matches. In this case, tell students to write new solutions for the cards.

8. Continue the activity by having each group make a set of three new cards, or by having the group members write three new solutions written as ordered pairs.

NEXT STEPS • Differentiate

👥 5-Day Instructional Plan:

PA 2, page 315—Students who are on the accelerated path, completing the activity for the first time, for additional practice

PM 2, page 318—All others students, to assess progress

👥 3-Day Instructional Plan:

PS 1, page 320—Students who are on the accelerated path, to develop problem-solving skills

PM 2, page 318—Students who are on the differentiated path, to assess progress

Practice Activities

PA 3 Playing the Domain and Range Game

Use with 5-Day Instructional Plan. In this activity, students calculate the range, given an equation and a value from the domain.

DIRECTIONS

1. Review the following terms with students:

   domain The possible values for x in a relation

   range The possible values for y in a relation

   relation A set of ordered pairs

2. Divide the class into two groups. Tell students that each group will work together for a team score. Name the groups Group 1 and Group 2.

3. Write $y = x - 4$ on the board.

4. Explain to students that Group 1 will give a domain value, and Group 2 will give the range using Group 1's value.

   Sample answer:

   If Group 1 chooses 8 to be the domain, Group 2 should find the range to be 4.

   If Group 1 chooses 35 to be the domain, Group 2 should find the range to be 31.

5. Tell students that when Group 2 gives the range, Group 1 must immediately say whether they agree or disagree with the range. Have only one student answer each time, giving each student a chance to answer. Each student is responsible for the group score when it is his or her group's turn.

6. Explain the scoring system to students.

   • Each time a group chooses the correct range on their turn, they receive 2 points.

   • Each time a group is correct in its check of the other team's range, they receive 1 point.

   • Each time a group deems the other group's range as incorrect when it is correct, or each time a group deems the other group's range as correct when it is incorrect, they lose 1 point.

7. Choose three more equations, and follow the same procedure. Rotate the tasks for the groups.

   Sample problems:

   $y = 10 + x$ $y = 3x + 7$

   $y = x + 16$ $y = 8 - x$

   $y = \frac{1}{2}x + 5$ $y = 4x - 2$

   $y = -2x - 3$

8. Mix difficult and easy equations, depending on the class.

9. After students work with linear equations, give them more difficult equations.

   Sample problems:

   $y = x^2 + 2$ $y + 7x = 0$

   $x \cdot y = -6$ $\frac{1}{2} \cdot x = y \cdot \frac{1}{2}$

   $\frac{x}{y} = 2$ $8x = y$

   $xy = 0$

   > **Variation: Challenge** Write the equation and have students in both groups solve for y in terms of x and give the domain and range.

NEXT STEPS • Differentiate

5-Day Instructional Plan:
PM 3, page 319—All students, to assess progress

Progress-Monitoring Activities

PM 1 Apply Skills 1

Use with 5-Day or 3-Day Instructional Plan.

MATERIALS

- *Interactive Text*, page 133

DIRECTIONS

1. Have students turn to *Interactive Text,* page 133, Apply Skills 1.

2. Remind students of the key term: *domain*.

3. Monitor student work, and provide feedback as necessary.

   Watch for:

   - Do students correctly identify the domain?

   - Given the domain for an equation, do students correctly find the range?

NEXT STEPS • Differentiate

👥 5-Day and 3-Day Instructional Plans:

PA 2, page 315—Students who demonstrate understanding of the concept, for additional practice

CD 2, page 313—Students who need additional concept development

---

Name_____ Date_____

APPLY SKILLS 1

Find the values for y if $y = \frac{1}{2}x + 2$.

Example:
$$y = \frac{1}{2}x + 2$$
If $x = -8$, then $y = \frac{1}{2}(-8) + 2$
$$y = -4 + 2$$
$$y = -2$$

1. If $x = 2$, then $y = $ __3__.   2. If $x = 0$, then $y = $ __2__.

3. If $x = 6$, then $y = $ __5__.   4. If $x = -2$, then $y = $ __1__.

5. The value we use for x is called the domain. The domain for this equation is __{2, 0, 6, −2}__.

6. Complete the table below for the equation $y = 2x - 4$. The domain is {−2, 0, 2, 4, 6}.

x	$y = 2x - 4$	y	(x, y)
Example:			
−2	$y = 2(-2) - 4$	−8	(−2, −8)
0	$y = 2(0) - 4$	−4	(0, −4)
2	$y = 2(2) - 4$	0	(2, 0)
4	$y = 2(4) - 4$	4	(4, 4)
6	$y = 2(6) - 4$	8	(6, 8)

7. Complete the table below for the equation $x + y = 8$. The domain is {−2, −1, 0, 2, 4}.

x	$x + y = 8$	y	(x, y)
Example:			
0	$0 + y = 8$	8	(0, 8)
−2	$-2 + y = 8$	10	(−2, 10)
−1	$-1 + y = 8$	9	(−1, 9)
2	$2 + y = 8$	6	(2, 6)
4	$4 + y = 8$	4	(4, 4)

Progress-Monitoring Activities

PM 2 Apply Skills 2

Use with 5-Day or 3-Day Instructional Plan.

MATERIALS

- *Interactive Text*, page 134

DIRECTIONS

1. Have students turn to *Interactive Text,* page 134, Apply Skills 2.

2. Remind students of the key terms: *domain, ordered pair, range,* and *relation.*

3. Monitor student work, and provide feedback as necessary.

   Watch for:
   - Do students correctly write ordered pairs?

   - Do students correctly identify the domain and the range given a set of ordered pairs?

NEXT STEPS • Differentiate

👥 5-Day Instructional Plan:

PS 1, page 320—Students who are on the accelerated path, to develop problem-solving skills

PA 3, page 316—Students who are on the differentiated path, for additional practice

👥 3-Day Instructional Plan:

PA 2, page 315—Students who are on the accelerated path, for additional practice

PM 3, page 319—Students who are on the differentiated path, for additional progress assessment

---

Name _____ Date _____

APPLY SKILLS 2

Solve the problems involving relations.

1. If the domain is {−5, −3, 0, 3, 5} for the relation $y = 5 − x$, find the ordered pairs that satisfy the relation.

   {(__−5__ , __10__), (__−3__ , __8__), (__0__ , __5__),
   (__3__ , __2__), (__5__ , __0__)}

2. Complete the table below for the domain of {−2, −1, 0, 1, 2}.

x	$2x − y = 4$	y	(x, y)
−2	$2(−2) − y = 4$	−8	(−2, −8)
−1	$2(−1) − y = 4$	−6	(−1, −6)
0	$2(0) − y = 4$	−4	(0, −4)
1	$2(1) − y = 4$	−2	(1, −2)
2	$2(2) − y = 4$	0	(2, 0)

3. Find five ordered pairs that satisfy the relation $y = 2x + 1$. Answers will vary.

   {(__−2__ , __−3__), (__−1__ , __−1__), (__0__ , __1__),
   (__1__ , __3__), (__2__ , __5__)}

4. What is the domain in Problem 3? {−2, −1, 0, 1, 2}

5. What is the range in Problem 3? {−3, −1, 1, 3, 5}

6. Find the ordered pairs below that satisfy the relation $y − x = 4$. Use the domain of {−3, −1, 0, 2, 4}.

   {(−3, __1__), (−1, __3__), (0, __4__), (2, __6__), (4, __8__)}

Objective 3
Progress-Monitoring Activities

PM 3 Apply Skills 3

Use with 5-Day or 3-Day Instructional Plan.

MATERIALS

- *Interactive Text*, page 135

DIRECTIONS

1. Have students turn to *Interactive Text,* page 135, Apply Skills 3.

2. Remind students of the key term: *ordered pair.*

3. Monitor student work, and provide feedback as necessary.

   Watch for:
   - Do students predict what the ordered pairs for an equation should look like, or do they check each possible set?

   - Do students simplify the equations before finding the possible solutions?

NEXT STEPS• Differentiate

5-Day Instructional Plan:
Objective 3 Posttest, page 323—All students

3-Day Instructional Plan:
Objective 3 Posttest, page 323—Students who are on the accelerated path

PS 1, page 320—Students on the differentiated path who demonstrated understanding on PM 1, to develop problem-solving skills

Objective 3 Posttest, page 323—All other students

APPLY SKILLS 3

Match the equation with the group of ordered pairs that represent solutions to the equation. The ordered pairs are in (x, y) form. Not all sets of ordered pairs are used.

1. $x + y = 9$ ___o___

2. $y = 2x - 3$ ___g___

3. $x - y = 2$ ___h___

4. $y = -x$ ___p___

5. $2x + y = 5$ ___k___

6. $2x + 2y = 2$ ___d___

7. $6x - 2y = 6$ ___i___

8. $y = -2x$ ___m___

9. $x = 5$ ___c___

10. $x + 2y = 8$ ___j___

a. {(1, 0), (0, 1), (0, 0)}

b. {(4, 5), (3, 0), (5, 4)}

c. {(5, 0), (5, 4), (5, −5)}

d. {(1, 0), (0, 1), (−1, 2)}

e. {(0, 5), (4, 5), (−5, 5)}

f. {(3, 3), (1, 1), (−1, −1)}

g. {(4, 5), (−1, −5), (1, −1)}

h. {(5, 3), (0, −2), (3, 1)}

i. {(1, 0), (2, 3), (0, −3)}

j. {(2, 3), (0, 4), (4, 2)}

k. {(2, 1), (−3, 11), (4, −3)}

l. {(3, −3), (−3, 3), (−3, 0)}

m. {(0, 0), (−2, 4), (1, −2)}

n. {(2, 1), (−3, −1), (4, 3)}

o. {(4, 5), (8, 1), (2, 7)}

p. {(3, −3), (4, −4), (0, 0)}

q. {(0, 0), (4, −2), (1, −2)}

Problem-Solving Activity

★PS 1 Calculating Weight on Earth Versus Neptune

Use with 5-Day or 3-Day Instructional Plan. In this activity, students express a relation as a math sentence and use it to predict values.

MATERIALS

- Blackline Master 59

DIRECTIONS

1. Tell students that a person who weighs 100 pounds on Earth would weigh 140 pounds on Neptune due to the difference in the force of gravity.

2. Have students work in groups of three to four to guess how much a person who weighs 150 pounds on Earth would weigh on Neptune. Next, give them some other weights to guess.

   Sample problems:

   > 150 pounds on Earth = 210 pounds on Neptune
   >
   > 300 pounds on Earth = 420 pounds on Neptune
   >
   > 75 pounds on Earth = 105 pounds on Neptune

3. Explain to students that if they write an equation for the force of gravity on Neptune, they can calculate anyone's weight on Neptune. Tell students to think about what they multiply by 100 to get 140.
   $100 \cdot 1.4 = 140$

4. Remind students that the number 100 represents the weight in pounds on Earth. Assign the variable e to this amount. Next, remind students that the number 140 represents the weight in pounds on Neptune. Assign the variable n to this amount. Have students write an equation in terms of e.
   $n = e \cdot 1.4$, or $n = 1.4e$

5. Write the equation $e \cdot 1.4 = n$ on the board. Have groups use the equation to solve for different weights on Earth. Remind students to check their work. Continue this process until students are able to use the equation confidently.

   Sample problems:

e	$n = e \cdot 1.4$	n
120	$n = 120 \cdot 1.4$	168
117	$n = 117 \cdot 1.4$	163.8
179	$n = 179 \cdot 1.4$	250.6
125	$n = 125 \cdot 1.4$	175

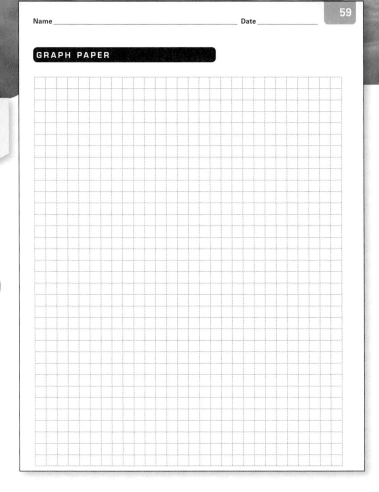

GRAPH PAPER

★ = Includes Problem Solving

6. Have each student choose any five Earth weights other than those already used and make a table to show the corresponding Neptune weights. Remind students to use the equation developed by the class.

7. Review the following terms with students:

    ordered pair Two numbers that name the coordinates of a point on a graph, with the horizontal coordinate listed first and the vertical coordinate listed second

    relation A set of ordered pairs

8. Distribute one copy of Blackline Master 59, Graph Paper, to each student. Tell students to write the relation of ordered pairs for the weights in their tables. Have them graph these ordered pairs on a coordinate plane. Discuss the scale for both the x- and y-axes and have students use the same scale for their graphs.

9. Next, give some weights on Neptune and have students find the corresponding weights on Earth.

    Sample problems:

e	$n = e \cdot 1.4$	n
200	$280 = e \cdot 1.4$	**280**
60	$84 = e \cdot 1.4$	**84**
30	$42 = e \cdot 1.4$	**42**
550	$770 = e \cdot 1.4$	**770**

NEXT STEPS • Differentiate

5-Day Instructional Plan:
PM 3, page 319—All students, to assess progress

3-Day Instructional Plan:
PM 3, page 319—Students who are on the accelerated path, to assess progress

Objective 3 Posttest, page 323—Students who are on the differentiated path

This page intentionally left blank

Ongoing Assessment

Objective 3 Posttest

Discuss with students the key concepts in Objective 3. Following the discussion, administer the Objective 3 Posttest to all students.

Using the Results

- Score the posttest and update the class record card.

- Provide reinforcement for students who do not demonstrate mastery of the concepts through individual or small-group reteaching of key concepts.

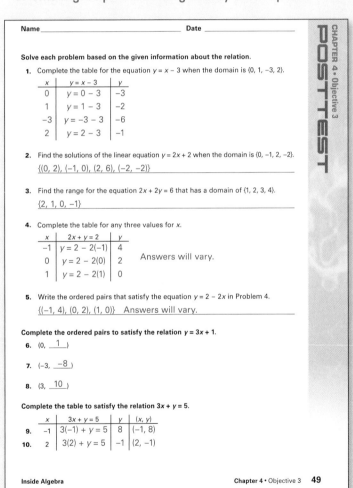

4 CHAPTER

Objective 4
Graph linear equations.

Objective 4 Pretest

Students complete the Objective 4 Pretest on the same day as the Objective 3 Posttest.

Using the Results

- Score the pretest and update the class record card.

- If the majority of students do not demonstrate mastery of the concepts, use the 4-Day Instructional Plan for Objective 4.

- If the majority of students demonstrate mastery of the concepts, use the 3-Day Instructional Plan for Objective 4.

Name _____ Date _____

Complete the table and construct the graph for each equation.

1. $y - 3x = 4$

x	$y - 3x = 4$	y	(x, y)
−2	$y - 3(-2) = 4$	−2	(−2, −2)
−1	$y - 3(-1) = 4$	1	(−1, 1)
0	$y - 3(0) = 4$	4	(0, 4)
1	$y - 3(1) = 4$	7	(1, 7)

2. Graph of $y - 3x = 4$

3. $4x + 2y = 6$

x	$4x + 2y = 6$	y	(x, y)
−1	$4(-1) + 2y = 6$	5	(−1, 5)
0	$4(0) + 2y = 6$	3	(0, 3)
2	$4(2) + 2y = 6$	−1	(2, −1)
3	$4(3) + 2y = 6$	−3	(3, −3)

4. Graph of $4x + 2y = 6$

5. $y = x$

x	$y = x$	y	(x, y)
3	$y = 3$	3	(3, 3)
0	$y = 0$	0	(0, 0)
−2	$y = -2$	−2	(−2, −2)

6. Graph of $y = x$

Name _____ Date _____

Make a table and construct the graph for each equation.

7. $x + y = 2$

x	$x + y = 2$	y	(x, y)
−1	$-1 + y = 2$	3	(−1, 3)
0	$0 + y = 2$	2	(0, 2)
1	$1 + y = 2$	1	(1, 1)

8. Graph of $x + y = 2$

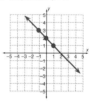

9. $y + 2x = 0$

x	$y + 2x = 0$	y	(x, y)
−1	$y + 2(-1) = 0$	2	(−1, 2)
0	$y + 2(0) = 0$	0	(0, 0)
1	$y + 2(1) = 0$	−2	(1, −2)

10. Graph of $y + 2x = 0$

Tables will vary depending on values for x.

Goals and Activities

Objective 4 Goals

The following activities, when used with the instructional plans on pages 326 and 327, enable students to:

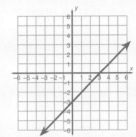

- Find the ordered pairs that satisfy the relation $y - 2x = -4$ for the domain of $\{-1, 0, 2, 4\}$ to be $\{(-1, -6), (0, -4), (2, 0), (4, 4)\}$

- Complete the table and construct the graph for $y = x - 3$

Objective 4 Activities

Concept Development Activities	
CD 1 Making Line Graphs, page 328	**★CD 2** Completing Linear and Nonlinear Equation Forms, page 330

Practice Activities	
★PA 1 Making and Sharing Graphs, page 332	**PA 2** Graphing Across the *x*-Axis and the *y*-Axis, page 333

Progress-Monitoring Activities		
PM 1 Apply Skills 1, page 334	**PM 2** Apply Skills 2, page 335	**PM 3** Apply Skills 3, page 336

★Problem-Solving Activities	
★PS 1 Checking Your Equation, page 337	**★PS 2** Determining a Straight or Curved Line, page 338

Ongoing Assessment
Posttest Objective 4, page 341
Pretest Objective 5, page 342

CD = Concept Development   PM = Progress Monitoring   PS = Problem Solving
PA = Practice Activity   ★ = Includes Problem Solving

4-Day Instructional Plan

Use the 4-Day Instructional Plan when pretest results indicate that students would benefit from a slower pace. This plan is used when the majority of students need more time or did not demonstrate mastery on the pretest. This plan does not include all activities.

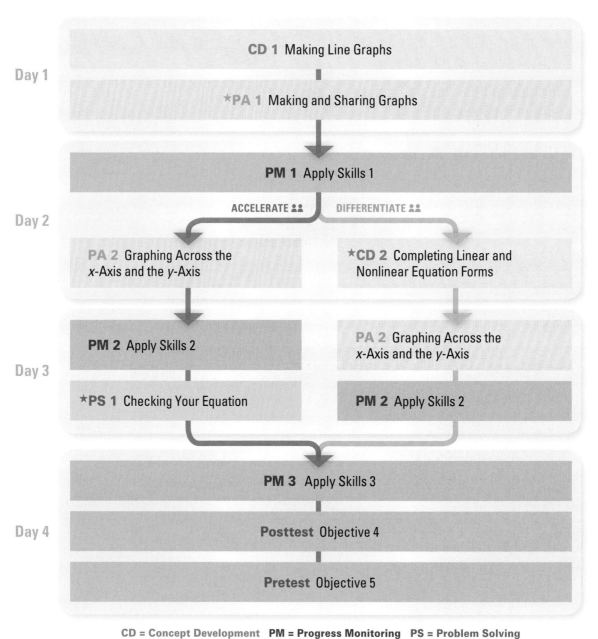

Day 1

CD 1 Making Line Graphs

★PA 1 Making and Sharing Graphs

PM 1 Apply Skills 1

ACCELERATE   **DIFFERENTIATE**

Day 2

PA 2 Graphing Across the *x*-Axis and the *y*-Axis

★CD 2 Completing Linear and Nonlinear Equation Forms

Day 3

PM 2 Apply Skills 2

★PS 1 Checking Your Equation

PA 2 Graphing Across the *x*-Axis and the *y*-Axis

PM 2 Apply Skills 2

Day 4

PM 3 Apply Skills 3

Posttest Objective 4

Pretest Objective 5

CD = Concept Development   PM = Progress Monitoring   PS = Problem Solving
PA = Practice Activity   ★ = Includes Problem Solving

3-Day Instructional Plan

Use the 3-Day Instructional Plan when pretest results indicate that students can move through the activities at a faster pace. This plan is ideal when the majority of students demonstrate mastery on the pretest.

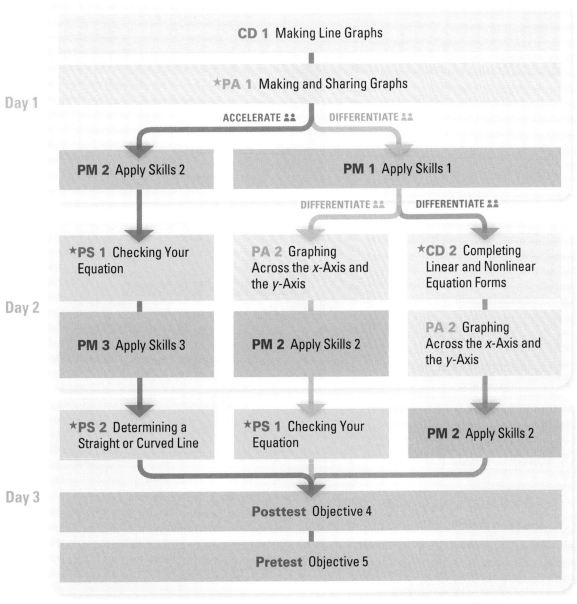

Day 1

CD 1 Making Line Graphs

★PA 1 Making and Sharing Graphs

ACCELERATE 👥   DIFFERENTIATE 👥

PM 2 Apply Skills 2   **PM 1** Apply Skills 1

DIFFERENTIATE 👥   DIFFERENTIATE 👥

Day 2

★PS 1 Checking Your Equation

PA 2 Graphing Across the x-Axis and the y-Axis

★CD 2 Completing Linear and Nonlinear Equation Forms

PM 3 Apply Skills 3

PM 2 Apply Skills 2

PA 2 Graphing Across the x-Axis and the y-Axis

★PS 2 Determining a Straight or Curved Line

★PS 1 Checking Your Equation

PM 2 Apply Skills 2

Day 3

Posttest Objective 4

Pretest Objective 5

CD = Concept Development   PM = Progress Monitoring   PS = Problem Solving
PA = Practice Activity   ★ = Includes Problem Solving

Concept Development Activities

CD 1 Making Line Graphs

Use with 4-Day or 3-Day Instructional Plan. In this activity, given an equation, students create a table and use the table to create a graph.

MATERIALS

- *Interactive Text*, pages 136–137

DIRECTIONS

1. Review the following term with students:

   ordered pair Two numbers that name the coordinates of a point on a graph, with the horizontal coordinate listed first and the vertical coordinate listed second

2. Write the equation **$y = 2x + 1$** on the board or an overhead transparency.

3. Ask students to discuss how a graph of this equation is made.

   Listen for:
   - We need ordered pairs to build a graph.
   - Making a table of values will give ordered pairs that satisfy the equation.
   - We need to choose appropriate scales and parts of the grid to make the graph.

4. Have students turn to *Interactive Text,* pages 136–137, Making Line Graphs. Have students complete the table for $y = 2x + 1$ in the *Interactive Text*. Discuss the completed table and correct ordered pairs.

5. Have students discuss how we make a graph from the table. Next, have each student make a graph for $y = 2x + 1$. Have one student show his or her graph and explain how it was constructed.

6. Remind students that a set of ordered pairs needs to be determined either by selecting some values for x and solving for y or by making a table. Tell students to use either method, as long as it determines correct ordered pairs.

Name _____ **Date** _____

MAKING LINE GRAPHS

To graph a linear equation, find three or four ordered pairs that satisfy the equation. Plot these points. If you are not sure of the graph, find more ordered pairs to complete the graph.

Complete the table to find the ordered pairs, then draw the graph.

1. $y = 2x + 1$

x	$y = 2x + 1$	y	(x, y)
−1	$y = 2(−1) + 1$	−1	(−1, −1)
−2	$y = 2(−2) + 1$	−3	(−2, −3)
0	$y = 2(0) + 1$	1	(0, 1)
2	$y = 2(2) + 1$	5	(2, 5)

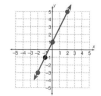

Make a table and sketch the graph of the equations.

2. $y = x + 3$ Tables will vary depending on the value of x. Sample answers are given.

x	$y = x + 3$	y	(x, y)
−1	$y = −1 + 3$	2	(−1, 2)
0	$y = 0 + 3$	3	(0, 3)
1	$y = 1 + 3$	4	(1, 4)

Name _____ **Date** _____

MAKING LINE GRAPHS   *(continued)*

3. $y = 2x$ Tables will vary depending on the value of x. Sample answers are given.

x	$y = 2x$	y	(x, y)
−1	$y = 2(−1)$	−2	(−1, −2)
0	$y = 2(0)$	0	(0, 0)
1	$y = 2(1)$	2	(1, 2)
2	$y = 2(2)$	4	(2, 4)

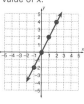

4. $2y − x = 4$

x	$y = \frac{1}{2}(x + 4)$	y	(x, y)
−2	$y = \frac{1}{2}(−2 + 4)$	1	(−2, 1)
0	$y = \frac{1}{2}(0 + 4)$	2	(0, 2)
2	$y = \frac{1}{2}(2 + 4)$	3	(2, 3)
4	$y = \frac{1}{2}(4 + 4)$	4	(4, 4)

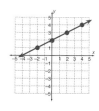

5. $x − y = 4$

x	$y = x − 4$	y	(x, y)
0	$y = 0 − 4$	−4	(0, −4)
1	$y = 1 − 4$	−3	(1, −3)
2	$y = 2 − 4$	−2	(2, −2)
3	$y = 3 − 4$	−1	(3, −1)

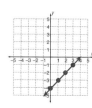

7. Review the process, and have students complete Problems 2–5.

8. Point out that all the equations graphed in this activity are straight lines. Ask students to discuss why they think this is true. Explain that any equation that can be written in the form $ax + by = c$ is a linear equation and the graph is a straight line.

NEXT STEPS • Differentiate

4-Day and 3-Day Instructional Plans:

PA 1, page 332—All students, for additional practice and problem solving

Concept Development Activities

★ CD 2 Completing Linear and Nonlinear Equation Forms

Use with 4-Day or 3-Day Instructional Plan. In this activity, students create a table from an equation and use the table to create a graph. Students determine the difference between linear and nonlinear equations and their graphs.

MATERIALS

- Blackline Master 59
- **Variation:** Gizmos
  Linear Functions

DIRECTIONS

1. Review the following term with students:

   ordered pair Two numbers that name the coordinates of a point on a graph, with the horizontal coordinate listed first and the vertical coordinate listed second

2. Have students work in groups of two or three. Give students two equations, one linear and one nonlinear.

   Sample problems:

   $x + y = 8$

   $xy = 8$

3. Have groups set up equation tables and find at least five ordered pairs for each equation. Remind students to use both positive and negative numbers and to always check to see what zero gives.

4. Discuss with students how the equation tables are the same and how they are different.

GRAPH PAPER

Sample answers:

x	x + y = 8	y	(x, y)
−2	−2 + y = 8	10	(−2, 10)
−1	−1 + y = 8	9	(−1, 9)
0	0 + y = 8	8	(0, 8)
1	1 + y = 8	7	(1, 7)
2	2 + y = 8	6	(2, 6)
3	3 + y = 8	5	(3, 5)

x	xy = 8	y	(x, y)
−2	−2 · y = 8	−4	(−2, −4)
−1	−1 · y = 8	−8	(−1, −8)
0	0 · y = 8	—	—
1	1 · y = 8	8	(1, 8)
2	2 · y = 8	4	(2, 4)
3	3 · y = 8	$2\frac{2}{3}$	$\left(3, 2\frac{2}{3}\right)$

★ = Includes Problem Solving

5. Distribute one copy of Blackline Master 59, Graph Paper, to each student. Have students graph the two equations. Talk about how the graphs are the same and how they are different.

$x + y = 8$

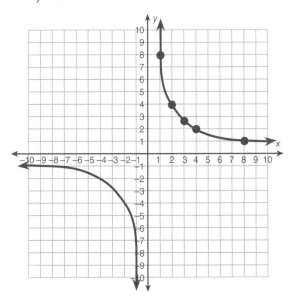

$xy = 8$

6. Tell students to think about how many ordered pairs they would need in order to know how a graph will look. Point out that for a linear equation they only need to find two points, but for a nonlinear equation they need more than two points.

7. Give the groups two more equations, one linear and one nonlinear. Have groups set up equation tables and find ordered pairs. Remind students to use positive and negative values in their equation tables.

Sample problems:

$$y = 2x - 1 \qquad y = x^2 - 1$$

8. Discuss with students how the equation tables are the same and how they are different. Answers will vary. Sample answer: For the equation $y = x^2 - 1$, the positive and negative x-values, such as $+2$ and -2, share the same y-value.

9. Have students graph the two equations. Talk about how the graphs are the same and how they are different. Answers will vary. Sample answer: The equation $y = 2x - 1$, is a linear equation, and $y = x^2 - 1$, is a nonlinear equation.

10. Have students discuss how many ordered pairs they would need to know to be certain of the shape of the graph. Answers will vary. Sample answer: You need at least three ordered pairs to know whether the graph is linear or nonlinear.

11. Complete this same activity a few more times until students understand the difference between a linear and a nonlinear equation and can identify the differences in the graphs.

> **Variation: Gizmos** Use the tables and graphs in the Gizmo *Linear Functions* to model and compare linear and nonlinear equations.

12. Tell students to work in their groups to come up with a linear and a nonlinear equation for another group to graph.

13. Instruct students to write what they see as the general form of a linear equation. Reinforce the idea of the infinite number of ordered pairs that work and lie on that straight line. $ax + by = c$, where a, b, and c are any real numbers

NEXT STEPS • Differentiate

4-Day and 3-Day Instructional Plans:
PA 2, page 333—All students, for additional practice

Practice Activities

★ PA 1 Making and Sharing Graphs

Use with 4-Day or 3-Day Instructional Plan. In this activity, students correctly graph linear equations.

MATERIALS

- Blackline Master 59

DIRECTIONS

1. Write the following equations on the board or overhead transparency:

   $y = ax + b$ where a and b are integers

   $ax + by = c$ where a and b are integers

   $x = ay + b$ where a and b are integers

2. Explain that a, b, and c can be any integers. Tell students to write an equation in the form $y = ax + b$. Discuss the equations, and check that students are following the directions.

   Sample answers:

   $y = -2x + 8$ where $a = -2$ and $b = 8$

3. Have students write one equation for $ax + by = c$ and one equation for $x = ay + b$. Check students' equations.

4. Distribute one copy of Blackline Master 59, Graph Paper, to each student. Tell students to make graphs of their equations.

5. Put students into groups of four. Have students exchange papers within their groups. Tell students to exchange the papers with the equations written on them, but not the graphs. Instruct students to make graphs of the equations they now have. Rotate the equation pages two more times. Each student should have a graph for all the equations in the group.

6. Have students compare their graphs and determine which graphs are correct if there are any differences.

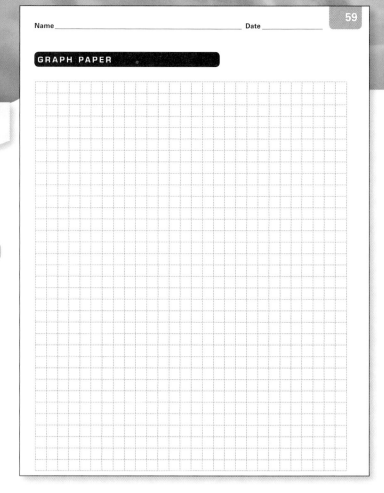

NEXT STEPS • Differentiate

4-Day Instructional Plan:
PM 1, page 334—All students, to assess progress

👥 **3-Day Instructional Plan:**
PM 2, page 335—Students who demonstrate understanding of the concept, to assess progress

PM 1, page 334—Students who need additional support, to assess progress

★ = Includes Problem Solving

Practice Activities

PA 2 Graphing Across the x-Axis and the y-Axis

Use with 4-Day or 3-Day Instructional Plan. In this activity, students will find the x- and y-intercepts of a line from its formula.

MATERIALS

• *Interactive Text*, pages 142–143

DIRECTIONS

1. Have students turn to *Interactive Text,* pages 142–143, x-Axis and y-Axis, and complete the problems on their own. Tell students they need to have another point, in addition to the intercepts, to be sure that all three points lie on the line.

2. Put students into groups of three or four, and have them discuss the answers. Tell groups to share how they know where the three points are and how this knowledge helps in graphing equations.

3. Have each group make up linear equations for other groups. With the new linear equations, tell groups to find where the line crosses the x-axis and y-axis.

NEXT STEPS • Differentiate

4-Day and 3-Day Instructional Plans:
PM 2, page 335—All students, to assess progress

---

x-AXIS AND y-AXIS

Find the three solutions to each equation, given the domain or range for each. Graph the equation and tell where the line goes through the x-axis and the y-axis.

1. $y = x - 4$

$(0, \underline{-4})$
$(\underline{4}, 0)$
$(5, \underline{1})$

2. $2x - y = 4$

$(0, \underline{-4})$
$(\underline{2}, 0)$
$(3, \underline{2})$

3. $y = 2x + 3$

$(0, \underline{3})$
$(\underline{-\frac{3}{2}}, 0)$
$(\underline{1}, 5)$

4. $3y = 2x$

$(0, \underline{0})$
$(\underline{0}, 0)$
$(3, \underline{2})$

5. $y = 3$

$(\underline{\quad}, 3)$
$(\underline{\quad}, 3)$
$(\underline{\quad}, 3)$

Answers will vary. Answer can be any value.

6. $x = 2$

$(2, \underline{\quad})$
$(2, \underline{\quad})$
$(2, \underline{\quad})$

Answers will vary. Answer can be any value.

---

x-AXIS AND y-AXIS *(continued)*

7. At the point where the graph goes through the y-axis, the domain is always _____zero_____.

8. At the point where the graph goes through the x-axis, the range is always _____zero_____.

9. Explain how you would graph any linear equation and how many points you would use.

Answers will vary. Sample answer: Choose any x-values, find the corresponding y-values, and draw a straight line through the points. Use at least two points.

Objective 4
Progress-Monitoring Activities

PM 1 Apply Skills 1

Use with 4-Day or 3-Day Instructional Plan.

MATERIALS

- *Interactive Text,* pages 144–145

DIRECTIONS

1. Have students turn to *Interactive Text,* pages 144–145, Apply Skills 1.

2. Remind students of the key term: *ordered pair.*

3. Monitor student work, and provide feedback as necessary.

   Watch for:
   - Do students correctly find ordered pairs that solve the equation?
   - Do students connect the pairs to graph the line?
   - Do students remember to put an arrow at each end of their lines?

NEXT STEPS • Differentiate

4-Day and 3-Day Instructional Plans:

PA 2, page 333—Students who demonstrate understanding of the concept, for additional practice

CD 2, page 330—Students who need additional concept development

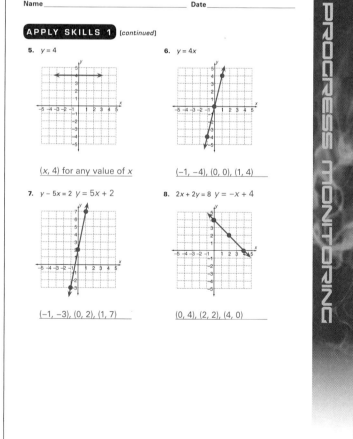

Objective 4
Progress-Monitoring Activities

PM 2 Apply Skills 2

Use with 4-Day or 3-Day Instructional Plan.

MATERIALS

- *Interactive Text*, pages 146–147

DIRECTIONS

1. Have students turn to *Interactive Text,* pages 146–147, Apply Skills 2.

2. Remind students of the key terms: *ordered pair, domain,* and *range.*

3. Monitor student work, and provide feedback as necessary.

   Watch for:
   - Do students correctly fill out the table for the equations?
   - Do students remember to put an arrow at each end of their lines?

NEXT STEPS • Differentiate

👥 4-Day Instructional Plan:

PS 1, page 337—Students who are on the accelerated path, to develop problem-solving skills

PM 3, page 336—Students who are on the differentiated path, for additional progress assessment

👥 3-Day Instructional Plan:

PS 1, page 337—Students who are on the accelerated path, to develop problem-solving skills

PS 1, page 337—Students on the differentiated path who demonstrated understanding on PM 1, to develop problem-solving skills

Objective 4 Posttest, page 341—All other students

APPLY SKILLS 2

1. Find the ordered pair solutions for $y = 2x - 1$ when the domain is {1, 2, 3, 4}. Graph these ordered pairs.

   {(__1__ , __1__), (__2__ , __3__), (__3__ , __5__), (__4__ , __7__)}

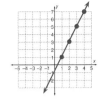

2. Complete the table and graph the equation $x - y = 4$.

x	$x - y = 4$	y	(x, y)
−2	−2 − y = 4	−6	(−2, −6)
0	0 − y = 4	−4	(0, −4)
1	1 − y = 4	−3	(1, −3)
2	2 − y = 4	−2	(2, −2)

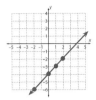

3. Choose any three values of x and find the range for the linear equation $2x + y = -3$. Graph these ordered pairs and the equation $2x + y = -3$.

   {(__−1__ , __−1__), (__0__ , __−3__), (__1__ , __−5__)}

   Ordered pairs will vary. All correct pairs yield the same graph.

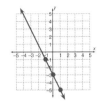

APPLY SKILLS 2 *(continued)*

4. If the domain is {−1, 0, 1, 2}, graph the relation $y = -2x + 4$.

x	y
−1	6
0	4
1	2
2	0

5. Complete the table and graph the equation $x + y = -2$.

x	$x + y = -2$	y	(x, y)
−4	x + 2 = −2	2	(−4, 2)
−2	x + 0 = −2	0	(−2, 0)
−1	−1 + y = −2	−1	(−1, −1)
0	0 + y = −2	−2	(0, −2)

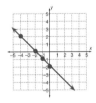

Progress-Monitoring Activities

PM 3 Apply Skills 3

Use with 4-Day or 3-Day Instructional Plan.

MATERIALS

- *Interactive Text*, pages 148–149

DIRECTIONS

1. Have students turn to *Interactive Text*, pages 148–149, Apply Skills 3.

2. Remind students of the key term: *linear equation*.

3. Monitor student work, and provide feedback as necessary.

   Watch for:
   - Do students understand how to recognize a linear equation?

   - Can students determine whether an equation will be a straight line without graphing?

NEXT STEPS • Differentiate

4-Day Instructional Plan:
Objective 4 Posttest, page 341—All students

3-Day Instructional Plan:
PS 2, page 338—All students, to develop problem-solving skills

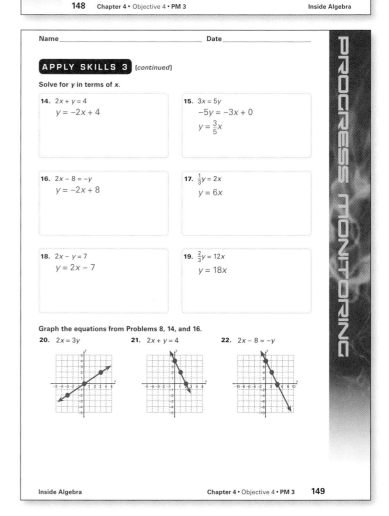

PROGRESS MONITORING

Name _____ Date _____

APPLY SKILLS 3

Tell whether each equation is a linear equation. Explain your answer.

1. $3x + 7y = 10$ _Yes; equation is of the form $ax + by = c$ (straight line)_

2. $\frac{1}{2}x = y + 5$ _Yes; straight line_

3. $y = x^2$ _No; curve_

4. $y = x^2 + 4$ _No; curve_

5. $x^2 + 2x = y$ _No; curve_

6. $xy = 12$ _No; curve (actually 2 curves)_

Tell whether the graph of each equation will be a straight line. Graph any that you are not sure of.

7. $y = 2x + 1$ _yes_   8. $2x = 3y$ _yes_   9. $x + 4 = 0$ _yes_

10. $4x + 3y = 6$ _yes_   11. $y = x^2$ _no_   12. $y = x^2 + 2x$ _no_

13. All equations that graph a straight line are called _linear_ equations.

148   Chapter 4 • Objective 4 • PM 3   Inside Algebra

Name _____ Date _____

APPLY SKILLS 3 (continued)

Solve for *y* in terms of *x*.

14. $2x + y = 4$
$y = -2x + 4$

15. $3x = 5y$
$-5y = -3x + 0$
$y = \frac{3}{5}x$

16. $2x - 8 = -y$
$y = -2x + 8$

17. $\frac{1}{3}y = 2x$
$y = 6x$

18. $2x - y = 7$
$y = 2x - 7$

19. $\frac{2}{3}y = 12x$
$y = 18x$

Graph the equations from Problems 8, 14, and 16.

20. $2x = 3y$ 21. $2x + y = 4$ 22. $2x - 8 = -y$

Inside Algebra   Chapter 4 • Objective 4 • PM 3   149

★ PS 1 Checking Your Equation

Use with 4-Day or 3-Day Instructional Plan. In this activity, students write an equation to represent each graph.

MATERIALS

- *Interactive Text,* page 150
- Graphing calculators

DIRECTIONS

1. Review the following term with students:

    ordered pair Two numbers that name the coordinates of a point on a graph, with the horizontal coordinate listed first and the vertical coordinate listed second

2. Have students turn to *Interactive Text,* page 150, Name Your Equation. Have students list some ordered pairs that satisfy each graph and guess at an equation for the graph. Tell students to document their guess by writing it down.

3. Put students in pairs, and tell them to check each other's equations. Have students try to convince their partners that they are correct by presenting facts about the graph and the equation.

4. Tell students to check the equations by using graphing calculators or by finding three ordered pairs for each equation and graphing these points.

5. Discuss the types of graphs that are easy to identify by their equations, such as $y = x$, $y = 3$, and $x = -2$.

6. Discuss the different equation forms that graphed the same line. Help students check if they are equivalent.

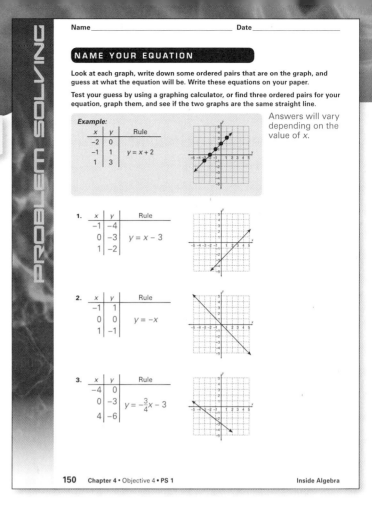

NEXT STEPS • Differentiate

4-Day Instructional Plan:
PM 3, page 336—All students, to assess progress

👥 **3-Day Instructional Plan:**
PM 3, page 336—Students who are on the accelerated path, to assess progress

Objective 4 Posttest, page 341—Students who are on the differentiated path

Objective 4
Problem-Solving Activities

★ PS 2 Determining a Straight or Curved Line

Use with 3-Day Instructional Plan. In this activity, given a word problem, students correctly identify the independent variable and determine whether the equation is linear.

MATERIALS

- *Interactive Text*, pages 151–153
- Blackline Master 59

DIRECTIONS

1. Review the following term with students:

   ordered pair Two numbers that name the coordinates of a point on a graph, with the horizontal coordinate listed first and the vertical coordinate listed second

2. Put students in groups of three or four, and distribute one copy of Blackline Master 59, Graph Paper, to each student.

3. Have students turn to *Interactive Text,* pages 151–153, Straight or Curved?, for this activity.

4. Tell students to graph each situation and determine whether the graph is a straight line. Have students set up a table and list at least four ordered pairs for each problem. Explain to students that they only need to write an equation for the graphs that are straight lines.

5. Tell students that it is okay to write equations for any of the problems. Point out that Problem 2 is the only one that does not have a simple equation that fits the data.

   Watch for:
   - Do students place the independent variable on the *x*-axis?
   - Do students write equations to show the dependent variable in terms of the independent variable?

★ = **Includes Problem Solving**

GRAPH PAPER

Name _____ Date _____

STRAIGHT OR CURVED?

Determine whether the situations will graph a straight line after setting up a table and a solution set of at least four ordered pairs. Sketch the graphs on graph paper. If the graph is a straight line, write an equation.

1. The area of a room is length times width (*l · w*). If the area is 40 square meters, make a table of four possibilities for the length and width, and graph the solutions.

   _____ curved _____

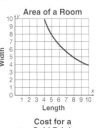
Area of a Room

2. Costs for a cold drink at the corner store are as follows:

   12 oz. drink costs $2.50
   18 oz. drink costs $3.50
   32 oz. drink costs $4.50
   64 oz. drink costs $5.50

   (When you graph these, be sure you make a scale for the ounces.)

   _____ curved _____

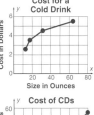
Cost for a Cold Drink

3. CDs are on sale at your favorite music store for $15, and with your coupon you get $5 off the total purchase. Make a table for buying one to four CDs.

   _____ straight, $y = 15x - 5$ _____

Cost of CDs

PROBLEM SOLVING

Inside Algebra   Chapter 4 • Objective 4 • PS 2   **151**

Objective 4
Problem-Solving Activities

NEXT STEPS • Differentiate

3-Day Instructional Plan:

Objective 4 Posttest, page 341—All students

STRAIGHT OR CURVED? *(continued)*

4. You have 40 cents in your pocket, and the coins are all nickels and dimes. Make a table of all possible combinations and graph it.

straight, $5n + 10d = 40$

Coins in Your Pocket

5. When I traveled to Alaska, I learned that the part of the iceberg that we see above water is only one-eighth the size of the whole iceberg. That means the iceberg is one-eighth above the surface of the ocean and seven-eighths below the surface of the ocean. Find out how much is below the ocean if the domain is 5,000 tons, 6,000 tons, and 7,000 tons above the ocean. Extend the graph so that we can read what is below for a 10,000-ton ice tip.

straight, $y = 7x$

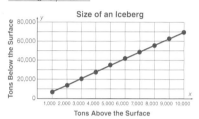

Size of an Iceberg

152   Chapter 4 • Objective 4 • PS 2   Inside Algebra

STRAIGHT OR CURVED? *(continued)*

Determine whether the situations will graph a straight line after setting up a table and a solution set of at least four ordered pairs. Sketch the graphs on graph paper. If the graph is a straight line, write an equation.

6. An advertisement for Internet access reads: "Internet access for $3.00 plus $0.20 per minute." Set up your table to find the cost in dollars for different numbers of minutes of access time, for example, 1 minute, 5 minutes, 10 minutes, etc.

straight, $c = 3 + 0.2m$

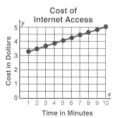

Cost of Internet Access

7. Every state has a certain way to figure out the cost of a speeding ticket on the highway. One state uses the formula: Ticket price = 10(speed of car − 55) + $40.

Figure the ticket price for a car going 60, 65, and 75 mph in that state. Set up a table and graph the results. Can you read the graph and figure out the ticket cost if you were going 90 mph or any other speed?

straight

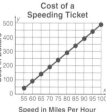

Cost of a Speeding Ticket

8. The area of a circle is $A = \pi r^2$. Find the area if the radius, r, is 2 feet, 4 feet, 6 feet, and 8 feet. Is the graph a straight line?

curved

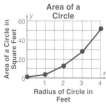

Area of a Circle

Inside Algebra   Chapter 4 • Objective 4 • PS 2   153

This page intentionally left blank

Objective 4
Ongoing Assessment

Objective 4 Posttest

Discuss with students the key concepts in Objective 4. Following the discussion, administer the Objective 4 Posttest to all students.

Using the Results

• Score the posttest and update the class record card.

• Provide reinforcement for students who do not demonstrate mastery of the concepts through individual or small-group reteaching of key concepts.

Complete the table and construct the graph for each equation.

1. $y - 2x = 3$

x	$y - 2x = 3$	y	(x, y)
-2	$y - 2(-2) = 3$	-1	(-2, -1)
-1	$y - 2(-1) = 3$	1	(-1, 1)
0	$y - 2(0) = 3$	3	(0, 3)
2	$y - 2(2) = 3$	7	(2, 7)

2. Graph of $y - 2x = 3$

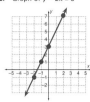

3. $2x + 3y = 10$

x	$2x + 3y = 10$	y	(x, y)
5	$2(5) + 3y = 10$	0	(5, 0)
2	$2(2) + 3y = 10$	2	(2, 2)
-1	$2(-1) + 3y = 10$	4	(-1, 4)
-4	$2(-4) + 3y = 10$	6	(-4, 6)

4. Graph of $2x + 3y = 10$

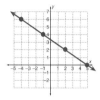

5. $y = 2x$

x	$y = 2x$	y	(x, y)
-2	$y = 2(-2)$	-4	(-2, -4)
0	$y = 2(0)$	0	(0, 0)
1	$y = 2(1)$	2	(1, 2)
3	$y = 2(3)$	6	(3, 6)

6. Graph of $y = 2x$

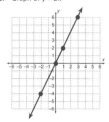

Inside Algebra   Chapter 4 • Objective 4   **53**

Make a table and construct the graph for each equation.

7. $x + 2y = -6$

x	$x + 2y = -6$	y	(x, y)
-2	$-2 + 2y = -6$	-2	(-2, -2)
0	$0 + 2y = -6$	-3	(0, -3)
2	$2 + 2y = -6$	-4	(2, -4)

8. Graph of $x + 2y = -6$

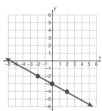

9. $x + y = 15$

x	$x + y = 15$	y	(x, y)
-5	$-5 + y = 15$	20	(-5, 20)
0	$0 + y = 15$	15	(0, 15)
5	$5 + y = 15$	10	(5, 10)
10	$10 + y = 15$	5	(10, 5)

10. Graph of $x + y = 15$

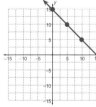

Tables will vary depending on values for x.

54   Chapter 4 • Objective 4   Inside Algebra

Objective 5
Determine whether a relation is a function, and find a value for a given function.

Objective 5 Pretest

Students complete the Objective 5 Pretest on the same day as the Objective 4 Posttest.

Using the Results

- Score the pretest and update the class record card.

- If the majority of students do not demonstrate mastery of the concepts, use the 5-Day Instructional Plan for Objective 5.

- If the majority of students demonstrate mastery of the concepts, use the 3-Day Instructional Plan for Objective 5.

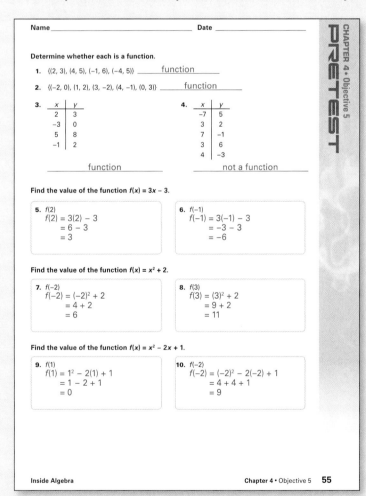

Name _____ Date _____

Determine whether each is a function.

1. $\{(2, 3), (4, 5), (-1, 6), (-4, 5)\}$ ___function___

2. $\{(-2, 0), (1, 2), (3, -2), (4, -1), (0, 3)\}$ ___function___

3.

x	y
2	3
-3	0
5	8
-1	2

___function___

4.

x	y
-7	5
3	2
7	-1
3	6
4	-3

___not a function___

Find the value of the function $f(x) = 3x - 3$.

5. $f(2)$
$f(2) = 3(2) - 3$
$\quad = 6 - 3$
$\quad = 3$

6. $f(-1)$
$f(-1) = 3(-1) - 3$
$\quad = -3 - 3$
$\quad = -6$

Find the value of the function $f(x) = x^2 + 2$.

7. $f(-2)$
$f(-2) = (-2)^2 + 2$
$\quad = 4 + 2$
$\quad = 6$

8. $f(3)$
$f(3) = (3)^2 + 2$
$\quad = 9 + 2$
$\quad = 11$

Find the value of the function $f(x) = x^2 - 2x + 1$.

9. $f(1)$
$f(1) = 1^2 - 2(1) + 1$
$\quad = 1 - 2 + 1$
$\quad = 0$

10. $f(-2)$
$f(-2) = (-2)^2 - 2(-2) + 1$
$\quad = 4 + 4 + 1$
$\quad = 9$

Inside Algebra   Chapter 4 • Objective 5   **55**

CHAPTER 4 • Objective 5 **PRETEST**

Goals and Activities

Objective 5 Goals

The following activities, when used with the instructional plans on pages 344 and 345, enable students to:

- Determine whether relation a. $\{(-1, 3), (0, 2), (-3, 6), (2, -4)\}$ or b. $\{(0, 0), (-1, 2), (0, 4), (2, -3), (-2, 4)\}$ is a function **Answer: a**
- Find the value of $f(5)$ if $f(x) = 2x - 1$ to be **9**
- Find the value of $f(2)$ if $f(x) = 3x - 8$ to be **-2**
- Find the value of $f(-2)$ if $f(x) = x^2 + 1$ to be **5**

Objective 5 Activities

Concept Development Activities

★CD 1 Explaining Relations as Functions, page 346	★CD 2 Determining Function Graphs, page 348	★CD 3 Determining the Function Value, page 350

Practice Activities

PA 1 Determining Whether a Relation Is a Function, page 352	PA 2 Playing Domain Roll to Solve Equations, page 353

Progress-Monitoring Activities

PM 1 Apply Skills 1, page 354	PM 2 Apply Skills 2, page 355

*Problem-Solving Activity

★PS 1 Determining Windchill Temperature, page 356

Ongoing Assessment

Posttest Objective 5, page 357

Review Chapter 4 Review, page 358

Chapter 4 Test, page 359

CD = Concept Development   PM = Progress Monitoring   PS = Problem Solving
PA = Practice Activity   ★ = Includes Problem Solving

Instructional Plans

5-Day Instructional Plan

Use the 5-Day Instructional Plan when pretest results indicate that students would benefit from a slower pace. This plan is used when the majority of students need more time or did not demonstrate mastery on the pretest.

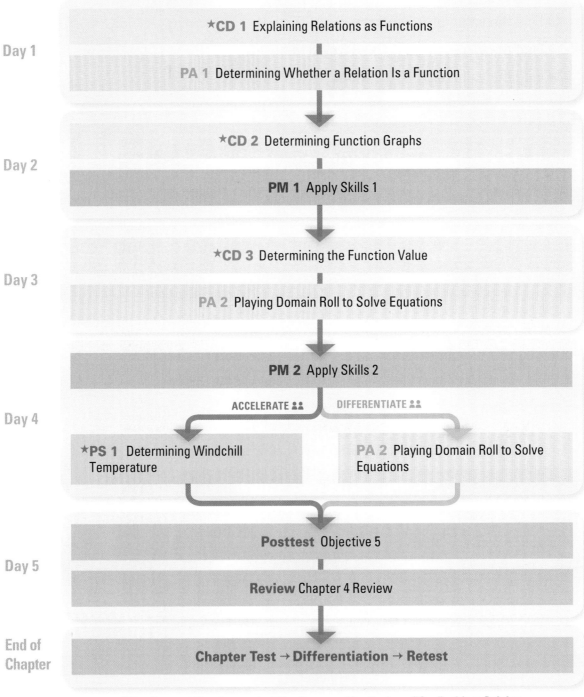

Day 1
★CD 1 Explaining Relations as Functions
PA 1 Determining Whether a Relation Is a Function

Day 2
★CD 2 Determining Function Graphs
PM 1 Apply Skills 1

Day 3
★CD 3 Determining the Function Value
PA 2 Playing Domain Roll to Solve Equations

Day 4
PM 2 Apply Skills 2
ACCELERATE 👥   DIFFERENTIATE 👥
★PS 1 Determining Windchill Temperature   PA 2 Playing Domain Roll to Solve Equations

Day 5
Posttest Objective 5
Review Chapter 4 Review

End of Chapter
Chapter Test → Differentiation → Retest

CD = Concept Development   PM = Progress Monitoring   PS = Problem Solving
PA = Practice Activity   ★ = Includes Problem Solving

3-Day Instructional Plan

Use the 3-Day Instructional Plan when pretest results indicate that students can move through the activities at a faster pace. This plan is ideal when the majority of students demonstrate mastery on the pretest.

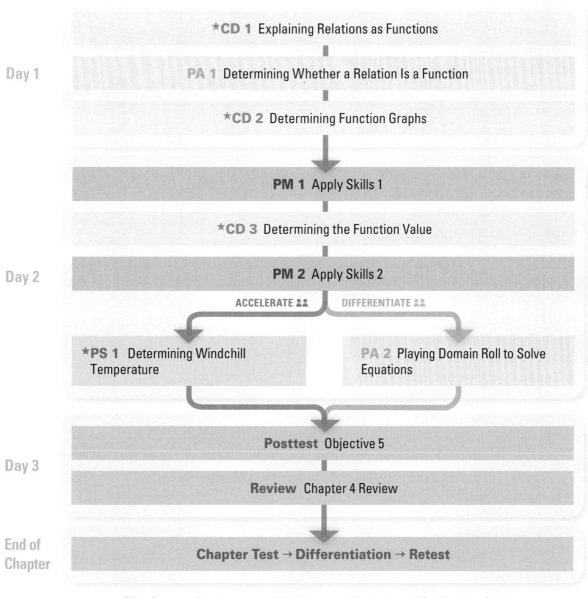

Day 1

★**CD 1** Explaining Relations as Functions

PA 1 Determining Whether a Relation Is a Function

★**CD 2** Determining Function Graphs

PM 1 Apply Skills 1

★**CD 3** Determining the Function Value

Day 2

PM 2 Apply Skills 2

ACCELERATE   DIFFERENTIATE

★**PS 1** Determining Windchill Temperature

PA 2 Playing Domain Roll to Solve Equations

Day 3

Posttest Objective 5

Review Chapter 4 Review

End of Chapter

Chapter Test → Differentiation → Retest

CD = Concept Development   PM = Progress Monitoring   PS = Problem Solving
PA = Practice Activity   ★ = Includes Problem Solving

★ CD 1 Explaining Relations as Functions

Use with 5-Day or 3-Day Instructional Plan. In this activity, students learn the definition of a function and calculate its range.

DIRECTIONS

1. Review with students the idea that in a relation the value of one variable depends on the value of another variable. This gives us a set of ordered pairs that are related.

2. Review the following terms with students:

   domain The possible values for *x* in a relation

   ordered pair Two numbers that name the coordinates of a point on a graph, with the horizontal coordinate listed first and the vertical coordinate listed second

   range The possible values for *y* in a relation

3. Discuss the following term with students:

   function A relation in which every element in the domain is paired with exactly one element in the range

4. Point out that a function is a special kind of relation in which each first value of the ordered pairs is paired with one and only one second value.

5. Challenge students to come up with a situation in which this would be true. Tell students to write the function and make a table for the function.

   Sample answer:

   > If a person on top of a building drops a coin from the roof, the distance the coin falls is a function of the time the coin is in the air. In the first second, the coin drops 16 feet. For each time there is one distance.
   >
   > $D(t) = 16t^2$
   >
   > | *t* (in seconds) | *D* (in feet) |
   > |---|---|
   > | 1 | 16 |
   > | 2 | 64 |
   > | 3 | 144 |
   > | 4 | 256 |

6. Challenge students to come up with a situation in which the relation would not be a function. Tell students to make a table for the situation.

   Sample answer:

   > The ticket price for a light rail train usually depends on the zones. The stops within a certain zone are all priced the same, even though their distances vary.
   >
   > | Station | Miles | Zone | Price of Ticket | Ordered Pair |
   > |---|---|---|---|---|
   > | Mt. Station | 12 | 5 | $6.00 | (12, 6) |
   > | Highland | 14 | 5 | $6.00 | (14, 6) |
   > | Church Road | 13 | 4 | $5.50 | (13, 5.5) |
   > | East Road | 12 | 4 | $5.50 | (12, 5.5) |
   > | Newtown | 10 | 2 | $4.50 | (10, 4.5) |

7. Have students practice writing relations as functions. Emphasize that one quantity is a function of the other, and that is why the notation is of the form *f*(*x*) instead of another letter, such as *y*.

   Sample problem:

   > At the post office, the total price is a function of the number of stamps you buy. Suppose the cost of a stamp is $0.44. **P(*x*)** = $0.44*x*
   >
   > | Number of Stamps | Price |
   > |---|---|
   > | 1 | $0.44 |
   > | 2 | $0.88 |
   > | 3 | $1.32 |
   > | 4 | $1.76 |
   > | 5 | $2.20 |

8. Have students set up a table for the function
$f(x) = 2x + 3$ for which the values of x are $\{-1, 0, 2, 3\}$.

x	$f(x) = 2x + 3$	Ordered Pairs
−1	$2(-1) + 3 = 1$	$(-1, 1)$
0	$2(0) + 3 = 3$	$(0, 3)$
2	$2(2) + 3 = 7$	$(2, 7)$
3	$2(3) + 3 = 9$	$(3, 9)$

9. Discuss the similarities and differences of each of the functions described in this activity.

10. Introduce more examples if students are struggling with the concept of a function.

Sample problems:

Earnings per hour; if $10.50 is earned per hour.
$E(h) = \$10.50(h)$

Phone rates per minute; if a call costs $0.16 per minute. $C(m) = \$0.16(m)$

Cost per pound; if beef is on sale for $2.30 a pound. $A(p) = \$2.30(p)$

NEXT STEPS • Differentiate

5-Day and 3-Day Instructional Plans:
PA 1, page 352—All students, for additional practice

Concept Development Activities

★ CD 2 Determining Function Graphs

Use with 5-Day or 3-Day Instructional Plan. In this activity, students determine whether a relation is a function from its graph.

MATERIALS

- *Interactive Text,* page 154
- Blackline Master 59

DIRECTIONS

1. Review the following terms with students:

   domain The possible values for *x* in a relation

   function A relation in which every element in the domain is paired with exactly one element in the range

   ordered pair Two numbers that name the coordinates of a point on a graph, with the horizontal coordinate listed first and the vertical coordinate listed second

   range The possible values for *y* in a relation

2. Put students into groups of two or three. Have students turn to *Interactive Text,* page 154, Function Graphs.

3. Have each group look at the graphs of relations in the *Interactive Text* and answer the questions.

4. Have groups determine the similarities of the graphs that are functions, and have them determine how these graphs differ from the ones that are not functions.

   Listen for:
   - Those that are not functions can have two dependent (*y*) values for the same independent (*x*) value.

5. Have each group write the definition of a function in their own words using the concepts of domain and range. Have groups share these definitions with the class. Look for common elements.

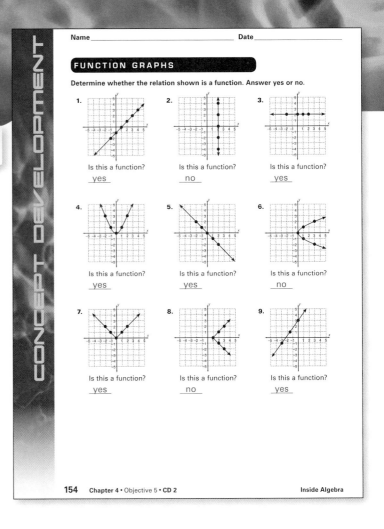

6. Show students the vertical line test by pointing out each of the functions on *Interactive Text,* page 154. We know these graphs are functions because each of them intersect the vertical lines no more than one time. Point out that the relations that are not functions intersect several vertical lines more than once.

7. Distribute one copy of Blackline Master 59, Graph Paper, to each student.

GRAPH PAPER

8. Put the following table on the board, and have students graph the information in the table. After students graph it, have them determine whether the relation is a function. Tell students to write the relationship of the function on their papers.

Example:

Number of People	Days Needed for Job
2	6
3	4
4	3

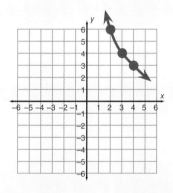

It is a function. The number of days needed to complete the job is a function of the number of people working on it.

9. Have each group develop three or four relations to give to another group. The other groups must complete and graph the relations to determine if they are functions. Tell groups to state the functions in terms of the relationship.

NEXT STEPS • Differentiate

5-Day and 3-Day Instructional Plans:
PM 1, page 354—All students, to assess progress

Concept Development Activities

★CD 3 Determining the Function Value

Use with 5-Day or 3-Day Instructional Plan. In this activity, students calculate values for the range of a nonlinear function.

DIRECTIONS

1. Review the following terms with students:

   domain The possible values for x in a relation

   function A relation in which every element in the domain is paired with exactly one element in the range

   ordered pair Two numbers that name the coordinates of a point on a graph, with the horizontal coordinate listed first and the vertical coordinate listed second

   range The possible values for y in a relation

2. Remind students that x represents the domain and y represents the range of the relation in a function. Explain that instead of using y, we use $f(x)$ to emphasize that one quantity is a function of the other quantity.

3. Present the function **$f(x) = 3x - 2$**, and have students find the value in the range that depends on 4 in the domain. Tell students to identify the ordered pair.

   Example:

   > **$f(4) = 3x - 2$**
   > $f(4) = 3(4) - 2 = 10$
   > The value in the range is 10.
   > The ordered pair is (4, 10).

4. Choose a few volunteers to write functions. Have the class find the range value that depends on a given domain value and write the ordered pair.

5. Give students two functions, and have them look at given values to determine which value the two functions have in common.

   Sample problem:

   > **$f(x) = x^2 - 5$**
   > **$f(x) = x + 1$**
   > Values: **$f(-2)$, $f(2)$, $f(-1)$**
   > The two functions have $f(-2)$ in common.

6. Give students a word problem that requires them to solve it by working with a function. Have students start by drawing a picture of the scenario. Encourage them to make a chart to organize the information.

   Example:

   > Pop Fligh hits a pitch that is 3.5 feet high. As the ball travels toward the outfield, its height can be represented by the function $f(x) = -0.005x^2 + 2x + 3.5$. Find the ball's height when the domain values are $f(0)$, $f(10)$, $f(30)$, $f(100)$, and $f(300)$.

   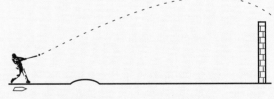

Feet From Home Plate	Height of the Ball in Feet
0	3.5
10	23
30	59
100	153.5
300	153.5

★ = Includes Problem Solving

7. Have students discuss why the heights for 100 and 300 feet are the same.

   Listen for:
   - The ball goes up and down.
   - The ball passes the same height on the way up and on the way down.

8. Tell students to work in pairs to figure out where a player should stand to catch a fly ball hit by Pop if they can catch a ball 10 feet in the air. $10 = -0.005x^2 + 2x + 3.5$; about 397 feet from home plate

9. Have students discuss other information they can figure out from the values.

   Sample problem:

   Could the ball go over a 10-foot fence 400 feet from the plate? No, the ball would be only $3\frac{1}{2}$ feet off the ground.

   > **Variation: Challenge** To extend this activity, have students graph the two functions in Step 5 to see where the two lines intersect.

NEXT STEPS • Differentiate

5-Day Instructional Plan:
PA 2, page 353—All students, for additional practice

3-Day Instructional Plan:
PM 2, page 355—All students, to assess progress

Practice Activities

PA 1 Determining Whether a Relation Is a Function

Use with 5-Day or 3-Day Instructional Plan. In this activity, students determine if a set of ordered pairs can belong to a function.

MATERIALS

- Blackline Master 61
- Game markers, one per student
- Blank wooden cubes, one per group

DIRECTIONS

1. Review the following terms with students:

   function A relation in which every value in the domain is paired with exactly one value in the range

   ordered pair Two numbers that name the coordinates of a point on a graph, with the horizontal coordinate listed first and the vertical coordinate listed second

2. Have students work in groups of three. Distribute one copy of Blackline Master 61, Function Board, to each group.

3. Make dice from the blank cubes with the six sides numbered 1, 2, 3, 1, 2, 3. Give one die to each group.

4. Explain the game rules to students.

   - The first player rolls the die and moves that many spaces. The student looks at the ordered pairs in the box, tells whether the relation is a function, and explains his or her answer.

   - The other players determine if he or she is correct.

   - If the player is correct, the player's marker stays on that spot. If the player is incorrect, the marker is moved back to the player's previous spot.

   - Play continues until someone reaches *END*.

5. Have each student select a marker as a game piece and place it on start. Have students roll the die to determine who will go first. The person with the highest number goes first, and the play will continue clockwise.

6. Circulate among the students, and review the rules if there is a conflict.

NEXT STEPS • Differentiate

5-Day and 3-Day Instructional Plans:
CD 2, page 348—All students, for additional concept development and problem solving

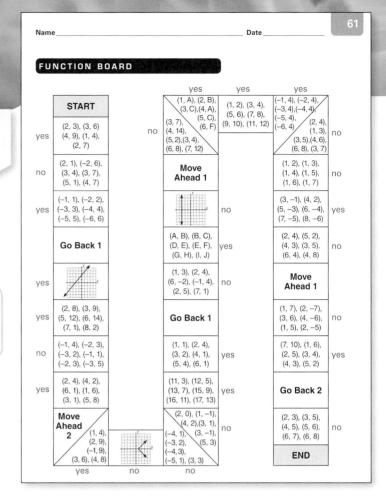

Practice Activities

PA 2 Playing Domain Roll to Solve Equations

Use with 5-Day or 3-Day Instructional Plan. In this activity, students increase their familiarity with finding the value of a function at a given point in the domain.

MATERIALS

- Dice, one per group

DIRECTIONS

1. Put students into groups of four. Give each group one die.
2. Write the equation $f(x) = 2x - 3$ on the board.
3. Explain the game rules to students.
   - Every person takes a turn to roll the die and use that number for the *x* value in the equation; for example, if a student rolls a 3, $f(3) = 2(3) - 3 = 3$.
   - All students check their group members' work.
   - For each correct answer, the student gets one point.
4. Tell students that each group must keep a tally for its players.
5. Continue the game with other equations after groups have completed one round. The equations may be used more than once.

   Sample problems:

$f(x) = 2x + 3$	$f(x) = -3x + 1$
$f(x) = 6 - x$	$f(x) = 3x + 2 - x$
$f(x) = -3 + 3x$	$f(x) = x^2$
$f(x) = 12 - x^2$	$f(x) = 7x + 2$

NEXT STEPS • Differentiate

5-Day Instructional Plan:
   PM 2, page 355—Students completing the activity for the first time, to assess progress

   Objective 5 Posttest, page 357—Students completing the activity for the second time

3-Day Instructional Plan:
   Objective 5 Posttest, page 357—All students

Objective 5
Progress-Monitoring Activities

PM 1 Apply Skills 1

Use with 5-Day or 3-Day Instructional Plan.

MATERIALS

- *Interactive Text*, page 155

DIRECTIONS

1. Have students turn to *Interactive Text*, page 155, Apply Skills 1.

2. Remind students of the key terms: *relation* and *function*.

3. Monitor student work, and provide feedback as necessary.

   Watch for:
   - Do students recognize that a function pairs exactly one element in the range with each element in the domain?

   - Can students identify the graph of a function using the vertical line test?

NEXT STEPS • Differentiate

5-Day and 3-Day Instructional Plans:
CD 3, page 350—All students, for additional concept development and problem solving

---

Name_____ Date_____

APPLY SKILLS 1

Determine whether the relation shown is a function.

1. {(2, −3), (3, 6), (5, −8), (1, 2)} yes

2. {(1, 5), (1, −2), (1, 0), (1, 3)} no

3. {(1, 4), (−2, 4), (3, 4), (0, 4)} yes

4.
x	y
−3	3
−2	4
2	4
0	2
4	4	yes

5.
x	y
−4	3
3	2
−4	1
−3	0
−4	0	no

6.
yes

7.
yes

8.
no

9.
no

10.
yes

Progress-Monitoring Activities

PM 2 Apply Skills 2

Use with 5-Day or 3-Day Instructional Plan.

MATERIALS

- *Interactive Text*, page 156

DIRECTIONS

1. Have students turn to *Interactive Text,* page 156, Apply Skills 2.

2. Remind students of the key terms: *relation* and *function*.

3. Monitor student work, and provide feedback as necessary.

   Watch for:
   - Do students understand that $f(x)$ is a way of writing y to show that it depends on x?

   - Do students correctly substitute values into a function?

NEXT STEPS • Differentiate

👥 **5-Day and 3-Day Instructional Plans:**

PS 1, page 356—Students who demonstrate understanding of the concept, to develop problem-solving skills

PA 2, page 353—Students who need additional practice

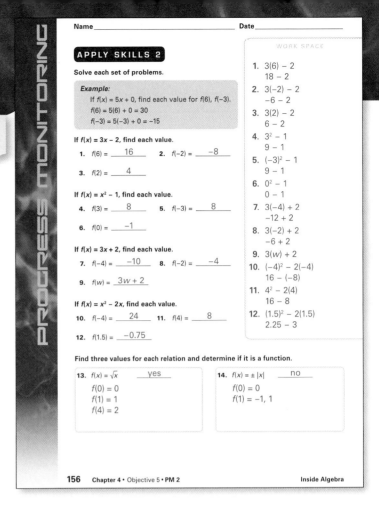

Name _____ Date _____

APPLY SKILLS 2

Solve each set of problems.

Example:
If $f(x) = 5x + 0$, find each value for $f(6)$, $f(-3)$.
$f(6) = 5(6) + 0 = 30$
$f(-3) = 5(-3) + 0 = -15$

If $f(x) = 3x - 2$, find each value.

1. $f(6) =$ ___16___   2. $f(-2) =$ ___−8___

3. $f(2) =$ ___4___

If $f(x) = x^2 - 1$, find each value.

4. $f(3) =$ ___8___   5. $f(-3) =$ ___8___

6. $f(0) =$ ___−1___

If $f(x) = 3x + 2$, find each value.

7. $f(-4) =$ ___−10___   8. $f(-2) =$ ___−4___

9. $f(w) =$ ___$3w + 2$___

If $f(x) = x^2 - 2x$, find each value.

10. $f(-4) =$ ___24___   11. $f(4) =$ ___8___

12. $f(1.5) =$ ___−0.75___

Find three values for each relation and determine if it is a function.

13. $f(x) = \sqrt{x}$ ___yes___
$f(0) = 0$
$f(1) = 1$
$f(4) = 2$

14. $f(x) = \pm|x|$ ___no___
$f(0) = 0$
$f(1) = -1, 1$

WORK SPACE

1. $3(6) - 2$
   $18 - 2$

2. $3(-2) - 2$
   $-6 - 2$

3. $3(2) - 2$
   $6 - 2$

4. $3^2 - 1$
   $9 - 1$

5. $(-3)^2 - 1$
   $9 - 1$

6. $0^2 - 1$
   $0 - 1$

7. $3(-4) + 2$
   $-12 + 2$

8. $3(-2) + 2$
   $-6 + 2$

9. $3(w) + 2$

10. $(-4)^2 - 2(-4)$
    $16 - (-8)$

11. $4^2 - 2(4)$
    $16 - 8$

12. $(1.5)^2 - 2(1.5)$
    $2.25 - 3$

156   Chapter 4 • Objective 5 • PM 2   Inside Algebra

Problem-Solving Activity

★ PS 1 Determining Windchill Temperature

Use with 5-Day or 3-Day Instructional Plan. In this activity, students increase their familiarity with finding the value of a function at a given point in the domain.

MATERIALS

- *Interactive Text,* page 157
- Graphing calculators, one per student

DIRECTIONS

1. Review the following terms with students:

   domain The possible values for *x* in a relation

   function A relation in which every value in the domain is paired with exactly one value in the range

   range The possible values for *y* in a relation

2. Have students turn to *Interactive Text,* page 157, Windchill Temperature. Explain that windchill temperature refers to the still-air temperature that would have the same cooling effect on your skin as the combination of the actual temperature and the wind. Thus, a very windy day that had an actual temperature of 20 degrees could have a windchill temperature well below zero.

3. Explain that the relation between windchill temperature and actual temperature depends on the wind speed. Point out that each wind speed will have a different relation. Tell students that the *y* variable, or the range, represents the windchill temperature and the *x* variable, or the domain, represents the actual temperature.

4. Instruct students to use a graphing calculator as they work on the windchill temperature chart.

5. Explain that the windchill temperature relation for a 10 mph wind is $f(x) = 1.2x - 21$, where *x* is the temperature. Ask students to find values for actual temperatures listed in the chart in the *Interactive Text.* Tell students to round the temperature off to the nearest whole number for the windchill temperature chart.

★ = Includes Problem Solving

356 Chapter 4 • Objective 5

Name_____ Date_____

WINDCHILL TEMPERATURE

Windchill represents the cooling effect of wind combined with actual temperature.

In the relation, the *y* variable (range) represents the windchill temperature and the *x* variable (domain) represents the actual temperature.

- The windchill function for a 10 mph wind speed is: $f(x) = 1.2x - 21$.
- The windchill function for a 40 mph wind speed is: $f(x) = 1.6x - 52.5$.

Using your graphing calculator, find the windchill values (to the nearest whole number) for the temperatures (30, 20, 5, 0, –10, –20).

Complete the chart below, then graph the two functions.

Windchill Temperature						
Temperature (Actual) Wind Speed	30	20	5	0	–10	–20
10	15	3	–15	–21	–33	–45
40	–4	–20	–44	–52	–68	–84

10 MPH Windchill 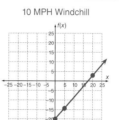   40 MPH Windchill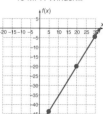

---

6. Now present the windchill temperature relation for a 40 mph wind as $f(x) = 1.6x - 52.5$. Ask students to find values for the actual temperatures listed in the chart.

7. Discuss with students the change in temperature when the wind is blowing faster or when the temperature is warmer or colder.

8. Have students use their graphing calculators to graph these two functions. Discuss the results they determine from the graphs.

   Variation: Different Numbers Have students research the relation for other wind speeds and calculate the temperatures.

NEXT STEPS • Differentiate

5-Day and 3-Day Instructional Plans:
Objective 5 Posttest, page 357—All students

Objective 5 Posttest

Discuss with students the key concepts in Objective 5. Following the discussion, administer the Objective 5 Posttest to all students.

Using the Results

- Score the posttest and update the class record card.

- Provide reinforcement for students who do not demonstrate mastery of the concepts through individual or small-group reteaching of key concepts.

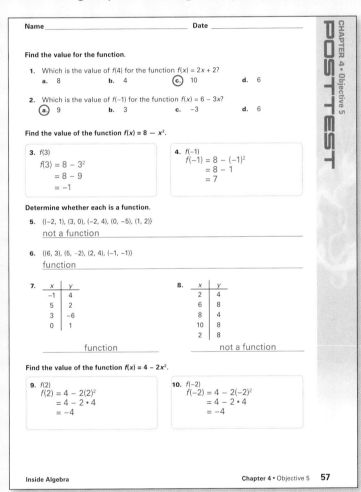

Name _____ Date _____

CHAPTER 4 • Objective 5
POSTTEST

Find the value for the function.

1. Which is the value of $f(4)$ for the function $f(x) = 2x + 2$?
   a. 8　　　b. 4　　　(c.) 10　　　d. 6

2. Which is the value of $f(-1)$ for the function $f(x) = 6 - 3x$?
   (a.) 9　　　b. 3　　　c. -3　　　d. 6

Find the value of the function $f(x) = 8 - x^2$.

3. $f(3)$
$$f(3) = 8 - 3^2$$
$$= 8 - 9$$
$$= -1$$

4. $f(-1)$
$$f(-1) = 8 - (-1)^2$$
$$= 8 - 1$$
$$= 7$$

Determine whether each is a function.

5. $\{(-2, 1), (3, 0), (-2, 4), (0, -5), (1, 2)\}$
   not a function

6. $\{(6, 3), (5, -2), (2, 4), (-1, -1)\}$
   function

7.
x	y
-1	4
5	2
3	-6
0	1

function

8.
x	y
2	4
6	8
8	4
10	8
2	8

not a function

Find the value of the function $f(x) = 4 - 2x^2$.

9. $f(2)$
$$f(2) = 4 - 2(2)^2$$
$$= 4 - 2 \cdot 4$$
$$= -4$$

10. $f(-2)$
$$f(-2) = 4 - 2(-2)^2$$
$$= 4 - 2 \cdot 4$$
$$= -4$$

Inside Algebra　　　　　　Chapter 4 • Objective 5　**57**

Chapter Review

Chapter 4 Review

Use with 5-Day and 3-Day Instructional Plans. In this activity, students review key chapter concepts prior to taking the Chapter Test.

MATERIALS

- *Interactive Text*, pages 159–160

DIRECTIONS

1. Have students turn to *Interactive Text*, pages 159–160, Chapter 4 Review.

2. Have students complete the review individually or in small groups. If the activity is completed individually, provide time for students to discuss their solutions as a class or in small groups.

3. Monitor student work, and provide feedback when necessary. If students complete the review quickly, pair them with other students or groups to discuss their answers.

Name_____ Date_____

OBJECTIVE 1

Use the graph to complete the problems.

1. Name the ordered pair for point A. (2 , −3)

2. Name the ordered pair for point B. (0 , 3)

3. Name a point in Quadrant II. __D__

4. Graph the ordered pair. E (4, 4)

5. Graph the ordered pair. F (0, −4)

6. Graph the ordered pair. G (−1, −2)

OBJECTIVE 2

Complete the statements about relations.

In Problems 7–9, the relation is {(1, 0), (2, 1), (0, −1), (−1, −2)}.

7. The domain of the relation is {1, 2, 0, −1}

8. The range of the relation is {0, 1, −1, −2}

9. The inverse of the relation is {(0, 1), (1, 2), (−1, 0), (−2, −1)}

OBJECTIVE 3

Solve each problem based on the given information about the domain and relation.

10. $2x + y = 6$

x	2x + y = 6	y	(x, y)
−4	−8 + y = 6	14	(−4, 14)
−3	−6 + y = 6	12	(−3, 12)
0	0 + y = 6	6	(0, 6)
7	14 + y = 6	−8	(7, −8)

11. Find the ordered pairs that satisfy the relation $x = y - 2$ when the domain is {4, 2, 0, −2}.

{(4, 6), (2, 4), (0, 2), (−2, 0)}

Name_____ Date_____

OBJECTIVE 4   Answers will vary depending on values for x.

Make a table of values and construct the graph for each equation.

12. $x - 2y = 4$

x	x − 2y = 4	y	(x, y)
−2	−2 − 2y = 4	−3	(−2, −3)
0	0 − 2y = 4	−2	(0, −2)
2	2 − 2y = 4	−1	(2, −1)
4	4 − 2y = 4	0	(4, 0)

13. Graph of $x - 2y = 4$

14. $x = y - 3$

x	x = y − 3	y	(x, y)
−1	−1 = y − 3	2	(−1, 2)
0	0 = y − 3	3	(0, 3)
1	1 = y − 3	4	(1, 4)
2	2 = y − 3	5	(2, 5)

15. Graph of $x = y - 3$

OBJECTIVE 5

Evaluate.

16. Given $f(x) = 2x^2 - 3x + 4$, find $f(-3)$.

$f(-3) = 2(-3)^2 - 3(-3) + 4$
$= 18 - (-9) + 4$
$= 31$

Determine whether each is a function relation.

17. {(2, 4), (3, −2), (0, −2), (5, 2)}   yes

18.

x	y
2	5
3	6
3	7
4	8

no

19.

x	y
0	11
1	14
−2	7
4	−3

yes

Ongoing Assessment

Chapter 4 Test, Form A

MATERIALS

- *Assessment Book*, pages 59–60

DIRECTIONS

1. Have students turn to *Assessment Book*, pages 59–60, Chapter 4 Test, Form A. Administer the Chapter Test to all students.

2. Score the test by objective and update the class record card.

3. Use the test data to determine differentiation needs.

Name _____ Date _____

Objective 1

Use the graph to complete the problems.

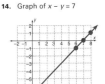

1. Name the ordered pair for letter A.
   (-3 , 2)

2. Name a point in Quadrant III. ___ C ___

3. Graph the ordered pair P (–1, 2).

4. Graph the ordered pair Q (3, 1).

Objective 2

In Problems 5–8, the relation is {(2, 1), (–1, 3), (5, 8), (0, 6)}.

5. The range of the relation is _____ {1, 3, 8, 6} _____

6. The inverse of the relation is {(1, 2), (3, –1), (8, 5), (6, 0)}

7. The domain of the relation is _____ {2, –1, 5, 0} _____

8. The domain of the inverse relation is _____ {1, 3, 8, 6} _____

Objective 3

Solve each problem based on the given information about the domain and relation.

9. $y = x - 3$

x	y
–2	–5
0	–3
3	0
8	5

10. $x + y = 7$

x	x + y = 7	y
–4	–4 + y = 7	11
–2	–2 + y = 7	9
0	0 + y = 7	7
2	2 + y = 7	5
4	4 + y = 7	3

11. $2x - 2y = 8$

x	2x – 2y = 8	y
–2	2(–2) – 2y = 8	–6
0	2(0) – 2y = 8	–4
4	2(4) – 2y = 8	0
8	2(8) – 2y = 8	4

12. Find the ordered pairs that satisfy the relation $y = 6 - x$ when the domain is {3, 6, 0, –5}.

   {(3, 3), (6, 0), (0, 6), (–5, 11)}

Inside Algebra   Chapter 4 • Test   59

Name _____ Date _____

Objective 4

Make a table and construct the graph for each equation.

13. $x - y = 7$

x	x – y = 7	y	(x, y)
8	8 – y = 7	1	(8, 1)
7	7 – y = 7	0	(7, 0)
6	6 – y = 7	–1	(6, –1)

14. Graph of $x - y = 7$

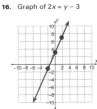

15. $2x = y - 3$

x	2x = y – 3	y	(x, y)
–2	2(–2) = y – 3	–1	(–2, –1)
0	2(0) = y – 3	3	(0, 3)
2	2(2) = y – 3	7	(2, 7)

16. Graph of $2x = y - 3$

Tables will vary depending on values for x.

Objective 5

Determine whether each relation is a function.

17. {(2, 3), (3, 4), (6, 7), (7, 6)} ___ yes ___

18. {(2, 8), (–2, 5), (0, 7), (–2, –5)} ___ no ___

19. 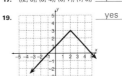 ___ yes ___

20. Given $f(x) = 4x - 12$, find $f(–4)$.
   $f(–4) = 4(–4) - 12 = –28$

60   Chapter 4 • Test   Inside Algebra

Differentiation

MATERIALS

- **Gizmos** *Linear Functions* Gizmo
- **Gizmos** Extension Activity pages
- **Gizmos** *Introduction to Functions* Gizmo
- **Gizmos** Reinforcement Activity page
- Additional Activities
- Algebra Skill Builders for Chapter 4
- Chapter Test, Form B

DIRECTIONS

1. Review Chapter 4 Test, Form A, with the class.

2. Use the results from Chapter 4 Test, Form A, to identify students for reinforcement or extension.

3. After students have been identified for extension or reinforcement, break students into appropriate groups. See pages 361–363 for detailed differentiated instruction.

Differentiation Planner

Students who demonstrated mastery on every objective posttest and scored 80% or above on the chapter test

Extend learning using:

- **Gizmos** Use the *Linear Functions* Gizmo with the Extension Activity. Have students work in pairs or individually to complete the activity.

Students who demonstrated mastery on every objective posttest but scored below 80% on the chapter test

Reinforce learning using:

- **Gizmos** Use the *Introductions to Functions* Gizmo with the Reinforcement Activity. Have students work in pairs or small groups to complete the activity.
- Additional Activities from the online resources.
- Algebra Skill Builders for Chapter 4 from the online resources.

Students who did not demonstrate mastery on any or all of the objective posttests or the chapter test

Reinforce learning using:

- **Gizmos** Present the *Introduction to Functions* Gizmo to students in small groups using the instruction on page 363.
- Additional Activities from the online resources.
- Algebra Skill Builders for Chapter 4 from the online resources.

Retest—Administer Chapter 4 Test, Form B, from the online resources to students who scored below 80 percent on Form A when time allows.

NEXT STEPS • Pretest

- Administer Chapter 5, Objective 1 Pretest, page 366, to all students.

Ongoing Assessment

Students who demonstrated mastery on every objective posttest and scored 80% or above on the chapter test

1. Divide students into pairs or allow them to work individually for this activity.

2. Distribute one copy of the Extension Activity from the online resources to each student.

3. Direct students to the Gizmo *Linear Functions* through the Inside Algebra Student Web site, http://insidealgebra. voyagerlearning.com.

4. Have students complete the Extension Activity.

5. **Peer Review.** If there is time, have students exchange papers with a peer. They should review and discuss each response, and be prepared to explain their thinking.

   Variation: If students do not have access to the Gizmo, provide them with grid paper so they can make the graphs asked for in the Extension.

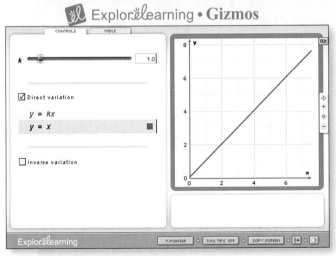

Explore learning • Gizmos

Linear Functions

Gizmos Extension Activity   Name _____   Date _____

LINEAR FUNCTIONS

Cole, Anna, and Marcus have each been saving money for a class trip. The table in Problem 1 shows the relationship between the week and dollars saved.

1.

Week	1	2	3	4	5
Cole's savings (dollars)	1	3	4	6	7
Anna's savings (dollars)	3	4	5	6	7
Marcus' savings (dollars)	2	4	6	8	10

Let x represent the week and let y represent the amount of savings.
Write ordered pairs (x, y) for each person's savings from Week 1 to Week 5.

Cole: {(1, 1), (2, 3), (3, 4), (4, 6), (5, 7)}

Anna: {(1, 3), (2, 4), (3, 5), (4, 6), (5, 7)}

Marcus: {(1, 2), (2, 4), (3, 6), (4, 8), (5, 10)}

2. Anna's ordered pairs form a relation. What are the domain and range of this relation?

Domain: {1, 2, 3, 4, 5}

Range: {3, 4, 5, 6, 7}

3. Start the *Linear Functions* Gizmo. Graph the ordered pairs for Cole's savings. Check "Show linear function test."

Is the relation for Cole's savings a function? yes

Can you draw a straight line through the points? no

Is the function a linear function? no

How much did Cole add to his savings from Week 1 to Week 2? $2

From Week 2 to Week 3? $1   From Week 3 to Week 4? $2

From Week 4 to Week 5? $1

Did Cole add the same amount each week? no

Gizmos Extension Activity   Name _____   Date _____

LINEAR FUNCTIONS (continued)

4. Click "Clear." Uncheck "Show linear function test." Graph the ordered pairs for Anna's savings. Check "Show linear function test."

Can you draw a straight line through the points? yes

Is the relation a linear function? yes

How much did Anna add to her savings from Week 1 to Week 2? $1

From Week 2 to Week 3? $1   From Week 3 to Week 4? $1

From Week 4 to Week 5? $1

Did Anna add the same amount each week? yes

5. Click "Clear." Uncheck "Show linear function test." Graph the ordered pairs for Marcus' savings. Check "Show linear function test."

Can you draw a straight line through the points? yes

Is the relation a linear function? yes

How much did Marcus add to his savings from Week 1 to Week 2? $2

From Week 2 to Week 3? $2   From Week 3 to Week 4? $2

From Week 4 to Week 5? $2

Did Marcus add the same amount each week? yes

6. Look at Problems 3–5. How are the linear functions alike?

The graphs are a straight line. For each function, the same amount of money is added each week.

How is the nonlinear function different from the linear functions?

The graphs are different. For a linear function, the same amount of money is added each week, but for the nonlinear function, the same amount is not added each week.

7. The equation for Anna's function is $y = x + 2$. Use this equation to find how much money Anna will have saved after Week 10. $12

8. The equation for Marcus' function is $y = 2x$. Use this equation to find how much money Marcus will have saved after Week 10. $20

Students who demonstrated mastery on every objective posttest but scored below 80% on the chapter test

1. Divide students into pairs or small groups.

2. Distribute one copy of the Individual Reinforcement Activity from the online resources to each student.

3. Direct students to the Gizmo *Introduction to Functions* through the Inside Algebra Student Web site, http://insidealgebra.voyagerlearning.com.

4. Have students complete the Reinforcement Activity.

5. **Peer Review.** If time permits, have students exchange papers with a peer to review and discuss each others responses. Remind students to be prepared to explain the reasoning behind their responses.

   Variation If students do not have access to the Gizmo, provide them with grid paper so they can complete Problems 7 and 8. Remind them that a relation is a function if every *x*-value is paired with only one *y*-value.

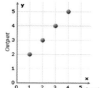

Gizmos
Reinforcement Activity   Name_____   Date_____

INTRODUCTION TO FUNCTIONS

1. Use the equation $y = x + 1$ to complete the table of values.

x	$y = x + 1$	y	(x, y)
1	$y = $ __1__ $ + 1 = $ __2__	2	(__1__ , __2__)
2	$y = $ __2__ $ + 1 = $ __3__	3	(__2__ , __3__)
3	$y = $ __3__ $ + 1 = $ __4__	4	(__3__ , __4__)
4	$y = $ __4__ $ + 1 = $ __5__	5	(__4__ , __5__)

2. Start the *Introduction to Functions* Gizmo. Check "Show ordered pairs" and "Show graph." Graph the points in the table in Problem 1 by dragging red points onto the grid.

3. What is the domain of the relation in Problem 1? *Hint:* The domain is all the *x*-values, or the inputs.
   {1, 2, 3, 4}

4. What is the range of the relation in Problem 1? *Hint:* The range is all the *y*-values, or the outputs.
   {2, 3, 4, 5}

5. What is the inverse of the relation in Problem 1? *Hint:* Switch the *x*-values and the *y*-values.
   {(2, 1), (3, 2), (4, 3), (5, 4)}

6. On the graph above, draw a straight line through the points on the graph. This is the graph of the linear function $y = x + 1$.

7. Click the "CLEAR ALL" button.
   Graph the ordered pairs in the relation {(1, 2), (2, 2), (3, 2), (4, 2), (5, 2)}.
   What kind of line is formed by the points in the graph? _____ horizontal line
   Click on the "Show function test" for each different display. Is the relation a function? ____ yes

8. What is the inverse of the relation in Problem 7? ____ {(2, 1), (2, 2), (2, 3), (2, 4), (2, 5)}
   Click the "CLEAR ALL" button. Graph the relation in the question above.
   What kind of line is formed by the points in the graph? _____ vertical line
   Click on the "Show function test" for each different display. Is the relation a function? ____ no
   Is the inverse of every function also a function? _____ no

Inside Algebra • Chapter 4 • Reinforcement **1**

Explore learning • Gizmos

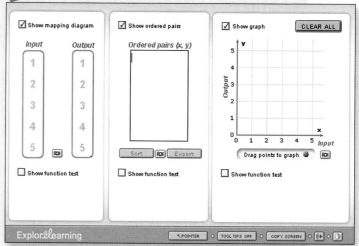

Introduction to Functions

Students who did not demonstrate mastery on any or all of the objective posttests or the chapter test

Note: The Gizmo is not needed for Problems 1 and 3–5.

1. Ask your students to complete a table of values. Arrange the table so the columns are x, $y = x + 1$, y, and (x, y). Give students these values for x: 1, 2, 3, 4. Use the following steps to scaffold instruction:

   - Complete the column for $y = x + 1$. For example, for $x = 1$, have students substitute 1 for x and write the expression. $y = 1 + 1$ Have them simplify. 2 Repeat for the rest of the x-values.

   - Ask students to state the y-value for each x-value and write the result in the table. 2, 3, 4, 5

   - Ask students to name the ordered pairs. (1, 2), (2, 3), (3, 4), (4, 5)

2. Start the *Introduction to Functions* Gizmo. Check "Show ordered pairs" and "Show graph." Graph the points as students tell you the ordered pairs from Problem 1.

3. Ask students to name the domain of the relation in Problem 1. Remind them that the domain is the set of x-values. {1, 2, 3, 4}

4. Ask students to name the range of the relation in Problem 1. Remind them that the range is the set of y-values. {2, 3, 4, 5}

5. Ask students to name the inverse of the relation in Problem 1. Remind them that the inverse is found by switching the x- and y-values. {(2, 1), (3, 2), (4, 3), (5, 4)}

6. Click "CLEAR ALL." Graph the points (1, 2), (2, 2), (3, 2), (4, 2), and (5, 2). Ask students to name the type of line formed by the points. horizontal Click "Show function test" for each display on the Gizmo. Ask students to tell whether the relation is a function. yes Point out that each input has only one output.

7. Click "CLEAR ALL." Graph the points (2, 1), (2, 2), (2, 3), (2, 4), (2, 5). Ask students to name the type of line formed by the points. vertical Click "Show function test" for each display. Ask students whether the relation is a function. no Point out that the input has more than one output.

   Variation: If students do not have access to the Gizmo, use a blackboard or overhead projector to complete the activity.

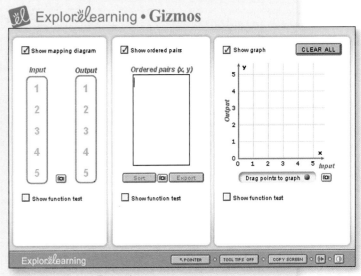

Introduction to Functions

4 CHAPTER

Ongoing Assessment

Chapter 4 Test, Form B

MATERIALS

- Chapter 4 Test, Form B, from the Online Resources, pages 1–2

DIRECTIONS

1. Have students turn to Chapter 4 Test, Form B, pages 1–2, from the Online Resources. Administer the Chapter Test to all students.

2. Score the test by objective and update the class record card.

Name _____ Date _____

Objective 1

Use the graph to complete the problems.

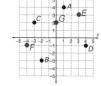

1. Name the ordered pair for letter A.
   (__1__ , __4__)

2. Name the ordered pair for letter B.
   (__−2__ , __−3__)

3. Name a point in Quadrant II. __C__

4. Graph the ordered pair E (3, 3).

5. Graph the ordered pair F (−4, −1).

6. Graph the ordered pair G (0, 2).

Objective 2

In Problems 7–9, the relation is {(1, 3), (2, 5), (0, 1), (−1, −1)}.

7. The domain of the relation is _____ {1, 2, 0, −1}

8. The range of the relation is _____ {3, 5, 1, −1}

9. The inverse of the relation is _____ {(3, 1), (5, 2), (1, 0), (−1, −1)}

Objective 3

Solve each problem based on the given information about the domain and relation.

10. $2x - y = 4$

x	$2x - y = 4$	y	(x, y)
−3	$-6 - y = 4$	−10	(−3, −10)
−1	$-2 - y = 4$	−6	(−1, −6)
1	$2 - y = 4$	−2	(1, −2)
3	$6 - y = 4$	2	(3, 2)

11. Find the ordered pairs that satisfy the relation $x = y + 3$ when the domain is {6, 3, 0, −3}.
    {(6, 3), (3, 0), (0, −3), (−3, −6)}

Inside Algebra   Chapter 4 • Test • Form B   **1**

Name _____ Date _____

Objective 4

Make a table and construct the graph for each equation.
Answers will vary depending on values for x.

12. $x + 2y = 8$

x	$x + 2y = 8$	y	(x, y)
−2	$-2 + 2y = 8$	5	(−2, 5)
0	$0 + 2y = 8$	4	(0, 4)
2	$2 + 2y = 8$	3	(2, 3)
4	$4 + 2y = 8$	2	(4, 2)

13. Graph of $x + 2y = 8$

14. $x = y - 5$

x	$x = y - 5$	y	(x, y)
−1	$-1 = y - 5$	4	(−1, 4)
0	$0 = y - 5$	5	(0, 5)
1	$1 = y - 5$	6	(1, 6)
2	$2 = y - 5$	7	(2, 7)

15. Graph of $x = y - 5$

Objective 5

Evaluate.

16. Given $f(x) = 3x^2 - 4x + 5$, find $f(-2)$.
    $f(-2) = 3(-2)^2 - 4(-2) + 5$
    $= 12 - (-8) + 5$
    $= 25$

Determine whether each relation is a function.

17. {(2, 4), (5, −3), (−4, −2), (0, 3)} __yes__

18.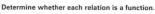

x	y	yes
3	7	
4	9	
8	−3	
15	7	

19.

x	y	no
0	6	
1	14	
−2	−7	
1	5	

Inside Algebra   Chapter 4 • Test • Form B   **2**

Analyzing Linear Equations

In this chapter, students explore characteristics of linear equations. They find the slope of a line and use the slope of two or more lines to determine if the lines are parallel or perpendicular. Students also write equations in standard, slope-intercept, and point-slope forms, and learn to convert from one form to another.

Objective 1
Determine the slope given a line on a graph or two points on the line.

Objective 2
Write the equation of a line in standard form given two points on the line.

Objective 3
Draw a best-fit line, and find the equation of the best-fit line for a scatter plot.

Objective 4
Write linear equations in slope-intercept form to find the slope, x-intercept, and y-intercept, and sketch the graph.

Objective 5
Use the slope of lines to determine if two lines are parallel or perpendicular.

Chapter 5 VOCABULARY

Objective 1
Determine the slope given a line on
a graph or two points on the line.

Objective 1 Pretest

Students complete the Objective 1 Pretest at least one day
before beginning Objective 1.

Using the Results

- Score the pretest and update the class record card.

- If the majority of students do not demonstrate mastery
  of the concepts, use the 5-Day Instructional Plan for
  Objective 1.

- If the majority of students demonstrate mastery of the
  concepts, use the 3-Day Instructional Plan for Objective 1.

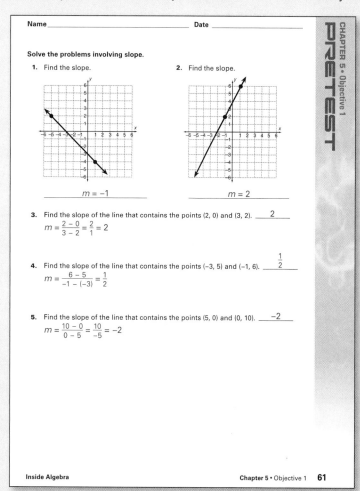

Name_____ Date_____

Solve the problems involving slope.

1. Find the slope.

$m = -1$

2. Find the slope.

$m = 2$

3. Find the slope of the line that contains the points (2, 0) and (3, 2). ___2___

$m = \dfrac{2 - 0}{3 - 2} = \dfrac{2}{1} = 2$

4. Find the slope of the line that contains the points (−3, 5) and (−1, 6). ___$\frac{1}{2}$___

$m = \dfrac{6 - 5}{-1 - (-3)} = \dfrac{1}{2}$

5. Find the slope of the line that contains the points (5, 0) and (0, 10). ___−2___

$m = \dfrac{10 - 0}{0 - 5} = \dfrac{10}{-5} = -2$

Inside Algebra   Chapter 5 • Objective 1   **61**

Goals and Activities

Objective 1 Goals

The following activities, when used with the instructional plans on pages 368 and 369, enable students to:

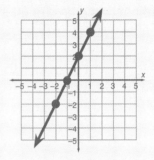

- Find the slope of the line in the graph as
  $m = 2$

- Find the slope of the line passing through the points $(2, -2)$ and $(-2, -1)$ as
  $m = -\frac{1}{4}$

Objective 1 Activities

Concept Development Activities

CD 1 Using a Ruler to Understand Slope, page 370

★CD 2 Discovering the Slope, page 373

CD 3 Looking at Slopes on Graph Paper, page 374

CD 4 Using Two Points to Find the Slope, page 376

Practice Activities

PA 1 Picking the Slope, page 378

★PA 2 Finding the Slope, page 379

Progress-Monitoring Activities

PM 1 Apply Skills 1, page 380

PM 2 Apply Skills 2, page 381

PM 3 Apply Skills 3, page 382

★Problem-Solving Activity

★PS 1 Finding Slopes in Newspapers and Magazines, page 383

Ongoing Assessment

Posttest Objective 1, page 385

Pretest Objective 2, page 386

CD = Concept Development PM = Progress Monitoring PS = Problem Solving
PA = Practice Activity ★ = Includes Problem Solving

Instructional Plans

5-Day Instructional Plan

Use the 5-Day Instructional Plan when pretest results indicate that students would benefit from a slower pace. This plan is used when the majority of students need more time or did not demonstrate mastery on the pretest.

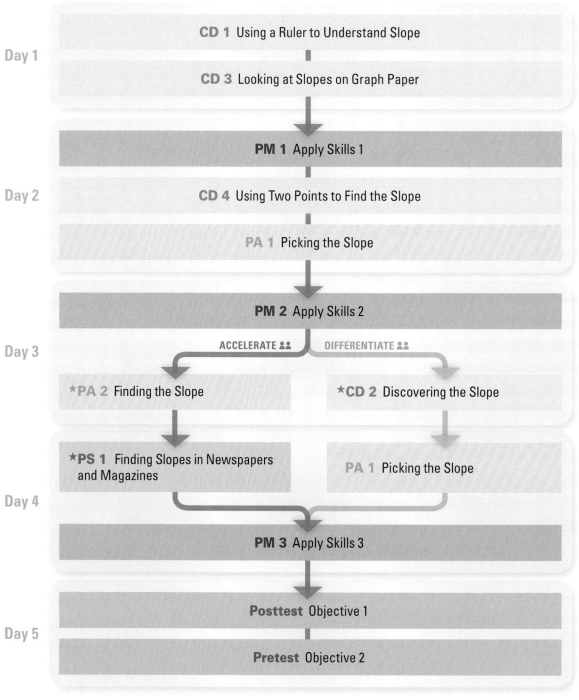

Day 1
- **CD 1** Using a Ruler to Understand Slope
- **CD 3** Looking at Slopes on Graph Paper

Day 2
- **PM 1** Apply Skills 1
- **CD 4** Using Two Points to Find the Slope
- **PA 1** Picking the Slope

Day 3
- **PM 2** Apply Skills 2
  - ACCELERATE — **★PA 2** Finding the Slope
  - DIFFERENTIATE — **★CD 2** Discovering the Slope

Day 4
- **★PS 1** Finding Slopes in Newspapers and Magazines
- **PA 1** Picking the Slope
- **PM 3** Apply Skills 3

Day 5
- **Posttest** Objective 1
- **Pretest** Objective 2

CD = Concept Development   PM = Progress Monitoring   PS = Problem Solving
PA = Practice Activity   ★ = Includes Problem Solving

3-Day Instructional Plan

Use the 3-Day Instructional Plan when pretest results indicate that students can move through the activities at a faster pace. This plan is ideal when the majority of students demonstrate mastery on the pretest. This plan does not include all activities.

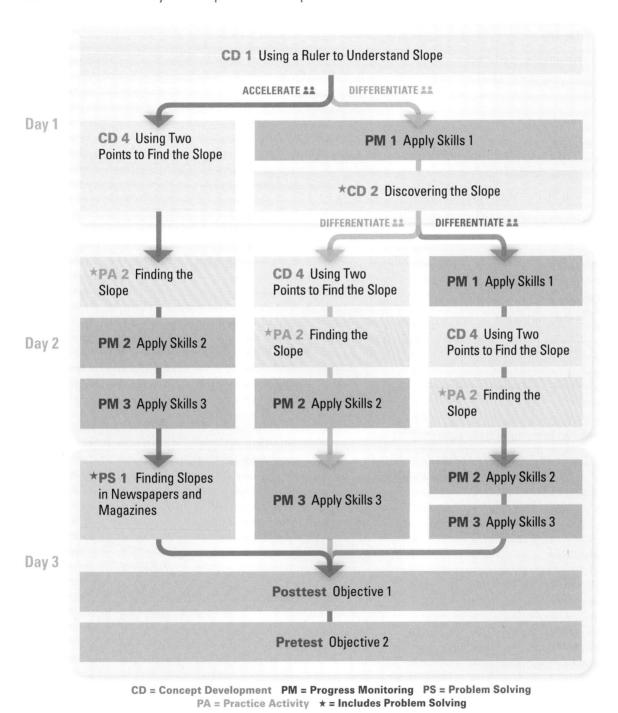

CD = Concept Development   PM = Progress Monitoring   PS = Problem Solving
PA = Practice Activity   ★ = Includes Problem Solving

Objective 1
Concept Development Activities

CD 1 Using a Ruler to Understand Slope

Use with 5-Day or 3-Day Instructional Plan.
In this activity, students calculate slope as $\frac{rise}{run}$.

MATERIALS

- Blackline Master 59
- Blank paper, one page per student
- Rulers, one per student

DIRECTIONS

1. Discuss the following terms with students:

   slope The steepness of a line

   rise The vertical distance traveled

   run The horizontal distance traveled

2. Distribute one ruler, one blank piece of paper, and one copy of Blackline Master 59, Graph Paper, to each student.

3. Have students draw a horizontal line on the blank piece of paper and mark off a distance of four inches. Tell students to mark and label 0", 1", 2", 3", and 4".

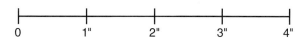

4. Have students put the end of their rulers on the first mark and raise the rulers up and down. Discuss the steepness of the ruler. Explain that the steepness is called the *slope* of the line.

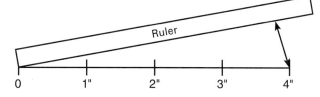

Example:

If a skier is going down a hill, which steepness, or slope, makes him go faster?
The more vertical the line, the faster the skier would be able to go.

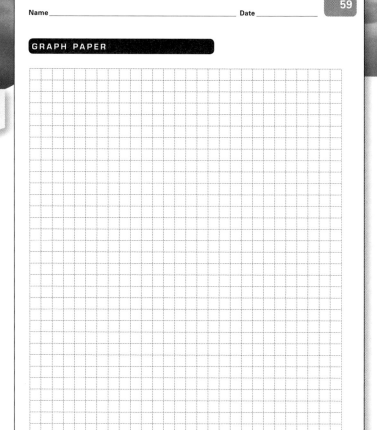

5. Put students in groups of two, and instruct them to share their rulers to accomplish the next task.

6. Have students put the end of one ruler on the first mark, laying it parallel to the line on the paper. Have them put the end of the other ruler at the 4" mark, holding it perpendicular to the line they drew. Make sure students place the ruler so the numbers increase vertically. Instruct students to raise the first ruler up 1", as in the figure.

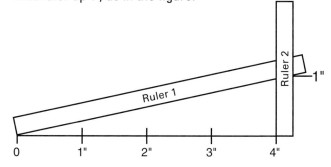

7. Explain that the slope is the distance the first ruler rises compared to the horizontal distance away from the starting point. Point out that the vertical distance is called the *rise* and the horizontal distance is called the *run*. Tell students to identify the slope of the first ruler.

Rise ___1"___

Run ___4"___

Slope ___$\frac{1}{4}$___

8. Have students raise the first ruler to 2" at the 4" mark on the line. Remind students that the slope of this hill, or line, is $\frac{rise}{run}$. Point out that the slope is $\frac{2}{4}$, or $\frac{1}{2}$. Explain that the line increases by 1 unit in the vertical direction for every 2 units in the horizontal direction.

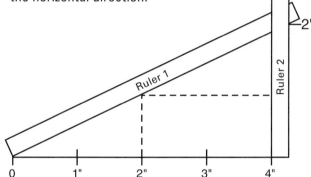

9. Make a transparency of Blackline Master 59, Graph Paper, and demonstrate how to graph a couple of lines on the overhead projector. Have students identify the slope of each line.

Sample problems:

Put a point on the origin (0, 0), count 4 units to the right (4, 0), then count up 1 unit (4, 1), and put a point here. Connect the two points by drawing a line.

Slope = $\frac{rise}{run}$ = $\frac{(4, 0) \text{ to } (4, 1)}{(0, 0) \text{ to } (4, 0)}$ = $\frac{1}{4}$

Put a point on the origin (0, 0), count 4 units to the right (4, 0), then count up 2 units (4, 2), and put a point here. Connect the two points by drawing a line.

Slope = $\frac{rise}{run}$ = $\frac{(4, 0) \text{ to } (4, 2)}{(0, 0) \text{ to } (4, 0)}$ = $\frac{2}{4}$ or $\frac{1}{2}$

10. Ask students to use the rulers to make a line that is 3" high at the 4" mark. Point out that the slope is $\frac{(4, 0) \text{ to } (4, 3)}{(0, 0) \text{ to } (4, 0)}$ = $\frac{3}{4}$.

11. Have students make a line that is 4" high at the 4" mark. Point out that the ratio is $\frac{4}{4}$ $\left(\frac{rise}{run}\right)$, and the slope is 1 $\left(\frac{1}{1}\right)$.

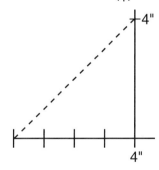

Concept Development Activities

12. On the overhead, graph a line that goes through (0, 0) and (4, 4). Show students that for every unit the line goes up, it goes over 1 unit (slope of $\frac{1}{1}$, or 1). Demonstrate how to compute the slope.

$$\frac{(4, 0) \text{ to } (4, 4)}{(0, 0) \text{ to } (4, 0)} = \frac{4}{4} = 1$$

13. Ask students to think about how we would get a slope of 2. Have students use their rulers to find a slope of 2. If students have difficulty, direct them to try moving the first ruler to a height of 8" at the 4" mark on the line. Show students that for every 2 units the line moves up, it moves horizontally 1 unit. Explain that the rise is 2 units, and the run is 1 unit.

14. Graph the line through (0, 0) and (4, 8) on the overhead. Show students that they can compute the slope with any two points on the line.

Example:

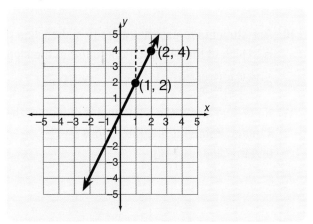

15. Have students use the graph paper to draw a slope of 3. They can draw a line through (0, 0) and (4, 12), for example.

16. Ask students to identify the slope for a vertical line. Students might describe the line as *straight down* or *no slope*. Explain that the slope is undefined. $\frac{\text{rise}}{\text{run}} = \frac{4}{0}$

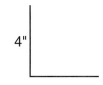

4"

17. Discuss the slope of a horizontal line at 4". Help students see that if the line is flat, there is no rise, and the slope is 0. $\frac{\text{rise}}{\text{run}} = \frac{0}{4}$

18. On the overhead, draw some lines that go through the origin, and discuss the slope of each line.

NEXT STEPS • Differentiate

5-Day Instructional Plan:
CD 3, page 374—All students, for additional concept development

👥 **3-Day Instructional Plan:**
CD 4, page 376—Students who demonstrate understanding of the concept, for additional concept development

PM 1, page 380—Students who need additional support, to assess progress

Objective 1
Concept Development Activities

★ CD 2 Discovering the Slope

Use with 5-Day or 3-Day Instructional Plan. In this activity, students define the slope of a line.

MATERIALS

- *Interactive Text*, page 163

DIRECTIONS

1. Review the following term with students:

   slope The steepness of a line

2. Have students turn to *Interactive Text*, page 163, Graphs and Related Numbers.

3. Point out that each coordinate graph has a number written in parentheses by the line. Explain that the number written on each graph has a specific relationship to that graph.

4. Divide students into groups of four or five.

5. Explain the game rules to students.

   - The object is to identify the relationship between the number in parentheses and the graph.

   - All students write several questions, then compare their questions within their group. Each group selects as many as three questions to ask the teacher.

   - Groups take turns asking the teacher questions about the number on each graph that can be answered yes or no.

   - After all groups have asked each of their questions, students work in their groups to discuss their ideas about the relationship between the number and the graph. Each group must agree on the relationship and write it down.

   - Groups are given additional opportunities to ask questions if they are unable to formulate a statement about the relationship.

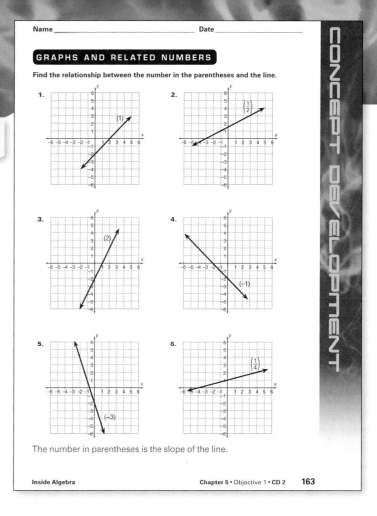

Name _____ Date _____

GRAPHS AND RELATED NUMBERS

Find the relationship between the number in the parentheses and the line.

1.
2.
3.
4.
5.
6.

The number in parentheses is the slope of the line.

Inside Algebra   Chapter 5 • Objective 1 • CD 2   **163**

- After all or most groups believe they have discovered the relationship, each group's conjectures are discussed one at a time. Several correct observations can relate the numbers to the graphs because there are several ways to find the slope.

6. As a class, form at least one generalization about the slope.

NEXT STEPS • Differentiate

5-Day Instructional Plan:
PA 1, page 378—All students, for additional practice

👥 3-Day Instructional Plan:
CD 4, page 376—Students who demonstrate understanding of the concept, for additional concept development

PM 1, page 380—Students who need additional support, to assess progress

★ = Includes Problem Solving

Objective 1
Concept Development Activities

CD 3 Looking at Slopes on Graph Paper

Use with 5-Day Instructional Plan. In this activity, students find the slope of the line in each graph and understand that a line going down has a negative slope.

MATERIALS

- *Interactive Text*, page 164
- Blackline Master 59

DIRECTIONS

1. Review the following terms with students:

   rise The vertical distance traveled

   run The horizontal distance traveled

   slope The steepness of a line

2. Make a transparency of Blackline Master 59, Graph Paper, and review the plotting of points on the overhead. Mark the *x*- and *y*-axes, and ask students to name some points. Plot the points they name. Make sure students identify the points by naming the ordered pairs.

3. Draw the graph of $y = x$. Do not tell students the equation. Have students discuss observations about the graph.

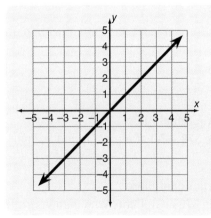

GRAPH PAPER

Sample questions:

What are some points on this graph?
(2, 2), (−3, −3), (4, 4)

What do you notice about this graph?

It bisects the *x*- and *y*-axes at a 45° angle.

The graph goes up 1 unit for each 1 unit it goes over. $\frac{\text{rise}}{\text{run}} = \frac{1}{1}$ or $\frac{4}{4}$

4. Have students turn to *Interactive Text*, page 164, Graphs. Point out that Problem 1 is the graph on the overhead. Have students locate the point (1, 1). Be sure students see that this graph has a slope of 1. If students have difficulty with this concept, have them move up one to (1, 2), then ask them how far over the line is. 1 unit

5. Have students look at Problem 2 and determine whether the slope is greater or less than the slope for Problem 1. Tell them to name a point on the graph and count the $\frac{rise}{run}$ to another point on the line. The slope for Problem 2 is less than the slope for Problem 1.

Example:

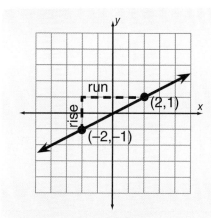

From (−2, −1), I count up 2, which is the rise, then I count to the right 4, which is the run.
Slope = $\frac{2}{4} = \frac{1}{2}$

6. Direct students' attention to Problem 3. Ask students whether the slope is more or less than the slope for Problem 1. Remind students to start by finding the slope for Problem 3. Have students draw the rise and run lines. Point out that the change in y is up 2, and the change in x is to the right 1. Problem 3 slope = $\frac{2}{1}$, or 2; the Problem 3 slope is greater than the Problem 1 slope.

7. Have students look at Problem 4 and find the slope. Have students draw the rise and run lines between two points on the graph. $\frac{rise}{run} = \frac{3}{1} = 3$

8. Have students find the slope of Problem 5. $\frac{rise}{run}$ is 1 to 4, or $\frac{1}{4}$

9. Ask students if they notice anything different about Problem 6. Make sure students see that the lines in Problems 1–5 slant from left to right going upward and the line in Problem 6 slants from left to right going downward.

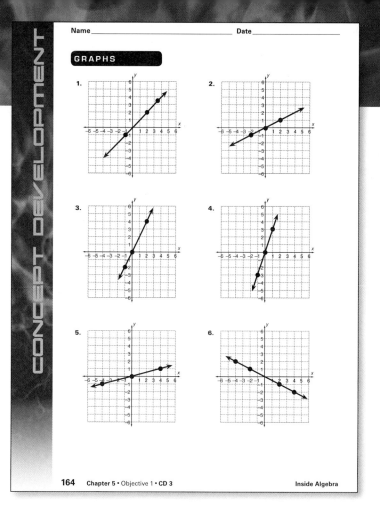

1.
2.
3.
4.
5.
6.

10. Have students find the slope for Problem 6. Point out that in Problems 1–5, they went up, which is a positive direction on the y-axis, and to the right, which is a positive direction on the x-axis.

11. Pointing to Problem 6, ask students to think about the direction we must go on the graph after we go up from any point on the graph. Help students to see that they go left 2 units, or in the negative direction on the x-axis. Point out that the $\frac{rise}{run}$ is $\frac{1}{-2}$, or $-\frac{1}{2}$. Problems 2 and 6 have the same slope but in a different direction. The line in Problem 2 slopes in the positive direction, and the line in Problem 6 slopes in the negative direction.

NEXT STEPS • Differentiate

5-Day Instructional Plan:
PM 1, page 380—All students, to assess progress

Objective 1
Concept Development Activities

CD 4 Using Two Points to Find the Slope

Use with 5-Day or 3-Day Instructional Plan. In this activity, students calculate the slope of a line from two given points without graphing.

MATERIALS

- Blackline Master 59
- **Variation:** Gizmos
  Slope-Intercept Form of a Line—Activity A

DIRECTIONS

1. Sketch a few different number lines on the board or overhead. On each number line, locate two points, and ask students to identify how far one point is from the other.

   Sample problems:

   How far is it from 8 to 6?

   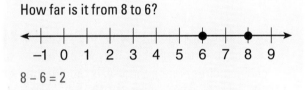

   $8 - 6 = 2$

   How far is it from 2 to –5?

   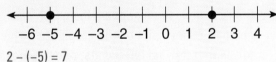

   $2 - (-5) = 7$

   How far is it from 4 to –3?

   $4 - (-3) = 7$

GRAPH PAPER

2. After several examples, have students come up with a rule on how to find the distance between any two points on a number line. Subtract the numbers.

3. Make a transparency of Blackline Master 59, Graph Paper, and sketch the graph of the line containing the points (1, 2) and (5, 5) on the overhead. Label the points (1, 2) and (5, 5) on the graph.

4. Review the following terms with students:

   rise The vertical distance traveled

   run The horizontal distance traveled

   slope The steepness of a line

5. Ask students to discuss how one finds the slope of a line containing the points (1, 2) and (5, 5). Help students to see that counting (change in y = 3 and change in x = 4) is not the only way to find the slope. Show them they can also find the change in y and the change in x by subtracting because the x- and y-axes are number lines.

Example:

Rise is from 2 to 5. $(5 - 2) = 3$

Run is from 1 to 5. $(5 - 1) = 4$

Slope is $\dfrac{\text{change in } y}{\text{change in } x} = \dfrac{\text{rise}}{\text{run}}$ $\dfrac{3}{4}$

Point out that we can find the slope without graphing if we know two points. Write the formula $m = \dfrac{(y_2 - y_1)}{(x_2 - x_1)}$ for points (x_1, y_1) and (x_2, y_2) on the board.

6. Demonstrate how to use the formula with other examples, then graph the points to check the slope you found. Point out that no matter what points are selected from a line, the slope is always the same for that line.

Sample problems:

Find the slope for a line with the points (2, 3) and (4, 7).

$x_1 = 2$; $y_1 = 3$; $x_2 = 4$; $y_2 = 7$

$\dfrac{(y_2 - y_1)}{(x_2 - x_1)} = \dfrac{(7 - 3)}{(4 - 2)} = \dfrac{4}{2} = 2$

The slope is 2.

Find the slope for a line with the points (–1, 2) and (7, 6).

$x_1 = -1$; $y_1 = 2$; $x_2 = 7$; $y_2 = 6$

$\dfrac{(y_2 - y_1)}{(x_2 - x_1)} = \dfrac{(6 - 2)}{[7 - (-1)]} = \dfrac{4}{8} = \dfrac{1}{2}$

The slope is $\dfrac{1}{2}$.

Find the slope for a line with the points (–3, –4) and (1, 0).

$x_1 = -3$; $y_1 = -4$; $x_2 = 1$; $y_2 = 0$

$\dfrac{(y_2 - y_1)}{(x_2 - x_1)} = \dfrac{[0 - (-4)]}{[1 - (-3)]} = \dfrac{4}{4} = 1$

The slope is 1.

Variation: Gizmos Use the tools in the Gizmo *Slope-Intercept Form of a Line—Activity A* to find and display the slope for each line.

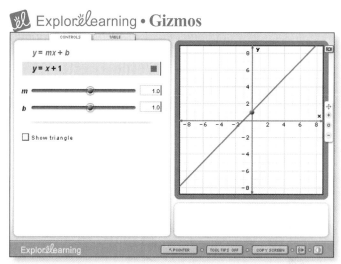

Slope-Intercept of a Line—Activity A

NEXT STEPS • Differentiate

5-Day Instructional Plan:
PA 1, page 378—All students, for additional practice

3-Day Instructional Plan:
PA 2, page 379—All students, for additional practice and problem-solving

Objective 1
Practice Activities

PA 1 Picking the Slope

Use with 5-Day Instructional Plan. In this activity, students calculate the slope of a line from two given points, both by graphing and by using the slope formula. Slopes can be fractional.

MATERIALS

- Blackline Master 59
- Dice of two different colors, two of each color per pair of students
- Paper bags, one per pair of students

DIRECTIONS

1. Put students in pairs, and give each pair one paper bag, two dice of one color, and two dice of another color. Designate one color to represent positive numbers and the other to represent negative numbers. Tell students to put the dice in a paper bag. Distribute one copy of Blackline Master 59, Graph Paper, to each pair of students.

2. Have one student in each pair select two dice from the bag without looking. Direct that student to roll the dice and use the numbers rolled to make an ordered pair. Tell students to put the dice back in the bag after they write the ordered pair.

   Example:

   Red die = negative numbers
   White die = positive numbers

   If the student selects two red dice and rolls a 1 and 4, he or she writes the point (–1, –4).

   If the student selects one white die and one red die and rolls 4 with the white die and 2 with the red die, he or she writes (4, –2).

3. The second student in the pair then repeats the same process to find another ordered pair.

4. Review the following terms with students:

   rise The vertical distance traveled

   run The horizontal distance traveled

   slope The steepness of a line

5. Have one student sketch a graph of a line containing the two points and find the slope. Have the other student calculate the slope using the formula $m = \frac{(y_2 - y_1)}{(x_2 - x_1)}$. Tell students to compare answers and check their work.

   Note: Many of the answers involve fractional slopes. Point out that a fractional slope is a good description of $\frac{\text{rise}}{\text{run}}$.

6. Have students reverse roles for finding the slope and continue the practice.

NEXT STEPS • Differentiate

5-Day Instructional Plan:

PM 2, page 381—Students completing the activity for the first time, to assess progress

PM 3, page 382—Students completing the activity for the second time, to assess progress

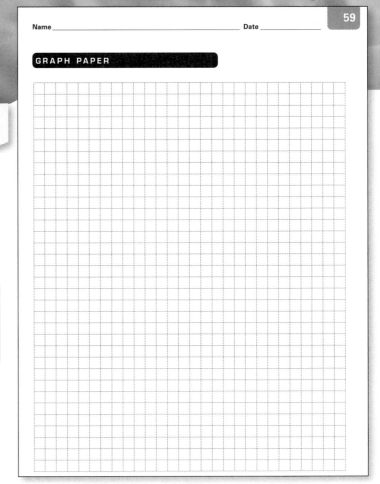

Name _____ Date _____

GRAPH PAPER

Objective 1
Practice Activities

★ PA 2 Finding the Slope

Use with 5-Day or 3-Day Instructional Plan. In this activity, students find the slope of the line on each graph. Slopes can be fractional.

MATERIALS

- Blackline Master 59
- Rulers, one per student

DIRECTIONS

1. Review the following term with students:

   slope The steepness of a line

2. Distribute one copy of Blackline Master 59, Graph Paper, to each student. Tell students to sketch a coordinate plane and label the *x*- and *y*-axes from −10 to 10.

3. Instruct each student to select any two points on the coordinate plane and label them. Tell students to use their rulers to draw the line that connects the points.

   Sample answer:

   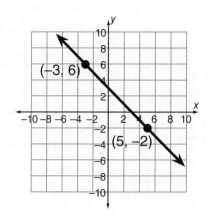

4. Have students work in groups of four to find the slope of each graph the four students drew. Have them estimate the slope from the graph, then compute the slope using the formula $m = \dfrac{(y_2 - y_1)}{(x_2 - x_1)}$. Instruct students to write their computations on a separate piece of paper.

★ = Includes Problem Solving

GRAPH PAPER

5. Have each group exchange the four graphs with another group and find the slopes. Have groups continue exchanging the graphs until time expires or all groups have found the slopes for all the graphs.

NEXT STEPS • Differentiate

5-Day Instructional Plan:
PS 1, page 383—All students, to develop problem-solving skills

3-Day Instructional Plan:
PM 2, page 381—All students, to assess progress

PM 1 Apply Skills 1

Use with 5-Day or 3-Day Instructional Plan.

MATERIALS

- *Interactive Text*, page 165

DIRECTIONS

1. Have students turn to *Interactive Text*, page 165, Apply Skills 1.

2. Remind students of the key terms: *rise*, *run*, and *slope*.

3. Monitor student work, and provide feedback as necessary.

   Watch for:

   - Do students understand that the slope of a line is its steepness?

   - Do students find the slope by using the formula $\frac{rise}{run}$?

NEXT STEPS • Differentiate

5-Day Instructional Plan:

CD 4, page 376—All students, for additional concept development

3-Day Instructional Plan:

CD 2, page 373—Students completing the activity for the first time, for additional concept development

CD 4, page 376—Students completing the activity for the second time, for additional concept development

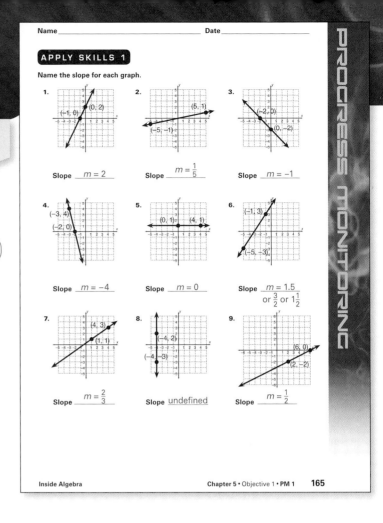

Objective 1
Progress-Monitoring Activities

PM 2 Apply Skills 2

Use with 5-Day or 3-Day Instructional Plan.

MATERIALS

- *Interactive Text*, page 166

DIRECTIONS

1. Have students turn to *Interactive Text*, page 166, Apply Skills 2.

2. Remind students of the key terms: *rise*, *run*, and *slope*.

3. Monitor student work, and provide feedback as necessary.

   Watch for:

   - Do students correctly find the slope without having two labeled points?

   - Do students correctly find the slope without using a graph?

   - Do students understand that the slope is the ratio of two distances?

NEXT STEPS • Differentiate

👥 **5-Day Instructional Plan:**

   PA 2, page 379—Students who demonstrate understanding of the concept, for additional practice and problem solving

   CD 2, page 373—Students who need additional concept development

3-Day Instructional Plan:

   PM 3, page 382—All students, for additional progress assessment

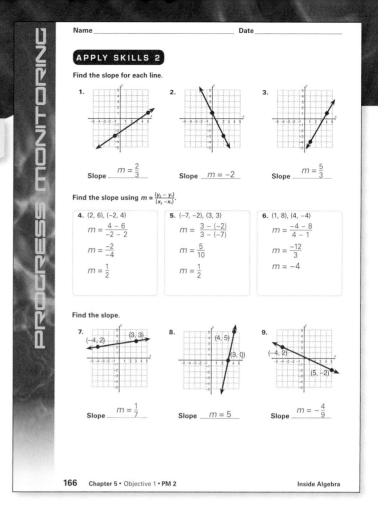

Name _____   Date _____

APPLY SKILLS 2

Find the slope for each line.

1.

Slope $m = \frac{2}{3}$

2.

Slope $m = -2$

3.

Slope $m = \frac{5}{3}$

Find the slope using $m = \frac{(y_2 - y_1)}{(x_2 - x_1)}$.

4. (2, 6), (−2, 4)

$m = \frac{4 - 6}{-2 - 2}$

$m = \frac{-2}{-4}$

$m = \frac{1}{2}$

5. (−7, −2), (3, 3)

$m = \frac{3 - (-2)}{3 - (-7)}$

$m = \frac{5}{10}$

$m = \frac{1}{2}$

6. (1, 8), (4, −4)

$m = \frac{-4 - 8}{4 - 1}$

$m = \frac{-12}{3}$

$m = -4$

Find the slope.

7. (−4, 2) (3, 3)

Slope $m = \frac{1}{7}$

8. (4, 5) (3, 0)

Slope $m = 5$

9. (−4, 2) (5, −2)

Slope $m = -\frac{4}{9}$

Objective 1
Progress-Monitoring Activities

PM 3 Apply Skills 3

Use with 5-Day or 3-Day Instructional Plan.

MATERIALS

- *Interactive Text*, page 167

DIRECTIONS

1. Have students turn to *Interactive Text*, page 167, Apply Skills 3.

2. Remind students of the key terms: *rise*, *run*, and *slope*.

3. Monitor student work, and provide feedback as necessary.

   Watch for:
   - Do students find the slope before or after graphing the equation?
   - Do students notice when a slope is negative?

NEXT STEPS • Differentiate

5-Day Instructional Plan:
Objective 1 Posttest, page 385—All students

3-Day Instructional Plan:
PS 1, page 383—Students who are on the accelerated path, to develop problem-solving skills

Objective 1 Posttest, page 385—Students who are on the differentiated path

---

APPLY SKILLS 3

Name the slope for each graph.

1. Draw the graph of $y + 3 = x$

   What is the slope?

   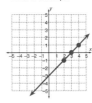

   Slope _____ $m = 1$

2. Draw the graph of $2x + y = 0$

   What is the slope?

   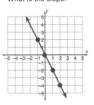

   Slope _____ $m = -2$

3. Draw the graph of $2y = 2x + 8$

   $y = x + 4$

   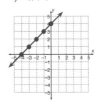

   Slope _____ $m = 1$

4. What is the slope of a line that contains (2, 5) and (3, 1)? Sketch the graph.

   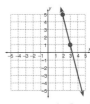

   Slope _____ $m = \dfrac{1-5}{3-2} = \dfrac{-4}{1} = -4$

Problem-Solving Activity

★ PS 1 Finding Slopes in Newspapers and Magazines

Use with 5-Day or 3-Day Instructional Plan. In this activity, students find the slope of a graph and explain what the slope represents.

MATERIALS

- Newspapers and/or magazines that have linear graphs

DIRECTIONS

1. Review the following term with students:

   slope The steepness of a line

2. Have each student find a linear graph in a newspaper or magazine.

3. Have students name two points that are on the graph and write an explanation of what the points mean, for example, sales over particular years.

4. Tell students to find the slope of the line represented in the graph. After they do so, ask them to write an explanation of what they think the slope has to do with the data on the graph; for example, a slope of $\frac{1}{4}$ for a line depicting sales over particular years means that sales are increasing by $\frac{1}{4}$ each year.

NEXT STEPS • Differentiate

5-Day Instructional Plan:
PM 3, page 382—All students, to assess progress

3-Day Instructional Plan:
Objective 1 Posttest, page 385—All students

★ = Includes Problem Solving

This page intentionally left blank

Ongoing Assessment

Objective 1 Posttest

Discuss with students the key concepts in Objective 1. Following the discussion, administer the Objective 1 Posttest to all students.

Using the Results

- Score the posttest and update the class record card.

- Provide reinforcement for students who do not demonstrate mastery of the concepts through individual or small-group reteaching of key concepts.

Name _____ Date _____

Solve the problems involving slope.

1. Find the slope.

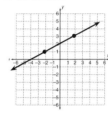

$$m = \frac{1}{2}$$

2. Find the slope.

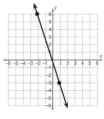

$$m = -3$$

3. Find the slope of the line that contains the points (3, 4), (2, 7).

$$m = \frac{7-4}{2-3} = \frac{3}{-1} = -3$$

4. Find the slope of the line that contains the points (10, 6), (2, 2).

$$m = \frac{2-6}{2-10} = \frac{-4}{-8} = \frac{1}{2}$$

5. Find the slope of the line that contains the points (−3, 4), (5, 6).

$$m = \frac{6-4}{5-(-3)} = \frac{2}{8} = \frac{1}{4}$$

Inside Algebra   Chapter 5 • Objective 1   **63**

CHAPTER 5 • Objective 1
POSTTEST

5 CHAPTER

Objective 2
Write the equation of a line in standard form given
two points on the line.

Objective 2 Pretest

Students complete the Objective 2 Pretest on the same day
as the Objective 1 Posttest.

Using the Results

- Score the pretest and update the class record card.

- If the majority of students do not demonstrate mastery
  of the concepts, use the 5-Day Instructional Plan for
  Objective 2.

- If the majority of students demonstrate mastery of the
  concepts, use the 3-Day Instructional Plan for Objective 2.

Name _____   Date _____

**Find the equation of each line from the given information. Write the equation in
standard form. Show your work.**

1.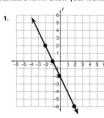

2.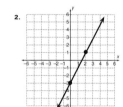

$$\underline{\quad 2x + y = -2 \quad}$$
$$y = -2x - 2$$

$$\underline{\quad 2x - y = 3 \quad}$$
$$y = 2x - 3$$

3. The line that contains the points (–1, 5) and (1, –3).

$$m = \frac{-3 - 5}{1 - (-1)} = \frac{-8}{2} = -4$$

$$y = -4x + 1$$
$$4x + y = 1$$

4. The line with a slope of 2 and that contains the point (1, 1).

$$y = 2x - 1$$
$$2x - y = 1$$

5. The line that contains the points (1, 6) and (3, 2).

$$m = \frac{2 - 6}{3 - 1} = \frac{-4}{2} = -2$$

$$y = -2x + 8$$
$$2x + y = 8$$

64   Chapter 5 • Objective 2   Inside Algebra

Goals and Activities

Objective 2 Goals

The following activities, when used with the instructional plans on pages 388 and 389, enable students to:

- Write in standard form the equation of the line that goes through (–2, 1) and (4, 3) as $x - 3y = -5$

Objective 2 Activities

Concept Development Activities

CD 1 Understanding Why We Find the Equation, page 390

★**CD 2** Discovering the Equation, page 392

Practice Activities

PA 1 Finding Another Equation, page 394

PA 2 Matching Them, page 395

Progress-Monitoring Activities

PM 1 Apply Skills 1, page 396

PM 2 Apply Skills 2, page 397

PM 3 Apply Skills 3, page 398

★Problem-Solving Activities

★**PS 1** Analyzing Airplane Miles, page 399

★**PS 2** Averaging Girls' Heights, page 400

Ongoing Assessment

Posttest Objective 2, page 401

Pretest Objective 3, page 402

CD = Concept Development PM = Progress Monitoring PS = Problem Solving
PA = Practice Activity ★ = Includes Problem Solving

5 | Instructional Plans

5-Day Instructional Plan

Use the 5-Day Instructional Plan when pretest results indicate that students would benefit from a slower pace. This plan is used when the majority of students need more time or did not demonstrate mastery on the pretest. This plan does not include all activities.

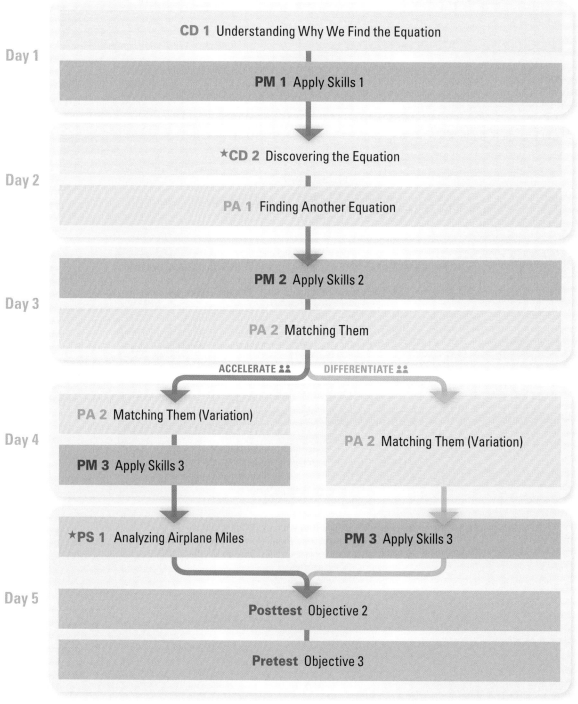

Day 1
CD 1 Understanding Why We Find the Equation
PM 1 Apply Skills 1

Day 2
★CD 2 Discovering the Equation
PA 1 Finding Another Equation

Day 3
PM 2 Apply Skills 2
PA 2 Matching Them

ACCELERATE 👥   DIFFERENTIATE 👥

Day 4
PA 2 Matching Them (Variation)
PM 3 Apply Skills 3

PA 2 Matching Them (Variation)

Day 5
★PS 1 Analyzing Airplane Miles
PM 3 Apply Skills 3
Posttest Objective 2
Pretest Objective 3

CD = Concept Development   PM = Progress Monitoring   PS = Problem Solving
PA = Practice Activity   ★ = Includes Problem Solving

3-Day Instructional Plan

Use the 3-Day Instructional Plan when pretest results indicate that students can move through the activities at a faster pace. This plan is ideal when the majority of students demonstrate mastery on the pretest.

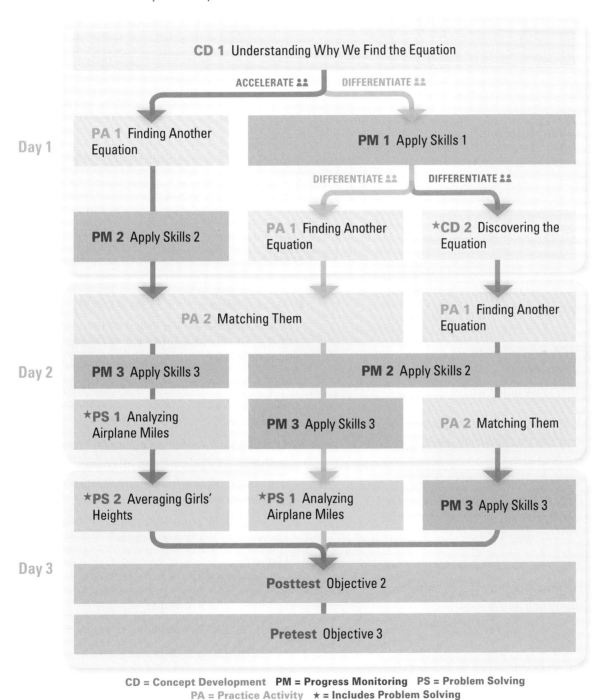

CD 1 Understanding Why We Find the Equation

ACCELERATE 👥   DIFFERENTIATE 👥

Day 1

PA 1 Finding Another Equation

PM 1 Apply Skills 1

DIFFERENTIATE 👥   DIFFERENTIATE 👥

PM 2 Apply Skills 2

PA 1 Finding Another Equation

★**CD 2** Discovering the Equation

PA 2 Matching Them

PA 1 Finding Another Equation

Day 2

PM 3 Apply Skills 3

PM 2 Apply Skills 2

★**PS 1** Analyzing Airplane Miles

PM 3 Apply Skills 3

PA 2 Matching Them

★**PS 2** Averaging Girls' Heights

★**PS 1** Analyzing Airplane Miles

PM 3 Apply Skills 3

Day 3

Posttest Objective 2

Pretest Objective 3

CD = Concept Development   PM = Progress Monitoring   PS = Problem Solving
PA = Practice Activity   ★ = Includes Problem Solving

Concept Development Activities

CD 1 Understanding Why We Find the Equation

Use with 5-Day or 3-Day Instructional Plan. In this activity, students understand that regardless of the order in which the points on a line are processed, the same slope is obtained.

MATERIALS

- Blackline Master 59
- **Variation:** Gizmos
  Defining a Line With Two Points

DIRECTIONS

1. Review the following terms with students:

> **rise** The vertical distance traveled
>
> **run** The horizontal distance traveled
>
> **slope** The steepness of a line

2. Discuss the following terms with students:

> **point-slope form** A linear equation in the form $y - y_1 = m(x - x_1)$
>
> **standard form** A linear equation in the form $ax + by = c$

3. Tell students this story about Andy.

> When Andy was 10 years old, his parents started giving him an allowance. He decided that he was going to save $2 a week so that he could buy items that cost more than he received in his allowance. Andy had $4 when he started. At the end of one week, he had $2 more for a total of $6. At the end of four weeks, he had saved $12.

Have students write ordered pairs to name how much money Andy had at the end of each week.

Examples:

> At the end of week one, Andy had saved $6.
> (1, 6)
>
> At the end of week four, Andy had saved $12.
> (4, 12)

4. Make a transparency of Blackline Master 59, Graph Paper, and sketch the graph on the overhead using the points **(1, 6)** and **(4, 12)**. Do not name other points. Keep the scales 1:1 on the *x*- and *y*-axes.

5. Explain that if you were to know the equation for this line, you could calculate how much Andy would save after 20 weeks or 52 weeks.

6. Explain that information collected in science, business, or medicine can often be graphed on a line. Point out that finding the equation of the line is an important step in making predictions. Ask students if they can name anything we already know about the line you drew.

Listen for:

- It starts at 4.
- It has a positive slope.
- We can find the slope.
- It keeps getting larger.

7. Review how to find the slope by using the line from Andy's story.

Examples:

From the graph: If the scales have been kept at 1:1, students can see that the graph rises 2 for each week. The slope is 2.

Using the two points: $m = \dfrac{(y_2 - y_1)}{(x_2 - x_1)}$

$m = \dfrac{(12 - 6)}{(4 - 1)} = \dfrac{6}{3} = 2$; Slope = 2

8. Demonstrate how to find the equation of this line using the information we know. Show students each form of the equation.

Example:

Use the point (1, 6) to find the equation.

Start with the slope equation: $m = \dfrac{(y_2 - y_1)}{(x_2 - x_1)}$

$2 = \dfrac{(y - 6)}{(x - 1)}$

Point-slope form: $y - y_1 = m(x - x_1)$

$y - 6 = 2(x - 1)$

y-coordinate x-coordinate

m or slope

Standard form: $ax + by = c$

$y - 6 = 2(x - 1)$

$y - 6 = 2x - 2$

$y - 2x = 4$

$2x - y = -4$

9. Show students that it does not make any difference which point is chosen when finding the equation.

Example:

Use the point (4, 12) to find the equation.

Point-slope form: $y - y_1 = m(x - x_1)$

$y - 12 = 2(x - 4)$

Standard form: $ax + by = c$

$y - 2x - 12 = -8$

$y - 2x = 4$

$2x - y = -4$

10. Demonstrate the process with a different line.

Example:

Find the slope and equation for a line that goes through (3, 5) and (4, 6).

Slope: $m = \dfrac{(y_2 - y_1)}{(x_2 - x_1)}$

$m = \dfrac{(6 - 5)}{(4 - 3)} = \dfrac{1}{1} = 1$

Point-slope form: $y - y_1 = m(x - x_1)$

$y - 5 = 1(x - 3)$

Standard form: $ax + by = c$

$y - 5 = 1x - 3$

$y - x = 2$

$x - y = -2$

> **Variation:** Gizmos Use the tools in the Gizmo *Defining a Line With Two Points* to demonstrate how to find the equation of a line.

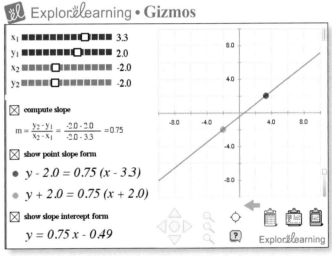

Defining a Line With Two Points

NEXT STEPS • Differentiate

5-Day Instructional Plan:
PM 1, page 396—All students, to assess progress

3-Day Instructional Plan:
PA 1, page 394—Students who demonstrate understanding of the concept, for additional practice

PM 1, page 396—Students who need additional support, to assess progress

Objective 2
Concept Development Activities

★CD 2 Discovering the Equation

Use with 5-Day or 3-Day Instructional Plan. In this activity, students find the equation of a line given two points on the line.

MATERIALS

- *Interactive Text*, page 168
- Blackline Master 59

DIRECTIONS

1. Review the following terms with students:

   point-slope form A linear equation in the form $y - y_1 = m(x - x_1)$

   slope The steepness of a line

   standard form A linear equation in the form $ax + by = c$

2. Have students turn to *Interactive Text*, page 168, What Is the Equation?, for this activity.

3. Discuss with students why it is important to find the equations of graphs (see Steps 3–6 of the Concept Development Activity, Understanding Why We Find the Equation). Tell students they are going to find the equation of the line on *Interactive Text*, page 168, by asking questions.

4. Have each student write three yes or no questions about the graph that might help in finding the equation.

5. Divide students into groups of four or five students each. Have them review the questions from each student and discuss which questions they want to ask. Circulate among the groups, and answer three questions from each group.

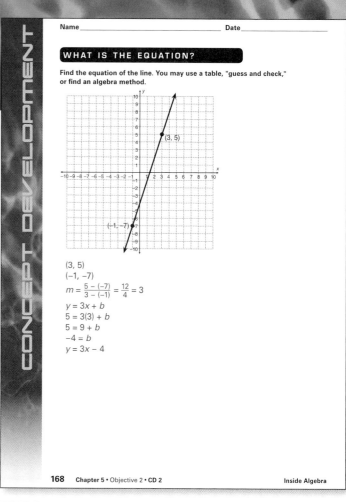

WHAT IS THE EQUATION?

Find the equation of the line. You may use a table, "guess and check," or find an algebra method.

(3, 5)
(−1, −7)
$m = \frac{5 - (-7)}{3 - (-1)} = \frac{12}{4} = 3$
$y = 3x + b$
$5 = 3(3) + b$
$5 = 9 + b$
$-4 = b$
$y = 3x - 4$

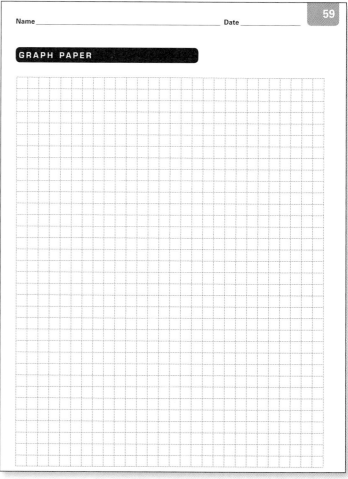

GRAPH PAPER

★ = Includes Problem Solving

6. Give the groups some time to work on finding the equation. If a group finds the equation, ask them if they can find the equation another way.

Examples:

Make a table of values from the graph, then use guess-and-check to determine the equation.

x	y
3	5
0	−4
−1	−7

Guess at rules until the equation is found.

$x + 2 = y$ No
$x − 6 = y$ No
$y = x − 4$ No
$y = 2x − 1$ No
$y = 3x − 4$ Yes

Note: There are several ways the equations can be found; this example is one of the ways.

7. Have groups present to the class any equations they found using an algebra method. Present the point-slope method of finding the equations if no group finds an algebra method. Students still find the method interesting and simple even if they work on finding the equation with no success.

Example:

$$m = \frac{(y_2 − y_1)}{(x_2 − x_1)}$$
$$m = \frac{[5 − (−7)]}{[3 − (−1)]} = \frac{12}{4} = 3$$
Slope = 3

$$3 = \frac{(y − 5)}{(x − 3)}$$
$$3(x − 3) = \frac{(y − 5)}{(x − 3)} \cdot (x − 3)$$
$$3(x − 3) = y − 5$$
Point-slope form: $y − 5 = 3(x − 3)$

8. Demonstrate how to write the equation in standard form.

Example:

$ax + by = c$
$y − 5 = 3x − 9$
$−5 = 3x − 9 − y$
$4 = 3x − y$
$3x − y = 4$

9. Make a transparency of Blackline Master 59, Graph Paper, and demonstrate how to find the equations for several more lines. Start by plotting the points **(0, −3)** and **(1, 6)**. Sketch the line, and show students how to find the equation.

Example:

$$m = \frac{(y_2 − y_1)}{(x_2 − x_1)}$$
$$m = \frac{[6 − (−3)]}{(1 − 0)} = \frac{9}{1} = 9$$

Substitute a point back into the slope equation.
$$m = \frac{(y_2 − y_1)}{(x_2 − x_1)}$$
$$9 = \frac{[y − (−3)]}{(x − 0)}$$
$$9 = \frac{y + 3}{x}$$
$$9x = y + 3$$
$$9x − y = 3$$

10. Answer any questions, then have students find equations in standard form for more points.

Sample problems:

(2, −1), (6, 7) $2x − y = 5$
(4, 2), (−2, 5) $x + 2y = 8$

NEXT STEPS • Differentiate

5-Day and 3-Day Instructional Plans:
PA 1, page 394—All students, for additional practice

Practice Activities

PA 1 Finding Another Equation

Use with 5-Day or 3-Day Instructional Plan. In this activity, students change equations from point-slope form to standard form.

MATERIALS

- Blackline Master 62

DIRECTIONS

1. Review the following terms with students:

   point-slope form A linear equation in the form $y - y_1 = m(x - x_1)$

   standard form A linear equation in the form $ax + by = c$

2. Distribute one copy of Blackline Master 62, Find Another Equation, to each student.

3. Instruct students to simplify each equation and put it in standard form. Write the equations **$2x + y = 6$** and **$-2x + y = 8$** on the board, and label the first "A" and the second "B." Tell students that every answer should simplify to one of these equations. Instruct students to name each equation on Blackline Master 62 either A or B.

4. Explain that the purpose of this activity is to help students work from the point-slope form to the standard form.

NEXT STEPS • Differentiate

5-Day Instructional Plan:
PM 2, page 397—All students, to assess progress

3-Day Instructional Plan:
PM 2, page 397—Students who are on the accelerated path, to assess progress

PA 2, page 395—Students on the differentiated path who demonstrated understanding on PM 1, for additional practice

PM 2, page 397—All other students, to assess progress

FIND ANOTHER EQUATION

Simplify each equation, and write it in standard form. The answer will be either (A) $2x + y = 6$ or (B) $-2x + y = 8$.

a. $y + 2 = -2(x - 4)$ A

b. $y - 6 = -2x$ A

c. $y - 12 = 2(x - 2)$ B

d. $y - 4 = 2(x + 2)$ B

e. $y - 8 = -2(x + 1)$ A

f. $y + 4 = -2(x - 5)$ A

g. $2x = 6 - y$ A

h. $2y - 12 = 4x + 4$ B

i. $y - 0 = 2(x + 4)$ B

j. $2x + 8 = y$ B

PA 2 Matching Them

Use with 5-Day or 3-Day Instructional Plan. In this activity, given two points or a point and a slope, students find the slope and the equation in both point-slope and standard forms.

MATERIALS

- Blackline Master 63

DIRECTIONS

1. Review the following terms with students:

   point-slope form A linear equation in the form $y - y_1 = m(x - x_1)$

   slope The steepness of a line

   standard form A linear equation in the form $ax + by = c$

2. Distribute one copy of Blackline Master 63, Match Them, to each student. Tell students to cut out the squares but keep them in their correct columns.

3. Explain to students that the object is to match one card from each column together. Thus, there will be eight sets of four cards each; each set includes one card from the *Points or Points and Slope* column, one card from the *Slope* column, one card from the *Point-Slope Equation* column, and one card from the *Standard Equation* column.

   Note: The advantage of this practice activity is that the answers are given. Students need to apply the formulas and use algebra to find the correct equations. This activity should also help reinforce the names of the equations (point-slope form and standard form).

   > **Variation:** Cut out the first and second columns, and have students match the points to the slopes. Cut out the third and fourth columns, and have students match the point-slope equations to the equivalent standard equations.

Name _____ Date _____

MATCH THEM

Points or Points and Slope	Slope	Point-Slope Equation	Standard Equation
a. $(2, 4), (4, 10)$	**b.** $m = 1$	**c.** $y + 2 = -1(x - 4)$	**d.** $x - y = -4$
e. $(-1, 3), m = 2$	**f.** $m = -1$	**g.** $y - 8 = -\frac{1}{2}(x - 8)$	**h.** $3x - y = 2$
i. $(2, 6), (-1, 3)$	**j.** $m = 2$	**k.** $y - 3 = 2(x + 1)$	**l.** $x + 2y = 24$
m. $(-1, 3), (4, -2)$	**n.** $m = -2$	**o.** $y - 6 = x - 2$	**p.** $2x + y = 5$
q. $(0, 5), m = -2$	**r.** $m = 3$	**s.** $y - 4 = \frac{1}{2}(x - 1)$	**t.** $2x - y = -5$
u. $(1, 4), m = \frac{1}{2}$	**v.** $m = -\frac{1}{2}$	**w.** $y - 5 = -2(x - 0)$	**x.** $4x + y = 2$
y. $(1, -2), (0, 2)$	**z.** $m = \frac{1}{2}$	**aa.** $y + 2 = -4(x - 1)$	**bb.** $x - 2y = -7$
cc. $(8, 8), (12, 6)$	**dd.** $m = -4$	**ee.** $y - 4 = 3(x - 2)$	**ff.** $x + y = 2$

Set 1: a., r., ee., h.   Set 3: i., b., o., d.   Set 5: q., n., w., p.   Set 7: y., dd., aa., x.
Set 2: e., j., k., t.   Set 4: m., f., c., ff.   Set 6: u., z., s., bb.   Set 8: cc., v., g., l.

NEXT STEPS • Differentiate

5-Day Instructional Plan:
PA 2 Variation, page 395—All students, for additional practice

5-Day Instructional Plan (Variation):
PM 3, page 398—All students, to assess progress

3-Day Instructional Plan:
PM 3, page 398—Students who are on the accelerated path, to assess progress

PM 2, page 397—Students on the differentiated path who demonstrated understanding on PM 1, to assess progress

PM 3, page 398—All other students, to assess progress

Objective 2
Progress-Monitoring Activities

PM 1 Apply Skills 1

Use with 5-Day or 3-Day Instructional Plan.

MATERIALS

- *Interactive Text*, pages 169–170

DIRECTIONS

1. Have students turn to *Interactive Text*, pages 169–170, Apply Skills 1.

2. Remind students of the key terms: *point-slope form* and *standard form*.

3. Monitor student work, and provide feedback as necessary.

   Watch for:
   - Do students correctly write the equation of a line in point-slope form?
   - Do students correctly write the equation of a line in standard form?

NEXT STEPS • Differentiate

5-Day Instructional Plan:
CD 2, page 392—All students, for additional concept development and problem-solving

3-Day Instructional Plan:
PA 1, page 394—Students who demonstrate understanding of the concept, for additional practice

CD 2, page 392—Students who need additional concept development

---

APPLY SKILLS 1

Solve.

Example:
Find the slope of the line.

$m = \frac{(y_2 - y_1)}{(x_2 - x_1)} = \frac{[0 - (-2)]}{(3 - 0)} = \frac{2}{3}$

Write the point-slope equation of the line using the slope and point (0, –2).

$y - y_1 = m(x - x_1)$

$y - (-2) = \frac{2}{3}(x - 0)$

$y + 2 = \frac{2}{3}x$

Write the equation in standard form, ($ax + by = c$).

$2x - 3y = 6$

1. Find the slope of the line.

   $m = \frac{3 - (-3)}{3 - 1} = \frac{6}{2} = 3$

2. Write the point-slope equation of the line $y - y_1 = m(x - x_1)$.

   $y - 3 = 3(x - 3)$ or $y - (-3) = 3(x - 1)$

3. Write the equation in standard form, $ax + by = c$.

   $3x - y = 6$

4. Given the slope of a line is –2 and it contains the point (4, 1), write the point-slope equation, $y - y_1 = m(x - x_1)$.

   $y - 1 = -2(x - 4)$

5. Write the equation in standard form, $ax + by = c$.

   $2x + y = 9$

Inside Algebra   Chapter 5 • Objective 2 • PM 1   **169**

APPLY SKILLS 1 *(continued)*

Find the equation of a line containing the points (–2, –4) and (1, 5). Use the given steps.

6. Find the slope of the line, $m = \frac{(y_2 - y_1)}{(x_2 - x_1)}$.

   $m = \frac{5 - (-4)}{1 - (-2)} = \frac{9}{3} = 3$

7. Write the equation in point-slope form, $y - y_1 = m(x - x_1)$.

   $y - (-4) = 3[x - (-2)]$ or $y - 5 = 3(x - 1)$

8. Write the equation in standard form, $ax + by = c$.

   $3x - y = -2$

9. Write the equation of the line containing the points (3, –1), (2, 2) in point-slope form and standard form.

   $y - 2 = -3(x - 2)$ or $y + 1 = -3(x - 3)$

   $3x + y = 8$

10. Write the equation of the line with slope 1 and containing the point (–1, –1) in point-slope form and standard form.

    $y + 1 = x + 1$

    $x - y = 0$

170 Chapter 5 • Objective 2 • PM 1   Inside Algebra

Objective 2
Progress-Monitoring Activities

PM 2 Apply Skills 2

Use with 5-Day or 3-Day Instructional Plan.

MATERIALS

- *Interactive Text*, pages 171–172

DIRECTIONS

1. Have students turn to *Interactive Text*, pages 171–172, Apply Skills 2.

2. Remind students of the key terms: *point-slope form* and *standard form*.

3. Monitor student work, and provide feedback as necessary.

   Watch for:
   - Do students correctly change equations from point-slope form to standard form?
   - Do students correctly identify the slope of an equation written in point-slope form?

NEXT STEPS • Differentiate

5-Day Instructional Plan:

PA 2, page 395—All students, for additional practice

3-Day Instructional Plan:

PA 2, page 395—Students who are on the accelerated path, for additional practice

PM 3, page 398—Students on the differentiated path who demonstrated understanding on PM 1, for additional progress assessment

PA 2, page 395—All other students, for additional practice

APPLY SKILLS 2

Write the equation in point-slope form, $(y - y_1) = m(x - x_1)$, for the line containing the point and slope given.

1. (3, 4), slope of −1

   $y - 4 = -1(x - 3)$

2. (−3, 1), slope of 2

   $y - 1 = 2(x + 3)$

3. (0, 0), slope of 6

   $y = 6x$

4. (3, 3), slope of $\frac{1}{2}$

   $y - 3 = \frac{1}{2}(x - 3)$

5. (−5, −1), slope of −4

   $y + 1 = -4(x + 5)$

6. (6, −3), slope of $-1\frac{1}{2}$

   $y + 3 = -\frac{3}{2}(x - 6)$

These equations are written in point-slope form. Rewrite them in standard form, $(ax + by = c)$.

7. $(y - 3) = 2(x + 2)$
   $y - 3 = 2x + 4$
   $2x - y = -7$

8. $(y + 2) = -1(x - 5)$
   $y + 2 = -x + 5$
   $x + y = 3$

9. $y - 6 = -3(x + 3)$
   $y - 6 = -3x - 9$
   $3x + y = -3$

10. $(y + 2) = -\frac{1}{2}(x + 6)$
    $y + 2 = -\frac{1}{2}x - 3$
    $2y + 4 = -x - 6$
    $x + 2y = -10$

APPLY SKILLS 2 *(continued)*

Write the equation in standard form for the line containing the point and slope given.

11. (2, 4), $m = 4$
    $y - 4 = 4(x - 2)$
    $y - 4 = 4x - 8$
    $y + 4 = 4x$
    $4x - y = 4$

12. (−1, 4), $m = -2$
    $y - 4 = -2(x + 1)$
    $y - 4 = -2x - 2$
    $y = -2x + 2$
    $2x + y = 2$

13. (−2, −4), $m = \frac{1}{4}$
    $y + 4 = \frac{1}{4}(x + 2)$
    $4y + 16 = x + 2$
    $4y + 14 = x$
    $x - 4y = 14$

14. $\left(\frac{1}{2}, 3\right)$, $m = 8$
    $y - 3 = 8\left(x - \frac{1}{2}\right)$
    $y - 3 = 8x - 4$
    $y + 1 = 8x$
    $8x - y = 1$

Objective 2
Progress-Monitoring Activities

PM 3 Apply Skills 3

Use with 5-Day or 3-Day Instructional Plan.

MATERIALS

- *Interactive Text*, page 173

DIRECTIONS

1. Have students turn to *Interactive Text*, page 173, Apply Skills 3.

2. Remind students of the key term: *standard form*.

3. Monitor student work, and provide feedback as necessary.

    Watch for:

    - Do students correctly account for negative slopes when writing equations?

    - Can students find the equation of a line given either two points or a point and a slope?

NEXT STEPS • Differentiate

5-Day Instructional Plan:

PS 1, page 399—Students who are on the accelerated path, to develop problem-solving skills

Objective 2 Posttest, page 401—Students who are on the differentiated path

3-Day Instructional Plan:

PS 1, page 399—Students who are on the accelerated path, to develop problem-solving skills

PS 1, page 399—Students on the differentiated path who demonstrated understanding on PM 1, to develop problem-solving skills

Objective 2 Posttest, page 401—All other students

Name _____ Date _____

APPLY SKILLS 3

Find the equation of each line given in the graphs below. Write the equation in standard form.

1.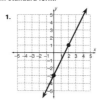

    $2x - y = 3$ _____

2.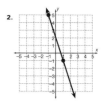

    $3x + y = 2$ _____

Find the equation of a line containing the two points. Write the equation in standard form.

3. $(4, 1), (3, 3)$

    $m = \frac{3 - 1}{3 - 4} = \frac{2}{-1} = -2$

    $y = -2x + 9$

    $2x + y = 9$

4. $(-1, 2), (-4, -4)$

    $m = \frac{-4 - 2}{-4 + 1} = \frac{-6}{-3} = 2$

    $y = 2x + 4$

    $2x - y = -4$

5. $(1, 7), (-4, 2)$

    $m = \frac{2 - 7}{-4 - 1} = \frac{-5}{-5} = 1$

    $y = x + 6$

    $x - y = -6$

6. $(-2, 3), (2, 5)$

    $m = \frac{5 - 3}{2 + 2} = \frac{2}{4} = \frac{1}{2}$

    $y = \frac{1}{2}x + 4$

    $\frac{1}{2}x - y = -4$ so $x - 2y = -8$

Find the equation of a line with the point and slope given below. Write the equation in standard form.

7. $(4, 6), m = \frac{1}{2}$

    $y - 6 = \frac{1}{2}(x - 4)$

    $2y - 12 = x - 4$

    $2y - 8 = x$

    $x - 2y = -8$

8. $(-1, -5), m = -2$

    $y + 5 = -2(x + 1)$

    $y + 5 = -2x - 2$

    $y = -2x - 7$

    $2x + y = -7$

Objective 2
Problem-Solving Activities

★PS 1 Analyzing Airplane Miles

Use with 5-Day or 3-Day Instructional Plan. In this activity, students find the equation of a line and use it to make predictions.

MATERIALS

- *Interactive Text*, page 174

DIRECTIONS

1. Review the following term with students:

   slope The steepness of a line

2. Tell students that in this activity, they answer questions by correctly interpreting a graph.

3. Have students work individually on this assignment.

4. Have students turn to *Interactive Text*, page 174, Airplane Miles, and solve the problems.

5. Encourage students to write in complete sentences when explaining what the slope and the equation represent. In Problem 1, students should realize that their slope of 0.5 corresponds to 500 miles per hour.

NEXT STEPS • Differentiate

5-Day Instructional Plan:
Objective 2 Posttest, page 401—All students

👥 3-Day Instructional Plan:
PS 2, page 400—Students who are on the accelerated path, for additional problem-solving

Objective 2 Posttest, page 401—Students who are on the differentiated path

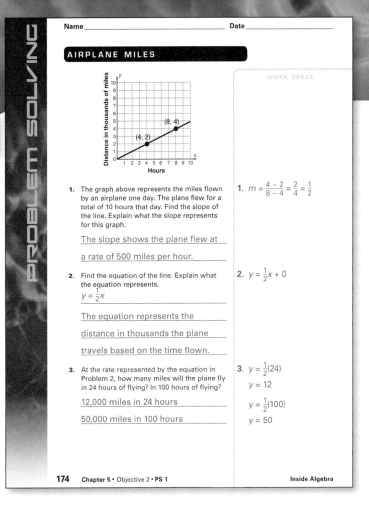

★ = Includes Problem Solving

Problem-Solving Activities

★ **PS 2** Averaging Girls' Heights

Use with 3-Day Instructional Plan. In this activity, students find the equation of a line segment and explain what the slope represents.

MATERIALS

- *Interactive Text*, page 175

DIRECTIONS

1. Review the following term with students:

   slope The steepness of a line

2. Tell students that in this activity, they correctly interpret a graph. Explain to students that they will see that some equations are valid only within a certain range of values.

3. Have students work individually on this assignment.

4. Have students turn to *Interactive Text*, page 175, Average Girls' Height, and solve the problems.

5. Encourage students to write in complete sentences when explaining what the slope and the equation represent. Check that students round their answers to two decimal places. Notice whether students understand why the equation is only valid within a certain subset of the domain.

NEXT STEPS • Differentiate

3-Day Instructional Plan:
Objective 2 Posttest, page 401—All students

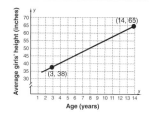

Name _____ Date _____

AVERAGE GIRLS' HEIGHT

WORK SPACE

1. The graph above represents the average girls' height from ages 2 years through 14 years. Find the slope of the line and explain what the slope represents. (Round off or approximate.)

   Girls grow about $2\frac{1}{2}$ inches per year from ages 3 to 14.

2. Find the equation of the line for this graph. What do you think the equation represents?

   $y = \frac{27}{11}x + \frac{337}{11}$ The equation represents height for ages 3 to 14.

3. What is the average height for a 10-year-old girl? Using the equation in Problem 2, what would you predict for the height for a 30-year-old female? Is this the height of a 30-year-old female? Explain.

   The average height of a 10-year-old is about 55 inches. The average height of of 30-year-old is about 104 inches. This is not the height of a 30-year-old since people do not grow indefinitely.

1. $m = \frac{27}{11} \approx 2.5$

2. $y - 38 = \frac{27}{11}(x - 3)$

   $y - 38 = \frac{27}{11}x - \frac{81}{11}$

   $11(y - 38) = 11\left(\frac{27}{11}x - \frac{81}{11}\right)$

   $11y - 418 = 27x - 81$

   $11y = 27x + 337$

3. $y = \frac{27}{11}(10) + \frac{337}{11}$

   $y \approx 55$

   $y = \frac{27}{11}(30) + \frac{337}{11}$

   $y \approx 104$

★ = Includes Problem Solving

Objective 2 Posttest

Discuss with students the key concepts in Objective 2. Following the discussion, administer the Objective 2 Posttest to all students.

Using the Results

• Score the posttest and update the class record card.

• Provide reinforcement for students who do not demonstrate mastery of the concepts through individual or small-group reteaching of key concepts.

Name _____   Date _____

CHAPTER 5 • Objective 2
POSTTEST

Find the equation of each line from the given information. Write the equation in standard form. Show your work.

1.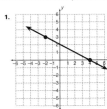

$x + 2y = 4$

$y = -\frac{1}{2}x + 2$

$\frac{1}{2}x + y = 2$

2.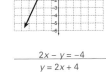

$2x - y = -4$

$y = 2x + 4$

3. The line that contains the points (1, 5) and (−3, 3).

$m = \frac{3 - 5}{-3 - 1} = \frac{-2}{-4} = \frac{1}{2}$

$y = \frac{1}{2}x + 4\frac{1}{2}$

$\frac{1}{2}x - y = -4\frac{1}{2}$

$x - 2y = -9$

4. The line with a slope of −1 and that contains the point (1, 3).

$y = -x + 4$

$x + y = 4$

5. The line that contains the points (1, 0) and (3, 6).

$m = \frac{6 - 0}{3 - 1} = \frac{6}{2} = 3$

$y = 3x - 3$

$3x - y = 3$

Inside Algebra   Chapter 5 • Objective 2   **65**

CHAPTER

Objective 3
Draw a best-fit line, and find the equation
of the best-fit line for a scatter plot.

Objective 3 Pretest

Students complete the Objective 3 Pretest on the same day
as the Objective 2 Posttest.

Using the Results

- Score the pretest and update the class record card.
- If the majority of students do not demonstrate mastery
  of the concepts, use the 4-Day Instructional Plan for
  Objective 3.
- If the majority of students demonstrate mastery of the
  concepts, use the 3-Day Instructional Plan for Objective 3.

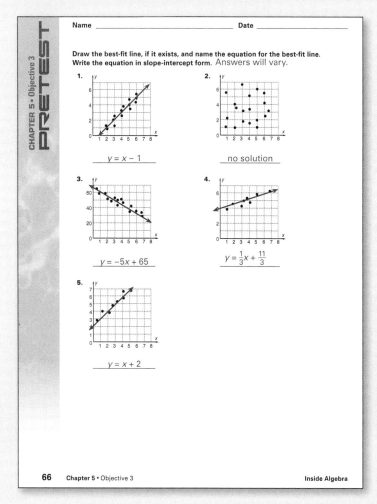

Goals and Activities

Objective 3 Goals

The following activities, when used with the instructional plans on pages 404 and 405, enable students to:

- Draw a best-fit line for the data below and determine the equation of the line to be $3x - y = 0$

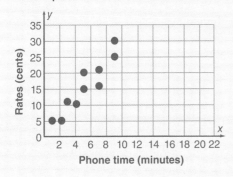

Objective 3 Activities

Concept Development Activities	
CD 1 Making Predictions, page 406	**CD 2** Writing the Best-Fit Line Equation, page 408

Practice Activity
PA 1 Matching the Graph, page 409

Progress-Monitoring Activities		
PM 1 Apply Skills 1, page 410	**PM 2** Apply Skills 2, page 411	**PM 3** Apply Skills 3, page 412

*Problem-Solving Activities	
★PS 1 Performing Dice Experiment 1: Separate Rolls, page 413	**★PS 2** Graphing Boys' Heights, page 414

Ongoing Assessment
Posttest Objective 3, page 415

Pretest Objective 4, page 416

CD = Concept Development   PM = Progress Monitoring   PS = Problem Solving
PA = Practice Activity   ★ = Includes Problem Solving

4-Day Instructional Plan

Use the 4-Day Instructional Plan when pretest results indicate that students would benefit from a slower pace. This plan is used when the majority of students need more time or did not demonstrate mastery on the pretest. This plan does not include all activities.

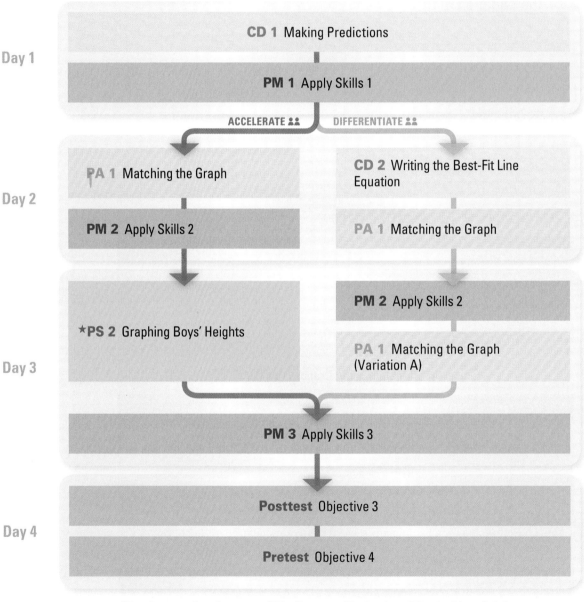

Day 1

CD 1 Making Predictions

PM 1 Apply Skills 1

ACCELERATE 👥   DIFFERENTIATE 👥

Day 2

PA 1 Matching the Graph

PM 2 Apply Skills 2

CD 2 Writing the Best-Fit Line Equation

PA 1 Matching the Graph

Day 3

★PS 2 Graphing Boys' Heights

PM 2 Apply Skills 2

PA 1 Matching the Graph (Variation A)

PM 3 Apply Skills 3

Day 4

Posttest Objective 3

Pretest Objective 4

CD = Concept Development **PM = Progress Monitoring** PS = Problem Solving
PA = Practice Activity ★ = Includes Problem Solving

3-Day Instructional Plan

Use the 3-Day Instructional Plan when pretest results indicate that students can move through the activities at a faster pace. This plan is ideal when the majority of students demonstrate mastery on the pretest.

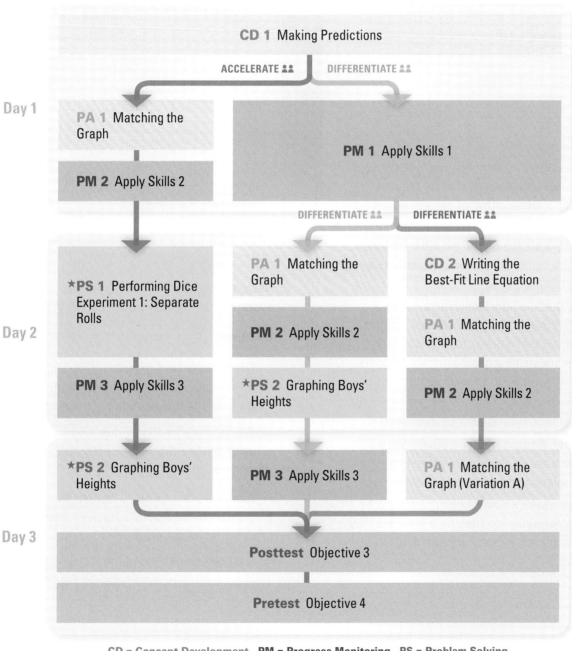

CD 1 Making Predictions

ACCELERATE   DIFFERENTIATE

Day 1

PA 1 Matching the Graph

PM 2 Apply Skills 2

PM 1 Apply Skills 1

DIFFERENTIATE   DIFFERENTIATE

Day 2

★PS 1 Performing Dice Experiment 1: Separate Rolls

PM 3 Apply Skills 3

PA 1 Matching the Graph

PM 2 Apply Skills 2

★PS 2 Graphing Boys' Heights

CD 2 Writing the Best-Fit Line Equation

PA 1 Matching the Graph

PM 2 Apply Skills 2

Day 3

★PS 2 Graphing Boys' Heights

PM 3 Apply Skills 3

PA 1 Matching the Graph (Variation A)

Posttest Objective 3

Pretest Objective 4

CD = Concept Development   PM = Progress Monitoring   PS = Problem Solving
PA = Practice Activity   ★ = Includes Problem Solving

Objective 3
Concept Development Activities

CD 1 Making Predictions

Use with 4-Day or 3-Day Instructional Plan. In this activity, students draw a best-fit line and understand that it gives an average of data that might not be exact.

MATERIALS

- *Interactive Text*, page 176
- Rulers, one per student
- Colored pencils, three different colored pencils per student

DIRECTIONS

1. Have students turn to *Interactive Text*, page 176, Phone Rates. Make sure each student has one ruler and a set of three different colored pencils.

2. Explain that this information represents the cost of making long-distance calls from different long-distance phone companies. Have different students explain each table.

3. Tell students that the information given allows them to predict the cost of a call for any length of time. Point out that a prediction is not exact, but it is close and gives a good estimate on costs. Tell students the prediction should represent an average cost.

4. Discuss the following term with students:

   scatter plot A number of coordinate pairs plotted on a graph; used to investigate a possible relationship between two variables

5. Have the class make a scatter plot of the data by plotting the information on the graph provided. Tell students to graph each company with a different colored pencil.

6. Ask students to think about how they can get an average cost and make predictions.

   Examples:

   The charges for 1 minute are 7¢, 15¢, and 10¢; the average is 10.7¢. Which point on the graph is closest to the average? 10¢, the middle one

   The average for 10 minutes is 69.7¢. Which point on the graph is closest to the average? 72¢, close to the middle

   Would the line using (1, 15) and (20, 136) be a good average, or fit? No, it is above the data, not in the middle.

   Is a line using (1, 7) and (14, 77) a good fit? No, it is too low, not in the middle.

Name_____ Date_____

PHONE RATES

Graph the points and draw the best-fit line.

Company A		Company B		Company C	
Time (min.)	Charge (cents)	Time (min.)	Charge (cents)	Time (min.)	Charge (cents)
1	7	1	15	1	10
2	12	2	20	3	29
3	17	5	38	5	45
4	23	8	55	7	57
5	30	10	63	10	74
10	72	14	77	13	92
15	101	18	99	16	110
20	133	20	110	18	122
				20	136

Best fit line will vary. Sample answer given.

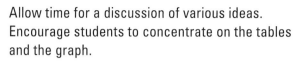

Allow time for a discussion of various ideas. Encourage students to concentrate on the tables and the graph.

Listen for:

- You can find the average charges for different times.

- To represent the average or best fit, the graph goes through the middle of the set of points.

7. Discuss the following term with students:

   best-fit line The line on a graph that will best connect the data or points

8. Tell students to use a ruler and draw the best-fit line. Circulate in the class to see if students draw the line through the center of the data.

9. Have students read the cost for 7 minutes from their graphed line. Note that a 7-minute call on the average would cost about 47¢.

10. Ask the class to discuss how we make predictions for a 30-minute call or a 60-minute call. Students should recognize that we need a rule or a formula. Make sure students notice that the formula is the equation of the line.

11. Review the following terms with students:

    point-slope form A linear equation in the form $y - y_1 = m(x - x_1)$

    slope The steepness of a line

12. Have students select two points on their graph that are close to the vertices on the best-fit line. Have them find the equation.

Example:

With the points (1, 11) and (5, 35):

$m = \frac{35 - 11}{5 - 1} = \frac{24}{4} = 6$

Slope = 6

Point-slope form

$y - 11 = 6(x - 1)$

$y - 11 = 6x - 6$

$-5 = 6x - y$

$6x - y = -5$

13. Collect several equations from the class. With the equations, check some rates with the class.

Example:

Equation: $6x - y = -5$

7-minute call

$6(7) - y = -5 \quad -y = -47 \quad y \approx 47¢$

30-minute call

$6(30) - y = -5 \quad -y = -185 \quad y \approx 185¢$

60-minute call

$6(60) - y = -5 \quad -y = -365 \quad y \approx 365¢$

14. Have students discuss the advantages of using a best-fit line.

Listen for:

- It gives an average of data.

- It allows predictions for equations.

- It is not exact for any one set of data.

- It simplifies the process and saves a lot of computation.

- It summarizes the data into an equation if there is a correlation between the points.

NEXT STEPS • Differentiate

4-Day Instructional Plan:
PM 1, page 410—All students, to assess progress

3-Day Instructional Plan:
PA 1, page 409—Students who demonstrate understanding of the concept, for additional practice

PM 1, page 410—Students who need additional support, to assess progress

Objective 3
Concept Development Activities

CD 2 Writing the Best-Fit Line Equation

Use with 4-Day or 3-Day Instructional Plan. In this activity, students create best-fit lines to explain nearly linear data.

MATERIALS

- *Interactive Text*, page 177
- Rulers, one per student

DIRECTIONS

1. Have students turn to *Interactive Text*, page 177, Electronic Calculator.

2. Review the following term with students:

   best-fit line The line on a graph that will best connect the data or points

3. Guide students through the process of drawing the best-fit line. First, ask students to think about whether they can connect all the points with one line.

4. Instruct students to draw a line so that some points are above the line and some points are below it. Point out that the average is more in the middle of the points. Have them start by making a light dashed line.

5. Have students check the dashed line to see if it comes close to the middle points. Direct students to redraw if necessary, then complete the line.

6. Next, guide students through the process of finding the equation of the best-fit line. Tell students to start by locating two points on the best-fit line for which they can name the coordinates.

7. Review the following terms with students:

   point-slope form A linear equation in the form $y - y_1 = m(x - x_1)$

   slope The steepness of a line

   standard form A linear equation in the form $ax + by = c$

8. Tell students to find the slope of the line using $m = \frac{(y_2 - y_1)}{(x_2 - x_1)}$. Have students use the slope to find the equation of the line. Tell them to start by finding the point-slope form, then simplify to find the standard form.

ELECTRONIC CALCULATOR

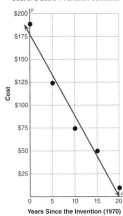

Cost of a Basic 4-Function Calculator

Answers will vary based on line. Sample answers given.

1. Draw the best-fit line.

2. Find the equation of the best-fit line.

   $8.7x + y = 180$ or $y = -8.7x + 180$

3. Predict the cost 12 years and 18 years after the invention.

   $75.60 in 12 years

   $23.40 in 18 years

Inside Algebra   Chapter 5 • Objective 3 • CD 2   **177**

CONCEPT DEVELOPMENT

Example:

Suppose (0, 180) and (15, 50) are on the line.

$$\frac{180 - 50}{0 - 15} = \frac{130}{-15} \approx -8.7$$

Slope $= -8.7$

Point-slope form: $y - y_1 = m(x - x_1)$

$y - 50 = -8.7(x - 15)$

Standard form: $ax + by = c$

$8.7x + y = 180.5$

$8.7x + y = 180$, depending on the point used because the slope is rounded off

9. Ask students to use the equation to find the cost 12 years after the invention; 18 years after. $75.60, $23.40

NEXT STEPS • Differentiate

4-Day and 3-Day Instructional Plans:

PA 1, page 409—All students, for additional practice

Practice Activity

PA 1 Matching the Graph

Use with 4-Day or 3-Day Instructional Plan. In this activity, given a set of points, students draw the best-fit line and find the slope and equation of the line.

MATERIALS

- Blackline Master 64
- Paper cutter or one pair of scissors per student
- Rulers

DIRECTIONS

1. Review the following terms with students:

    best-fit line The line on a graph that will best connect the data or points

    slope The steepness of a line

2. Distribute one copy of Blackline Master 64, Graphs and Equations, to each student. Have students cut out the squares with scissors.

    Note: If you want to save class time, cut the squares with a paper cutter ahead of time.

3. Have students make four sets of cards, each consisting of one card for each category: (1) points, (2) best-fit line, (3) slope, and (4) equation.

4. Instruct students to work individually to determine the slopes and the equations from the points and lines.

    | **Variation A:** Only give students the points cards. Have them draw the best-fit line, compute the slope, and find the equation. Give them the other cards to see how closely their answers match up.

    | **Variation B:** Give each student a best-fit line card. Have students find the points card that goes with the line. Have students compute the slope, and find the equation using the best-fit line card.

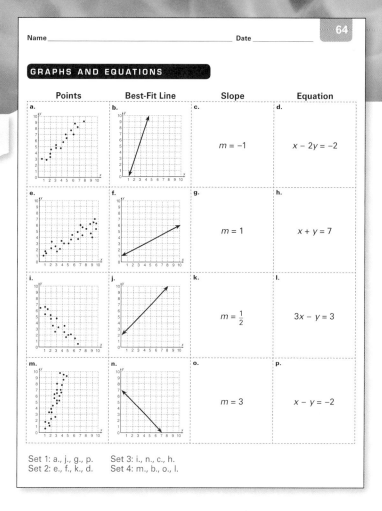

GRAPHS AND EQUATIONS

Points | Best-Fit Line | Slope | Equation

c. $m = -1$ d. $x - 2y = -2$

g. $m = 1$ h. $x + y = 7$

k. $m = \frac{1}{2}$ l. $3x - y = 3$

o. $m = 3$ p. $x - y = -2$

Set 1: a., j., g., p.   Set 3: i., n., c., h.
Set 2: e., f., k., d.   Set 4: m., b., o., l.

NEXT STEPS • Differentiate

4-Day Instructional Plan:
PM 2, page 411—All students, to assess progress

4-Day Instructional Plan (Variation):
PM 3, page 412—All students, to assess progress

3-Day Instructional Plan:
PM 2, page 411—All students, to assess progress

3-Day Instructional Plan (Variation):
Objective 3 Posttest, page 415—All students

PM 1 Apply Skills 1

Use with 4-Day or 3-Day Instructional Plan.

MATERIALS

- *Interactive Text,* page 178

DIRECTIONS

1. Have students turn to *Interactive Text,* page 178, Apply Skills 1.

2. Remind students of the key terms: *slope* and *best-fit line.*

3. Monitor student work, and provide feedback as necessary.

   Watch for:

   - Do students understand that the best-fit line for a scatter plot might or might not pass through any of the points?

   - Do students see that they can find the best-fit slope for a set of points even if those points do not lie on a line?

NEXT STEPS • Differentiate

👥 4-Day and 3-Day Instructional Plans:

PA 1, page 409—Students who demonstrate understanding of the concept, for additional practice

CD 2, page 408—Students who need additional concept development

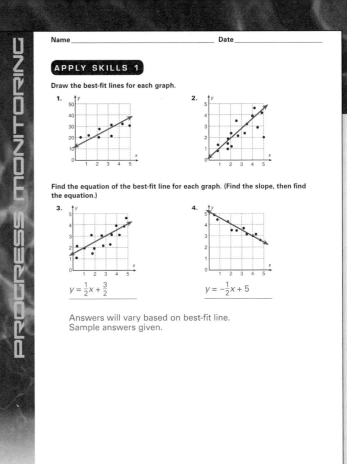

Progress-Monitoring Activities

PM 2 Apply Skills 2

Use with 4-Day or 3-Day Instructional Plan.

MATERIALS

- *Interactive Text,* page 179

DIRECTIONS

1. Have students turn to *Interactive Text,* page 179, Apply Skills 2.

2. Remind students of the key terms: *slope* and *best-fit line.*

3. Monitor student work, and provide feedback as necessary.

   Watch for:
   - Do students draw best-fit lines that go approximately through the middle of the points?

   - Do students choose best-fit lines that are approximately balanced from above and below?

NEXT STEPS • Differentiate

👥 4-Day Instructional Plan:

PS 2, page 414—Students who are on the accelerated path, to develop problem-solving skills

PA 1 Variation A, page 409—Students who are on the differentiated path, for additional practice

👥 3-Day Instructional Plan:

PS 1, page 413—Students who are on the accelerated path, to develop problem-solving skills

PS 2, page 414—Students on the differentiated path who demonstrated understanding on PM 1, to develop problem-solving skills

PA 1 Variation A, page 409—All other students, for additional practice

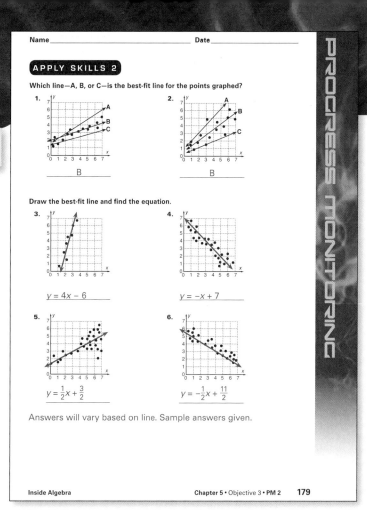

PM 3 Apply Skills 3

Use with 4-Day or 3-Day Instructional Plan.

MATERIALS

- *Interactive Text*, page 180

DIRECTIONS

1. Have students turn to *Interactive Text*, page 180, Apply Skills 3.

2. Remind students of the key terms: *slope* and *best-fit line*.

3. Monitor student work, and provide feedback as necessary.

   Watch for:
   - Do students write a concise description of what the equation represents?
   - Can students utilize the equation to make predictions?

NEXT STEPS • Differentiate

4-Day Instructional Plan:
Objective 3 Posttest, page 415—All students

3-Day Instructional Plan:
PS 2, page 414—Students who are on the accelerated path, to develop problem-solving skills

Objective 3 Posttest, page 415—Students who are on the differentiated path

---

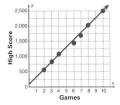

Name _____ Date _____

APPLY SKILLS 3

1. The information below represents the high scores earned on a video arcade game and the number of games played. Make a graph of the information.

Name	Game	High Score
Juan	8 games	2,000
Tim	2 games	600
Sally	10 games	2,500
Fran	6 games	1,400
Bill	7 games	1,700
Jordan	4 games	1,100
Andy	3 games	800

2. Draw the best-fit line for these data. What is the equation of the best-fit line?

   $250x - y = 0$ or $y = 250x$

3. Explain what the equation represents.

   Each game played adds about 250 points to the high score.

4. What would you predict for a high score if a person played 20 games?

   After 20 games we expect about 5,000 points.

Problem-Solving Activities

★PS 1 Performing Dice Experiment 1: Separate Rolls

Use with 3-Day Instructional Plan. In this activity, students understand that not all data have a correlation; events are not always related.

MATERIALS

- Blackline Master 59
- Dice, one per group of students

DIRECTIONS

1. Divide students into groups of five, and distribute one copy of Blackline Master 59, Graph Paper, to each group.

2. Explain that each student is going to roll one die 10 times and plot each roll on a graph. Tell students to follow the same process for each person in the group. Instruct students to plot all the group's points on the same graph.

Example:

Suppose a student gets a 4 on his or her first roll. The student plots the point (1, 4) on the graph.

Suppose he or she gets a 5 on the second roll. The point (2, 5) is plotted.

After each group completes the process, all the points are on the same graph.

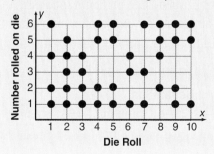

Name _____ **Date** _____

GRAPH PAPER

3. Review the following term with students:

   best-fit line The line on a graph that will best connect the data or points

4. Have each group show their graph to the class. Ask students if there is a correlation on each graph to where we can draw a best-fit line.

5. Have students discuss what they notice about correlations.

   Listen for:
   - A correlation occurs only in rare cases.
   - In some experiences, there is no correlation between events.
   - When scientists collect data, and there is no correlation, they can eliminate this outcome from their ideas and try something else.

NEXT STEPS • Differentiate

3-Day Instructional Plan:
PM 3, page 412—All students, to assess progress

★ = Includes Problem Solving

Objective 3
Problem-Solving Activities

★ PS 2 Graphing Boys' Heights

Use with 4-Day or 3-Day Instructional Plan. In this activity, students collect data and create a best-fit line to explain the data.

MATERIALS

- Blackline Master 59
- Tape measure

DIRECTIONS

1. Tell students that most doctor's offices have a chart on average growth, weight, and height of boys and girls. Ask students to discuss how they think this chart was developed. Make sure students recognize that a large set of data was collected by ages to find an average.

2. Indicate that this data set would be a good class project. Explain that the class is going to create a chart to show average boys' heights at various ages.

3. Discuss how the class can collect the data and age levels. Encourage students to get as large a sample of population and various ages as possible; for example, have one or two students visit an elementary school. Students need a tape measure to measure the boys' heights and a sheet of paper to record ages.

4. Have the class make a table of ages and heights that were collected.

5. Review the following terms with students:

   best-fit line The line on a graph that best connects the data or points

   scatter plot A number of coordinate pairs plotted on a graph; used to investigate a possible relationship between two variables

6. Distribute one copy of Blackline Master 59, Graph Paper, to each student. Have each student use the table to graph the points for each boy (age to height).

7. Divide students into groups of four or five. Have students compare their graphs of the data. Ask students which graph(s) they feel represent the data best. scatter plot

8. Have each group make a best-fit line and find the equation of the line.

9. Get reports from each group, and compare the equations.

10. Try some of the average age points for the data to see how they compare to the average from the equations.

11. Have the groups make predictions for some boys' heights not covered on the chart.

12. Discuss the limits of the equation for the average height of boys. Make sure students recognize that at a certain point, each boy will stop growing in height.

NEXT STEPS • Differentiate

4-Day Instructional Plan:
PM 3, page 412—All students, to assess progress

👥 3-Day Instructional Plan:
Objective 3 Posttest, page 415—Students who are on the accelerated path

PM 3, page 412—Students who are on the differentiated path, to assess progress

★ = Includes Problem Solving

Objective 3 Posttest

Discuss with students the key concepts in Objective 3. Following the discussion, administer the Objective 3 Posttest to all students.

Using the Results

• Score the posttest and update the class record card.

• Provide reinforcement for students who do not demonstrate mastery of the concepts through individual or small-group reteaching of key concepts.

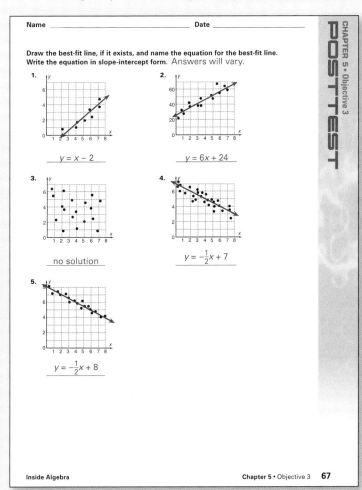

Name _____ Date _____

CHAPTER 5 • Objective 3
POSTTEST

Draw the best-fit line, if it exists, and name the equation for the best-fit line. Write the equation in slope-intercept form. Answers will vary.

1.

$y = x - 2$

2.

$y = 6x + 24$

3.

no solution

4.

$y = -\frac{1}{2}x + 7$

5.

$y = -\frac{1}{2}x + 8$

Inside Algebra   Chapter 5 • Objective 3   **67**

Objective 4

Write linear equations in slope-intercept form to find the slope, *x*-intercept, and *y*-intercept, and sketch the graph.

Objective 4 Pretest

Students complete the Objective 4 Pretest on the same day as the Objective 3 Posttest.

Using the Results

- Score the pretest and update the class record card.
- If the majority of students do not demonstrate mastery of the concepts, use the 5-Day Instructional Plan for Objective 4.
- If the majority of students demonstrate mastery of the concepts, use the 3-Day Instructional Plan for Objective 4.

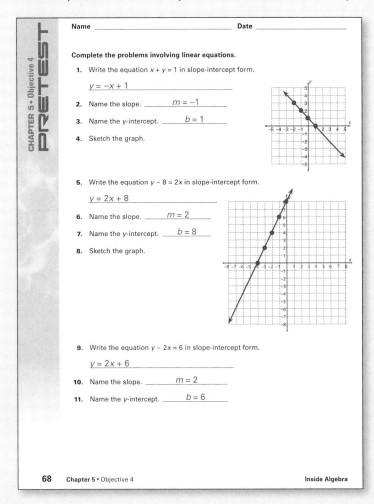

Goals and Activities

Objective 4 Goals

The following activities, when used with the instructional plans on pages 418 and 419, enable students to:

- Write the equation $2x - y = 7$ in slope-intercept form as
  $$y = 2x - 7$$

- Find the slope of the line to be
  2

- Find the y-intercept of the line to be
  −7

- Sketch the graph of $y = 2x - 7$ as

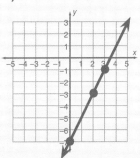

Objective 4 Activities

Concept Development Activities

CD 1 Identifying the x-Intercept and y-Intercept, page 420	★**CD 2** Discovering Slope-Intercept Form, page 422	**CD 3** Finding the Slope on a Graphing Calculator, page 423
★**CD 4** Discovering the Constant, page 424	**CD 5** Determining the Constant on a Graphing Calculator, page 426	**CD 6** Writing in Slope-Intercept Form, page 428

Practice Activities

PA 1 Naming the y-Intercept or Slope, page 430	★**PA 2** Playing Student Exchange, page 433

Progress-Monitoring Activities

PM 1 Apply Skills 1, page 434	**PM 2** Apply Skills 2, page 435	**PM 3** Apply Skills 3, page 436	**PM 4** Apply Skills 4, page 437

★Problem-Solving Activity

★**PS 1** Solving Linear Equations in Real-Life Situations, page 438

Ongoing Assessment

Posttest Objective 4, page 439

Pretest Objective 5, page 440

CD = Concept Development   PM = Progress Monitoring   PS = Problem Solving
PA = Practice Activity   ★ = Includes Problem Solving

5-Day Instructional Plan

Use the 5-Day Instructional Plan when pretest results indicate that students would benefit from a slower pace. This plan is used when the majority of students need more time or did not demonstrate mastery on the pretest.

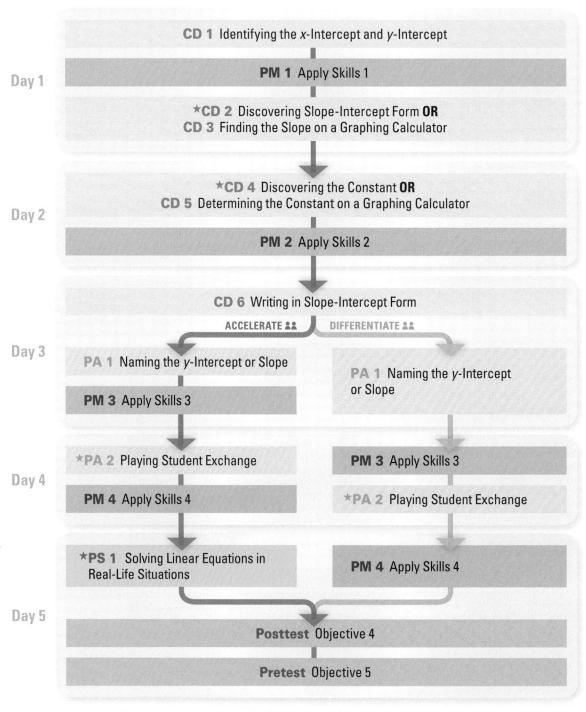

Day 1

CD 1 Identifying the x-Intercept and y-Intercept

PM 1 Apply Skills 1

★CD 2 Discovering Slope-Intercept Form **OR**
CD 3 Finding the Slope on a Graphing Calculator

Day 2

★CD 4 Discovering the Constant **OR**
CD 5 Determining the Constant on a Graphing Calculator

PM 2 Apply Skills 2

CD 6 Writing in Slope-Intercept Form

ACCELERATE 👥   DIFFERENTIATE 👥

Day 3

PA 1 Naming the y-Intercept or Slope

PM 3 Apply Skills 3

PA 1 Naming the y-Intercept or Slope

Day 4

★PA 2 Playing Student Exchange

PM 4 Apply Skills 4

PM 3 Apply Skills 3

★PA 2 Playing Student Exchange

Day 5

★PS 1 Solving Linear Equations in Real-Life Situations

PM 4 Apply Skills 4

Posttest Objective 4

Pretest Objective 5

CD = Concept Development   PM = Progress Monitoring   PS = Problem Solving
PA = Practice Activity   ★ = Includes Problem Solving

3-Day Instructional Plan

Use the 3-Day Instructional Plan when pretest results indicate that students can move through the activities at a faster pace. This plan is ideal when the majority of students demonstrate mastery on the pretest. This plan does not include all activities.

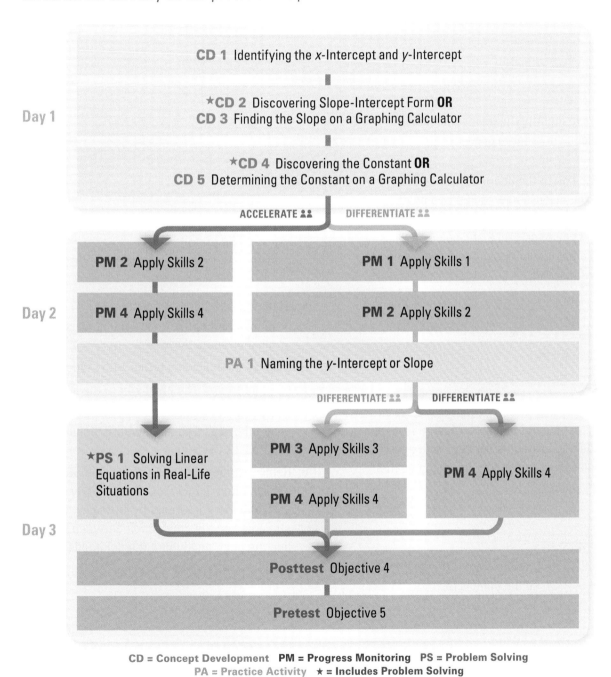

Day 1

CD 1 Identifying the *x*-Intercept and *y*-Intercept

★**CD 2** Discovering Slope-Intercept Form **OR**
CD 3 Finding the Slope on a Graphing Calculator

★**CD 4** Discovering the Constant **OR**
CD 5 Determining the Constant on a Graphing Calculator

ACCELERATE 👥   DIFFERENTIATE 👥

Day 2

PM 2 Apply Skills 2

PM 4 Apply Skills 4

PM 1 Apply Skills 1

PM 2 Apply Skills 2

PA 1 Naming the *y*-Intercept or Slope

DIFFERENTIATE 👥   DIFFERENTIATE 👥

Day 3

★**PS 1** Solving Linear Equations in Real-Life Situations

PM 3 Apply Skills 3

PM 4 Apply Skills 4

PM 4 Apply Skills 4

Posttest Objective 4

Pretest Objective 5

CD = Concept Development   PM = Progress Monitoring   PS = Problem Solving
PA = Practice Activity   ★ = Includes Problem Solving

Concept Development Activities

CD 1 Identifying the *x*-Intercept and *y*-Intercept

Use with 5-Day or 3-Day Instructional Plan. In this activity, students identify the x-intercept and y-intercept.

MATERIALS

- Blackline Master 59

DIRECTIONS

1. Ask students to identify the fewest number of points one needs in order to draw the graph of a linear equation. **2 points**

2. Write **y = 3x + 6** on the board. Have students think about and discuss how to find two points for the line easily. Make sure students recognize that substituting a value for *x* or *y*, and solving will allow them to find a point quickly. Point out that using zero for *x* and *y* works well.

Example:

> **y = 3x + 6**
> If $x = 0$, then $y = 6$
> $y = 3 \cdot 0 + 6$
> $(0, 6)$

3. Make a transparency of Blackline Master 59, Graph Paper, and demonstrate this concept with a few more examples. Find two points for each equation and graph the line.

Example:

> **y = 2x − 4**
> When $x = 0$, $y = -4$, so the point is $(0, -4)$.
> When $y = 0$, $x = 2$, so the point is $(2, 0)$.

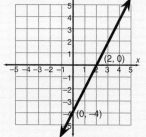

4. Make sure students notice that $(0, -4)$ is where the graph intersects the *y*-axis and $(2, 0)$ is where the graph intersects the *x*-axis.

5. Discuss the following terms with students:

   ***x*-intercept** The point where the line crosses the *x*-axis

   ***y*-intercept** The point where the line crosses the *y*-axis

6. Remind students of your example in Step 3, and explain that we find the *x*-intercept by letting $y = 0$ and the *y*-intercept by letting $x = 0$. Make sure students see the connection between your work to find the point and where the point falls on the graph.

7. Draw another graph on the overhead, and ask students to find where the line intersects the *x*-axis.

Sample problem:

y = *x* + 5

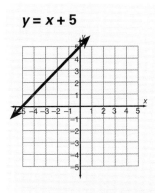

The line intersects the *x*-axis at (–5, 0).
The *x*-intercept is –5.

8. Demonstrate the process of finding the *x*- and *y*-intercepts. Show this on the graph. Repeat the rules from Step 6 if necessary.

Example:

y = *x* + 3

If $y = 0$, then $x = -3$.
$0 = x + 3$
The line intersects the *x*-axis at (–3, 0).
The *x*-intercept is –3.

If $x = 0$, then $y = 3$.
$y = 0 + 3$
The line intersects the *y*-axis at (0, 3).
The *y*-intercept is 3.

NEXT STEPS • Differentiate

5-Day Instructional Plan:
PM 1, page 434—All students, to assess progress

3-Day Instructional Plan:
CD 2, page 422—Students who work without graphing calculators, for additional concept development and problem-solving

CD 3, page 423—Students who work with graphing calculators, for additional concept development

Objective 4

Concept Development Activities

★ CD 2 Discovering Slope-Intercept Form

Use with 5-Day or 3-Day Instructional Plan. In this activity, students find the slope of an equation by solving for y.

MATERIALS

- Blackline Master 59

DIRECTIONS

1. Review the following term with students:

   slope The steepness of a line

2. Write the following equations on the board or overhead:

   $y = x$ $y = \frac{1}{2}x$ $y = -x$ $y = 2x$ $y = -2x$

3. Divide students into groups of five, and distribute one copy of Blackline Master 59, Graph Paper, to each student.

4. Have each group member graph a different equation so that all five equations will be graphed. Have students write the equation on their graph.

5. Ask each group to answer several questions about the graphs.

   Examples:

   What is the same about the equations? $y = mx$

   What is different about the equations?
   the coefficient of x (m)

   How do the graphs compare? different slopes; all go through origin

   How does the slope compare to the equation?
   $y = x$, slope 1; $y = \frac{1}{2}x$, slope $\frac{1}{2}$; the slope is m, or the coefficient of x when written $y = mx$

6. Discuss the following term with students:

   slope-intercept form A linear equation in the form $y = mx + b$

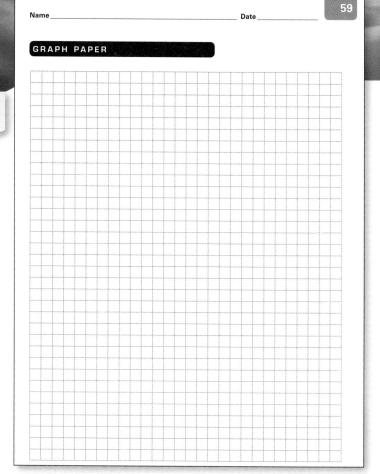

GRAPH PAPER

Name _____ Date _____

59

7. Ask students to predict the slope of several different equations. Point out to students that they might have to solve for y to find the slope on some of the equations.

Sample problems:

$y = 5x$ 5	$3y = 12x$ 4
$-2x = y$ -2	$x - y = 0$ 1
$y = \frac{1}{3}x$ $\frac{1}{3}$	$2y = x$ $\frac{1}{2}$
$x = y$ 1	

NEXT STEPS • Differentiate

👥 5-Day and 3-Day Instructional Plans:

CD 4, page 424—Students who work without graphing calculators, for additional concept development and problem-solving

CD 5, page 426—Students who work with graphing calculators, for additional concept development

★ **= Includes Problem Solving**

Concept Development Activities

CD 3 Finding the Slope on a Graphing Calculator

Use with 5-Day or 3-Day Instructional Plan. In this activity, students understand that given an equation in slope-intercept form ($y = mx + b$), a larger m *gives a steeper slope, and a negative* m *means the slope is downward.*

MATERIALS

- Graphing calculators, one per student

DIRECTIONS

1. Review the following terms with students:

   slope The steepness of a line

   slope-intercept form A linear equation in the form $y = mx + b$

2. Write the following equations on the board or overhead.

   $y = x$ $y = \frac{1}{2}x$ $y = -x$ $y = 2x$ $y = -2x$

3. Divide students into groups of five.

4. Have each group member graph one of the equations on his or her graphing calculator.

5. Ask each group to answer several questions about the graphs.

   Examples:

   What is the same about the equations? $y = mx$

   What is different about the equations?
   the coefficient of x (m)

   How do the graphs compare? different slopes; all go through origin

   How does the slope compare to the equation?
   $y = x$, slope 1; $y = \frac{1}{2}x$, slope $\frac{1}{2}$; the slope is m, or the coefficient of x when written $y = mx$

6. Ask students to predict the slope of several different equations. Point out to students that they might have to solve for y to find the slope on some of the equations.

   Sample problems:

$y = 3x$ 3	$y = -\frac{1}{2}x$ $-\frac{1}{2}$
$-3x = y$ -3	$x - y = 0$ 1
$y = 0.1x$ 0.1	$2y = x$ $\frac{1}{2}$
$y = 6x$ 6	

7. Next, have students graph the equations on their calculators.

NEXT STEPS • Differentiate

5-Day and 3-Day Instructional Plans:
   CD 4, page 424—Students who work without graphing calculators, for additional concept development and problem-solving

   CD 5, page 426—Students who work with graphing calculators, for additional concept development

Objective 4
Concept Development Activities

★ CD 4 Discovering the Constant

Use with 5-Day or 3-Day Instructional Plan. In this activity, students graph equations in slope-intercept form and might notice that graphs with the same slope and different y-intercepts are parallel.

MATERIALS

- Blackline Master 59
- Blackline Master 65

DIRECTIONS

1. Review the following terms with students:

   slope The steepness of a line

   slope-intercept form A linear equation in the form $y = mx + b$

   y-intercept The point where the line crosses the y-axis

2. Distribute one copy of Blackline Master 59, Graph Paper, and one copy of Blackline Master 65, Discover the Constant, to each student.

3. Divide students into groups of five. Have each student in a group graph one of the columns of equations so that each group graphs all five columns. Make sure students graph all four equations in their column on the same set of coordinates and label each line with its equation.

Example:

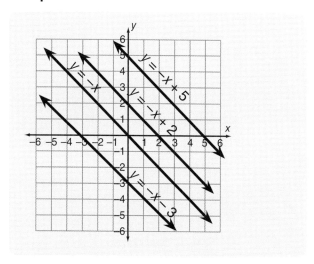

GRAPH PAPER

DISCOVER THE CONSTANT

A	B	C	D	E
$y = x$	$y = -x$	$y = 2x$	$y = \frac{1}{2}x$	$y = -\frac{1}{2}x$
$y = x + 3$	$y = -x + 2$	$y = 2x + 2$	$y = \frac{1}{2}x + 3$	$y = -\frac{1}{2}x + 2$
$y = x - 2$	$y = -x - 3$	$y = 2x - 1$	$y = \frac{1}{2}x - 4$	$y = -\frac{1}{2}x - 2$
$y = x + 6$	$y = -x + 5$	$y = 2x - 6$	$y = \frac{1}{2}x - 1$	$y = -\frac{1}{2}x + 5$

4. Have students work in their groups to discuss the graphs made by each group member. Make sure they focus on each column of graphs one at a time. Make suggestions about questions they can ask about each set of graphs.

Examples:

What is the same about the graphs within each column? The lines are parallel; they all have the same slope.

What is different about the graphs within each column? The numbers being added or subtracted (the constants); the x- and y-intercepts are different.

5. Have students discuss other examples of graphs.

Examples:

Explain how you can graph the equation $y = 3x + 2$. The slope is 3; the y-intercept is 2.

Explain how you can graph the equation $y = mx + b$. The slope is m; the y-intercept is b.

6. Have students graph the equation $y = 2x - 3$ without making a table of values. Ask them to identify the slope and the y-intercept. The slope is 2; the y-intercept is -3.

7. Have students determine the slope and y-intercept in other equations without graphing them.

Examples:

In the equation $y = -3x + 6$, what is the slope of the line? Where does the line intersect the y-axis? The slope is -3; the y-intercept is 6.

In the equation $y = mx + b$, what is the slope? Where does it intersect the y-axis? The slope is m; the y-intercept is b.

NEXT STEPS • Differentiate

5-Day Instructional Plan:
PM 2, page 435—All students, to assess progress

3-Day Instructional Plan:
PM 2, page 435—Students who demonstrate understanding of the concept, to assess progress

PM 1, page 434—Students who need additional support, to assess progress

★ = Includes Problem Solving

Objective 4

Concept Development Activities

CD 5 Determining the Constant on a Graphing Calculator

Use with 5-Day or 3-Day Instructional Plan. In this activity, students graph equations in slope-intercept form and might notice that graphs with the same slope and different y-intercepts are parallel.

MATERIALS

- Blackline Master 59
- Blackline Master 65
- Graphing calculators, one per student

DIRECTIONS

1. Review the following terms with students:

   slope The steepness of a line

   slope-intercept form A linear equation in the form $y = mx + b$

   y-intercept The point where the line crosses the y-axis

2. Divide students into groups of four. Make sure each student has a graphing calculator. Have each student graph one of the following equations on their calculators so that each group graphs all the equations.

   $y = x$ $y = x + 3$ $y = x - 2$ $y = x + 6$

3. Have group members compare their graphs and equations. If students need extra practice, distribute one copy of Blackline Master 59, Graph Paper, and have the group members sketch the graphs, labeling each line with its equation.

4. Ask each group to discuss the similarities and differences of the four graphs.

   Listen for:
   - They have the same slope.
   - They have different y-intercepts.

GRAPH PAPER

Name _____ Date _____

DISCOVER THE CONSTANT

A	B	C	D	E
$y = x$	$y = -x$	$y = 2x$	$y = \frac{1}{2}x$	$y = -\frac{1}{2}x$
$y = x + 3$	$y = -x + 2$	$y = 2x + 2$	$y = \frac{1}{2}x + 3$	$y = -\frac{1}{2}x + 2$
$y = x - 2$	$y = -x - 3$	$y = 2x - 1$	$y = \frac{1}{2}x - 4$	$y = -\frac{1}{2}x - 2$
$y = x + 6$	$y = -x + 5$	$y = 2x - 6$	$y = \frac{1}{2}x - 1$	$y = -\frac{1}{2}x + 5$

5. If students are having difficulty with the concept, distribute one copy of Blackline Master 65, Discover the Constant, to each student. Have each student graph all the equations from one column so that each group graphs all the equations.

6. Ask students to explain how to graph the equation $y = 3x + 2$. Have students sketch the graph on Blackline Master 59, Graph Paper, before they graph it on the graphing calculator. Have students compare the graphs and see if they are the same.

7. Have students sketch several more graphs, and discuss the slope and y-intercept of each graph. Be sure students understand that these equations are written in slope-intercept form.

Sample problems:

$y = x - 3$ slope = 1; y-intercept = –3

$y = 2x + 1$ slope = 2; y-intercept = 1

$y = -2x - 2$ slope = –2; y-intercept = –2

NEXT STEPS • Differentiate

5-Day Instructional Plan:
PM 2, page 435—All students, to assess progress

3-Day Instructional Plan:
PM 2, page 435—Students who demonstrate understanding of the concept, to assess progress

PM 1, page 434—Students who need additional support, to assess progress

Concept Development Activities

CD 6 Writing in Slope-Intercept Form

Use with 5-Day Instructional Plan. In this activity, students change linear equations from standard to slope-intercept form and understand that this makes the equations easier to graph.

MATERIALS

- Blackline Master 59
- **Variation:** Gizmos
  Slope-Intercept Form of a Line—Activity A

DIRECTIONS

1. Review the following terms with students:

   slope The steepness of a line

   slope-intercept form A linear equation in the form $y = mx + b$

   y-intercept The point where the line crosses the *y*-axis

2. Make a transparency of Blackline Master 59, Graph Paper. Review how to graph an equation that is in the slope-intercept form by demonstrating the process on the board or overhead projector.

   Example:

   $y = 3x - 1$
   The *y*-intercept is –1, and the slope is 3.

   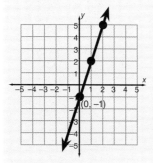

3. Have students plot more graphs using slope-intercept form.

   Sample problems:

   $y = x - 2$
   The *y*-intercept is –2, and the slope is 1.

   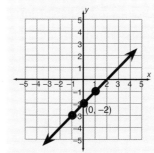

   $y = -2x + 4$
   The *y*-intercept is 4, and the slope is –2.

   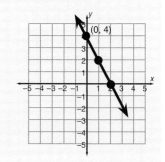

GRAPH PAPER

4. Point out how easy it is to graph equations when they are written in slope-intercept form. Without graphing, have students name the slope and y-intercept for several equations.

Sample problems:

$y = 3x + 1$ $m = 3, b = 1$

$y = -2x + 6$ $m = -2, b = 6$

$y = \frac{1}{2}x + 4$ $m = \frac{1}{2}, b = 4$

$y = 0.3x + 4.3$ $m = 0.3, b = 4.3$

5. Remind students that not all linear equations are written in slope-intercept form. Have students discuss how to take an equation and write it in slope-intercept form. Give students an example equation to work with, and have them find the slope and y-intercept.

Sample problem:

$x + y = 4$

$x + y - x = 4 - x$

$y = 4 - x$

$y = -x + 4$

$m = -1, b = 4$

6. Have students practice converting equations into slope-intercept form. Have them name the slope and the y-intercept for each equation. Discuss the techniques students use.

Sample problems:

$2x - y = 3$ $y = 2x - 3; m = 2, b = -3$

$y - x + 2 = 0$ $y = x - 2; m = 1, b = -2$

$2x + 2y = 8$ $y = -x + 4; m = -1, b = 4$

$2y + x = 6$ $y = -\frac{1}{2}x + 3; m = -\frac{1}{2}, b = 3$

$4x + 2y = 12$ $y = -2x + 6; m = -2, b = 6$

$x - 3y = 9$ $y = \frac{1}{3}x - 3; m = \frac{1}{3}, b = -3$

7. Have students graph the equations on the overhead or board. Remind them to find the y-intercept, then use the slope to find another point.

> **Variation:** Gizmos For this activity use the Gizmo *Slope-Intercept Form of a Line—Activity A* to demonstrate graphing and writing the equations in slope-intercept form.

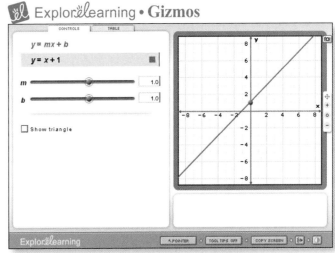

Slope-Intercept Form of a Line—Activity A

NEXT STEPS • Differentiate

5-Day Instructional Plan:
PA 1, page 430—All students, for additional practice

Practice Activities

PA 1 Naming the *y*-Intercept or Slope

Use with 5-Day or 3-Day Instructional Plan. In this activity, given an equation, students find the slope and y-intercept.

MATERIALS

- Blackline Master 66
- Blackline Masters 67–74 or blank cards
- Game markers to cover squares, one per student
- Blank wooden cubes, labeled 1, 2, 3, 1, 2, 3 on the six faces, one per group

DIRECTIONS

1. Review the following terms with students:

   slope The steepness of a line

   slope-intercept form A linear equation in the form $y = mx + b$

   y-intercept The point where the line crosses the *y*-axis

2. Put students in groups of three or four. Distribute one die and one copy of Blackline Master 66, Equation Board, to each group. Distribute one marker to each student to use on the game board.

3. Distribute one set of Blackline Masters 67–74, Name the *y*-Intercept or Slope, to each group, and have students cut out the cards. Make sure copies are made back-to-back: 67 and 68, 69 and 70, 71 and 72, and 73 and 74. Alternatively, have students copy the equations, slopes, and *y*-intercepts onto blank cards. Make sure students copy the correct slope and *y*-intercept with the corresponding equation. Tell students to place the deck of equation cards, equations facing up, in a pile.

4. Explain the game rules to students.

   - The first student, determined by the roll of a die, should take the top card, read the equation, then write the equation on his or her paper in slope-intercept form.

   - The student should then roll the die and move 1, 2, or 3 spaces on the game board. The space on which the

marker lands indicates whether the student should name the slope or *y*-intercept for that equation.

- The student provides the information, then turns the card over to see if he or she is correct. If incorrect, the student moves back to the last space he or she occupied. The card is placed at the bottom of the deck, equation side facing up.

- Students take turns rolling, providing the information, and checking the answers on the back of the cards.

- The game is over when all students reach the finish line.

NEXT STEPS • Differentiate

5-Day Instructional Plan:
PM 3, page 436—All students, to assess progress

3-Day Instructional Plan:
PS 1, page 438—Students who are on the accelerated path, to develop problem-solving skills

PM 3, page 436—Students on the differentiated path who demonstrate understanding of the concept, to assess progress

PM 4, page 437—All other students, to assess progress

EQUATION BOARD

67

Name _____ Date _____

NAME THE *y*-INTERCEPT OR SLOPE

$y = -2x + 7$ $m = -2$ $b = 7$	$x + y = 9$ $m = -1$ $b = 9$	$2x - y = 3$ $m = 2$ $b = -3$
$y = \frac{1}{2}x - 6$ $m = \frac{1}{2}$ $b = -6$	$6 + x = y$ $m = 1$ $b = 6$	$3 + 2y = x$ $m = \frac{1}{2}$ $b = -\frac{3}{2}$
$6x + 6y = 6$ $m = -1$ $b = 1$	$2x + y = 0$ $m = -2$ $b = 0$	$x + 3y = 6$ $m = -\frac{1}{3}$ $b = 2$

Name _____ Date _____

NAME THE *y*-INTERCEPT OR SLOPE *(continued)*

$m = 2$ $b = -3$	$m = -1$ $b = 9$	$m = -2$ $b = 7$
$m = \frac{1}{2}$ $b = -\frac{3}{2}$	$m = 1$ $b = 6$	$m = \frac{1}{2}$ $b = -6$
$m = -\frac{1}{3}$ $b = 2$	$m = -2$ $b = 0$	$m = -1$ $b = 1$

Name _____ Date _____

NAME THE *y*-INTERCEPT OR SLOPE *(continued)*

$y = 0.5x + 3.5$ $m = 0.5$ or $\frac{1}{2}$ $b = 3.5$	$0.5x - y = 2$ $m = 0.5$ or $\frac{1}{2}$ $b = -2$	$x + 0.5y = 1$ $m = -2$ $b = 2$
$y + 4 = x + 2$ $m = 1$ $b = -2$	$3x + 2y = 4$ $m = -\frac{3}{2}$ or $-1\frac{1}{2}$ $b = 2$	$y + 7 = 19 - x$ $m = -1$ $b = 12$
$3y - 4 = 6x + 8$ $m = 2$ $b = 4$	$2y - x = y + 6$ $m = 1$ $b = 6$	$2y + x = 5 - x$ $m = -1$ $b = \frac{5}{2}$

70

Name _____ Date _____

NAME THE *y*-INTERCEPT OR SLOPE *(continued)*

$m = -2$ $b = 2$	$m = 0.5$ or $\frac{1}{2}$ $b = -2$	$m = 0.5$ or $\frac{1}{2}$ $b = 3.5$
$m = -1$ $b = 12$	$m = -\frac{3}{2}$ or $-1\frac{1}{2}$ $b = 2$	$m = 1$ $b = -2$
$m = -1$ $b = \frac{5}{2}$	$m = 1$ $b = 6$	$m = 2$ $b = 4$

NAME THE *y*-INTERCEPT OR SLOPE *(continued)*

$y + 3 = 2x + 4$ $m = 2$ $b = 1$	$x + y = -3$ $m = -1$ $b = -3$	$2x + y = 6$ $m = -2$ $b = 6$
$y + 2y = 6x - 3$ $m = 2$ $b = -1$	$9 + x = y$ $m = 1$ $b = 9$	$\frac{1}{2}y + 2x = -4$ $m = -4$ $b = -8$
$3x + 3y = y + x - 6$ $m = -1$ $b = -3$	$0.6y - 1.2x = 2.4$ $m = 2$ $b = 4$	$0.5x + 0.3y = 0.2y + 0.4$ $m = -5$ $b = 4$

NAME THE *y*-INTERCEPT OR SLOPE *(continued)*

$m = -2$ $b = 6$	$m = -1$ $b = -3$	$m = 2$ $b = 1$
$m = -4$ $b = -8$	$m = 1$ $b = 9$	$m = 2$ $b = -1$
$m = -5$ $b = 4$	$m = 2$ $b = 4$	$m = -1$ $b = -3$

NAME THE *y*-INTERCEPT OR SLOPE *(continued)*

$2x - 3y = 9 - 4y$ $m = -2$ $b = 9$	$6y - 12 = 18x + 6$ $m = 3$ $b = 3$	$x - 2y + 7 = 3$ $m = \frac{1}{2}$ $b = 2$

NAME THE *y*-INTERCEPT OR SLOPE *(continued)*

$m = \frac{1}{2}$ $b = 2$	$m = 3$ $b = 3$	$m = -2$ $b = 9$

★**PA 2** Playing Student Exchange

Use with 5-Day Instructional Plan. In this activity, given an equation in standard form, students put it into slope-intercept form, find the slope and y-intercept, and sketch the graph.

MATERIALS

• Blackline Master 59

DIRECTIONS

1. Review the following terms with students:

   slope The steepness of a line

   slope-intercept form A linear equation in the form $y = mx + b$

   standard form A linear equation in the form $ax + by = c$

   *y***-intercept** The point where the line crosses the y-axis

2. Distribute a few copies of Blackline Master 59, Graph Paper, to each student.

3. Have students write an equation in standard form on the top of the paper, for example, $2x + y = 7$.

4. Have students exchange papers. On the paper they receive, instruct students to put the equation in slope-intercept form, name the slope and y-intercept, and sketch the graph. Circulate among the students, and check their work.

5. Have students use a new piece of graph paper to write another equation in standard form.

6. Have students repeat Step 4. Repeat the same process as time allows.

NEXT STEPS • Differentiate

5-Day Instructional Plan:
PM 4, page 437—All students, to assess progress

★ = Includes Problem Solving

Name _____ Date _____

59

GRAPH PAPER

PM 1 Apply Skills 1

Use with 5-Day or 3-Day Instructional Plan.

MATERIALS

• *Interactive Text*, pages 181–182

DIRECTIONS

1. Have students turn to *Interactive Text*, pages 181–182, Apply Skills 1.

2. Remind students of the key terms: x-*intercept* and y-*intercept.*

3. Monitor student work, and provide feedback as necessary.

   Watch for:

   • Do students understand that the *y*-intercept is where the line crosses the *y*-axis?

   • Do students find the *x*- and *y*-intercepts in an equation by setting the other variable to zero?

NEXT STEPS • Differentiate

👥 5-Day Instructional Plan:
   CD 2, page 422—All students, for additional concept development and problem-solving

   OR

   CD 3, page 423—All students, for additional concept development with calculators

3-Day Instructional Plan:
   PM 2, page 435—All students, to assess progress

Name _____ Date _____

APPLY SKILLS 1

Name the *y*-intercept and *x*-intercept (when *x* = 0 and when *y* = 0) in the graphs below. The *y*-intercept is the *y* value where the graph intersects the *y*-axis. The *x*-intercept is the *x* value where the graph intersects the *x*-axis.

Example:

$y = -\frac{1}{3}x + 1$

Let $x = 0 \rightarrow y = 1$
(0, 1)

Let $y = 0 \rightarrow x = 3$
(3, 0)

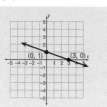

x-intercept = __3__
y-intercept = __1__

1.

y-intercept = __3__
x-intercept = __−1__

2.

y-intercept = __−4__
x-intercept = __2__

Name _____ Date _____

APPLY SKILLS 1 *(continued)*

Find the *y*-intercept and *x*-intercept for the equations.

3. $y = x + 6$
$y = 0 + 6$
y-intercept = 6
$0 - 6 = x + 6 - 6$
x-intercept = −6

4. $y = -2x + 8$
$y = -2(0) + 8$
y-intercept = 8
$-8 + 0 = -2x + 8 - 8$
$\left(-\frac{1}{2}\right)(-8) = -2x\left(-\frac{1}{2}\right)$
x-intercept = 4

5. $y = \frac{1}{2}x + 5$
$y = \frac{x}{2} + 5$
$y = 0 + 5$
y-intercept = 5
$-5 + 0 = \frac{x}{2} + 5 - 5$
$(2)(-5) = \frac{x}{2}(2)$
x-intercept = −10

6. $x + y = -2$
$0 + y = -2$
y-intercept = −2
$x + 0 = -2$
x-intercept = −2

7. $x + 2y = 10$
$0 + 2y = 10$
y-intercept = 5
$x + 0 = 10$
x-intercept = 10

8. $y - 2x = 6$
$y - 0 = 6$
y-intercept = 6
$0 - 2x = 6$
x-intercept = −3

Objective 4
Progress-Monitoring Activities

PM 2 Apply Skills 2

Use with 5-Day or 3-Day Instructional Plan.

MATERIALS

- *Interactive Text*, page 183

DIRECTIONS

1. Have students turn to *Interactive Text*, page 183, Apply Skills 2.

2. Remind students of the key terms: x-*intercept* and y-*intercept.*

3. Monitor student work, and provide feedback as necessary.

   Watch for:
   - Do students understand that knowing an intercept gives them a point on the line?

   - Can students find one intercept given the other intercept and the slope of the line?

NEXT STEPS • Differentiate

5-Day Instructional Plan:
CD 6, page 428—All students, for additional concept development

👥 3-Day Instructional Plan:
PM 4, page 437—Students who are on the accelerated path, to assess progress

PA 1, page 430—Students who are on the differentiated path, for additional practice

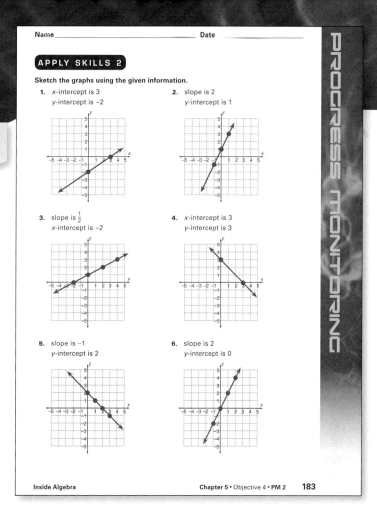

PM 3 Apply Skills 3

Use with 5-Day or 3-Day Instructional Plan.

MATERIALS

- *Interactive Text*, pages 184–185

DIRECTIONS

1. Have students turn to *Interactive Text*, pages 184–185, Apply Skills 3.

2. Remind students of the key terms: *slope*, *y-intercept,* and *slope-intercept form.*

3. Monitor student work, and provide feedback as necessary.

   Watch for:
   - When writing equations in slope-intercept form, do students set the coefficient of *y* to 1?
   - Do students see that the slope is the coefficient of *x* when the equation is in slope-intercept form?

NEXT STEPS • Differentiate

5-Day Instructional Plan:
PA 2, page 433—All students, for additional practice and problem-solving

3-Day Instructional Plan:
PM 4, page 437—All students, to assess progress

Name _____ Date _____

APPLY SKILLS 3

Write the linear equations in slope-intercept form ($y = mx + b$). Name the slope and y-intercept (when $x = 0$).

1. $x + y = 6$
$y = -x + 6$
$m = -1$
$b = 6$

2. $y + 3 = x$
$y = x - 3$
$m = 1$
$b = -3$

3. $4x + 4y = 20$
$y = -x + 5$
$m = -1$
$b = 5$

4. $x - y = 7$
$y = x - 7$
$m = 1$
$b = -7$

5. $x = y + 1$
$y = x - 1$
$m = 1$
$b = -1$

6. $x + 2y + 3 = 0$
$y = -\frac{1}{2}x - \frac{3}{2}$
$m = -\frac{1}{2}$
$b = -\frac{3}{2}$

7. $2x + 3y = 9$
$y = -\frac{2}{3}x + 3$
$m = -\frac{2}{3}$
$b = 3$

8. $\frac{1}{2}y = x - 4$
$y = 2x - 8$
$m = 2$
$b = -8$

9. $0.3x + y = 5$
$y = -0.3x + 5$
$m = -0.3$
$b = 5$

184   Chapter 5 • Objective 4 • PM 3   Inside Algebra

Name _____ Date _____

APPLY SKILLS 3 *(continued)*

Write the equations in slope-intercept form and sketch the graph.

10. $2x - y = 2$

$y = 2x - 2$

11. $2y + 4x - 6 = 0$

$y = -2x + 3$

12. $3y - 3 = 6x$

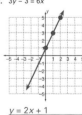

$y = 2x + 1$

13. $x + 0.5y = -1$

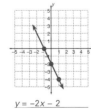

$y = -2x - 2$

Inside Algebra   Chapter 5 • Objective 4 • PM 3   185

Progress-Monitoring Activities

PM 2 Apply Skills 2

Use with 5-Day or 3-Day Instructional Plan.

MATERIALS

- *Interactive Text*, page 183

DIRECTIONS

1. Have students turn to *Interactive Text*, page 183, Apply Skills 2.

2. Remind students of the key terms: x-*intercept* and y-*intercept*.

3. Monitor student work, and provide feedback as necessary.

   Watch for:

   - Do students understand that knowing an intercept gives them a point on the line?

   - Can students find one intercept given the other intercept and the slope of the line?

NEXT STEPS • Differentiate

5-Day Instructional Plan:
CD 6, page 428—All students, for additional concept development

3-Day Instructional Plan:
PM 4, page 437—Students who are on the accelerated path, to assess progress

PA 1, page 430—Students who are on the differentiated path, for additional practice

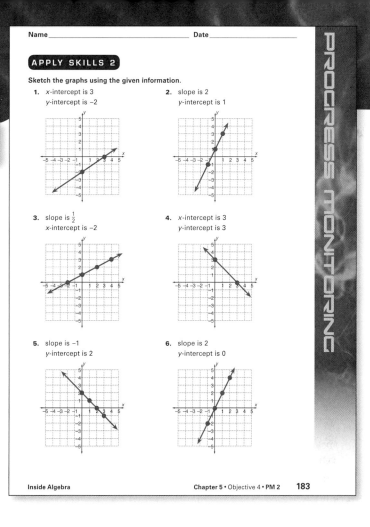

Name _____ Date _____

APPLY SKILLS 2

Sketch the graphs using the given information.

1. x-intercept is 3
   y-intercept is −2

2. slope is 2
   y-intercept is 1

3. slope is $\frac{1}{2}$
   x-intercept is −2

4. x-intercept is 3
   y-intercept is 3

5. slope is −1
   y-intercept is 2

6. slope is 2
   y-intercept is 0

Inside Algebra   Chapter 5 • Objective 4 • PM 2   **183**

Objective 4
Progress-Monitoring Activities

PM 3 Apply Skills 3

Use with 5-Day or 3-Day Instructional Plan.

MATERIALS

- *Interactive Text*, pages 184–185

DIRECTIONS

1. Have students turn to *Interactive Text*, pages 184–185, Apply Skills 3.

2. Remind students of the key terms: *slope*, *y-intercept,* and *slope-intercept form.*

3. Monitor student work, and provide feedback as necessary.

   Watch for:
   - When writing equations in slope-intercept form, do students set the coefficient of *y* to 1?

   - Do students see that the slope is the coefficient of *x* when the equation is in slope-intercept form?

NEXT STEPS • Differentiate

5-Day Instructional Plan:
PA 2, page 433—All students, for additional practice and problem-solving

3-Day Instructional Plan:
PM 4, page 437—All students, to assess progress

APPLY SKILLS 3

Write the linear equations in slope-intercept form ($y = mx + b$). Name the slope and *y*-intercept (when $x = 0$).

1. $x + y = 6$
   $y = -x + 6$
   $m = -1$
   $b = 6$

2. $y + 3 = x$
   $y = x - 3$
   $m = 1$
   $b = -3$

3. $4x + 4y = 20$
   $y = -x + 5$
   $m = -1$
   $b = 5$

4. $x - y = 7$
   $y = x - 7$
   $m = 1$
   $b = -7$

5. $x = y + 1$
   $y = x - 1$
   $m = 1$
   $b = -1$

6. $x + 2y + 3 = 0$
   $y = -\frac{1}{2}x - \frac{3}{2}$
   $m = -\frac{1}{2}$
   $b = -\frac{3}{2}$

7. $2x + 3y = 9$
   $y = -\frac{2}{3}x + 3$
   $m = -\frac{2}{3}$
   $b = 3$

8. $\frac{1}{2}y = x - 4$
   $y = 2x - 8$
   $m = 2$
   $b = -8$

9. $0.3x + y = 5$
   $y = -0.3x + 5$
   $m = -0.3$
   $b = 5$

APPLY SKILLS 3 *(continued)*

Write the equations in slope-intercept form and sketch the graph.

10. $2x - y = 2$

$y = 2x - 2$

11. $2y + 4x - 6 = 0$

$y = -2x + 3$

12. $3y - 3 = 6x$

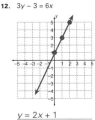

$y = 2x + 1$

13. $x + 0.5y = -1$

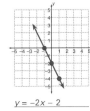

$y = -2x - 2$

Progress-Monitoring Activities

PM 4 Apply Skills 4

Use with 5-Day or 3-Day Instructional Plan.

MATERIALS

- *Interactive Text*, page 186

DIRECTIONS

1. Have students turn to *Interactive Text*, page 186, Apply Skills 4.

2. Remind students of the key terms: *slope*, y-*intercept*, and slope-*intercept form*.

3. Monitor student work, and provide feedback as necessary.

   Watch for:
   - When writing equations in slope-intercept form, do students set the coefficient of *y* to 1?

   - Do students see that the slope is the coefficient of *x* when the equation is in slope-intercept form?

NEXT STEPS • Differentiate

👥 5-Day Instructional Plan:

PS 1, page 438—Students who are on the accelerated path, to develop problem-solving skills

Objective 4 Posttest, page 439—Students who are on the differentiated path

👥 3-Day Instructional Plan:

PA 1, page 430—Students who are on the accelerated path, for additional practice

Objective 4 Posttest, page 439—Students who are on the differentiated path

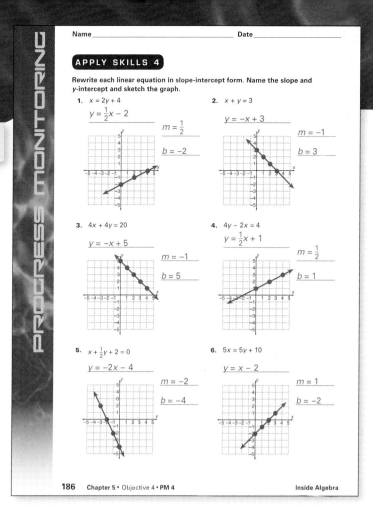

Objective 4
Problem-Solving Activity

★ PS 1 Solving Linear Equations in Real-Life Situations

Use with 5-Day or 3-Day Instructional Plan. In this activity, given a word problem with an equation, students explain what the slope and y-intercept represent.

MATERIALS

- *Interactive Text*, pages 187–188

DIRECTIONS

1. Tell students that in this activity, they answer questions by correctly interpreting an equation.

2. Have students work individually on this assignment. Have students turn to *Interactive Text*, pages 187–188, Long-Distance and Checking, and solve the problems.

3. Notice whether students correctly use dollar signs in Problems 5, 6, 12, and 13.

   Note: This activity tests whether students understand what is really going on in a linear equation and whether students can use equations to solve real-world problems.

NEXT STEPS • Differentiate

5-Day and 3-Day Instructional Plans:
Objective 4 Posttest, page 439—All students

★ = Includes Problem Solving

Name_____ Date_____

LONG-DISTANCE AND CHECKING

The long-distance phone rates for Company D are computed by using the formula $R = 0.07t + 0.26$, where R is the rate and t is the time in minutes. (*Hint*: Rewrite equations as cents instead of dollars.)

1. What is the slope of this line?

   0.07

2. What does the slope represent?

   The rate in dollars per minute
   _____

3. What is the R-intercept for this line? 0.26

4. What does the R-intercept represent?

   The minimum cost of a phone call
   _____

5. What is the rate for a 20-minute phone call?

   $1.66

6. What is the rate for a 30-minute phone call?

   $2.36

5. $R = 0.07(20) + 0.26$
   $R = 1.4 + 0.26$

6. $R = 0.07(30) + 0.26$
   $R = 2.1 + 0.26$

7. Sketch the graph of the equation.

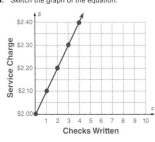

Rate in Cents vs. Time in Minutes

Inside Algebra   Chapter 5 • Objective 4 • PS 1   **187**

Name_____ Date_____

LONG-DISTANCE AND CHECKING (*continued*)

The service charge for a checking account at Bank K is figured by the following formula: $S = 0.1c + 2.00$, where S is the service charge and c is the number of checks written.

8. What is the slope of this line?

   0.1

9. What does the slope represent?

   The cost per check
   _____

10. What is the S-intercept for this line? $2.00

11. What does the S-intercept represent?

    The minimum service charge
    _____

12. What is the service charge if you write 6 checks?

    $2.60

13. What is the service charge if you write 15 checks?

    $3.50

12. $S = 0.1(6) + 2.00$
    $S = 0.6 + 2.00$

13. $S = 0.1(15) + 2.00$
    $S = 1.5 + 2.00$

14. Sketch the graph of the equation.

Service Charge vs. Checks Written

188   Chapter 5 • Objective 4 • PS 1   **Inside Algebra**

Objective 4 Posttest

Discuss with students the key concepts in Objective 4. Following the discussion, administer the Objective 4 Posttest to all students.

Using the Results

• Score the posttest and update the class record card.

• Provide reinforcement for students who do not demonstrate mastery of the concepts through individual or small-group reteaching of key concepts.

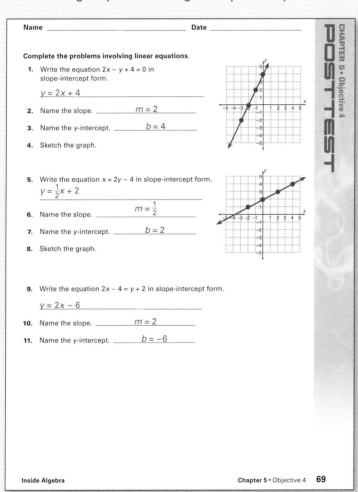

Name _____ Date _____

CHAPTER 5 • Objective 4
POSTTEST

Complete the problems involving linear equations.

1. Write the equation $2x - y + 4 = 0$ in slope-intercept form.

   $y = 2x + 4$

2. Name the slope. _____ $m = 2$

3. Name the y-intercept. _____ $b = 4$

4. Sketch the graph.

5. Write the equation $x = 2y - 4$ in slope-intercept form.

   $y = \frac{1}{2}x + 2$

6. Name the slope. _____ $m = \frac{1}{2}$

7. Name the y-intercept. _____ $b = 2$

8. Sketch the graph.

9. Write the equation $2x - 4 = y + 2$ in slope-intercept form.

   $y = 2x - 6$

10. Name the slope. _____ $m = 2$

11. Name the y-intercept. _____ $b = -6$

Inside Algebra   Chapter 5 • Objective 4   **69**

Objective 5

Use the slope of lines to determine if two lines are parallel or perpendicular.

Objective 5 Pretest

Students complete the Objective 5 Pretest on the same day as the Objective 4 Posttest.

Using the Results

- Score the pretest and update the class record card.
- If the majority of students do not demonstrate mastery of the concepts, use the 5-Day Instructional Plan for Objective 5.
- If the majority of students demonstrate mastery of the concepts, use the 3-Day Instructional Plan for Objective 5.

CHAPTER 5 • Objective 5
PRETEST

Name _____ Date _____

Indicate if the graphs of the two equations in each problem would be parallel, perpendicular, or neither.

1. $y = 2x + 3$
   $y = \frac{1}{2}x + 7$
   _____neither_____

2. $x + y = 4$
   $x - y = 2$
   _____perpendicular_____

3. $2x + 3y = 6$
   $3 - 2x = 3y$
   _____parallel_____

4. $x + y = 3x - 2$
   $2x = y + 4$
   _____parallel_____

5. $x - 2y = 4$
   $x - 2y = 6$
   _____parallel_____

6. $y - 1 = 3x$
   $3y - x = 6$
   _____neither_____
   $y = 3x + 1$
   $y = \frac{1}{3}x + 2$

7. $y = 2x + 8$
   $6 - 2y = x$
   _____perpendicular_____
   $y = 2x + 8$
   $y = -\frac{1}{2}x + 3$

8. $4x + 3y = 12$
   $3y = -4x + 9$
   _____parallel_____

9. $2x + y = 12$
   $\frac{1}{2}y = 6 - x$
   _____neither (same line)_____
   $y = -2x + 12$
   $y = -2x + 12$

10. $x + y = 4$
    $6 - y = x$
    _____parallel_____
    $y = -x + 4$
    $y = -x + 6$

70   Chapter 5 • Objective 5   Inside Algebra

Goals and Activities

Objective 5 Goals

The following activities, when used with the instructional plans on pages 442 and 443, enable students to:

- Determine whether the graphs of the equations $2x + y = 4$ and $y = -2x - 4$ are parallel, perpendicular, or neither
  parallel

- Determine whether the graphs of the equations $x + 3 = y$ and $y + x = 4$ are parallel, perpendicular, or neither
  perpendicular

- Determine whether the graphs of the equations $2y = 4x + 10$ and $2y = x - 6$ are parallel, perpendicular, or neither
  neither

Objective 5 Activities

Concept Development Activities			
CD 1 Determining Which Are Parallel, page 444	**CD 2** Determining Which Are Perpendicular, page 446	**CD 3** Looking at Parallel and Perpendicular Lines on the Graphing Calculator, page 448	*CD 4 Discovering Parallel and Perpendicular Line Graphs, page 450

Practice Activities	
PA 1 Naming the Equation, page 451	PA 2 Playing With Parallel-Perpendicular Cards, page 452

Progress-Monitoring Activities		
PM 1 Apply Skills 1, page 454	**PM 2** Apply Skills 2, page 455	**PM 3** Apply Skills 3, page 456

*Problem-Solving Activities	
*PS 1 Using Slope-Intercept Form, page 457	*PS 2 Plotting Two Ships, page 458

Ongoing Assessment
Posttest Objective 5, page 459
Review Chapter 5 Review, page 460

CD = Concept Development   PM = Progress Monitoring   PS = Problem Solving
PA = Practice Activity   ★ = Includes Problem Solving

5-Day Instructional Plan

Use the 5-Day Instructional Plan when pretest results indicate that students would benefit from a slower pace. This plan is used when the majority of students need more time or did not demonstrate mastery on the pretest. This plan does not include all activities.

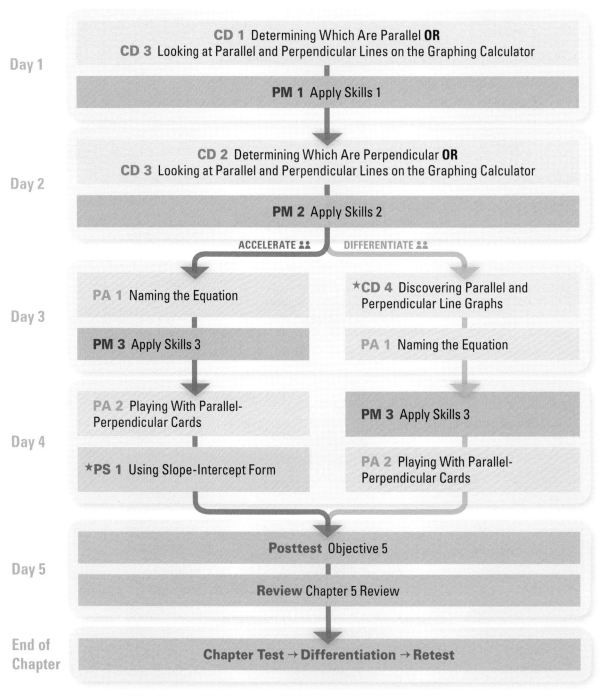

Day 1

CD 1 Determining Which Are Parallel **OR**
CD 3 Looking at Parallel and Perpendicular Lines on the Graphing Calculator

PM 1 Apply Skills 1

Day 2

CD 2 Determining Which Are Perpendicular **OR**
CD 3 Looking at Parallel and Perpendicular Lines on the Graphing Calculator

PM 2 Apply Skills 2

ACCELERATE ⠀ DIFFERENTIATE ⠀

Day 3

PA 1 Naming the Equation

PM 3 Apply Skills 3

★**CD 4** Discovering Parallel and Perpendicular Line Graphs

PA 1 Naming the Equation

Day 4

PA 2 Playing With Parallel-Perpendicular Cards

★**PS 1** Using Slope-Intercept Form

PM 3 Apply Skills 3

PA 2 Playing With Parallel-Perpendicular Cards

Day 5

Posttest Objective 5

Review Chapter 5 Review

End of Chapter

Chapter Test → Differentiation → Retest

CD = Concept Development   PM = Progress Monitoring   PS = Problem Solving
PA = Practice Activity   ★ = Includes Problem Solving

3-Day Instructional Plan

Use the 3-Day Instructional Plan when pretest results indicate that students can move through the activities at a faster pace. This plan is ideal when the majority of students demonstrate mastery on the pretest.

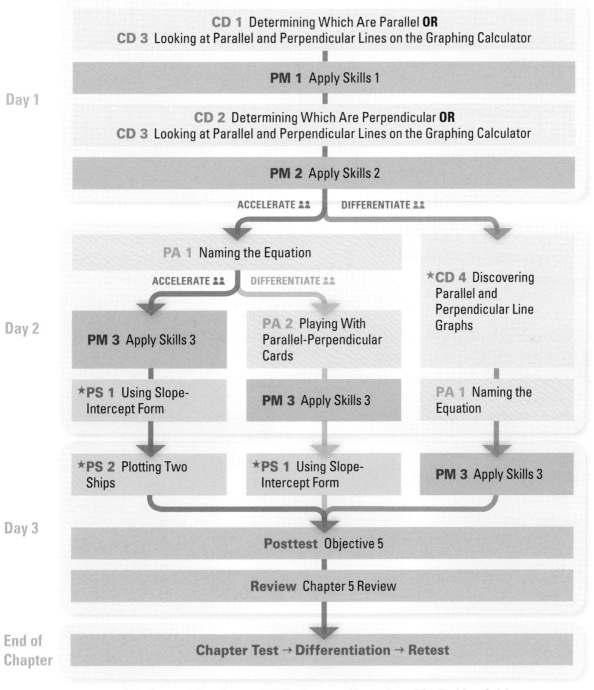

Day 1

CD 1 Determining Which Are Parallel **OR**
CD 3 Looking at Parallel and Perpendicular Lines on the Graphing Calculator

PM 1 Apply Skills 1

CD 2 Determining Which Are Perpendicular **OR**
CD 3 Looking at Parallel and Perpendicular Lines on the Graphing Calculator

PM 2 Apply Skills 2

ACCELERATE 👥   DIFFERENTIATE 👥

Day 2

PA 1 Naming the Equation

ACCELERATE 👥   DIFFERENTIATE 👥

PM 3 Apply Skills 3

★**PS 1** Using Slope-Intercept Form

PA 2 Playing With Parallel-Perpendicular Cards

PM 3 Apply Skills 3

★**CD 4** Discovering Parallel and Perpendicular Line Graphs

PA 1 Naming the Equation

Day 3

★**PS 2** Plotting Two Ships

★**PS 1** Using Slope-Intercept Form

PM 3 Apply Skills 3

Posttest Objective 5

Review Chapter 5 Review

End of Chapter

Chapter Test → Differentiation → Retest

CD = Concept Development   PM = Progress Monitoring   PS = Problem Solving
PA = Practice Activity   ★ = Includes Problem Solving

Objective 5
Concept Development Activities

CD 1 Determining Which Are Parallel

Use with 5-Day or 3-Day Instructional Plan. In this activity, students tell whether two equations describe parallel lines without graphing them, and students find the equation for a line that would be parallel to the given line.

MATERIALS

- Blackline Master 59

DIRECTIONS

1. Review the following terms with students:

   slope The steepness of a line

   y-intercept The point where the line crosses the y-axis

2. Write these three equations on the board or overhead:

   $y = 2x + 3$ $y = 2x$ $y = x + 2$

3. Distribute one copy of Blackline Master 59, Graph Paper, to each student. Instruct students to graph each equation and label each graph with its equation.

4. After students sketch all three graphs, ask them to identify which two graphs are parallel lines. $y = 2x + 3$ and $y = 2x$ are parallel lines

5. Ask students to discuss whether they can tell if the graphs of two linear equations will be parallel without making the graphs.

   Listen for:
   - You can tell if the graphs will be parallel without graphing them.
   - If two linear equations have the same slope and different y-intercepts, they will be parallel when graphed.

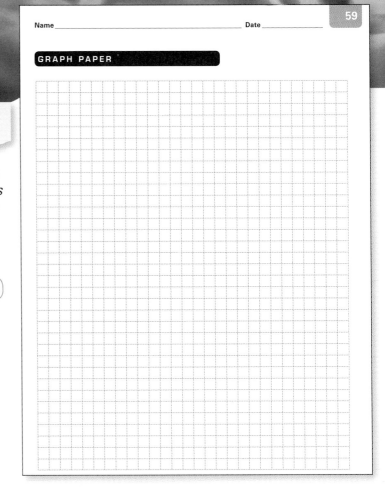

Name _____ Date _____

GRAPH PAPER

6. Give students several linear equations, and have students identify equations with parallel graphs. Have several students give their choices, then have students sketch the graphs to see if they are correct.

   Sample problem:

   $y = x + 4$

   $y = -x + 3$

   $y = x - 1$

   $y = x + 4$ and $y = x - 1$ are parallel

7. Name several more equations, and ask students to name an equation that would have a parallel graph to each of the equations. Sketch some of the graphs from students' equations to show whether the graphs are parallel.

Sample problems:

$y = 3x$ $y = 3x + 4$, or any equation with a slope of 3

$y = -x + 2$ $y = -x - 2$, or any equation with a slope of -1

$y = \frac{1}{2}x + 4$ $y = \frac{1}{2}x$, or any equation with a slope of $\frac{1}{2}$

NEXT STEPS • Differentiate

5-Day and 3-Day Instructional Plans:
PM 1, page 454—All students, to assess progress

Concept Development Activities

CD 2 Determining Which Are Perpendicular

Use with 5-Day or 3-Day Instructional Plan. In this activity, students tell whether two equations describe perpendicular lines without graphing them, and students find the equation for a line that would be perpendicular to the given line.

MATERIALS

- Blackline Master 59

DIRECTIONS

1. Review the following term with students:

   slope The steepness of a line

2. Write these three equations on the board or overhead:

   $y = 2x + 1$ $y = x + 1$ $y = -\frac{1}{2}x + 2$

3. Distribute one copy of Blackline Master 59, Graph Paper, to each student. Instruct students to graph each equation and label each graph with its equation.

4. After students sketch all three graphs, ask them to identify which two graphs are perpendicular lines.

   $y = 2x + 1$ and $y = -\frac{1}{2}x + 2$ are perpendicular lines

5. Ask students to discuss whether they can tell if the graphs of two linear equations will be perpendicular without making the graphs.

   Listen for:
   - You can tell if the graphs will be perpendicular without graphing them.
   - If two linear equations have slopes that are negative reciprocals, or the product of the slopes is –1, they will be perpendicular when graphed.

6. Give students several linear equations, and have students identify equations with perpendicular graphs. Have several students give their choices, then have students sketch the graphs to see if they are correct.

   Sample problem:

   $y = 3x + 2$

   $y = -\frac{1}{3}x + 1$

   $y = \frac{1}{3}x - 1$

   $y = 3x + 2$ and $y = -\frac{1}{3}x + 1$ are perpendicular

7. Name several more equations, and ask students to name an equation that would be perpendicular to each one. Sketch some of the graphs from students' equations to show whether the graphs are perpendicular.

Sample problems:

$y = x - 1$ $y = -x + 2$, or any linear equation with a slope of -1

$y = \frac{1}{2}x + 3$ $y = -2x + 1$, or any linear equation with a slope of -2

$y = 4x + 6$ $y = -\frac{1}{4}x - 2$, or any linear equation with a slope of $-\frac{1}{4}$

$y = -2x + 1$ $y = \frac{1}{2}x$, or any linear equation with a slope of $\frac{1}{2}$

NEXT STEPS • Differentiate

5-Day and 3-Day Instructional Plans:
PM 2, page 455—All students, to assess progress

Concept Development Activities

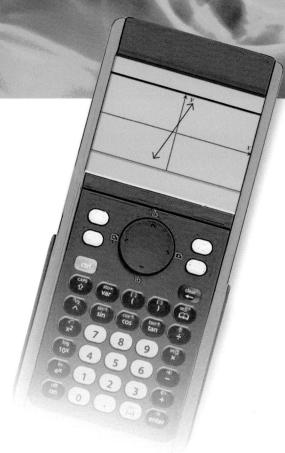

CD 3 Looking at Parallel and Perpendicular Lines on the Graphing Calculator

Use with 5-Day or 3-Day Instructional Plan. In this activity, students tell whether two equations describe parallel or perpendicular lines without graphing them, and students find the equation for a line that would be parallel or perpendicular to the given line.

MATERIALS

• Graphing calculators

DIRECTIONS

1. Review the following terms with students:

   slope The steepness of a line

   y-intercept The point where the line crosses the y-axis

2. Write the equations $y = 2x - 1$ and $y = 2x + 3$ on the board. Have students use graphing calculators to make the graphs of the two equations on the same axes.

3. Ask students what they notice about the graphs.

   Listen for:
   • They are parallel.
   • They do not intersect.

4. Ask students to explain why they think the graphs of these equations are parallel.

   Listen for:
   • They have the same slope.
   • They have different y-intercepts.

5. Give students the equation $y = -x + 1$ to graph using graphing calculators. Have students write an equation of a line they think will be parallel to it. Have them use graphing calculators to put the graph on the same axes to check their equation. $y = -x - 3$, or any linear equation with a slope of -1

6. Name several more linear equations, and have students name a parallel equation for each linear equation given. Have students graph each pair on their graphing calculators to see if they are correct.

Sample problems:

$y = 3x + 1$ $y = 3x + 4$, or any linear equation with a slope of 3

$y = x$ $y = x + 3$, or any linear equation with a slope of 1

$y = -\frac{1}{2}x + 2$ $y = -\frac{1}{2}x$, or any linear equation with a slope of $-\frac{1}{2}$

7. Write $y = 2x + 1$ and $y = -\frac{1}{2}x - 2$ on the board, and have students make the graphs using the graphing calculators.

8. Ask students what they notice about the graphs. Make sure they recognize that the graphs are perpendicular. Ask students why they think the graphs of these equations are perpendicular.

   Listen for:
   • The slopes are negative reciprocals.
   • The product of the slopes is -1.

9. Give students the equation $y = x + 3$ to graph using graphing calculators. Have students write an equation of a line they think will be perpendicular to it, and have them use their graphing calculators to put the graph on the same axes to check their equation. $y = -x + 2$, or any linear equation with a slope of -1

10. Give students several equations, and have them name an equation they think will have a perpendicular graph to each equation given. Have students graph each pair on a graphing calculator to see if they are correct.

Sample problems:

$y = 3x + 1$ $y = -\frac{1}{3}x + 1$, or any linear equation with a slope of $-\frac{1}{3}$

$y = -x + 2$ $y = x + 5$, or any linear equation with a slope of 1

$y = -\frac{1}{2}x + 1$ $y = 2x - 3$, or any linear equation with a slope of 2

$y = 2x + 14$ $y = -\frac{1}{2}x + 4$, or any linear equation with a slope of $-\frac{1}{2}$

NEXT STEPS • Differentiate

👥 5-Day and 3-Day Instructional Plans:
PM 1, page 454—Students who completed this activity instead of CD 1, to assess progress

PM 2, page 455—Students who completed this activity instead of CD 2, to assess progress

Concept Development Activities

★ CD 4 Discovering Parallel and Perpendicular Line Graphs

Use with 5-Day or 3-Day Instructional Plan. In this activity, students discover rules for how the equations of parallel and perpendicular lines in slope-intercept form are related.

MATERIALS

- Blackline Master 59

DIRECTIONS

1. Review the following terms with students:

   slope The steepness of a line

   slope-intercept form A linear equation in the form $y = mx + b$

   ***y*-intercept** The point where the line crosses the y-axis

2. Divide students into groups of three or four. Distribute one copy of Blackline Master 59, Graph Paper, to each group.

3. Instruct groups to write an equation in slope-intercept form, where m and b are integers. Tell them to sketch the graph of the equation.

4. Have groups draw any line parallel to the graphed line and find the equation for the parallel line.

5. Tell groups to analyze the two equations and write a rule telling when the graphs of two linear equations will be parallel lines. Slopes are the same, different y-intercepts.

6. Have two or three groups present their rule and give examples. Discuss the accuracy of the generalizations with the class.

7. Repeat Step 3 with the class.

8. Have groups draw any line perpendicular to the graphed line and find the equation for the perpendicular line.

9. Tell groups to analyze the two equations and write a rule telling when the graphs of two linear equations will be perpendicular lines. Slopes are negative reciprocals, or the product of the slopes is –1.

10. Have two or three groups present their rule and give examples. Discuss the accuracy of the generalizations with the class.

NEXT STEPS • Differentiate

5-Day and 3-Day Instructional Plans:
PA 1, page 451—All students, for additional practice

Name _____ Date _____

59

GRAPH PAPER

★ = Includes Problem Solving

Practice Activities

PA 1 Naming the Equation

Use with 5-Day or 3-Day Instructional Plan. In this activity, given the equation for a line, students find the equation for another line that would be parallel or perpendicular.

MATERIALS

- *Interactive Text*, page 189
- Blackline Master 59

DIRECTIONS

1. Review the following terms with students:

   slope-intercept form A linear equation in the form $y = mx + b$

   y-intercept The point where the line crosses the y-axis

2. Have students turn to *Interactive Text*, page 189, Name the Equation.

3. Have students look at Problems 1 and 2. Tell students to write equations in the other two columns that satisfy the headings.

4. Discuss correct responses for the first two problems. Make a transparency of Blackline Master 59, Graph Paper, and graph some equations if there is disagreement on correct responses.

5. Direct students to the equation in Problem 3. Review writing equations in slope-intercept form, then have students write equations in the other two columns that satisfy the headings.

6. Have students look at Problems 4 and 5. Point out that the perpendicular equation is given and the other two columns must be found. Demonstrate how to work backward to find the equation in Problem 4. Have students complete Problem 5 on their own.

7. Have students complete the table. They should write all the answers in slope-intercept form.

NAME THE EQUATION

Follow your teacher's instructions to fill in the table.

	Equation	Parallel Equation	Perpendicular Equation
1.	$y = x + 3$	$y = x - 1$	$y = -x + 2$
2.	$y = 2x - 1$	$y = 2x + 3$	$y = -\frac{1}{2}x + 4$
3.	$y = 2x + 4$	$y = 2x + 2$	$y = -\frac{1}{2}x + 1$
4.	$y = -3x - 5$	$y = -3x - 1$	$y = \frac{1}{3}x + 1$
5.	$y = -x - 7$	$y = -x + 1$	$x + 1 = y$
6.	$x + y = 6$	$y = -x$	$y = x + 3$
7.	$y = 2x + 4$	$y - 2x = 3$	$y = -\frac{1}{2}x - 9$
8.	$y = 2x - 2$	$y = 2x - 8$	$2y + x = 5$
9.	$\frac{1}{2}y + x = 3$	$y = -2x + 6$	$y = \frac{1}{2}x + 0$
10.	$y = 2x - 1$	$y + 6 = 2x + 1$	$y = -\frac{1}{2}x - 5$
11.	$2x + y = x - 1$	$y = -x + 3$	$y = x$
12.	$y = -2x - 5$	$y = -2x - 1$	$y + 3 = \frac{1}{2}x - 1$
13.	$y = -x + 8$	$2x + 2y = 6$	$y = x + 2$

The value of the y-intercept will vary.

NEXT STEPS • Differentiate

5-Day Instructional Plan:
PM 3, page 456—All students, to assess progress

3-Day Instructional Plan:
PM 3, page 456—Students on the accelerated path who demonstrate understanding, to assess progress

PA 2, page 452—Students on the accelerated path who need additional practice

PM 3, page 456—Students who are on the differentiated path, to assess progress

Practice Activities

PA 2 Playing With Parallel-Perpendicular Cards

Use with 5-Day or 3-Day Instructional Plan. In this activity, students identify parallel and perpendicular lines by looking at the linear equation for each line.

MATERIALS

- Blackline Masters 75–76 or blank cards

DIRECTIONS

1. Review the following terms with students:

   slope-intercept form A linear equation in the form $y = mx + b$

   y-intercept The point where the line crosses the y-axis

2. Divide students into groups of three or four. Distribute one set of Blackline Masters 75–76, Parallel-Perpendicular Cards, to each group. Have students cut out the cards. Alternatively, have groups write the equations on blank cards.

3. Have groups shuffle their own decks and deal four cards to each student. Tell students to use paper and pencil to put the equations in slope-intercept form.

4. Explain the game rules to students.

   - The dealer starts play.

   - On each student's turn, the other students each choose one card to lay faceup in front of them.

   - The goal is for the student whose turn it is to play one of the cards in his or her hand on one of the equations showing. He or she can play a card where the equation will be parallel or perpendicular to the equation showing.

   - The student whose turn it is states if the equation's graph is parallel or perpendicular to the one given, and why.

   - The group checks that the card played is correct.

   - If a student cannot play or is incorrect, that student should draw a card from the deck.

PARALLEL-PERPENDICULAR CARDS

$y = x + 3$	$y = x - 2$
$y = -x + 4$	$x + 2y = 4$
$x = 6 - 2y$	$3 + y = 2x$
$x + y = 1$	$x = 3 - y$
$y = x + 2$	$2x - y = 3$
$y = 2x$	$2 - 2y = x$
$y = \frac{1}{2}x + 1$	$2y - x = 2$
$y = -2x$	$2y - x = 4$

PARALLEL-PERPENDICULAR CARDS *(continued)*

$x = 6 + 2y$	$y + 2x = 1$
$y - 3x = 2$	$3x = 4 + y$
$3y + x = 6$	$3x + y = 0$
$4 - 3x = y$	$x = 9 + 3y$
$x + 3y = 6$	$3y = 2 - x$
$y - 3x = 2$	$y = \frac{2}{3}x + 1$
$3y - x = 3$	$y + 3x = 2$

- Play continues clockwise.
- The first player to play all his or her cards is the winner.

NEXT STEPS • Differentiate

5-Day Instructional Plan:

PS 1, page 457—Students who are on the accelerated path, to develop problem-solving skills

Objective 5 Posttest, page 459—Students who are on the differentiated path

3-Day Instructional Plan:

PM 3, page 456—All students, to assess progress

Progress-Monitoring Activities

PM 1 Apply Skills 1

Use with 5-Day or 3-Day Instructional Plan.

MATERIALS

- *Interactive Text*, page 190

DIRECTIONS

1. Have students turn to *Interactive Text*, page 190, Apply Skills 1.

2. Remind students of the key term: *slope*.

3. Monitor student work, and provide feedback as necessary.

   Watch for:

   - Do students determine which lines are parallel without drawing the graph?

   - Do students notice that any line is parallel to an infinite number of other lines?

NEXT STEPS • Differentiate

👥 5-Day and 3-Day Instructional Plans:

CD 2, page 446—All students, for additional concept development

OR

CD 3, page 448—All students, for additional concept development with calculators

---

Name _____ Date _____

APPLY SKILLS 1

1. Write the equations for the lines on the graph that are parallel.

   $y = 2x + 1, y = 2x - 2$

2. Can you tell by looking at the equations if the graph of the two lines will be parallel?

   Yes, they have the same slope.

In each problem below, circle the two equations whose graphs will be parallel. Sketch the graphs if necessary.

3. (y = x + 4)	(y = x − 10)	y = 4 − x
4. y = 3x + 6	(y = 2x − 8)	(y = 2x − 6)
5. (y = −x + 1)	y = x + 1	(y = −x + 3)
6. (x + y = 2)	(y = 3 − x)	y = x + 2
7. (2x − y = 4)	y = 4 + x	(y = 2x + 4)
8. (7x = y)	(y = 7x + 2)	y = 2x − 7

Name an equation whose graph will be parallel to the graph of the equation given.

9. $y = 2x \bigcirc 1$
   $y = 2x + b$

10. $y = 4x + \bigcirc 1$
    $y = 4x + b$

11. $x + y = \bigcirc 1$
    $y = -x + b$

12. $y = \bigcirc 3 - x$
    $y = -x + b$

13. $\bigcirc 4 - y = x$
    $y = -x + b$

14. $y = 9x + \bigcirc 0$
    $y = 9x + b$

Answers will vary based on student's choice for the variable *b*; any real number except the circled one is a correct choice.

Objective 5
Progress-Monitoring Activities

PM 2 Apply Skills 2

Use with 5-Day or 3-Day Instructional Plan.

MATERIALS

- *Interactive Text*, page 191

DIRECTIONS

1. Have students turn to *Interactive Text*, page 191, Apply Skills 2.

2. Remind students of the key term: *slope.*

3. Monitor student work, and provide feedback as necessary.

   Watch for:
   - Do students remember the concept of reciprocals?

   - Do students notice that any line is perpendicular to an infinite number of other lines?

NEXT STEPS • Differentiate

👥 5-Day and 3-Day Instructional Plans:

PA 1, page 451—Students who demonstrate understanding of the concept, for additional practice

CD 4, page 450—Students who need additional concept development

---

Name _____ Date _____

APPLY SKILLS 2

1. Write the equations for the lines on the graph that are perpendicular.

   $y = 2x - 1$, $y = -\frac{1}{2}x + \frac{3}{2}$

2. What relationship do you see between the slopes of lines that are perpendicular?

   The slopes are negative reciprocals of each other.

In each problem below, circle the two equations whose graphs will be perpendicular. Sketch the graphs if necessary.

3. $(y = 3x + 1)$	$y = x + 3$	$(y = -\frac{1}{3}x + 2)$
4. $(y = x + 4)$	$(y = -x + 1)$	$y = 2x - 3$
5. $(y = 2x + 1)$	$y = \frac{1}{2}x - 1$	$(y = -\frac{1}{2}x + 2)$
6. $(y + 2x = 4)$	$y - 2x = -4$	$(y = \frac{1}{2}x + 1)$
7. $(3 - 2y = x)$	$y = -2x + 4$	$(2x - y = 5)$
8. $y + x = \frac{1}{7}$	$(y = 7x - 3)$	$(y + \frac{1}{7}x = 1)$

Name an equation whose graph will be perpendicular to the graph of the equation given.

9. $y = \frac{1}{2}x + 3$
   $y = -2x + b$

10. $y = x + 1$
   $y = -x + b$

11. $y = \frac{1}{4}x - 4$
   $y = -4x + b$

12. $2x - y = 4$
   $y = -\frac{1}{2}x + b$

13. $x - 2y = 8$
   $y = -2x + b$

14. $5y + x = 10$
   $y = 5x + b$

Answers will vary based on student's choice for the variable *b*; any real number is correct.

Objective 5
Progress-Monitoring Activities

PM 3 Apply Skills 3

Use with 5-Day or 3-Day Instructional Plan.

MATERIALS

- *Interactive Text*, page 192

DIRECTIONS

1. Have students turn to *Interactive Text*, page 192, Apply Skills 3.

2. Remind students of the key term: *slope*.

3. Monitor student work, and provide feedback as necessary.

   Watch for:
   - Do students recognize functions as being parallel or perpendicular before graphing?
   - Do students see that the product of the slopes of perpendicular lines will be –1?

NEXT STEPS • Differentiate

5-Day Instructional Plan:

PA 2, page 452—All students, for additional practice

3-Day Instructional Plan:

PS 1, page 457—Students who are on the accelerated path, to develop problem-solving skills

PS 1, page 457—Students on the differentiated path who complete this activity on Day 2, to develop problem-solving skills

Objective 5 Posttest, page 459—Students who complete this activity on Day 3

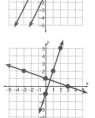

Name _____ Date _____

APPLY SKILLS 3

Answer the questions about each pair of equations.

1. Sketch the graphs of these two equations:

   $y = 2x - 1$

   $y = 2x + 3$

2. What can be said about the graphs of the equations in Problem 1?

   They are parallel.

3. Sketch the graphs of these two equations:

   $y = 3x - 1$

   $y = -\frac{1}{3}x + 1$

4. What can be said about the graphs of the equations in Problem 3?

   They are perpendicular.

Tell whether each pair of equations below is parallel or perpendicular.

5. $y = x + 1$ $y = -x + 2$ Perpendicular

6. $y = \frac{1}{2}x - 1$ $y = -2x + 3$ Perpendicular

7. $y = 5x + 4$ $y = 5x + \frac{1}{5}$ Parallel

8. $x + 2y = 4$ $2x - y = 4$ Perpendicular

9. Sketch the graphs of these two equations:

   $y = 2x - 3$

   $9 + 3y = 6x$

10. What can be said about the graphs of the equations in Problem 9?

    They are the same line.

192   Chapter 5 • Objective 5 • PM 1   Inside Algebra

Objective 5
Problem-Solving Activities

★PS 1 Using Slope-Intercept Form

Use with 5-Day or 3-Day Instructional Plan. In this activity, given the equation of a line, students find the equation of another line that is parallel or perpendicular and passes through a given point.

MATERIALS

- *Interactive Text*, page 193

DIRECTIONS

1. Review the following terms with students:

   slope The steepness of a line

   slope-intercept form A linear equation in the form $y = mx + b$

   y-intercept The point where the line crosses the y-axis

2. Tell students that in this activity, they write the equation of a line in slope-intercept form, given a point on the line. Explain that they also write the equation for a line that is parallel or perpendicular to the requested equation.

3. Direct students to work individually on this assignment. Have students turn to *Interactive Text*, page 193, Slope-Intercept, and solve the problems.

4. Have students begin each problem by finding the slope of the given line. Point out to students that writing the equation in slope-intercept form makes the task easier. Explain that if the line they want is parallel, this gives them the slope; if the line is perpendicular, they take the negative inverse of the slope.

   Note: Writing the equation in slope-intercept form gives a new equation with three variables (x, y, b). Make sure students understand that they should now plug in the given (x, y) coordinates and solve for b.

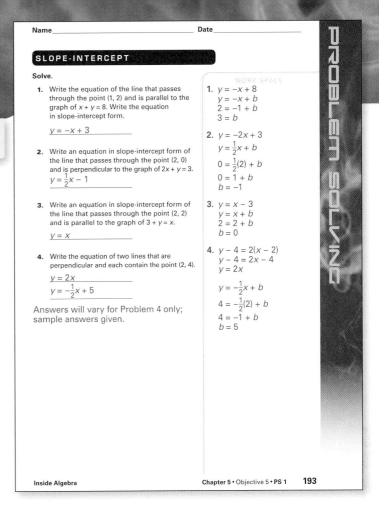

NEXT STEPS • Differentiate

5-Day Instructional Plan:
Objective 5 Posttest, page 459—All students

3-Day Instructional Plan:
PS 2, page 458—Students who are on the accelerated path, to develop problem-solving skills

Objective 5 Posttest, page 459—Students who are on the differentiated path

★ = Includes Problem Solving

Problem-Solving Activities

★PS 2 Plotting Two Ships

Use with 3-Day Instructional Plan. In this activity, given the graph of a line, students find the equation for a parallel line and a perpendicular line that intercepts the original line at a given point.

MATERIALS

- *Interactive Text*, page 194

DIRECTIONS

1. Review the following term with students:

   slope The steepness of a line

2. Tell students that in this activity, they use their knowledge of parallel and perpendicular lines to solve real-world problems.

3. Direct students to work individually on this assignment. Have students turn to *Interactive Text*, page 194, Two Ships, and solve the problems.

4. Circulate around the room to make sure students are completing the activity correctly. On Problem 1, ensure that students see any choice for *b* is valid, with the exception of $b = 2$. Notice if the slope of Ship C's course is the negative inverse of that for Ship B.

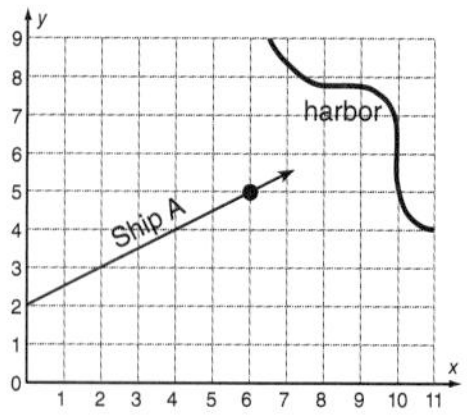

NEXT STEPS • Differentiate

3-Day Instructional Plan:
Objective 5 Posttest, page 459—All students

Name _____ Date _____

TWO SHIPS

Use the graph to answer the questions.

1. Two ships are traveling to the same destination. To be safe, the ships are given parallel routes so they will not collide if one goes faster than the other. Ship A has the route shown in the graph. What is the equation for a good route for ship B?

   $y = \frac{1}{2}x + b \qquad b \neq 2$

2. If two ships are going to cross each other's path, the best way is to cross at a 90° angle so the time is minimized when they could collide. If ship C is going to intersect ship A's path at (6, 5), what is the equation of the route ship C should follow through the point (6,5)?

   $y = -2x + 17$

WORK SPACE

2. $y = \frac{1}{2}x + 2$
   $y = -2x + b$
   $5 = -2(6) + b$
   $5 = -12 + b$
   $17 = b$

194   Chapter 5 • Objective 5 • PS 2   Inside Algebra

★ = Includes Problem Solving

Objective 5 Posttest

Discuss with students the key concepts in Objective 5. Following the discussion, administer the Objective 5 Posttest to all students.

Using the Results

• Score the posttest and update the class record card.

• Provide reinforcement for students who do not demonstrate mastery of the concepts through individual or small-group reteaching of key concepts.

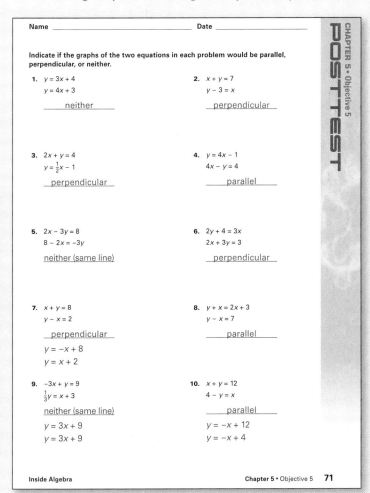

Name _____   Date _____

CHAPTER 5 • Objective 5
POSTTEST

Indicate if the graphs of the two equations in each problem would be parallel, perpendicular, or neither.

1. $y = 3x + 4$
    $y = 4x + 3$

    _____ neither _____

2. $x + y = 7$
    $y - 3 = x$

    _____ perpendicular _____

3. $2x + y = 4$
    $y = \frac{1}{2}x - 1$

    _____ perpendicular _____

4. $y = 4x - 1$
    $4x - y = 4$

    _____ parallel _____

5. $2x - 3y = 8$
    $8 - 2x = -3y$

    _____ neither (same line) _____

6. $2y + 4 = 3x$
    $2x + 3y = 3$

    _____ perpendicular _____

7. $x + y = 8$
    $y - x = 2$

    _____ perpendicular _____
    $y = -x + 8$
    $y = x + 2$

8. $y + x = 2x + 3$
    $y - x = 7$

    _____ parallel _____

9. $-3x + y = 9$
    $\frac{1}{3}y = x + 3$

    _____ neither (same line) _____
    $y = 3x + 9$
    $y = 3x + 9$

10. $x + y = 12$
    $4 - y = x$

    _____ parallel _____
    $y = -x + 12$
    $y = -x + 4$

Inside Algebra   Chapter 5 • Objective 5   **71**

Chapter Review

Chapter 5 Review

Use with 5-Day or 3-Day Instructional Plan. In this activity, students review key chapter concepts prior to taking the Chapter Test.

MATERIALS

- *Interactive Text*, pages 195–196

DIRECTIONS

1. Have students turn to *Interactive Text*, pages 195–196, Chapter 5 Review.

2. Have students complete the review individually or in small groups. If the activity is completed individually, provide time for students to discuss their solutions as a class or in small groups.

3. Monitor student work, and provide feedback when necessary. If students complete the review quickly, pair them with other students or groups to discuss their answers.

Name _____ Date _____

OBJECTIVE 1

Solve the problems involving slope.

1. Based on the graph, what is the slope of the line?

   $m = 2$

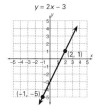

$y = 2x - 3$

2. Find the slope of a line that contains the points (0, –2), (3, 1).

   $m = \dfrac{(-2 - 1)}{(0 - 3)} = \dfrac{-3}{-3} = 1$

3. Find the slope of a line that contains the points (0, –2), (2, –8).

   $m = \dfrac{[-2 - (-8)]}{(0 - 2)} = \dfrac{6}{-2} = -3$

OBJECTIVE 2

Find the equation of each line from the given information. Write the equation in standard form. Show your work.

4. Write in standard form the equation of a line that has a slope of 3 and contains the point (0, 4).

   $3x - y = -4$

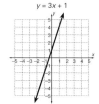

$y = 3x + 1$

5. Write in standard form the equation of a line that contains the two points (0, 3) and (4, 5).

   $x - 2y = -6$

6. Given the graph to the right, what is the equation of the line in standard form?

   $3x - y = -1$

Name _____ Date _____

OBJECTIVE 3

Draw the best-fit line, if it exists, and name the equation of the best-fit line. Write the equation in slope-intercept form. Answers will vary based on line.

7.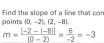

   $y = x - 2$

8.

   $y = -2x + 3$

OBJECTIVE 4

Answer the questions about the equation.

9. Write the equation $y - 4 = 2x$ in slope-intercept form. $y = 2x + 4$

10. What is the slope? ____2____

11. Sketch the graph.

OBJECTIVE 5

Indicate if the graphs of the two equations in each problem would be parallel, perpendicular, or neither.

12. $2x + y = 3$
    $2x + y = 7$
    _____parallel_____

13. $x = y + 4$
    $y - x + 1 = 0$
    _____parallel_____

14. $x + 2y = 6$
    $2x = y - 1$
    ___perpendicular___

5

CHAPTER

Ongoing Assessment

Chapter 5 Test, Form A

MATERIALS

- *Assessment Book*, pages 73–74

DIRECTIONS

1. Have students turn to *Assessment Book*, pages 73–74, Chapter 5 Test, Form A. Administer the Chapter Test to all students.

2. Score the test by objective and update the class record card.

3. Use the test data to determine differentiation needs.

Name _____ Date _____

Solve the problems involving slope.

1. What is the slope of the line?

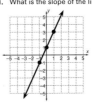

$m = 2$

2. Find the slope of a line that contains the points (5, 6), (1, 4).

$$m = \frac{4-6}{1-5} = \frac{-2}{-4} = \frac{1}{2}$$

Objective 2

Find the equation of each line from the given information. Write the equation in standard form. Show your work.

3.

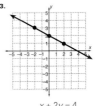

$x + 2y = 4$

4. The line that contains the points (3, 0) and (4, 6).

$$6x - y = 18$$
$$m = \frac{6-0}{4-3} = \frac{6}{1} = 6$$
$$y = 6x - 18$$

Name _____ Date _____

Objective 3

Draw the best-fit line, if it exists, and name the equation of the best-fit line. Write the equation in slope-intercept form. Answers will vary based on line.

5.

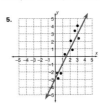

$y = 2x - 3$

6.

$y = -\frac{1}{2}x + 1$

Objective 4

Complete the problems involving the linear equation.

7. Write the equation $y - 2x = -3$ in slope-intercept form.

$y = 2x - 3$

8. Name the slope. $m = 2$

9. Name the y-intercept. $b = -3$

10. Sketch the graph.

Objective 5

Indicate if the graphs of the two equations in each problem would be parallel, perpendicular, or neither.

11. $y = 2x + 3$
    $x + 2y = -8$

    perpendicular

12. $6x - 2y = -8$
    $y + 2 = 3x$

    parallel

Chapter 5 • Ongoing Assessment   461

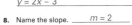

Differentiation

MATERIALS

- **Gizmos** *Distance-Time Graphs* Gizmo
- **Gizmos** Extension Activity pages
- **Gizmos** *Slope-Intercept Form of a Line—Activity A* Gizmo
- **Gizmos** Reinforcement Activity page
- Additional Activities
- Algebra Skill Builders for Chapter 5
- Chapter Test, Form B

DIRECTIONS

1. Review Chapter 5 Test, Form A, with the class.

2. Use the results from Chapter 5 Test, Form A, to identify students for reinforcement or extension.

3. After students have been identified for extension or reinforcement, break students into appropriate groups. See pages 463–465 for detailed differentiated instruction.

Differentiation Planner

Students who demonstrated mastery on every objective posttest and scored 80% or above on the chapter test

Extend learning using:

- **Gizmos** Use the *Distance-Time Graphs* Gizmo with the Extension Activity. Have students work in pairs or individually to complete the activity.

Students who demonstrated mastery on every objective posttest but scored below 80% on the chapter test

Reinforce learning using:

- **Gizmos** Use the *Slope-Intercept Form of a Line—Activity A* Gizmo with the Reinforcement Activity. Have students work in pairs or small groups to complete the activity.
- Additional Activities from the online resources.
- Algebra Skill Builders for Chapter 5 from the online resources.

Students who did not demonstrate mastery on any or all of the objective posttests or the chapter test

Reinforce learning using:

- **Gizmos** Present the *Slope-Intercept Form of a Line—Activity A* Gizmo to students in small groups using the instruction on page 465.
- Additional Activities from the online resources.
- Algebra Skill Builders for Chapter 5 from the online resources.

Retest—Administer Chapter 5 Test, Form B, from the online resources to students who scored below 80 percent on Form A when time allows.

NEXT STEPS • Pretest

- Administer Chapter 6, Objective 1 Pretest, page 468, to all students.

Ongoing Assessment

1. Divide students into pairs or allow them to work individually for this activity.

2. Distribute one copy of the Extension Activity from the online resources to each student.

3. Direct students to the Gizmo *Distance-Time Graphs* through the Inside Algebra Student Web site, http://insidealgebra.voyagerlearning.com.

4. Have students complete the Extension Activity.

5. **Peer Review.** If there is time, have students exchange papers with a peer. They should review and discuss each response, and be prepared to explain their thinking.

> **Variation:** If students do not have access to the Gizmo, for Problems 5 and 7b, have them conduct a mock race in class. Set a certain length of the classroom to represent 40 yards, then have two students "run" each race based on the description provided.

Explore learning • Gizmos

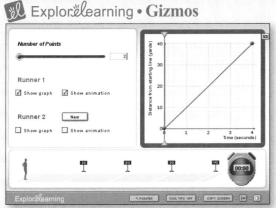

Distance-Time Graphs

Gizmos
Extension Activity   Name_____ Date_____

DISTANCE-TIME GRAPHS

Speed compares the change in a runner's distance to the change in time. A runner's speed is constant if he runs at the same pace during a race. Slope is a way to picture constant speed. Two runners are running the race described in the table.

		Starting Point	Ending Point	Slope
Runner A	Starts at the 0-yard line and runs to the 40-yard line in 4 seconds	(0, 0)	(4, 40)	$\frac{40}{4} = 10$
Runner B	Starts at the 20-yard line and runs to the 40-yard line in 4 seconds	(0, 20)	(4, 40)	$\frac{20}{4} = 5$

1. Ordered pairs name the time and distance of a runner at any instant. The ordered pair that names the starting point of Runner A is (0, 0). Write the ordered pair that names the starting point of Runner B in the table.

2. Write the ordered pairs that name the ending points of both Runner A and Runner B in the table.

3. Find the slope of the line that represents each runner. Write each slope in the table.

4. Which runner do you think will run faster? __Runner A__

5. Use the *Distance-Time Graphs* Gizmo to set up the race described in the table. Click and drag the starting and ending points to move them. Then click the green start button on the stop watch to have the runners actually run the race. Was your prediction correct? ___yes___

6. Explain how you could use the slope of the line for each runner to decide which runner will run faster.

   Answers will vary. Sample answer: The line with the steeper slope will be the faster runner.

Gizmos
Extension Activity   Name_____ Date_____

DISTANCE-TIME GRAPHS (continued)

7. Below is a part of a sports story that describes a race.
   Freshman Shelli Hernandez broke the school record for the 40-yard dash, sprinting to victory with a time of 3 seconds. A close second was taken by junior Rosa Embry with a time of 4 seconds.

   Use the description to complete the table.
   Is the story true based on the slopes of the lines for Shelli and Rosa? Explain.

   Answers will vary. Sample answer: The story is true because Shelli's line has a steeper slope.

	Starting Point	Ending Point	Slope	Equation of Line
Shelli	(0, 0)	(3, 40)	$\frac{40}{3} = 13.3$	$y = \frac{40}{3}x$
Rosa	(0, 0)	(4, 40)	$\frac{40}{4} = 10$	$y = 10x$

Use the Gizmo to model the race and sketch the graph.

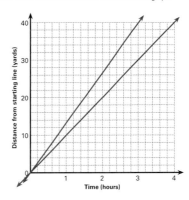

Ongoing Assessment

1. Divide students into pairs or small groups.

2. Distribute one copy of the Individual Reinforcement Activity from the online resources to each student.

3. Direct students to the Gizmo *Slope-Intercept Form of a Line—Activity A* through the Inside Algebra Student Web site, http://insidealgebra. voyagerlearning.com.

4. Have students complete the Reinforcement Activity.

5. **Peer Review.** If time permits, have students exchange papers with a peer to review and discuss each other's responses. Remind students to be prepared to explain the reasoning behind their responses.

   Variation: If students do not have access to the Gizmo, use the graph shown for Problems 1–4. For Problem 8, graph the equation **y = 0** on the board or overhead. For Problem 9, draw several lines with greater and greater slopes on the board or overhead. For Problem 10, draw the graph of a line with negative slope on the board or overhead. For Problem 11, draw several lines with different y-intercepts on the board or overhead.

Gizmos
Reinforcement Activity   Name_____   Date_____

SLOPE-INTERCEPT FORM OF A LINE—ACTIVITY A

1. Use the *Slope-Intercept Form of a Line—Activity A* Gizmo. With the sliders, set $m = 2$ and $b = 3$ to graph the equation $y = 2x + 3$. What ordered pair names the point on the graph? ___(0, 3)___

2. Locate one other point on the graph. Write the ordered pair that names this point. _____

You can use slope to describe the steepness of the line. Find the slope of the line using these steps.

3. Explain how you found the slope and y-intercept.
   Rise = ___2___ units as you move up.

4. Find the run, the horizontal distance between the points.
   Run = ___1___ units as you move to the right.

5. Write the ratio of the rise to the run. Slope = $m = \frac{rise}{run} = \frac{2}{1} = $ ___2___

6. Use the slope you found to write the equation in standard form. Start with the point-slope form.
   $(y - y_1) = 2(x - x_1)$ $(y - $ ___3___ $) = $ ___2___ $(x - $ ___0___ $)$

7. Rewrite the equation until you have it in standard form.
   $ax + by = c$ ___2___ $x - y = $ ___-3___

8. The point on the graph is the y-intercept. The y-intercept is the point for which the x-coordinate is ___0___. What is the y-intercept of the graph? ___(0, 3)___

9. Use the slope and the y-intercept to write the equation in slope-intercept form.
   $y = mx + b$ $y = $ ___2___ $x + $ ___3___

Use the Gizmo to graph the equation $y = 0$. (Hint: This is the same as the equation $y = 0x + 0$ using the sliders.)

10. What is the slope of this line? ___0___   11. What type of line is this? ___horizontal___

12. Use the m slider to increase the slope. What happens to the line as you increase the value of the slope, m?
    The line gets steeper from left to right.

13. Describe the graph of a line with a negative slope. Use the Gizmo to check your answer.
    The line goes down from left to right.

14. Use the b slider to change the value of b. how does the line change as you change the y-intercept, b?
    The line moves up or down the y-axis.

Explore learning • Gizmos

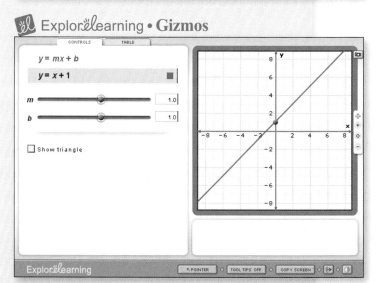

Slope-Intercept Form of a Line—Activity A

Students who did not demonstrate mastery on any or all of the objective posttests or the chapter test

1. Use the *Slope-Intercept Form of a Line—Activity A* Gizmo. Set the *m* slider to 2 and the *b* slider to 3 to graph the equation $y = 2x + 3$.

2. Ask students to write the ordered pair that names the point on the graph. (0, 3)

3. Ask students to write the ordered pair that names another point on the graph. Answers will vary. Example: (−2, −1)

4. Remind students that the slope describes the steepness of the line. Ask students to use the point (0, 3) and the other point they chose to find the slope of the line. Use these steps to scaffold instruction.

   • Ask students to define the rise. The vertical distance between the points Ask them to find the rise as they move up.

   • Ask students to define the run. The horizontal distance between the points Ask them to find the run as they move to the right.

   • Ask students to define the slope of a line. The ratio of the rise to the run Ask them to find the slope.

5. Remind students that in order to write an equation in standard form, they can start with point-slope form: $(y - y_1) = m(x - x_1)$. Have students name m, x_1, and y_1. Then remind them to use algebra to rewrite the equation in standard form: $ax + by = c$.

6. Ask students to define the *y*-intercept. The point for which the *x*-coordinate is 0 Ask them to name the *y*-intercept.

7. Ask student to use the slope and the *y*-intercept to write the equation in slope-intercept form: $y = mx + b$.

8. Use the Gizmo to graph the equation $y = 0$. Ask students to name the type of line shown. Horizontal Ask students to name the slope of this line. Zero

9. Ask students to predict what the graph of a line with a negative slope will look like. Use the Gizmo to graph a line with a negative slope.

   Variation: If teachers do not have access to the Gizmo, draw the graph shown for Problems 1–4. For Problem 8, graph the equation $y = 0$. For Problem 9, draw the graph of a line with a negative slope.

Explore**learning** • **Gizmos**

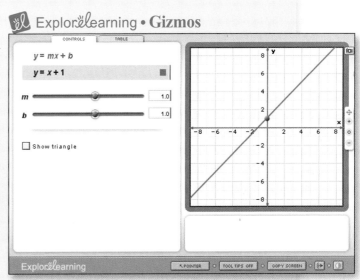

Slope-Intercept Form of a Line—Activity A

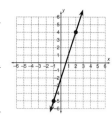

5 Ongoing Assessment

Chapter 5 Test, Form B

MATERIALS

- Chapter 5 Test, Form B, from the Online Resources, pages 1–2

DIRECTIONS

1. Have students turn to Chapter 5 Test, Form B, pages 1–2, from the Online Resources. Administer the Chapter Test to all students.

2. Score the test by objective and update the class record card.

Name_____ Date_____

Objective 1

Solve the problems involving slope.

1. What is the slope of the line? _____ $m = 3$

2. Find the slope of a line that contains the points (1, –3), (3, 3).

$$m = \frac{(-3 - 3)}{(1 - 3)} = \frac{-6}{-2} = 3$$

3. Find the slope of a line that contains the points (0, 4), (2, 0).

$$m = \frac{(4 - 0)}{(0 - 2)} = \frac{4}{-2} = -2$$

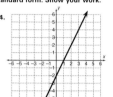

Objective 2

Find the equation of each line from the given information. Write the equation in standard form. Show your work.

4.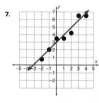

$2x - y = 2$

5. The line that has a slope of 2 and contains the point (0, 5)

$2x - y = -5$

6. The line that contains the two points (0, 2) and (3, 5)

$x - y = -2$

Name_____ Date_____

Objective 3

Draw the best-fit line, if it exists, and name the equation for the best-fit line. Write the equation in slope-intercept form. Answers will vary based on line.

7.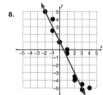

$y = x + 3$

8.

$y = -2x + 1$

Objective 4

Answer the questions about the equation.

9. Write the equation $y - 5 = 2x$ in slope-intercept form.

$y = 2x + 5$

10. What is the slope?

2

11. Sketch the graph.

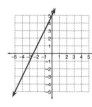

Objective 5

Indicate if the graphs of the two equations in each problem would be parallel, perpendicular, or neither.

12. $2x + y = 3$
    $0.5x - y = 7$

    perpendicular

13. $x = y + 2$
    $y - x + 6 = 0$

    parallel

14. $x + 3y = 4$
    $3x = y - 2$

    perpendicular

Solving Linear Inequalities

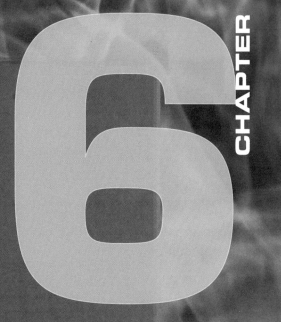

In this chapter, students explore inequalities in one and two variables. They solve and graph inequalities using one or multiple operations. Students also explore, solve, and graph compound inequalities and inequalities involving absolute value. At the end of the chapter, students learn to graph inequalities in two variables and recognize that the graph is the solution set for these inequalities.

Objective 1
Solve and graph the solution set of inequalities with addition and subtraction.

Objective 2
Solve and graph the solution set of inequalities with multiplication and division.

Objective 3
Solve and graph the solution set of inequalities using more than one operation.

Objective 4
Solve and graph the solution set of compound inequalities and inequalities involving absolute value.

Objective 5
Graph inequalities in the coordinate plane.

Chapter 6 VOCABULARY

Objective 1
Solve and graph the solution set of inequalities with addition and subtraction.

Objective 1 Pretest

Students complete the Objective 1 Pretest at least one day before beginning Objective 1.

Using the Results

- Score the pretest and update the class record card.
- If the majority of students do not demonstrate mastery of the concepts, use the 5-Day Instructional Plan for Objective 1.
- If the majority of students demonstrate mastery of the concepts, use the 3-Day Instructional Plan for Objective 1.

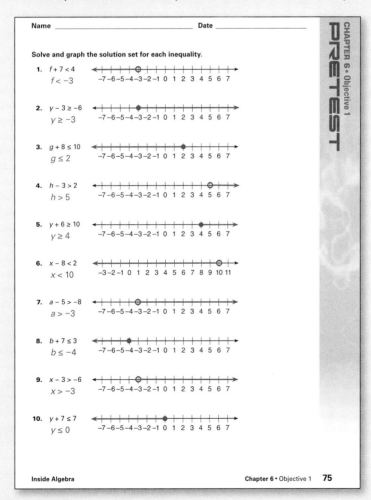

Name _____ Date _____

Solve and graph the solution set for each inequality.

1. $f + 7 < 4$
   $f < -3$

2. $y - 3 \geq -6$
   $y \geq -3$

3. $g + 8 \leq 10$
   $g \leq 2$

4. $h - 3 > 2$
   $h > 5$

5. $y + 6 \geq 10$
   $y \geq 4$

6. $x - 8 < 2$
   $x < 10$

7. $a - 5 > -8$
   $a > -3$

8. $b + 7 \leq 3$
   $b \leq -4$

9. $x - 3 > -6$
   $x > -3$

10. $y + 7 \leq 7$
    $y \leq 0$

Inside Algebra   Chapter 6 • Objective 1   **75**

CHAPTER 6 • Objective 1
PRETEST

Objective 1
Goals and Activities

Objective 1 Goals

The following activities, when used with the instructional plans on pages 470 and 471, enable students to:

- Solve the inequality $x + 9 < 6$ for x, and graph the solution as $x < -3$

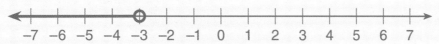

- Solve the inequality $h + 12 \leq 15$ for h, and graph the solution as $h \leq 3$

Objective 1 Activities

Concept Development Activities			
*CD 1 Understanding Inequalities, page 472	CD 2 Creating Inequality Graphs, page 473	CD 3 Demonstrating Inequalities on the Number Line, page 475	CD 4 Using a Balance Scale, page 477

Practice Activities	
PA 1 Writing and Solving an Inequality, page 479	PA 2 Playing Inequality Bingo, page 480

Progress-Monitoring Activities		
PM 1 Apply Skills 1, page 482	PM 2 Apply Skills 2, page 483	PM 3 Apply Skills 3, page 484

*Problem-Solving Activity
*PS 1 Asking Inequalities Questions, page 485

Ongoing Assessment
Posttest Objective 1, page 487
Pretest Objective 2, page 488

CD = Concept Development   PM = Progress Monitoring   PS = Problem Solving
PA = Practice Activity   ★ = Includes Problem Solving

Instructional Plans

5-Day Instructional Plan

Use the 5-Day Instructional Plan when pretest results indicate that students would benefit from a slower pace. This plan is used when the majority of students need more time or did not demonstrate mastery on the pretest.

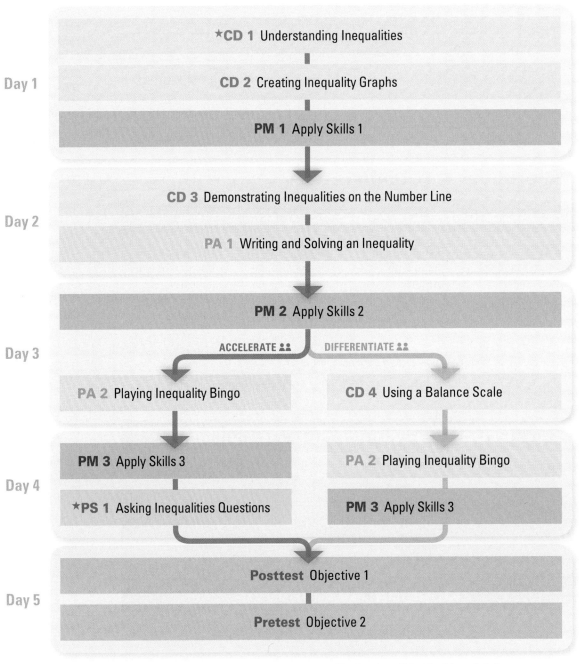

Day 1	★**CD 1** Understanding Inequalities	
	CD 2 Creating Inequality Graphs	
	PM 1 Apply Skills 1	
Day 2	**CD 3** Demonstrating Inequalities on the Number Line	
	PA 1 Writing and Solving an Inequality	
Day 3	**PM 2** Apply Skills 2	
	ACCELERATE	DIFFERENTIATE
	PA 2 Playing Inequality Bingo	**CD 4** Using a Balance Scale
Day 4	**PM 3** Apply Skills 3	**PA 2** Playing Inequality Bingo
	★**PS 1** Asking Inequalities Questions	**PM 3** Apply Skills 3
Day 5	**Posttest** Objective 1	
	Pretest Objective 2	

CD = Concept Development   PM = Progress Monitoring   PS = Problem Solving
PA = Practice Activity   ★ = Includes Problem Solving

3-Day Instructional Plan

Use the 3-Day Instructional Plan when pretest results indicate that students can move through the activities at a faster pace. This plan is ideal when the majority of students demonstrate mastery on the pretest. This plan does not include all activities.

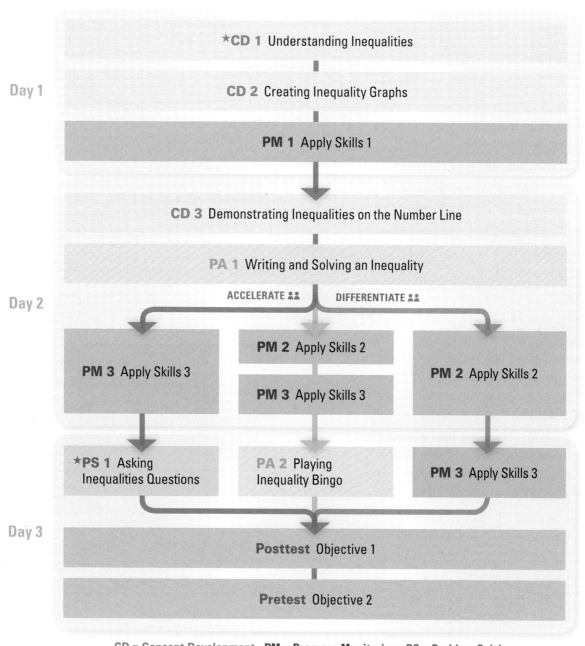

Day 1

★**CD 1** Understanding Inequalities

CD 2 Creating Inequality Graphs

PM 1 Apply Skills 1

Day 2

CD 3 Demonstrating Inequalities on the Number Line

PA 1 Writing and Solving an Inequality

ACCELERATE   DIFFERENTIATE

PM 3 Apply Skills 3

PM 2 Apply Skills 2
PM 3 Apply Skills 3

PM 2 Apply Skills 2

Day 3

★**PS 1** Asking Inequalities Questions

PA 2 Playing Inequality Bingo

PM 3 Apply Skills 3

Posttest Objective 1

Pretest Objective 2

CD = Concept Development   PM = Progress Monitoring   PS = Problem Solving
PA = Practice Activity   ★ = Includes Problem Solving

Objective 1
Concept Development Activities

★ CD 1 Understanding Inequalities

Use with 5-Day or 3-Day Instructional Plan. In this activity, students understand when to use open or filled circles when graphing inequalities on the number line and can tell whether a value is a solution to a given inequality.

MATERIALS

- *Interactive Text*, page 199

DIRECTIONS

1. Have students turn to *Interactive Text*, page 199, Introduction to Inequalities.

2. Discuss the following term and symbols with students:

   inequality A mathematical sentence that compares two expressions using one of the following symbols:

   > Greater than

   ≥ Greater than or equal to

   < Less than

   ≤ Less than or equal to

3. Select a student to read the directions and Problem 1 on *Interactive Text*, page 199. Explain to students that the set of numbers below each problem is the replacement set, or the set of numbers used to check for solutions.

4. Ask students if the first number in the replacement set satisfies the inequality. Explain that a number satisfies the inequality if it makes the inequality true. Have students circle the number if it satisfies the inequality.

5. Continue with each number in the replacement set until the class has checked every number.

6. Have students work individually to complete Problems 2–8. Discuss the answers as a class.

7. Put students in pairs. Have pairs complete Problems 9–13. Discuss the answers as a class.

8. Draw a number line on the board. Use a couple of the inequalities from Problems 1–8 to show that we use an open circle for < and > and a filled circle for ≥ and ≤.

★ = Includes Problem Solving

INTRODUCTION TO INEQUALITIES

Circle the numbers in the replacement set that make each inequality true.

1. $t < 7$
   {4, 7, 6, 8, 0, −6, 11}

2. $h > 4$
   {6, 2, 4, −7, −1, 4.5}

3. $a \le -4$
   {−1, 3, −7, −4, 0, 6}

4. $n \ge -5$
   {−10, 7, −1, −5, −6, −4}

5. $k + 5 < 9$
   {−1, 3, 4, 5, −2, 4.5, 3.5}

6. $y - 7 > 3$
   {−4, 2, 9, 10, 11, 10.01}

7. $u - 5 \ge -1$
   {4, 3, 5, −2, 4.1, 3.9}

8. $x + 3 \le -6$
   {−3, −9, −10, −8, −11, −9.6, −8.4}

9. Write four more numbers that would make the inequality in Problem 1 true.
   Answers will vary. Sample answer: −7, −1, $\frac{1}{2}$, 2

10. What is the largest number in the list of circled answers in Problem 2? __6__
    If you can, write a number that is larger than that number that will make Problem 2 true. ____any number > 6____

11. What is the largest number in the list of circled answers in Problem 3? __−4__
    If you can, write a number that is larger than that number that will make Problem 3 true. ____not possible____

12. What is the smallest number in the list of circled answers in Problem 5? __−2__
    If you can, write a number that is smaller than that number that will make Problem 5 true. ____any number < −2____

13. What is the smallest number in the list of circled answers in Problem 7? __4__
    If you can, write a number that is smaller than that number that will make Problem 7 true. ____not possible____

Inside Algebra   Chapter 6 • Objective 1 • CD 1   **199**

Examples:

$t < 7$

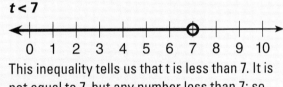

This inequality tells us that t is less than 7. It is not equal to 7, but any number less than 7; so we leave an open circle at 7.

$n \ge -5$

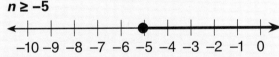

This inequality tells us that n is greater than or equal to −5. The number n could equal −5 or anything greater than −5; so we fill the circle.

NEXT STEPS • Differentiate

5-Day and 3-Day Instructional Plans:
CD 2, page 473—All students, for additional concept development

Objective 1
Concept Development Activities

CD 2 Creating Inequality Graphs

Use with 5-Day or 3-Day Instructional Plan. In this activity, students understand that inequalities graphed with filled circles have a unique largest (or smallest) value that satisfies the inequality, but those with open circles do not.

MATERIALS

- Blackline Master 27

DIRECTIONS

1. Draw a number line on the board, or make a transparency of Blackline Master 27, Number Lines. Label the number line as follows.

2. Review the following term and symbols with students:

    inequality A mathematical sentence that compares two expressions using one of the following symbols:

    > Greater than

    ≥ Greater than or equal to

    < Less than

    ≤ Less than or equal to

3. Write **x < 3** under the number line. Have a student volunteer read the sentence. *x is less than 3.*

4. Ask students to identify the number represented by Point A and whether that point satisfies the sentence x < 3. *Point A is –2, so –2 < 3 is true.*

5. Have students identify the number represented by Point B and whether that point satisfies the sentence x < 3. *Point B is 1, so 1 < 3 is true.*

6. Have students do the same for Points C and D. *Point C is 3, so 3 < 3 is false. Point D is 5, so 5 < 3 is false.*

7. Ask students to name other numbers that satisfy the sentence x < 3. Point out that infinitely many numbers are less than 3.

8. If students don't name 2 as a number that satisfies the sentence, suggest it as an answer. Ask students if 2 is the largest number that satisfies the sentence x < 3. Explain that 2 is the largest integer that satisfies x < 3 but there are other real numbers larger than 2 that satisfy x < 3. Have students name some real numbers that satisfy x < 3. Draw a number line to show the real numbers.

Sample answers:

$2\frac{1}{2}$, $2\frac{3}{4}$, 2.9, 2.99

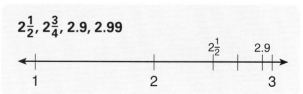

Concept Development Activities

9. Ask students to think of the largest number that satisfies $x < 3$. Guide students as they come to the conclusion that as we add more 9s to the right of the decimal point, the number gets closer to 3. 2.99, 2.999 Point out that all these decimal numbers satisfy $x < 3$, as long as the whole number is 2 or less.

10. Ask students how we picture $x < 3$. Discuss the use of the open circle for $x < 3$. Reinforce that the open circle means all numbers up to 3 but not including 3.

11. Discuss the following term with students:

    strict inequality An inequality that compares two expressions using only greater than (>) or less than (<)

12. Follow similar steps to discuss more graphs of inequalities. Show the linear graphs and write the corresponding inequalities.

Examples:

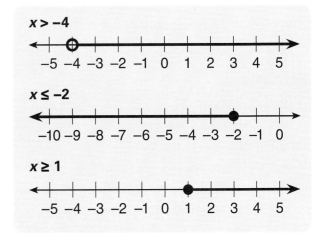

NEXT STEPS • Differentiate

5-Day and 3-Day Instructional Plans:
PM 1, page 482—All students, to assess progress

Objective 1
Concept Development Activities

CD 3 Demonstrating Inequalities on the Number Line

NUMBER LINES

Use with 5-Day or 3-Day Instructional Plan. In this activity, students understand that adding or subtracting the same value from both sides of an inequality does not change the inequality.

MATERIALS

- Blackline Master 27
- **Variation:** Gizmos *Solving Linear Inequalities Using Addition and Subtraction*

DIRECTIONS

1. Review the following terms and symbols with students:

   inequality A mathematical sentence that compares two expressions using one of the following symbols:

   > Greater than

   ≥ Greater than or equal to

   < Less than

   ≤ Less than or equal to

   strict inequality An inequality that compares two expressions using only greater than (>) or less than (<)

2. Make a transparency of Blackline Master 27, Number Lines, and label a number line with two points. Have students discuss which number is larger, which number is smaller, and how far apart the numbers are.

   Example:

   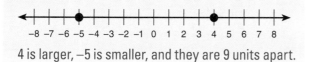

   4 is larger, −5 is smaller, and they are 9 units apart.

3. Ask students to write an inequality sentence for all numbers between the two points on your number line. Guide students to identify both a less than (<) inequality and a greater than (>) inequality.

   Sample answer:

   $4 > x > -5$ or $-5 < x < 4$

4. Have students choose another number to add to each of your original numbers. Demonstrate the addition on the number line. Have students reevaluate the inequality.

   Example:

   Is your inequality sentence still true?
   Yes, $-5 + 4 < x < 4 + 4$
   $-1 < x < 8$
   Are the two sums still the same distance apart?
   Yes, −1 and 8 are 9 units apart.

5. Discuss whether the same result would happen with any two numbers.

6. Demonstrate the process with two new numbers. Choose a negative number to add to the plotted points this time.

Example:

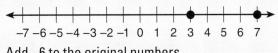

Add –6 to the original numbers.

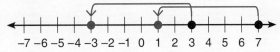

Is your inequality sentence still true?

Yes, $3 - 6 < x < 7 - 6$

$-3 < x < 1$

Are the two sums still the same distance apart?

Yes, –3 and 1 are 4 units apart.

7. Ask students to summarize this experiment. You can add or subtract the same numbers and it doesn't change the inequality.

> **Variation: Gizmos** For this activity use the number line in the Gizmo *Solving Linear Inequalities Using Addition and Subtraction* to model the process of solving and graphing inequalities.

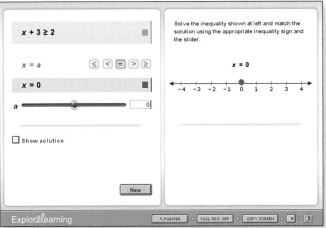

Solving Linear Inequalities Using Addition and Subtraction

8. Give students several situations in which numbers are added or subtracted within inequalities, and have them decide if the inequalities are true or false.

Sample problems:

> If $x > 3$, then $x - 3 > 3 - 3$, or $x - 3 > 0$. True
>
> If $x < 10$, then $x + 2 < 10 + 2$, or $x + 2 < 12$. True
>
> If $x - 3 < 4$, then $x - 3 + 3 < 4 + 3$, or $x < 7$. True
>
> If $x + 6 < 9$, then $x + 6 - 6 < 9 - 6$, or $x < 3$. True
>
> If $x + 2 \leq 7$, then $x + 2 - 2 \leq 7 - 7$, or $x < 0$. False

9. Point out that inequalities are like equations because the same quantity can be added to or subtracted from both sides without changing the inequality. Demonstrate how to solve an inequality using this idea.

Sample problem:

> $x - 4 > 6$
> $x - 4 + 4 > 6 + 4$
> $x > 10$

10. Have students solve some inequalities on their own. Discuss the addition or subtraction property used to solve each problem.

Sample problem:

> $x + 7 > 3 \quad x > -4$
>
> $x - 3 \leq 2 \quad x \leq 5$
>
> $x + 9 \leq 2 \quad x \leq -7$
>
> $7 \geq x + 2 \quad x \leq 5$

NEXT STEPS • Differentiate

5-Day and 3-Day Instructional Plans:

PA 1, page 479—All students, for additional practice

Objective 1
Concept Development Activities

CD 4 Using a Balance Scale

Use with 5-Day Instructional Plan. In this activity, students add or subtract the same value from both sides of an inequality to solve for the variable.

MATERIALS

- Elementary balance scale, one per group
- Weights for each balance (cubes, chips, paper clips—any uniform weight)
- Small paper bag, one per group

DIRECTIONS

1. Review the following term and symbols with students:

   inequality A mathematical sentence that compares two expressions using one of the following symbols:

   > Greater than

   ≥ Greater than or equal to

   < Less than

   ≤ Less than or equal to

2. Divide students into groups of four or five. Put nine weights in each paper bag and close the bags. Give each group one of the paper bags, a balance scale, and extra weights.

3. Explain that the paper bag has weights in it. Instruct students not to open the bags or try to feel the number of weights. Have groups put the paper bag on one side of the scale and three weights on the other side. Ask the class which is heavier. The paper bag

4. Tell students to let the paper bag be x, and have them write an inequality to represent the balance. Solicit answers to get $x > 3$. This can be interpreted to mean there are more than three weights in the paper bag.

5. Have the groups add two more weights to each side of the balance. Point out that nothing happened. Have students write an inequality to model what we did, and explain that because they added the same amount to each side, the inequality stayed the same. $x + 2 > 3 + 2$

6. Ask students to think about what will happen if we add 10 weights to each side, or if we add 100 weights to each side. Make sure students recognize that as long as we add the same amount to each side, the heavier side will remain heavier. Ask the class to summarize by writing an inequality with only variables. $x > y \rightarrow x + b > y + b$

Concept Development Activities

7. Have the groups remove the items from the balance, then put the paper bag (containing the same weights) on one side and five weights on the other side. Have students write the inequality on their papers. $x > 5$

8. Ask students to think about what would happen if we removed two weights from each side. $x - 2 > 5 - 2$; the side with the bag would still be heavier.

9. Point out that as long as the same amount is removed from each side, the heavier side will always remain heavier. Ask the class to summarize by writing an inequality with only variables. If $x > y$, then $x - b > y - b$.

10. Be sure students understand that this means you can add or subtract the same amount from an inequality and the inequality remains true.

11. Have the groups put the paper bag and three weights on one side ($x + 3$) and seven weights on the other.

12. Have students write the inequality modeled on the balance. Write the sentence on the board. $x + 3 > 7$

13. Have students discuss how to solve this inequality for x. Make sure students recognize that we take three away from each side. Write the inequality under the original problem.
$x + 3 - 3 > 7 - 3$
$x > 4$

NEXT STEPS • Differentiate

5-Day Instructional Plan:
PA 2, page 480—All students, for additional practice

PA 1 Writing and Solving an Inequality

Use with 5-Day or 3-Day Instructional Plan. In this activity, students correctly graph inequalities involving addition and subtraction.

MATERIALS

- Blank cards, two per student

DIRECTIONS

1. Review the following term and symbols with students:

    inequality A mathematical sentence that compares two expressions using one of the following symbols:

    > Greater than

    ≥ Greater than or equal to

    < Less than

    ≤ Less than or equal to

2. Give two blank cards to each student.

3. Instruct each student to write an inequality with addition on the first card; for example, $x + 9 \geq 3$.

4. Instruct each student to write an inequality with subtraction on the second card; for example, $x - 4 < 7$.

5. On the back of each card, have students copy the inequality from the front of the card, then solve it and graph the solution set.

    Sample answer:

    $$x + 9 \geq 3$$
    $$x + 9 - 9 \geq 3 - 9$$
    $$x \geq -6$$

    $$-7\ -6\ -5\ -4\ -3\ -2\ -1\ \ 0\ \ 1\ \ 2\ \ 3\ \ 4\ \ 5\ \ 6\ \ 7$$

6. Put students in groups of four or five.

7. Have students within each group exchange cards. Tell students to solve the inequality on the front of the cards they receive and graph the solution set on a separate sheet of paper.

8. When students finish the problems, they should check their answers with the answers on the back of the cards.

9. Have students exchange cards with someone else in their group and repeat Steps 7 and 8 until each student has solved the problems of every other student in the group.

10. Ask students to compare solutions in the group and agree on the correct solutions and graphs.

11. Have students exchange the cards with other groups and continue.

NEXT STEPS • Differentiate

5-Day Instructional Plan:
PM 2, page 483—All students, to assess progress

3-Day Instructional Plan:
PM 3, page 484—Students who demonstrate understanding of the concept, to assess progress

PM 2, page 483—Students who need additional support, to assess progress

Practice Activities

PA 2 Playing Inequality Bingo

Use with 5-Day or 3-Day Instructional Plan. In this activity, students solve inequalities involving addition and subtraction.

MATERIALS

- Blackline Master 38
- Blackline Master 77
- Game markers to cover squares

DIRECTIONS

1. Review the following term and symbols with students:

   inequality A mathematical sentence that compares two expressions using one of the following symbols:

   > Greater than

   ≥ Greater than or equal to

   < Less than

   ≤ Less than or equal to

2. Distribute one copy of Blackline Master 38, 4 × 4 Bingo Card, to each student.

3. Make a transparency of Blackline Master 77, Inequality Bingo, and show it on the overhead. Alternatively, copy the inequalities from Blackline Master 77 on the board. Have students write the inequalities in the squares of the bingo card in a random fashion.

38

Name _____ Date _____

4 × 4 BINGO CARD

<table>
<tr><td></td><td></td><td></td><td></td></tr>
<tr><td></td><td></td><td></td><td></td></tr>
<tr><td></td><td></td><td></td><td></td></tr>
<tr><td></td><td></td><td></td><td></td></tr>
</table>

77

Name _____ Date _____

INEQUALITY BINGO

1.	$x < 4$	$x + 5 < 9$
2.	$x > 4$	$x - 3 > 1$
3.	$x \geq -3$	$x + 7 \geq 4$
4.	$x \leq -3$	$5 + x \leq 2$
5.	$x > 2$	$7 + x > 9$
6.	$x < 2$	$x - 8 < -6$
7.	$x \leq 0$	$x - 9 \leq -9$
8.	$x > 0$	$x + 46 > 46$
9.	$x < 1$	$x - 9 < -8$
10.	$x < -1$	$x - 3 < -4$
11.	$x \geq 7$	$x + 6 \geq 13$
12.	$x < 7$	$x - 4 < 3$
13.	$x = 6$	$x + 2 = 8$
14.	$x > 10$	$x + 20 > 30$
15.	$x = 2$	$x + 6 = 8$
16.	$x < 10$	$14 > x + 4$

4. Select a problem at random from the problem list, and write it on the board or overhead. Tell students to solve the problem and use a marker to cover the square on the bingo card that corresponds to that answer.

Problem list:

$x + 5 < 9$	$x - 9 \leq -9$	$x + 2 = 8$
$x - 3 > 1$	$x + 46 > 46$	$x + 20 > 30$
$x + 7 \geq 4$	$x - 9 < -8$	$x + 6 = 8$
$5 + x \leq 2$	$x - 3 < -4$	$14 > x + 4$
$7 + x > 9$	$x + 6 \geq 13$	
$x - 8 < -6$	$x - 4 < 3$	

5. Repeat Step 4 until a student has four markers in a row horizontally, vertically, or diagonally. When a student has four markers in a row, he or she should shout "Bingo!"

6. Check to see if the student has the correct solutions covered.

7. If the solutions are correct, declare that student the winner, have all students clear their cards, and begin play again. Be sure to pick the problems from the problem list in a random fashion.

8. Repeat the game as time permits.

NEXT STEPS • Differentiate

5-Day Instructional Plan:
PM 3, page 484—All students, to assess progress

3-Day Instructional Plan:
Objective 1 Posttest, page 487—All students

Progress-Monitoring Activities

PM 1 Apply Skills 1

Use with 5-Day or 3-Day Instructional Plan.

MATERIALS

- *Interactive Text*, page 200

DIRECTIONS

1. Have students turn to *Interactive Text*, page 200, Apply Skills 1.

2. Remind students of the key term: *inequality*.

3. Monitor student work, and provide feedback as necessary.

   Watch for:
   - Do students use an open circle to indicate less than or greater than?
   - Do students use a filled circle to indicate possible equality?

NEXT STEPS • Differentiate

5-Day and 3-Day Instructional Plans:
CD 3, page 475—All students, for additional concept development

---

Name _____ Date _____

APPLY SKILLS 1

Construct the linear graph for each inequality.

Example:
$x < 8$

1. $x > 2$
2. $x \geq -4$
3. $x < 3$
4. $x \leq -1$
5. $x < -2$
6. $x < 10$
7. $x > 5$
8. $x \geq -2$
9. $x > -3$
10. $x \geq 4$

200   Chapter 6 • Objective 1 • PM 1   Inside Algebra

Progress-Monitoring Activities

PM 2 Apply Skills 2

Use with 5-Day or 3-Day Instructional Plan.

MATERIALS

- *Interactive Text*, pages 201–202

DIRECTIONS

1. Have students turn to *Interactive Text*, pages 201–202, Apply Skills 2.

2. Remind students of the key term: *inequality*.

3. Monitor student work, and provide feedback as necessary.

   Watch for:
   - Do students solve the equation before graphing?
   - Do students use open and filled circles correctly?

NEXT STEPS • Differentiate

👥 5-Day Instructional Plan:

PA 2, page 480—Students who demonstrate understanding of the concept, for additional practice

CD 4, page 477—Students who need additional concept development

3-Day Instructional Plan:

PM 3, page 484—All students, for additional progress assessment

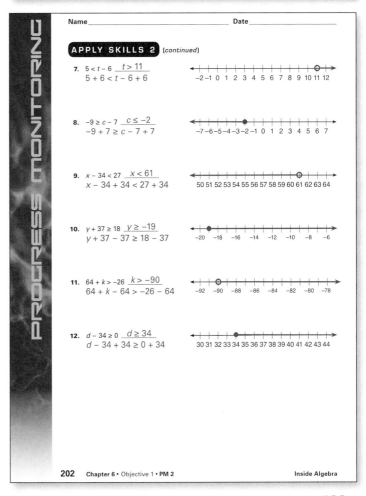

Objective 1
Progress-Monitoring Activities

PM 3 Apply Skills 3

Use with 5-Day or 3-Day Instructional Plan.

MATERIALS

- *Interactive Text*, pages 203–204

DIRECTIONS

1. Have students turn to *Interactive Text*, pages 203–204, Apply Skills 3.

2. Remind students of the key term: *inequality*.

3. Monitor student work, and provide feedback as necessary.

   Watch for:
   - Do students solve equations before graphing?
   - Do students use open and filled circles correctly?
   - Do students correctly locate rational values on the number line?

NEXT STEPS • Differentiate

👥 5-Day Instructional Plan:
PS 1, page 485—Students who are on the accelerated path, to develop problem-solving skills

Objective 1 Posttest, page 487—Students who are on the differentiated path

👥 3-Day Instructional Plan:
PS 1, page 485—Students who are on the accelerated path, to develop problem-solving skills

PA 2, page 480—Students on the differentiated path who completed PM 2 early, for additional practice

Objective 1 Posttest, page 487—All other students

Name _____ Date _____

APPLY SKILLS 3

Solve each inequality and graph the solution set on the number line.

Example:
$a - 7 \geq -3$ $a \geq 4$
$a - 7 + 7 \geq -3 + 7$

1. $x + 8 < 2$ $x < -6$
   $x + 8 - 8 < 2 - 8$

2. $w - 12 > -5$ $w > 7$
   $w - 12 + 12 > -5 + 12$

3. $17 \leq 13 + a$ $a \geq 4$
   $17 - 13 \leq 13 + a - 13$
   $4 \leq a$

4. $y + 7 \geq 13$ $y \geq 6$
   $y + 7 - 7 \geq 13 - 7$

5. $b + 4.5 > -2.6$ $b > -7.1$
   $b + 4.5 - 4.5 > -2.6 - 4.5$

6. $h - 1.9 \leq 4.3$ $h \leq 6.2$
   $h - 1.9 + 1.9 \leq 4.3 + 1.9$

Name _____ Date _____

APPLY SKILLS 3 *(continued)*

7. $2.5 < t - 5.8$ $t > 8.3$
   $2.5 + 5.8 < t - 5.8 + 5.8$
   $8.3 < t$

8. $-9 \geq c - 3.7$ $c \leq -5.3$
   $-9 + 3.7 \geq c - 3.7 + 3.7$
   $-5.3 \geq c$

9. $x - \frac{5}{8} < \frac{1}{2}$ $x < \frac{9}{8}$
   $x - \frac{5}{8} + \frac{5}{8} < \frac{1}{2} + \frac{5}{8}$

10. $y + \frac{1}{3} \geq \frac{5}{6}$ $y \geq \frac{1}{2}$
    $y + \frac{1}{3} - \frac{1}{3} \geq \frac{5}{6} - \frac{1}{3}$

11. $\frac{1}{4} + k > -\frac{2}{5}$ $k > -\frac{13}{20}$
    $\frac{1}{4} + k - \frac{1}{4} > -\frac{2}{5} - \frac{1}{4}$

12. $d - \frac{3}{4} \geq \frac{2}{3}$ $d \geq \frac{17}{12}$
    $d - \frac{3}{4} + \frac{3}{4} \geq \frac{2}{3} + \frac{3}{4}$

Objective 1
Problem-Solving Activity

★ PS 1 Asking Inequalities Questions

Use with 5-Day or 3-Day Instructional Plan. In this activity, students write inequalities that describe the number line.

MATERIALS

- *Interactive Text*, page 205

DIRECTIONS

1. Review the following terms and symbols with students:

   inequality A mathematical sentence that compares two expressions using one of the following symbols:

   > Greater than

   ≥ Greater than or equal to

   < Less than

   ≤ Less than or equal to

   strict inequality An inequality that compares two expressions using only greater than (>) or less than(<)

2. Tell students that in this activity, they learn to interpret descriptions of inequality graphs on the number line correctly.

3. Have students work individually on this assignment. Have students turn to *Interactive Text*, page 205, Inequalities Questions, and solve the problems. When they finish, discuss the problems as a class.

4. Notice whether students remember that a filled circle means the value at that location is included, while an open circle means a strict inequality.

NEXT STEPS • Differentiate

5-Day and 3-Day Instructional Plans:
Objective 1 Posttest, page 487—All students

★ = Includes Problem Solving

Name_____ Date_____

INEQUALITIES QUESTIONS

Read the sentences and respond.

1. Write an inequality if the graph of the solution set has a filled-in dot at 3 and an arrow to the right. $x \geq 3$

2. Write an inequality if the graph of the solution set has an open dot at 6 and an arrow to the left. $x < 6$

3. Write an inequality if the graph of the solution set has an open dot at −5 and an arrow to the right. $x > -5$

4. Write an inequality if the graph of the solution set has a filled-in dot at −8 and an arrow to the left. $x \leq -8$

5. Write an inequality with addition in it that has a solution of $n > 4$.

   Answers will vary. Sample answer: $n + 2 > 6$

6. Write an inequality with subtraction in it that has a solution of $n \leq -3$.

   Answers will vary. Sample answer: $n - 7 \leq -10$

7. Last year, a youth baseball player hit 32 home runs in a single season. This year, the same player hit 15 home runs in the first half of the season. Write an inequality that shows how many home runs the player needs to hit in the second half of the season to break his record from last season.

   $n + 15 > 32$ or $n > 17$

8. Another player hit 12 home runs in the first half of the season. Write an inequality that shows how many home runs he needs to hit to break the record of 32 home runs in a season.

   $n + 12 > 32$ or $n > 20$

9. Write an inequality for the graph below. $x < -1$

10. Write another inequality that would have the same graph as in Problem 9.

    Answers will vary. Sample answer: $x + 3 < 2$

11. Write an inequality for the graph below. $x \geq -3$

Inside Algebra   Chapter 6 • Objective 1 • PS 1   **205**

This page intentionally left blank

6

Ongoing Assessment

Objective 1 Posttest

Discuss with students the key concepts in Objective 1. Following the discussion, administer the Objective 1 Posttest to all students.

Using the Results

- Score the posttest and update the class record card.

- Provide reinforcement for students who do not demonstrate mastery of the concepts through individual or small-group reteaching of key concepts.

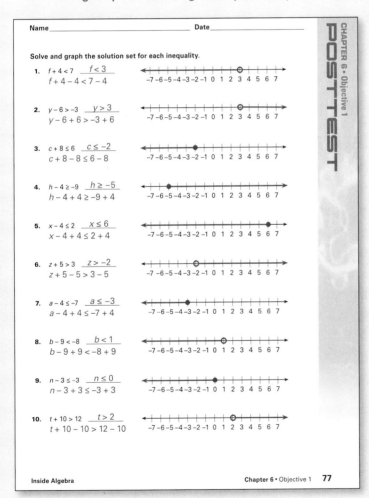

Objective 2
Solve and graph the solution set of inequalities with multiplication and division.

Objective 2 Pretest

Students complete the Objective 2 Pretest on the same day as the Objective 1 Posttest.

Using the Results

- Score the pretest and update the class record card.
- If the majority of students do not demonstrate mastery of the concepts, use the 4-Day Instructional Plan for Objective 2.
- If the majority of students demonstrate mastery of the concepts, use the 3-Day Instructional Plan for Objective 2.

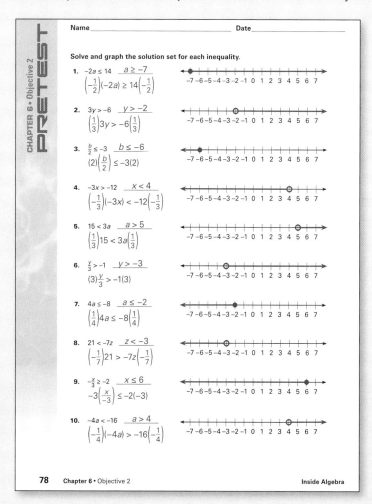

Goals and Activities

Objective 2 Goals

The following activities, when used with the instructional plans on pages 490 and 491, enable students to:

- Solve the inequality $3a < -6$ for a and graph the solution as **$a < -2$**

- Solve the inequality $-5h \leq 15$ for h and graph the solution as **$h \geq -3$**

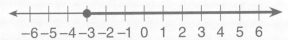

Objective 2 Activities

Concept Development Activities	
CD 1 Relating Multiplication and the Number Line, page 492	**★CD 2** Practicing With Numbers, page 494

Practice Activities	
PA 1 Playing Inequality Bingo, page 496	**PA 2** Playing Switch It, page 498

Progress-Monitoring Activities	
PM 1 Apply Skills 1, page 499	**PM 2** Apply Skills 2, page 500

★Problem-Solving Activity
★PS 1 Relating Equations and Inequalities, page 501

Ongoing Assessment
Posttest Objective 2, page 503
Pretest Objective 3, page 504

CD = Concept Development   PM = Progress Monitoring   PS = Problem Solving
PA = Practice Activity   ★ = Includes Problem Solving

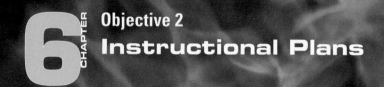
4-Day Instructional Plan

Use the 4-Day Instructional Plan when pretest results indicate that students would benefit from a slower pace. This plan is used when the majority of students need more time or did not demonstrate mastery on the pretest.

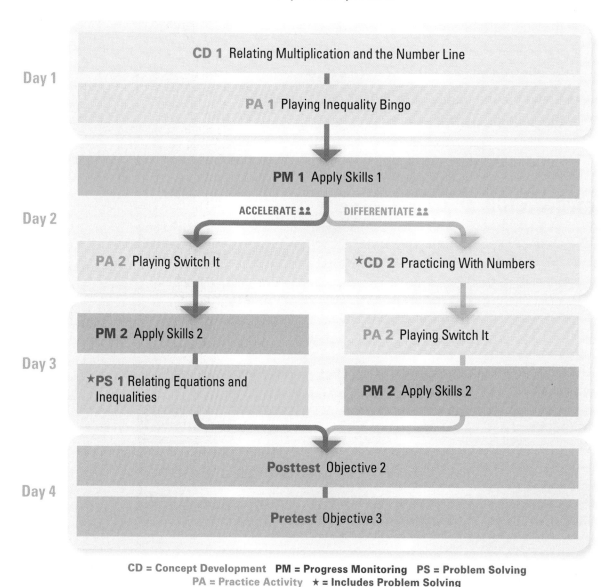

Day 1

CD 1 Relating Multiplication and the Number Line

PA 1 Playing Inequality Bingo

Day 2

PM 1 Apply Skills 1

ACCELERATE 👥   DIFFERENTIATE 👥

PA 2 Playing Switch It   **★CD 2** Practicing With Numbers

Day 3

PM 2 Apply Skills 2   **PA 2** Playing Switch It

★PS 1 Relating Equations and Inequalities   **PM 2** Apply Skills 2

Day 4

Posttest Objective 2

Pretest Objective 3

CD = Concept Development   PM = Progress Monitoring   PS = Problem Solving
PA = Practice Activity   ★ = Includes Problem Solving

3-Day Instructional Plan

Use the 3-Day Instructional Plan when pretest results indicate that students can move through the activities at a faster pace. This plan is ideal when the majority of students demonstrate mastery on the pretest.

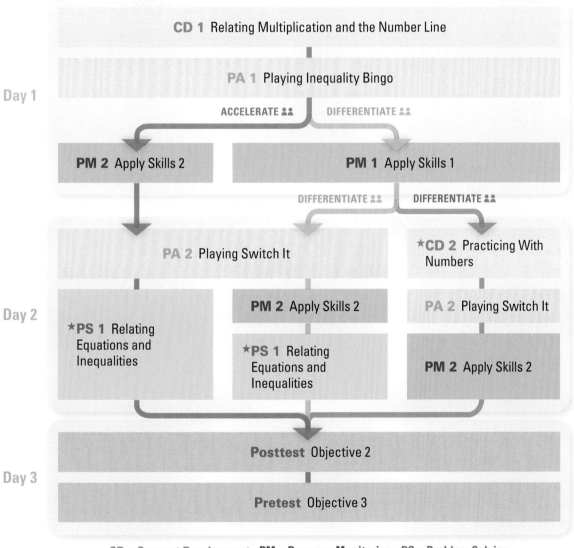

Day 1

CD 1 Relating Multiplication and the Number Line

PA 1 Playing Inequality Bingo

ACCELERATE   DIFFERENTIATE

PM 2 Apply Skills 2   **PM 1** Apply Skills 1

DIFFERENTIATE   DIFFERENTIATE

Day 2

★**PS 1** Relating Equations and Inequalities

PA 2 Playing Switch It

PM 2 Apply Skills 2

★**PS 1** Relating Equations and Inequalities

★**CD 2** Practicing With Numbers

PA 2 Playing Switch It

PM 2 Apply Skills 2

Day 3

Posttest Objective 2

Pretest Objective 3

CD = Concept Development   PM = Progress Monitoring   PS = Problem Solving
PA = Practice Activity   ★ = Includes Problem Solving

Objective 2
Concept Development Activities

CD 1 Relating Multiplication and the Number Line

Use with 4-Day or 3-Day Instructional Plan. In this activity, students understand that multiplying an inequality by a positive number does not change the inequality, and multiplying by a negative number reverses the inequality.

MATERIALS

- *Interactive Text*, page 206

DIRECTIONS

1. Have students turn to *Interactive Text*, page 206, Mapping Products on the Number Line.

2. Review the following term and symbols with students:

    inequality A mathematical sentence that compares two expressions using one of the following symbols:

    \> Greater than

    ≥ Greater than or equal to

    < Less than

    ≤ Less than or equal to

3. Have one student read aloud the inequality in Problem 1. Point out the 3 and the 7 plotted on the top number line.

4. Tell students to multiply both numbers by 2 and map the numbers to their products.

5. Ask students to identify the relation between 6 and 14. Demonstrate how the relation changed when each side was multiplied by 2.

    > **3 < 7**
    > **3 • 2 < 7 • 2**
    > **6 < 14**

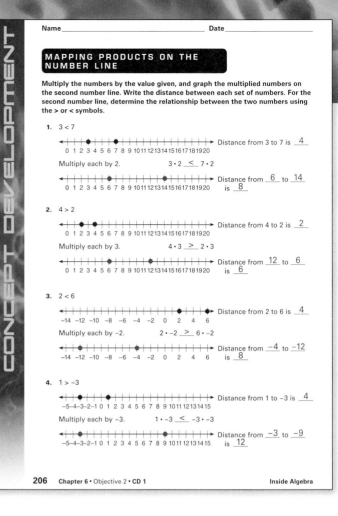

6. Discuss the distance from each of the original numbers to their products. Ask students what the relationship is between the distances.

    Listen for:
    - The distance from 3 to 7 is 4.
    - The distance from 6 to 14 is 8.
    - The second distance is twice as much as the first distance.

7. Explain that if you take two numbers in an inequality and multiply by 2 on each side, the numbers in the resulting inequality will be twice as far apart.

8. Have students repeat the process in Steps 3–6 for Problem 2.

9. Have one student read aloud Problem 3. Ask students what we get when each number is multiplied by −2. Have them map the numbers to their products and tell the new relation.

10. Be sure students see that −12 is smaller than −4. Demonstrate the change in the relation on the board or overhead.

> **2 < 6**
> **2 · (−2) > 6 · (−2)**
> **−4 > −12**

Note: The lines cross on the mapping. The relationship is reversed. When you multiply by a negative number, you reverse the relation. The larger number multiplied by a negative number becomes smaller than the smaller number multiplied by the same negative number.

11. Investigate with students the outcome of Problem 4. Help students see that the relation is reversed.

$1 > -3$
$1 \cdot (-3) < -3 \cdot (-3)$
$-3 < 9$

12. Ask students to write a generalization about inequalities and multiplication; for example, if $a < b$ and $c > 0$, then $ac < bc$; and if $a < b$ and $c < 0$, then $ac > bc$.

NEXT STEPS • Differentiate

4-Day and 3-Day Instructional Plans:
PA 1, page 496—All students, for additional practice

Concept Development Activities

★ CD 2 Practicing With Numbers

Use with 4-Day or 3-Day Instructional Plan. In this activity, students solve inequalities by dividing by the coefficient or multiplying by the inverse of the coefficient.

MATERIALS

- *Interactive Text*, pages 207–208
- **Variation:** Gizmos
  Solving Linear Inequalities Using Multiplication and Division

DIRECTIONS

1. Review the following term and symbols with students:

   inequality A mathematical sentence that compares two expressions using one of the following symbols:

   > Greater than

   ≥ Greater than or equal to

   < Less than

   ≤ Less than or equal to

2. Discuss the following term with students:

   coefficient A number or quantity placed before a variable, which indicates multiplication of that variable

3. Have students turn to *Interactive Text*, pages 207–208, Inequalities With Multiplication. Tell students to work independently to complete the activity.

4. Discuss all problems with students when everyone is finished. Start the discussion by calling on one student. Ask whether the first number in the replacement set for *a* in Problem 1 would make the inequality true. Call on a second student and ask about the second number in the replacement set for *a*. Repeat until all numbers in the replacement set for Problem 1 have been discussed.

★ = Includes Problem Solving

INEQUALITIES WITH MULTIPLICATION

Circle the numbers that make each inequality true, then read the sentences and respond. (An example of a mathematical sentence is "*a* < 3.")

1. $4a < 28$
   $a \in \{-6, -4, 0, 4, 6, 8, 7, 8, 11\}$
   List four more numbers that would make this inequality true. Answers will vary.
   Describe in words all the numbers that would make this inequality true.
   All numbers less than 7
   Write a mathematical sentence for these numbers. $a < 7$

2. $3h > -12$
   $h \in \{-7, -5, -4, -3, -1, 0, 4, 6\}$
   List four more numbers that would make this inequality true. Answers will vary.
   Describe in words all the numbers that would make this inequality true.
   All numbers greater than −4
   Write a mathematical sentence for these numbers. $h > -4$

3. $\frac{b}{2} \le -2$
   $b \in \{-8, -6, -4, -2, 0, 2, 4\}$
   List four more numbers that would make this inequality true. Answers will vary.
   Describe in words all the numbers that would make this inequality true.
   All numbers less than or equal to −4
   Write a mathematical sentence for these numbers. $b \le -4$

4. $4n \ge -20$
   $n \in \{-8, -6, -5, -4, -2, 0, 2, 4\}$
   List four more numbers that would make this inequality true. Answers will vary.
   Describe in words all the numbers that would make this inequality true.
   All numbers greater than or equal to −5
   Write a mathematical sentence for these numbers. $n \ge -5$

INEQUALITIES WITH MULTIPLICATION   *(continued)*

5. $-5g < 20$
   $g \in \{-8, -6, -4, -2, -1, 0, 2, 4\}$
   List four more numbers that would make this inequality true. Answers will vary.
   Describe in words all the numbers that would make this inequality true.
   All numbers greater than −4
   Write a mathematical sentence for these numbers. $g > -4$

6. $-4y > 12$
   $y \in \{-9, -7, -5, -3, -1, 3, 5\}$
   List four more numbers that would make this inequality true. Answers will vary.
   Describe in words all the numbers that would make this inequality true.
   All numbers less than −3
   Write a mathematical sentence for these numbers. $y < -3$

7. $-8z \ge -32$
   $z \in \{-2, 0, 2, 4, 6, 8, 9\}$
   List four more numbers that would make this inequality true. Answers will vary.
   Describe in words all the numbers that would make this inequality true.
   All numbers less than or equal to 4
   Write a mathematical sentence for these numbers. $z \le 4$

8. $-4x \le -36$
   $x \in \{-3, -1, 3, 5, 7, 9, 11, 13\}$
   List four more numbers that would make this inequality true. Answers will vary.
   Describe in words all the numbers that would make this inequality true.
   All numbers greater than or equal to 9
   Write a mathematical sentence for these numbers. $x \ge 9$

5. Point out that in Problem 1, all numbers less than 7 will work because $a < 7$. Write **$4a < 28$** and **$a < 7$** on the board. Ask students how we get from $4a < 28$ to $a < 7$. Divide by 4 or multiply by $\frac{1}{4}$.

6. Discuss Problems 2–4 in a similar fashion.

7. Ask a student which numbers he or she circled in Problem 5, and have the student describe the numbers that work. $-2, -1, 0, 2, 4;\ g > -4$

8. Explain that to get from $-5g < 20$ to $g > -4$, we must divide both sides by -5, or multiply by $-\frac{1}{5}$, then reverse the relation symbol.

$$-\frac{1}{5}(-5g) < -\frac{1}{5}(20)$$
$$g > -4$$

9. Discuss Problems 6–8 in a similar fashion.

10. Ask students to write a generalization for multiplying or dividing inequalities; for example, if $a < b$ and $c > 0$, then $ac < bc$ or $\frac{a}{c} < \frac{b}{c}$; and if $a > b$ and $c < 0$, then $ac < bc$ or $\frac{a}{c} < \frac{b}{c}$.

Variation: Gizmos For this activity use the number line in the Gizmo *Solving Linear Inequalities Using Multiplication and Division* to model the process of solving and graphing inequalities.

Explore learning • **Gizmos**

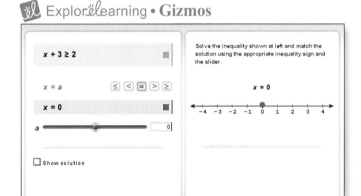

Solving Linear Inequalities Using Multiplication and Division

NEXT STEPS • Differentiate

4-Day and 3-Day Instructional Plans:
PA 2, page 498—All students, for additional practice

PA 1 Playing Inequality Bingo

Use with 4-Day or 3-Day Instructional Plan. In this activity, students solve inequalities by dividing by the coefficient or multiplying by the inverse of the coefficient.

MATERIALS

- Blackline Master 38
- Blackline Master 77
- Game markers to cover squares

DIRECTIONS

1. Review the following terms and symbols with students:

   coefficient A number or quantity placed before a variable, which indicates multiplication of that variable

   inequality A mathematical sentence that compares two expressions using one of the following symbols:

   > Greater than

   ≥ Greater than or equal to

   < Less than

   ≤ Less than or equal to

2. Distribute one copy of Blackline Master 38, 4 × 4 Bingo Card, to each student.

3. Make a transparency of Blackline Master 77, Inequality Bingo, and show it on the overhead. Alternatively, copy the inequalities from Blackline Master 77 on the board. Have students write the inequalities in the squares of the bingo card in a random fashion.

38

Name _____ Date _____

4 × 4 BINGO CARD

77

Name _____ Date _____

INEQUALITY BINGO

1.	$x < 4$	$3x < 12$
2.	$x > 4$	$-5x < -20$
3.	$x \geq -3$	$4x \geq -12$
4.	$x \leq -3$	$-3x \geq 9$
5.	$x > 2$	$7x > 14$
6.	$x < 2$	$18 > 9x$
7.	$x \leq 0$	$7x \leq 0$
8.	$x > 0$	$-5x < 0$
9.	$x < 1$	$-27x > -27$
10.	$x < -1$	$-9x > 9$
11.	$x \geq 7$	$-3x \leq -21$
12.	$x < 7$	$-5x > -35$
13.	$x = 6$	$-3x = -18$
14.	$x > 10$	$-\frac{1}{2}x < -5$
15.	$x = 2$	$-25x = -50$
16.	$x < 10$	$10x < 100$

---

4. Select a problem at random from the problem list, and write it on the board or overhead. Tell students to solve the problem and use a marker to cover the square on the bingo card that corresponds to that answer.

Problem list:

$3x < 12$	$7x \leq 0$	$-3x = -18$
$-5x < -20$	$-5x < 0$	$-\frac{1}{2}x < -5$
$4x \geq -12$	$-27x > -27$	$-25x = -50$
$-3x \geq 9$	$-9x > 9$	$10x < 100$
$7x > 14$	$-3x \leq -21$	
$18 > 9x$	$-5x > -35$	

5. Repeat Step 4 until a student has four markers in a row horizontally, vertically, or diagonally. Instead of shouting "Bingo!" the student could shout the name of the school mascot, or even just raise a hand.

6. Check to see if the student has the correct solutions covered.

7. If the solutions are correct, declare that student the winner, have all students clear their cards, and begin play again. Be sure to pick the problems from the problem list in a random fashion.

8. Repeat the game as long as you like. You may alter problems by multiplying both sides of the inequalities by the same positive number.

NEXT STEPS • Differentiate

4-Day Instructional Plan:
PM 1, page 499—All students, to assess progress

👥 3-Day Instructional Plan:
PM 2, page 500—Students who demonstrate understanding of the concept, to assess progress

PM 1, page 499—Students who need additional support, to assess progress

Practice Activities

PA 2 Playing Switch It

Use with 4-Day or 3-Day Instructional Plan. In this activity, students recognize when the inequality sign must be reversed to solve the inequality.

MATERIALS

- Blank cards, five per student

DIRECTIONS

1. Review the following term and symbols with students:

   inequality A mathematical sentence that compares two expressions using one of the following symbols:

   > Greater than

   ≥ Greater than or equal to

   < Less than

   ≤ Less than or equal to

2. Distribute five cards to each student.

3. Instruct students to write an inequality on each card, adhering to the following guidelines:

   - At least two of the inequalities should involve multiplication and at least two should involve division.

   - In at least one of the inequalities, the solution should involve a switch of inequality sign for each operation, and in at least one of the inequalities, the solution should not involve a switch of inequality sign for each operation.

4. Put students in groups of four. Have all students check every card in their group to see that they follow the instructions in Step 3.

5. Have each group exchange cards with another group.

6. Tell groups to shuffle the cards they received and place them equation-side down.

7. Explain the game rules to students.

   - The first player turns over a card so everyone in the group can see it.

   - The object of the game is to be the first one to recognize an inequality for which the solution involves switching the inequality sign. When such an inequality is spotted, the student says, "Switch it!" In turn, each of the players turns over a card.

   - The first player to say "Switch it!" gets all the cards played in that round.

   - If a player says "Switch it!" incorrectly, he or she must put three cards from his or her own stack at the bottom of the deck.

   - The student with the most cards when the deck is gone is the winner.

   | **Variation:** The groups exchange cards an extra time and solve the inequalities they receive. This exchange can continue among all the groups.

NEXT STEPS • Differentiate

4-Day Instructional Plan:
PM 2, page 500—All students, to assess progress

3-Day Instructional Plan:
PS 1, page 501—Students who are on the accelerated path, to develop problem-solving skills
PM 2, page 500—Students who are on the differentiated path, to assess progress

Objective 2
Progress-Monitoring Activities

PM 1 Apply Skills 1

Use with 4-Day or 3-Day Instructional Plan.

MATERIALS

- *Interactive Text*, page 209

DIRECTIONS

1. Have students turn to *Interactive Text*, page 209, Apply Skills 1.

2. Remind students of the key term: *inequality*.

3. Monitor student work, and provide feedback as necessary.

   Watch for:
   - Do students use multiplication and division to isolate the variable?
   - Do students reverse the inequality sign when multiplying or dividing by a negative number?

NEXT STEPS • Differentiate

👥 4-Day and 3-Day Instructional Plans:

PA 2, page 498—Students who demonstrate understanding of the concept, for additional practice

CD 2, page 494—Students who need additional concept development

---

Name_____ Date_____

APPLY SKILLS 1

Solve and graph the solution for each inequality.

Example:

$\frac{x}{2} \le -2$ $x \le -4$

$\frac{x}{2} \cdot 2 \le -2 \cdot 2$

1. $3x < 18$ $x < 6$

   $\left(\frac{1}{3}\right)3x < 18\left(\frac{1}{3}\right)$

2. $-4y \ge 8$ $y \le -2$

   $\left(-\frac{1}{4}\right)(-4y) \le 8\left(-\frac{1}{4}\right)$

3. $-\frac{z}{3} \le -5$ $z \ge 15$

   $(-3)\left(-\frac{z}{3}\right) \ge -5(-3)$

4. $\frac{a}{7} > 3$ $a > 21$

   $(7)\frac{a}{7} > 3(7)$

5. $6b > -36$ $b > -6$

   $\left(\frac{1}{6}\right)6b > -36\left(\frac{1}{6}\right)$

6. $-5c \ge -15$ $c \le 3$

   $\left(-\frac{1}{5}\right)(-5c) \le -15\left(-\frac{1}{5}\right)$

7. $\frac{d}{8} > -1$ $d > -8$

   $(8)\frac{d}{8} > -1(8)$

8. $\frac{f}{12} \le -2$ $f \le -24$

   $(12)\frac{f}{12} \le -2(12)$

9. $x - 12 < -15$ $x < -3$

   $x - 12 + 12 < -15 + 12$

10. $y + 15 \ge 9$ $y \ge -6$

    $y + 15 - 15 \ge 9 - 15$

Progress-Monitoring Activities

PM 2 Apply Skills 2

Use with 4-Day or 3-Day Instructional Plan.

MATERIALS

- *Interactive Text*, page 210

DIRECTIONS

1. Have students turn to *Interactive Text*, page 210, Apply Skills 2.

2. Remind students of the key term: *inequality.*

3. Monitor student work, and provide feedback as necessary.

   Watch for:
   - Do students correctly isolate the variable before graphing?
   - Do students reverse the inequality sign when multiplying or dividing by a negative number?

NEXT STEPS • Differentiate

4-Day Instructional Plan:

PS 1, page 501—Students who are on the accelerated path, to develop problem-solving skills

Objective 2 Posttest, page 503—Students who are on the differentiated path

3-Day Instructional Plan:

PA 2, page 498—Students who are on the accelerated path, for additional practice

PS 1, page 501—Students on the differentiated path who demonstrated understanding on PM 1, to develop problem-solving skills

Objective 2 Posttest, page 503—All other students

Name _____ Date _____

APPLY SKILLS 2

Solve and graph the solution for each inequality.

Example:
$4x < 32$ $x < 8$
$\frac{4x}{4} < \frac{32}{4}$

1. $7x < 56$ $x < 8$
   $\left(\frac{1}{7}\right)7x < 56\left(\frac{1}{7}\right)$

2. $-4y \geq 28$ $y \leq -7$
   $\left(-\frac{1}{4}\right)(-4y) \leq 28\left(-\frac{1}{4}\right)$

3. $-\frac{z}{6} \leq -8$ $z \geq 48$
   $(-6)\left(-\frac{z}{6}\right) \geq -8(-6)$

4. $\frac{a}{8} > -4$ $a > -32$
   $(8)\frac{a}{8} > -4(8)$

5. $9b > -36$ $b > -4$
   $\left(\frac{1}{9}\right)9b > -36\left(\frac{1}{9}\right)$

6. $-5c \geq -75$ $c \leq 15$
   $\left(-\frac{1}{5}\right)(-5c) \leq -75\left(-\frac{1}{5}\right)$

7. $-\frac{d}{7} > -9$ $d < 63$
   $(-7)\left(-\frac{d}{7}\right) < -9(-7)$

8. $\frac{f}{12} \leq -2$ $f \leq -24$
   $(12)\frac{f}{12} \leq -2(12)$

9. $x - 27 < -18$ $x < 9$
   $x - 27 + 27 < -18 + 27$

10. $y + 19 \geq 36$ $y \geq 17$
    $y + 19 - 19 \geq 36 - 19$

Problem-Solving Activity

★PS 1 Relating Equations and Inequalities

Use with 4-Day or 3-Day Instructional Plan. In this activity, students reverse the inequality sign in the correct situations.

DIRECTIONS

1. Review the following term and symbols with students:

   inequality A mathematical sentence that compares two expressions using one of the following symbols:

   > Greater than

   ≥ Greater than or equal to

   < Less than

   ≤ Less than or equal to

2. Write the following equations and inequalities on the board and have students solve them.

   $5x = 35$ $x = 7$ **$5x < 35$** $x < 7$

   $5x > 35$ $x > 7$ **$5x ≤ 35$** $x ≤ 7$

3. Ask students to describe the steps in solving the equation and the inequalities. Divide $5x$ by 5, and divide 35 by 5.

4. Ask students if there is any difference in the inequality sign. Tell students to explain the difference, if there is one. There is no difference in the sign.

5. Repeat Steps 2–4 for more problems.

   Sample problems:

   $\frac{x}{3} = 4$ $x = 12$ $\frac{x}{3} ≥ 4$ $x ≥ 12$

   $\frac{x}{3} < 4$ $x < 12$ $\frac{x}{3} ≤ 4$ $x ≤ 12$

   Multiply both sides by 3; no difference in signs

   $-4x = 16$ $x = -4$ **$-4x > 16$** $x < -4$

   $-4x < 16$ $x > -4$ **$-4x ≥ 16$** $x ≤ -4$

   Divide both sides by –4 and switch the inequality signs. The difference is that you must switch the inequality sign.

   $\frac{x}{-2} = -8$ $x = 16$ $\frac{x}{-2} ≤ -8$ $x ≥ 16$

   $\frac{x}{-2} < -8$ $x > 16$ $\frac{x}{-2} ≥ -8$ $x ≤ 16$

   Multiply both sides by –2 and switch the inequality signs. The difference is that if you multiply or divide by a negative, you must switch the inequality sign.

6. Make sure students recognize that whenever both sides are multiplied or divided by a negative number, the inequality sign must be reversed.

NEXT STEPS • Differentiate

4-Day and 3-Day Instructional Plans:
Objective 2 Posttest, page 503—All students

★ = Includes Problem Solving

This page intentionally left blank

Ongoing Assessment

Objective 2 Posttest

Discuss with students the key concepts in Objective 2. Following the discussion, administer the Objective 2 Posttest to all students.

Using the Results

• Score the posttest and update the class record card.

• Provide reinforcement for students who do not demonstrate mastery of the concepts through individual or small-group reteaching of key concepts.

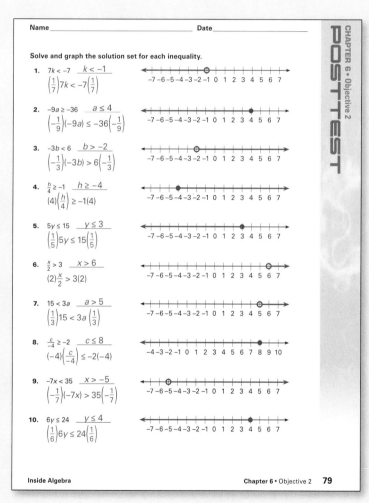

Name _____ Date _____

CHAPTER 6 • Objective 2
POSTTEST

Solve and graph the solution set for each inequality.

1. $7k < -7$ $k < -1$
$$\left(\frac{1}{7}\right)7k < -7\left(\frac{1}{7}\right)$$

2. $-9a \geq -36$ $a \leq 4$
$$\left(-\frac{1}{9}\right)(-9a) \leq -36\left(-\frac{1}{9}\right)$$

3. $-3b < 6$ $b > -2$
$$\left(-\frac{1}{3}\right)(-3b) > 6\left(-\frac{1}{3}\right)$$

4. $\frac{h}{4} \geq -1$ $h \geq -4$
$$(4)\left(\frac{h}{4}\right) \geq -1(4)$$

5. $5y \leq 15$ $y \leq 3$
$$\left(\frac{1}{5}\right)5y \leq 15\left(\frac{1}{5}\right)$$

6. $\frac{x}{2} > 3$ $x > 6$
$$(2)\frac{x}{2} > 3(2)$$

7. $15 < 3a$ $a > 5$
$$\left(\frac{1}{3}\right)15 < 3a\left(\frac{1}{3}\right)$$

8. $\frac{c}{-4} \geq -2$ $c \leq 8$
$$(-4)\left(\frac{c}{-4}\right) \leq -2(-4)$$

9. $-7x < 35$ $x > -5$
$$\left(-\frac{1}{7}\right)(-7x) > 35\left(-\frac{1}{7}\right)$$

10. $6y \leq 24$ $y \leq 4$
$$\left(\frac{1}{6}\right)6y \leq 24\left(\frac{1}{6}\right)$$

Inside Algebra   Chapter 6 • Objective 2   **79**

6 CHAPTER

Objective 3
Solve and graph the solution set of inequalities using more than one operation.

Objective 3 Pretest

Students complete the Objective 3 Pretest on the same day as the Objective 2 Posttest.

Using the Results

• Score the pretest and update the class record card.

• If the majority of students do not demonstrate mastery of the concepts, use the 5-Day Instructional Plan for Objective 3.

• If the majority of students demonstrate mastery of the concepts, use the 3-Day Instructional Plan for Objective 3.

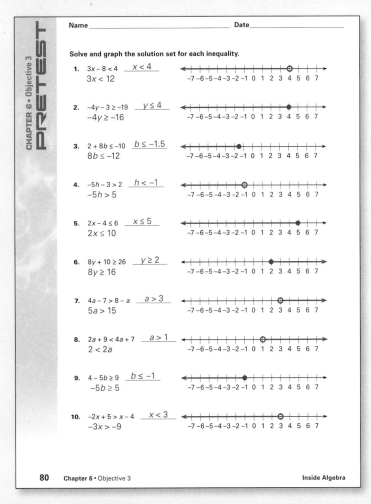

Goals and Activities

Objective 3 Goals

The following activities, when used with the instructional plans on pages 506 and 507, enable students to:

- Solve the inequality $-3x + 9 < -6$ for x and graph the solution as **$x > 5$**

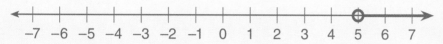

- Solve the inequality $-5 + 4h \leq 15 - h$ for h and graph the solution as **$h \leq 4$**

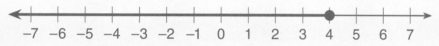

Objective 3 Activities

Concept Development Activities	
★**CD 1** Solving Inequalities and Equations, page 508	**CD 2** Solving Inequalities in More Than One Way, page 509

Practice Activities	
PA 1 Playing Solve and Graph, Beginning Version, page 511	**PA 2** Playing Solve and Graph, Experienced Version, page 513

Progress-Monitoring Activities		
PM 1 Apply Skills 1, page 515	**PM 2** Apply Skills 2, page 516	**PM 3** Apply Skills 3, page 517

★Problem-Solving Activities	
★**PS 1** Writing and Solving Inequalities, page 518	★**PS 2** Solving Inequality Word Problems, page 520

Ongoing Assessment
Posttest Objective 3, page 521
Pretest Objective 4, page 522

CD = Concept Development PM = Progress Monitoring PS = Problem Solving
PA = Practice Activity ★ = Includes Problem Solving

5-Day Instructional Plan

Use the 5-Day Instructional Plan when pretest results indicate that students would benefit from a slower pace. This plan is used when the majority of students need more time or did not demonstrate mastery on the pretest. This plan does not include all activities.

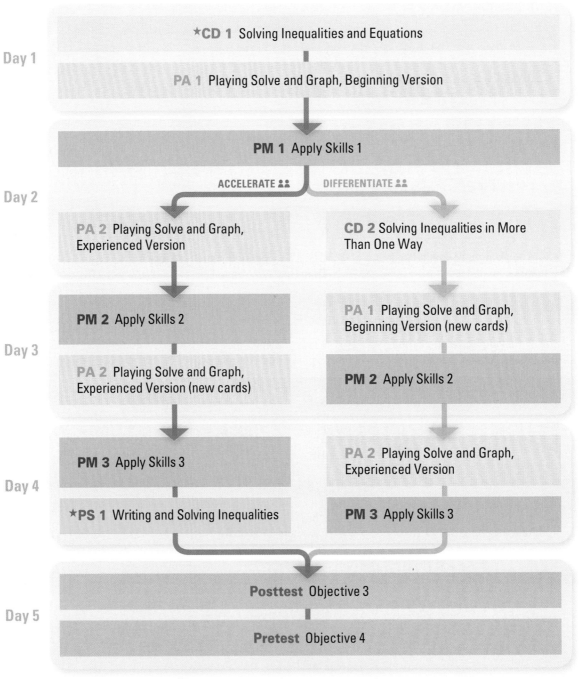

Day 1
★**CD 1** Solving Inequalities and Equations
PA 1 Playing Solve and Graph, Beginning Version

PM 1 Apply Skills 1

ACCELERATE   **DIFFERENTIATE**

Day 2
PA 2 Playing Solve and Graph, Experienced Version

CD 2 Solving Inequalities in More Than One Way

Day 3
PM 2 Apply Skills 2

PA 2 Playing Solve and Graph, Experienced Version (new cards)

PA 1 Playing Solve and Graph, Beginning Version (new cards)

PM 2 Apply Skills 2

Day 4
PM 3 Apply Skills 3

★**PS 1** Writing and Solving Inequalities

PA 2 Playing Solve and Graph, Experienced Version

PM 3 Apply Skills 3

Day 5
Posttest Objective 3

Pretest Objective 4

CD = Concept Development   **PM = Progress Monitoring**   **PS = Problem Solving**
PA = Practice Activity   ★ **= Includes Problem Solving**

3-Day Instructional Plan

Use the 3-Day Instructional Plan when pretest results indicate that students can move through the activities at a faster pace. This plan is ideal when the majority of students demonstrate mastery on the pretest. This plan does not include all activities.

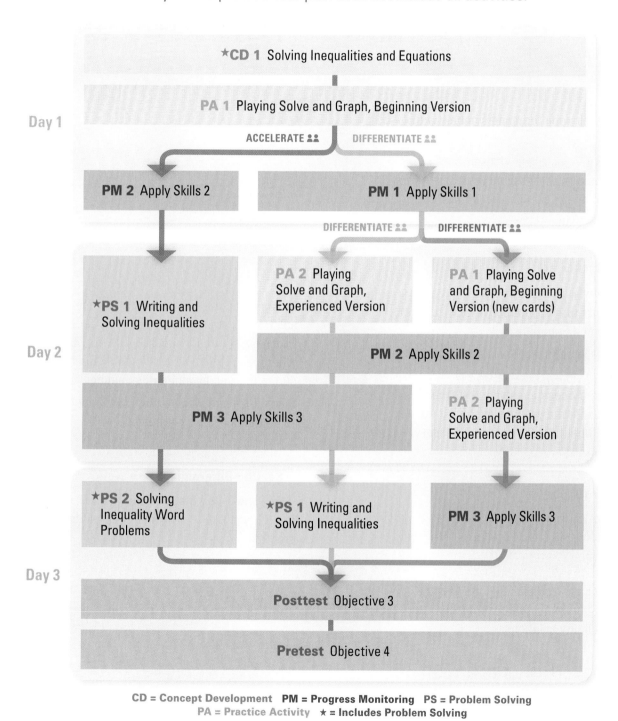

Day 1

★CD 1 Solving Inequalities and Equations

PA 1 Playing Solve and Graph, Beginning Version

ACCELERATE 👥   DIFFERENTIATE 👥

PM 2 Apply Skills 2   PM 1 Apply Skills 1

DIFFERENTIATE 👥   DIFFERENTIATE 👥

Day 2

★PS 1 Writing and Solving Inequalities

PA 2 Playing Solve and Graph, Experienced Version

PA 1 Playing Solve and Graph, Beginning Version (new cards)

PM 2 Apply Skills 2

PM 3 Apply Skills 3

PA 2 Playing Solve and Graph, Experienced Version

Day 3

★PS 2 Solving Inequality Word Problems

★PS 1 Writing and Solving Inequalities

PM 3 Apply Skills 3

Posttest Objective 3

Pretest Objective 4

CD = Concept Development   PM = Progress Monitoring   PS = Problem Solving
PA = Practice Activity   ★ = Includes Problem Solving

Objective 3
Concept Development Activities

★CD 1 Solving Inequalities and Equations

Use with 5-Day or 3-Day Instructional Plan. In this activity, students understand the difference between solving equations and inequalities.

MATERIALS

- *Interactive Text*, page 211

DIRECTIONS

1. Review the following term and symbols with students:

   inequality A mathematical sentence that compares two expressions using one of the following symbols:

   > Greater than

   ≥ Greater than or equal to

   < Less than

   ≤ Less than or equal to

2. Have students turn to *Interactive Text*, page 211, Inequalities and Equations.

3. Put students in pairs, and have each pair solve Problems 1–4.

4. Compare the process of solving the problems as inequalities with the process of solving them as equations. Substitute numbers if necessary.

   Examples:

   $4x + 7 = 19$ Solution: $x = 3$

   $4x + 7 < 19$ Solution: $x < 3$; therefore $x = 3$ will not work, but $x = 2$ will work as will any number less than 3.

5. Have pairs solve Problems 5–9. Review the relationship between the equation solution and the inequality solutions.

6. Have pairs solve Problems 10–14. Discuss the solutions to these problems. Point out that in Problems 1–9 the inequalities do not change, whereas in Problems 10–14 the inequalities change due to division by a negative number.

7. Summarize and write a good response to Problem 15 on the board or overhead.

NEXT STEPS • Differentiate

5-Day and 3-Day Instructional Plans:
PA 1, page 511—All students, for additional practice

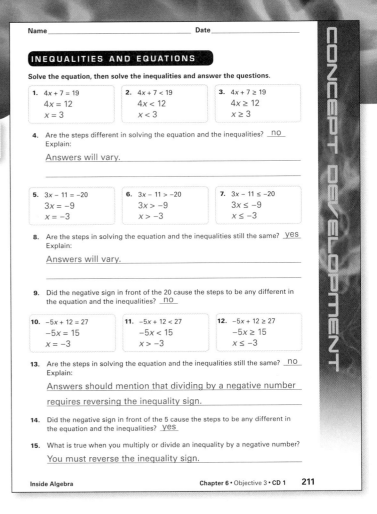

★ = Includes Problem Solving

Concept Development Activities

CD 2 Solving Inequalities in More Than One Way

Use with 5-Day Instructional Plan. In this activity, students solve inequalities by doing addition and subtraction before multiplication and division.

DIRECTIONS

1. Review the following term and symbols with students:

   inequality A mathematical sentence that compares two expressions using one of the following symbols:

   > Greater than

   ≥ Greater than or equal to

   < Less than

   ≤ Less than or equal to

2. Write **2x + 3 < 7** on the board or overhead. Ask students what operations must be performed to solve this inequality. Divide by 2 (or multiply by $\frac{1}{2}$) and subtract $\frac{3}{2}$, or reverse these operations.

3. Explain that the equations can be solved in two different ways.

   • Divide, then subtract

   • Subtract, then divide

4. Ask students to solve 2x + 3 < 7 using both ways.

$2x + 3 < 7$	$2x + 3 < 7$
$\frac{(2x+3)}{2} < \frac{7}{2}$	$2x + 3 - 3 < 7 - 3$
$x + \frac{3}{2} < \frac{7}{2}$	$2x < 4$
$x + \frac{3}{2} - \frac{3}{2} < \frac{7}{2} - \frac{3}{2}$	$\frac{2x}{2} < \frac{4}{2}$
$x < \frac{4}{2}$	$x < 2$
$x < 2$	

5. Point out that the answers are the same. Explain that the order in which the operations are done makes no difference.

6. Try another problem with the class by solving it in two different ways.

   Sample problem:

$3x - 7 > 5$	$3x - 7 > 5$
$\frac{(3x-7)}{3} > \frac{5}{3}$	$3x - 7 + 7 > 5 + 7$
$x - \frac{7}{3} > \frac{5}{3}$	$3x > 12$
$x - \frac{7}{3} + \frac{7}{3} > \frac{5}{3} + \frac{7}{3}$	$\frac{3x}{3} > \frac{12}{3}$
$x > \frac{12}{3}$	$x > 4$
$x > 4$	

7. Ask students to discuss which process seems easier. Make sure students recognize that adding or subtracting before dividing is easier in the type of equations used in the examples. Remind students that regardless of which method is easier, both methods will give the same answer.

Concept Development Activities

8. Give students more examples and have them think about which process is easier. Have volunteers discuss the steps they take for each problem.

Sample problems:

$5x - 9 \geq 6$	$5x - 9 \geq 6$
$\dfrac{(5x-9)}{5} \geq \dfrac{6}{5}$	$5x - 9 + 9 \geq 6 + 9$
$x - \dfrac{9}{5} \geq \dfrac{6}{5}$	$5x \geq 15$
$x - \dfrac{9}{5} + \dfrac{9}{5} \geq \dfrac{6}{5} + \dfrac{9}{5}$	$\dfrac{5x}{5} \geq \dfrac{15}{5}$
$x \geq \dfrac{15}{5}$	$x \geq 3$
$x \geq 3$	

$4x + 9 < -7$	$4x + 9 < -7$
$\dfrac{(4x+9)}{4} < -\dfrac{7}{4}$	$4x + 9 - 9 < -7 - 9$
$x + \dfrac{9}{4} < -\dfrac{7}{4}$	$4x < -16$
$x + \dfrac{9}{4} - \dfrac{9}{4} < -\dfrac{7}{4} - \dfrac{9}{4}$	$\dfrac{4x}{4} < -\dfrac{16}{4}$
$x < -\dfrac{16}{4}$	$x < -4$
$x < -4$	

9. Tell students to write a generalization about the process of solving any inequality of the form $ax + b > c$, where the $>$ sign could also be $<$, $\geq$, or $\leq$.

Listen for:

- Do any addition or subtraction before any multiplication or division.

- The main concept is to undo the operations by principal operator first.

10. Make sure students understand that in $ax + b > c$, the principal operator is addition ($ax + b$), so we undo the addition first by subtracting b: $ax > c - b$. Now the principal operator is multiplication (ax), so we undo the multiplication by dividing by a: $x > \dfrac{(c-b)}{a}$. Note that a is a positive number here; if it is negative, the inequality sign is reversed.

11. Ask students to use the easiest process to solve the problem **$3x - 4 > 14$**.

$3x - 4 + 4 > 14 + 4$

$3x > 18$

$x > 6$

NEXT STEPS • Differentiate

5-Day Instructional Plan:
PA 1 (new cards), page 511—All students, for additional practice

PA 1 Playing Solve and Graph, Beginning Version

Use with 5-Day or 3-Day Instructional Plan. In this activity, students follow the correct steps to solve simple inequalities.

MATERIALS

- Blank cards, five per student

DIRECTIONS

1. Review the following terms and symbols with students:

   coefficient A number or quantity placed before a variable, which indicates multiplication of that variable

   inequality A mathematical sentence that compares two expressions using one of the following symbols:

   > Greater than

   ≥ Greater than or equal to

   < Less than

   ≤ Less than or equal to

2. Give each student five blank cards.

3. Have students write a large **P** on one of their blank cards to identify the problem cards. Have them write an inequality problem on the back side of that card.

4. Have students write a large **S** on their four other cards to identify the solution cards. Explain to students that each of the four steps needed to solve and graph the problem they wrote on the problem card should be written on one of the four solution cards, one step per card.

5. Explain the directions for the solution cards, and have students complete their solution cards as you explain.

   - Solution Card 1: Add to both sides of the inequality the opposite of the constant term on the side with the variable.

   - Solution Card 2: Divide both sides of the inequality by the coefficient of the variable; if the coefficient is negative, reverse the inequality sign.

   - Solution Card 3: Write the solution.

   - Solution Card 4: Graph the solution set.

6. If students are having difficulty completing their sets of cards, demonstrate example sets.

   Examples:

Problem Cards	Solution Cards

   $2x + 3 < 5$
   Card 1 Add −3 to both sides (or subtract 3 from both sides)
   Card 2 Divide both sides by 2
   Card 3 $x < 1$
   Card 4

   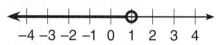

   $5 - 3x > -4$
   Card 1 Add −5 to both sides (or subtract 5 from both sides)
   Card 2 Divide both sides by −3 and reverse the inequality sign
   Card 3 $x < 3$
   Card 4

   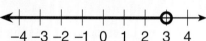

   $3x + 9 \geq 6$
   Card 1 Add −9 to both sides (or subtract 9 from both sides)
   Card 2 Divide both sides by 3
   Card 3 $x \geq -1$
   Card 4

   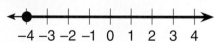

   $-4x - 7 \leq 9$
   Card 1 Add 7 to both sides
   Card 2 Divide both sides by −4 and reverse the inequality sign
   Card 3 $x \geq -4$
   Card 4

   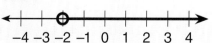

   $4 + \frac{x}{2} > 3$
   Card 1 Add −4 to both sides
   Card 2 Multiply both sides by 2
   Card 3 $x > -2$
   Card 4

7. Divide the class into groups of four or five. Be sure each student has a pencil and paper to work the problems. Give each group a deck of cards with four or five problem cards and the matching solution cards. Be sure all the problems in each group are different, although different groups can have the same problem sets.

8. Devise a method to determine who goes first in each group. One method would be to number the students in the group from 1 to 4 or 5 and to pick a random number by drawing a card or rolling a die.

9. Explain the game rules to students.

   - The person who is first shuffles all the solution cards and deals them all out, face down.

   - The person to the left shuffles all the problem cards and deals them all out, face down.

   - The person who is first starts the game by laying down his or her problem card. All students work the problem on paper.

   - The person who has the solution card with the first step of the solution then plays it.

   - Next, the person who has the next step of the solution plays that card.

   - Last, the person with the final solution plays that card.

   - The person with the correct solution graph plays that card.

   - The person who played the graph card begins the next round by playing his or her problem card. If he or she does not have a problem card, play continues with the next person in a clockwise direction who has a problem card.

   - The winner is the first person to play all his or her cards.

   - Cards can be shuffled to play again.

NEXT STEPS • Differentiate

👥 5-Day Instructional Plan:

   PM 1, page 515—Students completing the activity for the first time, to assess progress

   PM 2, page 516—Students completing the activity for the second time, to assess progress

👥 3-Day Instructional Plan:

   PM 2, page 516—Students completing the activity for the first time who demonstrate understanding of the concept, to assess progress

   PM 1, page 515—Students completing the activity for the first time who need additional support, to assess progress

   PM 2, page 516—Students completing the activity for the second time, to assess progress

Objective 3
Practice Activities

PA 2 Playing Solve and Graph, Experienced Version

Use with 5-Day or 3-Day Instructional Plan. In this activity, students follow the correct steps to solve inequalities that are more complex.

MATERIALS

- Blank cards, six per student

DIRECTIONS

1. Review the following term and symbols with students:

    inequality A mathematical sentence that compares two expressions using one of the following symbols:

    > Greater than

    ≥ Greater than or equal to

    < Less than

    ≤ Less than or equal to

2. Give each student six blank cards.

3. Have students write a large **P** on one of their blank cards to identify the problem cards. Have them write an inequality problem on the back side of that card.

4. Have students write a large **S** on their five other cards to identify the solution cards. Explain to students that each of the five steps needed to solve and graph the problem they wrote on the problem card should be written on the five solution cards, one step per card.

5. Explain the directions for the solution cards, and have students complete their solution cards as you explain.

    - Solution Card 1: Add to both sides of the inequality the opposite of the variable term on one of the sides of the inequality.

    - Solution Card 2: Add to both sides of the resulting inequality the opposite of the constant term on the side with the variable.

    - Solution Card 3: Divide both sides of the inequality by the coefficient of the variable; if the coefficient is negative, reverse the inequality sign.

    - Solution Card 4: Write the solution.

    - Solution Card 5: Graph the solution set.

6. If students are having difficulty completing their sets of cards, demonstrate example sets.

    Examples:

    Problem Card $3x - 4 < x - 5$

    Solution Cards   **Card 1** Add $-x$ to both sides (or subtract x from both sides)
    Card 2 Add 4 to both sides
    Card 3 Divide both sides by 2
    Card 4 $x < -\frac{1}{2}$
    Card 5

    Problem Card $6 - 3x > 2x - 4$

    Solution Cards   **Card 1** Add $-2x$ to both sides (or subtract $2x$ from both sides)
    Card 2 Add -6 to both sides (or subtract 6 from both sides)
    Card 3 Divide both sides by -5 and reverse the inequality sign
    Card 4 $x < 2$
    Card 5

    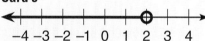

    Problem Card $4x + 7 \geq 6x + 15$

    Solution Cards   **Card 1** Add $-6x$ to both sides (or subtract $6x$ from both sides)
    Card 2 Add -7 to both sides (or subtract 7 from both sides)
    Card 3 Divide both sides by -2 and reverse the inequality sign
    Card 4 $x \leq -4$
    Card 5

    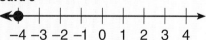

    Problem Card $x - 7 \leq 8 - 2x$

    Solution Cards   **Card 1** Add $2x$ to both sides
    Card 2 Add 7 to both sides
    Card 3 Divide both sides by 3
    Card 4 $x \leq 5$
    Card 5

    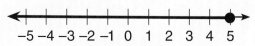

7. Divide the class into groups of four or five. Be sure each student has a pencil and paper to work the problems. Give each group a deck of cards with four or five problem cards and the matching solution cards. Be sure all the problems in each group are different, although different groups can have the same problem sets.

8. Devise a method to determine who goes first in each group. One method would be to number the students in the group from 1 to 4 or 5 and to pick a random number by drawing a card or rolling a die.

9. Explain the game rules to students.

   • The person who is first shuffles all the solution cards and deals them all out, face down.

   • The person to the left shuffles all the problem cards and deals them all out, face down.

   • The person who is first starts the game by laying down his or her problem card. All students work the problem on their paper.

   • The person with the solution card with the first step of the solution plays it.

   • Next, the person with the next step of the solution plays that card, and play continues until the final solution card is played.

   • The person with the correct solution graph plays that card.

   • The person who played the graph card begins the next round by playing his or her problem card. If he or she does not have a problem card, play continues with the next person in a clockwise direction who has a problem card.

   • The winner is the first person to play all his or her cards.

   • Cards can be shuffled to play again.

NEXT STEPS • Differentiate

👥 **5-Day Instructional Plan:**
   PM 2, page 516—Students on the accelerated path who are completing the activity for the first time, to assess progress

   PM 3, page 517—Students who are completing the activity for the second time, to assess progress

   PM 3, page 517—Students who are on the differentiated path, to assess progress

👥 **3-Day Instructional Plan:**
   PM 2, page 516—Students who demonstrated understanding on PM 1, to assess progress

   PM 3, page 517—All other students, to assess progress

Progress-Monitoring Activities

PM 1 Apply Skills 1

Use with 5-Day or 3-Day Instructional Plan.

MATERIALS

- *Interactive Text*, pages 212–213

DIRECTIONS

1. Have students turn to *Interactive Text*, pages 212–213, Apply Skills 1.

2. Remind students of the key term: *inequality*.

3. Monitor student work, and provide feedback as necessary.

   Watch for:
   - Do students reverse the inequality sign when multiplying or dividing by a negative number?
   - Do students remember to isolate the variable?

NEXT STEPS • Differentiate

👥 5-Day Instructional Plan:

PA 2, page 513—Students who demonstrate understanding of the concept, for additional practice

CD 2, page 509—Students who need additional concept development

👥 3-Day Instructional Plan:

PA 2, page 513—Students who demonstrate understanding of the concept, for additional practice

PA 1, page 511—Students who need additional practice

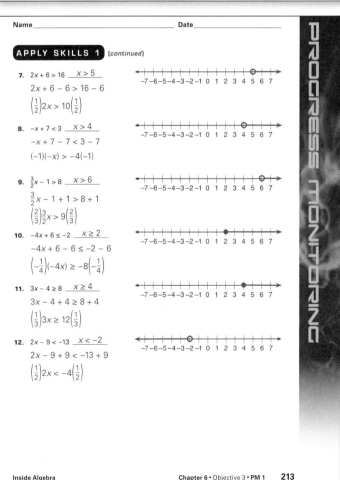

Progress-Monitoring Activities

PM 2 Apply Skills 2

Use with 5-Day or 3-Day Instructional Plan.

MATERIALS

- Interactive Text, pages 214–215

DIRECTIONS

1. Have students turn to Interactive Text, pages 214–215, Apply Skills 2.

2. Remind students of the key term: inequality.

3. Monitor student work, and provide feedback as necessary.

   Watch for:
   - Do students choose to add/subtract or multiply/divide first?
   - Do students isolate the variable on one side of the inequality sign?

NEXT STEPS • Differentiate

5-Day Instructional Plan:

PA 2, page 513—All students, for additional practice

3-Day Instructional Plan:

PS 1, page 518—Students who are on the accelerated path, to develop problem-solving skills

PM 3, page 517—Students on the differentiated path who demonstrated understanding on PM 1, to assess progress

PA 2, page 513—All other students, for additional practice

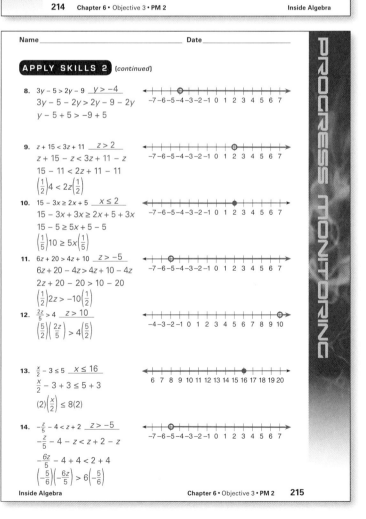

Objective 3
Progress-Monitoring Activities

PM 3 Apply Skills 3

Use with 5-Day or 3-Day Instructional Plan.

MATERIALS

- *Interactive Text*, pages 216–217

DIRECTIONS

1. Have students turn to *Interactive Text*, pages 216–217, Apply Skills 3.

2. Remind students of the key term: *inequality*.

3. Monitor student work, and provide feedback as necessary.

   Watch for:
   - Do students choose to add/subtract or multiply/divide first?
   - Do students isolate the variable on one side of the inequality sign?

NEXT STEPS • Differentiate

5-Day Instructional Plan:

PS 1, page 518—Students who are on the accelerated path, to develop problem-solving skills

Objective 3 Posttest, page 521—Students who are on the differentiated path

3-Day Instructional Plan:

PS 2, page 520—Students who are on the accelerated path, to develop problem-solving skills

PS 1, page 518—Students on the differentiated path who demonstrated understanding on PM 1, to develop problem-solving skills

Objective 3 Posttest, page 521—All other students

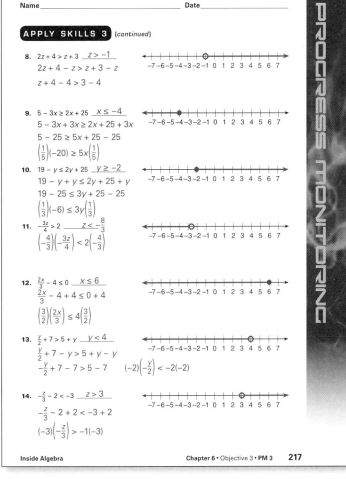

Problem-Solving Activities

★PS 1 Writing and Solving Inequalities

Use with 5-Day or 3-Day Instructional Plan. In this activity, students write inequalities for a given solution.

MATERIALS

- *Interactive Text*, pages 218–219

DIRECTIONS

1. Review the following term and symbols with students:

   inequality A mathematical sentence that compares two expressions using one of the following symbols:

   > Greater than

   ≥ Greater than or equal to

   < Less than

   ≤ Less than or equal to

2. Have students turn to *Interactive Text*, pages 218–219, Writing and Solving Inequalities. Be sure each student has pencil and paper.

3. Read Problem 1 aloud and have each student write an answer. On the board or overhead, write several of the inequalities that students volunteer. Point out that there are many different possible answers. Have the class solve several of the student-created problems to check that the solution is $x < 3$.

4. Have students work on the remaining problems independently, and monitor their progress. After most students have completed Problem 3, stop them and discuss some of the answers. Have the class solve several of the student-created problems.

5. After students complete all problems on *Interactive Text*, pages 218–219, ask them to exchange papers and check to see if the answers are correct solutions to the problems presented.

★ = Includes Problem Solving

Name_____ Date_____

WRITING AND SOLVING INEQUALITIES

Answers will vary. Sample answers are given.

1. Write an inequality that has the solution $x < 3$. The inequality problem must have a solution that involves multiplication (by something other than 1 or −1) and addition or subtraction of a constant.

   $3x + 11 < 20$

2. Write an inequality that has the solution $x > -2$. The inequality problem must have a solution that involves multiplication and a reversal of the inequality sign. It must also involve addition or subtraction of a constant.

   $-\frac{x}{2} - 1 < 0$

3. Write an inequality that matches the graph.

   The inequality problem must have a solution that involves multiplication and a reversal of the inequality sign. It must also involve addition or subtraction of a constant.

   $-4x + 12 \le 8$

4. Write an inequality that matches the graph.

   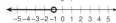

   The inequality problem must have a solution that involves multiplication. It must also involve addition or subtraction of a constant.

   $4x + 6 < 2$

5. Write an inequality that has the solution $x \le 4$. The inequality problem must have a solution that involves division. It must also involve addition or subtraction of a constant.

   $\frac{x}{2} - 7 \le -5$

Name_____ Date_____

WRITING AND SOLVING INEQUALITIES   *(continued)*

6. Write an inequality that has the solution $x \ge -3$. The inequality problem must have a solution that involves division and a reversal of the inequality sign. It must also involve addition or subtraction of a constant.

   $-\frac{x}{6} + 5 \le \frac{11}{2}$

7. Write an inequality that matches the graph.

   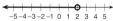

   The inequality problem must have a solution that involves division. It must also involve addition or subtraction of a constant.

   $8x + 9 < 25$

8. Write an inequality that matches the graph.

   The inequality problem must have a solution that involves division and a reversal of the inequality sign. It must also involve addition or subtraction of a constant.

   $-2x + 3 \le 5$

9. Write an inequality that has the solution $x < 3$. The inequality problem must have a variable term and a constant term on both sides of the inequality sign.

   $2x + 5 > 4x - 1$

10. Write an inequality that matches the graph.

    The inequality problem must have a variable term and a constant term on both sides of the inequality sign.

    $x - 4 \le 4x + 8$

5-Day Instructional Plan:

Objective 3 Posttest, page 521—All students

👥 3-Day Instructional Plan:

PM 3, page 517—Students who are on the accelerated path, to assess progress

Objective 3 Posttest, page 521—Students who are on the differentiated path

Problem-Solving Activities

★ PS 2 Solving Inequality Word Problems

Use with 3-Day Instructional Plan. In this activity, students solve word problems involving inequalities.

MATERIALS

- *Interactive Text*, pages 220–221

DIRECTIONS

1. Review the following term and symbols with students:

   inequality A mathematical sentence that compares two expressions using one of the following symbols:

   > Greater than

   ≥ Greater than or equal to

   < Less than

   ≤ Less than or equal to

2. Tell students that in this activity, they read word problems for information, then write and solve inequalities to represent the situation described.

3. Tell students to work individually on this assignment. Have students turn to *Interactive Text*, pages 220–221, Inequality Word Problems, and solve the problems.

4. Notice that Problem 5 asks how much Juanita needs to earn at her regular job only. This is $\frac{1}{52}$ of the difference between the amount she needs ($30,000) and the amount she makes at her part-time job ($4,000).

5. Notice whether students correctly orient the inequality sign in their equations.

NEXT STEPS • Differentiate

3-Day Instructional Plan:
Objective 3 Posttest, page 521—All students

★ = Includes Problem Solving

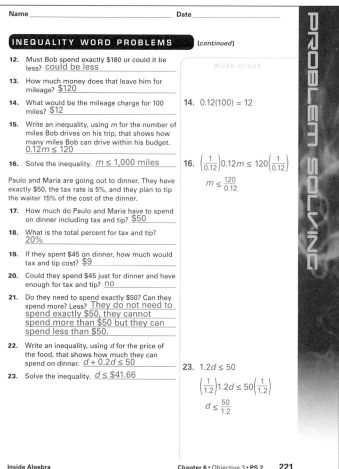

Name _____ Date _____

INEQUALITY WORD PROBLEMS

Juanita wants to buy a house. To qualify for a loan, she must earn at least $30,000 per year. She makes $4,000 a year in her part-time job at a specialty shop. In her regular job as a computer technician, she works 8 hours per day, 5 days a week. She works or gets paid vacation for all 52 weeks per year.

1. How much must Juanita earn per year to qualify for the loan? $30,000

2. How much does she earn in her part-time job? $4,000

3. How much must she earn from her regular job in one year to qualify for the mortgage? $26,000

4. Must Juanita's salary be exactly that amount or could she make more? could earn more

5. Counting 52 weeks in a year, how much would Juanita need to earn per week at her regular job? $500

6. If Juanita works 8 hours per day and 5 days a week, how many hours does Juanita work in a week? 40 hours

7. Write an inequality, using w for Juanita's hourly wage, that shows how much Juanita must be paid per hour to qualify for the loan. 40w ≥ 500

8. Solve the inequality. w ≥ $12.50

   8. $\left(\frac{1}{40}\right)40w \geq 500\left(\frac{1}{40}\right)$
   $w \geq \frac{500}{40}$

Bob is renting a car for the first time. Classic Rentals will rent him a car for $20 per day plus $0.12 a mile. He has a three-day trip planned and cannot spend more than $180 total for the rental car.

9. Write an inequality for how many miles he could drive in the three days. 60 + 0.12m ≤ 180

10. Without counting mileage, how much will Bob spend on the car in three days? $60

11. How much money does Bob have to spend for the car rental? $180

220   Chapter 6 • Objective 3 • PS 2   Inside Algebra

Name _____ Date _____

INEQUALITY WORD PROBLEMS (continued)

12. Must Bob spend exactly $180 or could it be less? could be less

13. How much money does that leave him for mileage? $120

14. What would be the mileage charge for 100 miles? $12

    14. 0.12(100) = 12

15. Write an inequality, using m for the number of miles Bob drives on his trip, that shows how many miles Bob can drive within his budget. 0.12m ≤ 120

16. Solve the inequality. m ≤ 1,000 miles

    16. $\left(\frac{1}{0.12}\right)0.12m \leq 120\left(\frac{1}{0.12}\right)$
    $m \leq \frac{120}{0.12}$

Paulo and Maria are going out to dinner. They have exactly $50, the tax rate is 5%, and they plan to tip the waiter 15% of the cost of the dinner.

17. How much do Paulo and Maria have to spend on dinner including tax and tip? $50

18. What is the total percent for tax and tip? 20%

19. If they spent $45 on dinner, how much would tax and tip cost? $9

20. Could they spend $45 just for dinner and have enough for tax and tip? no

21. Do they need to spend exactly $50? Can they spend more? Less? They do not need to spend exactly $50, they cannot spend more than $50 but they can spend less than $50.

22. Write an inequality, using d for the price of the food, that shows how much they can spend on dinner. d + 0.2d ≤ 50

23. Solve the inequality. d ≤ $41.66

    23. 1.2d ≤ 50
    $\left(\frac{1}{1.2}\right)1.2d \leq 50\left(\frac{1}{1.2}\right)$
    $d \leq \frac{50}{1.2}$

Inside Algebra   Chapter 6 • Objective 3 • PS 2   **221**

Objective 3 Posttest

Discuss with students the key concepts in Objective 3. Following the discussion, administer the Objective 3 Posttest to all students.

Using the Results

• Score the posttest and update the class record card.

• Provide reinforcement for students who do not demonstrate mastery of the concepts through individual or small-group reteaching of key concepts.

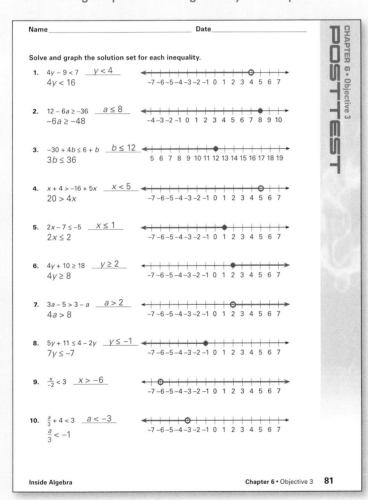

Name_____ Date_____

Solve and graph the solution set for each inequality.

1. $4y - 9 < 7$ $y < 4$
   $4y < 16$

2. $12 - 6a \geq -36$ $a \leq 8$
   $-6a \geq -48$

3. $-30 + 4b \leq 6 + b$ $b \leq 12$
   $3b \leq 36$

4. $x + 4 > -16 + 5x$ $x < 5$
   $20 > 4x$

5. $2x - 7 \leq -5$ $x \leq 1$
   $2x \leq 2$

6. $4y + 10 \geq 18$ $y \geq 2$
   $4y \geq 8$

7. $3a - 5 > 3 - a$ $a > 2$
   $4a > 8$

8. $5y + 11 \leq 4 - 2y$ $y \leq -1$
   $7y \leq -7$

9. $\frac{x}{-2} < 3$ $x > -6$

10. $\frac{a}{3} + 4 < 3$ $a < -3$
    $\frac{a}{3} < -1$

Inside Algebra   Chapter 6 • Objective 3   **81**

CHAPTER 6 • Objective 3
POSTTEST

6 CHAPTER

Objective 4
Solve and graph the solution set of compound inequalities and inequalities involving absolute value.

Objective 4 Pretest

Students complete the Objective 4 Pretest on the same day as the Objective 3 Posttest.

Using the Results

- Score the pretest and update the class record card.

- If the majority of students do not demonstrate mastery of the concepts, use the 5-Day Instructional Plan for Objective 4.

- If the majority of students demonstrate mastery of the concepts, use the 4-Day Instructional Plan for Objective 4.

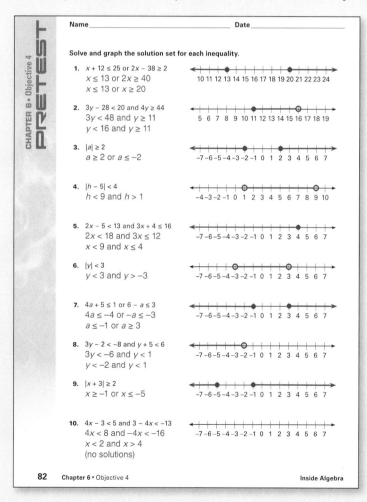

Name _____ Date _____

CHAPTER 6 • Objective 4 PRETEST

Solve and graph the solution set for each inequality.

1. $x + 12 \le 25$ or $2x - 38 \ge 2$
   $x \le 13$ or $2x \ge 40$
   $x \le 13$ or $x \ge 20$

2. $3y - 28 < 20$ and $4y \ge 44$
   $3y < 48$ and $y \ge 11$
   $y < 16$ and $y \ge 11$

3. $|a| \ge 2$
   $a \ge 2$ or $a \le -2$

4. $|h - 5| < 4$
   $h < 9$ and $h > 1$

5. $2x - 5 < 13$ and $3x + 4 \le 16$
   $2x < 18$ and $3x \le 12$
   $x < 9$ and $x \le 4$

6. $|y| < 3$
   $y < 3$ and $y > -3$

7. $4a + 5 \le 1$ or $6 - a \le 3$
   $4a \le -4$ or $-a \le -3$
   $a \le -1$ or $a \ge 3$

8. $3y - 2 < -8$ and $y + 5 < 6$
   $3y < -6$ and $y < 1$
   $y < -2$ and $y < 1$

9. $|x + 3| \ge 2$
   $x \ge -1$ or $x \le -5$

10. $4x - 3 < 5$ and $3 - 4x < -13$
    $4x < 8$ and $-4x < -16$
    $x < 2$ and $x > 4$
    (no solutions)

82 Chapter 6 • Objective 4   Inside Algebra

Objective 4 Goals

The following activities, when used with the instructional plans on pages 524 and 525, enable students to:

- Solve the compound inequality $x - 1 < 9$ or $4x - 23 \geq 37$ for x and graph the solution as **x < 10 or x ≥ 15**

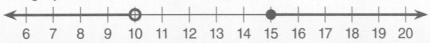

- Solve the compound inequality $4y - 24 \leq 28$ and $6y \geq 54$ for y and graph the solution as **y ≤ 13 and y ≥ 9**

- Solve the compound inequality $|c| \leq 4$ for c and graph the solution as **c ≤ 4 and c ≥ −4**

Objective 4 Activities

Concept Development Activities			
CD 1 Solving Compound Inequalities, page 526	**★CD 2** Understanding Absolute Value, page 528	**CD 3** Understanding Compound Inequalities, page 530	**CD 4** Solving Inequalities With Absolute Value, page 532

Practice Activities	
PA 1 Picking Your Poison, page 534	**PA 2** Making It and Sharing, page 535

Progress-Monitoring Activities				
PM 1 Apply Skills 1, page 536	**PM 2** Apply Skills 2, page 537	**PM 3** Apply Skills 3, page 538	**PM 4** Apply Skills 4, page 539	**PM 5** Apply Skills 5, page 540

★Problem-Solving Activities	
★PS 1 Graphing Compound Inequalities, page 541	**★PS 2** Investigating With Inequalities, page 542

Ongoing Assessment
Posttest Objective 4, page 543
Pretest Objective 5, page 544

CD = Concept Development   PM = Progress Monitoring   PS = Problem Solving
PA = Practice Activity   ★ = Includes Problem Solving

5-Day Instructional Plan

Use the 5-Day Instructional Plan when pretest results indicate that students would benefit from a slower pace. This plan is used when the majority of students need more time or did not demonstrate mastery on the pretest. This plan does not include all activities.

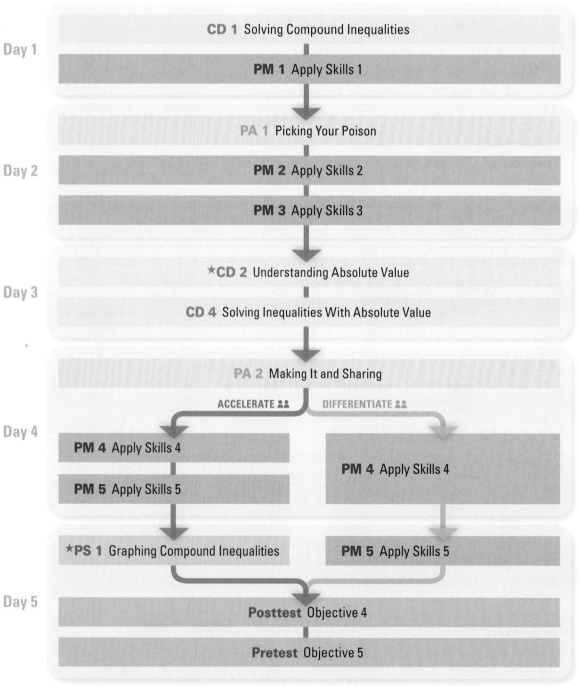

Day 1
- **CD 1** Solving Compound Inequalities
- **PM 1** Apply Skills 1

Day 2
- **PA 1** Picking Your Poison
- **PM 2** Apply Skills 2
- **PM 3** Apply Skills 3

Day 3
- **★CD 2** Understanding Absolute Value
- **CD 4** Solving Inequalities With Absolute Value

Day 4
- **PA 2** Making It and Sharing

ACCELERATE 👥   DIFFERENTIATE 👥
- **PM 4** Apply Skills 4
- **PM 5** Apply Skills 5
- **PM 4** Apply Skills 4

Day 5
- **★PS 1** Graphing Compound Inequalities
- **PM 5** Apply Skills 5
- **Posttest** Objective 4
- **Pretest** Objective 5

**CD = Concept Development   PM = Progress Monitoring   PS = Problem Solving
PA = Practice Activity   ★ = Includes Problem Solving**

4-Day Instructional Plan

Use the 4-Day Instructional Plan when pretest results indicate that students can move through the activities at a faster pace. This plan is ideal when the majority of students demonstrate mastery on the pretest. This plan does not include all activities.

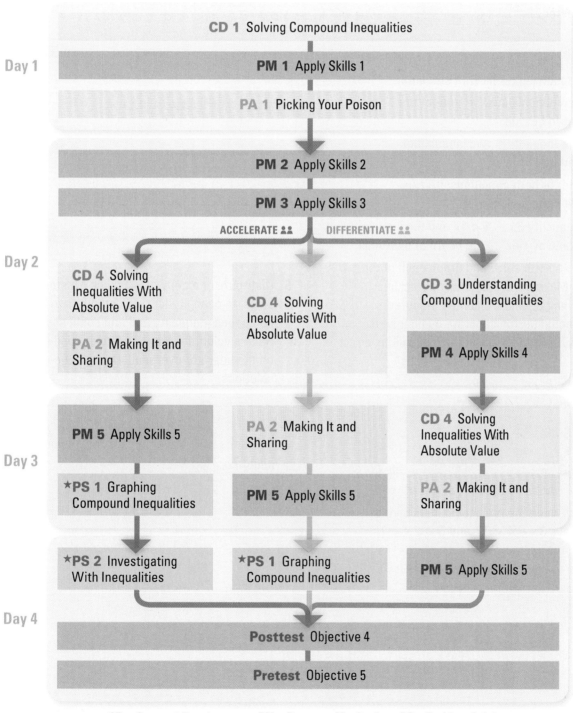

Day 1

CD 1 Solving Compound Inequalities

PM 1 Apply Skills 1

PA 1 Picking Your Poison

PM 2 Apply Skills 2

PM 3 Apply Skills 3

ACCELERATE 🔹🔹   DIFFERENTIATE 🔹🔹

Day 2

CD 4 Solving Inequalities With Absolute Value

PA 2 Making It and Sharing

CD 4 Solving Inequalities With Absolute Value

CD 3 Understanding Compound Inequalities

PM 4 Apply Skills 4

Day 3

PM 5 Apply Skills 5

★**PS 1** Graphing Compound Inequalities

PA 2 Making It and Sharing

PM 5 Apply Skills 5

CD 4 Solving Inequalities With Absolute Value

PA 2 Making It and Sharing

★**PS 2** Investigating With Inequalities

★**PS 1** Graphing Compound Inequalities

PM 5 Apply Skills 5

Day 4

Posttest Objective 4

Pretest Objective 5

CD = Concept Development   PM = Progress Monitoring   PS = Problem Solving
PA = Practice Activity   ★ = Includes Problem Solving

Objective 4
Concept Development Activities

CD 1 Solving Compound Inequalities

Use with 5-Day or 4-Day Instructional Plan. In this activity, students solve compound inequalities.

MATERIALS

- Blackline Master 27

DIRECTIONS

1. Discuss the following terms with students:

   and All conditions must be true for the statement to be true

   compound inequality Two inequalities connected by *and* or *or*

   or If either or both conditions are true, the whole statement is true

2. Write the inequality $3x - 4 < 17$ and the inequality $5 - 2x < 1$ side by side on the board or overhead.

3. Ask students how to solve and graph each of the inequalities. Make a transparency of Blackline Master 27, Number Lines, and have volunteers graph the inequalities on separate number lines. Alternatively, have them graph the inequalities on the board.

   $3x - 4 < 17$; $x < 7$

   $5 - 2x < 1$; $x > 2$

4. Write **and** between the two inequalities on the board so it says $3x - 4 < 17$ and $5 - 2x < 1$.

5. Distribute one copy of Blackline Master 27, Number Lines, to each student. Tell students to graph the compound inequality and find some solutions for it. Have a volunteer graph the compound inequality on the board or overhead. Discuss the possible solutions.

   Solutions will vary; they must be numbers between 2 and 7.

6. Write the inequalities **2x + 7 ≤ 13** and **5x − 19 ≥ 16** side by side on the board or overhead.

7. Solve and graph each inequality on the board.

2x + 7 ≤ 13; x ≤ 3

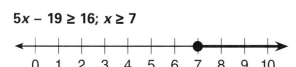

5x − 19 ≥ 16; x ≥ 7

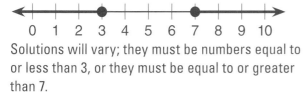

8. Write **or** between the two inequalities on the board so it says **2x + 7 ≤ 13 or 5x − 19 ≥ 16**. Ask students to graph the compound inequality and find some possible solutions. Have a volunteer graph the compound inequality on the board or overhead.

Solutions will vary; they must be numbers equal to or less than 3, or they must be equal to or greater than 7.

9. Explain that to solve a compound inequality, we need to solve each side of the conjunction *and* or *or*. Tell students we look at the conjunction and determine if it combines the solutions (or) or restricts them (and).

10. Work as a class to solve and graph more compound inequalities.

Sample problems:

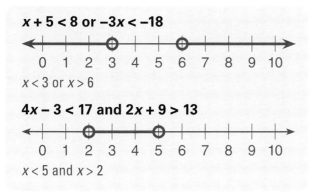

NEXT STEPS • Differentiate

5-Day and 4-Day Instructional Plans:
PM 1, page 536—All students, to assess progress

Concept Development Activities

★ CD 2 Understanding Absolute Value

Use with 5-Day Instructional Plan. In this activity, students understand that absolute value is the distance from zero and is always nonnegative.

MATERIALS

- Blackline Master 27

DIRECTIONS

1. Remind students of the key term: *absolute value*.

2. Make a transparency of Blackline Master 27, Number Lines, and label a number line from –10 to 10. Alternatively, draw a number line on the board.

3. Ask students to identify the absolute value of –7. Plot –7 on the number line, and have a volunteer find the distance by counting over from –7 to 0. The absolute value of –7 is 7.

4. Have a volunteer find the absolute value of 7 by plotting the number and counting over from 7 to 0. The absolute value of 7 is 7.

5. Review the following terms with students:

   and All conditions must be true for the statement to be true

   compound inequality Two inequalities connected by *and* or *or*

   or If either or both conditions are true, the whole statement is true

6. Ask students to think about how we solve an absolute value problem, such as $|x| = 4$. Explain that *x* is 4 units from 0. Demonstrate this concept on a number line. $x = 4$ or $x = -4$

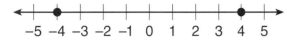

7. Write $|x| < 4$ on the board. Ask for some solution values, and have students graph the inequality. Make sure students see that the solution for *x* must be all numbers less than 4 units from 0 on the number line.

Sample answer:

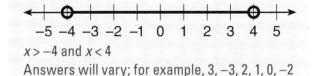

$x > -4$ and $x < 4$

Answers will vary; for example, 3, –3, 2, 1, 0, –2

★ = Includes Problem Solving

NUMBER LINES

8. Write **|x| > 4** on the board. Ask for some solution values, and have students graph the inequality. Make sure students see that the solution for *x* must be all numbers more than 4 units from 0 on the number line.

Sample answer:

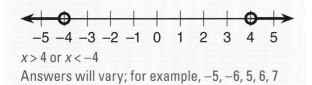

x > 4 or x < −4
Answers will vary; for example, −5, −6, 5, 6, 7

9. Tell students to write the compound inequality for **|x| > −2**. Discuss the solution and the graph. Solicit different explanations for how to arrive at the solution. Make sure students recognize that the absolute value of any number will be greater than a negative number.

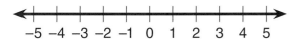

10. Repeat Step 9 with **|x| < 11**.

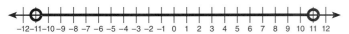

NEXT STEPS • Differentiate

5-Day Instructional Plan:
CD 4, page 532—All students, for additional concept development

Concept Development Activities

CD 3 Understanding Compound Inequalities

Use with 4-Day Instructional Plan. In this activity, students understand that or *means at least one condition must be true, while* and *means all conditions must be true.*

MATERIALS

• Blackline Master 27

DIRECTIONS

1. Review the following terms and symbols with students:

   and All conditions must be true for the statement to be true

   compound inequality Two inequalities connected by *and* or *or*

   inequality A mathematical sentence that compares two expressions using one of the following symbols:

   > Greater than

   ≥ Greater than or equal to

   < Less than

   ≤ Less than or equal to

   or If either or both conditions are true, the whole statement is true

2. Write **A number is less than 4 or greater than 10** on the board or overhead.

3. Ask students if the number could be 11. Solicit several numbers that work by suggesting other numbers, such as 7 and 3.8. 11 and 3.8 work; 7 does not

---

NUMBER LINES

---

4. Make a transparency of Blackline Master 27, Number Lines, and draw the graph of **x < 4 or x > 10**. Alternatively, graph the statement on a number line on the board. Discuss the numbers that work and the numbers that do not work by pointing them out on the number line.

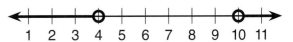

5. Write **n ≤ 6 or n ≥ 9** on the board or overhead. Solicit numbers that work for *n*, and draw the graph on the number line.

n ≤ 6 or n ≥ 9

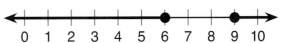

Sample numbers that work for *n*: 5, 5.9, 6, 9, 9.5, 10, and 23. Sample numbers that do not work for *n*: 6.2, 7, 8, and 8.9.

---

6. Write **x < 14 and x > 9** on the board or overhead. Solicit several numbers that work for the statement. Sample numbers that work: 9.3, 10, 11.6, 12, and 13.9. Sample numbers that do not work: 1, 5.8, 8, 14.5, 15, and 17.

7. Draw the graph of $x < 14$ and $x > 9$ on a number line on the board or overhead.

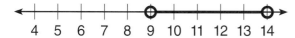

8. Present another example of a statement using *and*. Solicit numbers that work for the variable, and draw the graph on a number line on the board or overhead.

Sample problem:

> **x > −6 and x < 2**
>
> Sample numbers that work for *x*: −5, −4.3, −1, 0, 0.4, 1, and 1.7. Sample numbers that do not work for *x*: −10, −6.2, 2.2, 3, and 6.

NEXT STEPS • Differentiate

4-Day Instructional Plan:
PM 4, page 539—All students, to assess progress

Concept Development Activities

CD 4 Solving Inequalities With Absolute Value

Use with 5-Day or 4-Day Instructional Plan. In this activity, students solve inequalities involving absolute value.

MATERIALS

- *Interactive Text*, pages 222–227

DIRECTIONS

1. Have students turn to *Interactive Text*, pages 222–223, Absolute Value and Distance—Part 1, Equality. Make a transparency of *Interactive Text*, pages 222–227, so students can follow the explanation.

2. Review the following terms with students:

   and All conditions must be true for the statement to be true

   compound inequality Two inequalities connected by *and* or *or*

   or If either or both conditions are true, the whole statement is true

3. Remind students that $|7| = 7$ and $|-7| = 7$. Ask students what $|x - 4| = 5$ means. Discuss the graph and solution from *Interactive Text*, page 222.

4. Tell students to work Problems 1–3. Discuss the solutions as a class.

5. Ask students what $|x + 3| = 6$ means. Discuss the graph and solution from *Interactive Text*, page 223.

6. Tell students to work Problems 4–6. Discuss the solutions as a class.

7. Have students complete *Interactive Text*, pages 224–227, Absolute Value and Distance—Part 2, Less Than and Absolute Value and Distance—Part 3, Greater Than.

NEXT STEPS • Differentiate

5-Day and 4-Day Instructional Plans:
PA 2, page 535—All students, for additional practice

ABSOLUTE VALUE AND DISTANCE—PART 1, EQUALITY

Recall that $|x| = 5$ means x represents the numbers that are a distance of 5 from 0. An absolute value problem such as $|x - 4| = 5$ means that $x - 4$ represents the numbers that are a distance of 5 from 0, or simply that the distance from x to 4 is 5. On the number line, we can represent the problem as:

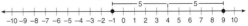

As an algebraic equation, we can write $|x - 4| = 5$ as the compound equation

$$x - 4 = 5 \quad \text{or} \quad x - 4 = -5$$

By adding 4 to both sides of these equations, we have

$$x - 4 + 4 = 5 + 4 \quad \text{or} \quad x - 4 + 4 = -5 + 4$$

Therefore, our solution is $\quad x = 9 \quad$ or $\quad x = -1$

Complete each problem, and graph the distance on the number line.

1. $|x - 1| = 4$

   The distance between x and 1 is __4__.
   On the number line, the problem can be represented by $x =$ __5__ or $x =$ __−3__.

2. $|x - 7| = 2$

   The distance between x and __7__ is 2.
   On the number line, the problem can be represented by $x =$ __9__ or $x =$ __5__.

3. $|x - 8| = 1$

   The distance between x and __8__ is __1__.
   On the number line, the problem can be represented by $x =$ __9__ or $x =$ __7__.

ABSOLUTE VALUE AND DISTANCE—PART 1, EQUALITY   *(continued)*

Recall now that since $|x| = 6$ means x represents the numbers that are a distance of 6 from 0, then $|x + 3| = 6$, which can be thought of as $|x - (-3)| = 6$, means that the distance between x and -3 is 6. On the number line, we can represent $|x + 3| = 6$ as:

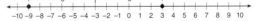

As an algebraic equation, we can write $|x + 3| = 6$ as the compound equation

$$x + 3 = 6 \quad \text{or} \quad x + 3 = -6$$

By subtracting 3 from both sides of these equations, we have

$$x + 3 - 3 = 6 - 3 \quad \text{or} \quad x + 3 - 3 = -6 - 3$$

Therefore, our solution is $\quad x = 3 \quad$ or $\quad x = -9$

Complete each problem, and graph the distance on the number line.

4. $|x + 2| = 5$

   The distance between x and -2 is __5__.
   On the number line, the problem can be represented by $x =$ __−7__ or $x =$ __3__.

5. $|x + 4| = 6$

   The distance between x and __−4__ is 6.
   On the number line, the problem can be represented by $x =$ __−10__ or $x =$ __2__.

6. $|x + 7| = 5$

   The distance between x and __−7__ is __5__.
   On the number line, the problem can be represented by $x =$ __−12__ or $x =$ __−2__.

   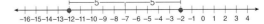

ABSOLUTE VALUE AND DISTANCE—PART 2, LESS THAN

Recall that $|x| < 5$ means x represents the numbers that are less than a distance of 5 from 0. An absolute value problem such as $|x - 4| < 5$ means that $x - 4$ represents the numbers that are less than a distance of 5 from 0, or simply that the distance between x and 4 is less than 5. On the number line, we can represent the problem as:

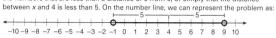

As an algebraic inequality, we can write $|x - 4| < 5$ as the compound inequality

$$x - 4 < 5 \quad \text{and} \quad x - 4 > -5$$

By adding 4 to both sides of these inequalities, we have

$$x - 4 + 4 < 5 + 4 \quad \text{and} \quad x - 4 + 4 > -5 + 4$$

Therefore, our solution is $\quad x < 9 \quad$ and $\quad x > -1$

Complete each problem, and graph the distance on the number line.

1. $|x - 1| < 4$

The distance between x and 1 is less than ___4___.
On the number line, the problem can be represented by $x <$ ___5___ and $x >$ ___-3___.

2. $|x - 7| < 2$

The distance between x and ___7___ is less than 2.
On the number line, the problem can be represented by $x <$ ___9___ and $x >$ ___5___.

3. $|x - 8| < 1$

The distance between x and ___8___ is less than ___1___.
On the number line, the problem can be represented by $x <$ ___9___ and $x >$ ___7___.

ABSOLUTE VALUE AND DISTANCE—PART 2, LESS THAN *(continued)*

Recall now that since $|x| < 6$ means x represents the numbers that are less than a distance of 6 from 0, then $|x + 3| < 6$, which can be thought of as $|x - (-3)| < 6$, means that the distance between x and -3 is less than 6. On the number line, we can represent $|x + 3| < 6$ as:

As an algebraic inequality, we can write $|x + 3| < 6$ as the compound inequality

$$x + 3 < 6 \quad \text{and} \quad x + 3 > -6$$

By subtracting 3 from both sides of these inequalities, we have

$$x + 3 - 3 < 6 - 3 \quad \text{and} \quad x + 3 - 3 > -6 - 3$$

Therefore, our solution is $\quad x < 3 \quad$ and $\quad x > -9$

Complete each problem, and graph the distance on the number line.

4. $|x + 2| < 5$

The distance between x and -2 is less than ___5___.
On the number line, the problem can be represented by $x <$ ___3___ and $x >$ ___-7___.

5. $|x + 4| < 6$

The distance between x and ___-4___ is less than 6.
On the number line, the problem can be represented by $x <$ ___2___ and $x >$ ___-10___.

6. $|x + 7| < 5$

The distance between x and ___-7___ is less than ___5___.
On the number line, the problem can be represented by $x <$ ___-2___ and $x >$ ___-12___.

ABSOLUTE VALUE AND DISTANCE— PART 3, GREATER THAN

Recall that $|x| > 5$ means x represents the numbers that are more than a distance of 5 from 0. An absolute value problem such as $|x - 4| > 5$ means that $x - 4$ represents the numbers that are more than a distance of 5 from 0, or simply that the distance between x and 4 is more than 5. On the number line, we can represent the problem as:

As an algebraic inequality, we can write $|x - 4| > 5$ as the compound inequality

$$x - 4 > 5 \quad \text{or} \quad x - 4 < -5$$

By adding 4 to both sides of these inequalities, we have

$$x - 4 + 4 > 5 + 4 \quad \text{or} \quad x - 4 + 4 < -5 + 4$$

Therefore, our solution is $\quad x > 9 \quad$ or $\quad x < -1$

Complete each problem, and graph the distance on the number line.

1. $|x - 1| > 4$

The distance between x and 1 is more than ___4___.
On the number line, the problem can be represented by $x >$ ___5___ or $x <$ ___-3___.

2. $|x - 7| > 2$

The distance between x and ___7___ is more than 2.
On the number line, the problem can be represented by $x <$ ___9___ or $x <$ ___5___.

3. $|x - 8| > 1$

The distance between x and ___8___ is more than ___1___.
On the number line, the problem can be represented by $x >$ ___9___ or $x <$ ___7___.

ABSOLUTE VALUE AND DISTANCE— PART 3, GREATER THAN *(continued)*

Recall now that since $|x| > 6$ means x represents the numbers that are more than a distance of 6 from 0, then $|x + 3| > 6$, which can be thought of as $|x - (-3)| > 6$, means that the distance between x and -3 is more than 6. On the number line, we can represent $|x + 3| > 6$ as:

As an algebraic inequality, we can write $|x + 3| > 6$ as the compound inequality

$$x + 3 > 6 \quad \text{or} \quad x + 3 < -6$$

By subtracting 3 from both sides of these inequalities, we have

$$x + 3 - 3 > 6 - 3 \quad \text{or} \quad x + 3 - 3 < -6 - 3$$

Therefore, our solution is $\quad x > 3 \quad$ or $\quad x < -9$

Complete each problem, and graph the distance on the number line.

4. $|x + 2| > 5$

The distance between x and -2 is more than ___5___.
On the number line, the problem can be represented by $x >$ ___3___ or $x <$ ___-7___.

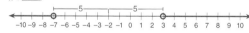

5. $|x + 4| > 6$

The distance between x and ___-4___ is more than 6.
On the number line, the problem can be represented by $x >$ ___2___ or $x <$ ___-10___.

6. $|x + 7| > 5$

The distance between x and ___-7___ is more than ___5___.
On the number line, the problem can be represented by $x >$ ___-2___ or $x <$ ___-12___.

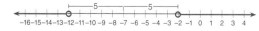

Practice Activities

PA 1 Picking Your Poison

Use with 5-Day or 4-Day Instructional Plan. In this activity, students create solutions and graphs for compound inequalities.

MATERIALS

- Blackline Masters 78–79

DIRECTIONS

1. Tell students that the goal of this game is to strengthen their skills of writing the solutions and graphs of compound inequalities.

2. Review the following terms with students:

    and All conditions must be true for the statement to be true

    compound inequality Two inequalities connected by *and* or *or*

    or If either or both conditions are true, the whole statement is true

3. Have students work in groups of four or five.

4. Distribute one copy of Blackline Masters 78 and 79, Pick Your Poison Card Game, to each group. Tell each group to cut out the cards, placing the number line cards in Deck 1 and the *AND* and *OR* cards in Deck 2.

5. Explain the game rules to students.

    - Each student draws two cards from Deck 1 and one card from Deck 2.

    - Students combine the cards they drew and write a compound inequality.

    - Each student writes the solution to the compound inequality and graphs it on a piece of paper.

    - When everyone is finished, have students check one another's solutions to make sure they are correct.

6. Have students shuffle the cards and repeat the game as long as time permits.

NEXT STEPS • Differentiate

5-Day and 4-Day Instructional Plans:
PM 2, page 537—All students, to assess progress

PICK YOUR POISON CARD GAME

PICK YOUR POISON CARD GAME *(continued)*

AND	OR
AND	OR
AND	OR
AND	OR
AND	OR

Practice Activities

PA 2 Making It and Sharing

Use with 5-Day or 4-Day Instructional Plan. In this activity, students solve compound inequalities and inequalities involving absolute value.

DIRECTIONS

1. Review the following terms with students:

   and All conditions must be true for the statement to be true

   compound inequality Two inequalities connected by *and* or *or*

   or If either or both conditions are true, the whole statement is true

2. Write $ax + b > c$ and $dx + e < f$ where a, b, c, d, e, and f are any integers $\neq 0$ on the board, and have students write an inequality according to your written instructions. Make sure students notice the word *and* in the compound inequality.

   Sample answer:

   $x + 6 > -5$ and $5x + 9 < 54$

3. Write $ax + b < c$ or $dx + e > f$ where a, b, c, d, e, and f are any integers $\neq 0$ on the board, and have students write an inequality according to your written instructions. Make sure students notice the word *or* in the compound inequality.

   Sample answer:

   $5x + 9 < 54$ or $x + 6 > -5$

4. Write $|ax + b| < c$ on the board, and have students write an inequality according to your written instructions.

   Sample answer:

   $|2x + 6| < 14$

5. Write $|ax + b| > c$ on the board, and have students write an inequality according to your written instructions.

   Sample answer:

   $|3x + 4| > 19$

6. Put students in groups of four. Have each group check all the group members' written inequalities to see if they are in the forms described. Tell students to help one another fix any incorrectly written inequalities. Explain to students that these inequalities become the problems for the group.

7. Have students trade papers on which the inequalities are written until everyone has worked all the problems. Tell students to write and do their work on their own paper, not on the problem sheets.

8. After each student has worked all the problems in the group, have students compare their solutions. If there is disagreement on a solution, tell the group to work the problem together and agree on the solution.

9. Tell students that each person in a group must have a set of problems and solutions to turn in at the end of the activity.

10. If time allows, have the groups exchange problems and repeat Steps 7–9.

NEXT STEPS • Differentiate

5-Day Instructional Plan:
PM 4, page 539—All students, to assess progress

4-Day Instructional Plan:
PM 5, page 540—All students, to assess progress

Objective 4
Progress-Monitoring Activities

PM 1 Apply Skills 1

Use with 5-Day or 4-Day Instructional Plan.

MATERIALS

- *Interactive Text,* pages 228–229

DIRECTIONS

1. Have students turn to *Interactive Text,* pages 228–229, Apply Skills 1.

2. Remind students of the key terms: *compound inequality, and,* and *or.*

3. Monitor student work, and provide feedback as necessary.

   Watch for:

   - Do students use arrows when plotting problems with an infinite number of solutions?

   - Do students use open circles for strict inequalities?

   - Do students realize that compound inequalities may have no solution?

NEXT STEPS • Differentiate

5-Day and 4-Day Instructional Plans:
PA 1, page 534—All students, for additional practice

Name _____ Date _____

APPLY SKILLS 1

Read each problem carefully and write the answer.

1. A number is less than 7 or greater than 15. Could the number be 11? __no__ 17? __yes__ 6.8? __yes__ 14.99? __no__

2. Name four more numbers that would make Problem 1 true. _Answers will vary._

3. Name four more numbers that would make Problem 1 false. _Answers will vary._

4. Plot, on the number line, all the points that make Problem 1 true.

   4 5 6 7 8 9 10 11 12 13 14 15 16 17 18

5. If a number is less than 10 and greater than 4, could it be 7? __yes__ 15? __no__ 10? __no__ 5.6? __yes__ 2? __no__

6. Name four more numbers that would make Problem 5 true. _Answers will vary._

7. Name four more numbers that would make Problem 5 false. _Answers will vary._

8. Plot, on the number line, all the points that make Problem 5 true.

   −4 −3 −2 −1 0 1 2 3 4 5 6 7 8 9 10

9. Problem 1 could also be written algebraically as $n < 7$ or $n > 15$. Does $n < 7$ or $n > 15$ mean the same thing as a number is less than 7 or greater than 15? __yes__

10. If $n < 3$ or $n > 9$, which of the following would make the compound inequality true? Circle the correct answers.
    −3, 0, 2.7, 3, 5, 8, 9, 9.2, 12, 15

11. Name four more numbers that would make Problem 10 true. _Answers will vary._

12. Name four more numbers that would make Problem 10 false. _Answers will vary._

13. Plot, on the number line, all the points that make Problem 10 true.

    −4 −3 −2 −1 0 1 2 3 4 5 6 7 8 9 10

14. Problem 5 could also be written algebraically as $y < 10$ and $y > 4$. Does $y < 10$ and $y > 4$ mean the same thing as a number is less than 10 and greater than 4? __yes__

228 Chapter 6 • Objective 4 • PM 1   Inside Algebra

Name _____ Date _____

APPLY SKILLS 1 *(continued)*

15. If $x < -5$ and $x > -1$, which of the following would make the compound inequality true? Circle the correct answers. _No numbers qualify._
    {−10, −7, −5, −4, −3, −1.5, −1.1, −0.7, 0, 2, 5}

16. Name four more numbers that would make Problem 15 true. _None exist._

17. Name four more numbers that would make Problem 15 false. _Any number is correct._

18. Plot, on the number line, all the points that make Problem 15 true.

    −7 −6 −5 −4 −3 −2 −1 0 1 2 3 4 5 6 7

19. If a number is between 10 and 20, could it be 4? __no__ 8? __no__ 10? __no__ 12? __yes__ 16? __yes__ 20? __no__ 24? __no__

20. Name four more numbers that would make Problem 19 true. _Answers will vary._

21. Name four more numbers that would make Problem 19 false. _Answers will vary._

22. Plot, on the number line, all the points that make Problem 19 true.

    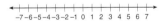
    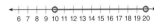
    6 7 8 9 10 11 12 13 14 15 16 17 18 19 20

Inside Algebra   Chapter 6 • Objective 4 • PM 1   **229**

Objective 4
Progress-Monitoring Activities

PM 2 Apply Skills 2

Use with 5-Day or 4-Day Instructional Plan.

MATERIALS

- *Interactive Text*, pages 230–231

DIRECTIONS

1. Have students turn to *Interactive Text*, pages 230–231, Apply Skills 2.

2. Remind students of the key terms: *compound inequality*, *and*, and *or*.

3. Monitor student work, and provide feedback as necessary.

   Watch for:
   - Do students use open and filled circles correctly?
   - Do students remember that *or* statements require at least one side to be true, while *and* statements require both sides to be true?

NEXT STEPS • Differentiate

5-Day and 4-Day Instructional Plans:
PM 3, page 538—All students, to assess progress

Name_____ Date_____

APPLY SKILLS 2

Solve and graph the given inequality.

1. $3x - 4 < 17$ ___$x < 7$___
   $3x - 4 + 4 < 17 + 4$
   $\left(\frac{1}{3}\right)3x < 21\left(\frac{1}{3}\right)$

2. $5 - 2x < 1$ ___$x > 2$___
   $5 - 2x - 5 < 1 - 5$
   $\left(-\frac{1}{2}\right)(-2x) > -4\left(-\frac{1}{2}\right)$

3. $2x + 7 \leq 13$ ___$x \leq 3$___
   $2x + 7 - 7 \leq 13 - 7$
   $\left(\frac{1}{2}\right)2x \leq 6\left(\frac{1}{2}\right)$

4. $5x - 19 \geq 16$ ___$x \geq 7$___
   $5x - 19 + 19 \geq 16 + 19$
   $\left(\frac{1}{5}\right)5x \geq 35\left(\frac{1}{5}\right)$

5. Now consider the compound inequality $3x - 4 < 17$ and $5 - 2x < 1$.

   The inequality on the left side of the "and" is the same as in Problem 1, and the inequality on the right side of the "and" is the same as in Problem 2. The solutions to Problems 1 and 2 gave easier forms of the solution to the compound inequality. The solution to the compound inequality in Problem 5 is the answers in Problems 1 and 2 linked with an "and."

   Write and graph the solution to Problem 5. ___$2 < x < 7$___

   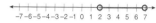

230   Chapter 6 • Objective 4 • PM 2   Inside Algebra

Name_____ Date_____

APPLY SKILLS 2 (continued)

6. Now consider the compound inequality $2x + 7 \leq 13$ or $5x - 19 \geq 16$.

   The inequality on the left side of the "or" is the same as in Problem 3, and the inequality on the right side of the "or" is the same as in Problem 4. The solutions to Problems 3 and 4 gave easier forms of the solution to the compound inequality. The solution to the compound inequality in Problem 6 is the answers in Problems 3 and 4 linked with an "or."

   Write and graph the solution to Problem 6. ___$x \leq 3$ or $x \geq 7$___

   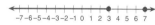

Solve and graph the compound inequalities.

7. $x + 5 < 8$ or $-3x < -18$ ___$x < 3$ or $x > 6$___

   $x + 5 - 5 < 8 - 5$ or $\left(-\frac{1}{3}\right)(-3x) > (-18)\left(-\frac{1}{3}\right)$

8. $4x - 3 < 17$ and $2x + 9 > 13$ ___$x < 5$ and $x > 2$___

   $4x - 3 + 3 < 17 + 3$ and $2x + 9 - 9 > 13 - 9$
   $\left(\frac{1}{4}\right)4x < 20\left(\frac{1}{4}\right)$ $\left(\frac{1}{2}\right)2x > 4\left(\frac{1}{2}\right)$

9. $7 - 2x \leq 1$ and $5x - 26 \leq 14$ ___$x \geq 3$ and $x \leq 8$___

   $7 - 2x - 7 \leq 1 - 7$ and $5x - 26 + 26 \leq 14 + 26$
   $\left(-\frac{1}{2}\right)(-2x) \geq (-6)\left(-\frac{1}{2}\right)$ $\left(\frac{1}{5}\right)5x \leq 40\left(\frac{1}{5}\right)$

10. $2x + 3 < x - 2$ or $5x - 6 \geq 2x + 3$ ___$x < -5$ or $x \geq 3$___

    $2x + 3 - x < x - 2 - x$ or $5x - 6 - 2x \geq 2x + 3 - 2x$
    $x + 3 - 3 < -2 - 3$ $3x - 6 + 6 \geq 3 + 6$
                                  $\left(\frac{1}{3}\right)3x \geq 9\left(\frac{1}{3}\right)$

Inside Algebra   Chapter 6 • Objective 4 • PM 2   231

Objective 4
Progress-Monitoring Activities

PM 3 Apply Skills 3

Use with 5-Day or 4-Day Instructional Plan.

MATERIALS

- *Interactive Text*, pages 232–233

DIRECTIONS

1. Have students turn to *Interactive Text*, pages 232–233, Apply Skills 3.

2. Remind students of the key terms: *compound inequality*, *and*, and *or*.

3. Monitor student work, and provide feedback as necessary.

   Watch for:
   - Do students remember that *or* statements require at least one side to be true, while *and* statements require both sides to be true?
   - Do students realize that compound inequalities may have no solution?

NEXT STEPS • Differentiate

5-Day Instructional Plan:
CD 2, page 528—All students, for additional concept development and problem solving

4-Day Instructional Plan:
CD 4, page 532—Students who demonstrate understanding of the concept, to extend understanding

CD 3, page 530—Students who need additional concept development

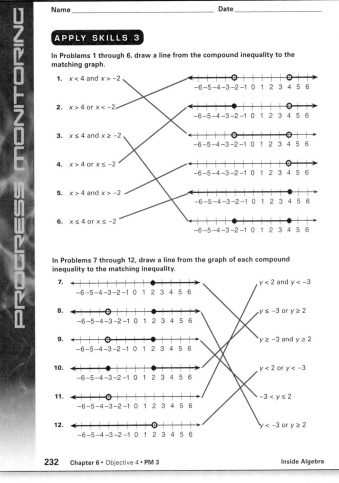

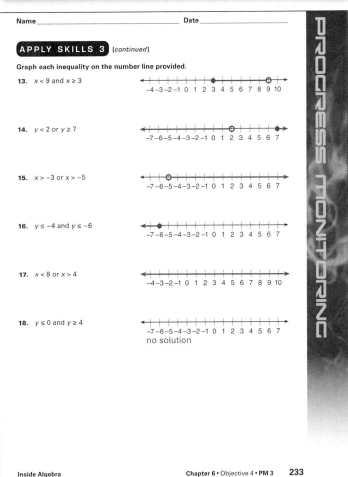

Objective 4
Progress-Monitoring Activities

PM 4 Apply Skills 4

Use with 5-Day or 4-Day Instructional Plan.

MATERIALS

- *Interactive Text*, pages 234–235

DIRECTIONS

1. Have students turn to *Interactive Text*, pages 234–235, Apply Skills 4.

2. Remind students of the key terms: *compound inequality*, *and*, and *or*.

3. Monitor student work, and provide feedback as necessary.

   Watch for:
   - Do students remember that *or* statements require at least one side to be true, while *and* statements require both sides to be true?

   - Do students reverse the inequality sign when multiplying or dividing by a negative number?

NEXT STEPS • Differentiate

5-Day Instructional Plan:
PM 5, page 540—All students, to assess progress

4-Day Instructional Plan:
CD 4, page 532—All students, for additional concept development

---

Name_____ Date_____

APPLY SKILLS 4

Solve each inequality and graph the solution set on the number line.

Example:

$2x - 7 < 1$ and $3x + 5 > -1$ $x < 4$ and $x > -2$

$2x - 7 + 7 < 1 + 7$ $\qquad$ $3x + 5 - 5 > -1 - 5$

$\qquad 2x < 8$ and $3x > -6$

$\qquad \dfrac{2x}{2} < \dfrac{8}{2} \qquad \dfrac{3x}{3} > -\dfrac{6}{3}$

1. $2x - 5 < 1$ and $3x > -9$ $x < 3$ and $x > -3$

   $2x - 5 + 5 < 1 + 5$

   $\left(\dfrac{1}{2}\right)2x < 6\left(\dfrac{1}{2}\right)$ and $\left(\dfrac{1}{3}\right)3x > -9\left(\dfrac{1}{3}\right)$

2. $4x - 9 > 7$ or $5 - 2x > 7$ $x > 4$ or $x < -1$

   $4x - 9 + 9 > 7 + 9 \qquad 5 - 2x - 5 > 7 - 5$

   $\left(\dfrac{1}{4}\right)4x > 16\left(\dfrac{1}{4}\right)$ or $\left(-\dfrac{1}{2}\right)(-2x) < 2\left(-\dfrac{1}{2}\right)$

3. $5x \le 10$ and $x + 6 \ge 4$ $x \le 2$ and $x \ge -2$

   $\left(\dfrac{1}{5}\right)5x \le 10\left(\dfrac{1}{5}\right)$ and $x + 6 - 6 \ge 4 - 6$

4. $3x + 4 \le 16$ or $5x - 9 \ge 16$ $x \le 4$ or $x \ge 5$

   $3x + 4 - 4 \le 16 - 4 \qquad 5x - 9 + 9 \ge 16 + 9$

   $\left(\dfrac{1}{3}\right)3x \le 12\left(\dfrac{1}{3}\right)$ or $\left(\dfrac{1}{5}\right)5x \ge 25\left(\dfrac{1}{5}\right)$

234　Chapter 6 • Objective 4 • PM 4 $\qquad$ Inside Algebra

Name_____ Date_____

APPLY SKILLS 4 *(continued)*

5. $-3x \le 9$ and $4x + 7 < 3$ $x \ge -3$ and $x < -1$

   $\left(-\dfrac{1}{3}\right)(-3x) \ge 9\left(-\dfrac{1}{3}\right)$ and $\begin{array}{c} 4x + 7 - 7 < 3 - 7 \\ \left(\dfrac{1}{4}\right)4x < -4\left(\dfrac{1}{4}\right) \end{array}$

6. $2x - 7 < 5x + 2$ or $12 - 2x \ge 22$ $x > -3$ or $x \le -5$

   $2x - 7 - 2x < 5x + 2 - 2x \qquad 12 - 2x - 12 \ge 22 - 12$

   $\begin{array}{c} -7 - 2 < 3x + 2 - 2 \\ \left(\dfrac{1}{3}\right)(-9) < 3x\left(\dfrac{1}{3}\right) \end{array}$ or $\left(-\dfrac{1}{2}\right)(-2x) \le 10\left(-\dfrac{1}{2}\right)$

7. $\dfrac{x}{3} \le 2$ and $5x - 9 \ge 11$ $x \le 6$ and $x \ge 4$

   $(3)\dfrac{x}{3} \le 2(3)$ and $\begin{array}{c} 5x - 9 + 9 \ge 11 + 9 \\ \left(\dfrac{1}{5}\right)5x \ge 20\left(\dfrac{1}{5}\right) \end{array}$

8. $3x - 4 < x + 2$ or $-\dfrac{x}{2} + 5 > 4$ $x < 3$ or $x < 2$

   $3x - 4 - x < x + 2 - x$

   $2x - 4 + 4 < 2 + 4 \qquad\quad -\dfrac{x}{2} + 5 - 5 > 4 - 5$

   $\left(\dfrac{1}{2}\right)2x < 6\left(\dfrac{1}{2}\right)$ or $(-2)\left(-\dfrac{x}{2}\right) < -1(-2)$

9. $3x - 7 > 8 - 2x$ and $14 - x > 3x + 14$ $x > 3$ and $x < 0$

   no solution

   $3x - 7 + 2x > 8 - 2x + 2x \qquad 14 - x + x > 3x + 14 + x$

   $5x - 7 + 7 > 8 + 7 \qquad\qquad 14 - 14 > 4x + 14 - 14$

   $\left(\dfrac{1}{5}\right)5x > 15\left(\dfrac{1}{5}\right)$ and $\left(\dfrac{1}{4}\right)0 > 4x\left(\dfrac{1}{4}\right)$

Inside Algebra $\qquad$ Chapter 6 • Objective 4 • PM 4　235

Objective 4
Progress-Monitoring Activities

PM 5 Apply Skills 5

Use with 5-Day or 4-Day Instructional Plan.

MATERIALS

- *Interactive Text*, pages 236–237

DIRECTIONS

1. Have students turn to *Interactive Text*, pages 236–237, Apply Skills 5.

2. Remind students of the key terms: *compound inequality*, *and*, and *or*.

3. Monitor student work, and provide feedback as necessary.

   Watch for:
   - Do students understand that the absolute value of a number is how far it is from zero?
   - Do students understand that the absolute value of a number cannot be negative?

NEXT STEPS • Differentiate

👥 5-Day Instructional Plan:

PS 1, page 541—Students who are on the accelerated path, to develop problem-solving skills

Objective 4 Posttest, page 543—Students who are on the differentiated path

👥 4-Day Instructional Plan:

PS 1, page 541—Students who are on the accelerated path, to develop problem-solving skills

PS 1, page 541—Students on the differentiated path who demonstrated understanding on PM 3, to develop problem-solving skills

Objective 4 Posttest, page 543—All other students

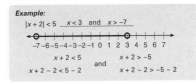

APPLY SKILLS 5

Solve each absolute value problem and graph the solution set on the number line.

Example:
$|x + 2| < 5$ $x < 3$ and $x > -7$

$x + 2 < 5$ and $x + 2 > -5$
$x + 2 - 2 < 5 - 2$ $x + 2 - 2 > -5 - 2$

1. $|x - 5| \le 3$ $x \le 8$ and $x \ge 2$

   $x - 5 + 5 \le 3 + 5$ and $x - 5 + 5 \ge -3 + 5$

2. $|x - 3| = 2$ $x = 5$ or $x = 1$

   $x - 3 + 3 = 2 + 3$ or $x - 3 + 3 = -2 + 3$

3. $|x - 4| > 1$ $x > 5$ or $x < 3$

   $x - 4 + 4 > 1 + 4$ or $x - 4 + 4 < -1 + 4$

4. $|x + 1| = 4$ $x = 3$ or $x = -5$

   $x + 1 - 1 = 4 - 1$ or $x + 1 - 1 = -4 - 1$

5. $|x + 2| \ge 2$ $x \ge 0$ or $x \le -4$

   $x + 2 - 2 \ge 2 - 2$ or $x + 2 - 2 \le -2 - 2$

APPLY SKILLS 5 *(continued)*

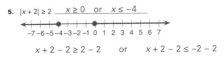

6. $|x + 3| < 1$ $x < -2$ and $x > -4$

   $x + 3 - 3 < 1 - 3$ and $x + 3 - 3 > -1 - 3$

7. $|2x - 5| = 3$ $x = 4$ or $x = 1$

   $2x - 5 + 5 = 3 + 5$ $2x - 5 + 5 = -3 + 5$
   $\left(\frac{1}{2}\right)2x = 8\left(\frac{1}{2}\right)$ or $\left(\frac{1}{2}\right)2x = 2\left(\frac{1}{2}\right)$

8. $|2x + 6| < 6$ $x < 0$ and $x > -6$

   $2x + 6 - 6 < 6 - 6$ $2x + 6 - 6 > -6 - 6$
   $\left(\frac{1}{2}\right)2x < 0\left(\frac{1}{2}\right)$ and $\left(\frac{1}{2}\right)2x > -12\left(\frac{1}{2}\right)$

9. $|3x - 9| \ge 6$ $x \ge 5$ or $x \le 1$

   $3x - 9 + 9 \ge 6 + 9$ $3x - 9 + 9 \le -6 + 9$
   $\left(\frac{1}{3}\right)(3x) \ge 15\left(\frac{1}{3}\right)$ or $\left(\frac{1}{3}\right)(3x) \le 3\left(\frac{1}{3}\right)$

10. $|2x - 3| \le 4$ $x \le 3.5$ or $x \ge -0.5$

    $2x - 3 + 3 \le 4 + 3$ $2x - 3 + 3 \ge -4 + 3$
    $\left(\frac{1}{2}\right)2x \le 7\left(\frac{1}{2}\right)$ or $\left(\frac{1}{2}\right)2x \ge -1\left(\frac{1}{2}\right)$

Problem-Solving Activities

★ PS 1 Graphing Compound Inequalities

Use with 5-Day or 4-Day Instructional Plan. In this activity, students name an inequality that has the given number line as its solution set.

MATERIALS

- Blackline Master 83

DIRECTIONS

1. Review the following terms with students:

   and All conditions must be true for the statement to be true

   compound inequality Two inequalities connected by *and* or *or*

   or If either or both conditions are true, the whole statement is true

2. Distribute one copy of Blackline Master 83, Compound Inequalities, to each student. Have students look at Problems 1–6 and tell them to name a compound inequality for each. Discuss students' answers as a class.

3. Have students look at Problems 7–12 and tell them to name an absolute value inequality for each. Discuss students' answers as a class.

4. Write solutions to compound inequalities on the board, and tell students to come up with a compound inequality with an *and* that has each of the solutions.

   Sample problems:

   > $x > 3$ Answers will vary; for example, $x > 1$ and $x > 3$.
   >
   > **an empty set** Answers will vary; for example, $x < 1$ and $x > 3$.
   >
   > $x \le -4$ Answers will vary; for example, $x \le -4$ and $x \le -2$.

5. Write solutions to compound inequalities on the board, and tell students to come up with a compound inequality with an *or* that has each of the solutions.

   Sample problems:

   > $x < 2$ Answers will vary; for example, $x < 2$ or $x < 1$.
   >
   > **all real numbers** Answers will vary; for example, $x < 3$ or $x > -3$.
   >
   > $x \ge -1$ Answers may vary; for example, $x \ge -1$ or $x > 2$.

NEXT STEPS • Differentiate

5-Day Instructional Plan:
Objective 4 Posttest, page 543—All students

4-Day Instructional Plan:
PS 2, page 542—Students who are on the accelerated path, for additional problem solving

Objective 4 Posttest, page 543—Students who are on the differentiated path

★ = Includes Problem Solving

Name _____ Date _____

83

COMPOUND INEQUALITIES

1. $x < -2$ or $x > 1$

2. $x \ge -3$ and $x \le 1$

3. $x > 1$ and $x < 5$

4. $x \le -3$ or $x \ge -1$

5. $x < -1$ or $x \ge 2$

6. $x > -4$ and $x \le 3$

7. $|x| < 2$

8. $|x| > 3$

9. $|x - 1| > 2$

10. $|x - 2| < 3$

11. $|x + 1| \le 2$

12. $|x + 2| > 1$

Problem-Solving Activities

★PS 2 Investigating With Inequalities

Use with 4-Day Instructional Plan. In this activity, students write inequalities to represent word problems.

MATERIALS

- Interactive Text, page 238

DIRECTIONS

1. Tell students that in this activity, they read word problems for information, then write inequalities to represent the situation described.

2. Review the following terms with students:

   and All conditions must be true for the statement to be true

   compound inequality Two inequalities connected by *and* or *or*

   or If either or both conditions are true, the whole statement is true

3. Tell students to work individually on this assignment. Have students turn to *Interactive Text*, page 238, Investigations With Inequalities, and solve the problems.

4. Notice whether students write compound inequalities for Problems 1, 2, 4, and 5. On Problem 2, be sure students remember from Problem 1 that the depth must be at least 24 feet. On Problem 6, be sure students write $|x - \$150,000|$ and not $|x - \$14,000|$.

NEXT STEPS • Differentiate

4-Day Instructional Plan:
Objective 4 Posttest, page 543—All students

PROBLEM SOLVING

Name _____ Date _____

INVESTIGATIONS WITH INEQUALITIES

The Baxters have just bought a lot on which they plan to build a house. The lot is rectangular and 80 feet across. It is 120 feet deep from front to back. The front faces the street.

80 feet

120 feet

1. The local building codes restrict the smallest building dimension to 24 feet. They also state that one cannot build closer than 10 feet to the side lot line. Write an inequality that represents the width of the house that will face the street.

   $24 \leq x \leq 60$

2. The building codes also state that the house cannot be closer than 25 feet from the street and must be at least 15 feet from the back lot line. Write an inequality that shows the possible depths of the house from front to back.

   $24 \leq x \leq 80$

3. The Baxters want a two-stall garage that will measure 20 feet by 25 feet. The cost of the garage is $20 per square foot. How much will the garage cost?

   $10,000

4. The Baxters have asked that the total cost of the house and garage be about $150,000, but they are willing to deviate from this price by $14,000. Write an inequality that shows how much they can spend on the house if they do not build the garage.

   $136,000 \leq x \leq 164,000$

5. Write an inequality that shows how much they can spend on the house if they do build the garage.

   $126,000 \leq x \leq 154,000$

6. Write the inequality for Problem 4 using absolute values.

   $|x - 150,000| \leq 14,000$

WORK SPACE

2. $120 - 25 - 15 = 80$

3. $20 \cdot 25 \cdot \$20$

4. $150,000 - 14,000 = 136,000$
   $150,000 + 14,000 = 164,000$

5. $136,000 - 10,000 = 126,000$
   $164,000 - 10,000 = 154,000$

238 Chapter 6 • Objective 4 • PS 2

Inside Algebra

Objective 4
Ongoing Assessment

Objective 4 Posttest

Discuss with students the key concepts in Objective 4. Following the discussion, administer the Objective 4 Posttest to all students.

Using the Results

• Score the posttest and update the class record card.

• Provide reinforcement for students who do not demonstrate mastery of the concepts through individual or small-group reteaching of key concepts.

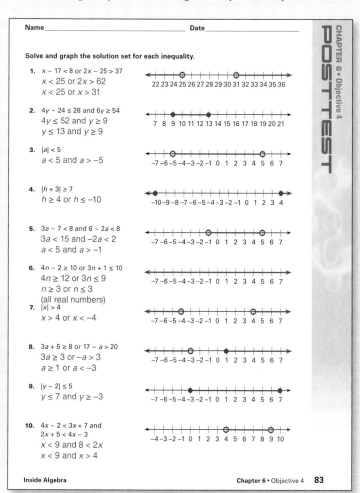

Name _____ Date _____

Solve and graph the solution set for each inequality.

1. $x - 17 < 8$ or $2x - 25 > 37$
   $x < 25$ or $2x > 62$
   $x < 25$ or $x > 31$

2. $4y - 24 \leq 28$ and $6y \geq 54$
   $4y \leq 52$ and $y \geq 9$
   $y \leq 13$ and $y \geq 9$

3. $|a| < 5$
   $a < 5$ and $a > -5$

4. $|h + 3| \geq 7$
   $h \geq 4$ or $h \leq -10$

5. $3a - 7 < 8$ and $6 - 2a < 8$
   $3a < 15$ and $-2a < 2$
   $a < 5$ and $a > -1$

6. $4n - 2 \geq 10$ or $3n + 1 \leq 10$
   $4n \geq 12$ or $3n \leq 9$
   $n \geq 3$ or $n \leq 3$
   (all real numbers)

7. $|x| > 4$
   $x > 4$ or $x < -4$

8. $3a + 5 \geq 8$ or $17 - a > 20$
   $3a \geq 3$ or $-a > 3$
   $a \geq 1$ or $a < -3$

9. $|y - 2| \leq 5$
   $y \leq 7$ and $y \geq -3$

10. $4x - 2 < 3x + 7$ and $2x + 5 < 4x - 3$
    $x < 9$ and $8 < 2x$
    $x < 9$ and $x > 4$

Inside Algebra   **Chapter 6 • Objective 4   83**

Objective 5
Graph inequalities in the coordinate plane.

Objective 5 Pretest

Students complete the Objective 5 Pretest on the same day as the Objective 4 Posttest.

Using the Results

- Score the pretest and update the class record card.

- If the majority of students do not demonstrate mastery of the concepts, use the 5-Day Instructional Plan for Objective 5.

- If the majority of students demonstrate mastery of the concepts, use the 3-Day Instructional Plan for Objective 5.

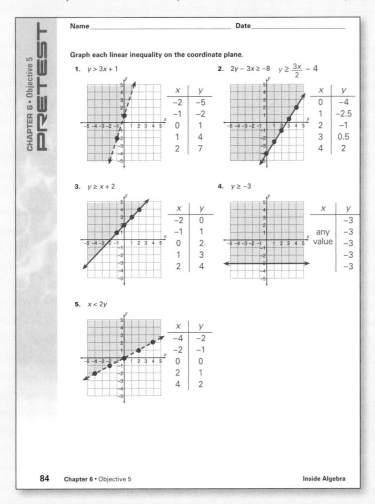

Goals and Activities

Objective 5 Goals

The following activities, when used with the instructional plans on pages 546 and 547, enable students to:

- Graph the inequality $y < 2x - 3$ as

- Graph the inequality $3x + 2y \geq 4$ as

- Graph the inequality $y < x + 3$ as

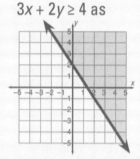
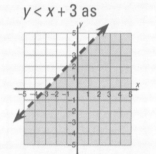

Objective 5 Activities

Concept Development Activities

★**CD 1** Predicting Points On and Not On a Line, page 548	**CD 2** Making Conjectures, page 549

Practice Activities

PA 1 Matching the Graph, page 551	★**PA 2** Sharing It, page 552

Progress-Monitoring Activities

PM 1 Apply Skills 1, page 553	**PM 2** Apply Skills 2, page 554	**PM 3** Apply Skills 3, page 555

★Problem-Solving Activities

★**PS 1** Graphing Situations, page 556	★**PS 2** Compounding the Compound, page 557

Ongoing Assessment

Posttest Objective 5, page 559

Review Chapter 6 Review, page 560

CD = Concept Development PM = Progress Monitoring PS = Problem Solving
PA = Practice Activity ★ = Includes Problem Solving

5-Day Instructional Plan

Use the 5-Day Instructional Plan when pretest results indicate that students would benefit from a slower pace. This plan is used when the majority of students need more time or did not demonstrate mastery on the pretest.

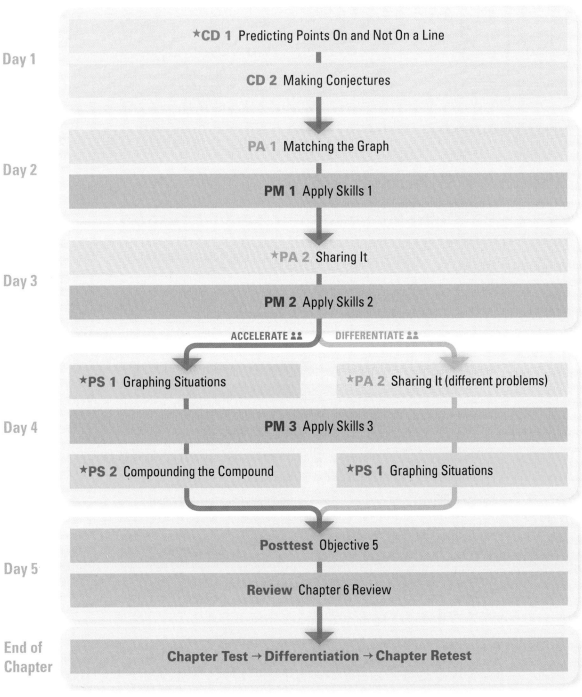

Day 1
- ★**CD 1** Predicting Points On and Not On a Line
- **CD 2** Making Conjectures

Day 2
- **PA 1** Matching the Graph
- **PM 1** Apply Skills 1

Day 3
- ★**PA 2** Sharing It
- **PM 2** Apply Skills 2

ACCELERATE 👥   DIFFERENTIATE 👥

Day 4
- ★**PS 1** Graphing Situations
- **PM 3** Apply Skills 3
- ★**PS 2** Compounding the Compound

- ★**PA 2** Sharing It (different problems)
- ★**PS 1** Graphing Situations

Day 5
- **Posttest** Objective 5
- **Review** Chapter 6 Review

End of Chapter
- **Chapter Test → Differentiation → Chapter Retest**

CD = Concept Development   **PM = Progress Monitoring**   PS = Problem Solving
PA = Practice Activity   ★ = Includes Problem Solving

3-Day Instructional Plan

Use the 3-Day Instructional Plan when pretest results indicate that students can move through the activities at a faster pace. This plan is ideal when the majority of students demonstrate mastery on the pretest.

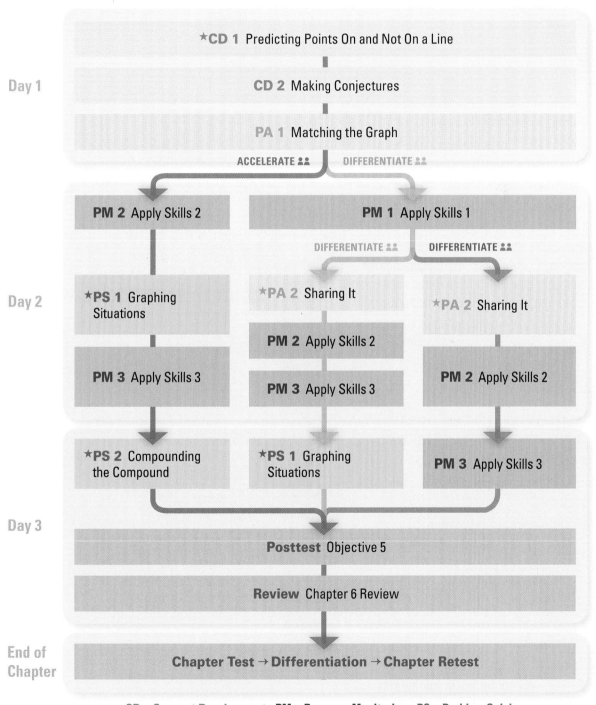

CD = Concept Development   PM = Progress Monitoring   PS = Problem Solving
PA = Practice Activity   ★ = Includes Problem Solving

Objective 5
Concept Development Activities

★ CD 1 Predicting Points On and Not On a Line

Use with 5-Day or 3-Day Instructional Plan. In this activity, students predict which side of a line on a graph contains points that satisfy the inequality.

MATERIALS

- *Interactive Text*, pages 239–240

DIRECTIONS

1. Have students turn to *Interactive Text*, pages 239–240, Points On and Not On a Line.

2. Put students in pairs. Tell students to complete Problem 1 with their partners.

3. Have one volunteer graph the line $y = 2x + 1$ on the overhead while the other students draw this graph at their seats.

4. Choose several different volunteers to graph the points in Problem 1 on the coordinate plane on the overhead. Instruct these students to label each point with **Y** if it is a solution to $y < 2x + 1$ or **N** if it is not.

5. Discuss the conjectures students make without correcting conjectures. Ask questions to get students to analyze their classmates' conjectures.

   Examples:

   > Do you think that might be true?
   >
   > Do the rest of you agree or disagree?

6. Ask students whether the point (2, 5) is part of the graph for $y < 2x + 1$.

7. Repeat the same process for Problem 9.

8. After both problems have been discussed, ask students if they were surprised about which side of the line for Problem 2 had the **Y** points after their conjecture about Problem 1.

NEXT STEPS • Differentiate

5-Day and 3-Day Instructional Plans:
CD 2, page 549—All students, for additional concept development

★ = Includes Problem Solving

POINTS ON AND NOT ON A LINE

Complete the problems given the inequality $y < 2x + 1$.

1. Tell which of the following points satisfy the inequality (state "yes" or "no").

   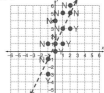

   (2, 6) _no_ (2, 5) _no_ (2, 3) _yes_

   (1, 3) _no_ (1, 1) _yes_ (1, 5) _no_

   (0, 0) _yes_ (0, 4) _no_ (0, 1) _no_

   (−1, −1) _no_ (−1, −3) _yes_ (−1, 1) _no_

2. Graph the line $y = 2x + 1$.

3. Plot the 12 points from Problem 1 on the graph. Label the ordered pairs and indicate whether they satisfy the inequality $y < 2x + 1$ with a "Y" for "yes" and an "N" for "no" according to Problem 1.

4. What do you observe about all the points that satisfy the inequality?
   They all lie below the line.

5. List four more ordered pairs that satisfy the inequality $y < 2x + 1$.
   Answers will vary.

6. Where are the points that satisfy $y = 2x + 1$?
   On the line

7. Where are the points that satisfy $y > 2x + 1$?
   Above the line

8. What points would be included if we changed $y < 2x + 1$ to $y ≤ 2x + 1$?
   The points on (and below) the line

POINTS ON AND NOT ON A LINE *(continued)*

Complete the problems given the inequality $x − y < 3$.

9. Tell which of the following points satisfy the inequality (state "yes" or "no").

   (2, −4) _no_ (2, −1) _no_ (2, 3) _yes_

   (1, 3) _yes_ (1, −2) _no_ (1, −4) _no_

   (0, −3) _no_ (0, −4) _no_ (0, 1) _yes_

   (−1, −4) _no_ (−1, −3) _yes_ (−1, −5) _no_

10. Graph the line $x − y = 3$.

11. Plot the 12 points from Problem 9 on the graph. Label the ordered pairs and indicate whether they satisfy the inequality $x − y < 3$ with a "Y" for "yes" and an "N" for "no" according to Problem 9.

12. What do you observe about all the points that satisfy the inequality?
    They lie above the line.

13. List four more ordered pairs that satisfy the inequality $x − y < 3$.
    Answers will vary.

14. Where are the points that satisfy $x − y = 3$?
    On the line.

15. Where are the points that satisfy $x − y > 3$?
    Below the line.

16. What points would be included if we changed $x − y < 3$ to $x − y ≤ 3$?
    The points on (and above) the line.

Concept Development Activities

CD 2 Making Conjectures

Use with 5-Day or 3-Day Instructional Plan. In this activity, students understand that the solution to an inequality with one variable is all values on one side of a point on a line, and the solution to an inequality with two variables is all points on one side of a line on a graph.

MATERIALS

- Blackline Master 59
- **Variation:** Gizmos
  Linear Inequalities in Two Variables—Activity A

DIRECTIONS

1. Compare a line on a plane to a point on a number line.

   - A point on the number line divides the line into three parts: the point, all the points on one side of the point, and all the points on the other side.

   - The solution to an equation with one variable is represented by just the point. The solution to an inequality with a less than sign is all the points on one side of the point. The solution to an inequality with a greater than sign is all the points on the other side of the point.

   - Similarly, a line divides the plane into three parts: the line, all the points on one side of the line, and all the points on the other side of the line.

   - The solution to an equation with two variables is represented by a line on a plane. The solution to an inequality with two variables is all the points on one side of the line.

2. Make a transparency of Blackline Master 59, Graph Paper. Discuss the steps to solving an inequality with two variables.

   - Graph the equation of the line with the inequality replaced by an equal sign.

   - Test a point on one side of the line to see if it satisfies the inequality. If it does, then all points on that side of the line satisfy the inequality, so shade that side of the line. If the point does not satisfy the inequality, shade the opposite side of the line.

Sample problems:

$y < 3x + 1$
Graph the line: $y = 3x + 1$.

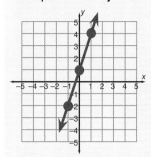

Check the point (2, 2) by substituting it in the inequality.

$2 < 3(2) + 1$
$2 < 6 + 1$
$2 < 7$

Find the point on the graph. Because (2, 2) satisfies the inequality, shade the side of the line that contains that point.

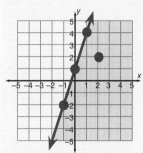

The line is intentionally not dashed, as students learn about this in the next step.

3. Point out to students that on a number line, if an endpoint is included in the inequality (greater than or equal to, less than or equal to), it is filled in; if it is not included (greater than, less than), it is represented as an open dot. Explain to students that on a coordinate graph, if the line is not included (greater than, less than), we use a dashed or dotted line. Explain that we use a solid line for a line that is included (greater than or equal to, less than or equal to). Fix your example from Step 2 to show a dashed line rather than a solid line.

Concept Development Activities

4. Provide more examples by graphing several inequalities with the class.

Sample problems:

$y > x - 2$

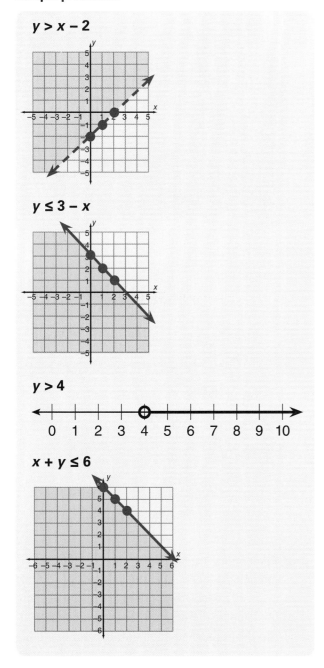

$y \leq 3 - x$

$y > 4$

$x + y \leq 6$

GRAPH PAPER

Variation: Gizmos For this activity use the graphing tool in the Gizmo *Linear Inequalities in Two Variables—Activity A* to model the process of graphing a linear inequality.

Explore Learning • Gizmos

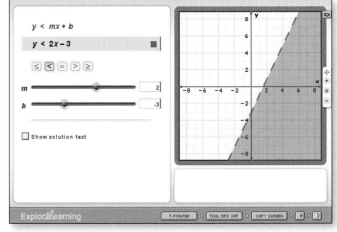

Linear Inequalities in Two Variables—Activity A

NEXT STEPS • Differentiate

5-Day and 3-Day Instructional Plans:
PA **1**, page 551—All students, for additional practice

PA 1 Matching the Graph

Use with 5-Day or 3-Day Instructional Plan. In this activity, students understand whether the graph of an inequality should have a solid or dotted line and which side of the line should be shaded.

MATERIALS

- Blackline Master 84
- Blank cards, 18 per pair of students
- Scissors

DIRECTIONS

1. Put students in pairs. Distribute 18 blank cards and one copy of Blackline Master 84, Match the Graph, to each pair of students.

2. Have each pair of students make two decks of nine blank cards each. For the first deck of cards, tell students to write one inequality from Blackline Master 84 on each card. For the second deck, tell students to tape each graph to one card.

3. Have students work with their partners to match each problem with the correct graph. Make sure students understand whether the line should be solid or dashed and which side of the line should be shaded.

> **Variation:** Have students work independently and write the correct inequality on each graph, rather than making cards.

NEXT STEPS • Differentiate

5-Day Instructional Plan:
PM **1**, page 553—All students, to assess progress

3-Day Instructional Plan:
PM **2**, page 554—Students who demonstrate understanding of the concept, to assess progress
PM **1**, page 553—Students who need additional support, to assess progress

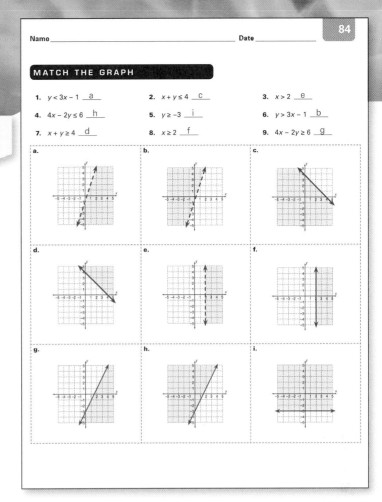

Practice Activities

★ **PA 2** Sharing It

Use with 5-Day or 3-Day Instructional Plan. In this activity, students correctly graph inequalities.

MATERIALS

- Blackline Master 59

DIRECTIONS

1. Write **ax + by ___ c** on the board and tell students to write two inequalities in this form. Explain that the blank can be any inequality symbol ($<$, $>$, $\leq$, or $\geq$) and a, b, and c are nonzero numbers. Instruct students to use different inequality symbols for each problem.

2. Distribute one copy of Blackline Master 59, Graph Paper, to each student. Tell students to draw the graphs for their two inequalities and label each graph with its equation.

3. Put students in groups of five. Have them exchange their inequalities within their groups. Tell students to keep their graphs. Have them graph the other students' inequalities. Remind them to label each graph with its equation. Tell students to continue exchanging problems until each person has graphed all 10 inequalities.

4. Have students compare their graphs and agree on the correct graphs for the problems.

NEXT STEPS • Differentiate

👥 5-Day Instructional Plan:
PM 2, page 554—Students completing the activity for the first time, to assess progress
PM 3, page 555—Students completing the activity for the second time, to assess progress

3-Day Instructional Plan:
PM 2, page 554—All students, to assess progress

★ = Includes Problem Solving

GRAPH PAPER

Objective 5
Progress-Monitoring Activities

PM 1 Apply Skills 1

Use with 5-Day or 3-Day Instructional Plan.

MATERIALS

- *Interactive Text*, page 241

DIRECTIONS

1. Have students turn to *Interactive Text*, page 241, Apply Skills 1.

2. Monitor student work, and provide feedback as necessary.

   Watch for:
   - Do students use solid lines to graph non-strict inequalities?
   - Do students choose a point on one side of the line to determine which side to shade?

NEXT STEPS • Differentiate

5-Day and 3-Day Instructional Plans:
PA 2, page 552—All students, for additional practice and problem solving

---

Name _____ Date _____

APPLY SKILLS 1

Graph the equation $y = x - 1$.

1. Plot the point $(-1, 2)$.

2. Plot the point $(3, -1)$.

3. For the inequality $y \leq x - 1$, which point makes it true, $(-1, 2)$ or $(3, -1)$? $(3, -1)$

4. Shade the part of the graph where $y \leq x - 1$ is true.

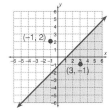

Graph the equation $y = 3 - x$.

5. Plot the point $(-1, 1)$.

6. Plot the point $(3, 3)$.

7. For the inequality $y \geq 3 - x$, which point makes it true, $(-1, 1)$ or $(3, 3)$? $(3, 3)$

8. Shade the part of the graph where $y \geq 3 - x$ is true.

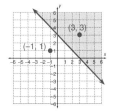

Graph the equation $x + y = 0$.

9. Plot the point $(2, 2)$.

10. Plot the point $(-2, -2)$.

11. For the inequality $x + y \geq 0$, which point makes it true, $(2, 2)$ or $(-2, -2)$? $(2, 2)$

12. Shade the part of the graph where $x + y \geq 0$ is true.

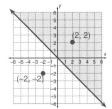

Inside Algebra   Chapter 6 • Objective 5 • PM 1   241

Progress-Monitoring Activities

PM 2 Apply Skills 2

Use with 5-Day or 3-Day Instructional Plan.

MATERIALS

- Interactive Text, pages 242–243

DIRECTIONS

1. Have students turn to Interactive Text, pages 242–243, Apply Skills 2.

2. Monitor student work, and provide feedback as necessary.

   Watch for:
   - Do students use solid lines to graph non-strict inequalities?
   - Do students use dotted lines to graph strict inequalities?

NEXT STEPS • Differentiate

👥 5-Day Instructional Plan:

PS 1, page 556—Students who demonstrate understanding of the concept, to develop problem-solving skills

PA 2, page 552—Students who need additional practice

👥 3-Day Instructional Plan:

PS 1, page 556—Students who are on the accelerated path, to develop problem-solving skills

PM 3, page 555—Students who are on the differentiated path, for additional progress assessment

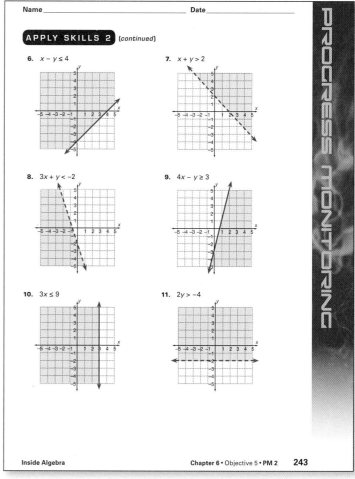

Objective 5
Progress-Monitoring Activities

PM 3 Apply Skills 3

Use with 5-Day or 3-Day Instructional Plan.

MATERIALS

- *Interactive Text*, pages 244–245

DIRECTIONS

1. Have students turn to *Interactive Text*, pages 244–245, Apply Skills 3.

2. Monitor student work, and provide feedback as necessary.

   Watch for:

   - Do students use solid lines to graph non-strict inequalities?

   - Do students use dotted lines to graph strict inequalities?

NEXT STEPS • Differentiate

👥 5-Day Instructional Plan:

PS 2, page 557—Students who are on the accelerated path, to develop problem-solving skills

PS 1, page 556—Students who are on the differentiated path, to develop problem-solving skills

👥 3-Day Instructional Plan:

PS 2, page 557—Students who are on the accelerated path, to develop problem-solving skills

PS 1, page 556—Students on the differentiated path who demonstrated understanding on PM 1, to develop problem-solving skills

Objective 5 Posttest, page 559—All other students

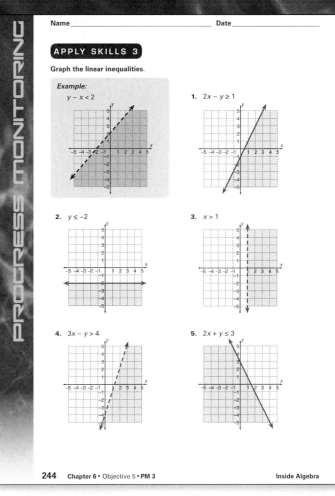

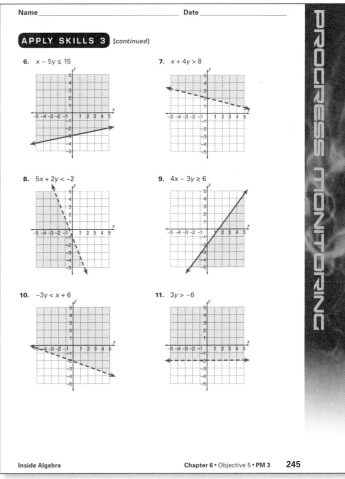

Objective 5
Problem-Solving Activities

★PS 1 Graphing Situations

Use with 5-Day or 3-Day Instructional Plan. In this activity, students write inequalities that describe the word problem and graph the inequality to show all possible solutions.

MATERIALS

- *Interactive Text*, page 246
- Blackline Master 59

DIRECTIONS

1. Tell students that in this activity, they read word problems for information, then write inequalities to represent the situation described and graph the results.

2. Complete this assignment as a class. Have students turn to *Interactive Text*, page 246, Graphing Situations, and follow along while you read the first problem. As you read, have students underline important points. When you finish, call on students for relevant points, and write them on the board.

3. Distribute one copy of Blackline Master 59, Graph Paper, to each student.

4. Have students solve Problem 1, writing an inequality and sketching a graph. Choose a student to write the inequality on the board and another student to sketch the graph. Ask students how to interpret the graph. Remind students that the answer to Problem 2 should be in complete sentences.

5. Repeat this procedure for Problems 3–4.

NEXT STEPS • Differentiate

👥 5-Day and 3-Day Instructional Plans:

PM 3, page 555—Students who are on the accelerated path, to assess progress

Objective 5 Posttest, page 559—Students who are on the differentiated path

★ = Includes Problem Solving

PROBLEM SOLVING

Name_____ Date_____

GRAPHING SITUATIONS

Write the inequality for each problem and graph the result, choosing an appropriate scale. Answer the question about each graph.

1. The ski club is going on a ski trip to Gold Mountain Resort. The lift tickets for students under the age of 17 cost $30; for people age 17 and older, the cost is $40. The ski club has at most $900 to spend on lift tickets. Write an inequality for the possible cost of the lift tickets in which x represents the number of lift tickets for those under age 17 and y represents the number of lift tickets for those age 17 and older.

   $30x + 40y \leq 900$

2. What might the graph mean?

   The ski club can buy any combination of tickets with numbers that fall on or under the line.

3. The jazz band wants to attend a concert. Tickets cost $40 for general admission and $60 for reserved seating. The jazz band can spend at most $1,000 on the concert. Write an inequality for the possible cost of the tickets in which x represents the number of general admission tickets and y the number of reserved seat tickets.

   $40x + 60y \leq 1,000$

4. What might the graph mean?

   The jazz band can buy any combination of tickets with numbers that fall on or under the line.

Name_____ Date_____   **59**

GRAPH PAPER

Objective 5
Problem-Solving Activities

★PS 2 Compounding the Compound

Use with 5-Day or 3-Day Instructional Plan. In this activity, students graph compound inequalities on a coordinate graph.

MATERIALS

- *Interactive Text*, page 247
- Blackline Master 59

DIRECTIONS

1. Make a transparency of Blackline Master 59, Graph Paper, and show a coordinate graph on the overhead. Alternatively, draw a coordinate graph on the board. Distribute one copy of Blackline Master 59, Graph Paper, to each student.

2. Write $y > \frac{1}{4}x + 2$ on the board. Have students graph the inequality on graph paper. When most students are finished, have one volunteer demonstrate how to graph the inequality on the board or overhead.

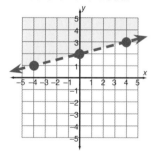

3. Review the following terms with students:

   and All conditions must be true for the statement to be true

   compound inequality Two inequalities connected by *and* or *or*

   or If either or both conditions are true, the whole statement is true

★ = Includes Problem Solving

Name _____ Date _____

GRAPH PAPER

Name _____ Date _____

COMPOUND THE COMPOUND

Graph each system of inequalities.

1. $x > y + 2$ and $x + y \geq 3$ and $5x > y - 5$

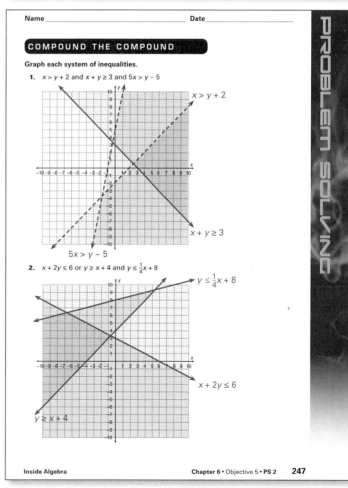

$x > y + 2$

$x + y \geq 3$

$5x > y - 5$

2. $x + 2y \leq 6$ or $y \geq x + 4$ and $y \leq \frac{1}{4}x + 8$

$y \leq \frac{1}{4}x + 8$

$x + 2y \leq 6$

$y \geq x + 4$

Problem-Solving Activities

4. Explain that compound inequalities on a coordinate graph are similar to those on a number line. Write **and** $y \leq 5x - 4$ on the board to the right of the first inequality. Tell students to graph this inequality on the same coordinate graph as the first inequality. Have students shade the area for the second inequality with a different type of shading; for example, students can shade it with a different color or pattern.

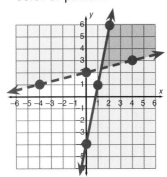

5. Have students identify the area where both types of shading are present. Explain that points in this area apply to the compound inequality and points in only one or none of the shaded areas do not apply to the compound inequality. Have students choose several points on the coordinate graph and substitute them in the inequalities to check that this is true.

Sample answers:

$y > \frac{1}{4}x + 2$ and $y \leq 5x - 4$

(4, 4) True
$4 > \frac{1}{4}(4) + 2$ and $4 \leq 5(4) - 4$
$4 > 1 + 2$ and $4 \leq 20 - 4$
$4 > 3$ and $4 \leq 16$

(0, 5) Not true; it is only true for $y > \frac{1}{4}x + 2$
$5 > \frac{1}{4}(0) + 2$ and $5 \nleq 5(0) - 4$
$5 > 0 + 2$ and $5 \nleq 0 - 4$
$5 > 2$ and $5 \nleq -4$

(6, 0) Not true; it is only true for $y \leq 5x - 4$
$0 \ngtr \frac{1}{4}(6) + 2$ and $0 \leq 5(6) - 4$
$0 \ngtr \frac{6}{4} + 2$ and $0 \leq 30 - 4$
$0 \ngtr 3\frac{1}{2}$ and $0 \leq 26$

6. Have students turn to *Interactive Text*, page 247, Compound the Compound, and complete the two problems. Circulate to make sure students correctly graph the compound inequalities.

NEXT STEPS • Differentiate

5-Day and 3-Day Instructional Plans:
Objective 5 Posttest, page 559—All students

Objective 5 Posttest

Discuss with students the key concepts in Objective 5. Following the discussion, administer the Objective 5 Posttest to all students.

Using the Results

• Score the posttest and update the class record card.

• Provide reinforcement for students who do not demonstrate mastery of the concepts through individual or small-group reteaching of key concepts.

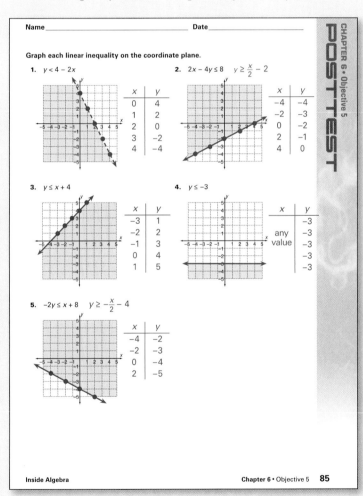

Name_____ Date_____

Graph each linear inequality on the coordinate plane.

1. $y < 4 - 2x$

x	y
0	4
1	2
2	0
3	-2
4	-4

2. $2x - 4y \leq 8$ $y \geq \frac{x}{2} - 2$

x	y
-4	-4
-2	-3
0	-2
2	-1
4	0

3. $y \leq x + 4$

x	y
-3	1
-2	2
-1	3
0	4
1	5

4. $y \leq -3$

x	y
	-3
	-3
any value	-3
	-3
	-3

5. $-2y \leq x + 8$ $y \geq -\frac{x}{2} - 4$

x	y
-4	-2
-2	-3
0	-4
2	-5

Inside Algebra   Chapter 6 • Objective 5   **85**

6 CHAPTER

Chapter Review

Chapter 6 Review

Use with 5-Day or 3-Day Instructional Plan. In this activity, students review key chapter concepts prior to taking the Chapter Test.

MATERIALS

- *Interactive Text*, pages 249–250

DIRECTIONS

1. Have students turn to *Interactive Text*, pages 249–250, Chapter 6 Review.

2. Have students complete the review individually or in small groups. If the activity is completed individually, provide time for students to discuss their solutions as a class or in small groups.

3. Monitor student work, and provide feedback when necessary. If students complete the review quickly, pair them with other students or groups to discuss their answers.

Name_____ Date_____

OBJECTIVE 1

Solve and graph the solution set for each inequality.

1. $x + 6 > 5$ $x > -1$
   $x + 6 - 6 > 5 - 6$

2. $3 + y \leq 6$ $y \leq 3$
   $3 + y - 3 \leq 6 - 3$

3. $x - 2 < -4$ $x < -2$
   $x - 2 + 2 < -4 + 2$

4. $n - 3.4 \geq -2.3$ $n \geq 1.1$
   $n - 3.4 + 3.4 = -2.3 + 3.4$

OBJECTIVE 2

Solve and graph the solution set for each inequality.

5. $3a > 15$ $a > 5$
   $\left(\frac{1}{3}\right)3a > 15\left(\frac{1}{3}\right)$

6. $-2x < 6$ $x > -3$
   $\left(-\frac{1}{2}\right)(-2x) > 6\left(-\frac{1}{2}\right)$

7. $\frac{n}{-2} < -1$ $n > 2$
   $(-2)\left(\frac{n}{-2}\right) > -1(-2)$

8. $\frac{2}{3}x \geq -2$ $x \geq -3$
   $\left(\frac{3}{2}\right)\frac{2}{3}x \geq -2\left(\frac{3}{2}\right)$

OBJECTIVE 3

Solve and graph the solution set for each inequality.

9. $2x > 4 + x$ $x > 4$
   $2x - x > 4 + x - x$

10. $-4x \leq 6 - x$ $x \geq -2$
    $-3x \leq 6$

Inside Algebra   Chapter 6 • CR 6   **249**

Name_____ Date_____

OBJECTIVE 3 (*continued*)

11. $14 - x \geq 9$ $x \leq 5$
    $-x \geq -5$

12. $\frac{1}{2}x - 5 \geq x - 3$ $x \leq -4$
    $-\frac{1}{2}x \geq 2$

OBJECTIVE 4

Solve and graph the solution set for each inequality.

13. $x + 2 > 3$ and $x - 1 < 3$
    $x > 1$ and $x < 4$

14. $\frac{x}{2} < -1$ or $4x > 20$
    $x < -2$ or $x > 5$

15. $|x| > 3$
    $x > 3$ or $x < -3$

16. $6 - x > 5$ and $2x > -12 - x$
    $x < 1$ and $x > -4$

OBJECTIVE 5   Answers will vary depending on values for *x*.

Graph the linear inequalities on the coordinate planes.

17. $x + y \geq 4$

x	y
−1	5
0	4
1	3
2	2

18. $x < 3 + 2y$

x	y
−3	−3
−1	−2
1	−1
3	0

19. $x = y - 3$

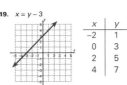

x	y
−2	1
0	3
2	5
4	7

20. $2y \geq 3x$

x	y
−2	−3
0	0
2	3
4	6

250   Chapter 6 • CR 6   Inside Algebra

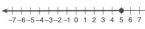

Ongoing Assessment

Chapter 6 Test, Form A

MATERIALS

- *Assessment Book*, pages 87–88

DIRECTIONS

1. Have students turn to *Assessment Book*, pages 87–88, Chapter 6 Test, Form A. Administer the Chapter Test to all students.

2. Score the test by objective and update the class record card.

3. Use the test data to determine differentiation needs.

Name _____ Date _____

Objective 1

Solve and graph the solution set for each inequality.

1. $x + 11 < 7$ $x < -4$

   ←+++++○+++++++++++++→
   −7 −6 −5 −4 −3 −2 −1 0 1 2 3 4 5 6 7

   $x + 11 - 11 < 7 - 11$

2. $y - 4 \geq -1$ $y \geq 3$

   ←++++++++++●++++++→
   −7 −6 −5 −4 −3 −2 −1 0 1 2 3 4 5 6 7

   $y - 4 + 4 \geq -1 + 4$

3. $a - 9 \leq -13$ $a \leq -4$

   ←+++●+++++++++++++→
   −7 −6 −5 −4 −3 −2 −1 0 1 2 3 4 5 6 7

   $a - 9 + 9 \leq -13 + 9$

4. $b + 17 > 21$ $b > 4$

   ←+++++++++++○+++++→
   −7 −6 −5 −4 −3 −2 −1 0 1 2 3 4 5 6 7

   $b + 17 - 17 > 21 - 17$

Objective 2

Solve and graph the solution set for each inequality.

5. $4a < -20$ $a < -5$

   ←++○++++++++++++++→
   −7 −6 −5 −4 −3 −2 −1 0 1 2 3 4 5 6 7

   $\left(\frac{1}{4}\right)4a < -20\left(\frac{1}{4}\right)$

6. $\frac{x}{3} \geq 2$ $x \geq 6$

   ←++++++++++++●++++→
   −7 −6 −5 −4 −3 −2 −1 0 1 2 3 4 5 6 7

   $3\left(\frac{x}{3}\right) \geq 2(3)$

7. $-5y < 15$ $y > -3$

   ←++++○++++++++++++→
   −7 −6 −5 −4 −3 −2 −1 0 1 2 3 4 5 6 7

   $\left(-\frac{1}{5}\right)(-5y) > 15\left(-\frac{1}{5}\right)$

8. $-3b \leq -12$ $b \geq 4$

   ←+++++++++++●+++++→
   −7 −6 −5 −4 −3 −2 −1 0 1 2 3 4 5 6 7

   $\left(-\frac{1}{3}\right)(-3b) \geq -12\left(-\frac{1}{3}\right)$

Objective 3

Solve and graph the solution set for each inequality.

9. $4x - 5 > 23$ $x > 7$

   ←++++++++++++++++○→
   −7 −6 −5 −4 −3 −2 −1 0 1 2 3 4 5 6 7

   $4x > 28$

10. $7 - 2b \leq 1$ $b \geq 3$

    ←+++++++++++●++++++→
    −7 −6 −5 −4 −3 −2 −1 0 1 2 3 4 5 6 7

    $-2b \leq -6$

11. $2y - 9 \leq -13$ $y \leq -2$

    ←+++++●++++++++++++→
    −7 −6 −5 −4 −3 −2 −1 0 1 2 3 4 5 6 7

    $2y \leq -4$

12. $4z - 7 > 7z - 4$ $z < -1$

    ←++++++○+++++++++++→
    −7 −6 −5 −4 −3 −2 −1 0 1 2 3 4 5 6 7

    $-3 > 3z$

Name _____ Date _____

Objective 4

Solve and graph the solution set for each inequality.

13. $3x + 2 < 5$ and $2x + 7 > 1$

    $x < 1$ and $x > -3$

    ←+++○++++++○++++++→
    −7 −6 −5 −4 −3 −2 −1 0 1 2 3 4 5 6 7

    $3x < 3$ and $2x > -6$

14. $4y \geq 20$ or $2y - 9 \leq -13$

    $y \geq 5$ or $y \leq -2$

    ←+++++●+++++++●++++→
    −7 −6 −5 −4 −3 −2 −1 0 1 2 3 4 5 6 7

    $2y \leq -4$

15. $|a| < 3$

    $a < 3$ and $a > -3$

    ←++++○++++++○+++++→
    −7 −6 −5 −4 −3 −2 −1 0 1 2 3 4 5 6 7

16. $|c - 4| \geq 3$

    $c \geq 7$ or $c \leq 1$

    ←++++++●+++++++●++→
    −5 −4 −3 −2 −1 0 1 2 3 4 5 6 7 8 9

Objective 5

Graph each linear inequality on the coordinate plane.

17. $y > 2x - 3$

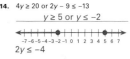

x	y
−1	−5
0	−3
1	−1
2	1
3	3

18. $y \leq 1 - 3x$

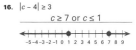

x	y
−1	4
0	1
1	−2
2	−5

19. $x - 2y \geq 6$ $y \leq \frac{x}{2} - 3$

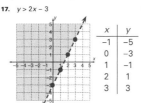

x	y
−4	−5
−2	−4
0	−3
2	−2
4	−1

20. $x < 4$

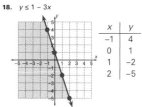

x	y
4	
4	
4	any value
4	
4	

Ongoing Assessment

Differentiation

MATERIALS

- **Gizmos** *Linear Inequalities in Two Variables—Activity A* Gizmo
- **Gizmos** Extension Activity pages
- **Gizmos** Reinforcement Activity page
- Additional Activities
- Algebra Skill Builders for Chapter 6
- Chapter Test, Form B

DIRECTIONS

1. Review Chapter 6 Test, Form A, with the class.

2. Use the results from Chapter 6 Test, Form A, to identify students for reinforcement or extension.

3. After students have been identified for extension or reinforcement, break students into appropriate groups. See pages 563–565 for detailed differentiated instruction.

Differentiation Planner

Students who demonstrated mastery on every objective posttest and scored 80% or above on the chapter test

Extend learning using:

- **Gizmos** Use the *Linear Inequalities in Two Variables—Activity A* Gizmo with the Extension Activity. Have students work in pairs or individually to complete the activity.

Students who demonstrated mastery on every objective posttest but scored below 80% on the chapter test

Reinforce learning using:

- **Gizmos** Use the *Linear Inequalities in Two Variables—Activity A* Gizmo with the Reinforcement Activity. Have students work in pairs or small groups to complete the activity.
- Additional Activities from the online resources.
- Algebra Skill Builders for Chapter 6 from the online resources.

Students who did not demonstrate mastery on any or all of the objective posttests or the chapter test

Reinforce learning using:

- **Gizmos** Present the *Linear Inequalities in Two Variables—Activity A* Gizmo to students in small groups using the instruction on page 565.
- Additional Activities from the online resources.
- Algebra Skill Builders for Chapter 6 from the online resources.

Retest—Administer Chapter 6 Test, Form B, from the online resources to students who scored below 80 percent on Form A when time allows.

NEXT STEPS • Pretest

- Administer Chapter 7, Objective 1 Pretest, page 568, to all students.

6 CHAPTER
Ongoing Assessment

Students who demonstrated mastery on every objective posttest and scored 80% or above on the chapter test

1. Divide students into pairs or allow them to work individually for this activity.

2. Distribute one copy of the Extension Activity from the online resources to each student.

3. Direct students to the Gizmo *Linear Inequalities in Two Variables—Activity A* through the Inside Algebra Student Web site, http://insidealgebra. voyagerlearning.com.

4. Have students complete the Extension Activity.

5. **Peer Review.** If there is time, have students exchange papers with a peer. They should review and discuss each response and be prepared to explain their thinking.

   Variation: If students do not have access to the Gizmo, provide them with grid paper so they can draw the graph in Problem 2.

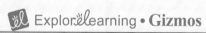

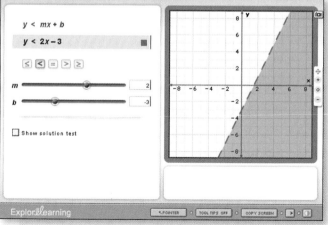

Linear Inequalities in Two Variables—Activity A

LINEAR INEQUALITIES IN TWO VARIABLES—ACTIVITY A

A group of friends are building a rectangular sandbox for a playground. They have 24 meters of wood to build the box that the sand will go in. The box will have only sides and no bottom.

1. Let x represent the width of the sandbox. Let y represent the length. The inequality $2x + 2y \le 24$ describes the different lengths and widths of rectangular sandboxes that can be made from using at most 24 meters of wood. Solve this inequality for y. $y \le -x + 12$

2. Start the *Linear Inequalities in Two Variables—Activity A* Gizmo. Graph the inequality from Problem 1. You can enter the values for m and b to the right of the sliders. You can click and drag on the graph to change the view or use the buttons to the right of the graph to change the view.

3. For this problem, can x be zero or negative? Can y be zero or negative? Explain your reasoning.

   No, because x and y represent the width and length of a rectangle and these measurements cannot be 0 or negative.

4. Draw the graph that represents the solution to Problem 1 on the coordinate plane at right.

5. What is the greatest whole number length the sandbox can be? What is the corresponding width? Explain how you found your answer.

   Sample answer: Because y represents the length and the greatest whole number y-value on the solution graph is 11, the greatest whole number length is 11 meters. The corresponding width is 1 meter, because the point (1, 11) is a solution of $y \le -x + 12$

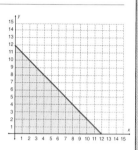

6. What is the perimeter of the rectangle from Problem 5? _____ 24 meters
   What is the area of the rectangle? _____ 11 square meters

7. What are the dimensions of the largest square sandbox that can be built? Explain how you found your answer.

   The largest square sandbox has a length and width of 6 meters because (6, 6) is the solution with the greatest x- and y-values that are equal.

Inside Algebra • Chapter 6 • Extension **1**

LINEAR INEQUALITIES IN TWO VARIABLES—ACTIVITY A (continued)

8. What is the perimeter of the sandbox in Problem 7? _____ 24 meters
   What is the area of the sandbox? _____ 36 square meters

9. What solutions on the graph represent the dimensions of the possible sandboxes that use all 24 meters of wood?

   The points on the line $y = -x + 12$

10. What solutions on the graph represent the dimensions of the possible sandboxes that do not use all 24 meters of wood?

    The points in the shaded area below the line $y = -x + 12$.

11. What are the dimensions of the largest possible square sandbox if not all 24 meters of wood are used? Explain how you found your answer.

    The largest square sandbox that does not use all the wood has a length and width of 5 meters because (5, 5) is the solution with the greatest x- and y-values that are equal, but are not on the line $y = -x + 12$.

12. What is the perimeter of the sandbox in Problem 11? _____ 20 meters
    How much wood is left over? _____ 4 meters
    What is the area of the sandbox? _____ 25 square meters

13. A landscaper is donating 6 cubic meters of sand. The sand in the box needs to be 0.2 meters deep. The number of cubic meters of sand needed is found by multiplying the area of the box by 0.2 meters. Which sandbox should the friends build, the box from Problem 7 or the box from Problem 11? Explain.

    The sandbox in Problem 7 needs 7.2 cubic meters of sand and the sandbox from Problem 11 needs 5 cubic meters. Because $5 < 6$ and $7.2 > 6$, the friends should build the smaller box.

Inside Algebra • Chapter 6 • Extension **2**

Students who demonstrated mastery on every objective posttest but scored below 80% on the chapter test

1. Divide students into pairs or small groups.

2. Distribute one copy of the Individual Reinforcement Activity from the online resources to each student.

3. Direct students to the Gizmo *Linear Inequalities in Two Variables—Activity A* through the Inside Algebra Student Web site, http://insidealgebra.voyagerlearning.com.

4. Have students complete the Reinforcement Activity.

5. **Peer Review.** If time permits, have students exchange papers with a peer to review and discuss each other's responses. Remind students to be prepared to explain the reasoning behind their responses.

   Variation If students do not have access to the Gizmo, provide them with graphs of $y = x + 3$, $y < x + 3$, $y > x + 3$, $y \le x + 3$, and $y \ge x + 3$ on an overhead or a blackboard for Problem 4.

---

el Gizmos Reinforcement Activity   Name_____   Date_____

LINEAR INEQUALITIES IN TWO VARIABLES—ACTIVITY A

1. Solve each inequality.

   $x + 8 > 7$ $x - 4 \le 1$

   $x > \underline{\ -1\ }$ $x \le \underline{\ 5\ }$

2. Complete the steps to solve each inequality, then graph each solution.

   $-3x > 12$ $\frac{x}{2} \ge -1$

   $-3x \div \underline{\ -3\ } < 12 \div \underline{\ -3\ }$ $\frac{x}{2} \cdot \underline{\ 2\ } \ge -1 \cdot \underline{\ 2\ }$

   $x < \underline{\ -4\ }$ $x \ge \underline{\ -2\ }$

   ‹—●——————→   ‹————●————→
   -5 -4 -3 -2 -1 0 1 2 3 4 5   -5 -4 -3 -2 -1 0 1 2 3 4 5

3. Solve each inequality, then circle the graph that represents the solution of $2x + 1 < 5$ and $3x - 1 > -7$.

   $2x + 1 < 5$ $3x - 1 > -7$

   $2x < \underline{\ 4\ }$ $3x > \underline{\ -6\ }$

   $x < \underline{\ 2\ }$ $x > \underline{\ -2\ }$

   ‹——○——○——→   ‹——○————○——→
   -5 -4 -3 -2 -1 0 1 2 3 4 5   -5 -4 -3 -2 -1 0 1 2 3 4 5

4. Start the *Linear Inequalities in Two Variables—Activity A* Gizmo. Graph the equation $y = x + 3$ by choosing the = button and using the *m* and *b* sliders.

   Graph the inequality $y > x + 3$. Is the solution above or below the line $y = x + 3$? _____above_____

   Graph the inequality $y < x + 3$. Is the solution above or below the line $y = x + 3$? _____below_____

   Graph the inequality $y \le x + 3$. How is this graph different from the graph of $y < x + 3$?

   The graph of $y \le x + 3$ includes the line $y = x + 3$, where the graph of $y < x + 3$

   does not.

   Graph the inequality $y \ge x + 3$. How is this graph different from the graph of $y > x + 3$?

   The graph of $y \ge x + 3$ includes the line $y = x + 3$, where the graph of $y > x + 3$

   does not.

Inside Algebra • Chapter 6 • Reinforcement   **1**

---

el Explore*learning* • Gizmos

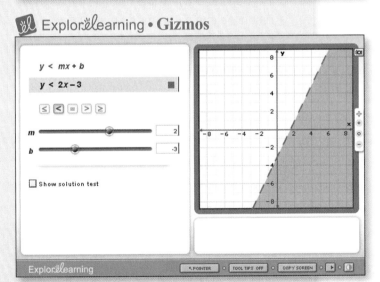

Linear Inequalities in Two Variables—Activity A

The Gizmo is not needed in Problems 1–3.

1. Ask students to solve $x + 8 > 7$. Use these steps to scaffold instruction.

   - Ask students how to undo the addition of 8. Subtract 8 from both sides.

   - Ask students to state the solution after subtracting 8. $x > -1$

   - Repeat the process above and have students solve $x - 4 \leq 1$. $x \leq 5$

2. Ask students to solve $-3x > 12$. Use these steps to scaffold instruction.

   - Ask students to describe how to undo the multiplication by −3. Divide by −3. Ask students what to do when multiplying or dividing both sides of an inequality by a negative number. Reverse the inequality symbol. Ask students to state the solution. $x < -4$

   - Graph $x < -4$ as students answer the following. Ask students where the endpoint should be. −4 Ask students if the point should be open or closed. open Ask students to which side of −4 the rest of the graph should be drawn. to the left

   - Repeat the process above and have students solve $\frac{x}{2} \geq -1$. $x \geq -2$

3. Ask students to solve the compound inequality $2x + 1 < 5$ and $3x - 1 > -7$. Use these steps to scaffold instruction.

   - Ask students to solve each inequality separately. $x < 2$; $x > -2$

   - Ask students to describe the graph of $x < 2$. all points to the left of 2 Draw this graph. Ask students to describe the graph of $x > -2$. all points to the right of −2 Draw this graph.

   - Ask students where on the graphs both inequalities are true. between −2 and 2 Draw this graph.

4. Start the *Linear Inequalities in Two Variables—Activity A* Gizmo. Graph the equation $y = x + 3$ by choosing the = button and using the *m* and *b* sliders. Graph all four inequalities that can be made from $y = x + 3$ and have students describe each graph as it relates to $y = x + 3$. (e.g. The graph of $y < x + 3$ is below the line $y = x + 3$.) Also have students compare the graphs of $y < x + 3$ and $y \leq x + 3$ (and the graphs of $y > x + 3$ and $y \geq x + 3$).

   Variation: If students do not have access to the Gizmo, use a blackboard or overhead projector to complete the activity.

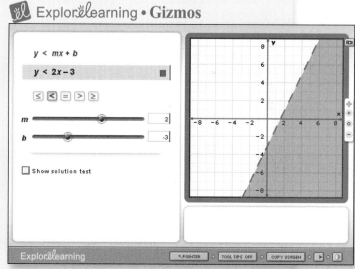

Linear Inequalities in Two Variables—Activity A

Ongoing Assessment

Chapter 6 Test, Form B

MATERIALS

- Chapter 6 Test, Form B, from the Online Resources, pages 1–2

DIRECTIONS

1. Have students turn to Chapter 6 Test, Form B, pages 1–2, from the Online Resources. Administer the Chapter Test to all students.

2. Score the test by objective and update the class record card.

Name _____ Date _____

Objective 1

Solve and graph the solution set for each inequality.

1. $x + 3 > 2$ $x > -1$

   -7 -6 -5 -4 -3 -2 -1 0 1 2 3 4 5 6 7

   $x + 3 - 3 > 2 - 3$

2. $4 + y \le 6$ $y \le 2$

   -7 -6 -5 -4 -3 -2 -1 0 1 2 3 4 5 6 7

   $4 + y - 4 \le 6 - 4$

3. $x - 1 < -2$ $x < -1$

   -7 -6 -5 -4 -3 -2 -1 0 1 2 3 4 5 6 7

   $x - 1 + 1 < -2 + 1$

4. $n - 5.1 \ge -2.7$ $n \ge 2.4$

   -7 -6 -5 -4 -3 -2 -1 0 1 2 3 4 5 6 7

   $n - 5.1 + 5.1 \ge -2.7 + 5.1$

Objective 2

Solve and graph the solution set for each inequality.

5. $4a > 12$ $a > 3$

   -7 -6 -5 -4 -3 -2 -1 0 1 2 3 4 5 6 7

   $\left(\frac{1}{4}\right)4a > 12\left(\frac{1}{4}\right)$

6. $-3x > 6$ $x < -2$

   -7 -6 -5 -4 -3 -2 -1 0 1 2 3 4 5 6 7

   $\left(-\frac{1}{3}\right)(-3x) < 6\left(-\frac{1}{3}\right)$

7. $-\frac{n}{3} < -2$ $n > 6$

   -7 -6 -5 -4 -3 -2 -1 0 1 2 3 4 5 6 7

   $(-3)\left(-\frac{n}{3}\right) > -2(-3)$

8. $\frac{3}{2}x \ge -6$ $x \ge -4$

   -7 -6 -5 -4 -3 -2 -1 0 1 2 3 4 5 6 7

   $\left(\frac{2}{3}\right)\frac{3}{2}x \ge -6\left(\frac{2}{3}\right)$

Inside Algebra   Chapter 6 • Test • Form B   **1**

Name _____ Date _____

Objective 3

Solve and graph the solution set for each inequality.

9. $-2x \le 3 - x$ $x \ge -3$

   -7 -6 -5 -4 -3 -2 -1 0 1 2 3 4 5 6 7

   $-x \le 3$

10. $12 - x \ge 9$ $x \le 3$

   -7 -6 -5 -4 -3 -2 -1 0 1 2 3 4 5 6 7

   $-x \ge -3$

11. $-3x - 4 \ge -x - 2$ $x \le -1$

   -7 -6 -5 -4 -3 -2 -1 0 1 2 3 4 5 6 7

   $-2x \ge 2$

12. $-3x > 4 + x$ $x < -1$

   -7 -6 -5 -4 -3 -2 -1 0 1 2 3 4 5 6 7

   $-3x - x > 4 + x - x$

   $\left(-\frac{1}{4}\right)(-4x) > 4\left(-\frac{1}{4}\right)$

Objective 4

Solve and graph the solution set for each inequality.

13. $x + 3 > 2$ and $x - 2 < 4$

   -7 -6 -5 -4 -3 -2 -1 0 1 2 3 4 5 6 7

   $x > -1$ and $x < 6$

14. $\frac{x}{3} < -1$ or $4x \ge 8$

   -7 -6 -5 -4 -3 -2 -1 0 1 2 3 4 5 6 7

   $x < -3$ or $x \ge 2$

15. $|x| > 1$

   -7 -6 -5 -4 -3 -2 -1 0 1 2 3 4 5 6 7

   $x > 1$ or $x < -1$

16. $3 - x > 5$ and $2x > -9 - x$

   -7 -6 -5 -4 -3 -2 -1 0 1 2 3 4 5 6 7

   $x < -2$ and $x > -3$

Objective 5

Graph each linear inequality on the coordinate plane.

17. $x + y \ge 2$ 18. $3x < 3 + 2y$ 19. $2x = y - 3$ 20. $3y \ge x$

Inside Algebra   Chapter 6 • Test • Form B   **2**

Appendix

Glossary

absolute value The distance of a number from zero on the number line; it is always a positive number (Chapter 2)

$$|-3| = 3 \text{ or } |9| = 9$$

acute triangle A triangle whose angles are all acute, or less than 90° (Chapter 3)

algebraic expression An expression that includes variables (Chapter 1)

$$9 - 2y$$

and All conditions must be true for the statement to be true (Chapter 6)

$$x \geq -1 \text{ and } x \leq 3$$

average The sum of the values in a set, divided by the number of values in the set (Chapter 2)

The average of the numbers 7, 19, 26, 31, and 42 is 25.

axis of symmetry The vertical line through the vertex (Chapter 10)

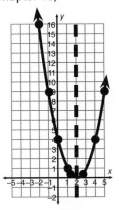

axis of symmetry: $x = 2$

best-fit line The line on a graph that will best connect the data or points (Chapter 5)

binary operation An operation that is applied to two operands; addition, subtraction, multiplication, and division are binary operations (Chapter 12)

$$\sqrt{x} \cdot \sqrt{y} = \sqrt{x \cdot y}$$

binomial An expression with two terms (Chapter 8)

$$10 + 6 \text{ or } x - 7$$

coefficient A number or quantity placed before a variable, which indicates multiplication of that variable (Chapter 6)

In $8x$**, the coefficent of** x **is 8.**

completing the square Adding to or subtracting from a quadratic equation to make it into a perfect square trinomial; a method used to find the solutions of a quadratic equation (Chapter 9)

$$x^2 + 6x + 5 = 0$$
$$x^2 + 6x + 9 - 4 = 0$$
$$(x + 3)^2 = 4$$
$$x = -1 \text{ or } -5$$

compound inequality Two inequalities connected by *and* or *or* (Chapter 6)

$$x > 0 \text{ and } x \leq 7$$
$$x < 3 \text{ or } x > 13$$

congruent Two angles that have the same measure (Chapter 12)

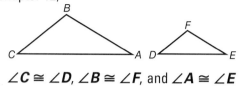

$\angle C \cong \angle D$, $\angle B \cong \angle F$, and $\angle A \cong \angle E$

---

consistent A system of equations that is always true (Chapter 7)

$$2x - y = 3$$
$$4x - 2y = 6$$
$$0 = 0$$

---

constant of proportionality The ratio between the lengths of the sides of two similar triangles (Chapter 12)

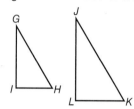

$\triangle GIH \sim \triangle JLK$

ratio ≈ 0.65 or 1.5

---

coordinate plane The plane determined by a horizontal number line, called the x-axis, and a vertical number line, called the y-axis, intersecting at a point called the origin (Chapter 4)

---

cube A number or variable raised to the third power (Chapter 1)

x^3 or 2^3

---

dependent variable A variable whose value is dependent upon the value of another variable (Chapter 4)

If you are traveling by car on a long stretch of highway with no gas stations, the distance you are able to travel is the dependent variable because it depends on the amount of gas you previously put in the car.

---

descending order Arranged from largest to smallest; decreasing (Chapter 8)

98, 87, 52, 31, 16, 4

$2x^5, 2x^3, 7x, 10$

---

difference of squares A binomial of the form $a^2 - b^2 = (a + b)(a - b)$ (Chapter 9)

$x^2 - 16 = (x + 4)(x - 4)$

---

domain The possible values for x in a relation (Chapter 4)

$y = 2x + 5$	
x	y
−1	3
0	5
3	11

---

elimination Removing one variable from a system of equations by adding or subtracting like terms with the same coefficients (Chapter 7)

$$x + 2y = 8 \qquad\qquad -3 + 2y = 8$$
$$-2x - 2y = -5 \qquad\qquad y = \frac{11}{2}$$
$$-x + 0 = 3$$
$$x = -3$$

---

equation A statement that two quantities or mathematical expressions are equal (Chapter 3)

$x + 1 = 8$

---

equilateral triangle A triangle whose three sides are equal in length and three angles are equal in measure; the angles are each 60° (Chapter 3)

Glossary

equivalent Equal in value (Chapter 3)

$$3 = 3$$
$$x + 1 = x + 1$$
$$\frac{7}{7} = 1$$

excluded value A value of a variable that results in a denominator of zero (Chapter 11)

$$\frac{3x}{9x^2}; \ x \neq 0$$

exponent The power to which some other quantity is raised (Chapter 8)

In x^y the exponent is y.

exponential function Any function in which a variable appears as an exponent and may also appear as a base (Chapter 10)

$$y = 2^x$$

extraneous root A root that is a solution to the derived equation but not the original equation (Chapter 12)

$$\sqrt{x + 2} + 4 = x$$
$$\boxed{x = 2} \text{ or } x = 7$$

 F

factor A monomial that evenly divides a value (Chapter 9)

Factors of 12: 1, 2, 3, 4, 6, 12

Factors of $2x^2 + 6x$: $2x$ and $x + 3$

false The statement is always incorrect (Chapter 1)

Five added to six is ten.

or $3 \cdot 8 = 16$

finite A set that contains a specific number of values (Chapter 2)

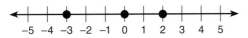

{−3, 0, 2}

function A relation in which every element in the domain is paired with exactly one element in the range (Chapter 4)

$$f(x) = x + 3$$

 G

greatest common factor (GCF) The largest factor that a set of monomials has in common (Chapter 9)

12: 1, 2, 3, ④, 6, 12
16: 1, 2, ④, 8, 16
The GCF of 12 and 16 is 4.

 H

hypotenuse The longest side of a right triangle, opposite the right angle (Chapter 12)

 I

inconsistent A system of equations that is never true (Chapter 7)

$$3x - 2y = 0$$
$$\underline{3x - 2y = -2}$$
$$0 = 2$$

independent variable A variable whose value does not depend upon the value of another variable (Chapter 4)

The length of your hair after a haircut depends on the length that you request to be cut from your hair, for example, 1 inch. The independent variable is the length cut from your hair.

inequality A mathematical sentence that compares two expressions using one of the following symbols (Chapter 6):

> Greater than
< Less than
≥ Greater than or equal to
≤ Less than or equal to

$x < 3$; $x \leq 7$

infinite A set that goes on forever (Chapter 2)

{2, 3, 4, 5...}

integer The set of whole numbers and their opposites (Chapter 2)

{...−2, −1, 0, 1, 2...}

inverse operations Pairs of operations that undo each other and share an inverse relation (Chapter 2)

inverse relation The set of ordered pairs obtained from switching the x- and y-values (Chapter 4)

The inverse relation for {(5, 8), (6, 9), (7, 10), (8, 11), (9, 12)} is {(8, 5), (9, 6), (10, 7), (11, 8), (12, 9)}.

irrational number A number that cannot be expressed as the ratio of two integers (Chapter 2)

$\sqrt{2} = 1.414213...$

isosceles triangle A triangle with two sides of equal length, and the angles opposite the equal sides are also equal (Chapter 3)

L

least common denominator (LCD) The lowest value that is a multiple of the denominators of more than one fraction (Chapter 11)

The LCD of $\frac{3}{5}$ and $\frac{1}{3}$ is 15.

$\frac{3}{5} \cdot \frac{3}{3} = \frac{9}{15}$ and $\frac{1}{3} \cdot \frac{5}{5} = \frac{5}{15}$

like terms Terms that have the same variables and exponents (Chapter 8)

x^2 and $2x^2$ or $6y$ and $3y$

linear equation The equation of a straight line (Chapter 3)

$y = 2x + 4$

M

median The center value in a set when all values are ordered by size (Chapter 2)

The median of the numbers 21, 18, 25, 26, and 17 is 21.

mode The value in a set that appears most (Chapter 2)

The mode of the numbers 29, 27, 23, 29, 26, and 25 is 29.

monomial An expression with only one term (Chapter 8)

24 or x

multiplicative inverse Numbers that multiply to equal one (Chapter 3)

$3 \cdot \frac{1}{3} = 1$

number line A tool used to represent numbers in graphic form (Chapter 2)

obtuse triangle A triangle with one obtuse angle, or angle that is greater than 90°; the longest side is always opposite the obtuse angle (Chapter 3)

open The truth of the statement cannot be determined without further information (Chapter 1)

> **An unknown number multiplied by six is thirty-six.**
>
> or $n(n + 3) = 40$

or If either or both conditions are true, the whole statement is true (Chapter 6)

> $x \leq -5$ or $x > -2$

ordered pair Two numbers that name the coordinates of a point on a graph, with the horizontal coordinate listed first and the vertical coordinate listed second (Chapter 4)

> (x, y) or $(5, 8)$

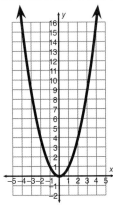

parabola The graph of a quadratic equation; the shape resembles the letter U (Chapter 10)

parallel Lines that do not intersect; they are always the same distance apart (Chapter 4)

percent A ratio whose second term is 100; percent means parts per hundred (Chapter 3)

> $\frac{56}{100} = 56\%$

perfect square The product of a monomial with itself (Chapter 9)

> $x^2, 16a^2,$ or 49

perfect square trinomial A polynomial of the form $a^2 + 2ab + b^2 = (a + b)^2$ or $a^2 - 2ab + b^2 = (a - b)^2$ (Chapter 9)

> $x^2 + 6x + 9 = (x + 3)^2$

perpendicular Lines that intersect at right angles (Chapter 4)

point-slope form A linear equation in the form $y - y_1 = m(x - x_1)$ (Chapter 5)

> **For the points (3, 7) and (0, −2), the point-slope form is** $y - 7 = 3(x - 3)$

polynomial An expression with two or more unlike terms (Chapter 8)

> $x^2 + 6x - 7$

power A number or variable that indicates repeated multiplication; x^y is the product of y copies of x (Chapter 1)

$$a^2 = a \cdot a \text{ or } 4^5 = 4 \cdot 4 \cdot 4 \cdot 4 \cdot 4$$

---

prime factorization The prime numbers and/or variables whose product is the desired expression, or the process of obtaining those values (Chapter 9)

---

principal square root The positive square root of a number (Chapter 2)

$$\sqrt{81} = \sqrt{9 \cdot 9} = 9$$

---

proportion An equation that states that two ratios are equal (Chapter 3)

$$\frac{2}{3} = \frac{4}{6}$$

Pythagorean theorem Formula relating the lengths of the sides of a right triangle, telling us that the sum of the squares of the legs is equal to the square of the hypotenuse (Chapter 12)

$$a^2 + b^2 = c^2$$

---

quadrant One of four regions on a coordinate plane formed by the intersection of the x-axis and the y-axis (Chapter 4)

---

quadratic formula

$x = \dfrac{-b \pm \sqrt{b^2 - 4ac}}{2a}$ where $ax^2 + bx + c = 0$ (Chapter 9)

---

quadratic polynomial A polynomial whose greatest power is 2 (Chapter 9)

$$x^2 - 4, \; x^2 + 9, \text{ or } x^2 + 3x + 2$$

---

quadratic trinomial A polynomial of the form $ax^2 + bx + c$ (Chapter 9)

$$x^2 + 4x + 3$$

---

radical A symbol that indicates that one is to determine the square root (Chapter 2)

$$\sqrt{}$$

---

range The possible values for y in a relation (Chapter 4)

$y = 2x + 5$	
x	y
−1	3
0	5
3	11

---

ratio A comparison of two numbers (Chapter 3)

$\frac{2}{3}$, 2:3, or **2 to 3**

---

rational expression Any expression that can be written as the quotient of two integers or polynomials (Chapter 11)

$\dfrac{1}{2}, \; \dfrac{1}{3x}$, or $\dfrac{x + 2}{x - 1}$

---

rational number A number that can be expressed as the ratio of two integers (Chapter 2)

$\dfrac{1}{8}$ or **−0.5**

---

reciprocal The reciprocal of a number a is a number b such that $a \cdot b = 1$ (Chapter 2)

The reciprocal of $\frac{5}{2}$ is $\frac{2}{5}$.

---

relation A set of ordered pairs (Chapter 4)

{(5, 8), (6, 9), (7, 10), (8, 11), (9, 12)}

Glossary

right triangle A triangle with one right angle, an angle that is exactly 90° (Chapter 3)

rise The vertical distance traveled (Chapter 5)

roots The solutions of an equation (Chapter 10)

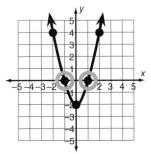

$x = -1$ and 1

run The horizontal distance traveled (Chapter 5)

scatter plot A number of coordinate pairs plotted on a graph; used to investigate a possible relationship between two variables (Chapter 5)

scientific notation A form of writing numbers as the product of a power of 10 and a decimal number greater than or equal to one and less than 10 (Chapter 8)

2.5×10^4

similar Triangles with congruent angles and proportional sides (Chapter 12)

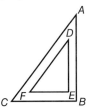

slope The steepness of a line (Chapter 5)

Slope: $\dfrac{2}{3}$

slope-intercept form A linear equation in the form $y = mx + b$ (Chapter 5)

$y = 4x + 1$

square A number or variable raised to the second power; the product of two equal factors (Chapter 1)

b^2 or $49 = 7 \cdot 7$

square root One of two equal factors of a given number (Chapter 2)

$5 = \sqrt{5 \cdot 5} = \sqrt{25}$

standard form A linear equation in the form $ax + by = c$ (Chapter 5)

$2x - y = -4$

standard notation A form of writing numbers with one digit for each place value (Chapter 8)

1,238,090

strict inequality An inequality that compares two expressions using only greater than (>) or less than (<) (Chapter 6)

$x > -2; x < 3$

---

substitution Removing one variable from a system of equations by rewriting the system in terms of the other variable (Chapter 7)

$x = 2y + 8$ and $2x + 2y = 4$

$2(2y + 8) + 2y = 4$

$4y + 16 + 2y = 4$

$6y = -12$ $x = 2(-2) + 8$

$y = -2$ $x = 4$

---

system of equations A set of two or more equations that use the same variables (Chapter 7)

$y = 2x - 3$ and $3y + 6 = x$

---

system of inequalities A set of two or more linear inequalities that use the same variables (Chapter 7)

$y \leq 2x - 3$ and $3y + 6 \leq x$

---

true The statement is always correct (Chapter 1)

Twenty-seven divided by nine is three.

or $2 \cdot 8 = 16$

---

variable A letter or symbol used to represent a value or set of values (Chapter 1)

x, y, a, b, n, or π

vertex The turning point of a parabola (Chapter 10)

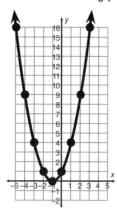

vertex: (-1, 0)

---

x-coordinate The horizontal distance from the point of origin of a graph; in an ordered pair, this value is always written first (Chapter 4)

---

x-intercept The point where the line crosses the x-axis (Chapter 5)

x-intercept: (2, 0)

---

y-coordinate The vertical distance from the point of origin of a graph; in an ordered pair, this value is always written second (Chapter 4)

y-intercept The point where the line crosses the y-axis (Chapter 5)

y-intercept: (0, 1)

zero pair A positive value and a negative value of equal magnitude that together equal zero (Chapter 2)

+4 + (−4) = 0 or +103 + (−103) = 0

zeros of a function The points at which the function crosses the x-axis (Chapter 10)

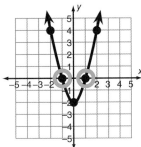

(1, 0) and (−1, 0)

Index

Index

drawing, and finding equation of for scatter plot, 402–415

graphing boys' heights, 414

predicting with, 406–407

problem-solving activities, 413, 414

writing equations for, 408, 409, 412

binary operation, 1042

bingo

Definition Bingo, 302

Dividing a Polynomial by a Binomial Bingo, 988–989

Equation Bingo, 211

Finding the Solution Bingo, 813

Four in a Row Bingo, 954–955

Inequality Bingo, 496–497, 512–513

Middle-Term Bingo, 752

Multiplication and Division Equation Bingo, 195

Operation Bingo, 27

Radical Bingo, 1049–1050

for scientific notation, 696

Square Root Roll It Bingo, 153

binomials. *See also* polynomials

defined, 729

dividing polynomials by, 980–995

factoring using algebra tiles, 790–791

Middle-Term Bingo for multiplying, 752

multiplying, and simplifying expression, including special products of $(a + b)(a + b)$ and $(a + b)(a - b)$, 742–757

multiplying monomials by, 729–730, 736

products of $(a + b)(a - b)$ as difference of squares $(a^2 - b^2)$, 829

products with middle term, 752, 757

special cases for multiplying, 751, 755

squaring to give perfect square trinomials, 827–828

using algebra tiles to understand product of two, 829

using Distributive Property with, 750

calculators. *See also* graphing calculators

experimenting with results involving exponents, 671

scientific notation and, 693–694

solving systems of equations using, 574

square root key on, 150

Card Match, 990

chance, ratios and, 242–243

coefficient

defined, 510

solving inequalities by dividing by, or multiplying by inverse of, 510–511

Commutative Property of Addition

applying, 64, 65, 66

Associative Property of Addition and, 54

defined, 53

formula, 55

identifying, 56, 59–60

Commutative Property of Multiplication

applying, 64, 65, 66

Associative Property of Multiplication and, 54

defined, 54

formula, 55

identifying, 56, 59–60

multiplying polynomials using, 731

completing the square

defined, 848

with negative middle terms, 853

solving equations by groups, 850

solving quadratic equations by, 844–856, 909–910

compound inequalities

and statements defined, 542

defined, 542

graphing, 534, 541, 557–558

or statements defined, 542

plotting systems of inequalities and, 647. *See also* systems of inequalities

solving/graphing inequalities involving absolute value and, 538–543

understanding, 546–547, 539

writing inequalities with, to represent word problems, 542

computing machine, using, 148

congruent angles, 1110, 1111

constant

determining on graphing calculator, 426–427

discovering, 424–427

constant of proportionality, 1110, 1111, 1112

Index

Index

hypotenuse. *See also* right triangles; similar triangles; triangles

    calculating length. *See* Pythagorean theorem

    defined, 1080

independent variables, 313, 338

indicated sum, 210

inequalities. *See also* systems of inequalities

    with absolute value, 548–533, 535

    alligator analogy to remember, 117

    and or *or* statements in. *See* compound inequalities

    balance-scale exercise, 493–494

    compound. *See* compound inequalities

    deciding if true or false, 42

    defined, 488

    dotted or solid lines on graphs and, 551, 553–555

    graphing, 121, 489–490, 499–500, 549–555, 556–558

    graphing in coordinate plane, 544–559

    making conjectures about points and lines with, 549–550

    multiplying by positives and negatives, 508–509, 515–516

    on number lines, 121, 489–490, 491–492, 499–500, 501, 508–509, 515–516

    order of rational numbers and, 116–117

    playing Solve and Graph, 527–530

    predicting points on and not on lines, 548

    ranking temperatures to understand, 118

    relating equations and, 517

    relating multiplication and number line, 508–509, 515

    reversing signs to solve, 508–509, 514, 515–516

    solving by dividing by coefficient or multiplying by inverse of coefficient, 510–511

    solving equations and, 524, 531

    solving in more than one way, 525–526, 532

    solving word problems, 536

    solving/graphing with addition and subtraction, 485–503

    solving/graphing with multiple operations, 520–537

    solving/graphing with multiplication and division, 504–519

    strict, 490, 491, 501, 536, 554, 555, 652

    symbols for, 488

    understanding, 488, 498

    writing, to represent word problems, 542

    writing and solving, 495, 499, 534–535

Inequality Bingo, 496–497, 512–513

Infinite

    defined, 82

    finite sets vs., 86

    intersecting lines and, 590, 594, 597–598, 631

    number of solutions, 599, 600, 602, 621, 632, 635, 636

    parallel lines and, 454

integers

    defined, 82, 135

    multiplying, 135, 138. *See also* multiplication

    on number lines. *See* number lines

    sets of, reviewing, 232

interpolation, geometric, 1066

inverse operations. *See also* Multiplicative Inverse Property

    defined, 134

    identifying domain, range, and inverse of relation, 294–307

    using, 134, 210

investments, calculating exponential growth of, 929–930, 932, 934, 935

irrational numbers, 151, 152, 157, 849, 1043, 1045, 1082

isosceles triangles, 229, 234, 1026

Jeopardy

    One, None, or Many, 597–598

    Perfect Squares, 832

Index

Index

Index

congruent angles and, 1110, 1111
equilateral, 229, 234
icosceles, 229, 234, 1026
obtuse, 229, 234
perimeter formula, 25
solving problems involving, 229–230. *See also*
Pythagorean theorem

true sentences
Addition Property of Equality and, 176–177
deciding between open, false and, 38–39, 41, 43–44
defined, 38, 176
Multiplication Property of Equality and, 193–194

variables
applying, 13
defined, 8, 10
dependent, 313, 338
elimination of. *See* elimination of variable
as exponents. *See* exponential functions
GCF of. *See* greatest common factor (GCF)
independent, 313, 338
retaining same value for entire problem, 608–609
substituting values for, 25, 41–42, 45
values that result in denominator of zero. *See*
excluded values

verbal expressions
creating closely related mathematical expressions
and, 16
evaluation process, 23
finding, for one mathematical expression, 6–8
matching mathematical and, 9–11
translating into mathematical equations, 183, 184
translating mathematical expressions into, and vice
versa, 2–17
writing equivalent mathematical and, 12–15

vertex. *See also* axis of symmetry; parabolas
as $(0, 0)$ for $y = ax^2$, 876–877
as $(0, c)$ for $y = x^2 + c$, 272–273
as $(b, 0)$ for $y = (x - b)^2$, 870–871
as (b, c) for $y = (x - b)^2 + c$, 874–875
defined, 869

as parabola turning point, 868–869
playing Quadratic Function Rummy to understand,
881–883
putting quadratic equation into form to easily find,
878–879

weight, calculating on Earth vs. Neptune, 320–321

***x*-coordinate**, 284, 291, 292, 298, 299, 391, 481, 1096. *See
also* ordered pairs
***x*-intercept**
defined, 420
identifying, 420–421, 434

***y*-coordinate**, 284, 291, 292, 298, 299, 391, 897, 1096. *See
also* ordered pairs
***y*-intercept**
defined, 420
identifying, 420–421, 434
naming/finding, 430–432

zero, variables resulting in denominators of. *See*
excluded values
zero pairs, 98–99, 105, 106, 174–175, 191, 208, 717, 748, 751
Zero Product Property, 795, 801, 811, 834, 896, 918
zeros of functions. *See also* quadratic equations
defined, 894
finding, by looking at graph, 894–895
relationship of roots to equation and, 896–897

A26 Appendix

Credits

Page F12 Group of friends ©istockphoto.com/Chris Schmidt.

Chapter 1 Blank unfolded newspaper ©istockphoto.com/Don Bayley.

Chapter 2 Blue book canvas ©istockphoto.com/Michelle Junior. Earth model: Asia view ©istockphoto.com/Jan Rysavy.

Chapter 3 The daily newspaper ©istockphoto.com/Henryk Falkiewicz. Newspaper stack ©istockphoto.com. Casino dice ©istockphoto.com/Sang Nguyen. Twenty-five cents ©istockphoto.com/Craig Wactor. Paper roll sideways ©istockphoto.com/Achim Prill. Happy young couple ©istockphoto.com/Angelika Schwarz.

Chapter 4 Compass 48 ©istockphoto.com. Blue book canvas ©istockphoto.com/Michelle Junior.

Chapter 5 Fake newspaper ©istockphoto.com/David Freund.

Chapter 6 Glass jam jar ©istockphoto.com. Red calculator and pencil ©istockphoto.com. Blank index card ©istockphoto.com.

Chapter 7 Blank unfolded newspaper ©istockphoto.com/Don Bayley. Colored markers ©istockphoto.com/Charles Brutlag. Twelve-inch wooden ruler ©istockphoto.com.

Chapter 8 Colored notepads ©istockphoto.com/Le Do. Pair of shoes ©1997 Artville, LLC.

Chapter 9 Blank index card ©istockphoto.com.

Chapter 12 Twelve-inch wooden ruler ©istockphoto.com. Clear protractor ©istockphoto.com/Matthew Rambo.

Student name _____   Teacher name _____

Grade level _____   School year _____

Inside Algebra   # Individual Record Card

Code on each line: X = mastered; / = instructed, not mastered; blank = not taught or mastered

---

Chapter 1 Variables and Expressions

_____ Obj 1 Verbal ↔ mathematical

_____ Obj 2 Order of operations

_____ Obj 3 Solve open sentences

_____ Obj 4 Mathematical properties

Chapter 2 Exploring Rational Numbers

_____ Obj 1 Graph rational numbers

_____ Obj 2 Add and subtract rational numbers

_____ Obj 3 Compare and order rational numbers

_____ Obj 4 Multiply and divide rational numbers

_____ Obj 5 Square root

Chapter 3 Solving Linear Equations

_____ Obj 1 With addition and subtraction

_____ Obj 2 With multiplication and division

_____ Obj 3 With one or more operations

_____ Obj 4 Word problems

_____ Obj 5 With proportions

_____ Obj 6 With percent problems

Chapter 4 Graphing Relations and Functions

_____ Obj 1 Graph ordered pairs and relations

_____ Obj 2 Domain, range, and inverse

_____ Obj 3 Determine the range

_____ Obj 4 Graph linear equations

_____ Obj 5 Find a value for a given function

Chapter 5 Analyzing Linear Equations

_____ Obj 1 Slope of a line

_____ Obj 2 Point-slope form

_____ Obj 3 Best-fit line

_____ Obj 4 Slope-intercept form

_____ Obj 5 Parallel or perpendicular

Chapter 6 Solving Linear Inequalities

_____ Obj 1 With addition and subtraction

_____ Obj 2 With multiplication and division

_____ Obj 3 With more than one operation

_____ Obj 4 Compound inequalities/absolute value

_____ Obj 5 Graph inequalities

Chapter 7 Solving Systems of Linear Equations and Inequalities

_____ Obj 1 By graphing

_____ Obj 2 One solution, no solutions, many solutions

_____ Obj 3 Using the substitution method

_____ Obj 4 Eliminating one variable

_____ Obj 5 Solve inequalities by graphing

Chapter 8 Exploring Polynomials

_____ Obj 1 Multiply and divide monomials

_____ Obj 2 Scientific notation

_____ Obj 3 Add and subtract polynomials

_____ Obj 4 Multiply a polynomial by a monomial

_____ Obj 5 Multiply two binomials

Chapter 9 Using Factoring

_____ Obj 1 GCF through prime factorization

_____ Obj 2 Factor polynomials and solve

_____ Obj 3 Factor quadratic trinomials and solve

_____ Obj 4 Perfect squares and differences of squares

_____ Obj 5 Solve by completing the square

Chapter 10 Exploring Quadratic and Exponential Functions

_____ Obj 1 Graph parabolas

_____ Obj 2 Estimate the roots of a quadratic equation

_____ Obj 3 Quadratic formula

_____ Obj 4 Graph exponential functions

Chapter 11 Exploring Rational Expressions and Equations

_____ Obj 1 Simplify rational expressions

_____ Obj 2 Multiply and divide rational expressions

_____ Obj 3 Divide a polynomial by a binomial

_____ Obj 4 Add and subtract rational expressions

_____ Obj 5 Solve rational equations

Chapter 12 Exploring Radical Expressions and Equations

_____ Obj 1 Simplify and perform operations

_____ Obj 2 Solve radical equations

_____ Obj 3 Use the Pythagorean theorem

_____ Obj 4 Find the distance between two points

_____ Obj 5 Similar triangles

Inside Algebra

Class List Record

Teacher: _____ Class: _____ Period: _____ # Students: _____ Date: _____

Student	Chapter 1 Objective				Chapter 2 Objective					Chapter 3 Objective						Chapter 4 Objective					Chapter 5 Objective					Chapter 6 Objective				
	1	2	3	4	1	2	3	4	5	1	2	3	4	5	6	1	2	3	4	5	1	2	3	4	5	1	2	3	4	5
1.																														
2.																														
3.																														
4.																														
5.																														
6.																														
7.																														
8.																														
9.																														
10.																														
11.																														
12.																														
13.																														
14.																														
15.																														
16.																														
17.																														
18.																														
19.																														
20.																														
21.																														
22.																														
23.																														
24.																														
25.																														

Inside Algebra

Class List Record

Teacher: _____ Class: _____ # Students: _____ Period: _____ Date _____

Student	Chapter 7 Objective					Chapter 8 Objective					Chapter 9 Objective						Chapter 10 Objective				Chapter 11 Objective					Chapter 12 Objective				
	1	2	3	4	5	1	2	3	4	5	1	2	3	4	5	6	1	2	3	4	1	2	3	4	5	1	2	3	4	5
1.																														
2.																														
3.																														
4.																														
5.																														
6.																														
7.																														
8.																														
9.																														
10.																														
11.																														
12.																														
13.																														
14.																														
15.																														
16.																														
17.																														
18.																														
19.																														
20.																														
21.																														
22.																														
23.																														
24.																														
25.																														